Contents

10   Local and Quasi-Government   248

11   The Judicial Power: Personnel and Practice   270

PART III   CIVIL LIBERTIES   289

12   Freedom of Association, Assembly and Expression   291

Preface

The election of the Labour government in May 1997 on a manifesto which promised a series of major constitutional changes has complicated the updating of this work. If the proposed changes are implemented they have the potential to be a constitutional revolution, or at least the most significant changes since the Glorious Revolution, just over 300 years ago. These proposals include:

- Devolution: the establishment of a Scottish Parliament and a Welsh Assembly subject to approval in referendums;
- Incorporation of the European Convention on Human Rights;
- Freedom of Information Act;
- Reform of the House of Lords;
- Proportional representation for elections to the House of Commons to be put to a referendum;
- Reform of local government in London with the possibility of an elected Mayor to be put to a referendum.

With the indulgence of my publishers I have been able to include the proposals in the Scottish and Welsh Devolution White Papers. The results of the referendums, will be known just before publication. White Papers are promised on incorporating the European Convention, and Freedom of Information. I have discussed some of the issues relating to incorporation but not Freedom of Information. I have not dealt with London. So far as the House of Lords is concerned, it seems Labour policy is clear only on removing the hereditary peers but not on how, or indeed whether, a second chamber should be elected. The election of the House of Commons by proportional representation is not addressed directly but details of the proposals for the Additional Member voting sytem for the Scottish Parliament and Welsh Assembly are given and the explanation of Northern Ireland's Single Transferable Vote system is retained in chapter 7.

I have updated the account of Northern Ireland to cover the reaction to the break-down of the IRA cease-fire in 1996 and its resumption in 1997. In the previous edition I was able to include details of the First Report of the Committee on Standards in Public Life. In this edition I cover the implementation of the report and the operation of the Committee on Standards and Privileges, including part of the saga of the former MP, Neil Hamilton. I also outline the recommendations in the Committee's two subsequent reports on local public spending bodies and local government. I have summarised some of the provisions from the Amsterdam Intergovernmental Conference and the Commission's proposals for enlargement of the European Union.

Having been involved elsewhere in a full consideration of Sir Richard Scott's report on the export of defence equipment to Iraq, I focus here upon the aspects relating to ministerial accountability and public interest immunity.

I have added a new section on fairness in judicial review which uses sentencing as a case study.

I wish to acknowledge with gratitude the assistance which I have received from the following: officials in the House of Commons Public Information Office, the House of Lords and Journals and Information Office, the Cabinet Office, the Department of Social Security, the Lord Chancellor's Department and the office of the Parliamentary Commissioner for Administration; Dr. Carsten Doerfert, Professor D. S. Greer and Kiron Reid.

The thanks I owe the team involved with publication are greater than ever given their assistance and cheerful coping with disruption, which facilitated the inclusion of the developments in July 1997.

Brian Thompson
September 1997

Table of Cases

NUMERICAL LIST OF CASES BEFORE THE EUROPEAN COURT OF JUSTICE

Table of Cases

Table of Statutes

PART I

CONSTITUTIONAL THEORY AND PRACTICE

Constitutional and administrative law is part of what is known as public law, which is the law regulating the relationship between the citizen and the State. One might say that constitutional and administrative law is the body of law which is concerned with government. Different countries have different types of government. Politics determines not only the type of government but also the constitution within which government is supposed to be conducted. The public law of a country is greatly influenced by politics, indeed, according to Craig (1990), a country's public law can only be understood properly in the light of its background political theory. Craig identifies some of the different theories of democracy and analyses their implications for principles of public law.

The discussion in chapter 1 focuses upon the idea of a constitution, its characteristics, purpose, and the range of provisions which it may contain. After this introduction, in which the experience of other countries is emphasised, we move to our consideration of the United Kingdom (UK). Chapter 2 provides an outline of the UK's constitutional jigsaw. This account will deal with history and politics, showing the building of the State and its structures of government from its four component nations. The sources of the UK's constitutional arrangements will be identified, including the external European elements: the treaties and legislation of the European Communities, and the European Convention on Human Rights.

The fundamental features of the UK's constitution and its constitutional law are discussed in the final two chapters in this part. In chapter 3 the legal doctrine of Parliamentary sovereignty, or legislative supremacy, is examined. The great power which this doctrine provides is offset in many States by constitutionalism and it will be suggested that, in the UK, this comprises the rule of law, the separation of powers and responsible government. The non-legal rules, or constitutional conventions, which are crucial in the operation of the UK's constitutional arrangements, are explored in chapter 4.

PART I

CONSTITUTIONAL THEORY AND PRACTICE

CHAPTER ONE

The Idea of a Constitution

1.1 DEFINING TERMS

Constitutional law can obviously be defined as the law relating to the constitution. This raises the question: what is a constitution? The usual answer to this is that a constitution is a document which contains the rules for the operation of an organisation. Organisations vary in size and complexity, ranging from bodies such as student unions and companies, to nation States and groupings of States, such as the United Nations Organisation or the European Communities. While these organisations are quite different from each other, their constitutions share the common feature of providing for the management of the organisation. Such arrangements may include the specifying of offices, the duties, powers and responsibilities which are attached to those positions, and the procedures which are to be followed in filling those positions.

Our subject is the political constitution of the United Kingdom of Great Britain and Northern Ireland. There is, however, a problem, because there is no document which is called the constitution of the United Kingdom. The absence of such a document has not prevented scholars from writing about British constitutional law. What they have done is to define a constitution as:

a body of laws, customs and conventions that define the composition and powers of the organs of the State and that regulate the relations of the various State organs to one another and to the private citizen (Hood Phillips and Jackson 1987, p. 5).

This approach proceeds upon the basis that since the UK has a system of government which is regulated by rules, which are partly legal and partly non-legal, then this is just as much a constitution as those documents in the United States of America and Ireland whose titles proclaim their status as the constitutions of those countries. This conception seems to be in keeping with the image of the pragmatic British. There is no requirement to codify the rules relating to government: what matters is that there are rules. Yet, as one commentator has noted, it seems only to be the British who do not accept that a constitution consists of 'the legal rules which govern the government of that country and which have been embodied in a document' (Wheare 1966, p. 2).

Is this an important difference? Some people think that it is. One of the aims of the pressure group Charter 88 is the creation of a written or codified constitution for the UK. They take the view that the present constitutional arrangements are unsatisfactory because the government has too much power. It is the case that all constitutions are concerned with power. Constitutions 'identify the sources, purposes, uses and restraints of public power' (Duchacek 1987, p. 142). The limiting of governmental power is usually regarded as a major feature of a constitution. The concept of *constitutionalism*, which has been defined as 'an institutionalised system of effective, regularised restraints upon governmental action' (Friedrich 1963, p. 217), by its very name emphasises the point that the control of governmental power is an extremely important function of a constitution. If one wants to increase the restraints upon governmental power in the UK, is it necessary to write a codified constitution? The answer to this is probably yes. The reasons may be found in the work of Ridley (1988, 1991) who has proposed a list of the characteristics of a constitution and therefore of constitutional law.

1.2   CHARACTERISTICS OF A CONSTITUTION

Ridley's suggestions for the characteristics of a constitution come from his analysis of a passage in which Bryce described a 'statutory' or written constitution:

> The instrument in which a constitution is embodied proceeds from a source different from that whence spring other laws, is regulated in a different way, and exerts a sovereign force. It is enacted not by the ordinary legislative authority but by some higher and specially empowered body. When any of its provisions conflict with the provisions of the ordinary law, it prevails and the ordinary law must give way (Bryce 1901, vol. 1, p. 151).

1.2.1   Constituent Act
The first characteristic is an obvious one, but it is also very important: a constitution establishes or constitutes a system of government. We can see this point not only in the constitutions of other States but also in bodies such as a students' union. Students in a college might group together to pursue certain objectives but it will only be after they have agreed a constitution that their organisation will have an official existence, which will allow access to funds.

The history of the UK explains why there is no constituent act or blueprint for the system of government. Instead of the constitution preceding and making the government, the arrangements for government came into being and subsequently developed. In other words the British constitution was not made, rather it has grown.

1.2.2 Constituent Power
The authority for the constituent act derives from a constituent power, i.e., an authority which is both outside and above the system which it establishes. In liberal democratic societies the people are normally the constituent power. This usually means that, only after the constitution has been approved by the people, will it take effect. Therefore in liberal democratic States the people's approval of the constitution legitimises the system which the constitution creates. This may be done directly by the people in a referendum, as occurred in Ireland in 1937, or indirectly, through the people's representatives. This is what happened in the USA. Although the preamble to the constitution of the USA begins with the words 'We the people', it was first agreed at a special convention and then approved by the elected representatives in the legislatures of the founding States.

1.2.3 Hierarchy of Law
It follows from the idea of a constituent power giving rise to a constituent act that there is a hierarchy of law. The constitution is a higher or fundamental law as it is the source or authorisation for all other law. It then follows that in order for these inferior laws to be valid, they must not be inconsistent with the higher law. This is the reasoning which led the US Supreme Court to assert that it possessed the power to review legislation for its conformity to the constitution, even though the constitution did not expressly confer this power upon the court (*Marbury* v *Madison* (1803) 5 US (1 Cranch) 137).

1.2.4 Entrenchment
The provisions of constitutions are usually entrenched so they may only be amended or repealed if special procedures are followed. The logic of this is that, since the constitution is higher law which is made by the constituent power, modification should be approved by the constitutent power. This is illustrated by the Irish constitution of 1937 which was adopted, and can only be modified, after ratification by a referendum of the people. Amendments to the constitution must first be approved by the two chambers of the legislature before submission to the people in a referendum.

1.3 CLASSIFICATION

Some people class constitutions according to whether they are written or not. This is not a particularly useful point on which to focus analysis, given that only the UK and Israel seem not to have a written constitution. In any event there are written rules relating to the UK constitution. As Bryce (1901, vol. 1, Essay III) indicated, a more significant feature which does provide an important basis for classification of constitutions is the ease or difficulty with which amendments may be made. Other means of classifying constitutions refer to the type of government established by a constitution.

1.3.1   Rigid/Flexible

In coining these terms to describe the amendment procedures for constitutions, Bryce distinguished between those which did require special processes, and those which did not (1901, vol. 1, Essay III). Used crudely, this classification is little different from written and unwritten, as very few constitutions join that of the UK in the flexible class.

If we pay more attention to the degree of rigidity, then it is possible to discern differences amongst rigid constitutions. Some of the possible variations include (a) specifying that the legislature's approval of an amendment must be by a particular majority, (b) approval by the legislature both before and after a general election, (c) approval by the legislature and the people in a referendum.

Wheare (1966, p. 17) points out that while reference to the particular amendment procedure tells us something about a constitution, it can mislead, as it does not tell us the reality of the amendment process. Constitutions of similar degrees of formal rigidity may differ in the number of amendments actually made because the people feel that the constitution suits them, or not, as the case may be. Wheare therefore suggests the use of rigid or flexible as classes to distinguish between constitutions on the basis of whether or not they are easily and often altered (p. 17).

1.3.2   Monarchical/Republican

Classifying constitutions according to whether they are monarchies or republics is not now regarded as being of general significance. The trend is for new constitutions to proclaim republics. Monarchs in Western Europe are no longer politically powerful. As heads of State their role is ceremonial and symbolic. Many presidents are heads of State, e.g., in Germany and Ireland, and they are similar to the modern constitutional monarchs. Other presidents, as in the United States, are also heads of government and then there are some presidents, as in France, whose powers are greater than the average head of State, but are not quite those of the typical head of government.

1.3.3   Federal/Unitary

In most countries there is provision for more than one tier of government; however, in a federal constitution, the allocation of powers between the federal or national government and the regions, States or provinces is akin to a sharing amongst equals. Each will have its own sphere of influence and certain matters can only be done in partnership. In a unitary State there is a hierarchical arrangement which may permit control of the other tiers by the national government. Again the formal provisions may not give an accurate picture of practice. For example, the relationship between the United Kingdom Parliament at Westminster and the Northern Ireland Parliament at Stormont before the outbreak of the 'troubles' in 1968, was characterised by minimal interference in Northern Ireland's affairs which was more in keeping with a federal constitution. The prorogation, or discontinuance, of the Northern Ireland Parliament in 1972, however, reflected the greater power of a national legislature in a unitary State.

1.3.4 Presidential/Parliamentary

The growth of the presidential executive was due to a belief that one of the ways in which government could be limited was by separating powers. As developed in the United States this meant that the executive branch of government was not part of the legislative branch. In a parliamentary executive, ministers are required to be members of the legislature. The stark contrast of these opposites has been blurred, particularly in Africa but also in France where the president, who is elected, shares power with the prime minister who is appointed by the president.

1.3.5 One-party State

The constitution of a State may stipulate that there is only one lawful political party. This was the case in some of the former communist countries of Eastern Europe before the advent of democracy.

1.4 CONTENTS

Wheare suggests that the answer to the question as to what a constitution should contain is 'The very minimum, and that minimum to be rules of law' (1966, p. 34). He notes that this is not what actually occurs, as some people regard a constitution as 'a sort of manifesto, a confession of faith, or statement of ideals' (1966, p. 32). That a constitution should contain aspirations or ideals is not surprising when one considers the circumstances in which constitutions are made. They may be made upon a country gaining independence from its colonial power, as was the case with the United States of America and Ireland. They may be the result of a terrible experience such as the constitution or Basic Law of the German Federal Republic, made after the Second World War. In dealing with the future, reference will be made to the past to mark the independence or other change.

According to Wheare, constitutions may contain rules of law and principles. These two types of constitutional provision may be used to achieve two purposes, the creation of a system of limited government and the announcement of certain ideals. Whilst it would seem that rules would be used to limit government and principles to express ideals, there can be a crossover between these provisions and purposes. Rules can be used to enforce ideals. For example, the 18th amendment to the US constitution prohibited the manufacture, sale, transportation, import and export of intoxicating liquor. This 1919 amendment was repealed by the 21st amendment in 1933 following widespread disregard of it, and the realisation, perhaps, that this was not the best way of achieving a particular goal.

The following analysis of types of constitutional provisions draws upon Wheare (1966) and Finer (1979). Examples will be drawn from two common law countries, the USA and Ireland, and two civil law countries, France and Germany. The constitution of the USA was drafted in 1787 and came into effect in 1788. The European constitutions were approved in 1937 (Ireland), 1949 (Germany) and 1958 (France).

1.4.1   Status of a Constitution

Included under this heading are the authority of a constitution and its amendment procedures.

1.4.1.1   Authority   We saw earlier (1.2) that constitutions derive their authority from the making of a constituent act by a constituent power. The modern trend is to hold that the people are the constituent power and that they may, either directly, or indirectly through an assembly of their representatives, approve a constitution. This may suggest that, if a constitution is meant to be paramount law, then the constitution is superior to the institutions it creates, and it therefore follows that legislation which is repugnant to the constitution must be void. This is the logic accepted in the US as enunciated by Chief Justice Marshall in *Marbury* v *Madison* (1803) 5 US (1 Cranch) 137. By this reasoning the US Supreme Court reached the conclusion that it had the power of constitutional review, i.e., the ability to strike down legislation. In other constitutions, such as the Irish one of 1937, it is clearly stated that the judges have this power. In France a special body, the Constitutional Council (*Conseil constitutionnel*), has the power to check legislation, and if it is found to be unconstitutional then it cannot be implemented (see further 1.4.3.3).

Another method of tracing the authority for a constitution would take one to a superior external body, such as the colonial power which agrees to the independence of its colonies. Thus the constitutions of many former British colonies are to be found in legislation passed by the Westminster Parliament. Canada's constitution was formerly the British North America Act 1867. This constitution required that amendments to it would have to be passed by Westminster. The Canadians wished to be able to amend their constitution without involving Westminster. This 'patriation' of the constitution to Canada had to be approved by the enactment of a Westminster statute, the Canada Act 1982. Similarly, the Australian constitution was patriated by the Australia Act 1986. In these statutes Westminster declared that it would no longer legislate for these countries.

1.4.1.2   Amendment   Most constitutions are rigid in the sense that they require a special procedure for amendment. Often it is the constituent power which approves amendments. In the USA the representatives of the people must approve an amendment and this requires a two-thirds majority in both Houses of the Congress, *and* the support of three-quarters of the legislatures in the States. In Ireland an amendment proposal must be passed by the legislature prior to being placed before the people in a referendum. The situation in France is that a measure is passed by both chambers of the legislature and takes effect after approval in a referendum. A referendum will not be held if the president decides to submit the proposed amendment to the legislature, which is convened as a congress. The congress must approve the amendment by a three-fifths majority of the votes cast. The French constitution also stipulates that it is not possible to amend the republican form of government.

The German Basic Law, which is a federal constitution, prohibits amendments relating to the division of the federation into *Länder* and the basic principles in arts 1 (protection of human dignity) and 20 (preservation of State order, the right to resist). Those parts of the Basic Law which may be amended require two-thirds majorities in both chambers of the federal legislature.

1.4.2 Territorial Division of Powers

If a State determines to have a federal structure then the division of powers amongst the different territories will be very important. The constitution will usually specify which powers may be exercised by the federal, and which by regional governments. This may be done by giving a list of the federal government's powers and/or a list of the regional governments' powers. There may be some topics for which there is concurrent jurisdiction, that is, both sets of governments may deal with them. The German Basic Law can illustrate this. The federal legislature's exclusive list of powers or competences includes, for example, foreign affairs, passports, immigration, extradition, customs and coinage. The regions, or *Länder*, may legislate on matters where the Basic Law has not conferred that power on the federal parliament. The catalogue of concurrent competences contains more items than the federation's exclusive list. Examples from this catalogue include civil and criminal law, public welfare, residence and establishment of aliens, promotion of agriculture and forestry, food safety and environmental protection. The *Länder* have the power to legislate on concurrent matters as long as, and to the extent that, the federation does not exercise the power to legislate. The Basic Law prescribes conditions which must be met before the federation may legislate on concurrent matters. These conditions are: (a) a matter cannot be effectively regulated by legislation of the individual *Länder*; or (b) regulation by one *Land* might prejudice the interests of the other *Länder* or of the people as a whole; or (c) the maintenance of uniformity of living conditions beyond the territory of any one *Land* necessitates such regulation.

One might compare these conditions with the definition of subsidiarity in the Treaty on European Union. This treaty, when ratified by all of the member States of the European Communities will insert into the Treaty Establishing the European Economic Community a provision to determine when matters should be the subject of action by the Community or left to the member States. This provision (art. 3b) states:

> In areas which do not fall within its exclusive competence, the Community shall take action, in accordance with the principle of subsidiarity, only if and insofar as the objectives of the proposed action cannot be sufficiently achieved by the member States and can therefore, by reason of the scale or effects of the proposed action, be better achieved by the Community.
>
> Any action by the Community shall not go beyond what is necessary to achieve the objectives of this Treaty.

There does seem to be a preference in federal constitutions for listing the competences of the federal government and giving the residue to the regions or the people. This was done in the US constitution, although not until the passage of the 10th amendment was it made clear that residual powers were given to the States or the people.

1.4.3 Branches of Government

A constitution will usually create three separate organs to exercise the three functions of government: executive, legislative and judicial. The idea of the separation of powers, of conferring upon each organ of government only one function is to be found in its purest form in the constitution of the United States of America. The aim behind this is to limit power, to create checks and balances on the exercise of governmental power.

1.4.3.1 Executive The membership and powers of the executive will be specified in a constitution. In a parliamentary system, the members of the executive will be members of the legislature, indeed, maintaining the legislature's confidence will be essential to the executive's continuance in office. In a presidential executive there is greater separation from the legislature. The French constitution of 1958 creates a mixture of a presidential-cum-parliamentary executive where the president appoints the prime minister, but if the government loses a motion of censure then ministers must tender their resignations to the president.

1.4.3.2 Legislature In addition to prescribing the membership and powers of the legislature, a constitution may stipulate the arrangements for elections. This will include the qualifications required for candidates and electors. The particular voting system may also be specified by the constitution. While the German Basic Law states that the method of voting will be regulated by federal law, the Irish constitution stipulates that elections to the legislature's lower chamber shall be by the single transferable vote system of proportional representation.

The constitution may state the normal duration of a legislature. In some systems this is a fixed term and in others, principally parliamentary ones, there will be provisions dealing with dissolution before the expiry of the maximum period.

The requirements for, and the types of, legislation may be prescribed. Arrangements relating to the control of finances are very important. Where a legislature has two chambers (bicameral), there may be differences between the powers given to the chambers where money Bills are concerned. Under federal constitutions the federal and regional parts may both be given taxation powers. There may also be provisions for the apportionment of tax revenues. In Germany, for example, the federation gets customs duties, the *Länder* take motor vehicle taxes, and they share equally income and corporation taxes.

1.4.3.3 Judiciary The constitution may stipulate the arrangements for appointing the judiciary, which in some cases may be by election. The qualifications to be a judge may be specified. In democracies it is usual to provide for the independence of the judiciary by setting out the terms of their tenure and, if it is possible to remove them, the provision of a special procedure and grounds for their dismissal. In the USA and Ireland judges hold office during good behaviour. French judges are irremovable, and in Germany judges can only be dismissed by a judicial decision and on a ground specified by law.

One of the most important aspects of a court's jurisdiction is whether or not it has the power of constitutional review. The French Constitutional Council is not a court. Its power to declare legislation unconstitutional is exercised before the laws are promulgated. Usually the constitutionality of legislation is raised in a dispute over the application of that law. This 'concrete' review occurs in the USA, Germany and Ireland. In Ireland it is possible for the president to refer to the Supreme Court a Bill which has been approved by the legislature, so that its constitutionality can be checked. This power does not apply to money Bills or any Bills proposing an amendment to the constitution.

1.4.4   Emergency Powers

The problem of what to do in time of emergency has usually been provided for by the framers of constitutions. The logical approach is first to define the circumstances of an emergency, and second to provide special powers for dealing with the situation. There is usually a concern to balance the exercise of emergency powers by the executive with oversight by the legislature. For example, the power to declare war is usually given to the legislature. In Germany the constitution prohibits preparations for an aggressive war but permits defence against attack. Such a state of defence is normally authorised by a two-thirds majority of the votes cast in the legislature.

States of emergency may include circumstances other than war. In France, if the institutions of the republic, the independence of the nation, the integrity of its territory or the fulfilment of its international commitments are threatened in a grave and immediate manner, or the regular functioning of the constitutional public authorities is interrupted, then the president may take emergency measures. The president must consult the prime minister and the presidents of the two houses of parliament and the Constitutional Council. The parliament will be convened and the lower chamber may not be dissolved during the exercise of emergency powers.

The Irish constitution confers very wide powers in an emergency. This is done by a provision which states that nothing in the constitution may be used to invalidate legislation passed to secure public safety and the preservation of the State in time of war or armed rebellion. Time of war is defined so as to include a situation in which there is an armed conflict in which Ireland is not a participating country, and both chambers of the legislature have resolved that a state of emergency has arisen out of the conflict and the emergency affects the vital interests of the State. This is indeed a wide power for it could authorise the suppression of the citizen's fundamental rights. It would theoretically be possible to rewrite the constitution without consulting the people during such an emergency.

1.4.5 Relations with Other States

Two aspects of a constitution's provisions concerning relations with other States will be examined, these are the conduct of foreign affairs and the status of international law.

1.4.5.1 Conduct of foreign affairs   The executive branch of government is usually given the power to conduct a State's foreign affairs. In France, Germany and the USA the president is given this task. The German president is involved at the formal level of representing the federation and concluding treaties, although the actual work will be done by ministers and officials.

The unusual French arrangement of a mixed presidential-cum-parliamentary executive requires specific allocation of the various responsibilities to the president and the ministers. The constitution details which treaties are to be ratified and approved by legislation. Examples of such treaties are peace treaties, treaties or agreements concerning international organisations and those which imply a commitment for the finances of the State. The Constitutional Council may declare that a treaty contains a clause contrary to the constitution, in which case it may only be ratified or approved following amendment of the constitution.

In the USA the president's power to make treaties is subject to the advice and consent of the Senate and a two-thirds majority vote is required to approve a treaty.

1.4.5.2 Status of international law   States can be divided into categories with respect to their law on the status of international law. If they are 'monist' then international law, including a concluded treaty, will become part of the State's domestic law without further action. In Germany the Basic Law provides that public international law shall take precedence over domestic laws and can create rights and duties for the inhabitants of Germany.

The other position, the 'dualist', accepts that there are two systems of law and that international law provisions will not become part of domestic law unless they are specifically incorporated. Ireland adopts this position. The Irish constitution provides that Ireland accepts, as its rule of conduct in its relations with other States, the generally recognised principles of international law. In addition it is stipulated that if an international agreement imposes a charge upon public funds then it will not be binding unless approved by the lower chamber of the legislature.

Ireland's membership of the European Communities has required amendments to the constitution. There was some surprise when it was held by the Irish Supreme Court that ratification of title III of the Single European Act could only be carried out if the constitution was amended. The majority of the court held that title III, which dealt with European political cooperation, was inconsistent with arts 1 and 5 of the constitution which gave full sovereignty to Ireland (*Crotty* v *Ireland* [1987] IR 713). The Treaty on European Union was ratified by Ireland after approval of the 11th amendment to the Irish constitution which provided the authority for this action.

1.4.6 Declarations of Rights

One of the most important aspects of a State's relations with its citizens is the declaration of the rights of the citizen. If such a declaration is part of a constitution which is fundamental law then this will mean that the rights can only be amended or removed by way of amendment to the constitution. Before Canada's Constitution Act 1982, which incorporates a Charter of Fundamental Rights and Freedoms, there was a statute called the Bill of Rights. This declaration of rights was not entrenched and therefore could be amended by ordinary legislation.

Where declarations of rights are entrenched as part of a constitution this does not mean that the rights are unqualified. If we take freedom of expression as an example, in Germany it may be limited by provisions of general laws, the provisions of laws for the protection of youth, and by the right to the inviolability of personal honour. In Ireland the limitations upon freedom of expression include prohibitions on the undermining of public order, morality or the authority of the State. It is an offence to publish or utter blasphemous, seditious or indecent matter. The German Basic Law also provides for the forfeiture of some of the basic rights, including freedom of expression, if they are abused by combating the free democratic order. This forfeiture and its extent shall be pronounced by the Federal Constitutional Court.

The types of right which are declared in liberal democratic constitutions are usually political rather than social and economic. The classic political rights include freedom of assembly, association, conscience and expression, protection of the person and property, and the right to due legal process, which includes the right to a fair trial. Social and economic rights refer to employment and accommodation and were to be found, for example, in the constitutions of the former communist countries of Eastern Europe.

The Irish constitution has been held to guarantee rights which are not specifically enumerated. This position was reached by the interpretation of art. 40.3, which declares in subsection 1 that the State will defend and vindicate the personal rights of the citizen. Subsection 2 stipulates that the State shall 'in particular' protect certain specified rights and this has been held to mean that subsection 2 does not exhaustively define the personal rights to be protected in subsection 1. Examples of the unspecified rights recognised by the judges are the right to strike, to privacy, to legal representation on criminal charges, and to travel. The sources from which the unspecified rights have been drawn include inferences from the constitution's specified rights, from the section in the constitution which details the directive principles of social policy, from common law, from human personality and from the democratic nature of the State.

1.4.7 Political Manifesto

It would be a mistake for lawyers not to recognise the significance of a constitution as a kind of political manifesto. This is because some of the provisions which deal with aspirations and ideals may be of assistance in interpreting the constitution's legal rules. Two aspects of the constitution as a charter of ideals are the forging of an identity for the State and proclaiming its values.

1.4.7.1 Identity   The French, German and Irish constitutions all describe their national flags. The French constitution stipulates the national anthem and the Irish constitution specifies that Irish is the first official language and that English is the second official language. It is further provided that where there is an ambiguity in the text of the constitution then the Irish-language version is the more authoritative.

The Irish constitution of 1937 was the second constitution, after the partition of the island of Ireland, for that part of Ireland which left the UK. Part of the reason for the making of this constitution was that it would have less of a British stamp upon it and reflect more of an Irish influence. This can be seen in the first article of the constitution:

> The Irish nation hereby affirms its inalienable, indefeasible, and sovereign right to choose its own form of government, to determine its relations with other nations, and to develop its life, political, economic and cultural, in accordance with its own genius and traditions.

The next article of this constitution is controversial. It is a claim that the national territory consists of the whole island of Ireland. For those people in Northern Ireland who wish to continue the union with Great Britain, this claim is a cause of great resentment. It had been thought that this provision was simply an aspiration for the unification of the island; however, the Supreme Court held that the reintegration of the national territory is a 'constitutional imperative' (*McGimpsey* v *Ireland* [1990] 1 IR 110 at p. 119 per Finlay CJ).

The German Basic Law of 1949 was a reaction to the rise of Hitler and the Second World War, and also the resulting partition of Germany by the Allied Powers. The preamble notes that this Basic Law is the work of some of the German people who have acted on behalf of those Germans to whom participation was denied. It called upon the entire German people to achieve in free self-determination the unity and freedom of Germany. After unification was achieved the preamble was amended to note that the unity and freedom of Germany had been achieved in free self-determination and that the Basic Law now applied to the people in 16 *Länder* rather than the 11 *Länder* of the former West Germany.

1.4.7.2 Values   A constitution can express the values which its framers have for their country. These values may be seen in the type of governmental institutions which are created, and in the declarations of rights of the citizens. Values will be found particularly in preambles. The preamble to the constitution of the USA has served as a model. It declares:

> We the People of the United States, in Order to form a more perfect Union, establish Justice, insure domestic Tranquillity, provide for the common

defence, promote the general Welfare, and secure the Blessings of Liberty to ourselves and our Posterity, do ordain and establish this Constitution for the United States of America.

The preamble to the Irish constitution, in addition to marking the independence of the nation, also proclaims the importance of religion to the people:

In the name of the Most Holy Trinity, from Whom is all authority and to Whom, as our final end, all actions both of men and States must be referred.

Part of Ireland's expression of its independence from Britain was a celebration of Catholicism which had been suppressed at various times under British rule. It was not therefore surprising to find aspects of Catholic doctrine informing the constitution. Until its removal through the 15th amendment in 1995 there had been a constitutional prohibition on divorce. Another specifically Catholic doctrine was added to the constitution by the eighth amendment in 1983. This sought to ban abortion by the State acknowledging the right to life of the unborn and seeking to defend and vindicate that right. The amendment placed the right to life of the unborn on an equal basis with the right to life of the mother and, as a consequence, the Supreme Court has ruled that an abortion was permissible where the mother, a 14-year-old rape victim, was threatening to commit suicide because of the pregnancy (*Attorney-General* v *X* [1992] 1 IR 1). This decision and others relating to the provision of information about abortion services in Great Britain led to the submission of three amendments to the people in a referendum in November 1992. The amendment which proposed that termination of the life of the unborn could not be carried out unless there was risk to the life, as opposed to the health of the mother, was rejected. The people approved the amendments which provided that the rights to travel to other States and to information relating to services lawfully available in another State were not limited.

The experience of Ireland on these issues of morality may be taken by some to endorse Wheare's view that they are not suitable for inclusion as rules of fundamental law in a country's constitution.

Reaction against Nazism is a significant part of the German Basic Law and can be seen in the preamble, which recited that the German people:

Conscious of their responsibility before God and man, Animated by the resolve to preserve their national and political unity and to serve the peace of the world as an equal partner in the united Europe, Desiring to give a new order to political life for a transitional period . . .

The creation of a democratic State was so important that art. 20 confers the right to resist those who seek to abolish that constitutional order should no other remedy be available. There is also a ban on aggressive war and authorisation of armed forces only for defence to the extent explicitly permitted by the Basic Law. There is also provision for control of the manufacture, transport and marketing of weapons designed for warfare.

After this survey of the constitutions of other countries, we turn to the constitutional arrangements of the UK. There are similarities but the most important difference is that these arrangements do not amount to fundamental law which prevails over inconsistent ordinary law.

CHAPTER TWO
The UK's Constitutional Jigsaw

In this chapter the constitutional arrangements in the UK are outlined. The metaphor of the jigsaw seems apt to describe the different component parts of these constitutional arrangements. In addition to the current institutions of government and the theories underlying them, i.e., what passes for a constitution in the UK, there are also the sources of this constitution and the nations which together make up the UK. Greater attention is paid to the arrangements for Northern Ireland as the attempts to resolve that area's problems have involved interesting constitutional innovations. The chapter will end with a discussion of decentralising reform proposals.

2.1 THE EVOLUTION OF THE CONSTITUTION

There is a view that history is written by the victors. Perhaps it would be more accurate to say that the victors write the first draft and that later drafts contain a less partial account of events and personalities. One influential view of the constitutional history of the UK may be called the Whig version. In this account the transfer of power in the government from the King to Parliament is presented as almost inevitable and a desirable thing. The proposition that Parliament is a representative institution, and is at the centre of the country's political life through its supervision of the ministers of the Crown, is not an accurate statement about the UK system of government. As we shall see there may have been a period in which the executive branch of government was amenable to the influence of Parliament but it is certainly not the case any more. Today the government controls the House of Commons which is the dominant partner in Parliament. The dominance of the, historically, lower chamber has come about because its members are elected by the citizens. Somewhat paradoxically the move to mass democracy has not increased the power of the elected representatives in their relationship with the government.

2.1.1 The Balanced Constitution

A comprehensive understanding of the constitution would necessitate a study of history which would take us back as far as the earliest records. It is not proposed to travel as far back as that. The 18th-century constitution resulted from the upheavals of the previous century in which there was civil war, out of which arose a republic, which was then succeeded by the restoration of the monarchy and then a so-called Glorious, but not bloodless, revolution in which King James II was replaced by William and Mary. The constitutional settlement of the end of the 17th century secured a transfer of power away from the King to Parliament. The Bill of Rights 1688 made Parliament the supreme legislator and confirmed that taxation required Parliamentary approval.

It must be remembered that Parliament in the 18th century was not a truly representative body. The electorate was restricted to men who owned property of a minimum value, and the constituencies bore no relation to the changes in demography which had occurred even before the onset of the industrial revolution. The constitution was termed a balanced one because of the equilibrium amongst the feudal estates of the King, aristocracy and clergy, and the middle classes. The House of Commons had gained in influence but the King had the power of patronage, and the aristocracy, through its control of some of the Parliamentary boroughs, could obtain support in the Commons for some of their proposals. Effective government therefore required the cooperation of all three of these groups.

It will be noted that the ordinary people did not have much of a part to play in this order of things. The idea of democracy, of giving a voice to everyone, was a deeply shocking one to the political elite. Such rights were too important to be given to anyone who did not have a stake in the country. Only men of property could be relied upon to act responsibly.

2.1.2 The Liberal Constitution

The successor to the balanced constitution has been termed 'liberal' (Dearlove and Saunders 1991, p. 24). The 18th century saw the progress of radical ideas both in the events leading to, and the aftermath of, two revolutions. The first of these was the War of Independence (1775–83) between Britain and her American colonies, and the second was the French Revolution (1789). Both revolutions were, in part, concerned with the relationship between rulers and elected representatives.

The Reform Act of 1832 signified a change much greater than the relatively small extension of the franchise which it brought about. This was because the topic of reform was really the only issue in the 1831 general election. Candidates supporting reform were returned and this mandate enabled the government to obtain from the King an assurance to create the number of peers necessary to secure the passage of the Bill through the House of Lords if it was initially rejected by the upper chamber. In these circumstances the opposition to the measure in the House of Lords was not pursued vigorously. The Act not only increased the numbers of male property owners who could vote, but also began a process of reforming the constituencies. Gradually the constituencies changed to take account of the new industrial towns. The 'rotten boroughs' which were controlled by the aristocracy were abolished and so this also helped to increase the power of the House of Commons in its relations with the King and the House of Lords. Thus the balanced constitution was replaced by the liberal constitution.

It is this particular set of constitutional arrangements which has lingered on as the description of government even though reality has changed. In this liberal constitution, relatively accurately analysed by Bagehot (1867) the House of Commons was no longer in a partnership with the King and the House of Lords; instead, the important relationship was between the Commons and the cabinet. The still restricted electorate voted for their representatives who, in the House of Commons, decided who should form the government. The ministers might be ministers of the Crown but it was no longer the King who chose them. The cabinet would have to work to carry the Commons. Compromises would have to be agreed otherwise the Commons' loss of confidence in the government would lead to its loss of office. This significant influence over the government by the House of Commons has given rise to the idea that it is the normal state of affairs between the government and the House of Commons. The efforts to increase democracy have led to a diminution of the influence of the Commons over the government and a new liberal-democratic constitution.

2.1.3 The Liberal-Democratic Constitution
The Reform Acts of 1867 and 1884 significantly increased the franchise, although it was not until 1918 that all male adults received the right to vote. At the same time women over the age of 30 were enfranchised. It was not until 1928 that universal adult suffrage was introduced. In addition to the extension of the franchise, the introduction of secret ballots in 1872 and legislation curbing electoral malpractices, plus the redistribution of constituencies from 1885, created the conditions which led to the growth of political parties. The change in electoral law transformed elections from a series of local contests into a national event fought by organised parties. Gradually party support became absolutely crucial to a person's chances of being elected as an MP. As party machines developed this also gave power to their leaders which enabled them to maintain fairly strict discipline. This firm party discipline then became the key to the government's dominance of Parliament. When the electorate voted in a party with a majority in the House of Commons, the leadership could rely upon their backbenchers to ensure that their programme was implemented.

Under the liberal constitution, in the middle of the 19th century, there was the idea of a chain of command through which the electorate had power over their representatives who, in turn, had power over the government. Strong party discipline reduced the influence of the House of Commons upon the government. The majority ensured that the sanction of a vote of confidence lost its sting. The votes that mattered now were those cast in the general election, rather than the votes in Parliament. This was because the former conditioned the latter.

According to Dearlove and Saunders (1991) the major theorist of the liberal democratic constitution is Dicey. His account highlighted the sovereignty of Parliament, the rule of law and the conventions of the constitution. The key idea of the liberal constitution was the shift of power from the King, giving sovereignty to Parliament. Dicey divided sovereignty into two aspects, legal and political, and allocated the former to Parliament and the latter to the people. Parliament is the supreme lawmaker but its exercise of that power 'should represent or give effect to the will of the political sovereign, i.e. of the electoral body, or of the nation' (Dicey 1959, p. 430). This is secured by constitutional conventions which are the code of constitutional morality.

One of the consequences of the constitution having evolved from the balanced version to the liberal democratic type is that the formal position and practice do not coincide. The King has lost the reality but not the appearance of power. Authority is still formally vested in the monarch, or the Crown. The government ministers, the civil service and the judges are all servants of the Crown and legislation requires the royal assent. The rule of law and the constitutional conventions place limits on what these constitutional actors may do.

2.2 SOURCES

The sources of constitutional law and practice comprise legislation, judicial decisions, the royal prerogative, Parliamentary law and custom, European treaties, authoritative writings and constitutional conventions. The place and operation of these conventions, as the non-legal rules of the constitution are known, will be scrutinised in chapter 4.

2.2.1 Legislation

One of the sources of constitutional law in countries which have codified constitutions is 'organic laws'. This body of law is legislation which is enacted to give detail to provisions in the constitution. An example of an organic law is legislation dealing with elections to a legislature (see 7.3 to 7.7). In the UK legislation provides not only organic laws, but also measures which would be present in a constitution. As we saw in 1.4, declarations of rights are a feature of many constitutions. Constitutional development in the UK has not produced an entrenched declaration of rights, as has happened in Germany and Ireland, but there are important pieces of legislation which have limited the power of the monarch. These include Magna Carta 1215, the Bill of Rights 1688, and an equivalent Scottish measure, the Claim of Right 1689. Other important pieces of legislation which have dealt with citizens' rights include the Public Order Act 1986, the Habeas Corpus Act 1679 and the Police and Criminal Evidence Act 1984 which deal with the freedom of the person (see chapter 13).

The period at the end of the 17th century and the start of the 18th was very important in the constitutional development of the UK. In addition to the Bill of Rights there was the Act of Settlement 1700, which not only dealt with the succession of the Crown but also secured the independence of the judiciary. The union of crowns in 1603 meant that the same person was the monarch in the two kingdoms of England and Scotland. This link was furthered by the Union with Scotland Act 1706 which established the United Kingdom of Great Britain (see further 2.3.2).

The field of administrative law provides important means of redress against officers, officials and agencies of the State, of which some significant statutes are the Crown Proceedings Act 1947 (see chapter 18), the Tribunals and Inquiries Act 1992 (see chapter 15) and the Parliamentary Commissioner Act 1967 (see chapter 15).

One statute with profound constitutional significance is the European Communities Act 1972. Through this piece of legislation the UK provided that Community law could become part of domestic law. Community law is itself an important source of constitutional law.

Statutes are primary legislation and, as this term suggests, there is another form of legislation, subordinate or secondary legislation, which includes measures made by ministers under power delegated by statute. There are different types of these measures, of which the most used is the statutory instrument. There are various degrees of Parliamentary oversight for statutory instruments and the other forms of subordinate legislation (see further 8.2.6).

A distinction may be drawn between the source of subordinate legislation and its form. The great majority of statutory instruments derive from powers granted in a statute but the royal prerogative is the source for Orders in Council which may take the form of statutory instruments (see 2.2.3).

2.2.2 Case Law

The decisions of the judges do more than decide a particular legal dispute, as they can provide general guidance. In the civil law countries of Western Europe much of the law has been codified and the place of decisions in which the judges have interpreted the code is not as important as the code itself. This is simply an aspect of the hierarchy of legal rules. In common law countries, however, the judges do more than interpret legislation, they also make law – the common law. In the hierarchy of legal rules in common law States, these judge-made rules are inferior to legislation and, if they possess one, the constitution. In the UK there are many areas of constitutional law in which the major source is the common law.

2.2.2.1 Common law Many of the significant constitutional cases have concerned the limits of governmental action affecting citizens. There is a series of cases in which it was held that the powers of arrest and search which were sought to be exercised by general warrants were illegal (*Entick* v *Carrington* (1765) 19 St Tr 1030; *Leach* v *Money* (1765) 19 St Tr 1002; *Wilkes* v *Wood* (1763) 19 St Tr 1153).

Some cases have dealt with the limits of the royal prerogative, such as the *Case of Proclamations* (1611) 12 Co Rep 74, in which it was held that the King could not alter the law of the land by a proclamation and that the King only had those prerogatives 'which the law of the land allows him'. On other occasions the King's claims were upheld by the judges. For example, in the

Case of Impositions (Bate's Case) (1610) 2 St Tr 371, the court accepted the argument that the King could tax goods entering the country without the consent of Parliament as this exercise of the prerogative related to the conduct of foreign affairs rather than raising revenue. Parliament responded to this with the Petition of Right 1627, and, as part of the Revolution settlement, the Bill of Rights 1688 made it quite clear that 'levying money for or to the use of the Crowne by pretence of prerogative without grant of Parlyament for longer time or in other manner than the same is or shall be granted is illegal' (art. 4).

The grounds of challenge in judicial review of administrative action have been entirely developed by the judges in the exercise of their inherent supervisory jurisdiction (see further chapter 16).

A final example of judge-made constitutional law is the doctrine of the legislative supremacy of Parliament, which is one of the UK's fundamental constitutional principles (see further 3.2).

2.2.2.2 Statutory interpretation When the judges are interpreting legislation they must bear in mind that such legal rules are at the top of the country's hierarchy of legal norms, and that the common law is therefore inferior. Yet the common law provides general constitutional principles and canons of construction which may be in opposition to the meaning of the legislation. This is not a problem if the legislation is expressed in clear language as the judges must loyally implement it. For example, in *R* v *Inland Revenue Commissioners, ex parte Rossminster* [1980] AC 952, the House of Lords upheld as valid search warrants issued under the Taxes Management Act 1970, s. 20C, even though the warrants did not specify any particular offences of which the company's officers were suspected. In *R* v *Secretary of State for the Home Department, ex parte Brind* [1991] 1 AC 696, the House of Lords upheld censorship provisions in the Broadcasting Act 1980 and the BBC's licence and agreement, pointing out that arguments based upon the European Convention on Human Rights were misplaced as the Convention had not been incorporated into domestic law.

Where the courts are dealing with subordinate legislation they have greater scope to argue that citizens' rights should not be adversely affected by anything other than the clear words of a statute. An example of this is *Director of Public Prosecutions* v *Hutchinson* [1990] 2 AC 783, which concerned some of the protesters against cruise missiles who had camped outside an RAF base (the 'Greenham Common women'). They had been charged with breaching by-laws made under the Military Lands Act 1892 which prohibited intrusion on to land. The House of Lords upheld the argument that, as the land in question was common land and the statute did not authorise the infringing of any rights in common, then the by-laws were unlawful and the convictions could not stand.

The courts have also held that it is unlawful to use subordinate legislation (a) to levy money (*Attorney-General* v *Wilts United Dairies Ltd* (1921) 37 TLR 884); (b) to restrict access to the courts to determine rights (*Commissioners of Customs and Excise* v *Cure and Deely Ltd* [1962] 1 QB 340); (c) to interfere with the liberty of the citizen (*Chester* v *Bateson* [1920] 1 KB 829).

One of the difficulties of construing legislation is that the courts are meant to give effect to the will of Parliament, but there was a rule that reports of proceedings in Parliament could not be used for guidance. This was overturned by the House of Lords in a tax case (*Pepper* v *Hart* [1993] AC 593). A panel of seven Law Lords held that it was permissible to refer to *Hansard* in order to discern the mischief aimed at, or the legislative intention behind, a provision which was ambiguous or obscure. Their lordships did not feel that to do this would be to breach either the Bill of Rights 1688, art. 9, or Parliamentary privilege. The purpose of art. 9 was to protect MPs when they took part in Parliamentary proceedings and this was not affected by the reference to *Hansard*, which did not impede those proceedings since the aim was to.seek guidance on legislation.

2.2.3   The Royal Prerogative

The royal prerogative is a residual source of authority which comprises power, privileges and immunities belonging to the Crown. The prerogative derives its authority from its recognition by the judges as common law. Part of the prerogative meant that royal proclamations provided authority for governmental actions. As we have seen, the scope of this prerogative power was limited in the *Case of Proclamations* (1611) 12 Co Rep 74 (see 2.2.2.1).

Foreign affairs is an aspect of government for which the authority comes from prerogative and this includes the signing of treaties and the declaration of war. The deployment of the armed forces is another prerogative power.

The prerogative also includes Orders in Council, which are a species of subordinate legislation. Recruitment to the civil service is regulated by such prerogative rules.

The aspects of the prerogative dealt with so far refer to power exercised on behalf of the government. Other parts of the prerogative are personal to the monarch and they include appointing the prime minister, assenting to legislation, dissolving Parliament, and conferring certain honours.

Finally, the prerogative also encompasses certain immunities such as the Crown is not bound by statute unless it is expressly provided or it is a necessary implication (see further 5.4.2).

The scope of prerogative power is declining because topics formerly regulated by prerogative have been superseded by legislation (see further 5.6 on the relationships between prerogative and (a) the courts, and (b) legislation).

2.2.4   Law and Custom of Parliament

Parliament is an extremely important institution which is very jealous of its powers and privileges. Some law relating to Parliament, such as electoral law, is statutory (see 7.3 to 7.7), but by and large most of the custom relating to the internal procedures of Parliament is outside the scope of legislation and the common law. Parliament is itself a court and the judges have been very careful not to intrude upon Parliament's internal affairs. There is, however, tension between the courts and Parliament as the courts hold that, as with the prerogative, they may determine the scope of Parliamentary privilege, whereas Parliament claims that it decides this matter (see further 7.8, especially 7.8.5).

2.2.5   European Sources

If the UK cannot be said to have its own codified constitution, it may be said that it does have an external constitution which comes from Europe and is shared with other signatories of (a) the treaties establishing the European Union, and (b) the European Convention on Human Rights.

2.2.5.1   Community law   Membership of the European Union has had a significant impact upon the UK's legal system and its substantive law, including constitutional and administrative law. Examples of this include (a) altering the fundamental doctrine of UK constitutional law, the legislative supremacy of Parliament; (b) improving the rights which citizens may enjoy in combating sex discrimination; and (c) adding to the grounds of challenge and available remedies in administrative law.

2.2.5.2   European Convention on Human Rights   Various rights have been protected in the UK, not by its national courts, but through the interpretation of the European Convention on Human Rights by the European Court of Human Rights which sits in Strasbourg. Under international law, States which have ratified the convention are bound to rectify breaches determined by the Strasbourg court, and it is this external obligation which has led to the vindication of rights, because the UK has no domestic declaration of rights and has not incorporated the convention into domestic law, so that its national courts cannot adjudicate upon it. The Labour government elected in May 1997 propose to enact incorporating legislation in the first session of the Parliament (see further chapter 12).

2.2.6   Authoritative Authors

Given the absence of a codified constitution, the writings of scholars and jurists on both the constitution of the UK and its law, may play an important part in our understanding of these matters. Some authors have produced works which have become very influential so that they are regarded as more than commentaries, indeed almost as substitutes for the UK's uncodified constitution. Bagehot, Dicey and Jennings are pre-eminent amongst those whose work is helpful on constitutional matters. Others include Anson, Bryce, Keith and Hood Phillips.

It must be remembered that, so far as the law is concerned, the authority of scholarly literature is only persuasive, though some academic writers really have influenced judges. This can be said of De Smith and the three editions of his book on judicial review of administrative action which were written before his death.

2.3   THE CONSTITUENT PARTS OF THE UK

The UK is a unitary State but it is also a multinational State containing three different legal systems. The UK consists of Great Britain and Northern

Ireland. England, Scotland and Wales constitute Great Britain. The largest of the UK's three legal systems is formed by England and Wales with the other two in Scotland and Northern Ireland.

The UK was formed in stages and we now consider the emergence of the union, looking at the situation in Wales, Scotland and Northern Ireland.

2.3.1 Wales

The defeat of Prince Llewellyn the Last in 1282 was the culmination of England's military conquest of Wales. Full union did not occur until the Laws in Wales Act 1536 was passed by the English Parliament. In the period between those two events Wales was subject to a variety of rulers. The principality, which did not consist of the whole of Wales, was administered on behalf of the Prince of Wales, while various local princes and lords governed in the remainder of the country. During this time the Welsh language, customs and laws coexisted with their English counterparts. There was a gradual process of integration which was furthered by the House of Tudor's succession to the Crown after the Wars of the Roses. Henry VII came from Welsh stock.

The 1536 statute brought about union between England and Wales by giving Wales representation in Parliament, requiring the English language to be used, and recasting the system of administration on the model of the English shires. Legislation passed in 1542 provided for a new legal system in which the Court of Great Session applied the English common law. This lasted until 1830 when the Welsh courts were assimilated into the English circuit system by creating two new circuits, Chester and North Wales, and South Wales. Monmouthshire was incorporated into the Oxford circuit.

In the 20th century central governmental bodies were given units designed to cater for Wales. The Welsh Disestablishment Act 1914 disestablished the Church of England in Wales. After the First World War greater decentralising steps were taken and a Minister for Welsh Affairs was created in 1951. This office was placed in the Home Office and then was transferred to the Ministry of Housing and Local Government in 1957. A Secretary of State for Wales was appointed in 1964 and this meant that there was now a separate Welsh Office whose ministerial head was a member of the cabinet. Examples of the responsibilities of the Welsh Office include local government, town and country planning, housing and transport.

The Welsh Language Act 1967 removed restrictions on the use of the Welsh language in official documents and in the courts in Wales. It also ended the rule that, in an Act of Parliament, England was deemed to include Wales (s. 4).

2.3.2 Scotland

Just as the English Crown had sought to take over Wales to the west, so it was with Scotland to the north. Hostilities between the two kingdoms were intermittent. The Scots secured an independence-saving victory at the Battle of Bannockburn in 1314 but a family relationship brought these neighbouring countries together when James VI of Scotland succeeded to the English crown and became that country's James I.

This union of the crowns did not immediately produce integration of the countries, their peoples and institutions. The King moved to London and the Scottish Parliament was managed by a committee known as the Lords of the Articles who were controlled by the King. It was in the final years of its life that the Scottish Parliament exerted a significant amount of independence following the abolition of the Lords of the Articles in 1690. Despite this tendency to independent action the Scottish Parliament decided to establish with their English counterpart a negotiating team of royal commissioners who were to work towards union. As in many important negotiations progress towards the desired outcome was not smooth. The Scottish Parliament passed an Act of Security in 1704 which provided that, on the death of Queen Anne, the succession to the Scottish throne would not be on the same basis as for England. The English Parliament retaliated with an Aliens Act 1705, the provisions of which would adversely affect the Scots in England and trade between the two countries unless Scotland also accepted that the succession to the two crowns should be the same. This exchange of legislative measures resulted in an agreement on union which came into being on 1 May 1707. Both Parliaments passed statutes giving effect to the Treaty of Union and in so doing voted for their own abolition. Article 1 provided for the union of the kingdoms of England and Scotland into the new kingdom to be known as the United Kingdom of Great Britain, and art. 3 established that this kingdom would be represented by the 'one and the same Parliament, the Parliament of Great Britain'. The Hanoverian succession to the monarchy of Great Britain was declared and arrangements were made for common matters, such as trade, weights and measures and coinage. The continuance of Scottish institutions including the courts and the administration of justice, the Presbyterian Church, the education system, and in particular the universities, were all guaranteed. While the Parliament of Great Britain could legislate upon public right, policy and civil government, alterations to private rights within Scotland could not be carried out except for 'evident utility'.

In the immediate post-union period there was a Secretary of State for Scotland in the government in London. An appointment to this office was not made after 1745; instead, responsibility for Scotland was given to other ministers. From 1782 it was the Home Office which was in charge of the Scottish portfolio. In practice the Lord Advocate, the chief Scottish law officer, was the person who exercised real power over Scottish affairs.

The Scottish Office was established in 1885 and its ministerial head has usually been in the cabinet since 1892. In 1926 the office of the Secretary of State for Scotland was made that of a Principal Secretary of State. Currently there are five departments within the Scottish Office: Home and Health, Education, Industry, Environment, Agriculture and Fisheries.

As the Scottish legal system differs from England and Wales, changes planned for the whole of the UK may require specific Scottish legislation. There are special Scottish standing committees in the House of Commons to which Scottish Bills will be committed as part of their passage through Parliament.

2.3.3 Northern Ireland

The discussion of Northern Ireland which follows will be longer than that given for Scotland and Wales. It will be a short summary of important constitutional points (see Hadfield (1989) on Northern Ireland's constitutional law).

2.3.3.1 Pre-union Before we deal with Northern Ireland, we must sketch in very briefly some of the history of Ireland as a whole.

Ireland's independence was weakened in the 12th century when the Normans 'invaded'. The English monarch, Henry II, added Lord of Ireland to his royal titles. The colonisation of Ireland was, however, a lengthy process. Although the Irish Parliament was prevailed upon to pass Poynings' Law in 1494, thereby giving the King and his Council in England a veto over Irish legislation, it was not until the Elizabethan period that Ireland was conquered. The military victory was consolidated by encouraging English and Scots settlers. The most successful of these 'plantations' was in the north-east of Ireland, in Ulster, which was somewhat ironic as that area had been the last to capitulate to the English.

The administration of Ireland during the 17th and most of the 18th centuries saw measures which advantaged Protestants, which included the English and Scots settlers, and a minority of the Irish. The Penal Laws were a series of measures which discriminated against Catholics, who formed the great majority of the native Irish. By the mid 18th century the elite class in Ireland were extremely dissatisfied with the various restrictions, in particular those relating to trade, which were imposed upon them by London. They desired more control over their own affairs and in this they were influenced by ideas and events in America. In 1782 their campaign was successful and the restrictions upon the powers of the Irish Parliament were removed, but the period of autonomy was short-lived. Doubts about the wisdom of granting 'home rule' to Ireland were confirmed by the failed rebellion of 1798. The cooperation between the rebels and the French had been especially worrying. Union between Great Britain and Ireland was felt to be desirable. The passage of the Act of Union through the Irish Parliament was secured by bribery, as it was rejected when first introduced into the Irish House of Commons. The union came into effect on 1 January 1801. The articles of the union first created a United Kingdom of Great Britain and Ireland in which the succession to the crown was on the same basis as that in the union between England and Scotland. To the existing Parliament were added Irish members, of which there were 100 MPs, four bishops and 28 temporal lords who were elected for life by the peers of Ireland. The Church of England and the Church of Ireland were united into the established Church of England and Ireland and the maintenance of this was 'deemed and taken to be an essential and fundamental part of the union' (art. 5). So far as trade was concerned, a few duties would be levied on some goods between Great Britain and Ireland for 20 years, otherwise the new UK was a single free trade area. The final two articles dealt with financial and legal matters.

2.3.3.2 Union and its dissolution The period of the union in Ireland was dominated primarily by two issues: first Catholic emancipation, and then home rule. It had originally been intended that Catholic emancipation would be part of the union legislation but this foundered upon the resistance of the Irish Parliament and a royal veto. Eventually, in 1829 the Catholic Emancipation Act was passed, which enabled Catholics to enter Parliament and hold civil and military positions.

Not only did home rule dominate Irish politics, but through the tactics of those Irish MPs who sought it, business in Parliament was conducted in its shadow. One of the consequences of this was the creation of new procedural rules (see 8.1.4).

It took three attempts before home rule was approved by Parliament in the Government of Ireland Act 1914, and then the statute was passed without the agreement of the House of Lords under the Parliament Act 1911 procedure. The first Home Rule Bill was defeated in the House of Commons in 1886 and the second was rejected by the House of Lords in 1893. Home rule was not wanted by the Protestant majority in Ulster and they determined to resist it by force of arms. The 1914 Act did not come into effect: it was suspended because of the First World War.

After the war the 1918 general election produced a Sinn Fein majority in all of Ireland except for the north-east. A provisional government was declared in Dublin and an Anglo-Irish War ensued with terrible atrocities on both sides. The next statute to deal with this constitutional issue was the Government of Ireland Act 1920 which partitioned Ireland and provided for two Parliaments in Dublin and Belfast. This was not liked by any of the parties in Ireland but the Unionists in the north preferred it to inclusion in an independent Ireland, which was the objective for the rest of the island. An Anglo-Irish Treaty was agreed in 1921 which gave to Ireland self-governing dominion status, equivalent to that of Canada, within the Commonwealth. There was an opt-out clause for Northern Ireland. This option was exercised and so Ireland was divided into the Irish Free State and Northern Ireland.

2.3.3.3 Devolution 1921–72 The Government of Ireland Act 1920 was the constitution for Northern Ireland. Under it there was a Parliament with a 52-member House of Commons, a 26-member Senate and a Governor who, as the representative of the Crown, could summon, prorogue and dissolve the Parliament as well as giving or withholding the royal assent to legislation. There were three categories of legislative power. Excepted matters were solely within the competence of Westminster, for which the criterion would seem to be the desirability of uniformity for the whole of the UK. Some of the excepted matters were foreign affairs, defence, naturalisation and weights and measures. A second category reserved some matters for Westminster. It would seem that the original intention behind the 1920 Act was that eventually these matters would be transferred to an all-Ireland parliament. The reality therefore became two classes of legislation outside the competence of the Northern Ireland Parliament. Amongst the reserved matters were the postal service, registration of deeds and the Supreme Court of Northern Ireland. The third category, known as transferred matters, was the general legislative power of the Northern Ireland Parliament. This was expressed as a power to make laws for 'peace, order, and good government . . . of Northern Ireland' (s. 4(1)).

These provisions made it clear that the Northern Ireland Parliament was a subordinate legislature but this was further emphasised by s. 75 which proclaimed the supreme authority of the Westminster Parliament over Northern Ireland notwithstanding any other provision in the 1920 Act.

During its life the Northern Ireland Parliament was dominated by one party, the Unionist Party. The major political issue was the constitutional one of the border: whether or not Northern Ireland should remain part of the UK or reunite with the rest of Ireland. The Unionists developed a siege mentality and sought to protect their position. A suspicion of those who sought a united Ireland led to discrimination against such people which could be justified because of their supposed disloyalty. There had been various campaigns of violence waged by those with nationalist aspirations but the great bulk of the minority community rejected violence.

In the 1960s sections of the minority community decided to turn to broader political issues and a campaign for civil rights was launched. The street demonstrations led to public order problems arising from the actions of some of their supporters and opponents to their cause. The disturbances escalated so that in 1969 the government in London consented to the request for the deployment of troops to aid the civil power in keeping order. This involvement of London continued as street disturbances were succeeded by more violent acts of terrorism. This involvement ended the convention that, so far as transferred powers were concerned, action by the UK government and Parliament would only be at the request of the Northern Ireland Parliament. The programme of reform was expanded and accelerated. The discrimination carried out by councils was dealt with by transferring their housing responsibilities to a new agency and by creating a special ombudsman, the Commissioner for Complaints, with the possibility of judicial enforcement of remedies (see 15.3.6). The local government franchise was changed from the basis of ratepayers, to one person, one vote. One council, which had notoriously gerrymandered (rigged) boundaries to produce a majority from a minority of the population, was disbanded.

The violence continued and in 1971 various 'suspects' were interned without trial under the Civil Authorities Special Powers Act (Northern Ireland) 1922. This action increased rather than diminished the violence as the internment of innocent people provided more recruits and sympathisers for the Irish Republican Army. Eventually in 1972 the Northern Ireland Parliament was prorogued and responsibility for Northern Ireland was moved from Belfast to London (Northern Ireland (Temporary Provisions) Act 1972).

2.3.3.4 Direct rule 1972–92 A new department was established to take over the government of Northern Ireland. It was hoped that the Northern Ireland Office would reduce its work by seeking a return to devolved government. This was reflected in the title and terms of the 1972 Act. The conditions for the establishment of a Northern Ireland government would not, however, be on the old basis of a simple majority, rather, such a government, or executive, would be required to be 'widely accepted throughout the community'. The legislative framework for this was conferred by the Northern Ireland Assembly Act 1973 and the Northern Ireland Constitution Act 1973. The first of these statutes provided for elections to the Northern Ireland Assembly. The Assembly was to have 78 members elected by the single transferable vote system of proportional representation. The 1973 Constitution Act stipulated the conditions for devolution as well as the powers that the Assembly and a Northern Ireland executive could exercise. This statute also contained a 'constitutional guarantee' to the effect that Northern Ireland would remain part of the UK unless a majority of its people voting in a poll consented to changed this status (s. 1, see Hadfield 1983; 1989, p. 105).

The legislative powers which could be devolved under the 1973 Act followed the tripartite classification used in the Government of Ireland Act 1920. Added to the original list of excepted matters were elections, the franchise in elections, special powers to deal with terrorism, and the appointment of magistrates and circuit judges. The basis for these additions was that the exercise of these powers by previous Northern Ireland governments had been controversial and divisive. Reserved matters included what might be termed law and order issues, such as the criminal law, the organisation and control of the police, and the maintenance of public order. These matters could be transferred to the Assembly if it had successfully established itself but the Assembly could legislate on these matters, exceptionally, if the Secretary of State for Northern Ireland and Westminster consented. All other matters fell into the transferred category which were within the competence of the Assembly.

The Assembly elections in June 1973 did lead to the creation of a three-party coalition which the Secretary of State felt could form an executive with widespread support in the community. Accordingly powers were devolved to the Assembly on 1 January 1974. This power-sharing executive did not last long. Its demise was brought about by a strike which, because of either the genuine or coerced support of the majority community, especially in the power stations, led the Unionist members to resign. The major cause of this discontent was the Sunningdale Agreement which had been negotiated in December 1973 by the UK and Irish governments and the Northern Ireland executive designate. The Unionist community was suspicious about the Agreement's provisions relating to the Council of Ireland, which was envisaged as an institution for the conduct of relations between Northern Ireland and the Republic of Ireland.

Direct rule was reintroduced by the Northern Ireland Act 1974. Under it and the 1973 Constitution Act, legislation for Northern Ireland, in the interim period, was to take the form of statutes for excepted matters, and Orders in Council for reserved and transferred matters. The use of the term 'interim period' makes clear that direct rule was once again envisaged as temporary.

A Constitutional Convention was to be elected so that the parties in Northern Ireland might try to come to an agreement which could lead to devolution. This was not reasonably foreseeable as the majority of the Unionist parties did not wish to have a power-sharing executive, nor an Irish dimension such as the Council of Ireland, whereas these were sought by the Social, Democratic and Labour Party (SDLP), the best-supported party in the minority community. Unsurprisingly the Constitutional Convention was unable to satisfy the widespread acceptability criterion for resuming devolution.

The next policy initiative was 'rolling devolution'. The intention behind the Northern Ireland Act 1982 was that an elected Assembly would have 'scrutinising, deliberative and consultative' functions and could make recommendations to the Secretary of State on how the Assembly could exercise all or any of the powers devolved under the 1973 Constitution Act. It was hoped by involving an Assembly in direct rule that the parties would be able to proceed gradually to the submission of proposals for a devolved executive which would either (a) have the support of 70 per cent of the members of the Assembly, or (b) be supported by the majority of members and be such as to satisfy the Secretary of State that they would command widespread acceptance throughout the community (Northern Ireland Act 1982, s. 1(4)). The Assembly did carry out a deliberative function and produced reports on proposals for legislation and other matters (see O'Leary, Elliott and Wilford 1988) but it did not lead to rolling devolution. Although the Assembly did consider how progress towards devolution might be made, this was done in the absence of the SDLP members who carried out their election promise of abstentionism.

The UK government became convinced that cooperation with the Irish government was an important factor in dealing with the political and terrorist aspects of the Northern Ireland problem. The two governments negotiated an Anglo-Irish Agreement in 1985 (Cmnd 9657). This Agreement sought to reassure both communities in Northern Ireland by recognising and respecting their identities and the right to pursue their aspirations by peaceful means. This was done in art. 1 by which both governments (a) affirmed that any change in the constitutional status of Northern Ireland would only come about with the consent of the majority of the people of Northern Ireland; (b) recognised that the present wish of the majority was for no change in the status of Northern Ireland; and (c) declared that in the future, if the people clearly wish for and consent to the establishment of a united Ireland, both governments would introduce and support legislation in their respective Parliaments to give effect to that wish.

Article 2 created an Intergovernmental Conference which would meet on a regular basis, at the level of either ministers or officials, to discuss political matters, security and related matters, legal matters (including the administration of justice), and the promotion of cross-border cooperation. The UK government accepted that the Irish government would put forward proposals within the remit of the Conference insofar as they were not matters transferred to a devolved administration within Northern Ireland. In art. 4(b) the Irish government accepted that it was the policy of the UK to seek a devolved administration in Northern Ireland which could command widespread acceptance.

It would seem that the combination of arts 2 and 4 is meant to encourage the Unionist parties in Northern Ireland to agree to a power-sharing executive by reducing the scope of the Intergovernmental Conference and the Irish government's consultative role in the governance of Northern Ireland. The fact that there is an irreducible role for the Irish government in the event of devolution is meant to reassure the nationalist community.

The Unionist parties were extremely unhappy about the Agreement, which affected them but about which they had not been consulted. They challenged it on several fronts: by resigning their seats at Westminster and fighting the ensuing by-elections as a kind of referendum on the Agreement; by a policy of non-cooperation with governmental bodies; and in the courts. Their application for judicial review of the Agreement in the High Court in London was unsuccessful (*Ex parte Molyneaux* [1986] 1 WLR 331). They argued that (a) the Agreement would impose fetters on the Secretary of State; (b) that this exercise of the treaty-making power with a foreign country would unlawfully differentiate between the rights enjoyed by the people of Northern Ireland and Great Britain, contrary to art. 6 of the Act of Union 1800; and (c) that the establishment of the Intergovernmental Conference in the UK for the purpose of influencing government was unlawful in the absence of implementing legislation. In dismissing the application it was held that (a) the discretion of the Secretary of State would not be fettered by the Agreement which stated that there be no derogation from the sovereignty of the UK government which retains responsibility for the decisions and administration of government within its own jurisdiction; (b) under the Ireland Act 1949 the Republic of Ireland was held not to be a foreign country and there would not be any differentiation between the rights of the people of Northern Ireland and Great Britain; (c) the Intergovernmental Conference was an international body rather than a body established in the UK and, as it had neither legislative nor executive powers, no implementing legislation was required; and (d) the court would not inquire into the exercise of the prerogative either in making or implementing the Agreement.

The challenge in the Irish courts was also unsuccessful (*McGimpsey* v *Ireland* [1990] 1 IR 110). It was argued that the Agreement was unconstitutional in that (a) the recognition of the present constitutional arrangements for Northern Ireland was inconsistent with arts 2 and 3 of the constitution which claim the whole of the island as part of the national territory; (b) that the Intergovernmental Conference fettered the power of the government to conduct foreign affairs contrary to arts 28 and 29; and (c) the Agreement committed the government to differentiate between the majority and minority communities in Northern Ireland contrary to art. 40 which guarantees equality of rights for citizens. The Supreme Court held that (a) whilst it was a constitutional imperative to seek the reintegration of the national territory, the *de facto* recognition of Northern Ireland did not entail an abandonment of the territorial claim; (b) the Agreement did permit the government to pursue its foreign policy in the manner it wished; and (c) the making of proposals in relation to the minority community did not amount to an abandonment of the majority community in Northern Ireland.

The unionists' opposition to the Agreement has not removed it. Instead they have recognised that they can only cancel it by negotiating a replacement. Such negotiations have been convened on two occasions in 1991 and 1992. They have had three strands: (a) relations between the parties in Northern Ireland; (b) relations between Northern Ireland and the Republic of Ireland and (c) relations between the Irish and UK governments. The negotiations have not resulted in a settlement. Accordingly direct rule continues and so does the machinery created under the Agreement.

2.3.3.5 Direct rule 1993–97 After the breakdown of the interparty talks the next initiative by the British and Irish governments was their Joint Declaration issued at Downing Street in December 1993 (Cm 2442; see Walker and Weaver 1994). In this Declaration the two governments gave various undertakings. The British government stated that it would uphold the democratic wish of a greater number of the people of Northern Ireland on whether they wished to remain in the UK or form a united Ireland (para. 4). The British government reaffirmed that it has 'no selfish strategic or economic interest in Northern Ireland' but its primary interest was in seeing peace, stability and reconciliation established by agreement among all the people who inhabit the island (para. 4). The Irish government stated that it would be wrong to attempt to impose a united Ireland, 'in the absence of the freely given consent of a majority of the people of Northern Ireland', and that any reintegration would have to be 'consistent with justice and equity, respect the democratic dignity and the civil rights and religious liberties of both communities' (para. 5). The Irish government also stated that, in the event of an overall settlement, it would 'as part of a balanced constitutional accommodation, put forward and support proposals for change in the Irish Constitution which would fully reflect the principle of consent in Northern Ireland' (para. 7). The two governments also made it clear that 'the achievement of peace must involve a permanent end to the use of, or support for, paramilitary violence', and if groups have a commitment to exclusively peaceful methods and show that they abide by the democratic process then they would be free to participate in democratic politics and 'to join in dialogue in due course between the Governments and the political parties on the way ahead' (para. 10).

The aims of the Declaration were to try to reassure the different political traditions in Northern Ireland that their rights, identities and aspirations would be protected; that consent would be necessary for any change in Northern Ireland's status and that such consent could not be coerced. If it was clear that aspirations could be achieved democratically then there was no place for violence. Accordingly, if paramilitary groups and their supporters gave up violence and demonstrated a commitment to the democratic process then they could play a part in future discussions on the way ahead.

In the period immediately after the Declaration there was not widespread acceptance of its principles. Hopes of peace were raised, however, in August 1994 when the IRA announced that it was ordering the cessation of its military activities and in October a similar announcement was made on behalf of loyalist paramilitary groups. Subsequently there has been some concern about the length of a 'quarantine' period in which groups who have previously supported violence demonstrate their commitment to the democratic process, before they may enter into talks. Representatives of Sinn Fein and of political parties closely associated with loyalist paramilitaries have had meetings with civil servants and a minister from the Northern Ireland Office.

In February 1995 the two governments produced a document entitled 'A New Framework for Agreement', which was accompanied by a document prepared by the British government entitled 'A Framework for Accountable Government in Northern Ireland'. The two documents deal with the different strands which had been the basis for discussion in the interparty talks in 1991 and 1992. 'A Framework for Accountable Government in Northern Ireland' deals with strand 1 and 'A New Framework for Agreement' is concerned with strands 2 and 3. In both documents it is made clear that the proposals are not meant to be blueprints to be imposed but points which can serve as a basis for discussion in future talks.

The British government's proposals for the creation of local institutions of government in Northern Ireland comprise:

(a)   A unicameral assembly with 90 members elected by proportional representation for a fixed four- or five-year term which would have responsibility for a range of topics at least as wide as that conferred upon the 1973 Assembly.

(b)   A system of committees of the Assembly would be established, to oversee the work of the Departments of the Northern Ireland Civil Service and other functions, the composition of the committees would be broadly in proportion to party strengths.

(c)   The Assembly would be complemented by a Panel, consisting of probably three persons elected from a single Northern Ireland constituency by proportional representation.

(d)   A system of checks and balances designed to secure confidence in the new institutions including, for example, that the Panel might nominate the Assembly members who would chair committees and also their deputies, who would be elected on weighted majorities, that the Panel might have the power to scrutinise legislation and refer it for judicial consideration; that legislation might require majority support in both a Committee and the Assembly, with provision in the case of contentious matters that approval be given by a weighted majority; that a Code of Practice could regulate the relationship between the Assembly and its Committees and also between the chairs of Committees and relevant Departments.

'A New Framework for Agreement' proposes new institutions to deal with relations between (a) the two parts of Ireland (the North–South axis) and (b) the British and Irish governments (the East–West axis). It is envisaged that a new North–South body would have the power to discharge or oversee delegated executive, harmonising or consultative functions over a range of matters which the two governments would designate in agreement with the parties, or which the administrations in the North and South of Ireland agreed to designate. The examples of possible executive matters which could be within the remit of the North–South body include sectors involving a natural or physical all-Ireland framework, EC programmes and initiatives and culture and heritage. Matters which were suggested as being candidates for the consultative function include agriculture and fisheries, industrial development, transport, energy and trade. It is envisaged that it would be a duty of service of posts in adminstration in the two parts of Ireland to participate in the North–South body (para. 25). There would be a framework of administrative support for the North–South body which would be drawn from the Northern Ireland and Irish civil services. The two governments expect that a Parliamentary Forum comprising representatives from agreed political institutions in Northern Ireland and from the Oireachtas (the Irish Parliament) would be established to consider matters of mutual interest.

The governments contemplate that the 1985 Anglo-Irish Agreement would be superseded by a new and more broadly based Agreement which would include an Anglo-Irish Intergovernmental Council, and an Anglo-Irish Intergovernmental Conference serviced by a permanent secretariat. The Conference would be the principal instrument for cooperation and partnership between the two governments on a wide range of issues concerning Northern Ireland and with relations between the parts of the island of Ireland. Matters which are transferred to the new political institutions in Northern Ireland would normally be excluded from consideration by the Conference. It is envisaged that there would be some association with the work of the Conference by representatives of the agreed political institutions in Northern Ireland.

In both framework documents reference is made to the protection of civil, political, social and cultural rights. Such rights could include freedom of political thought; freedom of, and expression of, religion, the pursuit of democratically national and political aspirations; the seeking of political change by peaceful and legitimate means; to live wherever one chooses without hindrance; and to equal opportunity in all social and economic activity regardless of class, creed, gender or colour. The protection of such rights would be in accordance with each State's constitutional arrangements and its international obligations. The adoption of a Charter or Covenant of Rights could be encouraged by the governments.

The aim of having talks involving all of the political parties proved difficult to realise. Some of the parties and the British government thought that the issue of the decommissioning of weapons held by paramilitary organisations should be carried out before talks. An international body chaired by the US Senator George Mitchell was charged with investigating and reporting on this issue. Its report in January 1996 found that those who had arms were not willing to dispose of them before entering negotiations. The report recommended that participation in negotiations must require adherence to six principles, which included the acceptance of being committed to exclusively democratic and peaceful means to achieving political ends and a willingness to engage in a process of decommissioning of arms which must be capable of verification by an independent commission. It was suggested that discussions on decommissioning might be considered in proceedings conducted in parallel with the general negotiations. Prime minister Major's response to the Mitchell Report in the House of Commons was that there seemed to be two ways to proceed to negotiations involving all of the parties; his preference was for decommissioning arms and then commencing talks, the other method drew on a point in the section of the Mitchell Report which dealt with confidence-building measures, in which it was noted that it had been suggested that an elective process could serve as the path to talks. Given the finding in the report about the unwillingness to accept the prior decommissioning, the British government proposed to explore an elective process. This was not well received by Irish nationalists and republicans. In the following month the IRA broke its ceasefire with a bomb in London's docklands. The British and Irish governments agreed to a plan which could lead to the holding of talks. The Northern Ireland (Entry to Negotiations) Act 1996 authorised the holding of elections to a Forum which would be a discussion body. Parties elected to it could then participate in negotiations which would deal with the various relationships identified in strands 1, 2 and 3.

The elections represented another innovation as they combined the normal single transferable vote system of proportional representation used in Northern Ireland with a regional list so that the 10 parties with the most votes would be entitled to have two representatives. This regional list enabled smaller parties which did not have any of their candidates elected in the multi-member constituencies to have representatives in the Forum and thus be eligible for participation in the talks. The additional criterion for such participation was that the parties were committed to exclusively peaceful means and would abide by the democratic process (Cm 3232, para. 8). Consequently whilst Sinn Fein had representatives elected they were barred from participating in the talks until the IRA declared a ceasefire.

A ceasefire was announced by the IRA in July 1997. Sinn Fein representatives would be eligible to take part in the talks if they agreed to the Mitchell principles, and the ceasefire had held for a minimum period of six weeks. It remains to be seen if the resumption of the talks in September 1997 will see all of the main parties participating, as two of the unionist parties withdrew in July, citing, amongst other things, unhappiness about the two governments' proposals for decommissioning. The Labour prime minister Tony Blair has stated that he hopes that the talks will have produced a settlement by May 1998 when their legislative authority expires. If a settlement is agreed amongst the parties it would then have to be approved by Parliament and in a referendum in Northern Ireland.

2.3.3.6 Analysis McCrudden (1989, 1994) has suggested that Northern Ireland exhibits two approaches to constitution making: (a) the pragmatic empiricist and (b) the constitutional idealist. The former approach is traditionally British and the latter is more common in the USA and Canada.

The Government of Ireland Act 1920 is an example of the pragmatic empiricist approach in that it sought to transplant to Northern Ireland the Westminster model of constitutional and political practice. The fact that the transplant did not work was because the legitimacy of Northern Ireland and its institutions was not accepted by a substantial section of its population who would have preferred to be citizens in an independent Ireland.

The constitutional idealist approach as identified by McCrudden has substantive and procedural aspects. The substantive aspect focuses upon the values of liberty, equality, justice and the institutions which are most likely to secure those values. The procedural aspect highlights institutions, process and methods. It is this latter facet of the constitutional idealist approach which has been used in the objective of trying to secure devolution which would command widespread acceptance. McCrudden argues it would be better to adopt the substantive aspect, for example, by creating a Bill of Rights which might address the problems faced by the minority community. Such a step might begin to answer the problem of legitimacy of the State and its institutions.

It would seem that the framework documents address McCrudden's point about substantive constitutional idealism, in that the proposed institutions and procedures are based on, and seek to promote, certain values. As Northern Ireland is a divided community, the two major identities should be given appropriate expression; the different political aspirations should be accorded parity of esteem; there should be equity of treatment and equality of opportunity; and constitutional change should be the result of consent.

As to McCrudden's suggestion that a Bill of Rights would be an appropriate measure for Northern Ireland, although the two governments do propose legislative protection of rights in the framework documents, the proposals appear to fall short of international human rights norms. Now that the new Labour government propose to incorporate the European Convention on Human Rights, this will presumably apply to Northern Ireland.

It seems that the scope of constitutional innovation in Northern Ireland was, under Conservative governments, confined by the concern that it could serve as an undesirable precedent for the rest of the UK. Conservative policy was against incorporation of the European Convention on Human Rights and devolution in Great Britain. The Labour government elected in May 1997 has a very different view on these issues. Devolution is considered in the next section.

2.4 DECENTRALISING REFORM PROPOSALS

Given that the formation of the UK was made from peoples in areas with distinctive identities, it is not surprising that there have been calls for devolution, or decentralisation. It is generally agreed that there should be a regional administration in Northern Ireland, but on the basis of cross-community support. The Labour and Liberal Democrat Parties wish to see widespread decentralisation to the nations and regions of the UK and such an arrangement is included in the Institute for Public Policy Research's proposal for a UK constitution (IPPR 1991).

2.4.1 Definitions
Before examining decentralisation proposals it would be sensible to define important terms. 'Devolution' is usually taken to mean that a superior body

grants powers to an inferior body and has the competence to override action taken by the inferior body within the range of transferred powers. The Kilbrandon Royal Commission (1973) identified three types of devolution: legislative, executive and administrative. If we take them in ascending order, administrative devolution could mean that the central government arranges for the execution or administration of policy to be carried out at a lower (regional) level. At the executive stage new institutions would be created which could devise polices and administer them but this would be done within a framework set by central government. Where legislative devolution is conferred the subordinate legislature has specified subjects transferred to it, which may be dealt with under a framework of its own design and it may legislate in addition to the powers exercised under the executive devolution model. As in Northern Ireland from 1921 to 1972, the superior legislature could intervene.

'Decentralisation' is a somewhat imprecise term. It seems to be preferred for this very reason as it can include transfers of power which might be devolution or which might be federal or somewhere in between. As we saw in 1.3.3 and 1.4.2, in a federal constitution the region may have exclusive competence over some subjects, none over other subjects, and share it with the federal body over further subjects.

2.4.2 Proposals: Past and Present

The rise of nationalism in Scotland and Wales in the 1960s led to the establishment of a Royal Commission on the Constitution in 1969. When they reported four years later, the commissioners were not unanimous in proposing a scheme for devolution, and two of them produced a substantial memorandum of dissent. They were, however, agreed in rejecting (a) separatism and the consequent break-up of the UK, and (b) federalism. The majority view was legislative devolution for Scotland and Wales, and administrative devolution for eight English regions.

A Scotland and Wales Bill was introduced into Parliament in 1976. It was rejected by the House of Commons. Two Bills, one each for Scotland and Wales were introduced in 1977 and, after important amendments had been made, were enacted. The Scotland Act 1978 provided for legislative devolution, and the Wales Act 1978 provided for executive devolution. Each of the directly elected assemblies was to be financed by a block grant from Westminster. The arrangements were to come into effect after a referendum was held in each country. The important amendment mentioned above required that the 'yes' vote must not only be a majority of those votes cast, but also amount to a minimum of 40 per cent of those entitled to vote. In neither country was this 40 per cent threshold reached. Voting took place on 1 March 1979 and the figures were as follows:

	Yes	No	Abstained
Scotland	32.5%	30.4%	37.1%
Wales	11.9%	46.5%	41.7%

The lack of enthusiasm for the devolution schemes in the 1978 statutes led to a reduction in the demand for decentralisation, although separatist nationalist candidates continued to be elected to Parliament in Scotland and Wales. The issue was placed back on the political agenda after the 1987 general election in which the Conservative Party, while gaining a large majority in England, only won 10 out of 72 seats in Scotland. After the publication by the Campaign for a Scottish Assembly of *A Claim of Right for Scotland* in 1988, which called for a Scottish Parliament, a Scottish Constitutional Convention was convened in 1989. This body drew its members from Scotland's elected representatives, the churches, business, industry, trade unions. It was, however, boycotted by the Conservative and Scottish National Parties. Their report, *Towards Scotland's Parliament* (Scottish Constitutional Convention 1990), recommended the creation of a directly elected Scottish Parliament which would have legislative powers for non-UK matters. Issues which related to the UK as a whole would remain with Westminster. The scheme was quasi-federal in that the consent of the Scottish Parliament was required to permit Westminster to amend the transferred powers. The Scottish Parliament's finance would come from tax revenue raised in Scotland plus equalisation payments made from the UK exchequer.

2.4.2.1 Current proposals The manifesto of the Labour government elected in May 1997 promised a Scottish Parliament and a Welsh Assembly and proposed facilitating the establishment of English regional assemblies where these were sought by local populations.

The Referendums (Scotland and Wales) Act 1997 reverses the approach used in the 1970s. On 11 and 18 September 1997 the people resident in Scotland and Wales, respectively, can vote for or against the principle of the relevant decentralising proposals and only if they are approved will legislation be brought before Parliament. To assist the voters details of the proposed schemes were outlined in White Papers published in July 1997 (*Scotland's Parliament*, Cm 3658, and *A Voice for Wales*, Cm 3718) and summaries will be delivered to every household. The referendum in Scotland will have two questions, with the second asking whether the Parliament should have a tax-varying power.

Broadly the current proposals are similar to their predecessors. Scotland would be given legislative devolution and Wales executive and administrative devolution. Members of the Scottish Parliament and Welsh Assembly would be elected by a combination of the traditional Westminster Parliament 'first past the post' (see 7.6) and an additional member system. Each voter would have two votes: one for an individual candidate using first past the post in the Westminster constituencies, and the other for a party. Each party would provide its list of candidates from which its share, if any, of the additional members would be drawn. These additional members would be linked to the European Parliamentary constituencies which consist of groups of Westminster constituencies. The additional members would be elected on the basis of the total votes cast for each party in the European Parliamentary constituencies divided by the total seats won by that party for the Scottish Parliament or Welsh Assembly within that European constituency plus 1. The party with the highest number of votes after this calculation would then be entitled to an additional member. This calculation would be repeated so as to elect the prescribed number of additional members for that European constituency, with the difference that in the subsequent counts a party which has any elected additional members will have that total added to its number of seats (the divisor in the formula). *A Voice for Wales* gave an example drawn from the votes cast at the May 1997 general election. Using one of the five European constituencies (Mid and West Wales) the eight Westminster constituencies within it returned 4 Labour, 2 Liberal Democrat and 2 Plaid Cymru MPs. Under the proposed system the party distribution of the 4 additional members would be 1 to Labour and 3 to the Conservatives.

In the event of a vacancy there would be a by-election where the former member was elected by first past the post. In the case of an additional member vacancy the party of the outgoing member would be able to nominate the successor.

It is not proposed to debar members of the Westminster or European Parliaments or local authorities from membership of the Scottish Parliament or Welsh Assembly.

The term of the two bodies will be four years although only the Scottish Parliament will have the power to dissolve itself before the expiry of that term. It is proposed that the first elections to the two bodies would take place in 1999, with the Welsh Assembly meeting later that year and the Scottish Parliament in 2000.

In both Scotland and Wales the financial arrangements would, predominantly, be a continuation of the current situation of a block grant in which changes are made according to the 'Barnett formula', which allocates funds to various programmes in Scotland and Wales (and Northern Ireland) on the basis of the comparable programmes in England. This arrangement favours the Scots and the Welsh (and the Northern Irish) as they enjoy higher per capita expenditure than the UK average. If the second question in the Scottish referendum is approved, the Scottish Parliament could increase or decrease, by a maximum of 3 pence in the pound of the basic rate of income tax levied in Scotland. The basic rate of income tax would continue to be set by Westminster. Both the Parliament and Assembly would have a role to play in scrutinising European Community legislative proposals, and also in forming UK policy on European issues.

The responsibility for the staff in the Scottish and Welsh Offices would be transferred to the Scottish Parliament and Executive, and the Welsh Assembly, but the staff would remain in the home civil service

2.4.2.2 Scotland Under the proposals in *Scotland's Parliament* there would be a total of 129 members of the Scottish Parliament (MSPs). Scotland has 72 Westminster constituencies, but it is proposed that the Shetland and Orkneys constituency should have representation from both groups of islands, making 73 MSPs to be elected by the first past the post system, and 56 additional members. The Scottish Parliament would have an executive drawn, it is envisaged, from one party. There would be a first minister appointed by the Queen on the advice of the Scottish Parliament's Presiding Officer, following nomination by the MSPs. The Presiding Officer, whose role would be equivalent to that of the Speaker of the House of Commons, would be elected by the MSPs, as would be two deputies. The basis for the division of powers between the Scottish and UK Parliaments would be roughly that matters which the Scottish Office deals with would be given to the Scottish Parliament. Unlike the Scotland Act 1978, the proposed new legislation would allocate the legislative competencies by listing those which would be reserved at Westminster. This is a more comprehensible approach than stipulating all those which are to be devolved. The White Paper envisages that powers retained at Westminster will include: UK constitutional issues; foreign and defence policy; the fiscal, economic and monetary system; common markets for UK goods and services, employment; social security and transport safety and regulation. The matters which the Scottish Parliament and executive could deal with would be: health; education and training; local government, social work and housing; economic development and transport; law and home affairs; the environment; agriculture, fisheries and forestry; sport and the arts.

The Presiding Officer would have the task of conducting pre-legislative scrutiny so as to ensure that Bills introduced into the Scottish Parliament are not *ultra vires*, that is, that they do not exceed the boundaries of the Parliament's legislative powers. The Executive would also be expected to ensure that Bills which they propose are not *ultra vires* and they would consult the Scottish executive law officers and perhaps seek other advice. Before legislation was given the royal assent there would be a pause so that the UK government could be assured that it is not *ultra vires*. Any unresolved dispute could be referred to the Judicial Committee of the Privy Council for determination. The Judicial Committee would be composed of Lords of Appeal in Ordinary (Law Lords), and would sit with a minimum of five. The Judicial Committee would also have jurisdiction to deal with other devolution disputes concerning secondary legislation or Acts of the Scottish Parliament which have received royal assent.

2.4.2.3 Wales According to *A Voice for Wales*, the Welsh Assembly will have a total of 60 members of which 20 will be elected under the additional member provisions. The Assembly's role will be that of taking over responsibility for policies and services currently exercised by the Secretary of State for Wales. These matters include economic development; agriculture, forestry, fisheries and food; industry and training; education; local government; health and personal social services; housing, the environment, planning, transport and roads; arts, culture and the Welsh language; the built heritage; sport and recreation. In respect of these matters the Assembly will set policies and standards, and allocate resources for the delivery of services in Wales, and will also monitor the work of unelected public bodies. The Assembly will also be able to act as a forum for debating issues of concern within Wales. Some of the decisions taken by the Assembly will be capable of implementation through its power to make Orders, which are a type of secondary legislation. There will be a series of subject committees and an Executive Committee comprised of the people who chair the various subject committees. The subject committees will consider, within their remit, policy and its administration The Audit Committee and the Secondary Legislation Scrutiny Committee will be chaired by members from minority parties. The Audit Committee will not usurp the role of the Public Accounts Committee (PAC) of the House of Commons (see 8.4.3). The PAC might delegate evidence-taking to the Audit Committee or pursue further an investigation about which the Audit Committee expressed concern. The Secondary Legislation Scrutiny Committee will consider draft Assembly Orders to ensure that they fall within the legislative powers of the Assembly. Orders will have to be approved by the Assembly as a whole but the relevant subject committee will be able to make amendments as well as being able to consult and to take expert evidence about them. These arrangements mean that the scrutiny such orders would receive will be more intensive than that currently given to secondary legislation at Westminster (see 8.2.6).

The Assembly will elect a Presiding Member and a deputy (who must be from a minority party). The leader of the Executive Committee will be chosen by the Assembly.

Primary legislation for Wales will continue to made at Westminster but the Assembly will have a consultative role. It is proposed that there be a requirement on the Secretary of State for Wales to consult the Assembly after the announcement of proposed legislation in the Queen's Speech. The Secretary of State can attend these sessions and answer questions but not vote.

2.4.3 Analysis

There are several difficult issues which must be considered in any scheme for decentralisation. Three of these will be discussed. Some general issues will be considered and then some points related to the current proposals.

2.4.3.1 Symmetry? Whilst the UK is made up of nations and regions, should all of these territorial units be treated in the same way? Scotland has been driving the decentralisation debate and it would seem that there is a large amount of support for a Scottish legislature. This does not seem to be true for Wales or for the English regions. Should Scotland be given a legislature and the rest of the UK executive and administrative devolution, or should all of the nations and regions have their own legislatures? In other words, should the decentralising arrangements be symmetrical, as in a federal State, with all of the regions given the same range of powers, or not? Advocates of 'decentralisation all round' argue that in a centralised State the regions suffer because central government is too remote and unresponsive to their needs and concerns. Decentralised government would be more efficient, effective, responsive and accountable and it could promote greater participation of citizens in decisions which affect them (Marquand 1989). Some supporters of asymmetrical or 'lopsided' decentralisation take the view that only in Scotland is the case for a legislature persuasive and that executive or administrative devolution is appropriate for Wales and the English regions. It would seem that the English regions, especially those neighbouring Scotland take the view that if Scotland was given a measure of autonomy then they would require the freedom to devise and implement their own industrial policies in order to be able to compete for inward investment.

Spain is one example of a country which has a system of 'lopsided' decentralisation.

2.4.3.2 'The West Lothian question' One of the reasons why some people support the idea of decentralisation all round is because of a point raised during the passage of the Scotland and Wales Bills by the MP for West Lothian, Tam Dalyell. He wanted to know whether it would be appropriate for Scottish MPs at Westminster to take part in debates and vote on matters which related only to England since the Assembly would be the Scottish legislature for such matters. This does seem to be a question of fairness. However, during the period of the Northern Ireland Parliament, few objected to the MPs representing Northern Ireland constituencies participating in matters which affected only Great Britain (see Mount 1992, p. 201). This may have been because there were only 12 MPs from Northern Ireland. The region's representation at Westminster had been reduced because of its Parliament. If there is a system of asymmetrical decentralisation the suggestion has been made that there could be new rules of procedure at Westminster which would exclude MPs who represent any area with a legislative assembly from participating in business relating to other parts of the UK which do not have decentralised legislative powers for those matters (Oliver 1991b, p. 103). This 'in and out' participation of some Westminster MPs would be untidy. 'The West Lothian question' does point out an anomaly but then the current arrangements are anomalous, with some in Scotland arguing that during the period 1979–97 Scotland sent a majority of Labour MPs to Westminster but was ruled by a Conservative government.

2.4.3.3 Finance One of the difficult practical problems for decentralising schemes concerns the arrangements for financing the regional bodies. The 1978 statutes provided that the Scottish and Welsh assemblies would be given block grants so that tax spending was devolved but not tax raising. Such an arrangement seems bound to create tension between the regional and central tiers of government, as the region will inevitably complain that the grant is insufficient to give it the ability to meet what it perceives to be its area's particular needs. The lack of responsibility for, and power to raise, finance will also cut against the suggested benefits of decentralisation, namely, improved accountability, responsiveness and effectiveness. If a region is given a tax-raising power it may discover that if the local economy is depressed its tax base is also insufficient to meet its needs, which could mean that the standard of public service provision varies from region to region. In a unitary State it is accepted that the richer areas will subsidise the poorer regions. If central government is to make equalisation payments, it will wish to specify their purposes and so we could again have a difficult relationship between the two tiers of government. There might be tension amongst the regions if decentralisation was lopsided, as those regions which were net contributors might not be willing to continue to support subsidy if they had a lesser degree of decentralisation.

Detailed proposals which have been put forward to deal with the financial aspect of decentralisation have supposed that the English regions would be included and this fresh-start approach makes it easier and essential to devise a formula which would govern initial allocations and equalisation payments (IPPR 1991; Constitution Unit 1996a).

2.4.3.4 Disputes Finance is only one area in which there might be disputes between the proposed Scottish and Welsh bodies and Westminster. As the Welsh Assembly has no tax-raising powers it can only argue that Wales should obtain more funds in its block grant. The Scottish Parliament may be given a tax-varying power, but the most it could raise is around £450 million, so it is likely that could lead to Scottish pressure to increase the block grant. There could be other disputes between these bodies. All would be political but there could be a legal dimension in that the Acts of the Scottish Parliament and the Orders of the Welsh Assembly could be subject to challenge as being *ultra vires*. Those who fear that decentralisation could lead to the break-up of the United Kingdom, especially Scots who do not desire an independent Scotland, suggest that the limits of the devolution would be tested in political and legal trials and that defeat in the courts might allow the Scottish National Party to gain support for the proposition that Scots must be allowed to govern themselves, that devolution is not enough and that independence is the solution.

A Voice for Wales does not elaborate on the mechanisms for challenging the *vires* of Assembly Orders, but it may be presumed that this would be through an application for judicial review (see chapters 16 and 17). *Scotland's Parliament* proposes that the Judicial Committee of the Privy Council would deal with Scottish devolution disputes. The Constitution Unit (1997a) suggested that despite the history of the Privy Council as a constitutional court for some Commonwealth countries, the nature of some of the cases raising devolution issues was such that they would also involve other matters of law which would otherwise be determined in the House of Lords. Accordingly they suggested that the House of Lords might be the better court to deal with all of the issues. This fits in with the generalist tradition, but consideration might be given to taking the opportunity to create a new constitutional court. The argument in favour of this is reinforced by the plan to incorporate the European Convention on Human Rights.

Jones (1997) makes a very important point that whichever court is given jurisdiction to determine devolution issues, it would be assisted by the listing of values in the devolution legislation, which would enable it to have a context to assist its interpretation so as to ensure that the vision behind, and the objectives of, devolution could be secured. Such a teleological, or purposive approach to interpretation is used by the European Court of Justice when considering the treaties which are the fundamental law of the European Union (see 9.4). In some cases it might be easy to determine that a Scottish Act went beyond the powers allocated to the Scottish Parliament, whereas in others it might be less clear. If the legislation listed, for example, the value of subsidiarity, i.e., the idea that power should be allocated to the lowest level, then this would aid the court. Jones also suggests that other values could include equality before the law, equivalence of rights of all UK citizens and freedom of trade. As was pointed out in the discussion on Northern Ireland, the traditional British pragmatic empiricist approach to constitution building has not focused heavily upon values (2.3.3.6). To include values in devolution legislation would be a welcome and necessary continuation of the trend which has recently been applied in policy on Northern Ireland. Its use would not be unusual in the Scottish context as the Act of Union 1707 contained values which were to underpin the union.

2.4.3.5 Prospects If the people in Scotland and Wales vote for the Parliament and Assembly then this would be a dramatic change in the UK's constitutional arrangements. Whether or not it leads to the break-up of the union, it will lead to the development of more constitutional law, to which a specialised court will be contributing case-law. If one adds to this the proposed incorporation of the European Convention on Human Rights, then the UK will have most of the elements to be found in written constitutions. Perhaps we are about to embark upon a process of 'constitution creep', whereby we gradually acquire a constitution through accumulation. Instead of creating a constitution afresh, we could consolidate and codify the various parts. Adoption by referendum could give us a constituent power and constituent act and signal a break from what is currently the most important of our fundamental constitutional principles and doctrine — legislative supremacy. We examine these fundamentals next.

CHAPTER THREE

Fundamental Principles and Doctrines of Constitutional Law

3.1 CONSTITUTIONAL AUTHORITY

Following Bryce and Ridley, we have defined a constitution according to the characteristics that it is a constituent act made by a constituent power comprising superior law which is entrenched (see 1.2). Such a constitution typically creates a system of law and government in which institutions are empowered to make, apply and interpret law. As the constitution is supreme law this means that it will not only provide criteria for determining the validity of any law, but also for allocating laws to different levels in a hierarchy of legal norms. Thus certain procedures may be stipulated for legislation to be recognised as law, though a measure may meet those criteria and still be denied legal effect because it is inconsistent with some provision of the constitution which is supreme law.

In this analysis the constitution supplies the authority for law and the operation of government, and the basis for the constitution itself is the constituent power. Generally, the people are regarded as having the authority to make a constitution and the institutions and powers which it creates. This is the idea of popular sovereignty. We saw this, for example, in Ireland and the USA. The Irish constitution of 1937 was adopted after a majority of the people voted for it in a referendum, while the US constitution was adopted by the representatives of the people in the legislatures of the various States.

If the people provide the authority for a constitution in the narrow sense of a document which is fundamental law, do the people in the UK provide the authority for their constitutional arrangements? As the UK is a State which considers itself to be a parliamentary democracy, in which representatives are elected to a body empowered to make legislation and which holds the government to account, it would appear that the operation of the system of government derives its legitimacy from the will of the people. But what are the origins of this system? As we saw in 2.1, constitutional arrangements in the UK have evolved from feudal notions of a monarch who wielded sovereign power through the balanced and liberal constitutions, to the current liberal democratic framework. This evolutionary process has not taken the form of a seamless web. At one time there was a document which was a constitution, the Instrument of Government, under which the Cromwells ruled in the short-lived 17th-century republican Commonwealth. It was the Glorious Revolution towards the end of the 1680s which saw a more lasting constitutional change, transferring power from the monarch to Parliament.

The work of theorists of law may assist us in determining the legal basis of our constitutional arrangements. Hart (1961) has suggested that in regarding law as a system of rules a distinction must be drawn between primary and secondary rules. Primary rules are rules of obligation whereas secondary rules provide the means for (a) recognising rules, (b) changing them through new enactments and repeal, and (c) adjudicating upon them. Rules of recognition provide the criteria for validity of laws and this may cope with hierarchies of superior and subordinate rules by the specification of a supreme criterion. Where a constitution is supreme law, then that constitution will operate as the supreme criterion for validity. If that constitution is capable of amendment then the rule of recognition will take that into account in providing the means for determining the validity of law.

In the UK it would appear that the rule of recognition is the legislative supremacy of Parliament. Not only does it provide the supreme criterion for validity, meaning that legislation is superior to any other source of law, but it also means that Parliament is unlimited in its lawmaking competence, a factor which marks out this legislature from most others in the world.

3.2 THE TRADITIONAL VIEW OF LEGISLATIVE SUPREMACY

The legislative supremacy of Parliament is a legal doctrine which refers to the relationship between the courts and Acts of Parliament. The nature of this relationship is that the courts must give effect to Acts of Parliament. They may not deny them legal effect, as could happen in the USA and Ireland, where incompatibility with the constitution is the basis on which the courts may strike down legislation. The judges accept this limitation. In *Pickin v British Railways Board* [1974] AC 765 Lord Reid said, at p. 782:

> In earlier times learned lawyers seem to have believed that an Act of Parliament could be disregarded insofar as it was contrary to the law of God or the law of nature or natural justice, but since the supremacy of Parliament was finally demonstrated by the Revolution of 1688 any such idea has become obsolete.

The classical exposition of this doctrine was given by Dicey (1959). He gave it the name 'Parliamentary sovereignty'. Unfortunately, 'sovereignty' is a term which has several meanings, including the political concept of ultimate power, or a State's independence in international law. In order to minimise confusion the doctrine will be referred to here as 'legislative supremacy', though Dicey's term is used by some writers and judges.

In Dicey's formulation, the legislative supremacy of Parliament had two aspects, the positive and the negative. The positive side is that Parliament can 'make or unmake any law whatever', and the negative aspect is that no person or body is recognised as having the 'right to override or set aside the legislation of Parliament' (Dicey 1959, p. 40).

3.2.1   Unlimited Legislative Authority

To say that Parliament can make or unmake any law whatsoever is to assert a major claim. There is evidence to show that Parliament has exercised significant legislative power. Examples of this omnicompetence will now be given relating to (a) the succession to the Crown, (b) Parliamentary terms, composition and procedures, (c) space; and (d) time.

3.2.1.1 Succession   The most important statute regulating the succession to the Crown is the Act of Settlement 1700, which limits the Crown to the Protestant heirs of the Princess Sophia. Today we have no reservations about the competence of Parliament to legislate upon this matter but, as Dicey pointed out, this was, at the time, a controversial action by Parliament. This was a period in which there were rival theories about kingship. The Stuarts inclined to the divine right of kings and this led to war and the execution of Charles I. After the restoration of the monarchy, James II took a different view about his powers from that of Parliament and this resulted in the Crown being taken away from him and given to William and Mary, which was confirmed by the Bill of Rights 1688. James II had not given up the throne, although his disposal of the Great Seal of the Realm in the River Thames and subsequent departure from the country could be construed as amounting to that. Matters were quite different when it was felt that it was inappropriate for King Edward VIII to remain on the throne if he married the American divorcee Mrs Simpson. He renounced his personal right, and that of any of his heirs, to the throne by His Majesty's Declaration of Abdication Act 1936. This clearly affirmed that an Act of Paliament was the proper method by which to carry out changes to the line of succession.

3.2.1.2 Parliamentary terms   Parliament has on several occasions prolonged its own life. This may be regarded as exceptional but justified when done during wartime (Prolongation of Parliament Acts 1940, 1941, 1942, 1943, 1944). The passage of the Septennial Act 1715 which extended the life of a Parliament from three to seven years was justified because of fears that conflict might be imminent with the Jacobites, the supporters of the Stuart pretenders to the throne. Dicey argues that the 1715 statute was important in demonstrating that Parliament was neither 'the agent of the electors nor in any sense a trustee for its constituents' (1959, p. 48). Opposition to the Septennial Act 1715 had made the argument that the House of Commons had been elected for three years and that MPs were no longer the representatives of the people when Parliament prolonged its existence. Their period in office beyond the original three years came about through Parliament's actions rather than the people's choice. It is this assertion by Parliament that it was not bound by such conceptions about its relationship with the electorate which is the significant point about this statute.

The Parliament Act 1911 reduced the life of a Parliament to five years (s. 7).

3.2.1.3 *Parliamentary composition*

The membership of Parliament has been regulated by statute. The biggest changes were brought about by the Acts of Union when Parliament became first that of the United Kingdom of Great Britain, and then the United Kingdom of Great Britain and Ireland (Union with Scotland Act 1706, Union with Ireland Act 1800).

The basis for membership of the House of Lords used to be hereditary but this was changed by the Life Peerages Act 1958. Under this statute individuals may be made Barons or Baronesses entitling them to sit and vote in the House of Lords, but this right ceases upon their death and does not pass to their heirs, in contrast to the position applying to hereditary peers (see further 7.2).

3.2.1.4 *Parliamentary procedures*

Statutes are made by the Queen in Parliament, a body which has three components, the Queen and both Houses of Parliament. The Parliament Act 1911 amended this so that under certain conditions the approval of the House of Lords was not required for a Bill to become an Act. In effect the House of Lords was given a suspensory veto. The period of this veto was reduced by the Parliament Act 1949 (see further 8.6).

Whilst the Parliament Act 1911 removed money Bills from the requirement of approval by the House of Lords (s. 1), it explicitly stipulated that if a Bill sought to extend the maximum duration of a Parliament beyond five years, then such a Bill could not be presented for royal assent following the observance of procedures which permit dispensing with the approval of the House of Lords (s. 2(1)).

The Regency Act 1937 provides for the functions of the monarch to be undertaken by a regent when the monarch is under 18 at the time of accession. These functions include giving assent to Bills, unless a Bill seeks to change the order of succession or to alter or amend legislation relating to the Protestant religion and Presbyterian church government in Scotland (s. 4(2)).

3.2.1.5 *Space*

One might think that the UK Parliament legislates only for the territory of the UK, but statutes have been passed which are intended to have effect beyond the boundaries of the State. This is partially explained by the legacy of a colonising history. There has been a pattern in which land is claimed in the name of the Crown and then, gradually, a measure of self-government is granted, though they are still subject to any legislation which might be enacted at Westminster. Usually the grant of independence would end the involvement of the Parliament at Westminster. This was not the arrangement with some of the countries which were accorded independence in the first half of the 20th century. In most respects these countries were independent States and it was agreed that the Westminster Parliament would only enact legislation concerning them at their request (Statute of Westminster 1931, s. 4). Two of these countries were Canada and Australia and amendments to their constitutions could only be validly made if Westminster enacted them. Patriation of their constitutions, that is, the transfer to a country of responsibility for all matters relating to its constitution, was achieved with the passage of the Canada Act 1982 and the Australia Act 1986.

Legislation can apply to subjects of the monarch outside the UK. It will only be when such persons return to this country that the courts would then be able to try issues relating to that legislation which occurred in other countries. The War Crimes Act 1991 allows the UK courts to try people accused of committing certain war crimes abroad if they were, on 8 March 1990, or have subsequently become, a British citizen, or resident in the UK, the Isle of Man, or any of the Channel Islands. This means that people who, at the time of the commission of the alleged war crime, were not British subjects or otherwise amenable to trial in UK courts, can now be tried in the UK. This is the closest that Parliament has come to the situation which Jennings used to illustrate the lack of territorial limits upon Parliament's legislative supremacy. He stated that Parliament could enact that smoking in the streets of Paris is a criminal offence. Such a UK law would not have any effect on French law or cause the French police to enforce it. If a French individual did come to the UK, however, then a prosecution for breach of this law could be heard in our courts.

An example of a case in which the courts have ruled that a statute has extraterritorial effect is *Mortensen v Peters* (1906) 14 SLT 227. The Herring Fishery Board for Scotland had exercised its powers under the Herring Fishery (Scotland) Act 1889, s. 7, to make by-laws regulating fishing in the Moray Firth. Part of the Moray Firth is in international waters and the appellant had been in international waters when he was arrested for a breach of the by-laws. He was convicted in the Sheriff Court. He appealed unsuccessfully against his conviction. The High Court of Justiciary held that the clear words of the legislation included all of the Moray Firth, and this could not be restricted by a presumption that Parliament would not legislate in contravention of the principles of international law.

3.2.1.6 Time Usually legislation will take effect after it has received the royal assent. Sometimes Parliament enacts a measure which is to take effect retroactively, that is, before the statute is passed. An example of this is the War Damage Act 1965. This measure was a response to the decision in *Burmah Oil Co. Ltd v Lord Advocate* [1965] AC 75 in which the House of Lords held that compensation was payable in respect of action taken by troops in Burma during the Second World War. The statute declares that no compensation will be payable by the Crown in respect of damage done 'whether before or after the passing of this Act, within or outside the United

Kingdom' where this was the result of acts lawfully done by, or on the authority of the Crown during, or in contemplation of the outbreak of a war (s. 1(1)). It was further stated that, where proceedings to recover compensation in such circumstances have been instituted before the passing of the Act, then the court can dismiss the proceedings subject only to determining any question relating to costs (s. 1(2)).

This is quite an extraordinary statute which surely offends against most people's sense of justice. Yet such is the legislative supremacy of Parliament that it seems the courts will ascribe retrospective force to Acts interfering with rights, unless it can be shown that the statute's language is too vague or that there is no necessary implication that this was the intention of Parliament (*Phillips v Eyre* (1870) LR 6 QB 1).

3.2.1.7 Indemnity The War Damage Act 1965 could be regarded as a variant of legislation which is passed to indemnify people who have broken the law. Once again, actions carried out in time of war provide examples of this: Indemnity Act 1920, War Charges Validity Act 1925. The action of the Secretary of State for Social Services and the actions of commissioners he had appointed had to be indemnified after the High Court held that his replacement of members of a regional health authority by commissioners was unlawful (*Lambeth London Borough Council* v *Secretary of State for Social Services* (1980) 79 LGR 61). The statute which regularised this situation was the National Health Service (Invalid Direction) Act 1980. It was passed within a month of the decision. The record for passage of a statute reversing an inconvenient decision is 24 hours. The Northern Ireland Act 1972 was enacted the day after *R (Hume)* v *Londonderry Justices* [1972] NI 91. The decision held that the Minister for Home Affairs in the Northern Ireland government had no power to make regulations enabling a member of Her Majesty's armed forces to order a crowd to disperse, as the Northern Ireland Parliament was prohibited from making laws relating to the armed forces (Government of Ireland Act 1920, s. 4(1)). The 1972 statute had retrospective effect, stipulating that the Government of Ireland Act 1920 did not prevent the making of laws involving the armed forces in relation to the peace, order or good government of Northern Ireland.

3.2.1.8 Summary This positive facet of legislative supremacy, of unlimited authority, indicates that Parliament may legislate on any matter, anywhere, at any time. The idea that there might be a distinction drawn between fundamental constitutional laws and ordinary laws is not supported in the case law.

3.2.2 No Legislative Rival
The second or negative aspect according to Dicey was that there was no authority which could override Parliament's legislation. Dicey's exposition of this aspect of legislative supremacy concentrated upon the fact that there was a hierarchy of laws and, as Parliamentary legislation was on the highest level, it must prevail over subordinate laws. Rival lawmakers would include the monarch, a single House of Parliament, international law and the courts.

3.2.2.1 Monarch The monarch had sought to make law through proclamations and to suspend the operation of law. The *Case of Proclamations* (1611) 12 Co Rep 74, made it clear that the monarch could not add to or amend legislation or common law by way of a proclamation. The prerogative powers relating to foreign affairs and defence of the realm were upheld as ways of circumventing the necessity of Parliament's consent for raising money in the *Case of Impositions (Bate's Case)* (1606) 2 St Tr 371 and *R v Hampden (Ship Money Case)* (1637) 3 St Tr 826. The Bill of Rights 1688 made it quite clear that it would be illegal for the King to attempt, without Parliamentary consent, (a) to impose taxes, (b) to suspend the operation of laws, and (c) to dispense with penalties (arts 4, 1, 2 respectively).

Since the Bill of Rights 1688, it is now abundantly clear that the prerogative power as a source of law can be reduced, or abolished, by legislation. An example of abolition is the Crown Proceedings Act 1947 which removed the Crown's immunity to be sued in contract and tort (see 18.2–3).

3.2.2.2 Parliamentary resolutions On occasions it would seem that Parliament has intended its resolutions to have legislative effect. Relations between the courts and Parliament are somewhat strained over the issue of Parliamentary privilege (see 7.8.5). It does seem to be clear, however, following the case of *Stockdale v Hansard* (1839) 9 Ad & El 1, that mere resolutions of either House of Parliament do not change the law. The episode of which this case was a part ended with the passage of the Parliamentary Papers Act 1840 which, in effect, enacted the Commons resolution at issue in *Stockdale v Hansard* (1839) 9 Ad & El 1, by providing that persons involved in the publication of Parliamentary Papers were privileged and thus immune from defamation actions.

3.2.2.3 Subordinate legislation This is a type of legislation which may, *inter alia*, be authorised by statute, predominantly in the form of a statutory instrument (see further on Parliamentary procedures for making statutory instruments, 8.2.6). The courts have held that if the power conferred by the enabling Act is exceeded or abused in making subordinate legislation, then the legislation so made may be struck down (see further on principles of judicial review chapter 16).

3.2.2.4 International law We have already seen in 3.1.2.5 that legislation which extends beyond the UK's territory into international waters, as defined by international law, will be applied by the courts (*Mortensen v Peters* (1906) 14 SLT 227). In *Cheney v Conn* [1968] 1 WLR 242, an attempt to argue that an income tax assessment made under the Finance Act 1964 was incompatible with an international treaty ratified by the UK, the Geneva Convention, was rejected. The argument was that under international law manufacture of nuclear weapons was prohibited, yet that purpose would be carried out by the UK government using tax revenue. As Ungoed-Thomas J said at p. 247:

What the statute itself enacts cannot be unlawful, because what the statute says and provides is itself the law, and the highest form of law that is known to this country.

Therefore the express words of a statute can override the presumption that legislation is in accordance with international obligations.

This view has implications for the UK's membership of the European Communities, as it is part of Community law that it should prevail over any inconsistent national law (see 9.4.3 and 9.6.2). In the White Paper which was produced at the time of the unsuccessful application for membership in 1967, it was proposed that this traditional view of legislative supremacy would not be changed. Instead the Parliament of the UK would ensure that there was no conflict between its legislation and Community law by refraining from legislating inconsistently with Community law obligations (Cmnd 3301, para. 28).

3.2.2.5   Courts   The judges are the source of common law which they recognise as being inferior to statute. They will give effect to clear words in an Act which would restrict a common law right (*R* v *Inland Revenue Commissioners, ex parte Rossminster Ltd* [1980] AC 952 in which search warrants which did not specify a particular suspected offence were upheld).

3.2.3   The Make-up of an Act of Parliament
In 3.2.2 it was suggested that there are no legislative rivals to Parliament. Some of these potential rivals included elements of the Queen in Parliament, the body which enjoys legislative supremacy. The Queen in Parliament comprises both Houses of Parliament and the Queen, and their approval of a Bill transforms it into an Act of Parliament. Since the passage of the Parliament Act 1911, it is now possible for a Bill to become a statute after being passed by the House of Commons and receiving the royal assent. This means that the rule of recognition in the UK – what the Queen in Parliament enacts is law – has two elements. How do the courts identify an Act of Parliament? A copy of the statute could be presented to the court. Each statute will, in its preamble, contain the enacting formula which indicates that the three necessary consents have been given. If there was no royal assent, or no approval by the House of Commons, then on the authority of *The Prince's Case* (1606) 8 Co Rep 1a, it would seem that the courts could say that the document was not an Act of Parliament. If the Act had been passed under the procedures of the Parliament Acts 1911 and 1949, then the enacting words are different and they specify that the provisions of those statutes have been followed. So the courts accept these words of enactment at face value.

3.2.3.1   The enrolled Act rule   On occasions a statute has been challenged on the basis that, whilst it may have been enacted, this was achieved improperly. In *Edinburgh and Dalkeith Railway Co.* v *Wauchope* (1842) 8 Cl & F 710, a dispute arose over a private Act of Parliament which the respondent alleged had not been passed in accordance with the House of Commons Standing Orders. Lord Campbell dealt with this point saying, at p. 725:

All that a court of justice can do is to look to the Parliamentary roll: if from that it should appear that a Bill has passed both Houses and received the royal assent, no court of justice can inquire into the mode in which it was introduced into Parliament, nor into what was done previous to its introduction, or what passed in Parliament during its progress in its various stages through both Houses.

The Parliamentary roll contained the official version of a statute. Today there are two official versions of every statute which are to be found in the library of the House of Lords and the Public Records Office.

The reasons why the courts would not investigate the processes which led to the making of a disputed statute were given in the House of Lords in *Pickin v British Railways Board* [1974] AC 765 which, like *Edinburgh and Dalkeith Railway Co. v Wauchope*, concerned private Acts relating to railways. Their lordships were of the view that the internal procedures of Parliament were solely a matter for Parliament. They were conscious of the relationship between the courts and Parliament and felt that there would be conflict if a court were to investigate the making of a statute.

3.2.4 Continuing Nature of Legislative Supremacy

If Parliament has unlimited legislative power, can it be exercised so as to deprive itself of that power? The continuing theory states that this is not possible. Under this variant of the doctrine of legislative supremacy, Parliament is 'free, at every moment of its existence as a continuing body, not only from legal limitations imposed *ab extra*, but also from its own prior legislation' (Hart 1961, p. 145).

Thus Parliament can do anything it likes apart from seeking to limit its successor's powers. This would appear to mean that if one Parliament enacted a statute which attempted to bind its successors, that legislation could be overridden by a subsequent statute. Attempts to bind a Parliament's successors could take these forms:

(a)   that a Parliament would not, in the future, legislate on a particular topic, for example, stating that it would no longer legislate for a country to which it had granted independence (Canada Act 1982, s. 2); or

(b)   stipulating that a particular procedure must be followed in legislating on a topic, for example, requiring a majority vote in a poll of the people in Northern Ireland favouring Northern Ireland's departure from the UK before legislating to remove Northern Ireland from the UK (Northern Ireland Constitution Act 1973, s. 1).

The alternative to this is the self-embracing theory under which Parliament can limit irrevocably the legislative competence of its successors. This theory would mean that a later Parliament would be legally bound by the examples given relating to Canada and Northern Ireland.

According to Hart there is no reason in logic to dictate which of these theories should apply to a State's rule of recognition.

3.2.4.1 Implied repeal There are some decisions by the courts which suggest that they accept the continuing theory of legislative supremacy. These cases involve the interpretation of inconsistent statutes. The Acquisition of Land (Assessment of Compensation) Act 1919 set out rules for assessing compensation in respect of land acquired compulsorily for public purposes. It was further stipulated that

> The provisions of the Act or order by which the land is authorised to be acquired, or of any Act incorporated therewith, shall in relation to the matters dealt with in this Act, have effect subject to this Act, and so far as inconsistent with this Act those provisions shall cease to have or shall not have effect. (s. 7(1).)

The rules for assessment of property compulsorily acquired for improvement or clearance schemes in the Housing Act 1925 were different from those in the 1919 Act and would produce lower compensation payments. Some landlords tried to argue that they were entitled to the higher payments under the 1919 Act and that the effect of s. 7(1) was to deprive the 1925 Act provisions of effect as they were inconsistent with the earlier statute. This argument was not accepted and the later statute was held to constitute an implied repeal of the earlier statute on the basis that it was the latest expression of the will of Parliament (*Vauxhall Estates Ltd* v *Liverpool Corporation* [1932] 1 KB 733). In a similar case, *Ellen Street Estates Ltd* v *Minister of Health* [1934] 1 KB 590, Maugham LJ said, at p. 597:

> The legislature cannot, according to our constitution, bind itself as to the form of subsequent legislation, and it is impossible for Parliament to enact that in a subsequent statute dealing with the same subject-mattter there can be no implied repeal. If in a subsequent Act Parliament chooses to make it plain that the earlier statute is being to some extent repealed, effect must be given to that intention just because it is the will of the legislature.

This dictum ranges further than was necessary to decide this case, which was concerned with the rules for assessment of compensation. Advocates of the continuing nature of legislative supremacy have argued that this dictum supports the point that Parliament may not stipulate the form of any subsequent legislation. The challenge to this viewpoint will be examined later (see 3.3.2).

3.3 REVISIONIST VIEWS OF LEGISLATIVE SUPREMACY

The traditional version of legislative supremacy has not been without its critics. A shared basis for their views is the self-embracing theory of legislative supremacy. Parliament, they contend, has the ability to limit its legislative power. Some believe that the Acts of Union created a new Parliament which did not inherit the unlimited authority which was an attribute of the Parliament of England (and Wales). Others claim that it is possible to entrench provisions in legislation by prescribing certain procedures which must be followed in order to amend or repeal them. Finally, the UK's membership of the European Communities does appear to have brought about a judicially accepted modification of the traditional version of legislative supremacy.

3.3.1 The Acts of Union

It has been suggested that the Parliaments which resulted from the Acts of Union with Scotland and with Ireland were limited legislatures. To put it in the phrase of one writer, that Parliament was 'born unfree' (Mitchell 1968, pp. 93–8).

3.3.1.1 Distinctive features The union between England (and Wales) and Scotland came about by the implementation of a treaty. Both the English and Scottish Parliaments passed legislation which created the new Parliament of the United Kingdom of Great Britain. In establishing this new Parliament they abolished its creators. The union legislation stipulated the succession to the Crown, preserved certain Scottish institutions, including the courts, church and universities, and stated that the union was to last for ever after.

The legislative union with Ireland was also accomplished by the passage of statutes in the two Parliaments, although they were not preceded by a treaty. Special arrangements were made for the church, as a new established United Church of England and Ireland was created.

Since the new Great Britain Parliament was created by legislation, could it not be argued that such legislation is constituent, and that it can set limits upon the Parliament's legislative capacity? Can it be said that within the union legislation there are provisions which are fundamental and cannot, therefore, be altered by this new Parliament? These arguments have been countered quite convincingly by Munro (1987, ch. 4). He argues that where the language of the union legislation suggests a fundamental nature through phrases indicating permanence, such as 'in all time coming', this was not evidence of an intention to bind successor Parliaments. Such phrases had been used in other pieces of legislation and had still been amended in both the Scottish and English Parliaments.

3.3.1.2 Subsequent legislative history If the Acts of Union were meant to be permanent and unalterable, then this has not been achieved. Not a single article of the Union with Ireland Act 1800 escaped change. The ultimate change was the dissolution of the union. The only argument about dissolution is not whether legislation could achieve it but whether it was brought about by the Irish declaration of independence or Westminster legislation. Before the dissolution of the union there was a dissolution of a different kind. This was the disestablishment of the Anglican Church in Ireland by the Irish Church Act 1869. Yet the United Church of England and Ireland created by the Union with Ireland Act 1800, art. 5, was to 'remain in full force for ever'.

Some of the provisions concerned with religion in the union with Scotland were also changed. The Protestant Religion and Presbyterian Church Act

1707 was incorporated into the union legislation. It provided that professors and masters in universities, colleges and schools were required to subscribe to the Confession of Faith. The Universities (Scotland) Act 1853 and the Parochial and Burgh Schoolmasters (Scotland) Act 1861 are examples of legislation which abolished or modified this religious test.

3.3.1.3 Judicial views The revisionist case is given some support by dicta, in particular the view expressed by the Lord President, Lord Cooper, in *MacCormick* v *Lord Advocate* 1953 SC 396. The case concerned a challenge to the title of Queen Elizabeth II. Scotland had never had a Queen Elizabeth I. Part of the argument was that the union legislation created a new State and that this title was in conflict with the legislation. At first instance it was held that (a) under the Royal Titles Act 1953 the Queen could adopt whatever title she chose; (b) there was no breach of the union legislation since it did not deal with royal titles; and (c) the petitioners had no title to sue as the use of the royal title did not infringe any of their rights. On appeal, points (b) and (c) were affirmed. The Lord President made some *obiter* comments on the union legislation. He noted that the unlimited legislative supremacy of Parliament was a distinctively English principle and he wondered why the 'new Parliament of Great Britain must inherit all the peculiar characteristics of the English Parliament but none of the Scottish Parliament'. He pointed out that some parts of the union legislation contain declarations that they 'shall be fundamental and unalterable in all time coming'. The fact that the Lord Advocate had conceded that Parliament could not repeal 'fundamental and essential conditions' seems to add to the idea that the union has some fundamental aspects. Yet the comfort which Lord Cooper offers to the revisionists is somewhat qualified by subsequent comments. He stated that the petitioners had a problem even assuming that what they were alleging was a breach of fundamental law. The problem was whether such a question was a justiciable issue in the courts of England or Scotland. He reserved his opinion on arts 18 and 19 dealing with the Court of Session and laws which concern private right. The question before the court was one of public right, on which the Great Britain Parliament could legislate, and he noted that there was no precedent for the view that a court had jurisdiction 'to determine whether a governmental act of the type here in controversy is or is not conform to the provisions of a Treaty' (at p. 413).

While the Lord President did not rule out the possibility that a court could have jurisdiction to determine whether legislation breached the union provisions on the Scottish courts or 'private right' (arts 18 and 19), he did not really give the revisionists judicial authority on which to hang their case. Another dictum which might be pressed into service is that of the Lord Ordinary, Lord Keith, in *Gibson* v *Lord Advocate* 1975 SLT 134. In a case about EEC fishing regulations the argument that they affected private right (art. 18) was dismissed because they were public law matters. The Lord Ordinary said that he agreed with Lord President Cooper and reserved his opinion on the question of a purported abolition of the Court of Session or the substitution of the whole of Scots private law by English law. He did commit himself on the issue of justiciability, where the question was whether the amendment of a particular aspect of Scots private law is or is not for the evident utility of the people of Scotland. He said, at p. 137:

> The making of decisions upon what must essentially be a political matter is no part of the function of the court, and it is highly undesirable that it should be.

A contrary view was given in *Stewart* v *Henry* 1989 SLT (Sh Ct) 134 by Sherriff Stewart who saw 'no absolute bar to a court's considering the question whether a particular change in the law is for the evident utility of the subjects in Scotland'. The case raised the question whether the earlier introduction of the community charge in Scotland than in England and Wales was compatible with the union legislation. This was also the basis for a case heard by the Court of Session, *Pringle* 1991 SLT 330. In particular, it was argued that the petitioner's liability to pay this tax breached art. 4 which he claimed required that there should be no difference in the rights, privileges and advantages enjoyed by citizens in Great Britain unless expressly provided for in the treaty. The claim failed but the Lord President, Lord Hope, said the fact there were differences in the two jurisdictions over local government taxation 'for the year in question would not be sufficient to persuade me, without a much more detailed inquiry into the overall effects of these differences, that there was a failure to do what this part of art. 4 intended should be done'. Could this mean that there might be circumstances in which he would be prepared to make such an inquiry, and that the court would have the competence to hold invalid legislation which was inconsistent with the union legislation (see Edwards 1992)?

There are no cases on the union with Ireland. There was a challenge to the Irish Church Act 1869 which was based on the Coronation Oath rather than the union legislation. The court took the view that the validity of an Act could not be questioned by any judicial body (*Ex parte Canon Selwyn* (1872) 36 JP 54).

Whilst the theory seems attractive that the Acts of Union could limit the legislative authority of the new Parliaments which they created, it would appear that there is little evidence to support the assertion that this was the intention. The best that might be said about the dicta of the Scottish judges is that they are open to the view that it might be possible for legislation to bind successor Parliaments.

3.3.2 Entrenchment and Redefinition

The proponents of what has been called the 'new view' propose that Parliament may be limited as to the form or making of legislation. The term 'entrenchment' conveys the idea that a particular topic may only be validly legislated on in accordance with a special procedure which is meant to be more difficult than the normal legislative process. The aim behind this is to protect, for example, a Bill of Rights, or to ensure that there is substantial support for change. Entrenchment is, therefore, a more evaluative term than 'redefinition', which simply states that the composition of Parliament has been changed for specified purposes. Both terms encompass requirements such as a special majority in the legislature, or joint meetings of both chambers of a legislature, or the holding of a referendum either as a condition precedent or subsequent to the passage of a Bill. Redefinition also deals with changes which can make it easier for legislation to be enacted, as with the Parliament Acts 1911 and 1949 which permit statutes to be made without the approval of the House of Lords.

3.3.2.1 Support The basis put forward for the idea of self-embracing legislative supremacy by Heuston is that a legislative body is created by rules which (a) identify it, (b) prescribe its procedures and (c) determine its legislative competence. He asserts that the courts may question the validity of statutes on (a) and (b), but not (c). In other words, Parliament can enact any law it wishes, as long as it follows the rules relating to the making of law (1964, pp. 6–7). The courts would not be flouting the will of Parliament but respecting the limits which it had established.

Jennings illustrated the ideas of continuing and self-embracing legislative supremacy by reference to a prince (1959, p. 152). In the first example he has supreme power and can make and unmake laws so that he could create a constitution which bound him not to make law without the consent of the legislature but then abolish the legislature without its consent and legislate by decree. The supposition in the second example is that the prince does not have supreme power but instead there is a rule that the courts accept as law that which is made in the proper form, then if the prince changes the law so that the legislature's consent is required for valid law, the courts will not accept as law decrees made by the prince alone. This is because the rule about form has changed and it can only be changed by law made in accordance with that rule.

The point that Jennings goes on to make is that it is not clear whether the legislative supremacy of Parliament corresponds to his first or second example. The fact that an Act of Parliament is superior to any rule of common law does not mean that the Queen in Parliament is like the prince who has supreme power. What it does mean is:

> as the law now stands Parliament can enact anything: but this of course means that Parliament can change the law which now stands. (Jennings 1959, pp. 160–1.)

Jennings and Heuston have pointed to cases which indicate that if a special process is not followed then the court will not give effect to such a purported law. In *Attorney-General for New South Wales* v *Trethowan* [1932] AC 526 a dispute arose over measures made by the legislature of New South Wales. This body was empowered by a Westminster statute (Colonial Laws Validity Act 1865, s. 5) to legislate for its own constitution, powers and procedure, provided that these laws were passed 'in the manner and form' required by the law in force at the time, whether it be imperial or colonial. The constitution (Constitution Act 1902) was amended by the Constitution (Legislative Council) Amendment Act 1929. The amendment inserted a new s. 7A which provided that (a) no Bill to abolish the Legislative Council could be presented to the Governor for royal assent until it had been approved by a majority of electors voting in a referendum; and (b) any Bill to abolish the referendum requirement must also be approved in a referendum. Subsequently both chambers of the New South Wales legislature approved Bills which sought to repeal s. 7A and to abolish the Legislative Council, and the government intended to present these to the Governor for the royal assent without holding a referendum. Some members of the Legislative Council successfully sought a declaration that the Bill could not be presented for the royal assent without their approval in a referendum as required by s. 7A. They were also granted an injunction restraining the presentation of the Bills. The Judicial Committee of the Privy Council held that the referendum requirements must be respected as the authority of the New South Wales legislature to deal with the constitution derived from the Colonial Laws Validity Act 1865, which specified that 'manner and form' requirements currently in force must be respected (s. 5).

Another case cited by both Jennings and Heuston is *Harris v Minister of the Interior* 1952 (2) SA 428, which dealt with a requirement in the South Africa Act 1909, s. 152, that certain matters, including the amendment or repeal of this provision, required the approval of a two-thirds majority of the members of the two chambers of the Union Parliament of South Africa, sitting together. This Parliament derived its powers from the 1909 Act and the Statute of Westminster 1931. The Status of the Union Act 1934 claimed that the Union Parliament was the supreme legislative power in South Africa. There was a challenge to legislation which sought to deprive certain people of their voting rights. It was argued that this measure should have been passed in a joint sitting of the Parliament under the South Africa Act 1909, s. 152. The court held that the Status of the Union Act 1934 did not change the manner and form for dealing with s. 152. This could be validly carried out, either by the joint sitting procedure, or by an Act of the Westminster Parliament. The Union Parliament had been established by higher law, Westminster legislation, and it was bound by the rules created by that higher law, until those rules were changed by the procedure which they stipulated.

A more recent Privy Council decision, *Bribery Commissioner v Ranasinghe* [1965] AC 172, concerned the appointment of a judicial body, the Bribery Commission, in Ceylon (now Sri Lanka). This was held to be unlawful as it was appointed by ordinary legislation rather than by a special majority as required by the constitution. Much attention has focused upon the following passage in the judgment delivered by Lord Pearce, at p. 198:

> But the proposition which is not acceptable is that a legislature, once established, has some inherent power derived from the mere fact of its establishment to make a valid law by the resolution of a bare majority which its own constituent instrument has said shall not be a valid law unless made by a different type of majority or by a different legislative process.

Marshall argues that Lord Pearce:

> seemed to imply . . . that both non-sovereign and sovereign legislatures may be made subject to procedural rules entrenching parts of the law from simple majority repeal. (1971, p. 55.)

3.3.2.2 Opposition Criticism of the new view attacks both the case law and the theory underpinning it. Certainly it is easy to suggest that the cases cannot support the weight which Jennings, Heuston and Marshall place upon them. In *Attorney-General for New South Wales* v *Trethowan* [1932] AC 526, it was explicitly stated in the Privy Council that the New South Wales legislature was a subordinate body limited in ways which the revisionists do not seek to suggest is true for the Westminster Parliament. The South African and Sri Lankan legislatures were also creatures of higher law. In *Bribery Commissioner* v *Ranasinghe* [1965] AC 172, Lord Pearce's dictum deals with a body which is subject to a constitutent instrument, but that is not true for the UK and invalidates the point which Marshall was seeking to make about entrenchment applying to all legislatures whether or not they are legislatively supreme.

Another point which might be made is that the cases upon implied repeal, which are cases from England and Wales, suggest that statutes which seek to bind successor Parliaments are no more special than any other legislation (*Vauxhall Estates Ltd* v *Liverpool Corporation* [1932] 1 KB 733; *Ellen Street Estates Ltd* v *Minister of Health* [1934] 1 KB 590). Whilst it is only *obiter*, Maugham LJ did say in *Ellen Street Estates Ltd* v *Minister of Health* that Parliament could not bind itself as to the form of subsequent legislation.

Wade has suggested a different theory for legislative supremacy which does not allow for Parliament to change the rules relating to form. He argues that the rule which requires the courts to obey statutes cannot be changed by an Act of Parliament. This rule is itself the authority for statute and it 'is the ultimate *political* fact upon which the whole system of legislation hangs', and it can only be changed by 'revolution' (1955, p. 187).

This theory seems quite similar to Hart's ultimate rule of recognition in suggesting that the basis of a legal system is the fact of acceptance of its ultimate rule of recognition by the judges, officials and the public. Wade seems, however, to be suggesting that legislative supremacy is continuing, whereas Hart allows that it may be either continuing or self-embracing.

3.3.2.3 Appraisal If we take the rival theories, the revisionists are claiming that legislative supremacy allows a body to bind itself to follow certain processes and that failure to do this can result in a court denying legal effect to the purported statute. Wade is contending that this cannot happen. The current constitutional order derives from the Glorious Revolution in which the courts accepted that what the Queen in Parliament enacts is law. Several revolutions occurred in the 17th century: the period of the Commonwealth was a break from the monarchy, the restoration of the monarchy was clearly a break from the Commonwealth, and the transfer of the Crown from James II to William and Mary was yet another break from the current constitutional order. Is it this historical survey which leads Wade to contend that change can only result from revolution? May not Parliament change the rules itself, or is every rule change to be regarded as a revolution? Parliament has redefined its composition on several occasions. These changes include: (a) the creation of new Parliaments by the Acts of Union; (b) expansion of the franchise, thereby enabling more men, and eventually women, to vote; (c) alteration of the qualifications of those entitled to become members of both Houses of Parliament (for example, the addition of life peers to the hereditary ones); and (d) modification of the Queen in Parliament by the Parliament Acts 1911 and 1949 so that statutes may be made without the consent of the Lords, and permitting a regent to give the assent in place of a monarch who is either under the age of 18 or is totally incapacitated (Regency Act 1937).

The redefinition of Parliament carried out by the Parliament Acts 1911 and 1949 is interesting because it does not alter the composition of Parliament where it relates to the making of a statute to prolong the life of a Parliament; the approval of both Houses of Parliament is required (Parliament Act 1911, s. 2(1)). This raises the question as to what would happen if a statute purporting to prolong a Parliament were enacted without the approval of the House of Lords. According to De Smith & Brazier (1994, p. 95), it might be possible for a court to deny legal effect to such a measure. They suggest that it would be possible to circumvent the prohibition on investigating the internal procedures of Parliament reaffirmed in *Pickin* v *British Railways Board* [1974] AC 765, because the defect would be apparent on the face of the statute as the words of enactment would indicate that Parliament (Queen and Commons) was not the body which is authorised to prolong the life of a Parliament (Queen, Lords and Commons). Perhaps *The Prince's Case* (1606) 8 Co Rep 1a, might serve as an authority.

The argument which states that an inconsistency between statutes implies a repeal of the earlier one by the later one, could be countered by the view that it was not clear that it was the intention of Parliament to bind its successors by the Acquisition of Land (Assessment of Compensation) Act 1919. As has been pointed out, the dictum of Maugham LJ on the impossibility of binding successors as to form of legislation was *obiter* (see 3.2.4.1).

An alternative reason for a court striking down such a measure might be that legislation passed without Lords' consent under the procedures of the Parliament Acts 1911 and 1949 is delegated legislation. If that is correct then it would be an unauthorised expansion of the delegate's authority to seek to prolong Parliament's life. The suggestion that the Parliament Acts produce delegated legislation has been made by Hood Phillips & Jackson (1987, pp. 89–90) and supported by Wade (1980, pp. 27–80). This is based on *The Prince's Case* (1606) 8 Co Rep 1a, which affirms that all three elements of the Queen in Parliament must approve a statute for it to be valid. Therefore the recognition of legislation passed without Lords' consent is like that given to a statutory instrument because it was authorised by an enabling Act passed in the usual way. There is no support in the case law for this view, although as an argument from first principles it is not without substance.

Both Wade and Hood Phillips have suggested how it might be possible to switch from continuing to self-embracing legislative supremacy. Wade thinks a Bill of Rights could be entrenched by changing the judicial oath of office so as to require its protection (1980, p. 37). Hood Phillips argues that it could be done by creating a constitution which established a limited legislature. This could be achieved in one of two ways (Hood Phillips 1970, pp. 156–7):

(a) A new constitution could be drawn up by Parliament and, after approval in a referendum, the old Parliament would be abolished and suceeded by a new limited Parliament.

(b) Parliament could transfer its powers to a constituent assembly which would then produce a constitution for approval.

The argument about entrenchment and redefinition, it would seem, is not whether it is possible, but about the circumstances in which it could happen and be recognised by the courts. The implied repeal cases suggest that Parliament must make its attempts to bind its successors very clear. This may have been done by the Parliament Act 1911, s. 2(1), with the exclusion of the prolongation of Parliament from Acts which may be passed without Lords' consent. In 3.3.3 it will be argued that the UK's accession to the European Communities has constituted a signal from Parliament to the courts that it now has a legislative rival.

3.3.3 Membership of the European Union

A fuller account of the European Union is given in chapter 9. For the present purposes it is sufficient to say that, as a member of the European Union and its Communities, the UK has joined a special legal order in which there is a rule which accords supremacy to Community law over inconsistent national law (see 9.4.3 and 9.6.2). This was known when the UK applied for membership and the view taken was that the continuing theory of legislative supremacy was the correct view. The consequence of this was that if Parliament legislated inconsistently with Community law, then the UK courts would follow the later UK statute rather than the earlier provision of Community law. All that Parliament could do would be to follow a kind of self-denying ordinance not to exercise its legislative supremacy so as to conflict with Community law (Cmnd 3301, para. 28).

The incorporation of Community law into UK law was carried out by the European Communities Act 1972. Under s. 2(1) existing and future Community law rights, obligations, remedies and procedure are given effect in UK law. Where future Community law has to be implemented in the UK, s. 2(2) provides for this to be done, mainly by subordinate legislation. Determinations of the European Court of Justice have produced principles which the courts are to use in interpreting Community law (s. 3(1)). The issue of conflict between Community and UK law is dealt with in s. 2(4) which states that '. . . any enactment passed or to be passed, other than one contained in this part of this Act, shall be construed and have effect subject to the foregoing provisions'. This is meant to give primacy to Community law. Does it bind successor Parliaments? Judicial opinion has varied over time. The traditional view that implied repeal operates found support from Lord

Denning MR in *Felixstowe Dock and Railway Co.* v *British Transport Docks Board* [1976] 2 CMLR 655. In *Garland* v *British Rail Engineering Ltd* [1983] 2 AC 751, the House of Lords said of s. 2(4) that it was a principle of construction to be used, wherever possible, to construe UK legislation consistently with Community law. The current position following *R* v *Secretary of State for Transport, ex parte Factortame Ltd* [1990] 2 AC 85, seems to mean that the traditional view of implied repeal no longer applies. The effect of s. 2(4) would appear to be that it implies into every piece of legislation a term that the legislation takes effect subject to directly enforceable Community law rights giving the courts the right under UK law and the duty under Community law to override inconsistent domestic law (this principle was applied in *R* v *Secretary of State for Employment, ex parte Equal Opportunities Commission* [1995] 1 AC 1; see further 9.6.2).

Perhaps this modification of the implied repeal rule has occurred because of a combination of Parliament's wish to limit itself, expressed in the European Communities Act 1972 and, as it were, the very clear rules of the club which this legislation enabled the UK to join. It would appear that if the UK wished to end its membership and Parliament indicated this by explicitly repealing s. 2(4) then the courts would revert to the practice of according Parliament legislative supremacy (*Macarthys Ltd* v *Smith* [1979] ICR 785, at p. 789 per Lord Denning MR).

This situation does seem somewhat strange as legislative supremacy would appear to vary depending upon whether or not the subject-matter of legislation involves Community law. If it does not then the traditional view continues to apply, and if it does then it is what might be termed 'semi-self-embracing', that Parliament is bound until it frees itself by explicit repeal.

If this is correct then it would seem that the UK has two ultimate rules of recognition, which seems a contradiction in terms. It has been suggested that Hart's theory can accommodate this on the basis that there are two legal orders in the one State. In the UK this would mean that there is the Community legal order and a national legal order. In the Community legal order the ultimate rule of recognition means that directly enforceable Community law prevails over inconsistent domestic law, and in the national legal order the ultimate rule of recognition is what the Queen in Parliament enacts (Starr 1977).

A summary of the doctrine of legislative supremacy might be that it is gradually evolving from the continuing version into a self-embracing variation and that, if this can happen in the field of Community law, there is no reason in principle why it could not happen in other fields, provided Parliament clearly signals this. Given the development of the UK constitution, it would be strange if legislative supremacy were immune from change (see Bradley 1994).

3.4 CONSTITUTIONALISM

The legislative supremacy of Parliament, whether in the traditional or revisionist conception, is the fundamental rule of the UK's constitutional arrangements. This would seem to endow Parliament with a large amount of power. Yet, as we saw in 1.1, one of the usual objectives of a constitution is to set limits or restraints upon governmental power. This function derives from the theory of constitutionalism, which is 'an institutionalised system of effective, regularised restraints upon governmental action' (Friedrich 1963, p. 217). Alder has suggested that four ways of restraining governmental action have been used in constitutions. These are (a) the formulation of principles of justice and declarations of rights which are policed by the courts; (b) the division of powers amongst governmental bodies according to functions and territory; (c) the adoption of representative institutions which allow the people to vote governments into and out of office; and (d) provision for direct participation by the people in governmental decision-making through, for example, a referendum (1989, pp. 39–40).

3.4.1 Constitutionalism and the UK

Elements of all of these approaches are to be found in the UK's current constitutional arrangements. Under the liberal democratic theory which underpins these arrangements, the election of a new Parliament every five years, at least, provides a political check. The importance placed on Parliament as both legislature and scrutiniser of the executive emphasises the representative nature of our democracy, which reduces the scope of more participation by the people. Referendums were held during the 1970s. The first of these was held in 1973 under the Northern Ireland (Border Poll) Act 1972 and it resulted in a majority wishing Northern Ireland to remain in the UK. The second referendum was held in 1975 and approved the renegotiated terms of membership of the European Communities. The final referendums were held in 1979 and rejected the arrangements for devolution contained in the Scotland and Wales Acts 1978.

These referendums were controversial. Some were opposed to them in principle, in that Parliament was elected to take decisions on behalf of the people. This was particularly true of the one on the European Communities, which was the only one to be held throughout the UK. Some took the view that Northern Ireland's membership of the UK was a matter for the whole of the UK, and not simply the people of Northern Ireland. Scots in favour of decentralising power were dissatisifed with the condition which required that, in order for the Scotland Act 1978 to take effect, the vote in favour had to reach a threshold of 40 per cent of those entitled to vote, rather than a simple majority of those who voted. There was a majority in favour but it did not reach this threshold (see 2.4.2).

Some of those who argue that referendums are alien to our representative democracy are not above arguing for them when they feel that the result would be to reject a change which they dislike. This has occurred in the debate about the (Maastricht) Treaty on European Union, and there is a precedent, for Dicey was at one stage against referendums but then argued in favour of them. It is not entirely clear if his vehement opposition to Irish home rule was the initial trigger for this change of view, but his belief that it was a check on the party system does not fit with his writings on the legislative supremacy of Parliament (see McEldowney 1985, pp. 49–52, 59).

The rejection of the Scotland and Wales Acts 1978, and the failure to achieve widespread support within Northern Ireland for decentralisation, seem to suggest that the UK does not have a significant domestic territorial division of governmental power. If one takes account of the UK's membership of the European Communities, there is a territorial-cum-functional division of powers. In the field of competition law, control of mergers may be dealt with by national authorities or by the European Commission. Mergers which have a Community dimension will be subject only to investigation by the Commission and not by any of the relevant national authorities (EEC Regulation 4064/89). Therefore on some topics there is a division of powers between UK institutions and those of the European Communities.

There is, domestically, a certain degree of functional division amongst governmental bodies, which is usually referred to as the doctrine of the separation of powers.

Finally, the policing by the courts of principles of justice and declarations of rights is also, to a degree, found in the UK's arrangements. There is no domestic declaration of rights but the UK has ratified the European Convention on Human Rights (ECHR). This has provided machinery for enforcement of the rights protected in the ECHR, even though it has not been incorporated into national law. (The Labour government elected in May 1997 does intend to incorporate the ECHR (see 12.6).) The UK's courts have, within the scope allowed by legislation, developed and applied principles of justice which can check the exercise of governmental power. This is an aspect of the rule of law.

The three major aspects of constitutionalism in the UK are (a) the rule of law; (b) separation of powers; and (c) responsible government, and each will now be discussed.

3.4.2 Rule of Law

The rule of law has a comforting ring to it. If we are concerned about restraining government then the idea of government by laws rather than men seems to be helpful, until we realise that laws are made by men and women. We may break down the idea of the rule of law into two aspects: a principle of legality and a political doctrine.

3.4.2.1 Legality This aspect of the rule of law simply means that the actions of government must have a basis in law. Ministers or officials should be able to refer to some source of law which authorises any decision or action they take. Where such action will have serious consequences for an individual, such as deprivation of liberty, the rhetoric of the judges is that their enforcement of legality will put the onus on officialdom to justify those consequences. They acknowledge that if clear words are used in legislation, then they must defer to the will of Parliament, the maker of the supreme legal rules (*R v Inland Revenue Commissioners, ex parte Rossminster Ltd* [1980] AC 952). Yet on occasions words in legislation are not clear, but nevertheless a power of arrest is approved by the courts (*Wills v Bowley* [1981] 1 AC 57).

The legality principle has also been applied by the courts where statute confers discretionary power, which gives a minister or an official freedom to decide how to act. The common law principles of judicial review of administrative action deal with the limits of the powers which legislation or prerogative confer. In determining the limits the courts will be comparing the action or decisions with the intention of Parliament. If the courts rule that the exercise of power goes beyond what they interpret as its limits, then that is illegal and can be invalidated. Thus the basis for much of judicial review is ensuring compliance with Parliament's will, which is the highest law, so that upholding legislative supremacy is also maintaining legality. This skates over the difficulty of discerning Parliament's intention and the fact that these principles have been applied to powers which have not been conferred by legislation (see further chapter 16 on grounds of judicial review).

3.4.2.2 Political doctrine The rule of law as a political doctrine is somewhat wider than the principle of legality. It connotes a preference for order and, as articulated by some legal theorists, requirements of a legal system. According to Raz (1977), the basic idea of the rule of law is that not only should law be obeyed, but that the law should be such that people will be able to be guided by it. From this he proposes eight principles, which are divided into two groups. The aim of the first group is to provide standards which are designed to enable law to guide action. If law or the procedures for making law are secret or vague, or law is retroactive or constantly changing, then people will have difficulty in conforming to it. Raz's second group of principles refer to the machinery for the enforcement of law and seek to ensure that it will not distort the law but supervise conformity to the rule of law and provide effective remedies where there is deviation from it. These principles require: the judiciary must have a guaranteed independence; there should be easy access to the courts, which should have the power to review the implementation of the other principles of the rule of law; procedures must be fair; and the discretion of crime prevention agencies must not be allowed to pervert the law.

These principles have a formal character, they do not dictate the contents of most laws, and Raz admits that these principles could be conformed to by undemocratic governments. In liberal democratic States the broader political doctrine of the rule of law does concern itself with the content of laws, the ends to which the exercise of governmental powers is the means. Unfortunately it is difficult to distill a consensus from the range of political views which subscribe to liberal democracy. Perhaps there may be agreement that it is impermissible to attack the basis of liberal democracy, for example, by infringing the civil and political rights relating to conscience, expression, assembly and association without which free elections would be an empty promise. It is therefore not surprising that in many liberal democracies there are declarations of such rights which are entrenched.

3.4.2.3 The UK The rule of law is not a robust check upon government. There is government according to law but the law can indemnify past illegalities and take retrospective effect. These are not everyday occurrences but they show that whatever is the check upon government it is not law.

3.4.3 Separation of Powers

A common understanding of the doctrine of the separation of powers is that it makes a differentiation of the various powers of government, executive, legislative and judicial, and separates the organs that exercise them so that they are dispersed. This, it is hoped, reduces the potential for the abuse of governmental power by avoiding its concentration in a single person or institution. Rarely has the physical separation been complete. From the basis of a greater or lesser degree of physical separation, there have been alternative developments. The position in the USA illustrates the arrangement where the power exercised by any organ of government is subject to checks and balances by the others. France exemplifies the opposing system of an organ being immune from interference in its work. In the USA the judiciary may review and deny legal effect to the acts and actions of the legislature. In France the executive and the legislature review themselves through the *Conseil d'État* and the *Conseil constitutionnel* respectively.

In the UK there is some degree of separation, civil servants may not be MPs, yet government ministers must sit in one of the two Houses of Parliament. The strongest aspect of separation is the independence of the judiciary from both the executive and the legislature, although the most senior judges, as members of the House of Lords, can be involved in making legislation (see chapter 11 on the judiciary).

The balancing and checking which occurs in the UK combines the French internal, and the American external. The legislative power of Parliament is not generally subject to external check by the courts, rather legislation is produced by the representative institution of a liberal democracy which succeeded another internal arrangement, balanced or mixed government, which was based on the estates or classes (monarchy, aristocracy and democracy). The actions of the executive are subject to the external checks of Parliament and the courts. Party discipline reduces the stringency of the checks which Parliament conducts upon the executive. The consequent dominance over Parliament enables the executive to make legislation and thus to pass the judicial check which is based upon the principle of legality. The exception to this is in the sphere of Community law where the courts can override inconsistent domestic legislation. See generally Barendt 1995 and Stevens 1997.

3.4.4 Responsible Government

Turpin suggests that there are two aspects to the responsibility of the government (1994, p. 113). The first of these is responsiveness. If the government can be persuaded, or influenced, to take a particular course of action then this amounts to a degree of control over the government. It is a priori, that is, prospective, forward-looking. The second aspect of responsibility is backward-looking, or a posteriori. Here we are dealing with accountability. The government accounts to Parliament after action has been taken. Such accountability may be explanatory or amendatory. The government may explain to Parliament what happened and, if an error occurred, then the government will be expected to amend or remedy the situation.

Responsible government is principally enforced through ministerial responsibility which is perhaps one of the most important constitutional conventions. These non-legal rules are dealt with in chapter 4, which includes an examination of the most important aspects of ministerial responsibility, that a government is sustained in office by the support or confidence of the House of Commons, and that ministers are responsible to Parliament for the actions of their departments.

These ideas are fundamental to the nature of our liberal democracy and yet they are not rules of law but non-legal obligations. They are obeyed because it is felt correct. It may be wondered if this provides a satisfactory restraint upon government. Of course a constitution in the sense used by the rest of the world does not guarantee that a government will operate according to the standards and values of liberal democracy but it is easier to deviate from them if they are not entrenched through fundamental law.

CHAPTER FOUR
Constitutional Conventions

In chapter 3, the part played by legal rules and the rule of law in the UK's constitutional arrangements was examined. This chapter deals with the non-legal rules of the constitution, or constitutional conventions, the term used by Dicey. As we shall see the distinction between these conventions and law is important. However, it must not be thought that a study of non-legal rules is unnecessary in a book about law. A failure to investigate the constitutional conventions will result in an imperfect understanding of our constitutional arrangements. Not only do the conventions supplement the legal rules, but some of them are significant constitutional rules.

4.1 THE NATURE OF CONSTITUTIONAL CONVENTIONS

Experience in the operation of rules and arrangements can lead to the identification of problems and their resolution. Sometimes formal rules may be altered and on other occasions they may be modified by informal practices. Such a practice may qualify or restrict the operation of a formal rule. This has occurred in the UK's constitutional arrangements so that some of the rules of law are applied in accordance with non-legal rules or constitutional conventions, a term popularised by Dicey.

4.1.1 Dicey's Definition
Dicey used the term 'convention' to include understandings, habits, practices (1959, p. 24), and also customs, maxims and precepts (p. 417). He was concerned to distinguish these conventions from law and he pointed out that laws were enforced by the courts, whereas conventions were not.

Despite not being enforced by the courts, conventions are very important as they regulate 'the whole of the remaining discretionary powers of the Crown' whether exercised by the sovereign or ministers (Dicey 1959, p. 426).

We will now examine the major elements of this formulation of constitutional conventions.

4.1.2 Function

For Dicey, conventions regulate the residual discretionary powers of the Crown. He did accept that, in addition to the prerogative, conventions also regulate the privileges of Parliament. Today we would regard the coverage of constitutional conventions as being wider than suggested by Dicey. In addition to the Crown's discretionary powers, which include, for example, relations between the sovereign and Parliament, and the sovereign and the government, we would include relations between the executive and Parliament, relations between the two Houses of Parliament, relations between the judiciary and both the government and Parliament, and relations between the UK and the other members of the Commonwealth.

Dicey focused upon the discretionary prerogative powers because the formal rules of our constitutional arrangements no longer reflect political reality. Constitutional development has moved power from the sovereign to the ministers, not as servants of the Crown, but as representatives of the people. The Bill of Rights 1688 and the Revolution Settlement shifted the balance of power from the sovereign to Parliament, and the Reform Acts 1832 and 1868 extended the franchise to most adult males and introduced real electoral politics. As the formal rules have not changed the conventions have developed so as to condition their exercise. For example, legislation requires approval either by the two Houses of Parliament and the sovereign, or the House of Commons and the sovereign, following the procedures in the Parliament Acts 1911 and 1949 (see further 8.6). The formal legal position is that a Bill could be refused the royal assent by the sovereign and thus not become a statute. It may well be that the sovereign would wish that certain Bills should not become statutes but it is now felt inappropriate that the royal assent should be denied. There is a convention to the effect that the royal assent should be given to Bills which have been approved by the Houses of Parliament. An alternative formulation of the convention stipulates that the sovereign should exercise this prerogative power following the advice of ministers. The reason why it is felt inappropriate for the sovereign to refuse the royal assent is that our constitutional arrangements take the form of a responsible and representative democracy. The sovereign is not responsible to the people and so the real exercise of power should be placed with those who are, the ministers.

Jennings had the advantage of writing after Dicey and could therefore take account of changes which had become more apparent in the 20th century. For Jennings it is not so much the prerogative which requires regulation, as cabinet government. The cabinet and the prime minister are conventional institutions. The formal rules of the constitution only deal with marginal aspects of these institutions. The Ministers of the Crown Act 1937 authorised different salaries for ministers depending upon whether or not they were members of the cabinet (see now Ministers of the Crown Act 1975 and 6.1.2). Indeed it is convention which recognises the role of the opposition. A reflection of this is that in Parliamentary debates the Speaker asks for contributions alternately from those on the government benches, and those on the opposition benches.

Jennings also had a gift for the use of metaphor. He wrote that conventions 'provide the flesh which clothes the dry bones of the law' (1959, p. 81). He also identified two basic functions of constitutional conventions. They 'enable a rigid legal framework – and all laws tend to be rigid – to be kept up with changing social needs and changing political ideas' (p. 101). Secondly, conventions enable those who govern to 'work the machines'. This aspect is a little different from the previous fundamental function of adapting to change. A convention which Jennings used illustrates this 'workability' function very well. The practice of 'pairing' involves an MP from the government party and an MP from an opposition party agreeing not to vote in divisions in the Commons. This arrangement means that neither party is disadvantaged as the absence of the paired MPs does not affect the result of a division. It eases life for those MPs who become paired bearing in mind that divisions usually take place in the evening at the end of debates.

4.1.3 Conventions and the Courts

Dicey maintained that conventions could be distinguished from law because the courts would not enforce conventions. The case law indicates that, while the courts do not enforce conventions, they do recognise them and, indeed, on occasion, use them as an aid to the construction of statutes.

The case of *Madzimbamuto* v *Lardner-Burke* [1969] 1 AC 645 is a clear example in which a court has refused to enforce a convention. The Judicial Committee of the Privy Council was asked to take account of the convention which stipulates that the Westminster Parliament would only legislate for a Commonwealth country at the request, and with the consent, of that country's government. The government of Southern Rhodesia (now Zimbabwe) had made an unlawful unilateral declaration of independence. In reaction to this the Southern Rhodesia Act 1965 was enacted at Westminster. This statute, which reasserted the right of the Westminster Parliament to legislate for Southern Rhodesia, had not been requested by the Southern Rhodesian government, nor was it consented to by that government. The case raised the legality of regulations made by the government of Southern Rhodesia. The Privy Council was faced with a conflict between the legislative supremacy of the Westminster Parliament and a convention. Unsurprisingly, the Privy Council held that the 1965 statute, although passed in breach of the convention, was valid.

In *Attorney-General* v *Jonathan Cape Ltd* [1976] QB 752, the literary executors of the late cabinet minister Richard Crossman wished to publish his diaries which discussed matters which had been before cabinet. The Attorney-General sought an injunction to prevent publication. The High Court acknowledged that there was a convention of confidentiality of cabinet business. However, any prohibition of publication would not be based on that convention. Instead the law on breach of confidence could be used. To invoke this one would have to show that material was confidential and that its disclosure would be contrary to the public interest. Lord Widgery CJ stated that cabinet matters were confidential and it could be in the public interest to prevent their disclosure. He held that the maintenance of the doctrine of joint responsibility of the cabinet is in the public interest. However, as some of the material was at least 10 years old, it would be permissible for it to be published as this would not harm the public interest. The convention was recognised and used to determine if the public interest could be prejudiced by the publication of the material.

The Judicial Committee of the Privy Council paid regard to a convention which referred to itself in an appeal from Canada (*British Coal Corporation* v *The King* [1935] AC 500). The committee hears appeals from Commonwealth countries which take the form of a petition. It then reports to Her Majesty in Council and the determination of the petition is given as an Order in Council. The question before the Committee in this case was whether it could really be regarded as a court. The committee took the view that the Judicial Committee Act 1833 which had established the committee did intend it to be a court, and there was a convention that the sovereign would always give effect to the committee's report.

The convention of ministerial responsibility was recognised in *Carltona Ltd* v *Commissioners of Works* [1943] 2 All ER 560. A factory was requisitioned by the commissioners. Part of the grounds of the challenge to the requisition was that the competent body had not directed its mind properly to the matter. An official had carried out the challenged action. The court, in dismissing the challenge, ruled that the matter had been properly considered. The official had acted under the minister's authority. 'Constitutionally, the decision of such an official is, of course, the decision of the minister. The minister is responsible. It is he who must answer to Parliament for anything that his officials have done under his authority' (per Lord Greene MR at p. 563).

One of the more important cases dealing with conventions was decided by the Supreme Court of Canada (*Reference re Amendment of the Constitution of Canada (Nos. 1, 2 and 3)* (1981) 125 DLR (3d) 1). The court was empowered to give advisory opinions and one was requested about the action of the federal government, which was proposing to seek enactment of legislation at Westminster for the patriation of the Canadian constitution. This would mean that all Canadian constitutional matters would be decided in Canada by Canadian institutions and no longer would a Westminster statute be required to give legal effect to certain changes. Some of the provincial governments in Canada had objected to the proposals which the federal government wished to have enacted by Westminster. They contended that there was a Canadian constitutional convention which required the agreement of the provinces where changes were proposed in the relations between the federal and provincial governments. The Supreme Court held there was a convention which required substantial agreement from the provincial governments to such changes but, as a matter of law, it could not be enforced by the courts. Following this ruling the federal government renegotiated an agreement which all of the provincial governments except Quebec accepted. It was duly enacted by Westminster as the Canada Act 1982.

4.1.4 Obedience to Conventions
As conventions are not court enforced, the question arises as to why they are obeyed. On this point there is disagreement amongst the commentators.

Dicey suggested that failure to obey conventions could lead to future legal difficulties. He illustrated this by referring to the convention that Parliament should assemble at least once a year. If Parliament did not sit for two years this would mean that the prohibition in the Bill of Rights 1688 against the keeping of a standing army would be breached. There must therefore be an annual authorisation for the Army. In Dicey's time such authorisation was provided by the Army (Annual) Act each year. Currently the Army and the Royal Air Force are authorised by the quinquennial Armed Forces Acts (most recently the Armed Forces Act 1996), and by the Appropriation Acts. In fact the Appropriation Acts are also crucial for all of government expenditure, as Jennings has pointed out (1959, p. 129). Not only does government require statutory authority to impose taxes, but also to spend this money. Whilst a government could exist without some of the taxes authorised annually, because of its ability to borrow, the Appropriation Acts permit expenditure (see further 8.4).

Dicey also suggested that legal difficulties would apply to the breach of the convention that a government must resign or seek a dissolution of Parliament if it loses the confidence of the House of Commons. This would be the case if the Commons continued to vote against the government. If the circumstances of the defeat on a motion of confidence were unusual, it might be possible for the government to be able to secure the passage of essential financial legislation.

Jennings rejected Dicey's legal difficulties sanction for the breach of conventions. He preferred the explanation that it was future political difficulties which served to secure obedience to conventions. He suggested that Dicey's explanation could only deal with conventions concerning relations between the cabinet and the House of Commons, and even then only if the Commons objected to the cabinet's breach.

Jennings's suggested theory may help explain why some ministers resign and others do not when a mistake is made by the departments for which they are responsible. It seems that ministers rarely resign over such matters, despite calls to do so by the opposition parties. As the scope and scale of governmental intervention has increased, the numbers of officials have grown and consequently ministers cannot be expected to have a full knowledge of everything which their officials do. Sir David Maxwell Fyfe outlined guidance to the House of Commons following the resignation of Sir Thomas Dugdale over the Crichel Down affair in which officials had failed to honour an undertaking given to the owner of land which had been compulsorily acquired. The guidance on the relationship between a minister and officials, and the former's responsibility for the latter, covered four situations. The minister is responsible if the official is following direct instructions, or acts in accordance with policy, and also when an official makes a mistake which is neither on an issue of policy nor where a claim to individual rights is seriously involved. In these circumstances the official is not exposed to public criticism. Where an official acts against policy and the minister has no prior knowledge, then the minister is not required to accept blame but must account to Parliament (Parliamentary Debates (Hansard), Commons vol. 530, cols

1285–7, 20 July 1954). This guidance does not help to explain the difference between those ministers who have, and those who have not, resigned. It is now accepted that Sir Thomas Dugdale did not resign simply because he accepted responsibility for his officials' action, but rather because he had lost the support of his party (Nicolson 1986).

Home Secretary William Whitelaw did not resign when an intruder breached security at Buckingham Palace and entered the Queen's bedroom. Northern Ireland Secretary James Prior did not resign when there was an escape of prisoners from the Maze Prison. He did in fact offer his resignation to the prime minister but it was not accepted and not made public at the time. Later, an inquiry blamed the prison governor for the escape.

The resignations of Foreign and Commonwealth Office ministers were accepted when the Argentines invaded the Falkland Islands but Defence Secretary John Nott's resignation was not accepted despite the perception that it was aspects of defence budget cuts which prompted the Argentines to invade.

Home Secretaries Kenneth Baker and Michael Howard did not resign when prisoners escaped from Brixton, Whitemoor and Parkhurst Prisons. The inquiries into all of these escapes did not place blame upon the ministers.

Findings of maladministration leading to injustice by the Parliamentary Commissioner for Administration against the Foreign and Commonwealth Office over compensation for former prisoners of war at Sachsenhausen Camp, and the Department of Trade and Industry for the losses of investors in the Barlow-Clowes company, did not lead to the resignations of the relevant ministers, George Brown and Nicholas Ridley. Both denied that their departments were at fault, although compensation was paid to the complainants.

The masterly analysis of ministerial resignations carried out by Finer (1956) concluded that resignation would occur if 'the minister was yielding, his prime minister unbending and his party out for blood'. This has been updated by Woodhouse (1993), who adds that errors must be serious and foreseeable and have serious consequences for people who enjoy public sympathy. These analyses meet the case of Northern Ireland Secretary Peter Brooke. He offered his resignation after he had been persuaded to sing a song on a television chat show in Dublin some hours after the sectarian killing of eight men in Northern Ireland by the IRA. The prime minister did not accept the resignation, and no doubt the cross-party support for the minister in the House of Commons explained his continuance in office.

Finer's explanation can also include situations of personal responsibility where ministers have relied upon prime-ministerial suport and survived (see 4.2.2.3 for the cases of William Waldegrave and Sir Nicholas Lyell, who survived strong criticism in the Scott report).

In addition to this disagreement with Dicey about the sanction which would explain obedience to conventions, Jennings also proposed that conventions and laws were both obeyed because people accepted the obligations which they imposed. This theory has been tellingly attacked by Munro (1987, p. 47) who points out that failure to obey a law does not mean that its status as law has been denied, whereas disobedience to a convention seems to imply that it has no binding force. Other commentators, such as Hood Phillips have stressed the importance of acquiescence in their definition of conventions as those 'rules of political practice which are regarded as binding by those to whom they apply' (Hood Phillips & Jackson 1987, p. 113).

4.2 EXAMPLES OF CONVENTIONS

4.2.1 Sovereign–Parliament Relations

The sovereign has various formal prerogative powers but their exercise is qualified by convention. We have already noted the convention which applies to the royal assent to legislation (see 4.1.2). This convention, in common with others which deal with the sovereign's relations with Parliament and the government, stipulates that the powers are exercised upon the advice of ministers. This formulation allows for the advice to be ignored. The circumstances in which advice could be ignored are unclear. The convention on royal assent may be regarded as having less scope for non-compliance with ministerial advice than others. Marshall suggests that if a Bill of Rights was enacted which stipulated certain procedural steps for its amendment, then the sovereign might wish to think very carefully about giving assent to amendments which did not comply with those procedural requirements (1984, p. 22).

4.2.1.1 Appointment of the prime minister Another personal prerogative is the sovereign's choice of prime minister. Whilst there are legal rules which determine the succession to the throne and thus who may become head of State (see 5.2), the conventions which regulate the appointment of the prime minister are not entirely clear. It does now seem to be the case that the person appointed should be an MP rather than a peer. This convention would appear to have become firmly established by 1963. In that year the prime minister, Harold Macmillan, resigned due to ill-health, and his successor as leader of the Conservative Party was the Earl of Home. He then disclaimed his peerage under the Peerage Act 1963, and arrangements were made to find a constituency for him to represent in the Commons. It may be supposed that it was the enactment of the Peerage Act 1963 which clearly established that the prime minister should sit in the Commons as the more important House of Parliament. The last prime minister who was a peer was Lord Salisbury, who resigned in 1902. An important step in the establishment of this convention was the appointment of Stanley Baldwin rather than Lord Curzon as prime minister in 1923.

As we shall see in 4.3.2 a hung Parliament could also present problems for the sovereign's exercise of this power of appointment.

4.2.1.2 Dismissal of ministers Ministers are appointed by the sovereign on the advice of the prime minister. The sovereign also has the power to dismiss the whole government. How likely is it that this power would be exercised? There are hardly any precedents in the UK. In both Australia and Canada the Governors-General, acting as the Queen's personal representatives, have dismissed governments. Generally this is regarded as an action of the last resort and that would appear to be the view taken by Sir John Kerr in Australia in 1975. What had happened was that the upper house of the federal Parliament, the Senate, refused to grant supply so that the executive was running out of money to carry on the government of the country. The prime minister, Gough Whitlam, refused to resign or to advise a dissolution. As the leader of the opposition was willing to advise a dissolution, the Governor-General decided to dismiss the government, and asked the leader of the opposition to become prime minister. He advised a dissolution and his party was returned with a majority in the ensuing election. Sir John's action divided Australia. Argument has continued over whether he had no alternative. As the day approached when the government's revenues would be spent, the Senate might have given way and approved supply. It is clear that the use of the dismissal power is likely to be very controversial.

4.2.1.3 Dissolution Although a Parliament may last for a maximum of five years, it is most unusual that this period will elapse before a general election is held. Accordingly, the Parliament must be dissolved and the power to do this is also a personal prerogative of the sovereign. A dissolution will usually be sought when the party in government judges that its chances of re-election are good.

There is some dispute over whether it is the government as a whole, or the prime minister, who takes the responsibility in advising the sovereign to dissolve Parliament. In the 19th century it was generally regarded that this was a collective decision for the government. The point at which it was suggested that it was a matter for the prime minister can be traced to 1918 and a speech in the Commons by Bonar Law (Parliamentary Debates (Hansard), Commons, vol. 11, col. 2227, 7 November 1918). Marshall suggests that this was a plainly mistaken assertion about previous practice made in circumstances in which certain politicians wished to have the responsibility for dissolving Parliament placed on David Lloyd George, the prime minister (1984, p. 50).

Whether the prime minister communicates the advice to dissolve as a personal matter or as a collective one, it seems that the sovereign may decline to accept the advice. Writing under the pseudonym of Senex, Sir Alan Lascelles, private secretary to King George VI, outlined in a letter published in *The Times* (2 May 1950) considerations which might justify the refusal of a dissolution. These were that (a) the existing Parliament was still vital and capable of doing its job; (b) a general election would be detrimental to the economy; and (c) the King could rely upon finding a prime minister who would be able to form a government with a working majority in the Commons which could function for a reasonable period of time. This advice had been given to the King when the 1950 general election gave Mr Attlee a working majority of six. An election was held in 1951 and the Conservatives were returned with a working majority.

Difficulties with dissolution occur, then, where the government is either a minority one or has a small majority. One commentator has proposed that the crucial factor in refusal of a dissolution would be that 'an alternative government is possible and able to carry on with the existing House' (Markesinis 1972, p. 120). Aspects of this will be examined in the discussion of problems with conventions in a hung Parliament (see 4.3.2).

4.2.2 Executive–Parliament Relations

The most important of the conventions regulating relations between the executive and Parliament is that of ministerial responsibility. It may be divided between those aspects which refer to the government as a whole, collective responsibility, and that which applies to individual ministers. There are three aspects of collective responsibility which Marshall has termed the confidence, confidentiality and unanimity rules (1984, p. 55). The latter two rules really refer to relations between ministers, rather than between the government and Parliament. They will be discussed later (see 6.4.1).

4.2.2.1 Confidence If a government loses a vote of confidence then the convention requires that it should either resign or seek a dissolution of Parliament. Marshall is of the view that the convention has changed to allow for alternatives, and that previously resignation was the obligation placed on the government (1984, p. 55). Another matter on which there has been change concerns the situation where a government loses a vote on an important issue of policy. Hood Phillips used to think that a government was obliged to resign in those circumstances. On the other hand Norton has argued that this was never the case and accordingly, when the Labour government lost such votes, its failure to resign was not in breach of the convention (1981).

This convention underscores the transfer of power from the sovereign to Parliament. The government is composed of the ministers of the Crown, but it is as representatives of the people that they hold office. To lose the confidence of Parliament is to lose the confidence of the people's representatives and the authority to govern.

4.2.2.2 Individual ministerial responsibility Ministers account for the actions of their departments. If something has gone wrong then the minister is responsible and will explain what happened and why. The minister will also be expected to rectify the situation. This may mean changing procedures, or bringing disciplinary action against some officials, or even resigning if the matter is one for which the minister accepts personal responsibility.

As was discussed earlier, ministers' responsibility for their departments does not now encompass acceptance of blame for the actions of officials of which they neither knew nor approved – the Maxwell Fyfe guidelines. (see 4.1.4.) This has been taken a little further by the promotion of the distinction between ministerial accountability and ministerial responsibility. As it was phrased in a Cabinet Office memorandum to a select committee, 'a minister is *accountable* for all the actions and activities in his department, but is not *responsible* for all the actions in the sense of being blameworthy' (HC 27-II of 1993–4). This might seem innocuous but if the convention of individual ministerial responsibility does embody this distinction, then it is a significant change and, it is suggested, a weakening.

The argument for the distinction is that the growth in government means that ministers cannot personally know of everything which their officials do and so they cannot be personally responsible for it, but as ministers they must come to Parliament and give an account of what their departments do. Sir Richard Scott who conducted the inquiry into the export of defence equipment and dual-use goods to Iraq was clear that if ministers were not personally responsible then they must give a full account to Parliament (HC 115 of 1995–6, K.8). Sir Richard's report, which was prompted by the collapse, in 1992, of the prosecution of three directors of the company Matrix Churchill for their breach of the ban on exports to Iraq of arms or products which could be adapted to military use, analysed the topic of ministerial accountability in great detail. One aspect of the investigation of ministerial accountability concerned the policy on defence-related exports to Iraq and Iran, the so-called 'Howe guidelines'. Scott formed the view, contested by the government, that the Howe guidelines had been changed so that they were less restrictive towards Iraq. This change had not been announced to Parliament. Answers given to Parliamentary questions and in correspondence on the Howe guidelines, by the junior Foreign Office minister, William Waldegrave, maintained that they remained unchanged. Scott found that the ministerial obligation to give a full account had not been properly discharged and in his report and in subsequent speeches he put forward possible reforms. Scott's report led the House of Commons Public Service Committee to revise the terms of reference of an inquiry it was conducting on ministerial accountability and responsibility. One of the recommendations it made was that the House of Commons should adopt a resolution on accountability. A resolution was approved by the House in March 1997, though it was not the draft proposed by the committee. One of the differences concerned the extent of the justification for ministers withholding information when providing an account to Parliament. The committee's version stated that withholding information should be done 'exceptionally'. The government's version stipulated that the refusal to provide information would only be justified when 'disclosure would not be in the public interest', which should be decided in accordance with the relevant statute and the government's *Code of Practice on Access to Government Information* (Parliamentary Debates (Hansard) Commons vol 292, cols 1046–7, 19 March 1997). The difficulty here is that the extent of the public interest is not well-defined, giving ministers significant scope for withholding information.

The obligation to provide information requires that ministers should not mislead. If a minister knowingly misleads the House then it is expected that the minister will make an offer to resign to the prime minister. Inadvertent errors should be corrected at the earliest opportunity. Again this is not as tight as it might appear. How great is the obligation upon ministers to ensure that they are not ignorant of matters? What happens after they have corrected an inadvertent error?

The Ministerial Code: A Code of Conduct and Guidance on Procedures for Ministers (Cabinet Office, 1997) has been revised in line with the Commons resolution, including the expectation of an offer of resignation from a minister who knowingly misleads Parliament. While the obligation to uphold collective responsibility is stipulated, there is no mention of personal ministerial responsibility.

How realistic is it to expect ministers to give a full account, if to do so would place them in an embarrassing position? Is it possible to enforce the obligation of accountability? Sir Richard Scott has made several reform proposals: (a) the enactment of a Freedom of Information Act; (b) revising the so-called Osmotherly Rules so as to permit officials to give evidence on their own behalf, rather than as the representatives of ministers, on matters of fact to a select committee investigating affairs in which something has gone wrong; (c) the creation of an officer of Parliament who would investigate claims by MPs that a minister had misled the House, and (d) placing the accountability obligation on a statutory basis (1996a). While the Labour government elected in May 1997 promised action on a Freedom of Information Bill, the timetable for this has slipped. Legislation will not be enacted until at least the second year of the Parliament. Anyway, everything will depend upon how extensive the obligation to provide information is, and how it is to be enforced. The experience of the current arrangements, in which a non-statutory code of practice is policed by the Parliamentary Commissioner for Administration, shows that the secretive Whitehall culture is very much alive and not very cooperative (see the reports of the Parliamentary Commissioner on complaints about the operation of the code of practice). We will consider the second proposal when dealing with the relationship between ministers and officials at 6.4.3.4. The obvious difficulty with the idea of a Parliamentary official enforcing ministerial accountability is that this would be intensely political and likely therefore to compromise the person holding the post. More mundanely, if the workload of the other Parliamentary Commissioners for Administration, the Health Service and Standards necessitated the creation of an entirely new officer, the public could well be confused about the responsibilities of these officers. Bogdanor, in commenting about the fourth proposal, simply said that the idea of putting the obligation to account on a statutory basis was, perhaps, the most unrealistic of the four reform proposals (1997, p. 82). He did not specify whether his comment referred to the likelihood of (a) any government proposing such legislation, or (b) success even if enactment was carried out.

It seems then that the growth in government has led to a reduction in ministerial responsibility. One explanation might be that the focus upon ministerial resignation as the price to be paid when something goes wrong has caused ministers to avoid such an unpleasant outcome. They have sought to do this by (a) reducing the area of their personal responsibility by shifting responsibility on to officials, which includes separating policy from operations and administration, with officials being responsible for the latter (see 6.4.3.4), and (b) seeking to provide a less than full account to Parliament on the basis that the less information Parliament has, the less likely it is that Parliament will be able to hold ministers responsible for the work of their departments. This diminished ministerial responsibility and accountability seems to be based on linked misapprehensions. First, that holding a minister responsible for departmental mistakes always requires ministerial resignation, rather than appropriate corrective action, and secondly the idea that in the past when governmental activities were not as extensive, ministers resigned for any error committed by their officials no matter how trivial.

As very few people, least of all ministers like to admit a mistake, whether trivial or grave, is it possible for ministers to accept more personal responsibility for their departments' actions? Woodhouse wonders if the trend towards emphasising accountability over responsibility and information over culpability might reduce the desire of MPs to allocate blame for departmental errors and demands for resignation (1997b, p. 281). She suggests that if Parliament is serious about its functions then withholding information and giving inadequate explanations should be regarded as more serious offences than making a mistake. She regards it is as overly optimistic to think that reducing the threat of resignation will induce ministers to be more open about mistakes. It would appear that it is the threat of embarrassment which may both keep ministers up to the mark and spur them on to seek to evade responsibility. One response to this, and strongly resisted by government, is for Parliament to move on to those who have had responsibility passed to them by ministers — their officials. As a delegation of responsibility has occurred with the creation of the Next Steps executive agencies, it would seem logical that their chief executives should have a direct relationship with select committees through which Parliament mainly exercises its oversight. This will be discussed at 6.4.3.4.

4.2.2.3 Relationship between collective and individual responsibility The operation of these two types of responsibility may be subverted by their relationship with each other. The reality of ministerial resignation was explained by Finer (1956) as being a political matter. If pressure for a resignation is overwhelming, then it will be made. Often a minister may rely upon the prime minister for support and the individual minister is shielded by collective responsibility. It also occurs the other way round and an individual minister may be sacrificed to save the government as a whole.

An example of individual ministerial responsibility being subverted by what was, in effect, collective responsibility is provided by the reception to the Scott report culminating in the debate on it in February 1996. Two ministers had been the subject of strong criticism. Mention has already been made of William Waldegrave, who, in Scott's view, had not discharged his obligation to give a full account about the status of the Howe guidelines. Sir Nicholas Lyell, who was the Attorney-General, was adjudged by Scott not to have performed his duties adequately, in particular, his failure to honour his promise to Michael Heseltine about informing the trial judge of Heseltine's reservations concerning the matters in the public interest immunity certificate which the Attorney had persuaded him to sign. Lyell took the view that he was not personally responsible but was constitutionally obliged to account for the work of his officials in dealing with the administration of public interest immunity certificates (Woodhouse 1997a, Thompson 1997, pp. 184–5). Both ministers declined to resign. They survived in office, as did the government following its one-vote majority in the adjournment debate on the Scott report. As this was, in effect, a vote of confidence, it was not surprising that the government won. What was surprising was that some backbenchers on the government's side either abstained or voted with the opposition, so that the majority was achieved by only a single vote.

It has been suggested that the resignation of Mr Leon Brittan during the Westland affair saved the government. He ordered one of his departmental officials to 'leak' to the press the confidential advice of the Solicitor-General as part of an attempt to discredit Mr Michael Heseltine, the former defence minister, who had resigned because his preference that the Westland Helicopter Company should become part of a European consortium rather than a wholly owned subsidiary of an American firm was at variance with the official governmental stance of neutrality. It seemed that Mr Brittan preferred the American option and this division in the government had weakened its authority, especially when Mr Heseltine, after his resignation, attacked the leadership style of the prime minister. Mr Brittan's actions gave the prime minister, the government and its backbenchers a scapegoat, even though there were allegations that the prime minister's staff had been involved in this leak. Subsequent inquiries did not link Mrs Thatcher or her staff to Mr Brittan's 'indiscretion'.

4.2.3 Parliamentary Conventions

Parliament has its own customs, but some of the constitutional conventions relate to its work, dealing with matters inside both Houses, and relations between the Houses.

4.2.3.1 Inter-House relations When Dicey first wrote on the conventions regulating the relations between the two Houses of Parliament in 1885, there was a convention that, in a conflict between them, the Lords should give way to the Commons. The Lords' rejection of the People's Budget led to the enactment of the Parliament Act 1911, which limited the powers of the Lords so that they could only delay and not veto the vast majority of Bills passed by the Commons. The period of delay was reduced by the Parliament Act 1949, which was itself passed under the provisions of the 1911 statute (see further 8.6). This legislation has not removed convention, which now refers to the degree of resistance which the unelected Lords may offer to the Commons. The Salisbury conventions provide that the Lords may not offer outright opposition to a measure which was in the election manifesto of the government. This, however, leaves quite a scope for conflict between the two Houses. The House of Lords does seem to exercise self-restraint in recognition of its inferior status as an unelected chamber. Relations between the two Houses are pragmatic, with the peers attempting to see what they 'can get away with'. Sometimes they back down and sometimes a compromise is agreed (see further 8.6).

4.2.3.2 House of Commons Mention has already been made of the practice of pairing, where MPs make arrangements not to vote in divisions without altering the numerical balance between the parties (see 4.1.2).

Another convention refers to the decision to hold a by-election for a seat which has become vacant. The writ for the by-election is moved by the chief whip of the party which held the seat. The relevant chief whip has discretion as to the timing of the by-election but it is usually done within three months of the occurrence of the vacancy.

4.2.3.3 House of Lords When the Law Lords sit as an Appellate Committee of the House, other peers, by convention, do not join them to participate in the hearing and determination of an appeal. The legislation which created the first life peerage, a Lord of Appeal in Ordinary, thereby ensuring that the House had properly qualified members for its judicial work, did not stipulate that lay peers were excluded from that work (Appellate Jurisdiction Act 1876).

4.2.4 The Commonwealth
Just as power has shifted from the sovereign to Parliament, the same process has occurred in relations between the UK as colonial power and the former colonies, now members of the Commonwealth. When colonies, these countries were legally subordinate to the UK and the Westminster, or Imperial, Parliament was the ultimate constitutional authority. By the early years of the 20th century relations between some of the colonies and the UK were becoming more like those of independent States, of equals rather than of superior and inferiors. The Balfour Declaration at an Imperial Conference in 1926 established conventions regulating relations between some of the colonies and the UK. While the constitutions of these countries were Westminster statutes, it was agreed that no legislation relating to any of those countries would be enacted at Westminster unless the government of that country had requested and consented to the legislation.

Subsequently the Statute of Westminster 1931 was enacted. This Act dealt with countries which were called 'dominions' (s. 1). Of the group of countries which were dominions for this Act, only Australia, Canada and New Zealand still remain in the Commonwealth (South Africa left and has rejoined). The parliaments of the dominions were given the power to legislate free from the restrictions of the Colonial Laws Validity Act 1865 (s. 2), and to make laws having extraterritorial operation (s. 3). The statute also declared that after its commencement, no Act of the UK Parliament would 'extend, or be deemed to extend, to a Dominion as part of the law of that Dominion, unless it is expressly declared in that Act that that Dominion has requested, and consented to, the enactment thereof' (s. 4).

In effect, these countries were acknowledged as independent States. After the Second World War most colonies were given their independence and new constitutions were drafted which reflected this change in status. Some countries, such as India, became republics. These countries could no longer have the British monarch as their own head of State; instead, the Queen has the title Head of the Commonwealth. Where countries retain the Queen as head of State they must be consulted and agree to, and enact any legislation which would alter the succession to the throne and the royal style and titles.

When Canada and Australia sought full independence, they wished to be able to deal with their constitutions using their own institutions and processes, so that they were no longer legally required to have an Act passed at Westminster to give final effect to such matters. They sought the 'patriation' of their constitutions and this required, for the final time, the passage of a statute at Westminster (Canada Act 1982, Australia Act 1986).

4.3 DIFFICULT ISSUES

The discussion of the nature of constitutional conventions has indicated that there are difficult issues. Some of the conventions are vague, and it is occasionally unclear if a particular convention has become established. Three issues will now be examined: (a) the establishment of conventions; (b) situations in which conventions seem to conflict; and (c) arguments for and against the codification of conventions.

4.3.1 Establishment of Conventions

Conventions may be established by specific agreement, and by practice. The making of conventions by agreement is illustrated by the Imperial Conferences out of which arose conventions regulating relations between dominions and the UK (see 4.2.4). It is also possible for agreements to modify conventions. At the Mauritius Constitutional Conference of 1965, an exception was agreed to the general conventions relating to the appointment and removal of a Governor-General. The government of Mauritius agreed that, upon independence, it would not ask for the removal of the Governor-General, save under a special provision dealing with medical incapacity.

Most conventions arise because a particular practice is followed in the future. Jennings took the view that neither practice nor precedent were themselves sufficient to establish a convention (1959, pp. 134–6). He argued that the fact that no monarch had refused a dissolution of Parliament for over a century did not establish that such ministerial advice must always be accepted. He supported this with material from memoirs which indicated that various monarchs had maintained their right to refuse a dissolution (1959, p. 135).

So far as precedent is concerned, he concluded that it was not clear that the preference for Mr Baldwin over Lord Curzon in 1923 created the precedent that the prime minister must always be an MP. Jennings suggested a set of questions which would assist in identifying conventions (1959, p. 136). First one must ask what are the precedents? Then, did the actors in those precedents believe that they were bound by a rule? Thirdly, is there a reason for the rule?

The second and third questions are not entirely easy to answer. It will not always be clear why people acted as they did. Jennings's insistence on a rule appears to derive from his view that conventions must have a normative character, that is, oblige people to act in certain ways. This comes about because of his two suggested objectives of conventions, that they seek compliance with the prevailing political philosophy, and that they ease the operation of the machinery of the State.

The third question which focuses on the reason for the rule would appear to have been very significant in the Canadian case where the Supreme Court adopted Jennings's questions in an attempt to determine if there was a convention to the effect that there should be agreement between the federal and provincial governments over amendments which would affect the relationship between these two tiers of government (*Reference re Amendment of the Constitution of Canada (Nos. 1, 2 and 3)* (1981) 125 DLR (3d) 1). By a majority the court found that there were precedents in which the actors did feel obliged to have substantial agreement about such changes to federal–provincial relations. Canada, as a federation, has two tiers of government which share power. This is different from a unitary state such as the UK. Devolved government could be established in Northern Ireland and it could also be removed as the Crown in Parliament is the ultimate constitutional power. In a federal constitution the two types of government are created at the same time and power allocated between them. This allocation is fundamental. Accordingly, the Canadian Supreme Court could decide that the reason for the convention requiring agreement for alterations to federal–provincial relations was 'to protect the federal character of the Canadian constitution'.

4.3.1.1 Crystallisation The Canadian Supreme Court did not accept the argument that a convention could crystallise into a rule of law which a court could enforce. Just as it followed Jennings in its identification of a convention, so it followed Dicey in maintaining enforcement by the courts as the distinction between conventions and rules of law. Conventions, it held, are neither judicial precedents nor statutory commands which courts must obey and follow.

In another case which derived from the patriation of the Canadian constitution, the English Court of Appeal rejected the contention of a group of native Canadian Indians that the convention of Canadian consent to legislation enacted at Westminster must be actual consent which had to be establisned (*Manuel v Attorney-General* [1983] Ch 77). The court, in rejecting the claim, pointed out that s. 4 of the Statute of Westminster 1931 only required that a statute enacted at Westminster concerning a dominion contain an express declaration that the statute had been requested by and consented to by the dominion. As Slade LJ stated, the wording of s. 4 precluded going behind the declaration in the enactment to discover if there had, in fact, been such consent. This would appear to have been done to stop cases such as this one from coming before the courts.

The Statute of Westminster 1931 and the Parliament Act 1911 are often described as being 'enacted conventions'. In fact in both instances the legislation did not reproduce the conventions (see *Manuel v Attorney-General* and De Smith and Brazier 1994, pp. 47–8).

4.3.2 Conflicting Conventions
Some conventions are imprecise but another problem can arise when it appears that there is a conflict between conventions. Such a situation could

occur in a hung Parliament, that is, a Parliament in which no party has an overall majority. A couple of scenarios will enable us to explore the possibilities. In the first example the Circle Party, which formed the government before the election, becomes the second largest party in Parliament after the election. The prime minister does not resign but negotiates an agreement with the Triangle Party, which is the third largest. The Circle and Triangle parties form a coalition government with a working majority. After six months the coalition partners are in dispute. The Triangle Party sought unsuccessfully an assurance on a point from the prime minister and leader of the Circle Party. The Triangle Party withdrew from the coalition but made it clear that if the Circle Party had a new leader, who would satisfy them about the point which had been in dispute, then they would be ready to form a coalition again.

The Circle Party carry on as a minority government and lose a vote on a major policy issue. The leader of the Square Party, which is the largest, calls for a dissolution. The Square Party have made it clear that they are not prepared to enter an agreement with the Triangle Party. There is a significant body of opinion in the Circle Party which would be prepared to meet the Triangle Party's terms for a new coalition. The Finance Bill is lost and the prime minister resigns. What should the sovereign do? The options are to appoint as prime minister someone from the Circle Party who would be prepared to work with the Triangle Party; to ask the leader of the Square Party to form a minority government; or to appoint someone who would advise a dissolution. Jennings seems to suggest that upon resignation, the leader of the opposition should be asked to form the government. The force of this is increased in this example because the Square Party is the largest. Against that it seems that a person might be found who could rebuild the coalition between the Circle and Triangle parties. For the sovereign to take such action could be construed as playing a real role in the battle between the parties. Could the resignation in this example be regarded as akin to those of Mr Wilson in 1976 and Mrs Thatcher in 1990, so that it is up to a majority to find its own successor to the leadership and thus a prime minister?

The reason behind the conventions restricting the personal prerogative powers is to remove the sovereign from party politics. If the outgoing leader of the Circle Party remains in that office it would be very difficult for the sovereign to appoint someone else from that party as prime minister. The leader of the Square Party wants a dissolution and it might be best to leave it to the people to decide if they want to elect a new House of Commons in which there is a party with an overall majority. The convention on dissolution of Parliament would seem to allow the sovereign to refuse it if a government with a working majority could be formed. As this Parliament is only six months old, this could also be a factor pointing against dissolution. It is suggested that in this situation the leader of the opposition should be appointed prime minister and if a dissolution is advised it should be granted. The Parliament is not stable so government with a majority is uncertain. The people should decide even though only six months have elapsed from the last election with its inconclusive result.

A better solution to this problem would be to remove the power of appointment of the prime minister from the sovereign and instead stipulate that the prime minister is to be elected by the House of Commons. This is a provision in one think-tank's proposed constitution for the UK (IPPR 1991). Such a provision is more in keeping with the UK's form of democracy. The people elect their representatives who in turn elect the head of government.

Let us return to the example and add some new facts. The coalition has broken up and the Appropriation Act has not been passed. The prime minister will neither resign nor advise a dissolution. Should the sovereign act as Sir John Kerr did in Australia in 1975, dismissing the government and appointing as prime minister the leader of the opposition who would seek a dissolution? Alternatively, should the sovereign await developments? Perhaps a vote of confidence might be tabled. It could be suggested that the power of dismissal is a reserve power which may be used to break a deadlock caused by action which is a breach of convention. However, perhaps it would be preferred to allow the people, rather than the sovereign, to resolve matters. Even if a prime minister refused to resign or advise a dissolution on losing a vote of confidence, it is suggested that it would be better to allow Parliamentary and public pressure to bring about compliance with the convention, rather than have the sovereign precipitate events.

Some commentators have argued for a principle of a kind of constitutional tit for tat, that it is permissible to infringe one convention in order to remedy the breach of another convention. Professor Wade proposed this in evidence before the Foreign Affairs Select Committee when it was conducting an investigation into another situation in which conventions came into conflict (HC 42 of 1980–81). This was the dispute between the Canadian federal and provincial governments over the federal government's request for legislation to be passed at Westminster to patriate the Canadian constitution. The select committee concluded that the Westminster Parliament was not bound by convention to comply automatically with requests from the federal government, even those which had unanimous support from the provincial governments. The committee took the view that Westminster retained the role of deciding whether or not a request for amendment or patriation of the British North America Act 1867 (the Canadian constitution) conveyed the clearly expressed view of Canada as a whole, bearing in mind the federal nature of Canada's constitutional system. Normally the federal request would be sufficient but if the opposition of the provincial governments is brought to the attention of Westminster then, the committee concluded, something more was required. This would mean, as the committee appreciated, that Westminster would not be acting in conformity with the usual formulation of the convention regulating the UK's response to a Commonwealth country's request for legislation. The reason for this was that it was in conflict with one of that country's own conventions.

The committee set limits to this discretion to refuse such a request. They were proposing that the manner of the request to alter the federal character should itself be in keeping with that federal character. The merits of any amendment or patriation requests were solely a matter for the Canadians.

The select committee's view was different from that of the UK government. It appeared that the UK government was prepared to comply with the federal government's request. It would be embarrassing for the UK government to reject such a request as it would entail meddling in Canadian affairs. Yet it was the case that this request breached a Canadian convention. As things turned out Westminster was spared this dilemma by the decision of the Canadian Supreme Court, which found as a matter of fact that there was the convention contended for by the unhappy provincial governments, but that as a matter of law the court could not enforce it. Although the federal government won on the law, they decided to renegotiate with the provincial governments and agreement was reached with all of them except Quebec. The request for legislation with this substantial agreement was granted by Westminster, which passed the Canada Act 1982.

It is suggested that this was a better solution than Westminster rejecting the request, even though this would have been motivated by concern to protect the federal nature of Canada. Surely this was a matter for Canadians? The reasons behind the convention concerning the UK's response to requests for legislation were that these were matters amongst equals, and the UK should not interfere in these countries' internal affairs.

4.3.3 Codification

We have seen that conventions are not always precise, that they sometimes conflict. Would it not therefore be better if they were codified? The objection to this is that the imprecision is desirable so as to allow conventions to be flexible, and thus to play their part of ensuring compliance with the prevailing constitutional philosophy. Would the setting down of conventions have this effect? Some of the conventions on UK–Commonwealth relations were specifically agreed at conferences. Why should a conference of MPs not set down agreed conventions? This has happened in Australia where elected representatives have met to 'recognise and declare constitutional conventions'. These representatives have usually come from both the government and opposition parties, in the federal and state legislatures. They have met since 1973 to discuss constitutional change. One of the matters which they considered was a compilation of constitutional conventions. The dismissal of the Whitlam government in 1975 by the Governor-General had added to the feeling that a list of generally agreed conventions would be a good idea. Sampford (1987) argues that this experiment is not likely to be a success. He noted that difficult issues, such as the relations between the Governor-General and the government, did not feature to any great extent in the list of conventions which had been 'recognised and declared'.

· Sampford's analysis of the Australian experience is thorough. Only a couple of points will be mentioned here. Not all of the existing conventions are included in the list, or code of conventions, and the formulation of some of the conventions in the code differs from the way they were expressed before the code was compiled. He suggests that the code will acquire a primacy, indeed that it may become regarded as being an authoritative list, as if it were a statute. This will mean that previous arguments about conventions, concerning their nature, existence or formulation will be changed to arguments about the meanings of the terms in the text of the code, their scope and intent and any qualifications or exceptions. Sampford argues that this is unfortunate because, while the code provides a means of identifying conventions, it does nothing to assist in the resolution of disputes about these conventions, nor does it cope with the changes which conventions may develop. He contrasts this situation with Canadian practice. The jurisdiction of the Canadian Supreme Court to give advisory opinions provides an adjudicatory institution. A rule of adjudication also gives rules for recognition and change. Sampford regards as a success the court's decision in the dispute over the convention on the amount of agreement which is required when modifications are proposed to the relations between the federal and provincial governments. This was a crisis and the court's finding that the convention existed led to a satisfactory outcome with proposals that all but one of the provincial governments supported.

It is not a new thing for the courts to acknowledge the existence of conventions but does the Canadian experience mean that they can be enforced by the courts? Strictly, this is not what happens. The Canadian Supreme Court ruled that the convention was not law and could not be enforced by the court. The federal government could, as a matter of law, have proceeded with its initial proposals but the court's recognition of the convention added to the political pressure which the government was under.

As for the impact this jurisdiction has on the courts, it is perhaps not particularly remarkable when a court has the jurisdiction to determine questions on the legal rules of the constitution. If Sampford feels that the Australian experiment should not be followed, can we follow Canada when the UK does not have a constitution in the sense accepted by most other liberal democracies?

4.4 RESOLVING CONFUSION

Conventions have an important part to play in the operation of constitutions, yet in the UK there is still much uncertainty surrounding their 'definition, scope and consequences' (Brazier 1992, p. 268). This is partially because constitutional conventions tend to be regarded as a group of non-legal rules which impose the same weight of obligation. Conventions are not equal in this regard. Distinctions have been drawn between rules and practices or usages (e.g., Wheare 1953, p. 10; Bradley and Ewing 1993, p. 28). Two attempts have been made to reclassify conventions or the non-legal constitution according to degree of obligation (Heard 1991 and Brazier 1992).

Heard's analysis of Canadian constitutional conventions divides them into three categories, which are superior to a fourth group of proposals of behaviour, which in turn rank above mere usages. Brazier proposes a threefold heirarchical classification of the non-legal constitution, which places constitutional practices at the bottom, constitutional conventions in the middle, and fundamental principles at the top.

Whilst Heard's analysis is focused upon Canada, it is derived from an insight made by a British academic and politician (Mackintosh 1977, pp. 20–1), and so it is not entirely inapplicable to the UK. Heard suggests that the factors which are involved in determining the allocation of informal rules to his suggested classes are (a) the importance of the principle or reason which lies behind the rule; (b) the degree of agreement in the community over the principle; (c) the degree of agreement over the specific terms of the rule; and (d) the closeness of fit between the terms of the rule and the principle which it is supposed to embody. He suggests as examples of his top tier of rules, or fundamental conventions, that the Queen's representatives (Governor-General and Lieutenant Governors) should act on constitutionally correct ministerial advice, the cabinet should resign or seek a general election if it loses a vote of confidence, and politicians should not try to influence the judges in their deliberations on a case. All of these are important principles in the constitution, so that their absence would mean that the constitution would be signficantly altered. As one moves down his hierarchy, the principles which the rules uphold will have decreasing support, at first because the specific details of the rule may vary, and later because the principle is controversial.

Brazier seeks to divide constitutional conventions from constitutional practices. Conventions limit the exercise of legal authority of those in each of the three branches of government, while practices are characterised by the fact that a constitutional actor will usually behave in a particular way despite the lack of an obligation to do so. A constitutional practice will limit the full effect of a legal rule and introduce a degree of predictability in areas not regulated by convention. Examples of constitutional practices include: (a) the consultation amongst colleagues by the prime minister when deciding upon the timing of a general election; (b) the custom of Commons select committees to try to operate on a consensual basis even though the government party has a majority on every committee; and (c) that persons elevated to the peerage are made life rather than hereditary peers. These practices are not invariably followed as Brazier notes (1992, pp. 270–2).

Constitutional practices may, as happened with the royal assent to legislation, change into a convention (Brazier 1992, pp. 269–70) and conventions could become practices if the obligation underlying the convention weakened.

Brazier also thinks that there is a place in the non-legal constitution for norms which are superior to conventions. He agrees with other commentators (McAuslan and McEldowney 1985, p. 8; Harden 1991, p. 502) that, because of the fundamental rule of the UK constitution, legislative supremacy, there ought to be restraints upon governmental power which would be derived from the fundamental values of the constitution. One such principle is constitutional propriety, which requires that constitutional actors exercise their legal powers with restraint. For governments this might mean that they must not legislate to subvert the democratic basis of the country, nor encroach upon the independence of the judiciary, but must resign or seek a dissolution if they lose a vote of confidence; and for the Queen it means that she must usually act on ministerial advice.

It will be seen that there is a great correspondence between Brazier's constitutional principles or super-conventions, and Heard's fundamental conventions, but there is a difference in how they see them being enforced. In Canada the Supreme Court could take them into account as it did with the convention which requires agreement over modifications in the relationship between the federal and provincial governments (*Reference re Amendment of the Constitution of Canada (Nos. 1, 2 and 3)* (1981) 125 DLR (3d) 1). Heard believes that the criteria underlying his classification of conventions mean that the important ones can be distinguished from the insignificant or controversial ones. Brazier seems to prefer a variant of the Australian approach. He proposes that politicians should, through a constitutional commission, seek agreement over the fundamental constitutional principles and then present them in an authoritative but non-legal text, or incorporate them in a statute. Brazier takes the view that since politicians as constitutional actors will be subject to such restraints, it is advisable to involve them in the process of formulating them (see Brazier 1991, for a general account of his pragmatic approach to securing constitutional reform).

Non-legal rules are necessary in any set of constitutional arrangements. Their purpose is to provide flexibility, to ensure the adaptation of the formal rules to the current constitutional orthodoxy. Inevitably there will be some ambiguity about the establishment of such informal rules, but there will also be some which are clear and fundamental to the operation of the constitution. Where possible it is suggested that such fundamental informal rules should be transformed into legal rules, for example, requiring that a government resigns or seeks a general election when it loses a vote of confidence, or requiring that the prime minister is elected by the House of Commons. Confusion over conventions can be reduced if it is appreciated that they are not a uniform group, and whether one creates classes of non-legal rules, or suggests that they form a continuum (Munro 1987, p. 60) effort should be directed to trying to separate the fundamental from the minor.

PART II

INSTITUTIONS OF GOVERNMENT

In this part we are concerned with the law and practice of the institutions of government. As chapter 4 showed, there is a discrepancy between form and function in our constitutional arrangements so that one of the roles of constitutional conventions is to bridge this gap by ensuring that the exercise of powers is taken by those who can be held to account. Chapter 5 explores further the changed circumstances in which a wide range of powers formally invested in the monarch are exercised on the advice of ministers. Chapter 6 focuses upon ministers and their officials, their relationship with each other and the changes brought about by the introduction of managerial reforms in the public service.

There are two chapters on Parliament. Chapter 7 deals with its composition and role, and chapter 8 examines the manner in which Parliament discharges its tasks and considers suggestions for reform. After these four chapters on central government in the UK we turn to Europe and in chapter 9 consider the supranational arrangements within the European Communities. This will include material on the origins and purposes of the Communities, as well as Community law and institutions and the increasing role they play in the UK. Chapter 10 returns to indigenous institutions of government which have been created because they have perceived advantages over central government. Local government's relationship with the centre has been one of confusion and change, especially with regard to its financing. The problems posed by quasi-government have received less attention but the distancing of executive power from accountability to the people and their elected representatives is one of fundamental importance.

Chapter 11, the final one in this part, deals with the judges, focusing upon their independence within our system of government.

CHAPTER FIVE

The Crown: Personality, Powers and Privileges

If we define democracy as government by the people, then the logic of representation could be taken to suggest that a president is to be preferred to a monarch on the grounds that a president is elected by the people and a monarch is not. The demands of logic are not always accepted and the UK is not the only country to retain the monarchical system. Within the European Union, for example, Belgium, Denmark, the Netherlands, Spain and Sweden all have monarchs, and Luxembourg, which is a Grand Duchy, may also be said to be a member of this group of countries with reigning royal families.

The position of these monarchs differs greatly from that of their forebears. Formerly the monarch was both head of State and head of government. Now the monarch is simply head of State and has much less power than the head of government. Yet the formal hierarchy still places the monarch above the prime minister. In the UK the difference between appearance and reality is quite pronounced because a wide range of powers is still vested in, and exercisable by, the monarch.

5.1 THE CROWN AS PERSON AND INSTITUTION

In the UK the concept of the State has not really been developed. Instead there has been an evolutionary process in which real loss of power from the monarch personally has been both signified by, and contained within, the institution of the Crown. As Lord Simon of Glaisdale said in *Town Investments Ltd v Department of the Environment* [1978] AC 359 at p. 398:

> . . . the Crown and 'Her Majesty' are terms of art in constitutional law. They correspond, though not exactly, with terms of political science like 'the Executive' or 'the administration' or 'the Government', barely known to the law, which has retained the historical terminology.

The institution of the Crown provides for both continuity and change. Power has flowed from the monarch to an executive composed, mainly, from the people's elected representatives, but the formal exercise of that power is performed by the monarch. The use of the term 'the Crown' signifies the continuing participation of the monarch even though this is now the role of a junior partner. Thus the government is Her Majesty's Government, and in the official opening of each session of Parliament the Queen in her 'gracious speech from the throne' announces the topics on which *her* government will present Bills to Parliament. Both ministers and their officials are Crown servants. The courts are the royal courts, in which criminal prosecutions are mounted in the name of the Queen by the Crown Prosecution Service. The publisher and printer of legislation and other official papers is Her Majesty's Stationery Office and the copyright in these publications is that of the Crown. These examples give an indication of the extent of the Crown as an institution. Quite often the legal authority for the government's actions will be provided for by statute. There are, however, some actions the authority for which is derived from the royal prerogative. Only the monarch is vested with prerogative power but the important powers are now only exercised by the monarch on the advice of ministers. Thus constitutional convention seeks to offset this departure from democratic theory. Other prerogative powers relate to what might be termed the ornamental, such as honours, some of which may be exercised solely at the discretion of the monarch.

5.1.1 The Privy Council
When the sovereign not only reigned, but ruled, the Privy Council was an important part of the machinery of government. As well as being an advisory body, it was also a means by which some actions took legal effect. Orders in Council are acts of the prerogative which is a source of powers and privileges peculiar to the sovereign (see further 5.4). Some legislation takes the form of Orders in Council (see 8.2.6.1). Since the prorogation of the Parliament of Northern Ireland, and the Northern Ireland Assembly, a majority of matters which would have been enacted as Acts of those subordinate legislatures, are now passed as statutory Orders in Council (see 8.2.7). It is felt that the preference for this type of legislation over 'ordinary' statutory instruments indicates a greater constitutional significance which is reflected in the participation of the sovereign. Certainly amendment of the constitutions of colonies is effected in this way.

The members of the Privy Council are, by convention, senior members of the royal family, cabinet ministers, the Archbishops of Canterbury and York, the Speaker of the House of Commons, the senior judiciary including the Lords of Appeal in Ordinary and the Lord Justices of Appeal, the leader of the opposition, and others who are distinguished in political or public service, such as non-cabinet ministers, and the leaders of some of the smaller political parties (currently the Liberal Democrats and Ulster Unionist Party leaders).

Meetings of the Privy Council occur wherever the sovereign is and so the members have to attend those palaces which are, as it were, the royal family's holiday homes, for example, Balmoral Castle. Usually about four ministers attend, including the Lord President of the Council, who is a senior minister usually without departmental responsibilities such as Leader of either of the two Houses of Parliament. The business conducted at a meeting is a formality. The sovereign has been briefed and gives oral assent to the title of the measure which the Lord President reads aloud. Usually the proceedings are conducted with everyone standing.

One of the functions of the Council is to give advice. There are advisory committees which deal with the Channel Islands, the universities, and a Political Honours Scrutiny Committee. This last committee, which is composed of 'elderly statesmen' from the three main national political parties, considers nominations for honours in respect of political service.

Another, technically, advisory committee is the Judicial Committee, which has an appellate jurisdiction from some Commonwealth countries and may also hear miscellaneous matters. Its opinions are promulgated as Orders in Council (see 11.1.2).

Occasionally an ad hoc inquiry to be conducted by Privy Councillors is created. As all members swear an oath to respect the confidentiality of Council proceedings, these inquiries can cover sensitive issues. One such example was the inquiry into the origin of the Falklands War. As this involved consideration of cabinet papers of different governments permission to see these papers was sought from the surviving prime ministers.

5.2 LEGAL CONSTRAINTS UPON THE SOVEREIGN

5.2.1 Succession
The line of succession to the throne is regulated by statute and common law. Only descendants of Sophia, Electoress of Hanover, are eligible. They must not, however, be Roman Catholics or marry a Roman Catholic. Not only does adherence to Roman Catholicism debar from the succession, but a person is not eligible unless he or she is able to, and does take communion in the Church of England. The Coronation Oath requires the sovereign to uphold the established churches, i.e., the Church of England and the Church of Scotland.

The line of succession passes according to rules relating to gender and age, so that males take precedence over females even if the females are older. If the sovereign has more than one son then the order of succession moves from the oldest to the youngest. Thus, a younger brother would succeed to the throne before an older sister. If all of the sovereign's children are female then the first born will succeed to the throne.

Prince Charles, the Prince of Wales, as the eldest son of the reigning sovereign, is the present heir apparent. Where the sovereign has no sons, the next in line to the succession is known as the heir/heiress presumptive because there is a possibility that a son might be born who would displace the presumptive heir or heiress.

5.2.2 Accession and Coronation
Following the death of the sovereign, the succession is immediate and automatic. Certain formalities are carried out. The successor will be

proclaimed at a specially convened Accession Council. This is usually composed of members of the House of Lords and other notable people who, in 1952, included some of the High Commissioners of Commonwealth countries. The proclamation will be approved at the first meeting of the Privy Council.

Several months may pass before the coronation is held. The coronation is quite a spectacle and also has symbolic significance. An important part of the ceremony is the taking of the Coronation Oath which stipulates the sovereign's duties to the subjects of the realm.

5.2.3 Royal Titles

It used to be the case that the Crown was single and indivisible. This theory has come under strain with developments in the Commonwealth, not least because of the inclusion of republics. Now each self-governing country in the Commonwealth can decide for itself the title which the sovereign will take in respect of that particular country. In the UK, and those territories whose foreign affairs are the responsibility of the UK, the current title of the sovereign is 'Elizabeth II by the Grace of God of the United Kingdom of Great Britain and Northern Ireland and of Her other Realms and Territories Queen, Head of the Commonwealth, Defender of the Faith' (Royal Titles Act 1953). The only title common to Her Majesty as Queen of Australia, Canada and New Zealand, is Head of the Commonwealth.

The proclamation of the royal titles was challenged in Scotland. This was on the basis that as Scotland had not previously had a Queen Elizabeth, the royal numeral, II, was a breach of the Treaty of Union between Scotland and England. The Court of Session rejected the challenge, holding that the royal numeral was not in contravention of the Treaty of Union; its legal derivation was from the proclamation of the accession, and that under Scots law a citizen had neither title nor interest to mount such a challenge (*MacCormick v Lord Advocate* 1953 SC 396, see 3.3.1.3).

5.2.4 Infancy and Incapacity

A new sovereign may be an infant, i.e., not have attained the age of majority (18). In such circumstances a regent will be appointed to carry out the sovereign's functions. A regent may also be appointed if the sovereign is unable to act due to some incapacity or infirmity. The Regency Acts 1937 to 1953 provide for these situations. Where the sovereign is suffering from a bodily or mental incapacity, there must be a written declaration to this effect made by any three or more of the following people: the sovereign's spouse, the Lord Chancellor, the Speaker of the House of Commons, the Lord Chief Justice, the Master of the Rolls (Regency Act 1937, s. 2(1)). Similarly a declaration must be made when the sovereign has returned to health and the regency is over. The person who can act as regent is the next in line to the succession who is of full age and is not disqualified on religious grounds. In addition the regent must be a British citizen who is resident in the UK. The regent can carry out all of the sovereign's functions apart from (s. 4(2)) giving the assent to any measure which would alter the succession to the throne or alter an Act of the Parliament of Scotland now known as the Protestant Religion and Presbyterian Church Act 1707.

If the sovereign intends to be absent temporarily from the realm or is suffering from an incapacity which would not justify a regency, then Counsellors of State may be appointed. The sovereign makes the appointment, the terms of which stipulate the royal functions which may be performed. Counsellors of State may not raise anyone to the peerage and may only dissolve Parliament if expressly instructed to do so by the sovereign. The Counsellors of State are to be the sovereign's spouse, the four persons next in line of succession and Queen Elizabeth, the Queen Mother. Disqualifications from the office of Counsellor of State include being the regent or absence from the realm (Regency Act 1937, s. 6).

5.2.5 Finances

The royal family are, as private individuals, wealthy. The separation of the sovereign's income into public and private began in the 18th century. Previously the sovereign financed government from the revenue of Crown lands and from such taxes as Parliament authorised. Eventually an exchange was agreed so that, in return for the sovereign handing over the Crown revenues, Parliament would grant the sovereign funds for the duration of the reign. The Civil List is the term for this Parliamentary allocation of funds. A Civil List Act is passed at the beginning of the reign to provide an annual amount which finances the expenses of the royal household and also of some of the other members of the royal family. The Civil List Act 1952 was amended by the Civil List Act 1972 allowing for an increase in the annual amount to be authorised by statutory instrument which is subject to annulment by the House of Commons. The Civil List Act 1975 provides for further supplementation of the Civil List by the Treasury approving payments to the Royal Trustees. The Civil List Acts 1972 and 1975, although dealing with increases to the Civil List, have the effect of moving towards annual Parliamentary approval of funds for the royal household, a situation which was rejected by the House of Commons Select Committee which inquired into the royal finances (HC 29 of 1971–2). The basic Civil List sum is paid out of the Consolidated Fund and so annual Parliamentary approval is not required (see further on financial procedures, 8.4).

Some of the royal household expenditure is borne by departments of State. For example, the Royal Yacht Britannia and the Queen's flight are included in the expenditure of the Ministry of Defence and the royal train is paid for by the Department of the Environment, Transport and the Regions.

In 1992 it was announced that the Queen would take responsibility for financing all of her relatives currently included in the Civil List apart from HM Queen Elizabeth the Queen Mother, and HRH the Prince Philip. As the Prince of Wales was not paid from the Civil List his position was unaffected. It was further announced that the Queen and the Prince of Wales would pay tax on their private income.

5.2.6 Royal Marriages

One archaic regulation affecting the royal family is the Royal Marriages Act 1772. Under this statute no descendant of George II under the age of 25 may marry without the consent of the sovereign. This does not apply to the issue of princesses who married into foreign families. Consent is not required if the descendant is 25 or over where a year's notice has been given to the Privy Council and Parliament has not expressed disapproval. The purpose of this is to guard against unsuitable marriages which could affect the succession to the throne (see Farran 1951).

5.3 THE ROYAL PREROGATIVE

The Crown enjoys various powers and immunities which derive from the royal prerogative. This is a source of legal authority which comes from customary law and is recognised by the common law. The prerogative evolved as the authority for some of the essential attributes of government including the conduct of foreign relations and the administration of justice. The prerogative was royal because medieval ideas about government were focused upon the King. This is no longer the case in modern liberal democracies and so the royal prerogative has become the prerogative of the government as a whole, although a few prerogatives remain personal to the sovereign (see 5.4).

5.3.1 The Nature of the Royal Prerogative

Blackstone, in seeking to emphasise the special nature of the royal prerogative, described it as being 'singular and eccentrical' (1825, vol. 1, p. 238). It could apply only to those rights and capacities which were unique to the King. This would include, for example, assenting to Bills, making treaties, creating hereditary peers. A less exclusive definition was proposed by Dicey who wrote that 'every act which the executive government can lawfully do without the authority of the Act of Parliament is done in virtue of the prerogative' (1959, p. 425). Is this difference between two of the most quoted authorities on the constitution significant? It was probably more significant when the courts were less inclined to review governmental action based on the prerogative. Since the House of Lords decision in *Council of Civil Service Unions* v *Minister for the Civil Service* [1985] AC 374, the worry that a claim of prerogative would immunise the government from scrutiny has been reduced (see further 5.6.2).

The majority of their lordships appeared to accept that employment of civil servants was based on the prerogative and, in an earlier case, that the creation of a scheme to make *ex gratia* payments of compensation to victims of criminal injuries was performed under the prerogative (*R* v *Criminal Injuries Compensation Board, ex parte Lain* [1967] 2 QB 864).

Despite these decisions on matters which anyone may do: employ staff and make payments, and which therefore appear to prefer Dicey to Blackstone, it is logical to maintain that some powers exercised by the Crown may not derive from statute, or the prerogative as defined by Blackstone. Harris has proposed a third source of authority for government action which is the freedom to do anything not prohibited by law (1992). He suggests that entering into contracts, establishing bodies to implement government policy and the distribution of written information are all examples of action based on the third source. An important factor about such action is that it will not override common law rights. Action founded on legislation or the prerogative does have the power to affect rights. This is not to say that action based on the third source may not have an important influence over individuals or institutions. Harris links his analysis with the work of Daintith (1979, 1982, 1989) on the methods which government may use to implement its policies. Daintith identified two broad mechanisms: *imperium*, which is the use of force; and *dominium*, which is the use of wealth. The achievement of an objective could be pursued by *imperium*, by commanding compliance, whereas *dominium*-based action might offer financial incentives, such as subsidies. For example, if one wished to promote the use of unleaded fuel in cars, one might forbid the use of leaded fuel, or ensure that unleaded fuel is much cheaper. In most cases *imperium* will require statute or prerogative, but *dominium* can be based on the third source, for example, the award of government contracts to implement a non-statutory wages policy in 1975–8 (Daintith 1994, p. 217).

The prerogative, it is suggested, should properly be regarded as consisting of a restricted number of rights, capacities and immunities which are necessarily part of the executive branch of government. The various aspects of the prerogative in relation to domestic and foreign affairs will now be examined.

5.4 THE PREROGATIVE AT HOME

While most of the prerogative is exercised on behalf of the government, there are some prerogative powers which are personal to the Queen. The appointment of a prime minister, the dismissal of ministers and the dissolution of Parliament are the most significant of these personal powers and are regulated by convention (see 4.2.1). The other domestic aspects of the prerogative may be classified according to their subject-matter: justice, immunities, appointments and honours, the armed forces, emergencies and miscellaneous.

5.4.1 Justice
The King was formerly the fountain of justice but since the decision in *Prohibitions del Roy* (1607) 12 Co Rep 63, that the King could not personally dispense justice, the administration of justice has been left to the judges. Criminal prosecutions are brought in the name of the Queen but the Attorney-General can stop them by entering a *nolle prosequi* under the prerogative. The Attorney-General is entitled to intervene in civil matters on the basis that this officer is concerned with the public interest, which is derived from the feudal notion of *parens patriae* (father of the country) which inhered in the King. The prerogative of mercy (by which a pardon or modification of punishment may be granted) is exercised on the advice of the Home Secretary and the Secretaries of State for Scotland and Northern Ireland.

New courts are generally created by statute but the prerogative could be used to establish new courts which administered the common law only (*Re Lord Bishop of Natal* (1864) 3 Moo PC NS 115).

Where a Commonwealth country has retained appeals to the Judicial Committee of the Privy Council, the grant of special leave to appeal by the Committee is itself a prerogative power (see 11.1.2).

5.4.2 Immunities

The feudal idea of the King as the fountain of justice gave rise to two related rules that the King could do no wrong and that the King could not be sued in his own courts. Today the Queen is personally immune from suit, but the Crown as the government may be sued, although the coercive remedies of an injunction or specific performance are not available, and a court may not order recovery of land against the Crown. Instead, the court may make a declaration as to the rights of the parties which it is assumed that the Crown will respect (Crown Proceedings Act 1947, s. 21(1); see further chapter 18).

Ministers are themselves Crown servants but they are amenable to review by the courts for their actions. In judicial review proceedings, coercive relief, including an injunction, is available against ministers in their official capacities (*Re M* [1994] 1 AC 377). Ministers could also be liable in contempt of court proceedings. In *Re M* the House of Lords assimilated the domestic position of the Crown as government to the position in European law (*R v Secretary of State for Transport, ex parte Factortame Ltd (No. 2)* (case C-213/89) [1991] 1 AC 603; see 17.3.4).

An important immunity enjoyed by the Crown is that it is not bound by legislation except by express words or necessary implication. The courts have not been eager to hold that binding the Crown is a necessary implication of legislation. In *Lord Advocate v Dumbarton District Council* [1990] 2 AC 580, the House of Lords held that a statute binds the Crown either generally or not at all, and that it is illogical to contend that the Crown is bound when acting without any right to do so, but not when the Crown does have such a right.

This general position has led to immunity for a Crown servant from conviction for exceeding a statutory speed limit (*Cooper v Hawkins* [1904] 2 KB 164), and for a National Health Service hospital from an abatement order which would require the cessation of a statutory nuisance (*Nottingham No. 1 Area Hospital Management Committee v Owen* [1958] 1 QB 50). Road traffic legislation now does expressly bind the Crown (see Road Traffic Regulation Act 1984, s. 130). It took an outbreak of food poisoning in a National Health Service hospital, which led to 19 deaths, to bring about removal of Crown immunity in respect of food hygiene and health and safety legislation only (National Health Service (Amendment) Act 1986, ss. 1 and 2).

Since taxation can only be authorised by legislation (Bill of Rights 1688, art. 4), it can only apply to the Crown if there are express terms, as with the Crown Private Estates Act 1862. While the Queen and the Prince of Wales may have volunteered to pay tax, it is unlikely that government departments will follow their lead.

5.4.3 Armed Forces

The armed forces are regulated both by prerogative and statute. While the maintenance of a standing army in peacetime requires the consent of

Parliament (Bill of Rights 1688, art. 6), the control, organisation and disposition of the armed forces is part of the prerogative. This covered forcible recruitment to the Royal Navy, or impressment, by the press-gangs. Conscription during the First and Second World Wars was carried out under legislation.

The declaration and the waging of war are exercises of prerogative power. Legislation was passed giving wide powers to the government during the two World Wars, but the Emergency Powers (Defence) Act 1939, s. 9, expressly saved the prerogative.

One of the actions which a government carries out in wartime is the requisitioning of ships. This was done during the Falklands War by prerogative legislation, the Requisitioning of Ships Order 1982 (see Turpin 1990, pp. 383–4).

5.4.4 Appointments and Honours

Ministers are appointed, officers in the armed forces are commissioned, and members of the judiciary are appointed by an exercise of the prerogative. Recruitment to the Home and Diplomatic Services is governed by Order in Council (see 6.2.1).

Honours and decorations are bestowed by the Queen. The vast majority are awarded on the advice of the prime minister who is assisted: (a) generally, by a special unit of officials in the Cabinet Office who deal with nominations for honours; and (b) specifically, by the Political Honours Scrutiny Committee, which is a group of three Privy Counsellors from the main national parties advising on honours given in respect of political service.

Some honours are in the personal gift of the Queen, such as the Order of the Garter, and the Order of Merit.

5.4.5 Miscellaneous

Included in this group of prerogative rights are treasure trove (the Crown's right to gold and silver which has been hidden and the owner of which cannot be traced), coinage, franchise rights to hold markets and fairs, the right to collect tolls from ferries and bridges, and the right to publish legislation, the Authorised Version of the Bible and the Book of Common Prayer.

5.5 THE PREROGATIVE ABROAD

The conduct of foreign relations is a classic example of a governmental task. It includes the conduct of international relations, and the negotiation and creation of international obligations. The lawful authority for these actions is the prerogative. In this section (a) treaties, (b) executive certificates, and (c) acts of State will be examined.

5.5.1 Treaties

International agreements may be negotiated between Heads of State, governments and international organisations. They may be bilateral (Anglo-Irish Agreement, see 2.3.3.4) or multilateral (the treaties establishing the European

Communities, see chapter 9), and they may cover, for example, political, economic, social and cultural matters. Parties to the agreements are bound by them in international law. Normally a treaty is signed by the parties, and then ratified, or formally accepted, by them. Usually the treaty becomes binding upon the parties on ratification, which in many countries is carried out by the legislature. In the UK, negotiation, signing and ratification of a treaty are all exercises of the prerogative. Membership of the European Communities has led, in respect of certain matters, to a modification of the general position regarding treaties (see 5.5.1.1).

The courts will not intervene in the treaty-making process (*Blackburn* v *Attorney-General* [1971] 1 WLR 1037 at p. 1041, which concerned the treaty of accession to the European Communities) or in their implementation (*Ex parte Molyneaux* [1986] 1 WLR 331 at p. 336 – the case concerned the Anglo-Irish Agreement).

Parliamentary approval is not normally required for a treaty. Under the 'Ponsonby rule' (Parliamentary Debates (Hansard), Commons, 5th ser., vol. 171, col. 2001, 1 April 1921), which is a constitutional usage, if not a constitutional convention, the text of a treaty is laid before both Houses of Parliament some 21 working days before ratification. This period may be reduced in cases of urgency.

Action by Parliament is required if the provisions of a treaty are to be given effect in UK domestic law (*The Parlement Belge* (1879) 4 PD 129, reaffirmed by *J. H. Rayner (Mincing Lane) Ltd* v *Department of Trade and Industry* [1990] 2 AC 418). This may be carried out by passing primary or subordinate legislation (see 5.5.1.1 for the European Communities). Treaties relating to the conduct of war or the cession of territory do not, it appears, require legislation to make them binding upon citizens (Shaw 1991, p. 115). Where incorporation is required it is more usually carried out before ratification.

Apart from Community law, a treaty will not be regarded as conferring rights in the UK which will be enforced by the UK courts (*Malone* v *Metropolitan Police Commissioner* [1979] Ch 344, in which there was an unsuccessful claim that telephone tapping by the police infringed the right of privacy protected in the European Convention on Human Rights, see 12.5). This is so even where a treaty is intended to benefit a particular group as, for example, where a foreign government provides funds from which amounts of compensation in respect of injury or loss may be paid (*Rustomjee* v *R* (1876) 2 QBD 69, a settlement between the Crown and the Emperor of China in respect of debts owed to British subjects by Chinese merchants). The position may be different if the Crown declared that it was acting as a trustee or agent for individuals (*Civilian War Claimants Association* v *R* [1932] AC 14 at pp. 26–27). The Foreign Compensation Commission is authorised to make payments of compensation to British subjects from sums given by foreign governments (Foreign Compensation Acts 1950 and 1969). As a matter of administrative law it is possible for a claimant before this Commission to challenge its determinations by way of a statutory appeal on a point of law (Foreign Compensation Act 1969, s. 3, following *Anisminic Ltd* v *Foreign Compensation Commission* [1969] 2 AC 147), but this does not enable a claimant to obtain a judicial declaration of entitlement to a specific amount since distribution of funds received in this way is regarded as a question of prerogative.

5.5.1.1 Community law and treaties   The UK's membership of the European Communities has modified the general law on treaties. Under the treaties establishing the European Community and Euratom, these two communities were given an express power to enter into treaties (EC Treaty, arts 113, 238; Euratom Treaty, art. 101). Where there is such an express treaty-making power it is regarded as exclusive and prevents the member States from entering into treaties for the same purposes, on their own account (*Opinion 1/75* [1975] ECR 1355). The Court of Justice of the European Communities has also held that the Communities may have an implied treaty-making capacity where the Community institutions have the power to legislate for member States in respect of common policies (*Commission* v *Council* (case 22/70) [1971] ECR 263).

In Community law some treaty provisions are capable of giving rise to rights which may be enforced in the member States' courts. Such provisions take effect in UK domestic law through the European Communities Act 1972, s. 2(1). Where a Community treaty has the effect of expanding the powers of the European Parliament then before that treaty can be ratified, it must first be approved by a statute (European Parliamentary Elections Act 1978, s. 6(1)). Otherwise new Community treaties can be authenticated by Orders in Council which will have to be approved in draft by resolutions of both Houses of Parliament if the UK is a party to them (European Communities Act 1972, s. 1(3)).

5.5.2 Executive Certificates

In the course of proceedings a court may seek from the executive a certificate on a matter related to foreign affairs. The information which the courts may seek includes:

(a)   if a person was an independent sovereign (*Mighell* v *Sultan of Johore* [1894] 1 QB 149);

(b)   whether or not a state of war still existed with Germany after her unconditional surrender (*R* v *Bottrill, ex parte Kuechenmeister* [1947] KB 41;

(c)   whether a State had been recognised by the Crown as an independent State (*Duff Development Co. Ltd* v *Kelantan* [1924] AC 797).

The answers to these questions can lead to the courts holding that a party has an immunity. For example, in *Mighell* v *Sultan of Johore* the certificate provided by the Colonial Office stated that the defendant was the Sultan of Johore and an independent sovereign, which led the court to conclude that he had sovereign immunity. Therefore the plaintiff could not pursue her action for breach of a promise to marry her against the Sultan, who had been living in this country under the name of Albert Baker.

Diplomats have certain immunities which have been agreed in international conventions and have been restated in statute (e.g., Diplomatic Privileges Act

1964, International Organisations Acts 1968 and 1981, Diplomatic and Other Privileges Act 1971). A certificate dealing with the question whether an individual has diplomatic status is now issued under the 1964 Act.

Sovereign and State immunity involve an exercise of the prerogative although this area is regulated by the State Immunity Act 1978.

Executive certificates are conclusive as to the facts but not the legal consequences to which they give rise. The courts seek these certificates on the basis that they provide the best authority on these questions of fact. In areas such as these which concern politically sensitive matters, it is considered reasonable for the courts to seek such information from the executive. Unlike other countries, the UK does not have a coherent and comprehensive basis for declaring points as non-justiciable, or outside the jurisdiction of the courts, because they comprise political questions. This means that issues which have political aspects may be decided with reference to the executive and on other occasions without such reference. Given the policy announcement in 1989 that the UK would no longer accord recognition to governments, as opposed to States, it is not clear if the courts would request certificates on such matters. The government may not wish to issue a certificate or declare conclusively that it recognises a government. This is because changes of government may occur by unconstitutional means and recognition could be taken to imply approval. It may be that the courts might have to determine for themselves what the status is of a new government (see Shaw 1991, pp. 134, 249–75).

5.5.3 Act of State

According to the late Professor E. C. S. Wade (1934, p. 103) an act of State is 'an act of the executive as a matter of policy performed in the course of its relations with another State, including its relations with the subjects of that State, unless they are temporarily within the allegiance of the Crown'. It would seem then that an act of State is an act of policy carried out in foreign affairs. While some acts of State are exercises of the prerogative, such as declaring war, or recognising a foreign government, others are not. This is particularly the case where, in proceedings taken against the Crown, an act of State is pleaded as a defence. If such a plea is successful it has the effect of ending the proceedings because the court has no jurisdiction to hear a claim made in respect of such an act. This is because the courts do not think it appropriate to interfere in the relations between governments. The discussion in this section is concerned with the pleading of act of State as a defence.

If the plea of act of State is to be successful, there must have been an act which was either authorised beforehand or subsequently adopted by the executive. An example of adoption is provided by *Buron* v *Denman* (1848) 2 Ex 167, in which a Royal Navy officer exceeded his instructions to suppress slavery by setting fire to the buildings of a slave owner and releasing his slaves. The slave owner brought an action in trespass but the officer's actions having been adopted by the executive were held to be an act of State and so the proceedings failed.

The pleading of an act of State is not accepted automatically by the courts, as they 'have the right to decide for themselves whether the act is, in this sense, an act of State' (*Nissan* v *Attorney-General* [1970] AC 179 at pp. 231–2). There is no clear test for an act of State. In *Nissan* v *Attorney-General* their lordships did not provide a clear and consistent view of the law relating to act of State. Perhaps it may be said that an act of State comprises high-level policy matters and actions expressly adopted by the executive.

The majority of the older cases on act of State come from the UK's imperial past, whereas the context of *Nissan* v *Attorney-General* – British soldiers engaged in peace-keeping duties in Cyprus – seems to be the likely setting for any future cases.

It seems that the defence cannot be pleaded within the territories of the Crown against those who: (a) owe allegiance to the Crown (*Walker* v *Baird* [1892] AC 491, British subject in Canada); or (b) are friendly aliens, i.e., nationals of another country with whom the Crown is not at war (*Johnstone* v *Pedlar* [1921] 2 AC 262, a US citizen in Ireland before partition). Where events have occurred outside the Crown's territories it is not entirely clear if the defence can be pleaded against a British subject. The House of Lords was divided on this point in *Nissan* v *Attorney-General*.

The remedy for foreign nationals against whom an act of State is successfully pleaded will lie in the political sphere at intergovernmental level.

5.6 THE BOUNDARIES OF THE PREROGATIVE

As the prerogative provides a source of lawful authority for governmental action it is important to discover how this executive power relates to the other branches of government.

5.6.1 Parliament and the Prerogative
The relationship between Parliament and the prerogative power can be subdivided into political scrutiny and the relationship with legislation.

5.6.1.1 Supervision The idea of responsible government means that the executive should account for its actions whatever the source of their authority. As the great majority of prerogative powers are exercised on ministerial advice, an account for their exercise can be demanded by Parliament from ministers. Not all of these matters are accounted for by ministers. This is the case in respect of those matters for which the Queen retains discretion, such as the dissolution of Parliament, and also other matters where she receives ministerial advice, including the prerogative of mercy and the appointment of bishops (Boulton (Erskine May) 1989, p. 288). On some other matters involving the exercise of the prerogative, ministers have consistently refused to answer questions on, for example, national security and relations with other States. Defence ministers do not answer questions on operational matters and the work of the Security and Secret Intelligence Services is not much discussed. In early 1993 the House of Commons Select Committee on Home Affairs had to accept a lunch as the guests of the Director of MI5 (the

Security Service) as a substitute for inviting her to attend their meetings to answer questions. The Security Service was only placed on a statutory basis in 1989 (Security Service Act 1989). The Intelligence Services Act 1994 did the same for the Secret Intelligence Service and the Government Communications Head Quarters.

Further evidence of the reduced accountability in respect of prerogative power is provided by the correlation between the prerogative and the list of matters excluded from the jurisdiction of the Parliamentary Commissioner for Administration. This includes action taken as part of inter-governmental relations, action taken in any country outside the UK on behalf of Her Majesty or the government for protection of the State, action taken in relation to the investigation of crime or for the protection of the security of the State, action in relation to the commencement of civil or criminal proceedings, action taken at the direction of a person acting in a judicial capacity, and matters relating to Crown employment (Parliamentary Commissioner for Administration Act 1967, sch. 3). This correspondence is, as Munro comments, striking (1987, p. 174).

5.6.1.2 Statute and the prerogative Given the legislative supremacy of Parliament, statute can abolish or restrict the operation of the prerogative. The Bill of Rights 1688 removed the suspending and dispensing powers and required the consent of Parliament for the imposition of taxation and the maintenance of a standing army in peacetime. Ratification of a Community treaty which extends the powers of the European Parliament must be preceded by an Act of Parliament (European Parliamentary Elections Act 1978, s. 6(1)).

Some statutes which deal with areas of prerogative power expressly provide that the prerogative is preserved (Emergency Powers (Defence) Act 1939, s. 9). The situation is less clear where legislation is passed to regulate an area formerly subject to prerogative power but the measure neither expressly abolishes nor retains the prerogative. Munro suggests that *Attorney-General* v *De Keyser's Royal Hotel Ltd* [1920] AC 508, provides the answer to this point. In that case it was held that statute superseded the prerogative to the extent of any inconsistency between them. Lord Atkinson said that the prerogative was in abeyance which, according to Munro, means that if the statute is subsequently repealed, the prerogative is returned to the situation which existed before the regulating statute was passed (1987, p. 172). Munro seeks to support this view further by suggesting that if the prerogative is not expressly abolished by the repealing statute, any argument contending that it has been abolished must be based on the idea of implied abolition. Not only are the courts reluctant to find abolition by implication, but they also construe statutes according to the prerogative-based idea that the Crown is not bound by statutes, except by express words or necessary implication. Thus, Munro suggests that the case for a superseded prerogative being revived on the repeal of the relevant statute is based on both principle and precedent.

A different view proposes that revival of a statutorily superseded prerogative should only occur if it is a major attribute of government (requisitioning power in wartime) or if it is otherwise in tune with contemporary conditions (De Smith & Brazier 1994, p. 145).

A different variation on the relationship between statute and prerogative was raised in *R* v *Secretary of State for the Home Department, ex parte Fire Brigades Union* [1995] 2 AC 513. The Criminal Injuries Compensation Scheme had been given effect by the prerogative. In the Criminal Justice Act 1988, ss. 108 to 117, sch. 6 and sch. 7, that non-statutory scheme was codified. It was to be brought into force on a day appointed by the minister by an order made by a statutory instrument, but until then the non-statutory scheme remained in force (s. 171(1)). No order was made, and compensation was paid, as before, under the prerogative. Subsequently the government decided to change the basis of compensation from common law damages to a tariff which would have the effect of reducing payments made under the scheme (Cm 2434). The government purported to bring the new tariff-based scheme into effect by the prerogative. This was successfully challenged in an application for judicial review. The House of Lords held unanimously that the minister was under no legally enforceable duty to bring the statutory scheme into effect because of the discretion in s. 171(1). By a majority of three to two they held that this discretion was not unfettered and that while ss. 108 to 177 and schs 6 and 7 were not in force, the minister was under a duty to consider if they should be brought into effect. The decision not to implement these provisions of the 1988 Act and to implement the tariff-based scheme was an abuse of power involving an exercise of the prerogative which was inconsistent with that duty. In other words, whilst the statute still provided for the implementation of the statutory scheme, only amending legislation and not the prerogative could displace it.

5.6.2 The Courts and the Prerogative

The Revolution Settlement in the final years of the 17th century established the supremacy of Parliament. Legislation was superior to the prerogative but the courts seemed to take the view that all they could do in respect of prerogative power was to satisfy themselves of its existence and not review the manner of its exercise. The continuance of such an approach given the development of the law on judicial review of administrative action was strange. The *ultra vires* principle which allows the courts to check that the exercise of statutory powers is confined within the limits of their grant, could also be applied to the exercise of the prerogative. The logic of this was accepted in *Council of Civil Service Unions* v *Minister for the Civil Service* [1985] AC 374 (the GCHQ case). In this case civil servants working at Government Communications Headquarters, Cheltenham, were deprived of the right to join independent trade unions. This was put into effect by a prerogative instrument made under the Civil Service Order in Council 1982. Lords Diplock, Roskill and Scarman were clear that the important factor in deciding if a court could exercise its review jurisdiction was the subject-matter of a power and not its source. Just as the exercise of statutory powers could be reviewed so could the exercise of the prerogative. The limitation is justiciability of the subject-matter – is it amenable to judicial review? Lord

Roskill suggested that the following prerogative powers could not be subjected to review: treaty-making, defence, mercy, honours, dissolution of Parliament and the appointment of ministers. This list was not exhaustive.

Alder (1989, pp. 190–1) suggests that the reasons for deciding that something is not justiciable include (a) deference to matters of high policy and to Parliament; (b) lack of judicial knowledge and effectiveness; (c) the absence of objective standards; (d) the need to trust the executive in an emergency; (e) the existence of other remedies; and (f) concern over impeding governmental efficiency. As Munro notes, the propriety of most exercises of prerogative power will continue to be irreviewable because they are non-justiciable. In the GCHQ case their lordships held that considerations of national security outweighed the fact that there had been a procedural irregularity in the exercise of the prerogative power. The issue of passports and aspects of the royal pardon have been declared reviewable (*R v Secretary of State for Foreign and Commonwealth Affairs, ex parte Everett* [1989] QB 811; *R v Secretary of State for the Home Department, ex parte Bentley* [1994] QB 349).

5.7 REFORM

The prerogative seems not to be subject to a satisfactory degree of accountability, either through Parliament or the courts. The reduced level of judicial review may be justifiable as some issues are not amenable to the judicial process, however, that does not mean that this is also true for the political process. The degree of secrecy which surrounds the work of the Security and Secret Intelligence Services is, it is suggested, excessive. The entire workings of the officers in these services need not be subjected to public scrutiny but there is scope to improve the level of accountability (beyond the limited joint committee of both Houses of Parliament in the Intelligence Services Act 1994) without impairing their work (see Lustgarten and Leigh 1989, 1994, and Norton-Taylor 1990 for discussion of supervision arrangements in Canada and Australia).

Some of the Queen's personal prerogatives could be taken from her and placed in others who could be rendered accountable. There is no necessity for the Queen to appoint the prime minister. It only becomes a real power when there is a hung Parliament. If the prime minister were to be elected by the House of Commons this would place responsibility where it should lie, in the people's representatives. This has been proposed by one constitutional reform group (IPPR 1991, art. 41).

Another personal prerogative which some think should be removed concerns the dissolution of Parliament. It is argued that this is exercised for party gain rather than in the public interest. It could be replaced by legislation fixing the life of a Parliament, with four years suggested as the appropriate period. Fixed-length Parliaments have been advocated by Munro (1987, p.183; IPPR (1991, art. 60) and the Hansard Society Commission (1991, paras 59–61). In the latter two groups' specific proposals there could be an election before the expiry of the four-year period if the government has lost a vote of confidence.

One other prerogative which might be removed is the rule that statute does not bind the Crown unless by express words or necessary implication. If the rule were reversed so that only exceptionally would the Crown not be bound, various unjustified immunities would in future have to be justified. Now that the Queen has agreed to pay tax, perhaps this change is possible.

CHAPTER SIX

The Government: Ministers and Officials

In chapter 5 we saw that much of the formal authority for the executive branch of government is still founded on the royal prerogative, including, for example, the appointment of the prime minister by the sovereign. The power of appointment may be vested in the sovereign but the real choice of which party will form Her Majesty's government is made by the people. Usually the 'first past the post' or plurality voting system results in one party having a majority of the elected MPs, which enables its leader to form the government.

It should not be surprising therefore that other aspects relating to Her Majesty's government should also retain a structure which has survived from earlier times. As we shall see, there are problems with the continuing adaptation of these ancient forms to changing circumstances. For example, can the doctrine of ministerial responsibility cope with the managerial revolution in public administration, where civil servants have been given greater powers in the new executive agencies hived off from departments of State?

Before addressing such issues we must first introduce the personnel in, and the machinery of, government.

6.1 MINISTERS

6.1.1 The Prime Minister

In the UK the head of government is the prime minister. If the UK had a codified constitution, then this position and its associated powers and responsibilities would be listed. In fact, there is very little mention of the office of prime minister in legislation. One of the first statutory appearances of the prime minister occurred in legislation dealing with the presentation of Chequers as the official 'country residence' of the prime minister (Chequers Estate Act 1917).

The rise of the prime minister and the waning of the sovereign took some time. Robert Walpole is usually considered to be the first prime minister in the modern sense of the real head of government, rather than the leading adviser to the sovereign. George II was the first sovereign not to attend cabinet, and it was only later that the real significance of this was appreciated as both an indication of, and factor in, the changing balance of power between sovereign and ministers.

The office of prime minister has developed out of a lesser known post, that of the First Lord of the Treasury. The prime minister is usually appointed to it because both posts are linked in the legislative authorisation for payment out of public funds (Ministerial and Other Salaries Act 1975, s. 1 and sch. 1).

The office of prime minister is now seen as the captain of the ministerial team, so that the prime minister has no departmental responsibility as such. This is so even though the prime minister formally has the Treasury post. The Chancellor of the Exchequer runs the Treasury.

There now seems to be a clear convention that the prime minister will be a member of the House of Commons. This would explain the action of Lord Home on his succession to Harold Macmillan as leader of the Conservative Party and prime minister. Lord Home disclaimed his hereditary peerage under the Peerage Act 1963 and a safe seat was found for him, so that he could become an MP. This is entirely proper given the greater importance of the Commons over the Lords, which derives from the fact that the Commons is an elected chamber, and therefore enjoys greater legitimacy. Other points which reflect this superior status of the Commons include the changes made by the Parliament Acts 1911 and 1949, allowing for the passing of legislation without the approval of the Lords, and the now weekly Commons ritual of prime minister's questions.

It has been suggested that one of the reasons why Churchill was appointed prime minister in succession to Chamberlain in 1940, was that he was an MP. King George VI, it is understood, preferred Lord Halifax but the King's advisers stated that it would be inappropriate for a peer to be prime minister. This followed the appointment of Stanley Baldwin as prime minister over Lord Curzon in 1923, which perhaps may be regarded as the precedent (De Smith and Brazier 1994, pp. 41–2).

6.1.1.1 The prime minister's powers   One of the most important powers enjoyed by a prime minister is the power of appointment. When the party in opposition moves into government there will usually be very little change between the 'shadow cabinet' and the real one. There is much sense in such continuity. However, so far as the Labour Party is concerned, its rules require that those people elected by the party into the shadow cabinet must be given a cabinet post if re-elected to Parliament.

The prime minister's choice in making ministerial appointments is not unconstrained. The different shades of opinion within the party should, out of prudence, be represented in the government. The Scottish and Welsh Offices should have ministerial teams from those countries. The current Labour Secretary of State for Wales is Welsh and has a Welsh seat, but his four Conservative predecessors all represented English constituencies. There has never been a Secretary of State for Northern Ireland from Northern

Ireland, but there has been a junior minister, Dr Brian Mawhinney, who was born and grew up there. He represents an English constituency. The Conservative Party is the only major UK party to organise in Northern Ireland. All of the MPs representing Northern Ireland seats belong to Northern Ireland parties.

Members of the government come from both Houses of Parliament. Whilst every department must have a minister in the Commons, ministers in the Lords may be required to speak on behalf of other departments. The task of speaking on behalf of the government in the Lords is also shared with the whips, something which does not occur in the Commons.

The major offices of State should be held by MPs rather than peers. Given the limited competence of the Lords in respect of financial matters, the Chancellor of the Exchequer must be an MP.

Every so often a prime minister reshuffles the members of the government. The reasons for such reshuffles are various. There may be serious disagreements between the prime minister and some colleagues. Rarely are dismissals openly acknowledged as such. The departing ministers tender letters of resignation and the prime minister replies thanking them for their splendid contribution to the work of the government. Sometimes reshuffles are caused by ministers who simply wish to retire for personal reasons, which may be that they wish to spend more time with their families, or that they want to be able to take up better paid employment. A prime minister may wish to introduce young blood into the government and therefore older ministers, or those perceived not to be working satisfactorily, may be moved out. It is sometimes suggested that a reshuffle is carried out to distract attention from the general performance of the government.

In addition to selecting ministers, the prime minister will be involved in making senior appointments to the judiciary, civil service and the armed forces, as well as bishops in the Church of England.

As head of government the prime minister will have a leading role in deciding the priorities within the government's programme. The prime minister chairs meetings of the cabinet and this provides the opportunity to control its agenda, which includes the allocation of business to committees, and determining the membership of these various committees. The setting up of a committee may be one way of dealing with interdepartmental disputes. The prime minister may also decide that the work of a particular department is so important that all of its papers must be copied to the prime minister.

The decision by the government to advise the sovereign to dissolve Parliament may be made by the prime minister alone. It is, however, unlikely that the prime minister would not consult some colleagues. This would be done out of prudence so that blame could be shared if they lost the consequential election (see 4.4 and Brazier 1992, pp. 270–1). In addition a wide range of information must be considered in taking the decision to call for a general election. The prime minister will want to know about the party's preparedness to wage an election campaign, and careful interpretation of the opinion polls will be required. The major parties, both in government and in opposition, regularly commission private polls, as well as paying close attention to those surveys carried out for the press and broadcasting organisations.

6.1.2 Other Ministers

Members of the government are generally known as 'ministers' even though only some of them have the official title of a minister. Similarly, ministers may work not only in ministries (Defence), but also in departments (Health), or in offices (Scottish). The better known ministerial posts are the political heads, and their junior colleagues, of the great departments of State, e.g., the Foreign and Commonwealth Office and the Home Office. These offices are each led by a Secretary of State, which was originally a position in the royal household. By 1782 there were two Secretaries of State whose responsibilities were allocated on the basis of an internal and overseas split, which is reflected in these two departments. Gradually the number of secretaries was increased, so that when a new department is established a Secretary of State is placed in charge of it. The strict position is that there is only one office of Secretary of State but that it can, and is, held simultaneously by many people (see Simcock 1992). The office of Secretary of State is a creation of the prerogative. Legislation, however, is needed to create other ministers who are to have new executive powers, and statute can also give additional powers to a Secretary of State. The legal status of a minister is that of a corporation sole and, under the Ministers of the Crown Act 1975, changes in the functions and designations of ministers, including the winding up of a department, are to be implemented by Order in Council.

Other less well-known ministerial posts also have their origin in positions closely associated with the sovereign and the royal household. The people who act as the leaders of the Commons and the Lords are often appointed as the Lord President of the Council, or the Lord Privy Seal. The post of the Chancellor of the Duchy of Lancaster entails the nominal oversight of the board which handles the duchy's affairs but it leaves the office-holder free to carry out the specific duties allocated by the prime minister. When the Conservatives are in government the position is sometimes given to the chairman of the Conservative Party who is often made a member of the cabinet. On other occasions it may be given to a person who is the second in command of a ministry when its leader is in the House of Lords, thus ensuring that the ministry has a senior spokesperson in the Commons. The current Chancellor of the Duchy of Lancaster heads the Office of Public Service which was created in 1992.

The whips, that is, the people who ensure that the party's MPs turn out for votes in the two Houses of Parliament, have offices linked to the royal household and the Treasury. The assistant whips in the Lords are known as Lords in Waiting, their chief and deputy hold the offices of Captain of the Honourable Corps of the Gentlemen-at-Arms, and Captain of the Queen's Bodyguard of the Yeomen of the Guard, respectively. Whips in the Commons may hold offices in either the Treasury or the royal household. The chief whip is the Parliamentary Secretary to the Treasury and some whips may be Lords Commissioners of the Treasury. The other offices which are held by whips are the Treasurer of HM Household, Comptroller of HM Household, and the Vice-Chamberlain of HM Household.

Where a Secretary of State heads a department the rest of the ministerial team will usually comprise a minister of State and at least two Parliamentary under-secretaries. If the head of the department is a minister, as is the case in the Ministry of Agriculture, Fisheries and Food then the title of Parliamentary secretary is given to the junior members of the ministerial team.

The office of minister of State is a relatively new one. It serves as an intermediate ministerial rank given to heads of small departments who are not in the cabinet, and also to signify the junior minister who may act as deputy to the Secretary of State. It appears that it is more seemly for a deputy at intergovernmental discussions to be called a minister rather than an under-secretary.

The Treasury is a little different from other departments. We have seen how it provides posts which are paid for out of public funds for the prime minister (First Lord) and the chief whip (Parliamentary Secretary). The actual head of the Treasury is the Chancellor of the Exchequer. The next in command is the Chief Secretary who is also a member of cabinet. The other junior Treasury ministers with specific titles are the Financial and Economic Secretaries.

The government must also appoint the law officers. These are the Attorney-General and Solicitor-General in England and Wales, and the Lord Advocate and Solicitor-General in Scotland. They act as the principal legal advisers to the government and will represent the government in major actions. While the English law officers are required to be MPs, this is not so for their Scottish counterparts (see further 11.5.3).

In both Houses of Parliament the leader of the opposition, that is, the leader of the largest party opposing the government, and that party's chief whip, are posts recognised and paid for out of public funds, and so is an assistant opposition whip in the Commons (Ministerial and Other Salaries Act 1975, s. 2).

6.1.2.1 *The size of government*   Legislation stipulates limits of (a) 105 for the total number of ministerial posts which may be paid for out of public funds, and (b) 21 who may receive cabinet-level salaries (Ministerial and Other Salaries Act 1975, s. 1(1) and sch. 1). The number of ministers who may sit and vote in the Commons is restricted to 95 (House of Commons Disqualification Act 1975, s. 2(1) and sch. 2). These limits have been broken so that some ministers have either not been paid at all or their salaries came out of party funds. This latter arrangement has been used in respect of the Chairman of the Party, who has often held office as the Chancellor of the Duchy of Lancaster in recent Conservative cabinets which had 22 members (see Watkins, *The Observer*, 2 February 1992).

The government, then, has what may be termed a 'payroll vote', all of whom are bound by collective ministerial responsibility. This is further increased by ministers appointing MPs as unpaid Parliamentary private secretaries who are also held to be bound by collective responsibility and must support the government. The task that they carry out is to be their ministers' 'eyes and ears' in the Commons, helping the ministers keep in touch with opinion on the backbenches.

6.1.2.2 Restrictions upon ministers   On taking up office ministers are required to ensure that there is no conflict of interest between their private affairs and public responsibilities. Accordingly if they are directors of companies they should resign from those offices. So far as financial interests are concerned the general guidance is that the interest should be disposed of, or alternative steps taken to avoid an actual or perceived conflict of interest. If the minister is unable or unwilling to dispose of a relevant interest then investments might be placed in a trust. Should this not be satisfactory then steps should be taken to ensure that the minister is not involved in relevant decisions by passing the decision or case on to another minister or official within the department, or to another Secretary of State. Should it not be possible to devise any mechanism to avoid possible conflicts then the minister should cease to hold the office in question (Cabinet Office 1997, paras. 109–28).

6.2 OFFICIALS

It is quite in keeping with the evolutionary nature of constitutional arrangements in the UK that there should be no statutory definition of a civil servant. As these officials have their origin in the royal household and as their regulation is conducted through the prerogative, it has not been felt necessary to place the civil service on a statutory basis. The definition of a civil servant which is commonly referred to comes from a Royal Commission on the Civil Service: 'servants of the Crown, other than holders of political or judicial office, who are employed in a civil capacity and whose remuneration is paid wholly and directly out of moneys voted by Parliament' (Tomlin 1931, para. 9). This definition covers a whole range of jobs carried out by people who work in the civil service. At the top there is the head of a department, a permanent secretary who is epitomised by the fictional character of Sir Humphrey Appleby in the television programme 'Yes Minister'. Sir Humphrey may well exhibit some of the characteristics of the most senior civil servants but clearly he cannot be representative of officials whose work ranges from processing claims in the Department of Social Security, to being a vet in the Ministry of Agriculture. Sir Humphrey exemplifies the civil servant who helps ministers to formulate policy, whereas the counter clerk in a social security office is involved in the implementation of policy. As we shall see there is a programme aimed at improving efficiency in the delivery of services to the public by officials, which seeks to emphasise the distinction between the formulation and implementation of policy.

6.2.1 Organisation of the Home Civil Service
The civil service consists of three services: the Home Civil Service, the Diplomatic Service and the Northern Ireland Civil Service (NICS). The Diplomatic Service comprises those officials working at home and abroad for

the Foreign and Commonwealth Office (FCO). The head of this service is the permanent secretary to the FCO. In Northern Ireland some officials work for the Home Civil Service which operates throughout the UK and some work for the NICS which was established there during the period of devolved government. The head of the NICS is usually the second permanent secretary in the Northern Ireland Office and this department is part of the Home Civil Service.

It has already been mentioned that there are a variety of jobs within the civil service. Whilst the great majority are administrators, there are specialists which include, for example, lawyers, accountants, computer scientists, civil engineers and forensic scientists. These professions and occupations within the service are organised into groups and categories with their own grades and salary scales. The largest group is the general group, which consists of administrators, librarians, information officers, economists and statisticians. In the uppermost ranks of the service there is a unified open structure comprising seven grades. A permanent secretary is grade 1 and the usual job title for grade 7 is principal officer.

The overall management of the Home Civil Service is shared by its head (who is also the permanent secretary to the cabinet) with the Treasury and the Office of Public Service. The Treasury is mainly responsible for the financial aspects of running the service.

As we have seen, officials are in Crown employment and the legal basis for the operation of the service continues to be the prerogative, even though other groups of public sector employees, especially the largest, the National Health Service, have a statutory basis. Orders in Council provide the legal instruments for the management of the service including the codes for the terms and conditions of employment.

Despite the great diversity of tasks and therefore of personnel in the service, it has been operated as a unitary organisation with common conditions throughout the country. Industrial relations are conducted through collective bargaining in the system of Whitley Councils, which operate at both national and departmental levels. The councils have two sides, the trade union and the official. The trade union side, formerly known as the staff side, represents the employees and is drawn from the relevant trade unions and staff associations. The official side, which represents the employer (the Crown), consists of senior civil servants. A member of the official side always takes the chair in these councils. If the councils cannot reach agreement, some matters may be settled by arbitration. A special commission, the Senior Salaries Review Body, deals with the salaries of 'top people' in the civil service, the armed forces and the judiciary.

In Government Communications Headquarters, Cheltenham (GCHQ), the right of employees to belong to independent trade unions was removed for reasons of national security by the Conservative government. For industrial relations purposes, these employees could join staff associations. Trade union rights have since been restored to GCHQ staff.

The continuation of the civil service as an organisation characterised by common arrangements is in doubt. This has come about because of the concern to improve efficiency through managerial reform (see 6.3.4). Two aspects of this programme of reform include the creation of semi-autonomous Next Steps Executive Agencies and contracting out to the private sector some tasks previously performed by the civil service. The breaking down of the civil service into smaller units has been accompanied by what amounts to a breaking up of the organisation. The civil service seems to be moving from a unitary to a federal structure, which is illustrated by the devolution of responsibility for pay and personnel to the agencies and the private-sector contractors (see the Civil Service (Management Functions) Act 1992).

This change has concerned some observers including the Treasury and Civil Service Select Committee. The Committee has been broadly in support of the .changes but has felt that the transformation of the civil service could (a) threaten the high standards of public administration because there is a danger that in a federal structure there is no longer a common culture, an ethos, which had developed in the unitary organisation (see Treasury and Civil Service Committee 1994); and (b) a concern that the external recruitment of senior staff, combined with the possibility that the growth of agencies would lead to barriers to transfers and staff development, thereby diminishing the likelihood of the civil service as a career and impeding civil servants acquiring both policy and managerial skills.

The government has stated that it expects most senior officials will have been career civil servants, but it is important that people with appropriate skills can be recruited from outside. A new Senior Civil Service has been created, which comprises all agency chief executives and staff in grades 1–5. The government hopes, and the Treasury and Civil Service Committee supports this, that the new Senior Civil Service could become more cohesive and would provide clear leadership in promoting the core values in those performing tasks of public administration.

6.2.2   Civil Service Recruitment

Today it is expected that civil servants will be recruited on the basis of ability. It was not always so. Posts could be exchanged for favours or money. The origins of the modern civil service may be traced back to the 1854 Northcote–Trevelyan Report which sought to establish the permanent civil service as a meritocratic organisation.

Civil Service Commissioners were established in 1855 to be responsible for overseeing recruitment and promotion. These commissioners were responsible for organising the open competitions for recruitment into the service. Evidence of educational attainment is now furnished by public examinations, such as GCSE and GCE, rather than the commissioners setting their own, as used to be the case. This is in contrast with the arrangements for applicants for the 'fast-stream' training posts who will have to sit a special examination, participate in role-playing exercises and undergo rigorous interviews. This process uses assessors from both inside and outside the service.

Since 1991 the Office of the Civil Service Commissioners is directly responsible for 'fast-stream' training posts and for oversight of appointments made at the level of grade 7 and above. The oversight process requires the written approval of the commissioners before appointment. The commissioners give advice to the Minister for the Civil Service who makes the rules relating to recruitment (Civil Service, and Diplomatic Service, Orders in Council 1991). The principal criterion for selection is merit, although the orders do provide that prescribed exceptions may be made to this requirement (art. 2(1)).

The commissioners are meant to be independent of government and, on occasions, they have been critical of the action of government in relation to some appointments (see Drewry and Butcher 1991, p. 103).

The actual recruitment of officials is carried out by departments and executive agencies themselves. The commissioners have delegated the operation of their recruitment responsibilities to the Recruitment and Assessment Services Agency which may also carry out this task for the departments and agencies.

6.2.2.1 Senior appointments The government has modified recruitment to the new Senior Civil Service. The Senior Appointments Selection Committee (SASC) will continue to advise the prime minister on these appointments but its membership of the Head of the Home Civil Service and some other permanent secretaries will also include the First Civil Service Commissioner, who will no longer hold that post as a serving civil servant. The SASC will consider whether posts at grades 1 to 5, and agency chief executives should be recruited from within the service or filled by open competition. The First Civil Service Commissioner will monitor and audit such appointments and will be responsible with the other Commissioners for promulgating guidance on selection on merit and auditing recruitment systems throughout the civil service. All appointments to the Senior Civil Service from outside the service are to be approved by the Commissioners. The government began implementing these changes from the summer of 1995 (see Cm 2627, Cm 2748).

The first advertisement for a permanent secretaryship at a mainstream department appeared in early 1995 for the vacancy at the Department of Employment. The person appointed was not a career civil servant but the chief executive of the Benefits Agency who had been recruited to that post from local government.

6.2.3 Terms and Conditions of Employment

It was often remarked of civil servants that they enjoyed great security in their employment. This popular perception was, and is, at variance with constitutional theory. A civil servant, as a servant, or employee, of the Crown may be dismissed at pleasure. The only lawful impediment to a civil servant being dismissed at will would be contrary statutory provision. In *Riordan* v *War Office* [1959] 1 WLR 1046, regulations made under the prerogative stipulated a period of notice before employment could be terminated; however, these were held to be ineffectual against the right of the Crown to dismiss at pleasure. It would appear that this power to dismiss is part of the prerogative which explains why only legislation is regarded as being capable of limiting it.

Most employees have a contract of service with their employer. The question whether those in Crown employment have a contract is somewhat unclear. It has been held that it is constitutionally possible for Crown servants to be employed under a contract but that the Crown's capacity to dismiss at will is unaffected by contract (*R* v *Civil Service Appeal Board, ex parte Bruce* [1988] 3 All ER 686). In *McClaren* v *Home Office* [1990] ICR 824, the Court of Appeal suggested that prison officers had a contract with the Home Office which derived from the Prison Act 1952, rather than the prerogative, and therefore some matters relating to their employment were part of private law.

While some employment protections are denied to Crown employees, such as the common law action for wrongful dismissal, statute has extended other rights to them, including those relating to discrimination on grounds of race and sex. What legislation can confer, legislation can also remove, as in the case of the statutory action for unfair dismissal. Staff at GCHQ lost this remedy when the government exercised the power of exception in the Employment Protection (Consolidation) Act 1978, s. 138(4). The basis for the exception is national security.

Therefore most civil servants have the general statutory employment rights. They also have their own internal procedures relating to discipline and dismissal which embody proper safeguards.

Civil servants would appear to have stronger employment rights than other types of Crown servant. It seems that, while civil servants may sue for arrears of pay upon dismissal (*Kodeeswaran* v *Attorney-General for Ceylon* [1970] AC 1111) this legal entitlement is denied to members of HM Armed Forces (*Leaman* v *R* [1920] 3 KB 663).

6.2.4 Political Activities

As the civil service is meant to be politically neutral, so that it can work for any party which forms the government, it is felt appropriate that there should be some restrictions upon the political activities of civil servants. Since participation in political activities is a civil liberty encompassing the human rights of freedom of conscience, association and expression, it ought to be important that the limitations upon it are no more than are reasonably justifiable. A system of categories has been developed which place curbs upon civil servants' political activities. These categories are (a) restricted, (b) intermediate, (c) unrestricted, and were devised following an official inquiry (Masterman 1949). Subsequently alterations were made to the scheme through a reallocation of officials from the restricted group to the intermediate category following an inquiry instigated by the representatives of the civil servants (Armitage 1978).

Officials in the restricted category may not participate in national politics. They may not hold office in a political party nor express views publicly on matters of political controversy. With the permission of their department they may involve themselves in local political activities. This is subject to their behaving with discretion, especially in matters connected with their department. The criteria for inclusion in this group are close contact with either ministers or the public. Where officials represent the department to the public as in, for example, social security and taxation, they must, as it were, submerge themselves in the department's policies as determined by the minister. Public confidence in the work of the department could be lessened where officials have a prominent profile in political life. The working relationship between ministers and their officials might also be adversely affected. Promotion decisions might take account of officials' personal views if they are known. Certainly, in the higher ranks of the service where there is greater contact with ministers, working relationships could be made very difficult if officials disclosed their political views. Following the Armitage Report the percentage of civil servants in this category was reduced from 26 per cent to 3 per cent (Parliamentary Debates (Hansard), Commons, 6th ser., vol. 64, written answers, col. 272, 19 July 1984).

Officials in the intermediate group may, with the consent of their department, participate in national and local politics. Again they should act discreetly but they may comment on controversial matters including those relating to their department. Such comments must not contain personal attacks upon their ministers.

The unrestricted class is the largest one of the three. Political activities may be engaged in with the proviso that this does not occur at the workplace or when wearing uniform (Treasury and Civil Service Committee 1986, vol. II, pp. 9–14).

No civil servant, whether permanent or temporary, may be an MP (House of Commons Disqualification Act 1975, s. 1(1)). Accordingly, civil servants who wish to stand for election as an MP must first resign from the civil service before announcing their candidature. If they are unsuccessful then only those who fall into the unrestricted category are elegible for possible reinstatement.

6.2.5 Security Provisions

In the period since the Second World War there have been a number of cases in which it was found that civil servants were passing on information to the intelligence organisations of foreign countries. This led to the introduction of a couple of procedures designed to counter potential threats to national security. The first measure was the purge procedure. This applied to civil servants whose work was considered vital to the State and was a means of allowing such officials to respond to allegations that they were 'unreliable' because they had inclinations towards communism or fascism, or that they associated with communist or fascist sympathisers. This permits the official to make representations to a tribunal known as the 'Three Advisers'. Two members of the tribunal are former senior civil servants, and a High Court judge usually takes the chair. Their role is purely advisory and so the relevant minister may act against their recommendation. This is by no means a fair hearing. While the candidate may be accompanied by a friend, this person does not have a right of audience. The candidate will rarely be given full details of the allegations, and will not be permitted to confront his or her accusers. This is justified on the basis that it could compromise the sources of the information.

The purge procedure was then followed by a more proactive system of scrutinising candidates for sensitive posts. This system is known as 'positive vetting' and was introduced in 1952. It involves a series of checks including interviews with these individuals and their relatives, friends and referees. Security clearance will be denied if the candidate is considered to be politically unreliable or has certain character defects which could lead to vulnerability to blackmail by foreign intelligence organisations. Unreliability, as we have seen, was originally conceived of as sympathy for fascism or communism. However, it was extended in 1985 to cover membership of, or sympathy for, subversive organisations, which are defined as bodies which seek to overthrow Parliamentary democracy in the UK by political, or violent or industrial means. Defects of character refer to drinking habits, drug-taking, sexual conduct, conviction for a serious criminal offence, financial difficulties and mental illness.

In the latest guidelines (Parliamentary Debates (Hansard), Commons, 6th ser., vol. 177, written answers, cols 159–61, 24 July 1990), reference is no longer made to communism or fascism. There are five levels of check rising from normal vetting covering reliability and counter-terrorism, through positive vetting (secret) and (top secret) to enhanced positive vetting which is applied to staff in the intelligence and security services and those who work on related matters in departments.

Where security clearance is denied upon the basis of character defect, the candidate may appeal to the head of the department whose decision is final. If it is alleged that the person has links with, or sympathy towards, a subversive organisation then the 'purge procedure' involving a hearing before the 'Three Advisers' may be invoked, although such a hearing has not been invoked since 1969 (Lustgarten and Leigh 1991, p. 621, and 1994, p. 139).

Members of the civil service who are regarded as having sympathy with extremist political views may be transferred to work which is not regarded as sensitive. If no appropriate transfer is possible, or can be agreed, the official will be permitted to choose between resigning and being dismissed.

The courts tend to defer to the government's assessment of national security and consequently the review of the government's action by the judges is not as rigorous as it might be in other contexts. In the GCHQ case the House of Lords upheld the government's changes in the employees' terms and conditions, including the removal of a right to join a trade union, despite the fact that the lack of consultations with the unions was a breach of their legitimate expectations (*Council of Civil Service Unions* v *Minister for the Civil Service* [1985] AC 374). In another case involving GCHQ, an employee disclosed that he was a homosexual. This led to his loss of security clearance on the basis that he was now vulnerable to blackmail. His challenge to this decision argued that it was irrational but the court declined to interfere (*R* v *Director, Government Communications Headquarters, ex parte Hodges* (1988) *The Times*, 26 July 1988). As Robertson (1993, p. 149) points out, the fact of disclosure of his sexual orientation should have negated any possibility of blackmail on that ground. In addition, the Security Commission, which advises the prime minister on national security matters in the public service, has recommended that homosexuality should not be an absolute barrier to security clearance.

In this decision there is some indication that while the courts will not probe national security considerations very deeply, they will seek to maintain a measure of procedural fairness (see Lustgarten and Leigh 1991, p. 624, and 1994, p. 145).

Lustgarten and Leigh conclude that the chances of successfully challenging vetting procedures under the European Convention on Human Rights are not high (1991, pp. 625–33, and 1994, p. 144).

Not only does positive vetting relate to those appointed to senior posts in the civil service, posts in the security and secret intelligence services, posts with access to highly classified information in the Ministry of Defence and the Atomic Energy Authority, but it also applies to companies allocated government contracts where the work has a secret element. One famous case involved ICI in 1955. The government required the company to dismiss one of its solicitors or else it would not be awarded any further contracts with sensitive aspects. The solicitor was deemed to be a security risk because his wife had been a member of the Communist Party, even though she had left the party before her marriage. In 1962 the Radcliffe Committee recommended that the 'Three Advisers' purge procedure be extended to independent contractors.

6.3   THE MACHINERY OF GOVERNMENT

The cabinet consists of the most important of the ministers, who also are in charge of the great departments of State. In this section we will look more closely at these parts of the machinery of government and also at a most significant development, the executive agencies.

6.3.1   Cabinet

In 6.1.2.1 we saw that there is a maximum of 105 ministers who may be paid for out of public funds. The senior group of ministers who form the cabinet are often perceived to be the government. The cabinet is the body which formulates governmental policy and exercises control over its implementation. In other words the cabinet is the apex of the executive branch of government. Bearing in mind the great range of activities in which governments involve themselves, what is the degree of influence that cabinet can exert? The current practice tends to be that cabinet meets once a week for three to five hours. Clearly this body cannot, in that amount of time, carry out the task of coordinating the government. The way that the cabinet can cope with its workload is by delegation.

6.3.1.1   Cabinet committees   The great impetus given to the development of a system of cabinet committees was the large amount of business which the Labour government under Attlee wished to implement, for example, the creation of the National Health Service and the programme of nationalising the railways and the coal and steel industries. This built upon a trend which had been increasing during the 20th century.

There are two types of cabinet committee: standing and ad hoc. The standing committees may create subcommittees. Usually governments have been extremely secretive about cabinet committees. This reticence was broken by prime minister John Major after winning the 1992 general election. He revealed in May 1992 that he had established 16 committees and 10 sub-committees. Mr Blair, the new Labour prime minister, has followed this precedent and announced in a written answer the cabinet committees which he had established at that point (Parlimentary Debates (Hansard) Commons vol 295, written answers, cols 302–10, 9 June 1997). The 11 full committees and the ministers who chair them are: defence and overseas policy, constitutional reform policy, intelligence services, Northern Ireland (Mr Blair); home and social affairs, environment, local government (Mr John Prescott, the deputy prime minister and Secretary of State for the Environment, Transport and the Regions); economic affairs, public expenditure (Mr Gordon Brown, Chancellor of the Exchequer); Queen's Speeches and future legislation, devolution to Scotland and Wales and the English regions (Lord Irvine of Lairg, Lord Chancellor); and legislation (Mrs Ann Taylor, President of the Council and Leader of the House of Commons). There are seven subcommittees: European issues, London, welfare to work, incorporation of the European Convention on Human Rights, drug misuse, health strategy, and women's issues. There is one ad hoc committee, MISC 1, which deals with food safety. It seems that in the life of a government many ad hoc committees may be created. In the 1987–92 Parliament some 140 were created. They may be established because of a particular problem and then, once that has been dealt with, the committee does not meet again.

Through the system of committees, meetings of cabinet can be reserved for discussion and decision on the most important matters. Accordingly the procedure is that when departments wish to propose an initiative it is considered by the relevant standing committee or one of its subcommittees. Some matters are determined by a committee rather than the full cabinet. Apparently a committee entitled MISC 7, comprising Mrs Thatcher and four other cabinet ministers, took the decision to replace Polaris with the Trident weapon system.

It is possible for a minister who has lost the argument in a committee to appeal to cabinet but normally this requires the agreement of the person who chaired the committee (Hogwood and Mackie 1985). The practice of committees reporting their decisions to cabinet was apparently ended by Mrs Thatcher (Kavanagh 1987). This increases the role and influence of committees.

Membership of these committees is not limited to cabinet ministers – their junior colleagues may represent the department, especially if the topic is not regarded as especially important. Sometimes the committees also have officials as members. It is more usual for the officials to attend to service the committee or to provide information.

Most of the main committees will have a 'shadow' one composed of officials, which will usually meet in advance of the cabinet committee. In the view of one minister, the purpose of these meetings was not to prepare advice and assistance for ministers but to 'pre-cook' or influence the outcome (Crossman 1975). Permanent Secretaries hold a weekly meeting amongst themselves.

There has been a tendency for some prime ministers to short-circuit cabinet committees and hold ad hoc ministerial meetings in order to decide matters. It is claimed that the decision to remove the right of trade union membership at GCHQ was taken in this way (Greenwood and Wilson 1989, p. 74).

6.3.1.2 The Cabinet Office It was not until 1917 that an office was created to serve the cabinet. The permanent secretary to the cabinet prepares the agenda for meetings in consultation with the prime minister. The office distributes the papers for cabinet meetings and is responsible for taking the minutes. These take the form of a note of the decisions made rather than a summary of discussion. Bodies which are affected by these decisions will be sent a copy of them. The office also services the various committees of cabinet.

According to Hennessy (1986) the cabinet secretariat has developed into six divisions: economic, overseas and defence, home affairs, science and technology, and European. This specialisation enables the staff to become knowledgeable and thereby efficient coordinators of the workload of the relevant committees. They will receive and distribute initiative papers from departments and, through a process of consultation, seek to resolve interdepartmental differences. They will also prepare briefing papers for the people who chair meetings which may suggest solutions to problems. These briefings are not made available to the ordinary members of the committees.

In addition to the secretariat, there are other units in the Cabinet Office. The Historical Section is responsible for the preparation of official histories. The Chief Scientific Officer is housed in the Cabinet Office as is the Efficiency Unit. The Efficiency Unit was first set up under Sir Derek (later Lord) Rayner with the brief of improving efficiency in central government. The unit has been responsible for introducing two important exercises: the Financial Management Initiative and the Next Steps project.

It is understandable that the Efficiency Unit should be in the Cabinet Office given that civil service matters have been allocated there. Since the 1981 abolition of the Civil Service Department, whose Permanent Secretary was the Head of the Home Civil Service, this post has either been held jointly or (as now) solely by the secretary to the cabinet. In 1987 the Office of the Minister for the Civil Service (OMCS) succeeded the Management and Personnel Office which had been established in the Cabinet Office following the reallocation of the Civil Service Department's functions between the Treasury and the Cabinet Office. The OMCS advised the prime minister, as Minister for the Civil Service, on duties and standards in the service as well as training and development. In 1992 those arrangements were replaced by the Office of Public Service which is headed by a cabinet minister, the Chancellor of the Duchy of Lancaster.

6.3.2 The Prime Minister's Staff
The prime minister does not, unlike most cabinet ministers, manage a department, but as the head of government there is a need to keep abreast of

developments both inside the governmental machine and outside in the country and abroad. To a certain extent the Cabinet Office can fulfil this function. While the prime minister does have a close relationship with the cabinet secretary – together they run cabinet – the secretariat works for the cabinet as a whole. Since 1974 all prime ministers have established a Policy Unit, which is a kind of think-tank for the prime minister. It will provide the prime minister with independent policy analysis. This may include monitoring the progress of some policies in departments or conducting work which may eventually become government policy (see Willetts 1987). The No. 10 Policy Unit is usually headed by a person who is brought in from outside and who shares the prime minister's political sympathies. Other members of staff are a mixture of career officials and people who become temporary civil servants during their employment in the Policy Unit. Such outsiders are special advisers. All ministers may recruit personnel. In addition to her Policy Unit Mrs Thatcher engaged other such advisers, for example, Sir Alan Walters on economics and Sir Anthony Parsons on foreign affairs.

The prime minister, like all ministers, has a private office composed of permanent civil servants who work as personal staff. The private office acts as the point of contact between a minister and the rest of the world. The private secretaries are usually 'high-flyers', i.e., officials who have been marked out as possible permanent secretaries and who are given the opportunity to work very closely with a minister. They organise the minister's diary and liaise with other departments and the outside world.

In the prime minister's private office the staff will have been seconded from other departments and some have the task of providing specialist advice on, and liaison with, their former department. For example, one of the private secretaries will have been seconded from the Foreign and Commonwealth Office, as foreign affairs is an area in which both the prime minister and the Foreign Secretary will represent the UK.

Every minister has a press office, which handles the minister's relations with the media. Normally press officers are permanent officials, part of the Government Information Service, but there has been a tendency for some prime ministers to appoint outsiders who then become civil servants.

The prime minister usually has another group of staff, the political office. The assistance they provide cannot be given by the civil service as it relates to the prime minister as a party politician rather than as a member of the government. They give political advice and help with the drafting of speeches which are delivered at party occasions such as the annual conference.

6.3.3 Departments

The work of the government is usually carried out in departments which are staffed by officials and led by ministers, although, as we shall see, some tasks have been given to non-departmental bodies or quangos (see 10.6). The major principle underlying the structure and organisation of, and the allocation of tasks amongst, departments is that of function or, as it was put in the report of the Committee on the Machinery of Government 'distribution according to services to be performed' (Haldane 1918). The committee preferred the functional to the clientele principle, or distribution of tasks according to the persons or classes to be dealt with. In the report 10 major services were suggested as being capable of being organised on a basis of separate administration: finance, national defence, external affairs, research and information, production, employment, supplies, education, health and justice. As the scope of government's activities has become greater, so the core services have increased to include, for example, social security.

If we take the first of the services, finance, then the relevant ministry is the Treasury. One would think that the two basic tasks of a finance ministry are (a) the collection of funds, which are (b) to be spent for public purposes. In fact tax collection is separated from the Treasury and entrusted to two bodies, the Board of Inland Revenue and the Board of Customs and Excise, whose day-to-day management is conducted by permanent officials. The reason for this is partly historical and partly to minimise the possibility of political intervention in individual cases.

These two bodies illustrate another organisational consideration, that of specialisation. As taxes have developed into those that deal with (a) the income of people and companies, and (b) with goods, so specialist bodies were created to administer them.

Another factor present in bureaucratic organisation is that of area. Where services are delivered all over the country then there will be a national network of field offices, as is the case with the Inland Revenue. This decentralisation within a department is rather different from territorial administration, which is to be found in the Scottish, Welsh and Northern Ireland Offices. These departments are responsible for administering several services to their areas. Education illustrates this point and the involvement of a different level of government. The basic policy framework is set by the territorial offices and the Department of Education and Employment but the delivery of the education service is administered by local governmental units.

Let us take the example of the Home Office to show the internal organisation of a ministry. Figure 6.1 depicts the directorates which deal with particular policy areas, such as criminal policy, immigration and nationality, and services such as corporate resources and planning and finance. The Home Office had a reputation for being a department which housed a somewhat disparate group of functions. Its former responsibilities for magistrates' courts and broadcasting were allocated to the Lord Chancellor's Department and the Department of Culture, Media and Sport respectively. It did seem inappropriate that a department with significant policing functions should also have responsibility for part of the judicial system. The Home Office has to liaise with organisations which actually deliver the services such as policing, probation, fire and emergency plannning — indeed it also has a role of inspection to ensure that the standards of those services are satisfactory. It is also the 'sponsoring' department for non-departmental public bodies such as the Commission for Racial Equality, the Equal Opportunities Commission, the Office of the Data Protection Registrar and the Gaming Board. The Home Office also has the Prison Service which is one of the most controversial of the executive agencies under the Next Steps programme (see further 6.3.4.2).

6.3.4 Managerial Reform

One particular criticism of the civil service refers to the lack of managerial training which civil servants receive. This may be explained by cultural factors. First, there is a general cult of the amateur in British life. Secondly, within the civil service greater emphasis has been placed on the policy advice role rather than the management of the delivery of public services. The Committee on the Civil Service chaired by Lord Fulton (1968) included these factors in its analysis. Some of its recommendations sought to raise both the status of management within the service and the general level of managerial skills of civil servants, as well as improving the position of specialist staff relative to their generalist colleagues. On the whole, the radical programme of reform advocated by Fulton was resisted by the civil service establishment (Kellner and Crowther-Hunt 1980, ch. 4).

During the period that Mrs Thatcher was prime minister an Efficiency Unit was recruited. At first its endeavours were concerned mainly with the economic aspects of efficiency, that is, reducing costs by rationalising procedures. This was done by a small team scrutinising selected parts of the civil service. A more general approach was adopted with the Financial Management Initiative (FMI).

6.3.4.1 Financial management   The idea behind FMI is that in order to obtain a better use of resources it is necessary to have a clear statement of objectives so that performance in achieving those objectives may be assessed. The basis of the FMI was conceived in the Efficiency Unit under Sir Derek Rayner who was the part-time head of the unit on secondment from Marks and Spencer. As Mrs Thatcher was eager to reduce the cost of public services the initiative was supported and the Treasury was involved in the team which oversaw the implementation of FMI.

One of the important aspects of FMI is the idea that the management of resources is improved by identifying cost centres and delegating responsibility to the managers of these units. Their closeness to the work should enable them to identify and implement improvements. They can do this if they are given budgetary control. The process of delegating responsibility to 'line managers' contrasts with the normal practice where a department's centralised finance and personnel sections determine budgets and staffing levels.

The identification of, and delegation of managerial authority to, cost centres, is a central feature of *Improving Management in Government: the Next Steps* (Efficiency Unit 1988). This report by the Efficiency Unit, then headed by Sir Robin Ibbs, reviewed the progress of the efficiency programme and recommended the creation within departments of executive agencies.

6.3.4.2 Executive agencies   The report, *Improving Management in Government: the Next Steps* (Efficiency Unit 1988), found that some progress had been made in efficiency. There was a greater consciousness of cost, and management systems were in place. There were, however, obstacles to further progress. Despite the fact that some 95 per cent of civil servants worked in delivery of services to the public, or executive functions, the attention paid to

Figure 6.1   Organisation chart of the Home Office

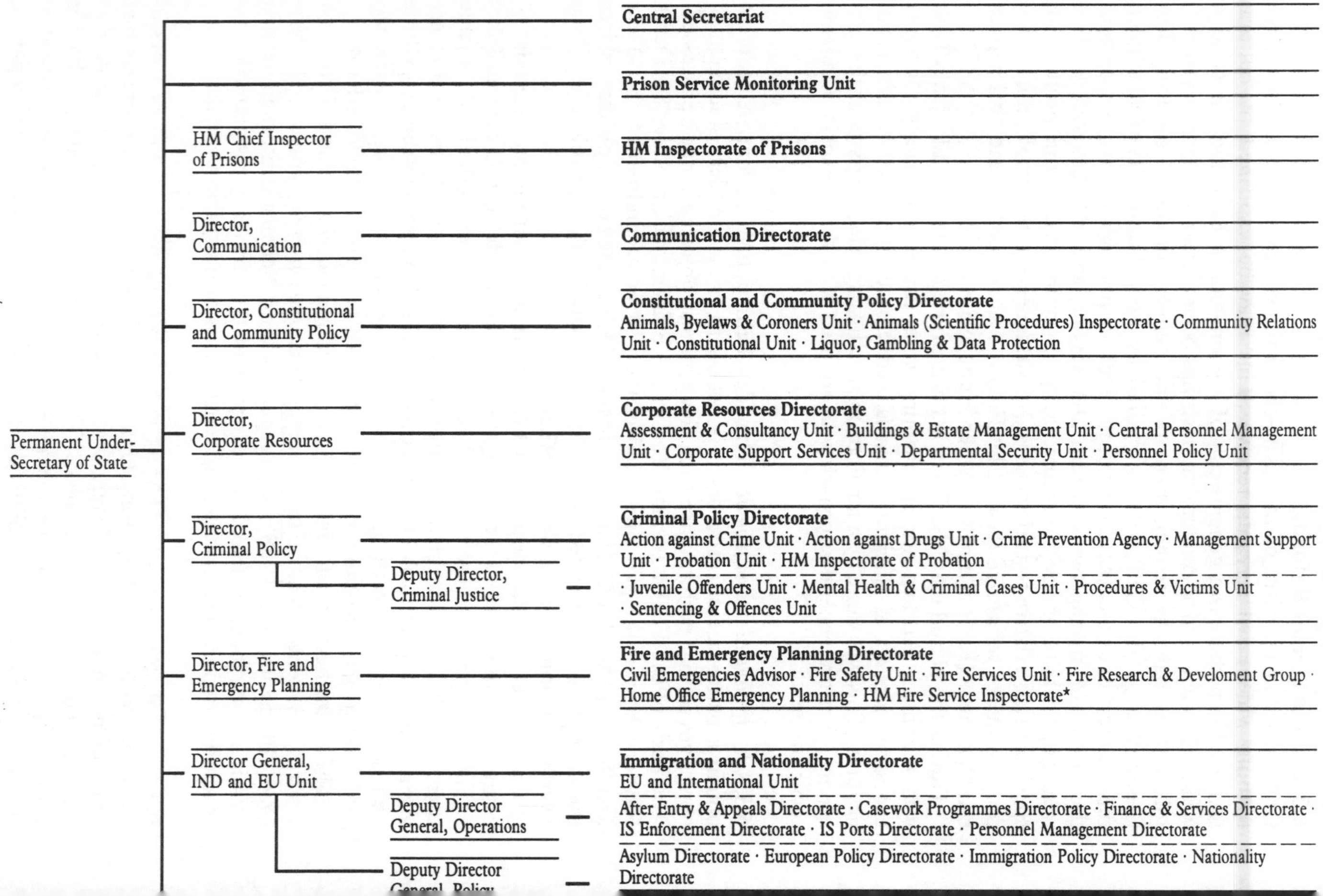

Permanent Under-Secretary of State

Central Secretariat

Prison Service Monitoring Unit

HM Chief Inspector of Prisons — **HM Inspectorate of Prisons**

Director, Communication — **Communication Directorate**

Director, Constitutional and Community Policy — **Constitutional and Community Policy Directorate**
Animals, Byelaws & Coroners Unit · Animals (Scientific Procedures) Inspectorate · Community Relations Unit · Constitutional Unit · Liquor, Gambling & Data Protection

Director, Corporate Resources — **Corporate Resources Directorate**
Assessment & Consultancy Unit · Buildings & Estate Management Unit · Central Personnel Management Unit · Corporate Support Services Unit · Departmental Security Unit · Personnel Policy Unit

Director, Criminal Policy — Deputy Director, Criminal Justice — **Criminal Policy Directorate**
Action against Crime Unit · Action against Drugs Unit · Crime Prevention Agency · Management Support Unit · Probation Unit · HM Inspectorate of Probation · Juvenile Offenders Unit · Mental Health & Criminal Cases Unit · Procedures & Victims Unit · Sentencing & Offences Unit

Director, Fire and Emergency Planning — **Fire and Emergency Planning Directorate**
Civil Emergencies Advisor · Fire Safety Unit · Fire Services Unit · Fire Research & Develoment Group · Home Office Emergency Planning · HM Fire Service Inspectorate*

Director General, IND and EU Unit — Deputy Director General, Operations / Deputy Director General, Policy — **Immigration and Nationality Directorate**
EU and International Unit
After Entry & Appeals Directorate · Casework Programmes Directorate · Finance & Services Directorate · IS Enforcement Directorate · IS Ports Directorate · Personnel Management Directorate · Asylum Directorate · European Policy Directorate · Immigration Policy Directorate · Nationality Directorate

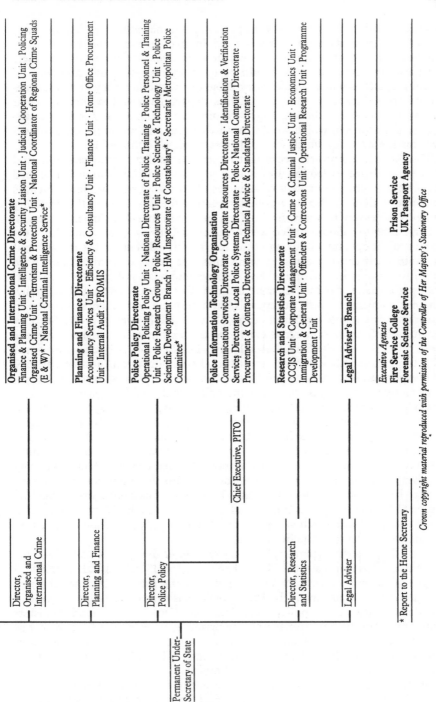

Organised and International Crime Directorate
Finance & Planning Unit · Intelligence & Security Liaison Unit · Judicial Cooperation Unit · Policing Organised Crime Unit · Terrorism & Protection Unit · National Coordinator of Regional Crime Squads (E & W)* · National Criminal Intelligence Service*

Planning and Finance Directorate
Accountancy Services Unit · Efficiency & Consultancy Unit · Finance Unit · Home Office Procurement Unit · Internal Audit · PROMIS

Police Policy Directorate
Operational Policing Policy Unit · National Directorate of Police Training · Police Personnel & Training Unit · Police Research Group · Police Resources Unit · Police Science & Technology Unit · Police Scientific Development Branch · HM Inspectorate of Constabulary* · Secretariat Metropolitan Police Committee*

Police Information Technology Organisation
Communication Services Directorate · Corporate Resources Directorate · Identification & Verification Services Directorate · Local Police Systems Directorate · Police National Computer Directorate · Procurement & Contracts Directorate · Technical Advice & Standards Directorate

Research and Statistics Directorate
CCCJS Unit · Corporate Management Unit · Crime & Criminal Justice Unit · Economics Unit · Immigration & General Unit · Offenders & Corrections Unit · Operational Research Unit · Programme Development Unit

Legal Adviser's Branch

Executive Agencies
Fire Service College   **Prison Service**
Forensic Science Service   **UK Passport Agency**

Director, Organised and International Crime

Director, Planning and Finance

Director, Police Policy

Chief Executive, PITO

Permanent Under-Secretary of State

Director, Research and Statistics

Legal Adviser

*Report to the Home Secretary

* Report to the Home Secretary

Crown copyright material reproduced with permission of the Controller of Her Majesty's Stationery Office this was insufficient compared with policy and ministerial work. Accordingly senior civil servants were inexperienced in management and in executive functions. The civil service was too large and diverse to manage as a single organisation. The next steps should be to reorganise executive functions by creating agencies which would carry these out within a policy and resources framework set by the department. Thus departments would change. Their core would consist of those engaged in ministerial support and those managing the department, which would mean devising and monitoring the objectives for the agencies which would deliver services to the public.

The Next Steps project seeks first to separate policy from execution, and then to improve execution by delegating responsibility within an agreed framework to chief executives of agencies. This responsibility should include personnel functions. Within a unified structure there is a loss in the flexibility which is necessary to assist the chief executives in meeting efficiency targets.

If we take the Home Office we can illustrate the way in which the Next Steps project operates. Looking at the organisational chart of the department (figure 6.1), it can be seen that some units are policy ones and others have executive functions.   Criminal law enforcement has a policy–executive split. Policy is a matter for the department both domestically and internationally. There is cooperation with European Union partners and others in relation to terrorism, drugs and organised crime. The lead UK agency is the Security Service which has had its remit expanded from counter-espionage to include these matters (Security Service Act 1996). The Security Service is associated with the Home Office, indeed when it seeks authorisation to intercept mail or telecommunications, it is the Home Secretary who must grant authorisation. Cooperation in justice and home affairs with our EU partners is done under the auspices of the 'third pillar' created by the Treaty on European Union. In addition to criminal matters, the cooperation also covers immigration and asylum, although the UK has not acceded to the Schengen agreement, which creates an area in which the group's first country of entry for travellers is responsible for conducting border control checks, allowing relatively free movement across the frontiers into the other countries of the group. Execution of policing is done by the various police forces but the Home Office has acquired operational groups such as the National Criminal Intelligence Service which are doing more than simply gathering information for dissemination to the police forces.

The UK Passport Agency is a good example of the type of unit which fits the Next Steps template of a body executing policy which can be given a degree of separation from its department enabling greater efficiency through delegation to its managers. The Prison Service is perhaps the best example of the deficiencies of the policy–executive split. On the one hand ministers would not want be held responsible for prison escapes, so they regard that as operational. Yet because crime is an important issue for the public it is important politically and therefore ministers will find it difficult to leave matters to the managers in the Prison Service.

As at the government's review of the agencies in 1996, there were 129 executive agencies (plus 24 Customs and Excise executive units and 25

Inland Revenue executive offices), with 10 candidates for agency status announced and 28 under consideration (Cm 3579).

6.3.4.3 Market testing As part of the government's drive for efficiency gains, a programme has been initiated which seeks to have tasks formerly carried out by civil servants in departments transferred to the private sector. It is hoped that the competition between existing staff and the private sector will lower the costs of delivering services.

At first, tasks such as catering and cleaning were subject to tender. This is to be expanded to professional services such as information technology, legal work, accounting and audit.

Compulsory competitive tendering was first used in local government (see 10.8.1) and is much further advanced there.

6.4   WORKING RELATIONSHIPS

The government is more than simply its personnel and machinery. The way in which the component parts work together is also very important. There are a couple of long-standing debates about the balance of power between (a) the prime minister and the cabinet, and (b) ministers and the civil service. In addition to these internal relationships, there is the external relationship of the government's accountability to the people through Parliament. We have already looked at aspects of the convention of ministerial responsibility, which relates to external relations (see 4.1.4). Individual ministerial responsibility, as it is traditionally understood, would appear to be under stress due to developments in the government's internal working relationships caused by the managerial reforms in the civil service.

Three sets of internal working relationships will be examined: between ministers, between the prime minister and cabinet, and between ministers and officials. The links between internal and external relationships will also be considered.

6.4.1   Inter-ministerial Relations
The convention of collective ministerial responsibility has been subdivided into three aspects: confidence, unanimity and confidentiality (Marshall 1984). The most important of these is confidence, the idea that the government must enjoy the confidence or support of the House of Commons in order to remain in office. This aspect of responsible government was dealt with in 4.2.2.1. Marshall (1984, p. 55) states that the unanimity and confidentiality rules relate to the way in which the members of the government behave whilst in office.

6.4.1.1 Unanimity Marshall (1984, p. 58) suggests that one of the reasons for the development of unanimity was to act as a shield for ministers. If the cabinet acted together then it was rather more difficult for the sovereign to take action against ministers who had incurred royal displeasure. Today unanimity seems to require that all ministers should publicly agree with government policy and if that is impossible should resign. Sir Geoffrey Howe resigned from his position as Leader of the House of Commons because he disagreed with Mrs Thatcher on the issue of the European Community. Ministerial resignations over policy differences are relatively few. Governments will always have some issues which do not have unanimous support. It will be a matter of political judgment not only whether or not a minister will publicly disagree with a policy, but also whether a resignation will be tendered. Before Mr Heseltine resigned from his position as Secretary of State for Defence, he could have been dismissed. The government's policy on the future of the Westland Helicopter Company was that it should choose whether it secured its future with an American company, or in a European consortium. Mr Heseltine was very active in advocating the European option. He resigned because he could not agree to all ministerial speeches being submitted to the Cabinet Office for clearance, and because he claimed that the prime minister had not honoured a commitment to hold a meeting on the matter.

European matters have produced occasions when Labour prime ministers have announced that they would suspend the operation of the unanimity aspect of collective responsibility. The first of these concerned the 1975 referendum on continued EC membership. Government policy was to continue but because the issue was one which divided households, and political parties, Mr Wilson said that ministers could participate outside Parliament in the campaign for a 'No' vote. In 1977 the issue concerned the Bill providing for direct elections in the UK to the European Parliament. Mr Callaghan, answering a question in the Commons on collective responsibility, said 'I certainly think that the doctrine should apply, except in cases where I announce that it does not' (Parliamentary Debates (Hansard), Commons, 5th ser., vol. 933, col. 552, 16 June 1977).

These suspensions have been criticised as devices designed to hold together a party which was divided. Does it really matter that a government's internal divisions should be openly acknowledged?

6.4.1.2 Confidentiality Clearly secrecy in government is related to maintaining its unanimity. However, confidentiality does involve more than cabinet solidarity. If we take the example of Richard Crossman's diaries, which led to a court decision (*Attorney-General* v *Jonathan Cape Ltd* [1976] QB 752), we can bring out the various elements. Crossman was a minister in the Labour governments 1964 to 1970. He was a former university teacher and had written an introduction to a new edition of Walter Bagehot's *The English Constitution* (1963). He had kept a full diary during his time as a minister with the intention that it should be published. Following his death the diaries were edited for publication, both in book form and in extracts in the *Sunday Times*. The publishers did not agree to all of the Cabinet Secretary's suggested cuts and proceeded towards publication of the first volume of diaries and their newspaper serialisation, which the government sought to stop. The Attorney-General argued that a permanent injunction should be granted because the material was confidential and that the public interest would be prejudiced if the dealings of ministers and their officials could be published. The government did not resort to the official secrets legislation, nor to an argument based on the oath which every Privy Councillor takes, which prohibits disclosure of Privy Council matters. Strictly speaking, the consent of the sovereign should be sought through the Cabinet Office where cabinet material is to be published. The court did accept that there was a convention of confidentiality and that publication could be prevented but did not grant the injunction sought. This was primarily on the basis that the material was 10 years old and its confidential nature had diminished with time. The danger that current cabinet discussions could be adversely affected by disclosures relating to 10-year-old material was dismissed. This to some extent missed the point that contemporary cabinets might be affected in what they do by the knowledge that ministerial memoirs could be published. The danger is that the fear of possible publication constrains ministers and their officials, so that advice and views are not given because of their supposed unpopularity or incompatibility with cherished policies.

The case led to the creation of a committee which reported on guidelines for ministerial memoirs (Radcliffe 1976). This restricted ministers to writing about events at least 15 years old. However, as there is no real sanction, these guidelines are breached. There is only a market for ministerial memoirs if they do reveal hitherto secret material and publishers are attempting to ensure in publishing contracts that the memoirs will contain interesting or controversial material.

Former ministers writing their memoirs are permitted to see cabinet papers which they dealt with when in office. The Cabinet Office acts as the guardian of these papers. When a minister or former minister wishes to see papers from the government formed from a different party, permission must be sought from the prime minister of that government or, if that person is dead, the current leader of that party (see further Hunt 1982).

Revelations about cabinet proceedings are made much closer to the event than in ministerial memoirs. All ministers, including prime ministers, unattributably disclose material to journalists. During the Westland affair, ministers did 'leak' stories to the press. Indeed, Mr Leon Brittan, who was then Secretary of State for Trade and Industry and was on the opposite side of the argument to Mr Heseltine, resigned for the 'crime' of leaking correspondence from the Solicitor-General. Advice from the law officers supposedly attracts the highest degree of confidentiality.

These two topics of unanimity and confidentiality play an important role in the debate about whether or not we have prime ministerial government.

6.4.2 Prime Minister and Cabinet

The debate about the balance of power between the prime minister and the cabinet is not new. The period of Mrs Thatcher's premiership was seen by some as further evidence supporting the thesis that we have prime ministerial government rather than cabinet government. Indeed some of the statements made by the contenders for the leadership of the Conservative Party, and thus the job of prime minister, following Mrs Thatcher's resignation in November 1990, indicated a preference for a more collegial style of government. On the other hand it has been said that this evidence tells us more about Mrs Thatcher's style and personality than it does about structural features of central government in the UK.

The case for prime ministerial government focuses upon the powers available to the prime minister. Briefly, these are the powers of appointment and patronage, within the ministerial and the official ranks of government and through the honours system, as well as the control of the agenda of cabinet and the allocation of business to, and the membership of, cabinet committees (see 6.1.1.1). In addition to this are the aspects of collective responsibility considered above unanimity and confidentiality. The prime minister will decide if transgressions of these rules will be punished or not. The practice of widespread delegation to small committees plus collective responsibility commits ministers to decisions on which they may not have been consulted, and indeed may not even have been officially informed of.

Against this it may be argued that the prime minister alone does not constitute the government. The influence of the prime minister upon cabinet is great but by no means total. Ministerial colleagues must be carried along, and if they are not then the prime minister's wishes will not prevail. Even Mrs Thatcher was not successful on every issue.

On the assumption that the concentration of power in the prime minister means that this is a much better hand of cards than those dealt to the other ministers around the cabinet table, what may be done to reduce this imbalance? One could embark upon a series of changes which would seek to reduce the power currently enjoyed by a prime minister. This could involve a written constitution which would constrain the power of a government with a majority in the House of Commons, or a chipping away at the patronage given to a prime minister.

Another aspect of cabinet government which concerns some observers is its inability to act as a collective entity at the top level of government. When items come to cabinet from a department, its minister is, understandably, partisan. As most members of cabinet have departments to run, they have little time to consider government policy as a whole and so do not have sufficient information to be able to take a considered view on a topic. This has been identified as a weakness by a former Permanent Secretary to the Treasury and Joint Head of the Home Civil Service, Sir Douglas Wass (1984) in his Reith Lectures. He took the view that the preferred method of addressing this matter was to create a body which would act as a think-tank for the whole cabinet. This body should check how a government's pro-grammes fitted into its strategic objectives, researching and reporting upon the implications of departmental proposals. The model which Sir Douglas has for this body is the Central Policy Review Staff (CPRS), which was abolished in 1983, the year in which he delivered his lectures. He would adapt the body to this particular remit and urge that it had the resources to carry out this task and that it be involved in the annual survey of expenditure proposals.

As well as improving the collective capacity of the government to govern, such a body would strengthen the hand of cabinet against the prime minister.

6.4.3 Ministers and Officials

There are several aspects to the relationship between ministers and officials. One of these has formed the major theme in the television programmes 'Yes Minister' in which the clever permanent secretary usually manages to persuade the minister to follow his advice, even if this is exactly the opposite of the minister's stated objective. This exaggerates a view which contends that permanent officials do have a 'departmental' view which they are reluctant to concede to their temporary ministerial leader. This 'domination by officials' view is reversed in a second aspect of the minister–official relationship, which is concerned that officials are too much at the beck and call of their ministers, with the possibility that ministers may abuse the loyalty owed to them by civil servants.

The final aspect of the relationship between ministers and officials to be considered here refers to the strain which managerial reforms in the civil service place upon ministerial responsibility and accountability to Parliament.

6.4.3.1 Officials in charge? It is a fact of political life that ministers come and go but the civil service is permanent. In these circumstances it might be expected that officials, who have worked on a topic for some time, will become knowledgeable about it. What if the 'departmental knowledge' changes into a 'departmental view', and what if that view is the basis on which officials seek to block the policies of ministers? Some ministers have claimed that their officials seemed to work against, and not for, them (e.g., Benn 1980). Under our system of democracy the ministers have been elected to govern us and this confers legitimacy upon their policies. The officials' views lack such legitimacy. Yet, as Kellner and Crowther-Hunt (1980) point out, it is unrealistic to expect that the bureaucrats will neither have nor exercise power, given the greater experience of, and expertise in, topics which officials possess.

Just as there are ministers who complain of bureaucratic power, so there are others who say that the problem is really that of weak ministers, rather than dominant officials (Heath 1977). If a minister is strongly committed to a set of policies, then this leadership is followed by officials. Where a minister does not give a lead then the officials will, as it were, fill this policy vacuum.

It is not possible to give a definitive judgment on the issue of whether officials have too much influence over ministers. An important point to bear in mind is that not all ministers gain support from their colleagues for their plans. It is claimed that the obstruction Tony Benn complained of derived from the prime minister who disagreed with him, and not the civil service (Young and Sloman 1982).

6.4.3.2 Duties and responsibilities Clive Ponting was unsuccessfully prosecuted for a breach of the official secrecy legislation. He passed on material to an MP who was asking questions about the circumstances of the sinking of the *Belgrano* during the Falklands War. Ponting did this because he believed that his minister, the Defence Secretary, was misleading Parliament. The minister's conduct was, in Ponting's view, wrong and he felt that this justified his action, which was itself a breach of trust. Following this prosecution the Head of the Home Civil Service issued guidance entitled *The Duties and Responsibilities of Civil Servants in Relation to Ministers*. In this it was stated that officials are servants of the Crown. In practice this means that they owe loyalty to the government of the day, and, in particular, the ministers in their department. Accordingly they must carry out their ministers' wishes, whether or not they agree with them. Officials should not be asked to do anything which might breach the law. If they feel that such a request has been made, then this should be reported to a superior or the Principal Establishments Officer, who may refer the matter to the departmental legal adviser. If officials find that they have problems of conscience in executing lawful tasks then they should consult their superiors. If these consultations do not resolve the matter then officials have to choose between resigning or performing their duties.

The guidance has been considered by the Treasury and Civil Service Committee on a couple of occasions (1986, 1994). On the first occasion the report was triggered by the issue of the guidance, and the investigation coincided with the Westland affair in which a civil servant was ordered by her minister, the Secretary of State for Trade and Industry, to leak a letter from the Solicitor-General to the Press Association. The second report was a general one on the role of the civil service in the new era of executive agencies and market testing. In both reports the Committee was concerned that the duties and responsibilities of civil servants *and* ministers ought to be clear. The government had published *Questions of Procedure for Ministers* which in para. 55 makes it clear that ministers must not ask their officials to do anything unlawful or improper. Somewhat anecdotal evidence given to the Committee suggested that there had been an increase in complaints by officials that some ministers were asking them to carry out improper actions, such as doing work for a minister which was party political in nature rather than governmental and that there was deep reluctance to use the internal appeal procedures due, in part, to a fear of adverse consequences (see Treasury and Civil Service Committee 1994, paras 87–117).

In its report on the role of the civil service the Committee felt that a code of conduct for civil servants was required in order to ensure that proper standards were clearly articulated. Between the two reports the Committee's views had changed on whether there should be an independent appeals procedure which could be used where officials felt that their minister's requests were improper, or raised an issue of conscience. The Committee now favoured an independent procedure. This change of mind was not confined to the Committee. The government in its evidence to the Committee had stated that an independent appeals procedure was not required but in its response to the report stated that the Head of the Home Civil Service should be substituted by the First Civil Service Commissioner as the person to whom officials could go when dissatisfied with the response by their departmental superiors. The government also accepted that there should be a code of conduct for officials and proposed minimal changes to the draft code prepared by the Committee, which simply brings together various points previously to be found in different documents (see Thompson 1995b). It is narrower than the code of ethics advocated by the First Division Association — the association of senior civil servants. The Committee's draft code does state that it should be read in the context of *Questions of Procedure for Ministers* in which ministerial obligations are specified, including: (a) accountability to Parliament, (b) the duty to give to Parliament and the public full information and not to deceive or knowingly mislead, (c) the duty to give due weight and consideration to the informed and impartial advice of civil servants, and (d) the duty to comply with the law, including international law and treaty obligations, and to uphold the administration of justice.

Civil servants must act with impartiality, integrity, honesty and objectivity. They must act so as to deserve the confidence of ministers, and be able to establish the same relationship with those whom they might serve in a future administration.

The code, whilst it stresses the two-way relationship between ministers and officials is not law. The Committee had advocated a statutory basis for the regulation of the civil service, which would also deal with these important matters. The provisions of a statute would be legally enforceable and would be a stronger safeguard against possible abuse. The government in its response did not rule out such a possibility, accepting that it would be 'an effective means of expressing and entrenching general agreement on the non-political nature of the civil service', for which the necessary conditions would appear to be widespread support for narrowly based legislation (Cm 2748, para. 2.16).

The government's response is a little encouraging but the draft code does not really grasp the important issue of the constitutional position of the civil service. While it acknowledges that officials should 'speak truth unto power' in giving advice to ministers, it evades the issue of whether civil servants have a loyalty and duty to the State/Crown, which is higher than that owed to ministers. To a degree this may be said to underpin the procedures for raising questions of propriety with their new independent element. This is another illustration of pragmatic, incremental development of constitutional arrangements rather than starting from first principles.

6.4.3.3 Standards The Committee on Standards in Public Life was primarily established because of concerns about the propriety of some behaviour by MPs (see 7.8.7) and of non-departmental public bodies or quangos (see 10.8.2.2). In its first report the Committee dealt with ministers and civil servants. In effect there were two aspects to the recommendations made in this area: codes of conduct whilst in service, and arrangements dealing with employment after leaving office.

Just as there is a code of conduct for officials, so should one be produced for ministers and either be issued separately or as a section in *Questions of Procedure for Ministers*. If the latter course is chosen then it should be renamed

Conduct and Procedure for Ministers to reflect more accurately its scope (now entitled *Ministerial Code A Code of Conduct and Guidance on Procedures for Ministers*). Ministers must decide how they must act in order to uphold the high standards applicable to them. It will be for the prime minister to decide if ministers have failed to meet them. There should be careful consideration given to the conduct of investigations of allegations of failure to meet these standards. Perhaps they should not be carried out by officials like the Secretary to the Cabinet. The code for officials should be implemented immediately, without waiting for legislation, but after having been revised to take into account circumstances in which an official is aware of, although not personally involved in, wrongdoing or maladministration. The details of the appeals system should be widely disseminated and the Civil Service Commissioners should report all successful appeals to Parliament. The Cabinet Office should monitor the best practice on the maintenance of standards of conduct and revise civil service arrangements accordingly. There should be regular surveys in departments and agencies of staff awareness and understanding of ethical standards, and where these highlight problem areas, remedial action including additional training should be taken. The new performance pay arrangements for the senior civil service should be structured so as to maintain political impartiality.

Similar arrangements to those for civil servants in relation to appointments in the business world should be applied to ministers. Cabinet ministers, like permanent secretaries, should have an automatic three-month waiting period before they can consider an appointment. If the Advisory Committee on Business Appointments advises a former minister or civil servant that a proposed appointment would not be appropriate then it should be able to publicise that advice if it is not followed. Where the advisory committee recommends that there should be an additional waiting period, this should be for a maximum of two years from the date of leaving office. There should be a right of appeal for former ministers to the prime minister who could reduce the waiting period or relax any conditions. Special advisers to ministers should also be subject to the business appointment rules. The operation, observance and objectives of the rules should be subject to review. Departments should maintain records of hospitality accepted by ministers in their official capacity, in addition to those that deal with gifts.

The recommendations were implemented.

6.4.3.4 Managerialism and accountability

6.4.3.4 *Managerialism and accountability* The aim of the managerial reforms in the civil service is to improve the efficiency of the delivery of services to the public. It is felt that effective management is achieved within a framework which is close to those who carry out the work. Accordingly, appropriate work units have been identified and their line managers have been delegated budgetary control and responsibility for the resources which they have been allocated. The logic of this means that the managers are responsible within their delegated remit. Yet the traditional understanding of ministerial accountability (see 4.1.4 and 4.2.2) states that officials are responsible to ministers who account to Parliament. If ministers are still to be fully responsible this requires that they must exercise oversight. Such scrutiny seems to be at odds with the idea of delegation. Can managers really be permitted to play the full part which the theory of delegation suggests, if ministers are still to account to Parliament for every operational detail? Would managers really be responsible if ministers, following the logic of their accountability to Parliament, felt impelled to intervene?

The Efficiency Unit had recognised that executive agencies really did not fit into the traditional accountability framework and suggested that the chief executives of the agencies be subject to scrutiny by select committees for operations. Ministers would still be responsible for the policy within which the agencies worked. At first this was rejected by the government, which stated that the usual chain of command should apply. Subsequently it accepted that there would be a convention that chief executives would answer on behalf of ministers for operational matters and that the chief executives would be, where appropriate, the accounting officers for their agencies and thus responsible for the agencies' expenditure of public funds.

From the implementation of the FMI, the select committees had recognised that delegated management would mean that such managers would be best placed to answer their questions about operational matters, and so they sought the ability to take evidence from them on these matters rather than from ministers. The government's view has been that it does not wish to see ministerial responsibility abridged. The point is, however, that ministers cannot answer about matters of operational detail, and the insistence on ministerial responsibility actually impedes the accountability of the executive to Parliament. It is as if the relationship between the ministers, officials and select committees is a kind of bureaucratic 'Bermuda Triangle' in which accountability disappears.

The separation of policy and administration is very difficult, if not a chimera. Political sensibilities will cause ministers both to intervene and to 'pass the buck'. Ministers tend to regard prison escapes as operational matters. Yet on the other hand Greer writes of how ministers took an interest in the layout of social security offices including whether there should be glass screens, which would seem preeminently to be an operational matter (1994, p. 88).

O'Toole and Chapman (1995) suggest that the agencies' evolving accountability relationship to ministers is, in some respects, like that of the old nationalised industries, in that ministers decided those matters for which they were, or were not, responsible. One example of how complicated matters are involves the Child Support Agency (CSA). The Chief Executive of the CSA took on a very high profile as its work came under attack. As the report of the Parliamentary Commissioner for Administration (1995) made clear there were operational and administrative shortcomings but as the Social Security Select Committee indicated difficult policy issues had been fudged (1994). The Chief Executive resigned but no minister has been a casualty despite a policy U-turn involving amending legislation.

There is one other aspect to this triangular relationship. During the Defence Select Committee's investigation of the Westland affair, they were unable to take evidence from civil servants who were very much involved. There was a dispute between the select committees and the government over the matters on which committees were permitted to interrogate officials. A compromise was agreed in that officials could be asked about their actions but not their conduct. Actions were defined as 'activities carried out on the instructions of, or are consistent with, the policies of the ministers concerned'. Conduct was not within the definition of actions and as conduct could include misconduct, the government took the view that it was not a matter for select committees. Officials could be asked about factual matters, but where a select committee's questions were directed towards the assignment of blame or criticism of individual civil servants then they were not to answer. The committees, if their inquiries took them into this area, should inform the minister who would then conduct an investigation and make a report.

The Public Service select committee has made recommendations to improve matters (HC 313 of 1995–6), but not all of them have been accepted by the government. It seems that the government is concerned that if chief executives were to be able to account to Parliament on their own behalf, and not as ministerial representatives, there would be a danger of confusion about who was responsible for what. What can be wrong in allowing chief executives to speak on their own behalf about responsibilities allocated to them by the framework agreements, which set down the relationships between the ministers and the agencies? The cynical answer is that it would reduce the freedom of manoeuvre to evade responsibility which ministers can enjoy by, for example, privately intervening in agency operations without public accountability for this, either from them or the chief executives (see generally Woodhouse 1997b).

This aspect of the working relationship between ministers and officials, like the whole practice of responsible government, is regulated by convention. Thus the advantage lies with the executive as Parliament must seek to wring concessions from it. For example, select committees do not have the power to require the attendance of ministers or officials. The executive's cooperation is itself a convention. Only Parliament as a whole can require the production of people and papers, and Parliament is, of course, dominated by the party of the government. Such is the way in the UK's constitutional arrangements which facilitates government rather than its scrutiny.

CHAPTER SEVEN
Parliament: Role, Composition and Privileges

In this chapter three aspects of Parliament are considered. First, the role of the institution is outlined. Secondly its composition is examined which, in the case of the House of Commons, includes the qualifications of those who can be MPs, as well as the rules of the electoral system through which membership is obtained. Finally, the system of privileges enjoyed, and standards required, by Parliament will be explained.

7.1 ROLE OF PARLIAMENT

When Bagehot described the British constitution it was during a period in which Parliament might be said to have enjoyed its 'golden age'. Once the electorate was widened to include most adult men, the political parties began their transformation from somewhat loose factions into much more tightly disciplined organisations. The voters having made their choice, the majority party formed the government at the formal invitation of the sovereign. In the party of government, the back-bench members supported their front-bench colleagues, rather than combine with the opposition in order to exercise control over the government. In fact, the period between the first and third Reform Acts was atypical in the amount of influence which Parliament was able to wield over the government.

If Parliament does not control the government what does it do? Norton (1985), identifies three primary functions for Parliament. These are (a) government formation, (b) legitimisation, and (c) scrutiny and influence.

7.1.1 Government Formation
The Queen's ministers are drawn from the majority party in the House of Commons, and the same party in the House of Lords. If a minister is not

already an MP or a peer, then convention requires that, before long, the person must succeed in winning a by-election for a seat in the House of Commons, or be made a peer, and thus a member of the House of Lords.

7.1.2 Legitimisation

The theory of the separation of powers matched organs and functions of government. Under this theory the lawmaking function should only be carried out by the legislature. Parliament is the UK's domestic legislature, though it is different in respect of European Community matters (see 9.2.2). Why then is lawmaking not specifically mentioned as a role of Parliament? The answer is that the initiative under the UK's arrangements lies with the government. As we shall see, public legislation may be instigated by any member of the two Houses of Parliament (see 8.2.1.3 and 8.5.2.2), and corporate bodies such as universities and local authorities may promote private legislation to be enacted by Parliament. Thus Parliament legitimises the government's policies and programmes by approving the legislation which will enable them to be implemented. Norton terms this manifest legitimisation. In contrast, latent legitimisation describes the political authority which the government enjoys through its election to (and domination of) the House of Commons. Latent legitimisation also embraces those actions of government which do not require the approval of Parliament, such as the conduct of foreign affairs, the legal authority for which is the prerogative (see, for example, 5.5.1 on treaties).

Whilst the House of Commons has legitimacy because it is elected, the House of Lords relies upon tradition and convention. Thus, where there is a dispute between the two chambers, the elected composition of the Commons should permit its will to prevail.

7.1.3 Scrutiny and Influence

As Parliament does not control the government, what it may do is to seek to influence the government. We may divide the substance of the process of scrutiny into legislative proposals and administration, and the levels at which it operates into the macro and micro. There tends to be an association between legislation and the macro level, and administration and the micro level. At the macro level Parliament is concerned with the policy of the government which underpins the legislation which is presented for its approval, whereas, at the micro level MPs are usually acting on behalf of their constituents seeking redress for grievances which they have sustained in their dealings with the executive. Micro-level scrutiny will also occur in the legislative process as interest groups affected lobby MPs in the hope of shaping the final form of the statute. A select committee's investigation of a department may focus on both micro and macro levels. For example, micro-level scrutinies could include the examination of departments' expenditure by the Public Accounts Committee, or the investigation of the 'salmonella in eggs' affair by the Agriculture Select Committee. The Treasury and Civil Service Select Committee's examination of the government's public expenditure proposals is conducted at the macro level.

7.2 HOUSE OF LORDS

The House of Lords is no longer the senior partner of the two chambers of Parliament. It may be referred to as the 'upper' House, which reflects the period when the Lords were more important than the Commons. We have moved on from a feudal conception of estates of the realm representing the nation to a more democratic ideal in which everyone, no matter their status, is supposed to be equal.

The old division between the lords spiritual and temporal is outdated. While it distinguishes between categories of membership of the House – the lords spiritual are not peers – it has been replaced by the difference between regular attenders and infrequent attenders or those who have leave of absence. The regular attenders mainly comprise those who are life peers, although some hereditary peers, more particularly in the Conservative Party, participate fully in the work of the House.

Not every peer wishes to become involved in Parliamentary work and so a peer may apply for leave of absence. Those peers who did not attend in the previous session of Parliament, or who had been granted leave of absence, receive a written inquiry from the Lord Chancellor asking if they wish to be excused for the coming session. If they answer in the affirmative, or do not reply, they are granted leave. If they change their minds, the leave may be cancelled after the expiry of a period of notice of one month. There are no formal rules which prevent a peer on leave of absence from attending, and voting on, the business of the House.

This system does seem to prevent normally absent peers, or 'backwoodsmen' from turning up to vote. In June 1997, 59 peers out of a total membership of 1,222 were on leave of absence (House of Lords 1997).

We may identify four separate categories of membership of the House of Lords: hereditary peers, life peers, lords spiritual and law lords.

7.2.1 Hereditary Peers

The history of the country is reflected in the peerage. Depending upon when the peerage was granted, the realm of which a person is a peer is England or Scotland (pre-1707); or Great Britain (1707–1800); or the United Kingdom (1801 onwards). Since 1922 Irish peers are no longer qualified for membership of the House of Lords, though this means that they may, if successful at an election, become an MP.

The proportions of peers according to the period of their creation are approximately: pre-1800, 18 per cent; 19th century, 14 per cent; and 20th century, 68 per cent (Gunn 1993). These figures would appear to indicate that hereditary peers continue to be created. In June 1997 there were 754 peers by succession and 10 hereditary peers of first creation (House of Lords, 1997). The passage of the Life Peerages Act 1958 has radically changed the category of membership of new peers (see further 7.2.2). There appeared to be a consensus during the period 1964–83 that no new hereditary peers would be created apart from the Royal Family. In 1983 the prime minister Mrs Thatcher recommended hereditary peerages for her deputy William

Whitelaw and the retiring Speaker of the House of Commons, George Thomas. As Viscount Whitelaw has no sons, and Viscount Tonypandy has no children, their peerages cease to exist upon their deaths. In 1984 Mrs Thatcher recommended a hereditary earldom for former prime minister Harold Macmillan. Following Mrs Thatcher's resignation from the leadership of the Conservative Party and the prime ministership, her husband was made a hereditary baronet. It had been the custom for former prime ministers to be created hereditary earls when they left the House of Commons. The current custom for former prime ministers is to become life peers on leaving the House of Commons.

At the beginning of each Parliament all peers entitled to sit in the House are issued a writ of summons by the Crown to attend Parliament. Where a person has established a rightful claim to a peerage during a Parliament, then the peer may sit in the House after a writ of summons has been issued. Peers are disqualified from sitting if they are under 21, or are aliens, or are bankrupt, or have been convicted of treason and have not been pardoned or served their sentences.

A person succeeding to a hereditary peerage has the right to disclaim it. This change was provided for in the Peerage Act 1963 which resulted, in the main, from a campaign by Tony Benn. He was an MP who did not wish to succeed to his father's title and consequently be disqualified from membership of the Commons. Under the statute's provisions a person succeeding to a peerage has a year in which to decide whether or not to disclaim the title. If the person is an MP at the time of succession, then the period for disclaimer is one month. When the disclaiming peer has died the peerage may be succeeded to by the rightful heir.

In June 1997 there were 11 persons who had disclaimed peerages for life but two of them sit in the House of Lords by virtue of other titles (House of Lords, 1997).

7.2.2 Life Peers

The category of life peer simply means that those who are awarded it become entitled to sit in the Lords. The title and membership of the Lords granted by a life peerage ends with the death of the person ennobled. This category of membership has widened the range of backgrounds of members of the Lords. In June 1997 there were 407 life peers (House of Lords, 1997). The largest single group of life peers are former MPs, often ministers who have decided to leave, or failed to be re-elected to, the Commons. Some of these people fall into the category of 'working peers', i.e., people who have been recommended by the prime minister (who consults with the leader of the opposition) because it is expected that they will play a full part in the Parliamentary work of the chamber. The allocation of such 'working peers' amongst the parties reflects the dominance of the two-party system, with the party in government gaining the biggest share.

7.2.3 Lords Spiritual

Twenty-six bishops of the Church of England have seats in the House of Lords and they are known collectively as the lords spiritual. Five of these seats are reserved ex officio for the Archbishops of Canterbury and York, and the Bishops of London, Durham and Winchester. The other 21 seats are taken by the bishops on the basis of seniority of appointment.

These lords are not peers and their entitlement to membership of the Lords ceases with their retirement from office at the age of 70. Usually the retiring Archbishop of Canterbury is created a life peer.

Bishops are appointed by the Crown on the advice of the prime minister. The prime minister chooses from one of two names forwarded from a Commission of the Church.

One of the functions which is carried out by the bishops is the leading of prayers at the start of each day's business in the House.

Leaders of the other churches are not automatically members of the Lords. Occasionally other clerics are created life peers, e.g., the Methodist Lord Soper, and Lord Jakobovits, when he was Chief Rabbi.

7.2.4 Law Lords

The House of Lords as well as being a House of Parliament is also the highest court of the land (except in relation to European Community matters). It is only by convention that lay peers do not participate in the appellate jurisdiction of the House. The law lords comprise the serving and retired Lords of Appeal in Ordinary as well as the current or former holders of other high judicial office. In June 1997 the House had 25 law lords (House of Lords, 1997).

Lords of Appeal in Ordinary are created specifically to determine appeals heard in the House. Although they retire from judicial office at 70, they are peers and so are members of the Lords for life. The maximum number of the serving Lords of Appeal in Ordinary is 12, of whom two are, by convention, Scottish judges and, in what might be an emerging convention, one from Northern Ireland.

The other 'automatic' law lords are the Lord Chancellor and the Lord Chief Justice. They too continue to be members of the House after retirement. If the Master of the Rolls was not already a law lord (as were Lord Denning and Lord Woolf) then the post holder may be made a peer (e.g., Lord Donaldson of Lymington).

7.3 PARLIAMENTARY CANDIDATES

Members of the House of Commons must fulfil only one qualification, that of being elected. There are, however, various disqualifications which can lead to the unseating of a person who obtained a majority of votes in an election. In addition, certain requirements must be met for a valid nomination in order to become a candidate in an election.

7.3.1 Disqualifications

7.3.1.1 General There are some disqualifications common to both Houses of Parliament. These are that the person is under 21 years of age, is an alien (here defined as not being a British, Commonwealth or Irish citizen), or is an undischarged bankrupt.

7.3.1.2 Mental illness Where an MP has been detained under the Mental Health Act 1983, s. 141, the Speaker must be informed. A report is made to the Speaker by two specialists. If the MP is still detained after six months then a further report is obtained. The seat will be vacated if this report states that the MP is detained because of mental illness.

7.3.1.3 Peers A peer may not be an MP but may be a local councillor or Member of the European Parliament. An Irish peer is not entitled to sit in the Lords but may be an MP (Richard Needham was an MP and junior minister while holding the title (which he did not use) of 6th Earl of Kilmorey).

7.3.1.4 Ministers of religion Not every minister of religion is disqualified from membership of the Commons. The House of Commons (Disqualification) Act 1801 and the Roman Catholic Relief Act 1829 exclude clergy ordained by bishops, and clergy in the established Church of Scotland. When the Church in Wales was disestablished, its clergy were permitted to become MPs (Welsh Church Act 1914, s. 2(4)). Clergymen in other non-conformist churches may become MPs.

This situation is illogical, for example, the two established churches are treated differently as the Church of England has guaranteed places in the House of Lords to offset the disqualification from the House of Commons, but this is not so for the Church of Scotland.

7.3.1.5 Holders of certain public offices The broad principle underlying this class of disqualifications seems to be incompatibility between being an MP and a holder of certain other public offices. The incompatibility would appear to be derived either from the idea of political impartiality or reasons such as time or location which militate against the proper discharge of responsibilities. People employed in the following positions are disqualified: full-time members of the judiciary including those who chair some administrative tribunals, members of HM armed forces, the police, civil servants, members of corporations receiving funds from ministers or nominated to their posts by ministers, and members of non-Commonwealth legislatures (House of Commons Disqualification Act 1975, s. 1 and sch. 1).

7.3.1.6 Limiting ministerial appointments Only 95 MPs may be appointed to certain ministerial posts (House of Commons Disqualification Act 1975, s. 2(1) and sch. 2). If this number is exceeded then either some of these ministers are created peers or enabling legislation must be passed.

7.3.1.7 Offences Disqualification applies to people who have been convicted of certain electoral offences (Representation of the People Act 1983, ss. 159, 160, 173 and 174) or have been sentenced to a term of imprisonment of a year or more (Representation of the People Act 1981, s. 1). If, in the latter case a sitting MP receives such a sentence, then disqualification operates for the period of the sentence and the person can return to the Commons after it has been served, provided that the person has not been expelled following a resolution of the House. Where the winner at an election has such a sentence, the election is void.

7.3.1.8 Expulsion One of the privileges of the House of Commons is the power to expel a member for any reason. Usually a seat will be declared vacant because the MP is subject to a disqualification. (See further on privilege 7.8).

7.3.1.9 The Chiltern Hundreds MPs cannot resign their seats. One way in which a sitting MP could leave the Commons was to apply to the Chancellor of the Exchequer for the offices of the steward or bailiff of the Chiltern Hundreds or the manor of Northstead. Such applications were always granted. Disqualification arose because they were offices of profit under the Crown. This method of 'resignation' has been preserved as a disqualification (House of Commons Disqualification Act 1975, s. 4).

When 15 Unionist MPs representing Northern Ireland seats wished to protest at the Anglo-Irish Agreement signed by the UK and Irish governments, they applied for these offices on 15 December 1985, so as to force by-elections. The intention was to use the elections, in all but two of Northern Ireland's constituencies, as a mini-referendum on the Agreement.

7.3.2 Nomination of Candidature
A person wishing to stand as a Parliamentary candidate must submit a nomination form to the returning officer. This form must be signed by a proposer and a seconder, as well as eight other electors from the constituency. The candidate must also submit a form signifying consent to the nomination. The consent form must also be signed by a witness.

Candidates must also deposit £500, which will be returned if they secure 5 per cent of the valid votes cast in the election (Representation of the People Act 1985, s. 13). The purpose of the deposit is to discourage frivolous candidates. While elections are serious matters, it would be unfortunate if levity was to be banished. A more serious point is that the system of deposits can act as a barrier to new political parties which wish to contest seats throughout the country.

7.3.3 Party Selection
Nowadays if people wish to be elected to Parliament, they must be selected as a candidate by a political party. Only in elections to local councils are some independent candidates successful (see 7.8.7.4 for an exception). While nomination is regulated by law, the selection of nominees is left to the rules of political parties and the whims of individuals outside the parties.

At present, Parliament is dominated by two parties, Conservative and Labour. In Northern Ireland, where politics are dominated by the constitutional question of whether the union with Great Britain should be maintained or dropped in favour of a united Ireland, only the Conservative Party, in a few constituencies, competes with the local parties.

A realistic, aspiring MP has to decide whether to become a member of the Conservative or Labour parties, and then join the round of others who apply for selection as a party's prospective Parliamentary candidate (PPC) in a safe constituency, i.e., one in which that party's candidates have consistently been returned with sizeable majorities. While both these parties maintain lists of approved candidates, it is open to the constituency party to select someone not included on these lists.

In both theory and practice a constituency Labour party's choice is subject to veto by the National Executive Committee (NEC). The NEC has refused to approve people who have been nominated for consideration by a constituency party, and has imposed its nominees to fight elections as the party's candidates. In the Conservative party the Central Office would very rarely fail to ratify the local party's choice.

Having been adopted as a PPC the person will 'nurse' the constituency, visit it regularly and become acquainted with its local issues and seek to become known to the electorate. The great majority of PPCs do not live in the constituency when adopted. The PPC will want to build up a good relationship with the active members of the constituency party as their help is essential when fighting the election. The other benefit of being a PPC for one of the larger parties is that they have a number of people who are at least quite experienced, if not full-time election agents. Their expertise and the general support available from the party headquarters are very important to a candidate, even to sitting MPs.

It is possible that a sitting MP may fall out with the local party and not be reselected. In the Labour Party there is a formal process of reselection for MPs during each Parliament, and some have not maintained the confidence of their constituency parties.

7.4 CONSTITUENCIES

The basis for representation in the Commons now is that of broadly equivalent numbers of electors living in defined areas or constituencies throughout the country. Previously representation was tied to units of local government, the county and the borough, and while there is now permanent machinery to review the boundaries of constituencies and take account of population changes, local government boundaries still play an important part. Representation, then, is of communities which together constitute the nation, rather than a division of the nation into numerically equal units.

7.4.1 The Boundary Commissions
The statutory authority for the Boundary Commissions for England, Scotland, Wales and Northern Ireland is the Parliamentary Constituencies Act 1986, s. 2, under which they are to keep under review the distribution of seats at Parliamentary elections in their areas. Each commission has two ordinary

members, a deputy chairperson and an ex officio chairperson, the Speaker of the House of Commons. The actual supervision of the work of the commissions is carried out by the deputy chairpersons who are High Court judges in England, Wales and Northern Ireland, and a judge of the Court of Session in Scotland. The commissions may call upon the expert assistance of the Ordnance Survey.

The commissions are to review the boundaries of constituencies so that they comply with the rules for the redistribution of seats. They may make general reports for their areas in which they submit either (a) proposals for change to the boundaries of constituencies, or (b) state that no change is necessary, so as to meet the requirements of the rules for redistribution. These reports are to be made within periods of eight to 12 years since their last report (see Boundary Commissions Act 1992, s. 2). They may also make interim reports on reviews of particular localities.

During the course of their reviews the commissions prepare provisional recommendations. These are to be made available for inspection and the arrangements publicised. Representations about the recommendations are invited. If either a local authority or 100 electors object, then a local inquiry must be held at which an assistant commissioner discovers local opinion, hearing comments upon, and objections to, the provisional recommendations as well as counter-proposals. The assistant commissioner reports to the commission and this report may contain entirely different proposals if they seem to command greater support. The commission deliberates upon the report and any other relevant material and makes its final recommendations. If these are different from the provisional recommendations then the inspection and representation process is to be carried out again. Although a second local inquiry is not required, it may be held if it is felt necessary. The final recommendations are then presented to the Secretary of State. The minister must lay the commissions' reports before Parliament as well as draft Orders in Council which are designed to implement the boundary changes as recommended or in a modified form. If approved by Parliament the new boundaries take effect at the next general election.

7.4.2 Rules for Redistribution of Seats

The redistribution rules are contained in the Parliamentary Constituencies Act 1986, sch. 2. The legislation does not stipulate a maximum number of constituencies for the UK. It does provide that the number of seats for Great Britain shall not be substantially greater or less than 613, of which Scotland is to have at least 71 seats, and Wales at least 35 seats. Northern Ireland is to have 17 seats, but this may be varied to 16 or 18. The current total of seats in the House of Commons is 659 with England having 529, Scotland 72, Wales 40 and Northern Ireland 18.

Local government boundaries are to be respected so that, generally, in England and Wales, no constituency containing a county shall include part of another county. The same general provision applies in respect of London boroughs (rule 4). The electorate of any constituency shall be as near the electoral quota as is practicable bearing in mind the previous rules. This quota is calculated by the commission dividing the total electorate in their region by the existing number of constituencies in the region (rule 5). The quota can also be deviated from if there would be excessive disparities between it and the electorate of any constituency, or between neighbouring constituencies. The commissions are permitted to depart from the strict application of rules 5 and 6 if considerations relating to the size, shape and accessibility of the constituency appear to them to render a departure desirable (rule 6). The commissions must take account of inconveniences which might follow alterations as well as the breaking of local ties (rule 7).

7.4.3 Implementation of Redistribution Reports

It is perhaps not surprising that redistribution has been controversial. Changes in the boundaries can cause local discontent as well as give rise to concern about their impact upon the result of future elections. The Labour Party has more of its supporters located in urban areas and the shift of population out of such areas has worried it. The reports submitted in 1969 proposed changes which it was thought might lead to the Labour Party losing some 10 seats in the next election if they were implemented. The Labour Home Secretary presented the reports to Parliament but did not lay draft legislation to implement the changes. It was explained that, as there was a reorganisation of local government in England and Wales in progress, most of the alterations to Parliamentary boundaries should be deferred. A Bill was presented which proposed alterations to some boundaries. This measure was approved by the Commons but not by the Lords. The government decided not to proceed with that measure. The Home Secretary did lay the draft legislation which would implement the reports before the Commons after a litigant had initiated proceedings for mandamus requiring this action, however, the government used its majority to reject the proposals. The election of 1970 was fought on the old boundaries. The Conservatives won that election and secured the passage of the legislation implementing the alterations.

The review in 1983 was also disliked by the Labour Party, which challenged the English Commission's recommendations in an unsuccessful application for judicial review (*R* v *Boundary Commission for England, ex parte Foot* [1983] QB 600). The basis for the challenge was that the commission had not produced substantially equal constituencies, and had failed to exercise its discretion to propose constituencies which crossed local government boundaries. The Court of Appeal upheld the Divisional Court. Its construction of the rules held that the commission was not required to produce substantially equal constituencies and that the large amount of discretion conferred upon the commission made a challenge very difficult to sustain.

7.5 THE ELECTORATE

The principle of one person one vote for Parliamentary elections was enacted in the Representation of the People Act 1948. This statute abolished the business and university franchises which had enabled certain people, including university graduates, to have more than one vote. The basis for entitlement to vote in a Parliamentary election is that a person has been included in the electoral register.

7.5.1 Inclusion in the Electoral Register
A person who meets the conditions relating to age, citizenship, residence, and is not subject to any disqualifications, will be included in the register (Representation of the People Act 1983, s. 1).

7.5.1.1 Age A person must either be over 18 years of age on the qualifying day (10 October in Great Britain), or reach that age within 12 months of the publication of the register.

7.5.1.2 Citizenship The types of citizenship which qualify a person for voting are British, British Dependent Territories, and British Overseas. If a person is a citizen of a Commonwealth country or of the Irish Republic, this also meets the citizenship qualification.

7.5.1.3 Residence In Great Britain a person need only establish residence on the qualifying date. In Northern Ireland residence must be established for a three-month period. The English and Scottish courts seem to differ on what counts as residence. In *Fox* v *Stirk* [1970] 2 QB 463, the Court of Appeal held that students could be registered at their term-time address on the basis that their residence at that address had a considerable degree of permanence. The court clearly accepted that a person may have two residences. Some people's second residence is a holiday home. The question of whether a person could be registered in respect of a holiday home was considered in two Scottish cases. The period of residence spent at these homes was every weekend between April and September and throughout July and August in *Ferris* v *Wallace* 1936 SC 561, and three and a half months each year in *Scott* v *Phillips* 1974 SLT 32. The courts held that staying in these holiday homes was incidental to their main residence. This approach focuses upon the nature and purpose, rather than the length, of the residence and is also found in another Scottish case, *Dumble* v *Electoral Registration Officer for Borders* 1980 SLT (Sh Ct) 60, in which the reason for a person spending every weekend at a particular house was his 'nursing of the constituency' for which he was a PPC.

The physical aspect of residence has also been before the courts. In *Hipperson* v *Newbury District Electoral Registration Officer* [1985] QB 1060, the Court of Appeal held that women who were members of the 'peace camp' beside the air-force base at Greenham Common and lived in tents, vehicles and the open air could be regarded as resident there and so included in the register. The court also held that the electoral registration officer did not have to consider whether or not the residence was a breach of property law.

7.5.1.4 Disqualifications The scope of disqualification is wider than the various qualifications to vote. Thus aliens, those under 18, and peers are not eligible to vote, though one may be validly included in the register and subsequently become disqualified. This could happen with a person who succeeds to a peerage (but not an Irish one) or who is created a life peer. Similarly a person could be on the register but will be disqualified from voting if serving a sentence of imprisonment. A person who has escaped from prison is also disqualified. A person is also disqualified if convicted of either illegal or corrupt practices at an election. In both cases the person cannot vote for five years. An illegal practice at an election is a lesser offence and so the disqualification only relates to the constituency in which the offence was committed.

7.5.2 Compiling the Register

Responsibility for the compilation of the register lies with the electoral registration officer who is usually the chief executive of the local authority, except in Northern Ireland where there is one such officer for that jurisdiction. Compilation is an annual process with a fixed timetable. The electoral registration officer has to ascertain those who are elegible for inclusion on the qualifying day (10 October, 15 September in Northern Ireland). By 28 November (30 November in Northern Ireland), a provisional register should be published and publicised so that it may be checked. Objections, either as to inclusion or exclusion should be submitted to the electoral registration officer by 16 December. Any objections should be heard and determined by the electoral registration officer and the appropriate corrections made. The electoral registration officer's decisions may be appealed to the county court and a further appeal on a point of law lies to the Court of Appeal. The decision of the electoral registration officer or the circuit judge may also be the subject of an application for judicial review. The register, as amended, comes into force on 16 February for any election held in the following 12 months.

7.5.2.1 Special categories of electors In the register certain categories of elector must be given special attention. This may be because they qualify for inclusion in a special way, such as those who may not actually be in residence on the qualifying day, including those in Crown service, merchant seamen and those entitled to vote although living abroad. Those who will attain the age of 18 during the life of the register should have that date included in their entry.

7.5.2.2 Service voters Members of HM forces, and Crown servants and employees of the British Council who are working abroad may be included in the register if they make a service declaration, otherwise they may not be registered. Such a declaration means that registration continues until cancelled or the qualification ceases. It refers to the residence where the person would be but for the service. The spouse of such a person may choose either to make a service declaration or be subject to the usual registration requirements.

7.5.2.3 Overseas electors British citizens living abroad may be registered at the last address at which they were resident in the UK (Representation of the People Act 1985, ss. 1 to 4). To qualify they must have been included in the register for that address and lived there within the previous five years. Such people must make an overseas elector's declaration in which they state that they do not intend to reside permanently outside the UK. Registration as an overseas elector must be renewed annually by the making of the declaration. There were 34,454 people registered as overseas electors in 1991 (Hansard Society 1991, p. 114).

7.5.3 Absent Voting

Normally electors will personally cast their votes by secret ballot at the appropriate polling station on election day. It is possible to vote in an election even though absent from the constituency on polling day. The absence may be because a person is working abroad on Crown service, or at sea, or because a person has moved to a new address outside the constituency, or because a person is blind or suffers from a physical disability which prevents personal attendance at the polling station. Such people may vote either by proxy or through a postal vote.

Absent voters may be divided into two categories, the indefinite and the temporary.

7.5.3.1 Indefinite To be included in the indefinite section of the absent voters' list a person must fall into the following elegibility categories: (a) service vote, (b) overseas elector, (c) the physically incapacitated, and (d) those who cannot be expected to attend the polling station because of the nature of their employment (Representation of the People Act 1985, s. 6). Applications must be supported by attestations from medical practitioners and employers in respect of groups (c) and (d) respectively.

7.5.3.2 Temporary The criterion for eligibility as a temporarily absent voter is that one 'cannot reasonably be expected to vote in person'. The list of such people can include those who are on holiday at the time of the election, or people who have moved to an address in a new constituency. Students are entitled to a temporary absence vote in respect of their home or parental address even though they may also have been included in the register applicable for their term-time address.

7.5.3.3 Manner of voting Persons registered as absent voters may choose to vote by proxy or use a postal vote. Postal ballot papers, however, will only be sent to an address within the UK. Thus service voters, overseas electors and persons who will be holidaying abroad on polling day can only vote by proxy. Those holidaying within the UK may have the postal ballot paper sent to their holiday address.

7.6 THE VOTING SYSTEM

On the day of a Parliamentary election any person who is not on the list of absent voters may go to an appropriate polling station and will be permitted to vote if on the register. Only in Northern Ireland must a voter produce evidence of identity, which may include a driving licence or an NHS card

(Elections (Northern Ireland) Act 1985). This is to counter attempts to commit the offence of personation, where an individual attempts to cast a vote claiming to be someone else.

The elector is given a ballot paper which is then stamped. Then the elector votes by placing a cross (X) beside the name of one of the candidates. The ballot paper is then placed into a ballot box.

After the polls close, at 10 p.m., the sealed ballot boxes are taken to the place in the constituency where the votes will be counted. The postal ballot papers and proxy votes will be included in the count. The candidate who obtains the highest number of valid votes is then declared elected by the returning officer who supervises proceedings at the count.

This system of voting is known as relative majority, or 'first past the post'. A candidate does not have to receive more than 50 per cent of the valid votes cast in order to be elected. The system has come under criticism for its unfairness to small parties. It is argued that the votes cast at an election are not properly reflected in the composition of the House of Commons. The evidence in table 7.1 supports this claim.

Table 7.1   General Election Results 1979 to 1997

Date	Party	Number of votes (millions)	(%)	Number of seats won	(%)
1979	Conservative	13.7	43.9	339	53.4
	Labour	11.5	36.9	268	42.2
	Liberal	4.3	13.8	11	1.7
	Others	1.7	5.5	17	2.7
1983	Conservative	13.0	42.4	397	61.1
	Labour	8.5	27.6	209	32.2
	Liberal-SDP	7.8	25.4	23	3.5
	Others	1.4	4.6	21	3.2
1987	Conservative	13.7	42.2	376	57.8
	Labour	10.0	30.8	229	35.2
	Liberal-SDP	7.3	22.6	22	3.4
	Others	1.4	4.4	23	3.5
1992	Conservative	14.1	42.3	336	51.6
	Labour	11.5	34.8	271	41.6
	Lib-Dem	6.0	18.1	20	3.1
	Others	1.9	1.9	24	3.7
1997	Conservative	9.5	29.2	165	25.0
	Labour	13.5	41.2	418	63.4
	Lib-Dem	5.2	15.9	46	7.0
	Others	4.5	13.7	30	4.6

The number of seats was increased from 635 to 650 between the 1979 and 1983 elections, to 651 for 1992 and to 659 for 1997.

It can be seen that when a party has a majority in the House of Commons it has never received more than 44 per cent of the votes cast. The 1997 election strikingly illustrates the discrepancy between votes received and seats won. The table does not show that in Scotland and Wales the Conservatives did not a win a single seat despite obtaining 17.5 per cent of the votes cast in Scotland and 19.6 per cent in Wales, nor that the Referendum Party obtained 810,778 votes throughout Great Britain, about 2.5 per cent, but did not win a single seat.

Despite the improvement in their fortunes in 1997 the Liberal Democrats still wish to have a system of proportional representation used in elections to the House of Commons and in a pre-election understanding with Labour they have agreed that a body will recommend a version of proportional representation, which will be the subject of a referendum.

The 1999 elections to the European Parliament are to be conducted using proportional representation. While Northern Ireland will continue to use STV, the rest of the country will use a variant of the list system. The White Papers for the Scottish Parliament and Welsh Assembly propose a combination of first past the post with additional members drawn from a party list (see 2.4.2.1).

In fact when Northern Ireland was given its devolved Parliament, the method of voting for it was proportional, but the legislation also allowed the Parliament to change this arrangement (Government of Ireland Act 1920, s. 14). Proportional representation was subsequently replaced by Westminster's first past the post method (House of Commons (Method of Voting and Redistribution of Seats) Act (Northern Ireland) 1929). Elections in Northern Ireland for local councils and also the European Parliament are by the single transferable vote (STV) variety of PR (Local Elections (Northern Ireland) Order 1985 (SI 1985/454); European Parliament Elections Act 1978, s. 3). In such a system a constituency elects more than one candidate. On the ballot paper the elector may mark the candidates in order of preference 1, 2, 3 and so on. The elector may or may not choose to put a preference for every candidate on the list. As parties put up more than one candidate, supporters of a party may indicate their preference amongst that party's candidates and not bother voting for other candidates. Suppose there are 15 candidates standing, of whom three represent the Rainbow Party. An elector could assign the preferences 1, 2, 3 amongst those candidates and stop, or continue assigning preferences 4 to 15 amongst the remaining candidates.

Once the votes have been counted the electoral quota is calculated. The formula for this is to divide the total of valid votes by the number of members to be elected in the constituency plus one, and then add one to that. For example, 120,000 votes are cast in a constituency which elects five members. The quota is 20,001 (i.e., 120,000/(5 + 1) + 1). The first-preference votes are counted and any candidate who meets or exceeds the quota is elected. An elected candidate's second-preference votes are redistributed amongst the remaining candidates. If after this no candidate is elected, then the candidate with the lowest votes is eliminated. This person's second-preference votes are then redistributed. The process continues in this way; a candidate meets the quota and second preferences are redistributed, and if this redistribution does not produce another candidate reaching the quota, then the one at the bottom is eliminated and second-preference votes are redistributed. It may be that one or more candidates are elected without reaching the quota simply because the other candidates have been elected or eliminated.

Clearly the successive counts take time, and it may be two days after the polling day before the final result is known.

Another system proposed to replace the first past the post method is the alternative vote system. This can be used in a single-member constituency. The aim is to produce a candidate who has acquired more than 50 per cent of the vote. Again voting is by numbering preferences. If, on the count of first preferences, a person does not have 50 per cent, then the person with the fewest votes is eliminated and that person's second preferences are redistributed. This process continues until a candidate reaches the quota of over 50 per cent of the votes.

7.7   THE ELECTION CAMPAIGN

As with other aspects of electoral matters, the election campaign is subject to a strange mix of legal regulation and absence of such control. This is partially because the legal framework for election campaigns has its origins in the last quarter of the 19th century and subsequent political, social and technological developments have been imperfectly considered. For example, the focus of the law on expenditure in elections is upon the individual candidate in the constituency. Anomalies and uncertainties have arisen because of national campaigning by parties and television coverage.

7.7.1   Expenditure Rules

Every candidate must appoint an election agent who is to be responsible for making the election return, which is an account of the expenses incurred in the campaign. Candidates may incur reasonable personal expenses on travelling and accommodation. If this totals more than £600 then the agent is responsible for the excess, but that amount is not counted in the sum which may be spent in the constituency (Representation of the People Act 1983, s. 74). The maximum which may be spent in a constituency is composed of two elements. The first is a flat amount of £4,965, and the second is a sum for every registered elector in the constituency (s. 76). The additional rate is 5.6p in a county constituency and 4.2p in a borough or burgh constituency (SI 1997/879).

Candidates may not spend money in attempts to treat, or bribe or exercise undue influence over electors. It is a corrupt practice for expenditure to be incurred to promote a candidate who was not authorised by the election agent (Representation of the People Act 1983, s. 75).

7.7.1.1   Expenditure rule difficulties   There are various difficulties with the rules on expenditure. We shall discuss those relating to their commencement, third-party expenditure and broadcasting.

7.7.1.2 Commencement The rules on constituency expenditure cover that which is incurred 'on account of or in respect of the conduct or management of the election' (s. 76). Does this mean that the rules apply from (a) the dissolution of Parliament, (b) the issue of the writ for the election, (c) the formal adoption of a Parliamentary candidate, or (d) the deadline for receipt of nomination of candidates? One 1981 unreported case dealing with local council elections held that expenses ran from the party's formal adoption of the candidate (*Richmond* (1981) Rawlings 1988, p. 142). This contrasts with the *Dorsetshire Eastern Case* (1910) 6 O'M & H 22, which held that an agreement between a candidate and the incumbent MP two years before the election was called triggered the start of the election and the expenditure rules.

De Smith and Brazier (1994, p. 277) suggest that the announcement of a dissolution may signal the commencement of the election on the basis that the election broadcasting rules use that starting-point (s. 93). Rawlings (1988, p. 141) refers to the conventional wisdom of the political parties in Parliamentary elections that a PPC, a person selected but not yet adopted as a Parliamentary candidate, may incur expenses outside the rules until the dissolution of Parliament or the issue of a writ for a by-election. If a PPC appoints an election agent then it seems that could initiate the application of the rules (*Rochester Case* (1892) 4 O'M & H 156).

7.7.1.3 Third-party expenditure If money is spent to promote a candidate without authorisation that is an offence. In *R v Tronoh Mines Ltd* [1952] 1 All ER 697, a mining company placed an advertisement in *The Times* newspaper which attacked a Labour Party policy. The company, its secretary and The Times Publishing Co. were charged with breaching the rules in the constituency where the newspaper was printed. McNair J directed an acquittal on the basis that the material was general political propaganda which was outside the scope of the rules, even though a particular candidate might be assisted by it. The decision underscores the distinction, already noted, between the campaigns at the levels of the individual constituency, and the nation. Thus it would seem that general political propaganda through poster and press advertisements is outside the constituency rules.

This would seem to favour the wealthiest political party. Indeed in submissions to the Hansard Society Commission on Election Campaigns (1991, para. 70), only the Conservative Party stated that it was happy with the rules on national campaigns. Most of the other parties wished to see some restrictions introduced. The Hansard Commission (1991) took the view that the discrepancies of resources amongst the parties were not as great as they might seem, because all parties benefited from subsidies in kind, including free party election broadcasts, free postage for election addresses and free hiring of publicly-owned premises for election meetings.

Another aspect of press advertisements arose in *Director of Public Prosecutions v Luft* [1977] AC 962. In this case advertisements were placed in papers circulating in three constituencies. The material was aimed against candidates standing for the National Front. It was held that this amounted to the promotion of the other candidates standing in those constituencies without the requisite authorisation.

7.7.1.4 Broadcasting The issue of unauthorised third-party expenditure was also raised in the sphere of broadcasting in *Grieve* v *Douglas-Home* 1965 SC 315. Here one of the defeated candidates opposing the then prime minister, Sir Alec Douglas-Home, argued that party election broadcasts featuring the prime minister as leader of the Conservative Party were caught by the expenditure rules. The contention was rejected, the court holding that the programmes had the objective of informing the public on matters of importance rather than promoting Sir Alec's candidacy.

This was very important because had the decision gone the other way the cost of such broadcasts by all of the party leaders would have taken their expenditure beyond their limits, even assuming they had authorised it in order to promote themselves rather than their parties. Legislation was passed affirming this decision (now the Representation of the People Act 1983, s. 75(1)(c)).

7.7.2 Media Coverage

The advent of broadcasting has posed problems which strain the framework of the law on election campaigns. Sometimes legislation is passed, such as that on the expenditure of party election broadcasts. Sometimes legislation is not introduced so that the responsibility for the allocation of party election broadcasts is left to the broadcasting authorities. Sometimes the legislation has unintended consequences as with the candidate's veto over broadcasts (Representation of the People Act 1983, s. 93).

7.7.2.1 Print media Regulation of election coverage in the press is minimal. Editorials may recommend readers to vote for a particular party. Advertising space may be sold or not to the parties and other groups in accordance with the preferences of the press's proprietors. Only if advertising material deals with individual constituencies does legislation relating to expenditure apply. This is all very different from the regulated world of the broadcasting organisations.

7.7.2.2 General political broadcasting rules The Independent Television Commission and the Radio Authority, as the regulators of television and radio broadcasting, are required to police the companies to which they award licences. These companies are required to be impartial in their presentation of news and matters of political controversy (Broadcasting Act 1990, ss. 6, 90). The BBC does not have such duties imposed upon it in its Licence and Agreement, but it has given undertakings to observe such restraints.

In their news coverage of elections the broadcasters employ 'stopwatch' coverage giving the parties time allocations based on the arrangements for party election broadcasts. Channel 4 News is of the view that this arrangement is over-rigid and in need of reform (Hansard Society 1991, para. 107).

7.7.2.3 Special election broadcasting rules The primary provision is the Representation of the People Act 1983, s. 93 which requires (a) that candidates must consent to being broadcast in material which involves their active participation, and (b) that material relating to the coverage of a constituency is subject to the consent of all of the candidates. The idea behind this legislation was to protect candidates, to permit them to change their minds about an interview being broadcast. The second limb of the provision has the effect of allowing one or more candidates to veto coverage of the campaign in a constituency and this has been used by candidates to deny coverage to their opponents. The Hansard Society Commission recommend the repeal of s. 93, arguing that it unduly interferes with election coverage and could be in breach of the freedom of expression protected by art. 10 of the European Convention on Human Rights (1991, para. 105).

7.7.2.4 Unregulated broadcasts Mention has already been made of party election broadcasts. These are not regulated by law but are the subject of negotiation between the broadcasting authorities and the major political parties through an unofficial body, the Committee on Political Broadcasting. This committee does not contain representatives of all of the political parties and in the elections of 1983 and 1987 it was unable to agree arrangements for the allocations of broadcasts. This left the broadcasting authorities to determine the issue. Since 1945 various criteria have been used to determine allocation of time. These have included: a threshold of 50 candidates standing for election, the number of seats in the dissolved Parliament, the number of votes obtained at the previous election. The criteria relating to previous electoral performance operate against new parties coming into existence between elections. The rise of the Social Democratic Party and its unhappiness with the criteria led to the breakdown in the committee in 1983.

Problems also arise with parties fighting in Scotland and Northern Ireland where rules relating to the whole of the UK are inapplicable. The Hansard Society Commission recommended that this matter should be formalised so that all affected interests are involved in negotiations to secure adequate access to broadcasting time for all political parties (1991, para. 109).

7.7.3 Election Petitions

The validity of a Parliamentary election may be challenged by unsuccessful candidates or electors by making an election petition to an election court. The arrangements are now found in Part III of the Representation of the People Act 1983. The court is composed of two judges from the Queen's Bench Division. Before 1868 disputes about elections were dealt with by the House of Commons itself as matters within its privilege, because the issue related to its membership.

Today, election petitions are rare occurrences. This may partially be explained by the format of such a petition. It is a private action brought by the petitioner against the respondent. The petitioner must give a security of £5,000 when presenting the petition (see Graham 1984 for an account of a petition in Northern Ireland).

7.7.3.1 Grounds for petitions A petitioner may allege (a) that a successful candidate was ineligible for membership of the Commons, (b) that corrupt or illegal practices had been committed during the campaign, and (c) that there was an administrative irregularity during the election.

A peer is ineligible for membership of the Commons. When Tony Benn succeeded to the peerage, the Commons resolved to expel him. He successfully contested the ensuing by-election and the runner-up submitted a petition claiming that, as Viscount Stansgate, Tony Benn could not become an MP. The petition was successful (*Re Parliamentary Election for Bristol South East* [1964] 2 QB 257). Subsequently Mr Benn was able to disclaim his title under the Peerage Act 1963 and return to the Commons representing that Bristol constituency.

Corrupt practices include treating, and illegal practices include the breaching of expenditure rules. A candidate may apply for relief in respect of an illegal practice. The court is to decide if the illegal practice arose through accident and that the candidate did not lack good faith. In *Re Bedwellty Constituency Parliamentary Election, ex parte Finch* (1965) 63 LGR 406, relief from exceeding the expenditure limit was sought where carelessness led to the offence.

The administration of the election has tended to give rise to the majority of election petitions. The irregularities will only cause the election to be declared invalid if it was not conducted substantially in accordance with the law or the irregularities affected the result (Representation of the People Act 1983, s. 23(3), as interpreted in *Morgan* v *Simpson* [1975] QB 151). Generally, petitions on these grounds are more likely to be submitted in local council elections. This is because it will be easier to show that an irregularity, such as the returning officer wrongly deciding upon the validity of ballot papers, has affected the result where the poll is low.

In a petition relating to a European Parliament election, the complaint was that a candidate had sought to confuse electors by describing himself as a Literal Democrat. The petition by the Liberal Democrats was unsuccessful as the candidate had identified himself properly by giving his name and address. The party description as not unlawful (*Sanders* v *Chichester* (1994) *The Independent*, 16 November 1994).

7.7.3.2 Outcome of petitions If a petition is successful then the election may be declared void or another candidate may be deemed to have won. The latter outcome occurred in the Tony Benn case. As the issue of his ineligibility due to his succession to the peerage had been brought to the attention of the voters, it was held that they must have appreciated the situation and, in effect, thrown away their votes. The runner-up was accordingly declared the winner.

7.8 PARLIAMENTARY PRIVILEGE

Both Houses of Parliament have certain rights and immunities known as Parliamentary privilege. The purpose of this privilege is to protect the Houses collectively, and their members individually, from any obstruction or interference in the performance of their functions, thereby maintaining Parliament's independence and authority.

The various privileges form part of the law and custom of Parliament and, as such, are recognised by the courts as part of the common law. Legislation is required to extend existing privileges and to create new ones.

Parliament has reserved the right to deal with those who breach this privilege and are therefore in contempt of Parliament. In the exercise of this penal jurisdiction Parliament has a range of penalties which may be imposed upon contemnors.

In the following discussion attention will be focused upon the Commons, as issues of privilege tend to be concerned with that particular House.

7.8.1 Individual Rights and Immunities
At the start of each session the Speaker claims some of the House's 'ancient and undoubted rights and privileges'. The Speaker will usually mention specifically the freedom of speech and the freedom from arrest in the petition to the Queen, to which assent is always given.

7.8.1.1 Freedom of speech This is by far the most important privilege. Parliament is the forum for debate about the nation and its government, as well as being a lawmaking body. The deliberations of members, and therefore the institution as a whole, could be impeded if their speeches were susceptible to any outside sanctions. The view is taken that members must be free to say what they want. Originally the freedom could have been interfered with by the sovereign which is why, as part of the Revolution Settlement, this freedom is to be found in art. 9 of the Bill of Rights, which provides that the freedom of speech and debates or proceedings in Parliament ought not to be impeached or questioned in any court or place outside Parliament. The effect of this is that MPs cannot be sued for defamation in respect of proceedings in Parliament because such matters are absolutely privileged. Evidence of what was said in Parliament may not be used to support an action arising from events which occurred elsewhere (*Church of Scientology of California* v *Johnson-Smith* [1972] 1 QB 522).

This aspect of Parliamentary privilege is akin to a shield, but, following the Defamation Act 1996, s. 13, an MP is enabled to waive privilege. This amendment of the Bill of Rights was done so as to enable Mr Neil Hamilton to continue a libel action against the *Guardian* newspaper. The action had been stayed because the judge ruled that following the Privy Council decision in *Prebble* v *Television New Zealand Ltd* [1995] 1 AC 321, which held that it would be a breach of the Bill of Rights 1688, art. 9, for a party to a legal action to question words or action in Parliamentary proceedings with a view to suggesting that they were untrue or misleading, the newspaper would be deprived of the ability to base part of its defence on activities in Parliament.

The effect of the amendment is to transform privilege from a shield into a sword at the MP's choosing. This seems to go beyond the constitutional justification for the shield, which is to enable MPs to be free from intimidation in the conduct of their Parliamentary duties, and offer them an extra benefit.

The manner in which this amendment was passed was unusual. Lord Hoffmann, a Law Lord, was prevailed upon to introduce it in the House of Lords, but he subsequently felt unhappy about it as he did not vote in favour of it. Officially the Conservative government did not support, nor seek to generate support for, the amendment, but there is some evidence to suggest that Mr Hamilton did enjoy government support and that the motivation of some MPs to vote for the amendment was a feeling that this might be a chance to exact a sort of revenge upon newspapers.

The Parliamentary Papers Act 1840 extends Parliamentary privilege to reports of the Houses and their committees, as well as papers published by Parliamentary order. It also seems that prosecutions under the Official Secrets Acts will not lie in respect of proceedings in Parliament as the Commons would regard that as a breach of privilege (case of Duncan Sandys MP, HC 146 of 1937-8).

There is some confusion about the scope of the meaning of 'proceedings in Parliament', and therefore the scope of the freedom. It clearly covers speeches in debates and in committee. Some correspondence is included as where, for example, a minister writes to an MP about a matter tabled as a question to be asked in Parliament. If communications do not relate to any matter before the House, then it would seem that this is not a proceeding in Parliament. In the case of *G.R. Strauss MP* (HC 305 of 1956-7), the MP had written to a minister complaining about the actions of an area board of a nationalised industry. The minister passed the letter on to the board as it related to operational matters for which the minister did not take responsibility. The board was outraged by the letter and threatened to sue the MP for libel. The MP raised the matter in the House which referred it to the Committee of Privileges. The committee concluded in its report that the MP's letter was a proceeding in Parliament and recommended that the board's threat of litigation was a breach of privilege. In deciding what to do the House divided along party lines and resolved by 218 votes to 213 to reject the report and its finding that the letter constituted a proceeding in Parliament. Such a decision does not bind the House, however. A subsequent select committee report recommended that it be reversed by legislation (HC 34 of 1967-8).

7.8.1.2 Freedom from arrest   This freedom relates only to arrest in connection with civil matters. It was of greater significance when debtors could be imprisoned.

Where an MP is imprisoned following conviction for a criminal offence the Speaker is informed, who then reports to the House. The member may then be expelled from the House as being considered unworthy of continued membership.

7.8.2 Corporate Rights and Immunities
The House of Commons regards certain matters as being within what may be termed its corporate privilege, which includes controlling its composition and managing exclusively its internal affairs.

7.8.2.1   Controlling composition   The House of Commons determines for itself whether members are disqualified or if they should be expelled for any reason. There is nothing to stop an expelled member who is not disqualified from standing for election. There have been cases in which a member has been expelled and then won the by-election and then been expelled again. This happened with John Wilkes in the 18th century and Mr Bradlaugh (about whom more later in 7.8.2.2) in the 19th century.

As we have seen (7.7.3), the Commons has transferred the determination of election petitions to a judicially staffed election court. The House 'rubber stamps' the court's finding and then the matter is entered into the Journal of the Commons which records resolutions on issues of privilege.

7.8.2.2   Exclusive cognisance of internal affairs   Mr Bradlaugh was involved in a case which illustrates another aspect of the House's corporate privilege, which is its claim to deal exclusively with its internal affairs. *Bradlaugh* v *Gossett* (1884) 12 QBD 271 concerned Bradlaugh's election to the House. His election was challenged and the seat was vacated. He was re-elected and was not permitted to take the oath of allegiance. An MP who sits or votes without taking the oath or making an affirmation may be liable to penalties and the seat may be vacated. The House also resolved that he should be excluded from it until he undertook not to disturb its proceedings. Bradlaugh sought a declaration to challenge the resolution and an injunction to prevent the Serjeant-at-Arms from excluding him. The court held that despite the fact that the interpretation of the Parliamentary Oaths Act 1866 was involved it did not have jurisdiction to intervene because the matter related to the House's internal affairs.

The extent of this privilege is not so great that it includes absolutely anything which occurs within the precincts of Parliament. If a criminal offence is committed within Parliament then the usual criminal justice process will be followed. It may be that the offence might also constitute a contempt of Parliament so that the courts and Parliament would have concurrent jurisdiction but, as in the case of the person who threw a canister of CS gas into the chamber, a criminal prosecution will be initiated rather than proceedings for contempt of Parliament.

7.8.3   Parliament's Penal Jurisdiction

The House of Commons has various disciplinary measures which may be used against its members. These include suspension and expulsion. Where breaches of Parliamentary privilege are concerned, the House asserts its right to punish those found to have committed them, whether they be members or non-members ('strangers' in Parliamentary parlance). A breach of privilege is a contempt of Parliament. However, contempt also embraces 'offences' which are wider than breaches of any particular privilege.

7.8.3.1   Contempts   The idea underlying contempt of Parliament is that it is something which directly or indirectly impedes or obstructs a House or its members in the discharge of their responsibilities. The fact that there is no precedent for an alleged contempt is not a barrier as the categories of contempt are not closed. This contrasts with privilege which can only be expanded by legislation. In fact the distinction between a contempt in the wider sense and breach of privilege is blurred.

Examples of contempts include refusing to answer a select committee's questions, leaking, or publishing leaked, information from a select committee, disrupting the proceedings of the House or a select committee, or molesting a member. The editor of a newspaper was found to have committed the contempt of molestation by publishing the telephone number of a MP and inviting readers who disagreed with the member's views to telephone him. As a result the MP was deluged with calls.

7.8.3.2 Punishment Members and strangers may be committed (imprisoned), or admonished or reprimanded for contempt of Parliament. It seems that the House no longer has the power to impose a fine. The last imprisonment occurred in 1880. Where this punishment was ordered it would automatically cease when Parliament was prorogued at the end of the session.

The recent practice is that punishment will only be inflicted if it is essential for the reasonable protection of the House and its members from interference. Often it will be resolved that no action be taken and this is very likely if the contemnor has apologised.

7.8.4 Privilege Procedure
A member who thinks that an issue might constitute a breach of privilege must raise the matter with the Speaker. If the Speaker thinks that a prima facie case has not been established, that will be the end of the matter. Should the Speaker be of the view that there is a prima facie case then the matter is reported to the House which may refer it to the Committee of Standards and Privileges. This committee usually has senior MPs serving on it. It then investigates the matter. The process followed is not a very settled one. Defendants may or may not be asked to give evidence, and if they do give evidence they will not usually be allowed representation by counsel. It is not unknown for the committee to condemn people unheard. In the *Strauss* case (see 7.8.1.1) the area board was not asked to give evidence and it was severely criticised in the committee's report. It has been recommended to the House that procedural reforms be made which would improve the position of those involved in such investigations. The report proposed to give participation rights to those involved, including the right to make submissions, to call and cross-examine witnesses and to have legal representation and legal aid (HC 34 of 1967–8). These reforms have not been implemented.

The House considers the report made by the committee and it may resolve to act in a manner contrary to the committee's recommendations. This is what happened in the *Strauss* case when the House resolved to take no action.

7.8.5 The Courts and Parliamentary Privilege
Parliament takes the view, not only that it has exclusive cognisance of its internal affairs, but also that it alone can determine the scope of its privileges.

While Parliamentary privilege is part of the law and custom of Parliament, it is part of the common law, and the courts do not accept that Parliament can exclusively decide its limits. The last occasion on which this was the cause of conflict between the courts and Parliament was in the middle part of the 19th century. In the case of *Stockdale* v *Hansard* (1839) 9 Ad & El 1, the plaintiff had published a book containing illustrations of the human reproductive system. In a report by prison inspectors concerning the circulation of the book amongst prisoners, adverse comments were made about the book. The plaintiff issued a writ for defamation against the publishers of the report which had been published by order of Parliament. The judge did not accept the defence that the report was covered by Parliamentary privilege.

The courts having squared up to Parliament on that point then backed down somewhat in a subsequent case. Stockdale wished to recover his damages and the Sheriff of Middlesex sought to execute this against the defendant company. This led to the Sheriff being committed by order of the Speaker. The Sheriff tried to test the validity of his detention by seeking habeas corpus, but the court would not question the general warrant issued by the Speaker (*Sheriff of Middlesex's Case* (1840) 11 Ad & El 273). Parliament then passed the Parliamentary Papers Act 1840 which did give privilege to papers published by order of Parliament.

This clash between Parliament and the courts is unresolved. Parliament has not dropped its claim nor have the courts conceded it. The two act with caution trying not to provoke a confrontation. It does, however, seem wrong that Parliament should claim, without legislation, the exclusive right to decide the scope of its privileges when this may lead to adverse consequences for citizens.

7.8.6   Abuse of Privilege?

There is, it would seem, an attitude amongst some MPs that their privileges must not only be protected, but also vindicated, even if it is embarrassment which is at stake. There have been occasions on which committee proceedings have been leaked to the press and the chair of the committee has demanded action against the newspaper. As journalists do not disclose a confidential source, even when this could lead, in other circumstances, to contempt of court, the person who leaked cannot be found. This issue was examined by the Committee of Privileges (HC 555 of 1984–5). The committee recommended that only leaks which had, or were likely to cause, substantial interference with the functions of the House or a committee should be pursued. In such cases the member who had leaked, and the journalist who received the leak should be punished. This was accepted by the House. The first case to be dealt with under the new arrangements concerned a leak published in *The Times* about the Environment Committee's report on radioactive waste. The Committee of Privileges took the view that this was a serious contempt and wanted (a) to have the journalist excluded from the Lobby for six months, and (b) to deprive the newspaper of one of its Lobby passes for a similar period. The House amended the motion to accept the report by saying that while it would be proper to punish a member who leaked, 'it would be wrong to punish a journalist merely for doing his job'. This approach seems sensible.

One of the privileges which may be abused by MPs is their immunity from defamation for statements made in proceedings in Parliament. Serious allegations have been made about individuals under the protection of privilege, some of which have been proved and others have not been substantiated. This is a question of balance. On occasions important matters might not be raised if it were not for the immunity, but yet a great injustice may be done to those falsely accused. It is true that the immunity only arises within Parliamentary proceedings and that the House can police itself, as the misuse of the immunity is itself a breach of privilege. Some may feel that given the attitude of some MPs on the general issue of privilege, the readiness to initiate contempt proceedings and the manifest unfairness of those proceedings, that effective self-regulation is unlikely. The question is which is more undesirable: the impairment of Parliament or possible abuse of the privilege?

7.8.7   Standards and Self-regulation

With the relevation by the *Sunday Times* newspaper that two MPs had accepted fees in return for putting down Parliamentary questions, the issues of the standards of MPs and their system of self-regulation were brought to the centre of public attention. The prime minister announced on 2 October 1994 the creation of a Standing Committee on Standards in Public Life which was charged to make an interim report in six months. The Committee was chaired by the Law Lord, Lord Nolan. Their first report was published in May 1995 and dealt with three issues: MPs' interests; ministers and officials, including employment taken up when ministers leave office, and quangos (Cm 2850). Consideration here will be given to the first of these points (see 6.4.3.3 and 10.8.2.2, respectively, for the second and third issues).

7.8.7.1   The previous regime on financial interests   The House of Commons had resolved in 1695 that it was a crime to offer an MP money or another advantage to promote a matter which had to be transacted in Parliament, and in 1858 that it would be improper for MPs to promote or advocate in the House a measure or proceeding in which they had a pecuniary interest. In 1947 the House, following a Committee of Privileges investigation (*Brown* HC 118 of 1946–7), resolved that it would be improper for an MP to 'enter into any contractual agreement with an outside body controlling or limiting the member's complete independence and freedom of action in Parliament or stipulating that he should act in any way as the representative of such outside body in regard to any matters to be transacted in Parliament' (Parliamentary Debates (Hansard) Commons vol. 440, col. 284, 15 July 1947).

It had been the custom of the House that: (a) MPs should not vote on matters in which they had a direct pecuniary interest, and (b) MPs should declare personal financial interests when speaking in debate in the chamber, or in standing committees. Custom became a more extensive rule when the

House resolved in 1974 that, both in proceedings before the House, and in dealing with other MPs, ministers or their officials, MPs must disclose any pecuniary interest or other benefit, whether direct or indirect, which they have had, have, or may expect to have.

This was followed the next year by the establishment of a compulsory register of members' interests in which MPs were to record financial or other interests they may receive, which might be thought to affect their conduct or influence their actions, speeches or votes in Parliament. The types of interest which are recorded include company directorships, employment, profession, trade, financial sponsorships including the payment of election expenses, contributions towards overseas visits other than from public funds or the MP's own resources, the names of companies in which MPs with their spouses and children who are still minors own more than 1 per cent of the shares, the ownership of land of a substantial value, and payment or other benefits from foreign governments or organisations. The register is maintained by a senior clerk of the House of Commons and is overseen by the Select Committee on Members' Interests. If interests have not been, or were falsely, recorded, then the matter may be regarded as a contempt. The two MPs who were named by the *Sunday Times* were, on the recommendation of the Committee of Privileges, suspended from the House and 'fined' their salaries for their periods of suspension.

7.8.7.2 The Nolan report In its May 1995 report the Committee on Standards in Public Life (Cm 2850) noted that there was a public perception that standards were lower than in fact the evidence tended to suggest. Nonetheless it was important to take corrective measures and prevent the public's anxiety and concern giving way to disillusion and growing cynicism. This was to be done by working within, and supplementing, the current regime.

It was felt right that MPs should be able to have paid employment unrelated to their role as MPs. The Committee recommended that MPs should be prohibited from entering into any agreements in connection with their role as Parliamentarians to undertake services for, or on behalf of, organisations which provide paid Parliamentary services to multiple clients, or from maintaining any direct or active connections with firms, or parts of larger firms, which provide such Parliamentary services. Other types of agreement which relate to the provision of services in the capacity of MPs should not only be declared in the register, but the remuneration received or expected should be listed, this would be acceptable if done in bands rather than exact amounts. If benefits in kind are given, including support services, then an estimate of their monetary value should be declared. Such contracts should be deposited and be available for public inspection.

It seemed that there was uncertainty about what should be declared in the register, indeed, the Committee noted that there was an inconsistency between the 1947 resolution of the House and the terms of the register. Accordingly there should be clarification of the rules and a code of conduct and induction sessions. The register should be maintained by an independent person, who would also investigate complaints. The model for this post would be other officers of the House — the Comptroller and Auditor General, and the Parliamentary Commissioner of Administration. While the new Parliamentary Commissioner for Standards would investigate complaints of misconduct and have powers to send for persons and papers, sanctions would remain a matter for the House. Where the Commissioner recommended that a case be considered further, this should be done by a subcommittee of the Committee of Privileges, which would normally conduct its hearings in public. It would report to the full Privileges Committee and in effect this would amount to a right of appeal for an MP. Only the most serious cases should need to be considered by the whole House.

7.8.7.3 Reaction The public's reaction to Lord Nolan's recommendations on MPs was generally favourable although some felt that more stringent controls should have been proposed. In the debate on the report there was a division of views. The opposition parties were generally in favour and wished to see implementation, whereas a majority of Conservative back-benchers who spoke were more critical of the report. The government announced that a special committee of MPs would be set up to consider ways in which the recommendations would be implemented.

The select committee did not recommend total implementation of the Nolan committee's recommendations. They took the view that there could be confusion in applying the Nolan suggestions, given that they were directed at the types of outside bodies with which MPs might have a paid relationship. How simple would it be to distinguish multi-client from single-client lobbying? The select committee recommended a complete ban on paid advocacy but would allow payment for advice, which would be strictly regulated, and would require transparency in all paid activities related to Parliament. They agreed with the Nolan recommendations of having a code of conduct with guidance and a Parliamentary Commissioner who would investigate allegations of misconduct and be responsible for offering advice on the code and also for compiling the register of members' interests (HC 816 of 1994–5). This was accepted by the House.

A code of conduct and associated guidance have been produced. They focus upon (a) registration of interests, (b) declaration of interests and (c) the advocacy rule. Interests to be entered in the register include: directorships; remunerated employment; sponsorships which provide an amount in excess of 25 per cent of election expenses, and/or funds linked to the member's candidacy at an election or financial or material benefits, e.g., free or subsidised research assistance or subsidised accommodation; gifts, benefits or hospitality; overseas visits; overseas benefits and gifts; land and property; shareholdings and miscellaneous. Employment agreements which relate to services provided in the capacity of being an MP are to be deposited with the Parliamentary Commissioner for Standards as well as being registered. If such an agreement is not in written form then it is to be put into writing and then deposited. MPs should declare any relevant interest when participating in proceedings. Declarations should include, in addition to current interests, past ones and those which the MP is expecting to have. The rule banning paid advocacy covers the initiation of a Parliamentary proceeding which includes presenting a Bill, presenting a petition, tabling and asking a Parliamentary question, initiating or seeking to initiate a debate, tabling or moving a motion, tabling or moving an amendment to a Bill.

The procedure for complaints is that anyone, MP or member of the public, may contact the Parliamentary Commissioner for Standards alleging that the conduct of an MP is incompatible with the code. It will be at the discretion of the Commissioner whether or not a complaint is accepted for investigation. If it is taken up then the MP will be contacted and after a preliminary investigation the Commissioner will report to the Select Committee on Standards and Privileges. If the Commissioner's conclusion is that there is no prima facie case, this will be reported briefly to the committee. If there is a prima facie case then the Commissioner's report will contain the facts and conclusions. The committee can call for persons, papers and records. It usually sits in private but may take evidence in public session, in which case it may refuse permission for the session to be broadcast.

7.8.7.4 Operation of the new arrangements The Commissioner has been busy, particularly in connection with complaints made by the owner of Harrods, Mr Mohamed Al Fayed and the *Guardian* against 25 MPs and former MPs. Attention has been focused on one person in particular, the Conservative MP Mr Neil Hamilton because he began a libel action against the newspaper, which was stayed and then resumed and then withdrawn. Following the collapse of the libel action the newspaper made very serious allegations about Mr Hamilton. He came to personify a general disquiet about Parliament and he was defeated in the 1997 general election by a former BBC journalist who ran as an independent, on an anti-corruption platform.

In summary form the allegations may be grouped into four categories: (a) cash payments had been made to MPs for Parliamentary services on behalf of Mr Al Fayed or his company the House of Fraser, which payments either came directly from Mr Al Fayed or via Mr Greer, who ran a lobbying organisation; (b) financial interests were persistently not registered; (c) financial interests were not declared in Parliamentary proceedings or in representations to ministers or contacts with civil servants; and (d) other actions incompatible with standards to be expected of MPs including taking commissions to introduce constituents to lobbyists, or soliciting business on behalf of lobbyists in the hope of obtaining a commission. The MPs could be placed in three groups (a) five MPs in a lobbying group, working on behalf of Mr Al Fayed, organised by Mr Greer; (b) three MPs associated with Mr Greer but not working for Mr Al Fayed; and (c) a group of 18 MPs alleged to have failed to have registered receipt of contributions towards election expenses from Mr Greer.

After a long investigation, during which the Commissioner hired a QC to assist in the inquisitorial procedure adopted, a report was made to the select committee (HC 30 of 1997–8). It concluded in respect of the lobbying group that four of them had received payments and failed to make entries in the Register of Members' Interests and to make declarations. The fifth member of this group was adjudged not to have complied with the spirit of registration. In the second group two were found to have no case to answer but a third was held to have failed to register and to declare interests. None of the group of 18 were found to have a case to answer in respect of election expenses, but the Commissioner did conclude that the relevant rules should be clarified.

Five of the six persons whom the Commissioner had criticised exercised the right to submit a written statement to the select committee. Of those five only Mr Hamilton challenged the facts in the Commissioner's report, as opposed to the interpretation of the facts. The select committee has reported its determination about all of these people, apart from Mr Hamilton, whose case it is still considering (HC 240 of 1997–8). The committee's function is to examine the Commissioner's report, to determine the extent to which the House's rules were infringed and to determine whether the conduct fell below the standards which the House and the public are entitled to expect. They did not conclude that Sir Peter Hordern fell below the standards but of the other four they did so conclude and in the case of two that they fell seriously short of these standards. Had any of these four still been MPs they would have recommended suspension from the service of the House, with the period being substantial for those adjudged to have seriously fallen short of the expected standards. The committee has indicated that it will in a subsequent report offer advice on the appropriate sanctions and penalties for MPs, former MPs and other persons involved in unacceptable behaviour.

7.8.7.5 Appraisal While the public reaction to Nolan was favourable, not all MPs agreed with it. The public disquiet with sleaze would have gone further than Nolan and sought to prohibit MPs from having any outside interests. Some of the MPs' antipathy was grounded in principle, that the House of Commons is different, which is why it has certain privileges. Nolan did not destroy their self-regulation, but the idea of the outside investigator was an attempt to give it some credibility. It may well be that the spirit of the times has changed so that with the clearer articulation of standards the incidence and seriousness of inappropriate behaviour by MPs will fade away, rendering redundant worries about the effectiveness of investigation by the Commissioner and the possible sanctions. It may be that concern about the lack of a sanction for former MPs is unnecessary as the very fact that they are no longer MPs is a satisfactory outcome. On the other hand there may be a concern that investigations do not conform to standards of due process.

The view put forward that the effect of Nolan would be a barrier to good people presenting themselves for election is worrying if it implied that measures taken to maintain standards would deter potential MPs. If people are not prepared to conform to the highest standards then they are no loss to public life. If the view was expressing a concern about the reduction in the opportunities for MPs to take up employment in addition to their Parliamentary duties then it may be that such people should reflect if they are qualified to be the people's representatives when their views are so much at variance with the majority of the electorate.

Given the disturbing ease with which the Bill of Rights was amended by the Defamation Act 1996 to allow MPs to waive their right to Parliamentary privilege and thus to have their cake and eat it, the creation of a joint party committee to review Parliamentary privilege and its relationship with the courts is entirely appropriate and useful, given that the Home Office is reviewing the law on corruption including bribery of MPs.

The House of Commons is in danger of losing touch with the electorate, adding to the current level of dissatisfaction with political parties and institutions of government.

CHAPTER EIGHT
Parliament at Work

In chapter 7 it was suggested that Parliament performed three roles: government formation, legitimisation and scrutiny of the executive's policy and administration. We know that government formation is normally a simple matter because one party usually has a majority in the House of Commons and convention requires the sovereign to appoint the leader of that party as prime minister. Thus the government has latent legitimisation because of the election result. Its policies and their implementation are then given manifest legitimisation because they must be approved by Parliament after scrutiny. Parliament thus has an important role, but party discipline ensures that the government's majority in the Commons will secure the necessary approval.

In examining the procedures and processes used in Parliament we can assess the quality of the scrutiny given to policy and administration, the making of law and the oversight of the nation's finances.

8.1 THE ORGANISATION OF PARLIAMENT

8.1.1 Meeting of Parliament
Once the House of Commons is elected that Parliament lasts for a maximum of five years (Septennial Act 1715 as amended by the Parliament Act 1911, s. 7). The Parliament may be dissolved before the end of the five-year period by the sovereign on the advice of the prime minister. The dissolution is contained in a proclamation of the Council which will also state the date for the summoning of the new Parliament. The elections are held on the authority of writs served to all returning officers.

By convention there are annual sessions of Parliament. The fact that the authorisation for taxation and expenditure, the maintenance of the army and the air force, and discipline of all of the armed forces are renewable annually, means that Parliament must meet every year.

Each session of Parliament begins with the Queen's speech which is given by the sovereign from the throne in the House of Lords. The speech is written by the government and outlines the measures which they will bring before Parliament for enactment.

The current practice is that the second and subsequent sessions begin in November. A session usually finishes with the completion of business which was not dealt with before, and the debating of issues which may have arisen during, the summer recess. If a Bill has not been through all of its stages before the end of the session then it lapses and, if it is to become law, will have to begin afresh in the next session. Normally, legislation initiated by the government will have been enacted before the prorogation, or ending of the session by the sovereign.

8.1.2 House of Commons' Staff

8.1.2.1 The Speaker of the House of Commons The Speaker chairs proceedings in the chamber of the Commons. The Speaker is elected by the House and thereafter is impartial, no longer being an active member of a party. This means that if the Speaker seeks re-election as an MP in the next Parliament, it will not be as a party candidate but as the Speaker.

In addition to chairing debates, which includes the determination of points of order, the Speaker also deals with disciplinary matters, applications for emergency debates, and certifying a Bill as a money Bill under the Parliament Act 1911.

8.1.2.2 The Deputy Speakers There are three Deputy Speakers who have most of the powers of the Speaker. They are also required to remove themselves from the party political battle, but not quite to the same extent as the Speaker. They do not vote unless it is to make the casting vote when in the chair. They assume these posts through their election as the chair and first and second deputy chair of the now defunct Ways and Means Committee of the House. The practice has arisen that the Speaker and the three deputies are drawn equally from the government and opposition sides of the House.

8.1.2.3 The Departments of the House of Commons The House of Commons (Administration) Act 1978 created the House of Commons Commission which oversees the work of the senior officers of the House and their departments. This commission consists of the Speaker, who chairs it, the Leader of the House, a person nominated by the leader of the opposition, and three back-bench MPs. The commission is responsible for the finances of the House and prepares the estimates, or budget, for its operation. It has delegated many powers to a board of management, which comprises the heads of the Commons departments.

8.1.2.4 The Clerk's Department The Clerk of the House is the principal adviser to the Speaker on the procedures and privileges of Parliament. The staff in the Clerk's Department are concerned with the administration of the business of the House and are organised into offices which deal with particular functions: public Bills, private Bills, the tabling of questions, and the preparation of the records of the House's business.

8.1.2.5 The Serjeant-at-Arms' Department This department is responsible for security, ceremonial and housekeeping duties, which include matters such as cleaning and repairs.

8.1.2.6 The Department of the Library In addition to maintaining a reference collection, the staff in this department also provide a research service for MPs and information about the House for the public. The Vote Office provides and distributes papers required by MPs and staff.

8.1.2.7 The Department of the Official Report The official report, or Hansard, is the verbatim report of proceedings in the chamber and in committees. The department is responsible for producing it, normally by the following day.

8.1.2.8 The Administration Department This department deals with the financial aspects of the administration of the House, and also serves as the personnel department for the House's staff.

8.1.2.9 The Refreshment Department This department operates the restaurants, tearooms and bars for the use of the MPs, staff, the press and guests.

8.1.3 Facilities for MPs

Compared with some legislatures, especially the US Congress, MPs do not have a large amount of support to assist them. The staff in the research division of the library will deal with queries for information. All MPs receive an office costs allowance which may be used for office and secretarial expenses and for the employment of a research assistant. However, some research assistants will work for little or no pay as they welcome the experience which the job provides.

Travel expenses for journeys within the triangle of London, the MP's home and the constituency are paid. The spouses and children of MPs may also have this benefit of free travel for a limited number of journeys. Research assistants may recover costs of up to nine return journeys between Westminster and the MP's constituency.

MPs have to pay for their own office equipment, although filing cabinets are provided, and telephone calls and postage from the House are free. They do have access to communal facilities such as photocopiers and computer terminals in the library, which are linked to various databases. An MP's own computer may be linked to these facilities.

The accommodation which an ordinary MP has is slowly improving. Some MPs have to share offices, this is especially so in the Palace of Westminster where accommodation is at a premium. Other buildings are used and the inconvenience of being a little distant from the House is compensated for with larger accommodation.

8.1.4 Parliamentary Procedure

The basis for much of the business conducted in both Houses is that a motion is moved, debated and then, after the question is put, there is a vote, or division. It may be a motion, for example, which asks for approval of a recent action of the government, or a Bill. Amendments may be proposed. Normally the government's majority will see to it that opposition amendments are defeated and the original motion, or clause in a Bill, is approved.

The Houses have agreed standing orders to regulate their business. Whilst these give priority to business initiated by the government, the rights of the opposition and back-benchers are also safeguarded.

Another source of procedure is the rulings made by the Speaker. These include, for example, the regulation of the admissibility of amendments to Bills and the interpretation of standing orders.

Debate may be brought to an end by a closure which is a motion 'that the question now be put'. The Speaker decides if this is an abuse of procedure or if it would infringe the rights of the minority. If the Speaker permits it then the House must approve it. Another procedural device which restricts debate is the allocation of time order, or the guillotine. This can set a limit to the amount of time which may be spent on a particular stage or stages of a Bill. It was a response to the filibustering tactics of Irish MPs who were causing a large amount of the time of the House to be spent on the consideration of the Criminal Law (Amendment) Bill in 1887. When the House approved an allocation of time on this Bill the previous 35 sitting days had been spent on it and some of those sittings had gone on after midnight.

When a guillotine is moved a timetable for consideration of the parts of the Bill may be included in the motion or left to the Business Committee of the House to decide.

The record for the number of Bills guillotined in a session is 10, which happened in the 1988–9 session.

8.1.5 The Parliamentary Timetable

There is a clear structure to the work of Parliament. Within the framework of the session and daily sittings it is possible to deal with urgent matters. The Leader of the House is responsible for organising the business of the Commons. Consultations are conducted between the government and opposition through the 'usual channels' or the whips' offices.

8.1.5.1 A session The new session begins with the formal opening ceremony and the Queen's speech, which is delivered in the Lords. When the MPs return to the Commons they deal with some preliminary business and then begin a five-day debate on the government's programme outlined in the speech. Specific topics will be allocated to debate on particular days agreed through the usual channels.

Following this debate the government will introduce some of its Bills so that consideration of them can be well underway by Christmas. Since December 1993 the previously separate public expenditure plans and taxation proposals have been presented together. The combined presentation contains the Treasury's latest forecast for the economy and announcement of the next three years' public expenditure plans for the various departments.

The Budget sets out the estimated income from taxes for the forthcoming financial year. Changes in taxation policy may be announced, and eventually such changes must be included in the Finance Act, which should be enacted by May (see Cm 1867).

After Christmas more Bills are introduced and most will be considered in committee. The amount of financial business increases as Parliament is asked to approve estimates for departmental expenditure as well as the Finance Bill.

Friday is different from other days in the Parliamentary week. It is the quietest day as MPs leave for their constituencies. It is also the day on which a significant amount of the business is initiated by private members rather than the government. In the period after Christmas some Fridays are set aside for Bills promoted by private members. If they are to become law the government must be favourably disposed so that sufficient time, and even assistance with drafting by Parliamentary counsel, may be provided.

By Easter most Bills introduced in the Commons will have passed their stages and will go to the Lords, and the Commons will then consider Bills which have been passed by the Lords. As the Lords may amend Bills the government has to decide whether or not to accept them. The end of the session, after the summer recess, is a time when such amendments will be considered.

8.1.5.2 The Parliamentary day

The House of Commons normally sits from 2.30 p.m. on Monday to Thursday, and from 9.30 a.m. on a Friday. Business could end at 10 p.m., or 2.30 p.m. on a Friday, with an adjournment debate, but often it does not. Everything will depend upon the importance of the business being dealt with, and, if a Bill, the particular stage which has been reached. Business stops when the House votes to adjourn. The House sits on Wednesday mornings so as to free some Fridays of business and to reduce the amount of business transacted late at night (see HC 20 of 1991–2).

Committees are often held in the mornings of Tuesday to Thursday. The morning start to business in the chamber on a Friday is to allow MPs to return to their constituencies.

The day in the chamber begins with prayers and by 2.45 questions for oral answer are dealt with. Ministerial statements are often made after question time, if the Speaker has been given sufficient advance notice. Other matters not involving a vote may be taken at this point. Next comes what is in the order paper under the heading 'At the Commencement of Public Business'. This includes the presentation of public Bills by ministers, motions to refer some matters to committees, motions to vary procedure for specified business, and motions to introduce '10-minute-rule Bills'.

The main business of the day is dealt with next. This may be a debate on a Bill or a motion. These items will be on the day's order paper.

At 10 p.m. business may be interrupted and a vote or division held. The House may then be adjourned after holding a short debate. Alternatively the House may agree to continue with other business. Some business is exempt from interruption at 10 p.m.

8.2 LEGISLATION

Parliament is a legislature but less than half of its time is spent on legislative procedures. In the 1996–97 session 38 per cent of House of Commons' time was devoted to legislation.

8.2.1 Types of Legislation

An Act of Parliament is the type of legislation most people have heard of. An Act may affect everyone, in which case it is known as a public general Act, or it may be concerned with only a few people or institutions, in which case it is a private Act. Some public Acts are termed hybrid, because they affect particular people's interests in a fashion which is different from the interests of similar categories of people. Different procedures are used for these various Bills when considered by Parliament.

8.2.1.1 Delegated legislation   Acts, or statutes, are primary legislation. Secondary or delegated legislation consists of rules or regulations dealing with details which it is inappropriate to include in a statute. Delegated legislation may also be justified because it can be made more quickly and so it is possible to make a rapid response to an emergency.

A 'parent' or enabling statute provides for the making of such legislation and various procedures may be used in its consideration by Parliament.

8.2.1.2 European Communities legislation   European Communities Regulations become part of UK law without Parliamentary approval (see further 9.2.2.1). Member States implement EC Directives by whichever domestic means they choose (see further 9.2.2.2). Parliament has made special arrangements for the consideration of EC measures (see further 8.2.8).

8.2.1.3 Private members' Bills   The great majority of public Bills are introduced by the government, but a few are initiated by private members. This is a reversal of the state of affairs before the middle of the 19th century. Those members who are drawn in the first six places in the ballot under Standing Order 13 have the best chance of steering a Bill on to the statute book, as they are guaranteed the first slot on the days set aside for private members' Bills. There are two other procedures which MPs may use to introduce a Bill, but the success rate is very much lower than for those who secured a high place in the ballot.

Private members' Bills may deal with issues which a government may not want to introduce because they are too controversial. Some such matters may then receive support from the government which is essential if they are to be enacted, e.g., Murder (Abolition of Death Penalty) Act 1965, Abortion Act 1967, Divorce Reform Act 1969. Some measures are suggested to MPs who did well in the ballot. Such measures may deal with minor amendments which a department was unable to place in the government's legislative programme.

8.2.2   Pre-Parliamentary Stage

Whilst amendments may be successfully moved to Bills during their passage through Parliament, there is generally no significant change made. Accordingly the realist will regard the pre-Parliamentary stages of legislation as crucial. Miers and Page (1990) suggest that there are four steps for legislation. These are the identification of an issue, the investigation of the issue, consultation with interested parties, and the final drafting of the measure.

Most topics for legislation are identified by the governmental machine. The political parties may propose items in their manifestos at election time, but the great bulk of legislation derives from the momentum of government. Sometimes this will be from fine-tuning of government programmes and policies. On occasions major initiatives will follow on from an investigation by a royal commission (Police and Criminal Evidence Act 1984 see further chapter 13) or a special inquiry (War Crimes Act 1991). Sometimes major initiatives will take account of inquiries as happened, for example, with the report of the inquiry into child abuse in Cleveland (Butler-Sloss 1988) aspects of which were incorporated in the Children Act 1989. Occasionally legislation will follow a great public outcry about a particular topic. Concern about horrific attacks on children by dogs led, after initial reluctance by the Home Office, to the Dangerous Dogs Act 1991.

A department, after having convinced its ministers that legislation is required on a topic, must secure agreement from cabinet committees. Eventually the Legislation Committee will decide which proposals will be included in the legislative programme for a session. This committee also monitors the progress of Bills through Parliament.

Departments will not only consult with other departments – the Treasury is always consulted when there are financial aspects to a measure – but also with outside bodies. The nature of this consultation will vary. If cooperation is needed then the consultation will be quite full and action will be taken on the feedback received. This is more likely to happen with delegated legislation than with Bills because of the detailed nature of the rules contained in delegated legislation.

The department will draw up a memorandum of instructions for the Parliamentary counsel who will draft the Bill. They normally work in teams of two on each Bill (Miers and Page 1990). Once a draft has been agreed then the measure will take its place in the legislative programme assigned by the Legislation Committee.

8.2.3   Parliamentary Stages of Public Bills

Public Bills may be introduced in either House of Parliament. Normally only uncontroversial Bills begin in the Lords. Where it is felt constitutional issues are involved then convention dictates that the Bill should begin in the Commons. The lack of competence of the Lords in respect of financial matters means that Bills involving taxation or a charge upon public funds should begin in the Commons, although since 1972 it is now possible for such measures to be introduced in the Lords. Major financial legislation is still introduced in the Commons (see further 8.4).

8.2.3.1 First reading This is a purely formal stage where a clerk reads out the short title of a measure introduced by a minister or member. After this a date is set for the next stage and the Bill is ordered to be printed.

8.2.3.2 Second reading The various stages of a public Bill's progress through Parliament are meant to provide opportunities for different types of scrutiny. At second reading the House considers the principle of the Bill. The minister or MP will outline the Bill's provisions as well as its justification. Normally a Bill is unopposed at this stage but it is not unknown for the opposition to vote against granting a second reading. This was the case with the Northern Ireland (Emergency Provisions) Act 1991 because the Labour Party took the view that the special powers given to the security forces were greater than was necessary and seriously infringed civil liberties.

Usually the second reading is taken on the floor of the House but it may be taken in a special committee in two circumstances. The first of these is that a minister moves for referral to a second reading committee and fewer than 20 MPs object. This committee considers the Bill and recommends to the House if it should be read a second time. Only uncontroversial Bills are likely to be referred to this committee and agreement through the usual channels would be a prerequisite.

The second circumstance is that a Bill which has been certified by the Speaker as one relating exclusively to Scotland may be referred to a committee of all the MPs representing Scottish seats, the Scottish Grand Committee, provided that fewer than 10 MPs object. Similarly this committee reports to the House which votes on the measure.

8.2.3.3 Money resolution Where a Bill involves expenditure the House must approve its financial provisions. Only a minister can move a money resolution and so this requirement is another barrier to private members' Bills.

8.2.3.4 Committee It is in committee that the Bill will have its closest scrutiny as each clause is considered separately. Most public Bills will be considered in a standing committee. This committee may contain up to 50 MPs and its composition reflects the House as a whole so the government has a majority.

As Standing Order 42 directs that public Bills should be considered in a standing committee, the House will have to approve alternative arrangements. This must be done after the second reading vote. Where a Bill is regarded as being of constitutional importance or where the government wishes to rush it through as quickly as possible, the committee may be one of the whole House. The rationale for this is that it permits all MPs who wish to participate in this stage to do so.

Another variation is that a Bill may have its major clauses scrutinised in a committee of the whole House, and the others considered in a standing committee. This procedure is used for the annual Finance Bill.

The committee which considers the Bill may be a select committee. This would allow the committee to take evidence about the Bill from witnesses.

Only a few Bills have been sent to a select committee as the scrutiny is somewhat longer than that given by other committees. The Armed Forces Bill which authorises the maintenance of the army and the air force every five years is sent to a select committee.

The final committee stage variation is that of a special standing committee. This is a standing committee which may use up to four of its sittings as a select committee and take evidence. Only a minister may move referral to a special standing committee. The procedure was recommended by the Select Committee on Procedure (HC 588 of 1977–8). The select committee took the view that this could improve the scrutiny of a Bill by giving an opportunity for the acquisition of more information about the measure. Indeed the select committee hoped that this method would become the preferred method of committee stage consideration. This has not proved to be the case as very few Bills have been referred to a special standing committee.

In committee stage the idea is to examine closely the detail of the Bill. This should be a technical scrutiny but it is often coloured by the political battle between the parties. The opposition parties can swing from constructive criticism to attempts to wreck the measure. Members of the committee may be lobbied by interest groups to press for certain amendments. The government may accept the tenor of some criticism and promise that they will come back with their own amendments designed to meet the point. Sometimes the government will be defeated because some of their back-benchers have joined with the opposition. If the government is unhappy about this it will, at a later stage, seek to move amendments to restore the original clause and hope that party discipline will allow them to prevail.

Where a Bill is a controversial one and a guillotine has been imposed, the opposition may not consider it according to the government's suggested timetable and thus parts of the Bill may not be considered at all in committee.

8.2.3.5 Report At this stage the chairman of the committee which considered the Bill reports to the House. This report will inform the House if the Bill has been amended and so enable the House to consider the revised Bill. It is normally at this stage that the government will seek to correct any reverses it suffered during committee, as well as implementing any undertakings by proposing amendments.

If a Bill was unchanged during committee then there would not be any debate on report unless amendments were tabled at this stage. Where a Bill is unchanged after consideration by a committee of the whole House, there is no report stage and the Bill proceeds straight to third reading.

8.2.3.6 Third reading This final stage in the Commons is usually taken immediately after the conclusion of the report stage. Whilst amendments may be moved they may not alter the substance of the Bill because this stage, like second reading, is concerned with the principle of the Bill. Once the motion that the Bill be read a third time is carried, the Bill has completed its passage in the Commons and is then forwarded to the Lords for their consideration. The stages in the Lords are the same but the details vary a little (see further 8.5.2).

8.2.3.7   Royal assent   After a Bill has been passed by both Houses, or by the Commons under the Parliament Acts (see further 8.6), it must receive the royal assent before becoming law. Normally the sovereign does not give the assent in person, rather it is done through commissioners who notify each House (Royal Assent Act 1967).

8.2.4   Parliamentary Stages of Private Bills

Usually a private Bill seeks to confer rights and powers beyond those covered by public Acts or the common law. There may be objections to this and so it is required that adequate notification of the promotion of a private Bill be carried out. This may be done in newspapers, the official gazettes and by writing to those who are likely to be affected by the Bill. When the Bill is presented to Parliament it must be accompanied by an explanatory memorandum. Presentation is by petition and it should normally be done by 27 November.

Private Bills are examined by officers of the Houses of Parliament to check that they conform with the requirements of Standing Orders. As with public Bills, the first reading stage is a formality. Thereafter the procedure followed depends upon whether or not objections have been made to the Bill. If it has been objected to then there must be a debate on the Bill. At committee stage there is an opposed committee and an unopposed committee. In both committees the procedure resembles a court as the promoters of a Bill will be represented by counsel who puts the case for the Bill. If it is opposed the procedure is somewhat more formal as the objectors, who may be represented by counsel, make their case against the Bill. The membership of the opposed committee includes four MPs who are impartial. They must sign a declaration that they have no interest in the Bill and that there is no local interest amongst their constituents.

In committee the first stage is akin to the second reading in a public Bill. The committee must be satisfied that there is a need for the Bill. If the preamble of the Bill is proved then more detailed consideration follows. If it is not proved then the Bill has been rejected. Where a need has been proved for the Bill, the consideration of amendments will focus upon the extent of the powers sought by the promoters and the protection of the interests of those who object.

Objections are made by way of petition. Petitioners may be individuals who can show that they are affected other than as a member of a community. Petitions on behalf of communities may be made by a town or parish council or an amenity society. A Court of Referees composed of senior back-bench MPs determines the right of petitioners to be heard where this is questioned by the promoters of the Bill.

There is no report stage for a private Bill. If it has been amended the new version of the Bill will be printed and the third reading may be objected to or amendments moved. If the Bill has been read a third time it proceeds to the Lords where it follows a similar process, which may also include an opposed committee.

Should a private Bill not pass through all of its stages in one session then, unlike the case with a public Bill, it is possible for the promoters to request a suspension. This means that in the following session the Bill is formally taken through those stages which were completed in the previous session and then the remaining stages are begun.

8.2.5 Parliamentary Stages of A Hybrid Bill
The Channel Tunnel Act 1986 which authorised the construction of the tunnel to France is an example of a Bill which was considered by the Parliamentary procedures used for hybrid Bills. While the statute is a public one, it was hybrid because it particularly affected the private rights and interests of people living in the area of the tunnel.

All Bills, whether public or private, are examined to check their conformity with Standing Orders. Where a Bill is a government one any element of 'hybridity' should have been noticed so that appropriate steps will have been taken. These will include notification procedures. If the requisite steps have not been taken then it will not proceed to second reading.

After the second reading a hybrid Bill will be sent to a select committee which will carry out a detailed examination if objectors have properly submitted petitions. This committee will act like an opposed committee scrutinising a private Bill, except that because of the second reading, the need for the Bill has been proved. The determination of the *locus standi* of petitioners is done by the committee itself rather than by the Court of Referees.

The petitioners put their objections first, then the promoters reply. Both may call witnesses who give their evidence on oath. Sometimes the select committee will visit the sites of the works proposed in the Bill.

The committee will then examine the clauses of the Bill and may agree amendments. On report, the Bill may go normally to either a committee of the whole House or to a standing committee. The remaining stages follow the same format as for a public Bill.

If a hybrid Bill was not objected to, it is not considered by a select committee but committed either to a committee of the whole House or to a standing committee and dealt with as if it were an ordinary public Bill.

It is possible for hybrid Bills, like private Bills, to be suspended from one session to the next.

8.2.6 Delegated Legislation
So far we have been concerned with primary legislation, the amount of which is far surpassed by delegated legislation. The justification for this legislation, which does not normally receive the scrutiny accorded to Bills, is efficiency. Parliamentary time does not allow for the full consideration of every legislative measure which comes before it. The basic distinction between primary and delegated legislation is supposed to be that the principle is contained in the former, and the fine detail in the latter. This distinction is not always maintained in practice.

Apart from sparing Parliament the burden of coping with the technical details of schemes to be implemented using delegated legislation (which most MPs would not have the expertise to understand), other reasons which support its use are that it is flexible and speedy. It may be that in providing for a scheme, it is appreciated that not all contingencies have been foreseen. If a minister is given the power to make regulations then new and unforeseen developments can be dealt with as they arise. Some delegated legislation takes the form of commencement orders. These formally bring a statute, or parts of it, into operation. The delay between the passage of a statute and its coming into force enables the preparations to be made for the implementation of the scheme authorised in the statute. At the other end of the time-scale, where a fast response is required to deal with emergencies, delegated legislation facilitates this aspect of government. It was the making of regulations under the Defence of the Realm Acts, which were enacted in 1914 and 1915, during the First World War, which led to concern about the width of this particular legislative power and the potential for abuse which it offered government. The 1932 report of the Committee on Ministers' Powers (Donoughmore) supported the use of, indeed, the necessity for, delegated legislation, and also proposed some safeguards, which included the creation of special scrutinising committees in both Houses of Parliament.

8.2.6.1 Varieties of delegated legislation The most common type is the statutory instrument, which is the name given by the Statutory Instruments Act 1946 to measures subject to its provisions. Orders in Council are the form prescribed by some parent statutes for delegated legislation. The choice between a statutory instrument and an Order in Council seems to be made on the basis that more important measures should take the more dignified form of an Order in Council. Most legislation for Northern Ireland is carried into effect by Orders in Council (Northern Ireland Constitution Act 1973 and Northern Ireland Act 1974; see further 2.3.3.4 and 8.2.7).

8.2.6.2 Consultation The practice of government departments with respect to the making of delegated legislation is that consultation is the norm. In some cases the parent statute requires that certain bodies are consulted, e.g., the Social Security Advisory Committee (Social Security Administration Act 1992, s. 172).

8.2.6.3 Statutory instruments The criteria set down in the Statutory Instruments Act 1946 (s. 1) for the identification and regulation of statutory instruments relate to form rather than substance. With respect to powers to make delegated legislation conferred after 1947, if the parent Act stipulates that the legislative power is exercisable by (a) the Queen in Council, or (b) a minister by statutory instrument, then they are statutory instruments. Prior to 1947 delegated legislation is to be identified as statutory instruments if they are legislative rather than executive in character.

The Statutory Instruments Act 1946 requires that all statutory instruments shall be numbered and then published (ss. 2(1) and 3(1)). Some instruments are exempted from the publication requirement. These include local and temporary instruments, and those which it would be contrary to the public interest to publish before they came into operation (Statutory Instruments Regulations 1947 (SI 1948/1), rr. 5–8).

8.2.6.4 Approval procedures   Statutory instruments are usually laid before
Parliament. The great majority of those which are not presented to Parliament are local instruments. There are four broad groups of methods by which
delegated legislation is made. Under the first two groups the measure may be
made but not laid before Parliament, whereas in the second group the
measure is laid before Parliament. Under the third group of methods, the
negative procedure, Parliament may withhold approval for a measure by
moving a prayer for its annulment within a period which is usually 40 sitting
days. There are two variations to this procedure: the measure may already be
made, and takes effect when it is laid before Parliament so that a prayer does
annul it, or it may be laid in draft so that a prayer would stop it from being
made. The former of these negative procedures is the most common method.
The affirmative procedure is the fourth basic method under which Parliament
must vote to approve a measure within a certain time. Again a measure may
be laid before Parliament in draft or final form. If it is laid before Parliament
in its final form it may either come into effect immediately or not come into
effect until approved. If it came into effect immediately but was not approved
within the stipulated time, it would lapse but without prejudice to any action
taken under it before lapsing. This method is used infrequently and tends to
be applied to measures altering the rates of taxes or duties.

The issue of Parliamentary time is the essential difference between the
affirmative and negative procedures. Under the affirmative procedure the
government must make time to approve the measure, whereas under the
negative procedure those opposed to a measure must find time to move, and
secure support for, a prayer in order to annul it. Not surprisingly governments
have been unwilling to limit their discretion by conceding that there is a clear
principle which would regulate the allocation of measures to these procedures. It is quite difficult to find time to debate prayers for annulment.
Standing Order 15(d) provides that the question must be put at 11.30 p.m.,
and usually debate will not have begun before 10 p.m. The control which
Parliament has is blunt: it can only approve or reject a measure as laid before
it, because it is most unusual for a parent Act to provide for the possibility of
amendment.

8.2.6.5 Parliamentary scrutiny   Due to the pressures of time, one cannot
really say there is much scrutiny of delegated legislation on the floor of the
House. The real oversight of these measures, such as it is, takes place in
committees of which there are two types: select and standing. There is a joint
committee of both Houses, the Joint Select Committee on Statutory Instruments which deals with technical matters. This committee was created in
1973 by merging committees which had originally been established in the
Lords in 1925 and the Commons in 1944. Both Houses provide seven
members who are assisted by counsel to the Speaker, and the Lord Chairman
of Committees. The MPs are also members of a Commons select committee
whose remit covers measures which are only subject to that House's proceedings. The joint committee is charged with examining measures and bringing
to the attention of the Houses those which raise any of the following points:

(a)   the imposition of taxes or charges,

(b)   the parent Act excludes the measure from judicial review,

(c)   the measure purports to have retrospective effect despite the absence of authority for this in the parent Act,

(d)   there appears to have been unjustifiable delay in publication or laying before Parliament,

(e)   the measure came into operation prior to being laid before Parliament and there has been unjustifiable delay in complying with the notification requirements to the Lord Chancellor and the Speaker under the Statutory Instruments Act 1946, s. 4(1),

(f)   there are doubts about whether or not the measure is *intra vires*, or it makes unusual or unexpected use of the powers conferred by the parent Act,

(g)   the measure requires elucidation,

(h)   the drafting appears to be defective, or

(i)   any ground which does not impinge on its merits or on the policy behind it.

If the joint committee is minded to draw attention to a particular measure, the relevant department must be given a chance to present its views.

On the whole, observers comment that the work of the joint committee has been beneficial despite the fact that the period in which a prayer for annulment may be moved could have expired before attention has been drawn to a measure. Miers and Page (1990, p. 124) suggest that the committee's effectiveness derives from its status and its discussions with departments rather than votes in Parliament following its scrutiny.

Standing committees (or 'merits' committees) were created in 1973 to deal with instruments which were neither controversial nor of interest to many MPs (Griffith and Ryle 1989, p. 246). Instruments which were subject to the affirmative procedure could be referred to a standing committee on the motion of a minister provided that fewer than 20 MPs objected. The committee has one and a half hours to discuss the instrument and then report that it has been considered. Approval of the instrument must be made in the House. If an instrument subject to the negative procedure is referred to a standing committee, it is unlikely that time will be found afterwards for the House to vote on the prayer for annulment. There is no need for the government to find time to debate the prayer as the instrument will come into effect unless the prayer for annulment is successful. In the 1985–6 session 96.4 per cent of all prayers for annulment were not debated, either in standing committee or on the floor of the House. The government has gained valuable Parliamentary time by the removal of this business to the standing committees from the crowded schedule on the floor of the House, but the voting opportunities on delegated legislation have not been increased.

Parliamentary oversight of delegated legislation is less than stringent but the whole point is that this legislative power has been delegated by Parliament to departments. The substantial amount of consultation does mean that these measures are subjected to outside scrutiny and, unlike primary legislation, they may be challenged in, and struck down by, the courts.

8.2.7   Northern Ireland Legislation

Following the collapse of the Northern Ireland Assembly in June 1974, Northern Ireland has been governed by 'direct rule'. Under this system, the great bulk of legislation is made as Orders in Council. This means that measures which would be passed as primary legislation in England, Scotland and Wales become law as delegated legislation, with a rather limited opportunity for Parliamentary oversight.

This system was intended to be temporary, an interim stage until new arrangements for devolved government could be agreed. As such agreement has not been achieved, the Order in Council procedure is renewed by statutory instrument for maximum periods of 12 months (Northern Ireland Act 1974, s. 1(4)).

To offset the lack of proper Parliamentary scrutiny, most Orders in Council are published in draft, allowing for consultation. The comments can lead to changes, which is important as Parliament cannot amend the Order. It is either accepted or rejected.

These Orders are infrequently referred to the standing committees for their merits to be considered. Instead the Order comes before the whole House, usually after 10 p.m., for debate. Usually the Orders are subject to the affirmative procedure (Northern Ireland Act 1974, sch. 1, para. 4). This procedure may be deviated from in two circumstances. First, under the 'urgency procedure' an Order is made and then laid before Parliament. It will cease to have effect if not approved within 40 days (para. 1(4)(b)). The second circumstance concerns measures enacted first in the rest of the UK and which are intended to be applied to Northern Ireland. The statute implementing such provisions will authorise the Northern Ireland Order to be made under the negative procedure.

The joint committee does not carry out its technical scrutiny on these Orders, on the basis that they are really primary legislation and so matters of *vires* are not applicable.

There is a standing committee of the House, the Northern Ireland Committee, to which matters relating exclusively to Northern Ireland may be referred. It is used to debate proposals for draft Orders for Northern Ireland. As Orders cannot be amended this process does enable feedback to be taken into account.

When Northern Ireland Orders are debated in the 'merits' committees, there is an extra hour allocated to the proceedings.

These arrangements for Northern Ireland are unsatisfactory. It is entirely wrong that a measure which concerns a matter of great significance such as the removal of the 'right to silence', i.e., permitting adverse inferences to be made about a defendant who declines to offer any evidence in a trial, should be passed using a procedure involving a minimum of Parliamentary scrutiny (Criminal Evidence (Northern Ireland) Order 1988 (SI 1988 No. 1987)) (see Hadfield 1989; 1990).

8.2.8   European Communities' Legislation

The arrangements for the oversight of European Communities' matters in the House of Commons are divided between general matters and proposals for legislation. Following the report of the procedure select committee (HC 622 of 1988–9), changes were accepted by the government (Cm 1081). Every six months, white papers on developments in the European Communities are published. These used to be subjected to debate. It has been agreed that debate on Community matters should be more forward-looking and so more general debates will take place before the twice-yearly meetings of the European Council.

The Select Committee on European Legislation examines various Community documents and reports to the House on their political and legal consequences. Its remit was expanded to include documents which are not specific proposals for legislation. Where this committee recommends that further consideration should be given to a particular matter, this is now referred to one of two new European standing committees which were created after the procedure committee's report. The allocation of work between these committees is based on the responsibilities of UK departments. Committee A takes matters relating to the Departments of Agriculture, Fisheries and Food, Environment, Transport, and the Forestry Commission and their Scottish, Welsh and Northern Irish equivalents. Committee B considers items relating to the other departments. A subsequent procedure committee report has urged that there should be a third European standing committee (Select Committee on Procedure 1992).

Of the two and a half hours of debate before these committees, up to one hour can be used for a statement by, and questioning of, a minister.

The government has agreed to accept various Commons resolutions to the effect that they will not approve proposals for legislation in the Council of Ministers if they are awaiting consideration by the House or are still subject to scrutiny. Ministers may, however, agree to proposals which:

(a)   are subject to scrutiny if they are confidential, routine, trivial or substantially the same as an item which has been scrutinised;

(b)   are awaiting consideration but the select committee has indicated that agreement could be given; or

(c)   are either awaiting consideration or are still subject to scrutiny, and the minister has special reasons why agreement should be given, provided that these reasons are given at the first opportunity (Parliamentary Debates (Hansard), Commons, vol. 178, col. 399, 24 October 1990).

8.2.9 Deregulation Orders

A new variety of delegated legislation has been created by the Deregulation and Contracting Out Act 1994. One of the aims of this statute is to reduce the burdens on business and, as this includes obligations imposed by legislation, it follows that further legislation will be required to remove or ease these requirements. The Parliamentary timetable would not allow for this to be achieved by passing statutes, so it was proposed that delegated legislation could be used, which would include the power to repeal primary legislation. Such provisions, which are sometimes known as 'Henry VIII clauses', are generally regarded as being undesirable because substantial changes could be

brought about, which would be subjected to the lower degree of Parliamentary oversight accorded to the making of delegated legislation. New procedures have been established by statue and Parliament's Standing Orders to
deal with the passage of deregulation orders (see Select Committee on
Procedure 1994a, 1994b).

8.2.9.1 Before Parliamentary consideration Under the Deregulation and
Contracting Out Act 1994, s. 1(1), a minister may amend or repeal an Act
by order where the minister considers (a) that it imposes a burden affecting
any person in the carrying on of a trade, business or profession or otherwise;
and (b) that by amending or repealing the enactment concerned it would be
possible, without removing any necessary protection, to remove or reduce
that burden. Section 1(5) defines 'burden' as including:

> a restriction, requirement or condition (including one requiring the pay-
> ment of fees), together with —
>   (i)   any sanction (whether criminal or otherwise) for failure to
> observe the restriction or to comply with the requirement or condition; and
>   (ii) any procedural provisions (including provisions for appeal)
> relevant to the sanction.

The minister is obliged to conduct consultations with organisations representative of those with interests which would be substantially affected by the
minister's proposals and such other persons as the minister thinks appropriate
(s. 3(1)).

8.2.9.2 Parliamentary consideration of a proposal If, after the completion of
the consultations, the minister considers it appropriate to proceed with the
making of an order, then a proposal containing a draft of the order and a
report will be laid before Parliament (s. 3(3)). The report will spell out:

(a)   the burden which it is proposed to remove or reduce;
(b)   whether there is necessary protection under the existing provision and
how it is proposed to be continued;
(c)   whether cost savings are expected, and if so, the estimated amount;
(d)   the other benefits expected to flow from the removal or reduction of
the burden;
(e)   details of the consultation exercise, including representations received, and any resulting changes made (s. 3(4)).

A period of 60 days for Parliamentary consideration runs from the laying
of the draft order and the report, and this can include further representations
from interested parties.
    In the House of Commons the Deregulation Committee, appointed under
Standing Order 124A, considers deregulation proposals. This Committee will
check if the proposal:

(a)   makes an inappropriate use of delegated legislation;
(b)   removes or reduces a burden;
(c)   continues necessary protection;
(d)   has been the subject of, and has taken appropriate account of, adequate consultation;
(e)   imposes a charge;
(f)   purports to have retrospective effect;
(g)   gives rise to doubts about whether or not it is *intra vires*;
(h)   requires elucidation or appears to be inadequately drafted; or
(i)   appears to be incompatible with any obligation arising from membership of the European Union.

The Deregulation Committee reports to the House of Commons after it has considered these matters and this may include the taking of any oral or written evidence which the Committee considers necessary. In its report the Committee must declare whether:

(a)   a draft order in the same terms as the proposal should be laid before the House; or
(b)   the proposal should be amended before a draft order is laid before the House; or
(c)   the order-making power should not be used in respect of the proposal.

If the Committee is minded to take the second or third of those options, it must give the government an opportunity of giving written or oral evidence before doing so.

8.2.9.3   Parliamentary consideration of a draft order   At the end of the consideration period the minister may lay a draft order for approval which must be accompanied by a statement detailing reports, representations and resolutions made during the consideration period and any resulting changes made. The Committee will once again apply the checklist outlined in 8.2.9.2, and will also consider how far the minister has taken into account its views and any representations made during the consideration period. Within 15 sitting days the Committee must report to the House whether the draft order should be approved, and if yes, whether there was a division upon it in the Committee. If the Committee is minded to recommend rejection, then the government should be given an opportunity for explanation before doing so.

The House has three options:

(a)   If the Committee recommended approval without a division, then the question on the approval is put forthwith.
(b)   If the Committee recommended approval after a division, a motion to approve the draft may be debated for up to $1\frac{1}{2}$ hours.
(c)   If the Committee recommended rejection, but the government wished to proceed, then the government must put down a motion to disagree with the Committee's report and this may be debated for up to 3 hours and if this

motion is approved, the question on the approval of the draft may be put forthwith.

There are equivalent procedures in the House of Lords where the relevant committee's title is the Select Committee on the Scrutiny of Delegated Powers. Approval of orders is required from both Houses.

8.2.9.4 Settling in The two Committees have produced reports on how they see the new procedures operating, stating their requirements from the government in terms of copies of materials (including the specification of word-processing software) and timing of submissions, and how best those who would be likely to be affected by orders might be informed about the Parliamentary part of the process. They have urged, and it has been accepted, that, in the settling-in period, the government should only submit a few proposals as part of a monthly forward look in which details are supplied of proposals at their various stages (Deregulation Committee 1995 and House of Lords Select Committee on the Scrutiny of Delegated Powers 1995). The first proposal to be considered by the Deregulation Committee was the Deregulation (Greyhound Racing) Order 1995, which was eventually approved after amendment. During the 1995–96 and 1996–97 sessions, 19 and 11 Orders respectively were approved.

8.3   SCRUTINY OF POLICY AND ADMINISTRATION

There are a variety of procedures by which Parliament may conduct an examination of the non-legislative work of the government. We can identify three broad classes of Parliamentary inspection. First, there are the opportunities for the opposition front bench and all back-benchers on the floor of the House. Secondly, there is the more searching scrutiny performed by the select committees which are composed of back-benchers. The third class is that of correspondence, which is the main method by which MPs carry out the task of seeking redress of their constituents' grievances against central government and anybody else about whom they have a complaint.

8.3.1   The Floor of the House
Most of the procedure on the floor of the House of Commons relates to debate. Question time, which lasts for about 45 minutes, has, because of broadcasting, especially television, become the most well-known procedure.

8.3.1.1   General debate We have seen (8.1.4) that the basic Parliamentary procedure is the debate. Debate allows for the expression of views on a matter. The government will have to explain what it is doing and why. The opposition will point out what it thinks are weaknesses or faults and may propose alternatives. Both front benches will wish to show their collective (and individual) competence as the government wishes to remain in office and the opposition wishes to replace it.

While the government can usually rely upon party discipline to provide a majority in the divisions, or votes, it must carry its supporters and so careful attention will be paid to the speeches and the reception given to them in order to assess the mood of the House.

The standard and level of debate can vary enormously, from the petty and political point scoring, to the measured and informed contribution.

There are the great set-piece debates following the Queen's speech, and the combined Budget and expenditure statement. Every six months there is usually a debate on recent developments in the European Union. The government will table motions seeking approval of its actions. Thus two days were set aside to debate the outcome of the intergovernmental conferences in Maastricht on political, economic and monetary union within the EC.

The opposition parties can initiate debate. Apart from tabling motions of censure of the government, the two largest opposition parties have 20 opposition days on which they choose the topics for debate. The allocation of these days is 17 for the bigger, and 3 for the smaller, party.

8.3.1.2 Adjournment debates Adjournment debates do not result in a formal decision as they are a device which enables the House to discuss a matter which is within the responsibility of a minister. The motion, from which they take their name, is 'That the House do now adjourn'. There are four types of adjournment debate. Under the first, the government includes the motion on the day's order paper and then may choose the topic for debate. Under Standing Order 20 an emergency adjournment debate may be asked for. The Speaker must have, where possible, a reasonable amount of advance notice of the request and, in deciding whether or not to grant it, will take into account its urgency, the availability of other means of bringing the matter before the House reasonably quickly, and whether its importance justifies the interruption of business. Given these criteria, it is not surprising that few requests are granted. If a request is granted then the matter will be debated as the first item of business on the following day. Exceptionally it could be debated at 7 p.m. on the same day (Standing Order 20(2)).

The final two types of adjournment debates involve ballots which determine who will be able to initiate the debate. The most frequent of these is the short daily adjournment debate. These enable an MP to gain a certain amount of public exposure for an issue. Sometimes the topic may concern problems experienced by a constituent. The Speaker personally chooses the topic for the adjournment debate on Thursday. On the day before each recess of Parliament more MPs, perhaps eight, have the chance to raise an issue as most of the day's business is given over to adjournment motions. As with the ordinary daily adjournment debate, the debates on each topic are short – about 30 minutes.

Finally, there are the adjournment debates which follow the passage of the (usually three) Consolidated Fund Bills during each session. These are all-night sittings and the topics are debated for a longer period than is the case with the daily adjournment debates.

8.3.1.3 Early day motions Early day motions are set down for debate but are rarely debated. The purpose behind them is to indicate the strength of concern on a particular matter. The support for an early day motion is indicated by the number of MPs who subsequently add their signatures to it. Some early day motions are all-party ones, others are initiated by a group within a party, e.g., government back-benchers who seek to change the government's policy on a topic.

The only early day motions which do get debated are those which pray against (object to) a statutory instrument, or which are motions of censure against the government.

8.3.1.4 Question time Parliamentary questions are divided between those which are for oral and those for written answers (see 8.3.3.2 for written answers). Each department has a place in the rota for question time and the prime minister has one 30 minute period on Wednesday, a change made by Mr Blair from the previous arrangements of two 15-minute slots on Tuesdays and Thursdays. The character of question time has changed over the years, especially prime minister's questions. The occasion is now primarily one for point scoring. This trend has accelerated because of the broadcasting of proceedings. The key point to question time is that while the minister has notice of the question, the questioner is entitled to ask a supplementary, for which there is no warning. It is the supplementary which has the great potential for point scoring. At prime minister's questions the leader of the opposition does not table Parliamentary questions but is called by the Speaker to ask supplementaries (up to a maximum of four). This confrontation between the prime minister and the prime minister-in-waiting is keenly anticipated, with supporters of each party urging on their leaders.

Another trend in Parliamentary questions, particularly to the prime minister, has been the open question in which, for example, the questioner asks for the list of the prime minister's engagements for the day. In this way there is even less of a clue to what the supplementary will be about. It is, however, quite likely that it will concern one of the current 'hot' topics so that the prime minister will be well-briefed and able to refer to a prepared reply in a folder.

All ministers take question time very seriously and their staff will carry out research so as to prepare their ministers for both the tabled Parliamentary questions and the supplementaries. They will know the particular concerns of some MPs and so will be able to guess the probable direction of the supplementary.

The Speaker will penalise an MP putting a very vague open question to a minister, other than the prime minister, by not allowing a supplementary unless there is some indication in the tabled question of the matter about which the MP is interested.

There are quite a few restrictions on the scope of Parliamentary questions. When a question is presented to the clerks at the Table Office they will check that it conforms to these rules and suggest ways in which it can be made more acceptable. A Parliamentary question must request factual information or urge action by the government. Ministers will not answer questions which are outside their responsibilities. There are differences amongst ministers on the issue of nationalised industries. Mr M. Rifkind will answer some questions about train services even though these matters are the responsibility of the British Railways Board (HC 178 of 1990–1). Ministers will not answer questions relating to security matters or operations of the armed forces. A Parliamentary question may pass at the Table Office but the minister may still refuse to answer it on the grounds of excessive cost. In 1989–90 the average cost of answering a Parliamentary question for oral answer was £53 (Select Committee on Procedure).

While the Opposition may hope to score points off ministers, this is not usually the case with government-party back-benchers. These MPs may ask 'planted' questions suggested to them by a minister's PPS. Such a question enables the minister to give a statement on a particular topic. This will often be on what the minister considers to be the government's successes in that area.

Some MPs do ask Parliamentary questions to obtain information, although if it is not on a controversial matter, it is more usual to ask for a written answer. Matters about which an MP and a minister have corresponded may be the topic of a Parliamentary question. The aim here is to publicise the matter. This is probably a last resort as, if the matter relates to a constituent's grievance, redress can usually be obtained through correspondence (see further 8.3.3).

If a Parliamentary question down for oral answer on the Order Paper has not been reached by the end of question time, then it will be answered in writing.

8.3.1.5 Private notice questions As with debates, standing orders provide for the possibility of questions dealing with urgent matters of public importance. The Speaker must receive a request for a private notice question before midday. The request will be granted if the matter is sufficiently urgent and important and it could not be raised under a question already on the order paper.

The usual rules on ministerial responsibility apply but the Speaker will normally permit a greater number of supplementaries.

8.3.2 In Committee

The work of the few select committees of the House which examined the work of departments received a boost when there was a rearrangement in 1979 which created a proper system of departmental committees. This reform was largely based on the report of the Select Committee on Procedure (1978). The idea was that 12 departments would be subject to the scrutiny of a select committee on policy administration and expenditure. Each departmental select committee would be able to call for papers and take evidence from witnesses. In addition, they could engage specialist advisers and would have a budget which would pay for the cost of research, including any trips which the committee might be minded to make.

The original 12 committees were, in alphabetical order: Agriculture; Defence; Education, Science and Arts; Employment; Energy; Environment;

Foreign Affairs; Home Affairs; Social Services; Trade and Industry; Transport; and Treasury and Civil Service. Subsequently in 1979 Scottish Affairs and Welsh Affairs Committees were established. They had not been proposed in the Procedure Committee's report as the creation of devolved assemblies in Edinburgh and Cardiff had been government policy. With the rejection of devolution in the referendums (see 2.4), it was felt appropriate to create these committees. When the Department of Health and Social Services split, Health and Social Security Committees were eventually created to monitor the new departments. The establishment of a new Department of National Heritage in 1992 was followed by a select committee to monitor it. That year also saw the establishment of the Science and Technology Committee to oversee part of the newly created Office of Public Service and Science.

It was felt inappropriate for a committee to monitor the Lord Chancellor's Department on the basis that judicial independence might be impaired. Eventually it was recognised that this would not necessarily follow from having a select committee scrutinising the departments responsible for the operation of the legal system, and the remits of the Home Affairs and Scottish Affairs Committees were amended in 1991 (see 11.3.1). No committee was created to oversee the Northern Ireland Office as government policy is to create an acceptable form of devolved government there in which local committees would be established. This did occur during the life of the Northern Ireland Assembly (1982–6). Subsequently a Northern Ireland Committee was created in 1994.

A Liaison Committee composed of the MPs who chaired the new select committees was also created. Its function is to consider general matters relating to the work of the departmental committees.

The departmental select committees established at the start of the new Parliament are Agriculture; Culture, Media and Sport; Environment, Transport and Regions (with subcommittees on Environment and Transport); Defence; Education and Employment (with subcommittees on Education and Employment); Foreign Affairs; Health; Home Affairs; International Development; Northern Ireland; Public Administration; Scotland; Social Security; Trade and Industry; Treasury; Wales.

Select committees may also be set up for ad hoc purposes. The first such one of this Parliament deals with the modernisation of the House of Commons.

The remit of the departmental select committees is broadly similar to an existing select committee, the Public Accounts Committee. The former Select Committee on the Parliamentary Commissioner for Administration has been incorporated into the Public Administration Committee created in July 1997. These two committees work with officers of the Commons, the Comptroller and Auditor General, and the Parliamentary Commissioner for Administration, the Parliamentary ombudsman (see further 8.4.3 and 15.3 respectively).

8.3.2.1 The committees in operation Each committee's membership is chosen by the House's Committee of Selection and gives the party of government a majority. Some of the committees are chaired by opposition

MPs. While some of the chairmen have been former ministers, most have been fairly senior back-benchers who are regarded by their parties as safe. One exception to this is Mr N. Winterton who was elected to chair the newly established Health Committee in 1990–1 by the members of the committee against the wishes of the government whips. Subsequently controversy has continued to attach itself to this particular committee.

While the committees have expenditure within their remit, they have tended to prefer examining departmental policies and administration over financial matters (see Robinson 1989b, p. 307). They have carried out inquiries into relatively controversial and topical matters such as the Westland affair (investigated by both the Defence and the Trade and Industry Committees), salmonella in eggs and bovine spongiform encephalopathy (BSE) (investigated by the Agriculture Committee), export of prohibited items to Iraq (investigated by the Trade and Industry Committee), and National Health Service trusts. The committees have also conducted investigations into more mundane, but no less important matters, such as airport security (the Transport Committee), part-time employment (the Employment Committee), and developments in the Next Steps programme (the Treasury and Civil Service Committee).

On the whole, the committees have tended to seek a consensus rather than divide along party lines. This has been done in the belief that it will give more force to their reports and recommendations. One example of party voting involved the Health Committee in which a critical draft prepared by the chairman was softened by a series of amendments proposed and voted through by the Conservative majority after a copy of it had been leaked to the Secretary of State's PPS.

8.3.2.2 Problems faced by the committees The major problem which the committees have is that whilst witnesses may be compelled to attend, they cannot be compelled to answer questions. Not that witnesses frequently resort to silence. Messrs Ian and Kevin Maxwell attended the Social Security Committee with counsel and through them indicated that they would not answer questions. The committee was perturbed by this and in a special report stated that there was no right to silence before a select committee and that it could adversely affect the future conduct of inquiries by committees (Social Security Committee 1992). Its hope that a successor committee and the House of Commons would call the Maxwells to account was not realised.

Lack of cooperation can also be achieved by stonewalling. This was observed in the cross-examination of former junior minister Mrs E. Currie over salmonella in eggs, and by former minister Mr L. (now Sir Leon) Brittan, and the then Secretary to the Cabinet and Head of the Home Civil Service Sir Robert (now Lord) Armstrong over the Westland affair. Mrs Currie initially refused to attend the committee and Sir Robert attended instead of five other named officials whose attendance was vetoed by the government.

Another problem, discussed in 6.4.3.3, is the tension between the traditional understanding of ministerial responsibility and the proper accountability of the government to Parliament. Officials are responsible to their ministers who account to Parliament. When officials attend select committees they act under their ministers' instructions, which may stipulate that certain questions are not to be answered. As the select committees are now the major method of investigating departments, they are very conscious of the difficulty which the current interpretation of ministerial responsibility imposes upon their work. The Treasury and Civil Service Committee has long been aware of this and the intensification of it which will follow from the government's managerial efficiency reforms, especially the creation of executive agencies under the Next Steps programme. The Treasury and Civil Service Committee takes the view that ministerial responsibility must and will change to take account of these developments.

8.3.2.3 Assessment of the committees There has been a strong temptation to regard the departmental select committees as akin to the investigative committees in the US Congress. In such a comparison Washington scores more highly than Westminster. This is not surprising because the systems in the two countries are quite different. As Drewry reminds us, the select committees are part of a Parliamentary system in which they scrutinise and do not govern (1989, pp. 426–7). If we apply the correct criterion of scrutiny, then how effective have the committees been? The answer is not very. Allowing for the problems of agreeing a report from a body composed of party political rivals, and these problems can influence greatly the choice of investigation topics, the committees' reports are not as hard-hitting as they could be. The influence which these reports have upon government is also mixed. Whilst the government responds to every report, this can vary from the two extremes of lofty dismissal to constructive dialogue. The reports' influence could be increased if they were debated in the Commons, but the pressure on Parliamentary time militates against this.

Even where issues examined by select committees have a high profile, this does not ensure that the government will act upon the committees' suggestions. The public reaction to the announcement of pit closures led to proposals made by the Trade and Industry Committee which were successfully ignored by the government, in part because public interest was not rekindled. On the other hand the changes which the government has made to the policy and practice of the Child Support Act 1991 and the practice of the Child Support Agency probably owe more to the countrywide campaign of opposition than the thorough reports of the Social Security Committee. The government can also be forced into change, not because of committees but because of the courts. The criticism of the provision of aid for the Malaysian Pergau Dam and Hydroelectric Project by the Public Accounts and Foreign Affairs Committees did not trouble the government, but the finding in *R* v *Secretary of State for Foreign and Commonwealth Affairs, ex parte World Development Movement Ltd* [1995] 1 WLR 386 that it was *ultra vires* the Overseas Development and Cooperation Act 1980 meant that the funding for it and three other aid programmes would have to be paid for out of other funds approved by Parliament.

We come back to the issue that the committees' effectiveness depends upon how much they can discover, but they obtain less than full accounts from ministers, they may not be able to require the attendance of named officials and, if they do, an official will give evidence on his or her minister's behalf and instructions in accordance with the rules. The comparison between the investigation by the Trade and Industry Committee into the Iraqi 'supergun' or Project Babylon, and the inquiry by Sir Richard Scott is very instructive. The committee had identified witnesses it wished to question, but not all of them gave evidence. The committee realised that it was not getting all of the story but, as is apparent from the Scott report, the missing part was rather larger than they imagined. Sir Richard's inquiry, although not created under the Tribunals of Inquiry (Evidence) Act 1921, which would have given him the powers of the High Court in requiring the attendance of witnesses and the production of documents, was given the assurance of the prime minister that ministers and officials would give him the fullest cooperation. Sir Richard has been criticised for the length of time his inquiry took, but it was thorough. By accumulating files he was able to follow a paper trail which led him to more documents and to individuals who could be questioned and thus uncover the details. One of the points made in the Liaison Committee report (HC 323 of 1996–7), which shows both a weakness and readiness to think about it but also reflects the current political and practical realities of Parliamentary scrutiny, is a suggestion from the Trade and Industry Committee, supported by the Public Service Committee, that a Parliamentary Commission be established. Such a body would gather factual information on complex issues which would otherwise take up too much time of an individual select committee. The Liaison Committee stated that it had not had sufficient time to consider this 'radical' proposal but thought that it was a worthwhile topic for the Procedure Committee to examine in the new Parliament (HC 323 of 1996–7). The Liaison Committee's view was that the major constraint upon select committees was the pressure of time on their members. They had noted that most committees had not requested greater research assistance, which they partially explained by saying that the topics of committees' investigations were 'member-driven', that is to say the committees responded to topical issues (or personal whims or hobby horses). This was recognition of reality that the committees will only devote time to matters which interest them. This was balanced by a recommendation that in the next Parliament the committees devote more time in general to examining the annual reports of the departments they monitor, and in particular to scrutinising financial information.

It would be wrong to dismiss the committees as a failed experiment but neither are they as good as the Select Committee on Procedure claimed in its review (1990; see Judge 1992, for a critical assessment of this review). Their performance has been a little disappointing but perhaps we may compare them to the Joint Committee on Delegated Legislation in that they have become part of the system and that their very existence will promote an improvement in the work of the departments they monitor.

8.3.3 Correspondence

The previous two sections have dealt with Parliamentary procedures by which MPs may subject the government's policies and its administration to scrutiny. In this section attention is paid to correspondence. By using correspondence an MP can carry out general scrutiny of the government as well as seek to redress the grievances of constituents. Letters from MPs to ministers about a constituent's grievance will usually be dealt with at a higher level within a department than the constituent's own letter of complaint. Correspondence is also a Parliamentary procedure, as MPs may table Parliamentary questions for written answer.

8.3.3.1 Redressing grievances MPs tend to take very seriously their role as someone to whom their constituents can turn for help with problems. This is not because of the altruism of MPs. They think that constituency casework will assist re-election. Rawlings (1986, pp. 128–9) has identified different roles which MPs may play in chasing constituents' grievances. These include gatekeepers, which means that they filter out complaints; letter-boxes, where they pass on complaints; or advocates who actively take up a complaint and personally seek to secure a satisfactory resolution for the constituent.

In their dealings with ministers about constituents' grievances, it would appear that MPs' intervention does not result in a decision being changed or a new course of action being pursued (Page 1985). This is because departments treat like cases alike and the intervention of an MP is not a valid distinguishing factor which would justify differential treatment. This is not to say that MPs' intervention never leads to an acceptable outcome for a constituent. However, Page notes that it is not apparent that this result could not have been obtained without the MPs' action.

It is clear from the amount of mail MPs receive that they do fulfil a need in attempting to redress grievances. As it is not entirely successful this raises the question whether the MPs should be aided to increase their effectiveness in redressing constituents' grievances, or whether this task should be given to others who might be more effective. The Parliamentary Commissioner for Administration works with MPs in redressing complaints against central government institutions (see further para. 15.3). As we shall see one may question the effectiveness of the Parliamentary Commissioner for Administration and the Commissioners for Local Administration, but this has more to do with the framework they work in rather than their personal adequacy to perform the task.

8.3.3.2 Written answers Questions which MPs table for written answers tend to be designed to elicit factual information, which is often quite detailed. The purpose behind the questions posed by opposition MPs may be to accumulate information which may then be used to criticise the government, or to assist in the formulation of policy. Such questions may be used by MPs of all parties as part of a campaign to assist a particular cause.

As with Parliamentary questions for oral answers, the government may find that the use of written answers is a convenient Parliamentary tactic.

Statements on quite important matters may be given in the form of a written answer. If ministers made an oral statement to the House they would be subjected to questions. The written answer avoids immediate questions.

8.4 FINANCIAL PROCEDURES

The control of the public purse has often been the cause of disputes in constitutional history. When the sovereign was very much more active in the government of the country, Parliament would attempt to negotiate arrangements by threatening to withhold supply or money which would be used for public expenditure. Some of the important constitutional cases revolved around the issue of whether or not the sovereign had a right to certain taxation powers (*Case of Impositions (Bate's Case)* (1606) 2 St Tr 371, and *R v Hampden (Ship Money Case)* (1637) 3 St Tr 826). It was stipulated in the Bill of Rights 1689, art. 4, that the levying of money for the use of the Crown without the grant of Parliament was illegal. Parliament must also approve public expenditure. Although taxation and expenditure decisions require Parliamentary approval, this does not mean that Parliament controls the nation's accounts. The framework for Parliamentary supervision of public finance decisions is formal rather than real.

One aspect of the government's firm grasp on financial affairs is the requirement that only the Crown can propose measures to the Commons which involve taxation or expenditure. Thus, money resolutions can only be moved by ministers.

The government has several accounts. These are the Consolidated Fund (Consolidated Fund Act 1816), the National Transactions Capital Account, the National Loans Fund (National Loans Fund Act 1968) and the Contingencies Fund (Contingencies Fund Act 1974). The first two accounts contain most tax revenue and are used for most public expenditure. The third account is used for government borrowing and lending. The fourth account may be drawn on for unforeseen items of expenditure. The amount in this fund is set at 2 per cent of the previous year's authorised expenditure.

The basic outline of financial procedure is that departments prepare estimates for their proposed expenditure in the next financial year, which in this context runs from 1 April to 31 March. After the estimates have been approved in resolutions by Parliament, legislation must be passed to authorise the withdrawal of money from the Consolidated Fund. There are two types of statute which permit this, Consolidated Fund Acts and Appropriation Acts.

The authority for taxation is the annual Finance Act which renews those taxes which are not permanently authorised and implements any variations in the rates of taxes and duties.

In addition to approving the government's financial proposals, Parliament conducts an audit of the way in which the money was spent. This is done by the staff of the National Audit Office, headed by the Comptroller and Auditor General, and a select committee, the Public Accounts Committee.

8.4.1 Supply

Public expenditure is part of a government's general management of the economy as well as part of particular policies, such as social security or education. The Treasury plays an important part in coordinating the proposals of the various spending departments. Every year, from November to May, the Public Expenditure Survey Committee, composed of officials from spending departments and the Treasury, carries out a survey of departments' spending plans for the next four years. A report is made to the Chancellor of the Exchequer. During the summer the Chief Secretary to the Treasury negotiates with the spending ministers the amounts for their departments. An outline of the public expenditure plans is given in the Chancellor's Autumn Statement, usually in November. As from December 1993 the public expenditure plans will be presented in combination with the Budget. Around February the departments will present their detailed estimates along with reports on their planned expenditure. The major piece of legislation which authorises the government drawing upon funds is the Consolidated Fund (Appropriation) Act. This is usually passed by early August and specifically allocates amounts to departments according to the estimates. As the financial year begins in April, authorisation for expenditure between then and the enactment of the Appropriation Act is required. This is done by approving a vote on account which allows the government to spend around 35 per cent of the estimates for the forthcoming financial year. This will then be included in one or more Consolidated Fund Bill passed before the start of the new financial year. The balance is then withdrawn on the authority of the Appropriation Act.

In order to cope with overspending, a department may prepare supplementary estimates. These may be submitted in February, July and November and, after approval, will be incorporated into the next Consolidated Fund or Appropriation Bill. If a department overspent but did not obtain an approved supplementary estimate during that financial year, an excess vote may meet that amount. Excess votes are considered first by the Public Accounts Committee which then reports to the House.

The Contingencies Fund may be used for expenditure before an authorising statute has been enacted. The expenditure may not occur before the relevant Bill has received its second reading.

In the past a lot of Parliamentary time was taken up with the consideration of estimates but this was taken as an opportunity to debate policy or administration rather than finances. Gradually procedures were changed so that Consolidated Fund and Appropriation Acts, as well as the estimates, were approved without debate. In return, opportunities were given for debate initiated by the opposition and backbenchers to compensate for the loss involved in the now formal consideration of supply. These debating opportunities are the 20 opposition days (see 8.3.1.1) which were formerly called supply days, and the adjournment debates which follow the uncontested passage of the three Consolidated Fund Bills (see 8.3.1.2). Three days are, however, given over to the debate of certain estimates, which are chosen by the Liaison Committee.

Public expenditure may be classed as either supply services, or Consolidated Fund services. Annual approval is required for the former but not for the latter. It is felt inappropriate that certain expenditure such as the Civil List, or the remuneration of the judiciary and the Speaker, should be considered annually.

8.4.2 Taxation

Some taxes, such as income tax, are only authorised a year at a time, whereas others, including customs and excise duties, are authorised permanently. The arrangements for tax collection are permanent (Income and Corporation Taxes Act 1988, and the Taxes Management Act 1970). The Board of Inland Revenue and the Board of Customs and Excise are the two major tax collection agencies, which are under the authority, but not the operational control, of the Chancellor.

Formerly, the Chancellor presented the Budget in March or April but it will, from December 1993, be combined with public expenditure proposals. The Budget details the levels of taxation and any new taxes, and has contained a general statement on the economy. Traditionally, the Budget speech is kept a close secret with cabinet being informed of its contents only hours before it is delivered.

When the Chancellor sits down the House will be asked to approve the measures contained in the Budget speech. These resolutions can then be implemented by virtue of the Provisional Collection of Taxes Act 1968. This legislation sets a timetable for the passage of the Finance Act which renews taxation for the current tax year, which runs from 6 April to 5 April. If this timetable is not met then taxes levied in the new tax year will have been collected unlawfully. Prior to 1913 it was assumed that the Parliamentary resolutions could authorise tax collection until the enactment of the Finance Act. A successful challenge to this practice was made in *Bowles* v *Bank of England* [1913] 1 Ch 57, which reaffirmed older authorities, such as *Stockdale* v *Hansard* (1839) 9 Ad & El 1, that mere resolutions of Parliament could not change the law. The courts have generally been vigilant in ensuring that charges upon the citizen have the correct authorisation (*Attorney-General* v *Wilts United Dairies Ltd* (1921) 37 TLR 884; *Congreve* v *Home Office* [1976] QB 629).

As has been mentioned (8.2.3.4) the committee stage of the Finance Bill is usually divided between a committee of the whole House and a standing committee. While it is important to the government that the Finance Bill should not be altered, amendments will be accepted if they resolve difficulties which became apparent during scrutiny.

The House of Lords, by convention, does not object to the Finance Bill. If a Bill has been certified by the Speaker as a money Bill, then the Lords can only delay it for one month under the Parliament Acts 1911 and 1949 (see further 8.6).

8.4.3 Audit

If Parliamentary oversight of taxation and expenditure proposals is less than rigorous, the same is not true of the scrutiny of how the money was actually

·spent. The audit of the departmental accounts is conducted by the National Audit Office which was created by a private member's statute (National Audit Act 1983). This office is a strengthened version of the former Exchequer and Audit Department. It has been strengthened by improving the independence of the Comptroller and Auditor General, who heads the office, and by increasing the scope of the audit from financial irregularities to the examination of the economy, efficiency and effectiveness of a department's use of resources in carrying out its functions. The office is also empowered to inspect other bodies which are wholly, or partially, in receipt of public funds, such as the National Health Service and the universities, but not the nationalised industries or local government (see further 10.5.3).

The appointment of the Comptroller and Auditor General is made by the Crown after a Commons resolution moved by the prime minister, and with the approval of the MP who chairs the Public Accounts Committee (National Audit Act 1983, s. 1(1)). To ensure the independence of the Comptroller and Auditor General, the office, like that of a judge, is held during good behaviour (Exchequer and Audit Departments Act 1866, s. 3), and the remuneration is a charge on the Consolidated Fund (National Audit Act 1983, s. 4).

The Comptroller and Auditor General reports to the Public Accounts Committee which then selects bodies which it will investigate. It will call the accounting officer, who is usually the permanent secretary in a central government department or the chief executive of an executive agency, to give evidence. When it is examining witnesses the Public Accounts Committee is assisted by the presence of the Comptroller and Auditor General.

The Public Accounts Committee is regarded as a very important committee which operates in a non-partisan way and it is chaired by an opposition MP. Its reports are always debated by the Commons. The Public Accounts Committee's investigations have exposed various shortcomings in departments' affairs, from inadequate monitoring of projects to programmes which produced poor value for money. Topics which were reported upon in 1993–4 included the Pergau Dam Hydroelectric Project (HC 155 of 1993–4) and a general critique of the proper conduct of public business (HC 154 of 1993–4).

The Comptroller and Auditor General has other important functions to perform. These concern the oversight of the Consolidated Fund and the National Loans Fund, checking that revenue is paid into them and authorising withdrawals from them.

Finally, the new select committees may consider the expenditure of their departments. It was hoped that they might examine the estimates but this has not really been done. One committee which has reported regularly on financial matters is the Treasury and Civil Service Committee. In the opinion of one observer this committee has improved the flow and quality of financial reporting to the Commons (Robinson 1989a, p. 283).

8.5 THE HOUSE OF LORDS

Unlike the lower House, the battle amongst the parties is not a major feature of the work of their lordships' House. Whilst the upper House carries out much the same functions as the lower one, lawmaking and scrutiny of the government, there is a different emphasis to these proceedings, as well as variations in procedure. Their lordships' dealings with financial legislation are purely formal.

8.5.1 Organisation and Senior Personnel of the House

The difference in atmosphere and the approach to work between the two Houses is reflected in the self-discipline exercised by their lordships. The Lord Chancellor may preside over the House but does not have disciplinary powers over peers as the Speaker has in the Commons. As the Lord Chancellor is a member of the cabinet, it is not surprising that party considerations are not forsworn, unlike the Speaker. The Lord Chancellor may join in debate and vote in divisions, and so does not have a casting vote. When the House of Lords is in a committee of the whole House, proceedings are chaired by the Chairman of Committees, or Lord Chairman, who is the first Deputy Speaker. The Chairman of Committees is, however, expected neither to speak nor vote on politically controversial matters. The Lord Chairman is the ex officio chairman of the House's select committees unless it orders to the contrary. This has been done in the case of the European Communities Committee which is chaired by the Principal Deputy Chairman of Committees, who generally assists the Lord Chairman. There are panels of Deputy Speakers and Deputy Chairmen of Committees but, unlike the Lord Chairman and Principal Deputy Chairman, they do not receive a salary for this work.

The Leader of the House of Lords carries out some of the functions performed by the Speaker of the Commons, principally, advising the House on matters of procedure and order. This role can conflict somewhat with the job of being the leader of the government in the Lords and, accordingly, a member of the cabinet.

The departmental administration of the House is shared between the Clerk of the Parliaments and the Gentleman Usher of the Black Rod. These officers, who have responsibilities equivalent to those of the Clerk of the House and the Serjeant-at-Arms in the Commons (see 8.1.2.4 and 8.1.2.5), sit on the Lords Offices Committee, which is chaired by the Chairman of Committees. This committee reports to the House and delegates control to sub-committees dealing with administration, computers, the library, the refreshment department, the House's staff, and works of art.

Only a few members of the House of Lords receive a salary, the rest may claim a daily attendance allowance, which is intended to cover accommodation subsistence, and secretarial expenses.

8.5.2 Legislation

Bills, and delegated legislation which is subject to the Lords' procedures, are dealt with using the same stages as in the Commons. There are, however, a few differences, which are dealt with below. The major difference between the Houses is that it has come to be accepted that the role of the Lords is that of a revising chamber. As a consequence more amendments to Bills are accepted in the Lords. This occurs for several reasons. In some cases the government tables amendments either to keep promises made in the Commons, when the business managers wished to rush a Bill through that House, or to implement second thoughts which the sponsoring department has had. The government's representatives in the Lords are also more amenable to amendments than their Commons counterparts so that pressure from peers succeeds either in amending points or causing a change in policy.

8.5.2.1 Public Bills Usually, all stages of public Bills are taken on the floor of the House. However, Bills are occasionally committed to a select committee. There is no guillotine, but there is a Standing Order which sets a timetable for the various stages. This can be overridden, especially near the end of a session, as their lordships work their way through Bills which originated in the Commons.

8.5.2.2 Private members' Bills There are greater opportunities for peers to initiate private members' Bills than for MPs. Although quite a few of these Bills may be passed by their lordships, they usually fall in the other House. It has happened that measures which began as private members' Bills in the Lords were eventually passed when taken up as a private member's Bill by an MP in the following session, e.g. the Abortion Act 1967 and the Sexual Offences Act 1967.

8.5.2.3 Private Bills Bills enabling marriage always begin in the Lords, while Bills promoted by nationalised industries, or which are mainly financial in nature, are usually first introduced in the Commons. Normally all private Bills are taken in a committee of the whole House but an opposed private Bill is considered by a select committee. Otherwise procedures are the same in both Houses.

8.5.2.4 Delegated legislation The Parliament Acts 1911 and 1949 (see further 8.6) do not cover delegated legislation, which opens up the possibility of conflict between the Houses. Their lordships' opposition to these measures, however, does not usually lead to rejection. Instead, they pass motions which seek amendments to the measures, rather than their annulment. In this way their lordships can make the government take notice of their views.

8.5.3 Scrutiny

As the Lords play the lesser role in relation to legislation, and especially finance, their lordships tend to initiate debate about the government's policies. The system of select committees is not organised on a departmental basis but their investigations tend to be longer and fuller than those conducted in the Commons.

8.5.3.1 Debate The quality of debate is often said to be higher in the Lords than in the Commons. On occasions this is due to the wide range of expertise which has been brought into the House by the life peers. Certainly the atmosphere is less highly charged and political point scoring is much lower. The great majority of the members of the government are in the Commons and this also helps to lower the temperature of proceedings.

In the organisation of the business of the House, government business does not have priority.

The Lords do not vote as often as the Commons. The Leader of the Lords and the chief whip can gauge the mood of the House from the speeches.

8.5.3.2 Questions As in the Commons there are questions for oral and written answers. Starred questions are the equivalent of questions for oral answer in the Commons. They have increased in number and supplementaries may be taken from peers other than the original questioner.

Unstarred questions are the Lords equivalent of the daily adjournment debates, but are not subject to a time-limit.

Private notice questions are even rarer occurrences in the Lords than in the Commons. In the three sessions from 1991–92 to 1993–94, a total of five were permitted.

8.5.3.3 Select committees The Lords have two types of select committee which examine policy and administration. These are the sessional and the *ad hoc*. Currently, there are two sessional committees which deal with the European Communities, and Science and Technology. Both may appoint subcommittees, of which the EC Committee has six and the Science and Technology has three. The EC Committee's remit requires it to consider all Community proposals whether in draft form or otherwise, and to report on those which it feels raise important points of policy or principle, or other points to which the House's attention should be drawn. During the 1990–91 session the committee made 17 reports, one of which dealt with the development and future of the common agricultural policy.

The six subcommittees cover (a) finance, trade and industry and external relations; (b) energy, transport and technology; (c) social and consumer affairs; (d) agriculture and food; (e) law and institutions; and (f) environment. The subcommittee covering law and institutions is chaired by one of the law lords and has the assistance of the second counsel to the Chairman of Committees and a legal assistant.

The EC Committee may also establish ad hoc subcommittees to investigate particular topics. One recent example was economic and monetary union and political union.

The Science and Technology Committee is the other policy and administration sessional select committee. It focuses its attention upon scientific and technological issues which have a political or social content. Some eminent scientists are life peers and so this committee's membership has impressive expertise. It tends to produce an average of three reports annually. Two of its reports dealt with nuclear power and hazardous waste disposal.

The ad hoc select committees are established to conduct an investigation into a particular Bill or topic. There have not been many of these committees, and those dealing with public Bills have outnumbered those on topics of public interest. While the Bill committees report within a session, the topic committees have taken at least two sessions to produce their reports. Only one Bill committee has been established to inquire into a government Bill with the result that it was killed (Hare Coursing 1976). Other examples of Bill reports include a Bill of Rights (1977–8), and the Infant Life (Preservation) Bill (1986–7), neither of which was enacted, and the Anti-Discrimination (No. 2) Bill (1972–3), which was eventually enacted as the Sex Discrimination Act 1975. One topic report which caused a controversy was the 1985 report on overseas trade. This was very critical of government policy and the Secretary of Trade and Industry issued a statement which rejected the committee's findings.

8.6   INTER-HOUSE DISSENSION

We have seen that the development of democracy has accorded primacy to the elected House of Commons over the hereditary and appointed House of Lords. By the start of the 20th century conventions had developed with respect to disputes about legislation. The Lords would give way on non-financial matters if the Commons was representing the will of the people, for which the precedent was the great Reform Act 1832. So far as financial legislation was concerned, the Lords accepted the Commons' claim that taxation and public expenditure measures would originate in the Commons, and that they would not amend them or financial clauses in other Bills. The Lords, however, claimed the right to reject such measures. The combination of the election of a reforming Liberal government in 1906 and these competing claims produced a recipe for dissension between the two Houses. Eventually a full-scale conflict occurred with the Lords' rejection of the Finance Bill in 1909. This gave the impetus to the Liberals to produce legislation to curb the Lords. After two general elections in 1910, and the knowledge that George V was prepared to create sufficient Liberal peers for them to form a majority, the Lords passed the Parliament Act 1911.

Under this statute public Bills might be enacted into law without the consent of the Lords. If their lordships were not minded to pass a public Bill, all they could do would be to suspend its passage for two years, i.e., over three successive sessions (s. 2). The 1911 Act was amended by the Parliament Act 1949 so that the Commons must pass, and the Lords reject, a Bill in two successive sessions, and there must be an interval of a year and one month between the second reading of the Bill in the first session and its third reading in the second session, before it can be presented for the royal assent. It is also required that the Speaker certifies that the Bill complies with the Parliament Acts.

If a Bill is intended to shorten the life of a Parliament then the Parliament Act's provisions for enactment without the consent of the Lords would not apply (s. 2(1)).

The 1911 statute also deals with money Bills, which are defined as those which, in the Speaker's opinion contain provisions exclusively relating to central government taxation, expenditure or loans (s. 1(2)). If a Bill is certified by the Speaker as a money Bill prior to its transmission from the Commons to the Lords, then it can proceed to royal assent after it has been before the Lords for one month (s. 1(1)). The Speaker should, if practicable, consult two members of the Commons' Chairmen's Panel before issuing such a certificate (s. 1(3)).

The Parliament Acts procedures have only been invoked on four occasions to enact Bills which the Lords had rejected. These measures were the Welsh Church Act 1914, the Government of Ireland Act 1914, the Parliament Act 1949 and the War Crimes Act 1991. Usually the two Houses are able to agree a Bill. Sometimes the Commons accepts some of the Lords' amendments (as with the Aircraft and Shipbuilding Act 1977: this was the second attempt to pass the Bill, the Lords' opposition having killed off the first Bill). On other occasions the Lords do not press their opposition and accept the Bill which has had the Lords' amendments removed by the Commons (the Environmental Protection Act 1990 where the Lords had initially inserted an amendment providing for a compulsory dog registration scheme). Agreement is sometimes reached on the basis that the government accepts defeat by the Lords and does not make another attempt to enact a measure (the Local Government (Interim Provisions) Bill in 1984).

The basis for this relative lack of conflict between the two Houses lies in the Salisbury conventions which are designed to take account of the wishes of the electorate by stipulating that there should not be outright opposition to a Bill which was part of the government's election manifesto. The Lords could, according to these guidelines amend or seek to delay such a Bill when it came before them for second reading. The War Crimes Act 1991 was regarded by some peers as being outside the conventions because it had not been in the manifesto and it had been passed under free votes in the Commons. Other peers took the view that their lordships' House did not have the legitimacy to resist the will of the elected House of Commons, rather their role was to allow time for reflection on the matter by the public and their representatives. A majority of their lordships felt that the Bill was so bad that they rejected it at second reading twice, even though they knew on the second occasion that the Parliament Acts would be invoked. Ganz (1992) notes that the issue was a non-party one and that the Lords, in insisting on voting according to their consciences, were claiming to be equal with the Commons. As she says, this is not the case because the Commons is a representative body and the Lords is not. This crucial difference explains why there was no constitutional crisis over the Houses' treatment of the War Crimes Act 1991, as the Lords is very much the junior partner in Parliament.

8.7 REFORM

There have been many proposals to reform various aspects of Parliament. In this section attention will be paid to those which deal with the issues of representation and improving Parliamentary procedures.

8.7.1 Representation

Parliament is supposed to be a representative institution, yet the House of Lords is an unelected body, and the elected representatives in the Commons are not representative of the nation(s). The imperfect representation affects both territories and peoples. Thus Scotland and Wales are overrepresented compared with England, and the revision of constituency boundaries lags behind the various population shifts. Women and the ethnic groups are underrepresented. The representation of parties is not proportional to the votes cast (see 7.6, especially table 7.1).

The most radical proposals are those proposed by the Liberal Democrats (1990) and the Institute for Public Policy Research (1991). Both of these groups have prepared draft constitutions which provide for three tiers of government, none of which would be elected by the first past the post method, and the House of Lords would be changed into an elected second chamber. The Liberal Democrats also propose that the boundaries of the English regions be drawn up by a boundary commission. The IPPR wishes to create an electoral commission which would take over the work of all of the boundary commissions, and also keep under review election campaigning, including finance, broadcasting and advertising.

Two academics have also produced reform proposals which are less ambitious (Brazier 1991; Oliver 1991b). Brazier's proposals are made on the premise that radical constitutional reform is unlikely and so he seeks reform which has a realistic chance of implementation.

The House of Lords is, perhaps, the greatest anomaly of the UK's constitutional arrangements due to its unelected composition. As Brazier (1991) points out, there is a paradox because the Lords' functions, at least adequately, as a reviser of Bills. The experience and expertise of the life peers are probably greater than would be the case if they were elected. Brazier wonders if the current part-time pool of talent would be matched by a second chamber of elected, and therefore full-time, politicians. With two elected chambers the relationship between them will be crucial. The second chamber will either have meaningful powers which will lead to greater conflict with the Commons, or it will have limited powers which may well reduce the attraction of the job and perhaps also a reduction in the calibre of people willing to stand for election to the second chamber.

Brazier's proposals for 'gradualist' reform of the Lords seek to retain the current expertise, and improve its representativeness. He suggests that the procedures for selecting life peers should be altered so as to increase the numbers of women and people from ethnic groups and religions other than the Church of England. It would still be the case that various occupations, including industry, commerce and education, would be represented in the House but the average age of the peers could also be reduced by including age amongst the criteria for selection.

Oliver (1991b) canvasses both radical and gradualist approaches to reform of the Lords. She offers a similar scheme to Brazier's in her more evolutionary proposals but she would end hereditary membership. There would be a transitional period in which existing hereditary peers would be entitled to attend and speak but not vote.

Having quickly considered the reform proposals of those not in government, we turn our attention to the significant constitutional reform programme of the Labour government elected in May 1997. Devolution was discussed at 2.4. It is proposed that if the Scottish Parliament and Welsh Assembly are approved, the voting system should consist of both first past the post and additional member. Proportional representation will also be introduced for the 1999 European Parliament elections and a commission will recommend a system of proportional representation for the House of Commons, which will then be put before the people in a referendum. Should proportional representation be accepted for the Commons it is likely that it would not produce a single party enjoying a majority of seats and so coalitions would have to be formed. This would be likely to have a substantial impact upon our system of government.

The Labour government's proposals for reform of the Lords have changed. The current position appears to be that it is committed to removing the hereditary peers. It is not clear what further change would follow. It might implement an earlier policy of creating an elected second chamber with limited powers or it might keep it as the largest quango in the country. It does seem odd to replace one body with dubious democratic credentials with another similarly flawed. The preamble to the Parliament Act 1911 referred to the creation of a second chamber on a popular basis. We are still waiting and while it is urged that we should not wait for much longer, the hereditary peers should not be expelled until we have a scheme for an elected second chamber. Expelling them first is not a halfway house to an elected second chamber, it would mean that we have lost our way towards a democratic destination.

8.7.2 Procedures

Reform of Parliamentary procedure seems much less radical than changing the voting system and the second chamber. It can, however, produce valuable improvements. Some of the present procedures do not realise their potential because of a lack of time, e.g., reports of select committees, prayers for annulment of statutory instruments. Other procedures are flawed, e.g., the consideration of public finances both in respect of the two aspects of taxation and spending, and the relationship between them despite the unified budget. Parliament does not make legislation, it tinkers with the government's Bills.

An extremely thorough critique of the legislative process was presented in the Hansard Society's report (1993). The recommended changes were premised upon the ideas that legislation affects the people, therefore they must have access to it, be able to understand it and play a part in its making if they are directly affected by it. Legislation would be improved if there were better and open consultation involving affected interests and Parliament. Thus, select committees could inquire into Green and White Papers. This could result in policy issues being better understood before a Bill was presented to Parliament and so the Bill's details and their implications could be picked up and resolved. Perhaps scrutiny might be enhanced if there were greater timetabling so as to ensure that more of a Bill was given fuller consideration. One example of a Bill which was poorly scrutinised was the Child Support Bill enacted in 1991, even though (or because?) there was general support for the basic principle behind the measure.

A theme which is common to Parliament's role as scrutiniser of Bills and administration, is that it would be improved if the culture of Whitehall was more open. This requires a Freedom of Information Act enforced in the courts rather than the code policed by the Parliamentary Commissioner for Administration (see 15.3.7) and it is unfortunate that the Labour government will not be enacting it in the first session of the new Parliament.

In previous editions of this work I have not been hopeful about the likelihood of procedural reform. However, the Parliament elected in 1997 contains so many new members who are not familiar with the current way of doing things, that I am now cautiously optimistic. The major reason for this is the Select Committee on the Modernisation of the House of Commons and its first report on the legislative process (HC 190 of 1997–8). The committee wishes to see improvements in pre-legislative scrutiny and consultation, programming of a Bill to ensure that all parts of it receive better scrutiny, changes in the legislative process, improved post-legislative scrutiny and amendments to the sessional cycle.

Given that the President of the Council and the Leader of the House chairs this committee, it is not surprising that there is some realism as well as openness in the report. In stating the criteria for reform the first is that the government of the day must be assured of getting its legislation through in reasonable time. This can conflict with the opposition's agenda. It must be right that a Bill is thoroughly considered and in an ideal world this could be achieved through an agreed timetable, rather than the government imposing a guillotine which can result in large parts of a Bill not being adequately scrutinised. The committee recommends as an experiment that there should be formal and open arrangements which will lead to a programme (timetable) for selected Bills. The programme should ensure that there is sufficient time for consideration of all parts of the Bill, that the rights of the opposition parties are taken into account, and that there should also be time for consultation with those outside Parliament.

The committee welcomes the intention of the Labour government to publish in draft seven Bills which can be subject to consultation and scrutiny before being brought before the House for enactment. Scrutiny could be by an ad hoc select committee, or an ad hoc joint select committee with the House of Lords, or by the relevant departmental select committee.

There could be greater recourse to existing variations to the usual practices in considering Bills. These include using a first reading select committee, which would be appropriate for a Bill not published in draft; greater use of special standing committees; and splitting consideration of part of a Bill between the floor of the House and a committee (this procedure is used in the consideration of Finance Bills). The standing committee which considered a Bill might have referred to back to it government amendments at report stage, or Lords amendments, thereby making use of its familiarity with the Bill and the relevant issues.

The committee proposes that departmental select committees could conduct post-legislative scrutiny by considering the operation of legislation which has recently come into force. If a measure crossed the remits of several committees then a special ad hoc select committee might be appointed to undertake such a monitoring role.

The committee would like to see an evening out of the legislative load and suggest that a Bill which was not passed by the end of a session could be carried over to the next one, as is the case with hybrid Bills.

Future topics for the committee's consideration include voting procedures, the parliamentary calendar, scrutiny of European legislation and the conduct of debate. Whether it is because of the influx of new MPs, or the change of government, or the approaching millennium, the prospects for more sensible procedures look bright. They are welcome because they should have a beneficial effect upon government.

CHAPTER NINE

The European Union

9.1 ORIGINS AND PURPOSES

The task of reconstructing Europe after the Second World War was a crucial factor in the development of the European Communities. For some, the first objective was to revive the economies of the countries, to rebuild housing and factories and the necessary infrastructure. Others had a more visionary outlook which focused upon ways in which the European continent might be prevented from embarking upon another destructive conflict in the second half of the 20th century. International cooperation was recognised as an important process by which these objectives could be furthered and, for some, such cooperation in the economic sphere could lead to increased political cooperation which could lessen the possibility of another devastating war.

The first project of significant international economic cooperation was the Benelux Union. This came into effect from the beginning of 1948 when Belgium, the Netherlands and Luxembourg established a customs union which entailed the removal of customs barriers amongst themselves and the creation of a common customs tariff for goods entering into the territory of these States from other countries. Gradually cooperation was extended to other parts of their economies. They agreed to adopt common policies on most customs and excise duties and, by permitting the free movement of both capital and people within the boundaries of the participating States, they created a common market.

9.1.1 The Treaty of Paris

The first European Community to be established was the European Coal and Steel Community (ECSC). This Community was created by the Treaty of Paris signed on 15 April 1951 by Belgium, France, Germany, Italy, Luxembourg and the Netherlands. The immediate objective of the ECSC was to create a common market in coal and steel. This was seen as a stage in a process which would lead to much greater political cooperation. The ECSC arrangements included common taxes on the production of coal and steel, and measures which would regulate competition, unemployment and investment in these industries. The ECSC went further than a simple customs union in coal and steel because the member States agreed to the creation of institutions — a High Authority, a Council of Ministers, an Assembly, a Court of Justice, and a Consultative Committee to the High Authority, which were given significant powers — and this took the character of the international cooperation to a supranational level.

9.1.2 . The Treaties of Rome

The member States of the ECSC decided that they should expand their cooperation beyond coal and steel into a kind of economic union. This idea was explored at first by other bodies and countries, including the UK. As this process developed, it was the six members of the ECSC who pursued it seriously, and they agreed to create two new Communities. The European Economic Community (EEC) and the European Atomic Energy Community (Euratom) were established by two separate Treaties of Rome signed on 25 March 1957. These two Communities came into effect on 1 January 1958 after the treaties had been ratified by the member States.

Euratom, like the ECSC, makes common arrangements for a particular economic sector, in this case atomic energy. As the research costs are so high, it was sensible to share them. This Community provides a framework within which atomic energy research and development are conducted, and controls distribution of such energy within the member States.

The EEC is more than a customs union, more than a common market. It is also a process leading to economic integration and political union. The preamble to the EEC Treaty envisages political cooperation when it refers to an ever closer union among the peoples of Europe.

9.1.3 The Development of the Communities

As the EEC and Euratom were modelled upon the ECSC, it was agreed that there should be a merger of the institutions rather than have three Communities, each with its own separate institutions. This was done in two stages. At first only the Assembly and Court served all three Communities. Eventually a Merger Treaty was signed in May 1965 which created a single executive body, the Commission, and a merged Council of Ministers.

9.1.4 The UK and the Communities

The fact that the UK was not a member of the Communities was due to a number of reasons, and not because exclusion was desired by the founding six countries. The UK had not suffered from the war to the same extent as the original six members had. The history of the UK had led to the forging of special political and trading relations with the countries of the Commonwealth and the USA. The establishment of the EEC prompted the founding of the European Free Trade Area (EFTA), which was a very much looser framework for international economic cooperation. The UK had played a prominent role in creating EFTA but by the early 1960s the Macmillan government decided to apply to join the EEC, ECSC and Euratom. Mr Edward Heath led the UK's negotiating team. The application failed because of a veto by France. Similarly a bid for membership by the Wilson government was thwarted by the French President, General De Gaulle in 1967. Finally, the Heath government successfully applied for membership and, along with Denmark and Ireland, the UK joined the Communities with effect from 1 January 1973.

9.1.5 Widening and Deepening of the Communities

Since the original six member States increased to nine, there has been not only a further expansion of membership, but also a move towards greater integration within the Communities. Greece became a member State from January 1981, Spain and Portugal joined in 1986, and Austria, Finland and Sweden in 1995.

Progress towards a closer integration has been halting. The Assembly was renamed the European Parliament, and enhanced in 1979 when its members were elected to it rather than appointed from the legislatures of the member States.

9.1.5.1 The Single European Act Although there had been various reports, e.g., those chaired by Dooge and Werner, which had, in varying degrees, proposed closer integration of the member States within the Communities, nothing much was done. The major economic change was the establishment of the European Monetary System which included a system to regulate exchange rates. The UK did not enter into this fully. In 1986 a treaty, the Single European Act (SEA), was signed which did advance the integration of the member States. The SEA's provisions included a timetable for the completion of the single, or internal, market, an increase in the powers of the Assembly, which was renamed the European Parliament, and the creation of European political cooperation, which sought to achieve a common position in the foreign policies of the member States.

9.1.5.2 The Treaty on European Union In December 1991 there were two intergovernmental conferences dealing with economic and monetary union (EMU) and political union. These conferences led to the signing of the Treaty on European Union (TEU) on 7 February 1993. The TEU seeks to further European integration. It creates a new entity, the European Union which has a three-pillar structure. The first pillar comprises the three Communities, in which the EEC is renamed the European Community (EC). Cooperation here is on the basis of the new legal order created by the earlier treaties. A timetable is stipulated for the single currency, although the treaty provides that the UK can decide if it wishes to join this venture. Cooperation in two other areas is provided for in two further pillars: a common foreign and security policy, and in the field of justice and home affairs. In these two pillars the governments of the member States agree to cooperate with each other outside the framework of the three Communities.

Ratification of the TEU took much longer than was expected. In Denmark a referendum was held which rejected ratification. This led to clarifications being made about the treaty enabling the Danish government to resubmit a ratification proposal in a second referendum, which was approved. In the UK the passage of the European Communities (Amendment) Act 1993 was complicated by the government's narrow majority, the fact that a significant number of its own backbenchers were opposed to the treaty, and the preference of the two major opposition parties to have the Agreement on Social Policy applied to the UK. In the TEU the Protocol on Social Policy provides that all of the member States apart from the UK can use the institutions, procedures and mechanisms of the treaty for giving effect to the Agreement on Social Policy. This is popularly known as the UK's 'opt-out' on social policy. The tactics of the opposition and the government party's dissidents had led to the inclusion in the statute of a requirement that it would come into effect when each House of Parliament had 'come to a resolution on motion tabled by a Minister of the Crown considering the adoption of the Protocol on Social Policy' (s. 7). In the Commons the resolution tabled by the government was defeated and a subsequent motion was approved only when it was indicated by the government that the issue was one of confidence. Faced with the prospect of a general election, the government's rebels came into line (see Rawlings 1994). Before the UK government formally ratified the TEU it had to wait for the outcome of a judicial review sought by a peer of the realm. This was unsuccessful at first instance (*R v Secretary of State for Foreign and Commonwealth Affairs, ex parte Rees-Mogg* [1994] QB 552) and when the applicant decided not to appeal, the instruments of ratification of the TEU were deposited in Rome.

A legal challenge also delayed the ratification of the TEU in Germany. The Bundesverfassungsgericht (Federal Constitutional Court) upheld the TEU as being compatible with the Grundgesetz (Basic Law) but indicated that there could be constitutional limitations to Germany's participation in certain aspects of European integration (*Brunner v Treaty on European Union* [1994] 1 CMLR 57).

9.1.5.3 The European Economic Area Agreement

Before Austria, Finland and Sweden joined the EU in January 1995, they had an association with the EU member States with the coming into effect of the European Economic Area Agreement in January 1994. This agreement created a free trade area between the EC States and the EFTA States. In this area some of the EC policies were to apply, such as with regard to competition.

The agreement has had a troubled life. It has been before the ECJ twice. The ECJ initially found that its judicial provisions were incompatible with the EC treaties (*Opinion 1/91* [1991] ECR I-6079) but after renegotiation it was approved (*Opinion 1/92* [1994] ECR I-2821). Switzerland withdrew from it after ratification was rejected in a referendum, and now the only participating EFTA States are Iceland, Liechtenstein and Norway. Norway would have become a member State of the EU if the people had approved the proposal in 1994. This was the second time that the Norwegian people had voted in a referendum to reject membership. The previous occasion was in 1972.

9.1.5.4 The Treaty of Amsterdam The TEU was to be reviewed and agreement on this was reached at the Intergovernmental Conference at Amsterdam in June 1997. It is envisaged that after technical work the text of a new treaty will be ready for signing in October 1997. The Amsterdam treaty did not meet the hopes of those who wished for greater integration, reform of institutions and procedures, and preparations for enlargement. The price for agreement was that of agreeing to differ and the continued use, rather than the rolling back, of 'opt-outs'.

The Union is committed to fighting discrimination and in particular gender and disability discrimination. Concern for employment and competitiveness has led to the proposal of new provisions to be added to the TEU and the EC Treaty. The common foreign and security policy is in its separate pillar although improved cooperation is sought. More agreement was reached on the third Maastricht pillar so that a new title is proposed in the EC Treaty on free movement of persons, asylum and immigration. This would lead to common arrangements on these matters, but in a protocol the UK and Ireland have opted out so that they can maintain their border controls. There is also a protocol on the special position of Denmark. There is to be greater judicial cooperation in cross-border civil and commercial matters.

On the issue of making institutional reform in preparation for enlargement, agreement was reached in principle on a reduction in the number of Commissioners to one for each member State and on changing the weighting of votes in the Council of Ministers so as to permit a move away from unanimity, which will be even more difficult to achieve in an enlarged Union. It is proposed to extend the number of measures to which the co-decision legislative procedure (EC Treaty, art. 189b) applies and also to streamline it. This procedure adjusts the balance of power between the Council and the Parliament by giving more to the Parliament (see figure 9.2 for the existing art. 189b procedure).

As it is proving difficult to achieve unanimity, the idea of flexibility is to be included so that those countries which wish to pursue closer cooperation may do so, provided that such cooperation does not relate to matters which are within the exclusive competence of the EU and would adversely affect EU policies.

9.1.5.5 Agenda 2000 After Amsterdam the Commission put forward its plans to the Parliament, entitled *Agenda 2000: For a Stronger and Wider Union*. It proposed that, of the states seeking membership, negotiations should be opened with Hungary, Poland, Estonia, the Czech Republic and Slovenia, as well as Cyprus. It was adjudged that the criteria for membership were not yet met by Bulgaria, Romania, Latvia, Lithuania and Slovakia, but entering into partnerships with them would assist them in their preparations for membership.

The Commission states that agreement is required on the institutional reforms not concluded at Amsterdam, i.e., reduction of the number of Commissioners, the weighting of votes in the Council of Ministers and agreement on greater use of qualified majority voting. The Commission notes that there will be costs in enlargement but that these may be met on certain assumptions which do not raise the expenditure ceiling. There are to be further reforms of the common agriculture policy and the continuance of economic and social cohesion through more effective use of the structural funds.

9.1.6 The Work of the Communities

As this is not a book on Community law, the purposes and work of the Communities will not be detailed at length. However, an understanding of the UK's constitutional arrangements will be aided by knowing something about the range of the EC's activities.

9.1.6.1 Treaty policies Article 2 of the EC Treaty sets the tasks of the creation of a common market, the progressive approximation of the member States' economic policies and the promotion of harmonious development of economic activities. Some of the methods by which those objectives may be pursued include the elimination of customs duties amongst the member States, the creation of a common customs tariff, the abolition of obstacles to the freedom of movement for persons, services and capital within the territory of the Community, the adoption of common policies for agriculture and transport, and the institution of a framework to ensure that competition in the common market is not distorted (EC Treaty, art. 3).

9.1.6.2 Freedom of movement of goods In a common market it is clear that producers should be able to sell their goods in any member State. Not only are customs duties eliminated (EC Treaty, arts 9–17), but measures having an equivalent effect to quantitative restrictions upon trade are also prohibited (EC Treaty, arts 30–5). Examples of equivalent measures are some health inspection charges (*Marimex SpA* v *Ministero delle Finanze (No. 2)* (case 29/72) [1972] ECR 1309) and storage charges prior to completion of customs formalities (*Commission* v *Belgium* (case 132/82) [1983] ECR 1649).

There are permitted exceptions to the freedom which are based on grounds of morality, public policy and national security (EC Treaty, art. 36). Public morality was considered by the ECJ in two cases from the UK. In *R* v *Henn* (case 34/79) [1981] AC 850, a prohibition on importing pornographic material was justified as there was no lawful trade in such products in the UK so that the prohibition was not discriminatory. Contrast the decision in *Conegate Ltd* v *Customs and Excise Commissioners* (case 121/85) [1987] QB 254, where a ban on the import of life-size rubber 'love dolls' from Germany was held to be discriminatory because the sale of these products was restricted but not prohibited in the UK.

9.1.6.3 Freedom of movement of persons Just as goods should not be restricted in a common market neither should workers. There are two aspects to this particular freedom of movement. The first is the more obvious one relating to immigration control. The second concerns provision of social security. Member States should not operate immigration controls upon citizens of other member States which impose discrimination on nationality grounds in respect of employment, conditions of work or pay (EC Treaty, art. 48). Again there is the possibility of derogating from this freedom on grounds of public policy, public security and public health. In *R* v *Secretary of State for the Home Department, ex parte Santillo* [1981] QB 778, it was held that the simple fact of a criminal conviction was insufficient to invoke the derogation. Regard must be had to the type and seriousness of the offence.

Workers will not enjoy real freedom of movement if they cannot qualify for their home country's social security benefits because they have been working in another member State. Regulation 1408/71 deals with aggregate apportionment and overlapping of social security benefits so that workers are not disadvantaged by living and working in a member State of which they are not nationals.

9.1.6.4 *Freedom of establishment* People may move amongst the member States not only as workers or employees, but as self-employed persons or professionals (EC Treaty, arts. 52–8), and as the providers of services (EC Treaty, arts 59–66). Differing national systems of qualifications would be a barrier to the free movement of such workers. This has been dealt with by seeking the harmonisation of such qualifications. This means that when a Dutch national living in Belgium qualifies as a lawyer under Belgian arrangements, the fact of that nationality should not prevent the practice of that profession in Belgium (*Reyners* v *Belgium* (case 2/74) [1974] ECR 631).

9.1.6.5 *Freedom of movement of capital* It is clear that a common market must permit the free transfer of money and the EC Treaty provides for this in relation to capital and connected current payments (EC Treaty, arts 67–73). The treaty deals with exchange controls amongst the member States and between them and other countries. The types of transactions which nationals should be able to carry out in all member States are transfers of funds relating to investments in real estate and capital markets.

9.1.6.6 *Agriculture* A common policy for agriculture (CAP) was stipulated as part of the common market (EC Treaty, art. 3(d)) and is dealt with in more detail in arts 38–47. The objectives of the CAP include improving productivity of, techniques for, and labour in agriculture, and the standard of living for agricultural workers; stability is to be brought to the agricultural markets; and the supply of agricultural products to the consumer at reasonable prices is to be ensured (EC Treaty, art. 39). Part of the way in which this is done is to guarantee prices to producers so as to keep up production and ensure that they receive a fair return. The member States' producers are also to be protected from their competitors outside the Community.

9.1.6.7 *Competition* The EC Treaty identifies specific practices which are regarded as distorting competition (EC Treaty, arts 85–90). Where undertakings, whether private or public, agree to practices which may affect trade between member States and which have the object of preventing, or restricting or distorting competition, then this is incompatible with the common market (EC Treaty, art. 85). An abuse of an undertaking's dominant position in the market is also prohibited (art. 86). This provision does not prohibit monopolies as such, simply an abuse of that market position. The treaty goes on to provide the authority for the making of legislation which will give effect to these prohibitions, including powers to impose fines (EC Treaty, art. 87). Regulation 4064/89 provides for the control of mergers, or 'concentrations' in the terminology of the measure. As the merger of undertakings could have significant effects upon competititon both where the undertakings are in the same member State, or where they are in different member States, the regulation provides criteria for demarcating control by the EC authorities and the national authorities.

The EC Treaty also deals with actual or threatened distortion to competition which may be caused by a member State government giving aid to industry (EC Treaty, arts 92–4). When the UK government sold the car company, Rover, to British Aerospace, the Commission decided that some aspects of the deal, the so-called 'sweeteners', tax concessions and delayed payment, constituted an unlawful State aid. The Commission's action was successfully challenged on grounds of procedural irregularity (*British Aerospace plc* v *Commission* (case C-294/90) [1992] ECR I-493) but the Commission has reinstituted proceedings against the undertakings.

9.1.6.8 Environment It was not until the SEA amended the EC Treaty that there was an explicit basis for environmental action by the Communities. Under the amended EC Treaty, action relating to the environment may be taken to preserve, protect and improve the quality of the environment, to protect human health and to ensure a prudent and rational utilisation of natural resources (EC Treaty, art. 130R). The treaty also distinguishes between action which may be taken at the Community level and by the member States. Where action would be better taken at the Community level to attain these objectives then the Community is empowered to take it. Community action has included, for example, setting levels for water quality and requiring that environmental impact assessments be made in respect of major development proposals (Directive 85/337/EEC, implemented originally by the Town and Country Planning (Assessment of Environmental Effects) Regulations 1988 (SI 1988/1199), as amended by the Town and Country Planning (Assessment of Environmental Effects) (Amendment) Regulations 1990 (SI 1990/367)).

9.2 SOURCES OF COMMUNITY LAW

The following discussion of the sources of Community law will focus on the EC.

9.2.1 Treaties
Treaties comprise the major primary source of Community law. The treaties which founded the three Communities are the original primary sources of

Community law. These treaties have been amended by various other treaties. The amending treaties include the three treaties of accession by which the membership of the Communities was increased. There are treaties which have dealt with specific matters such as the merger of institutions and budgetary matters. The SEA significantly amended the founding treaties by, for example, adding to the Communities' areas of competence, and changing the Assembly's title to Parliament, as well as increasing its powers. The TEU created the European Union, added the two new pillars and set a timetable for a single currency (see 9.1.5.2).

9.2.2 Legislation

The treaties provide that the Council and Commission may make three types of binding secondary legislation: Regulations, Directives and Decisions (EC Treaty, art. 189). All of these measures must state the reasons on which they are based, and refer to any procedural requirements in the treaty (EC Treaty, art. 190).

While the decisions of the court may be regarded as a source of Community law, it is unlikely that this status may be given to recommendations and opinions made by the Commission and Council which are non-binding · measures (EC Treaty, art. 189). The ECJ, however, said in *Grimaldi* v *Fonds des Maladies Professionnelles* (case 322/88) [1989] ECR 4407 that national courts should take recommendations into account.

9.2.2.1 Regulations These measures are defined as being 'binding in their entirety and directly applicable in all member States'. They must be published in the *Official Journal* and specify the date on which they come into effect or, if no date is specified, they come into effect on the 20th day after publication (EC Treaty, art. 191).

The member States do not need to take any action for a Regulation to become part of their national law. This is what is meant by 'directly applicable'.

9.2.2.2 Directives A Directive, in contrast to a Regulation, becomes part of the law of a member State because of action taken by the member State. It is binding on the member States to which it is addressed, and they may choose the form and method of implementation (EC Treaty, art. 189). Directives are often used to bring about harmonisation of law in the member States under arts 100 and 100A of the EC Treaty. A Directive, therefore, stipulates the objective to be achieved and the member State must achieve it. If a member State does not implement the Directive, the Commission can enforce this treaty obligation under art. 169 of the EC Treaty.

A Directive is not required to be published in the *Official Journal* but this is always done.

9.2.2.3 Decisions These measures are binding in their entirety on those to whom they are addressed. Decisions may be addressed to a member State, or an individual or a company. They must be notified to the addressee and they become effective upon notification (EC Treaty, art. 191).

The character of Decisions can vary, encompassing those which simply execute a Community policy and also those which are quasi-judicial. Examples of the latter type include the imposition of a penalty for an infringement of competition policy, and a determination by the Commission that a member State has failed to fulfil a treaty obligation under art. 169 of the EC Treaty.

9.2.3 International Agreements
The treaties provide the Communities with the power to enter into treaties with non-member States (EC Treaty, art. 228). There are other articles which confer treaty-making powers (e.g. EC Treaty, arts 111, 113, 114). If such agreements are within the scope of the authorisation of the founding treaties, then they are part of Community law.

9.2.4 Judicial Decisions
The law of the Communities is based on civil law. In this legal system the interpretations of the codes given by the courts do not have the importance of judicial decision in the common law system. This does not mean that the decisions of the ECJ are unimportant. Indeed the ECJ has developed general principles, such as proportionality and fundamental rights, and significant doctrines, such as supremacy and direct effect, and has also fashioned Community law into a distinctive legal order (see further 9.4).

The familiar common law doctrine of *stare decisis* may develop now that the ECJ hears appeals on certain matters from the Court of First Instance (see 9.3.5.1).

9.3 INSTITUTIONS

The major institutions of the EC are created in art. 4 of the EC Treaty. More detail is put on this framework in part 5 of the treaty.

9.3.1 The Commission
The traditional classification of the organs of government – executive, legislature and judiciary – cannot easily be applied to the Communities' institutions. The Commission is, to a certain extent, an executive body, but it does have some lawmaking powers and it has some quasi-judicial powers too. The Commission's range of activities includes coordination, implementation, making proposals and enforcement.

The Commission is made up of 20 members. Each member State supplies at least one commissioner and a maximum of two (EC Treaty, art. 157). The five largest member States, France, Germany, Italy, Spain and the UK, all provide two commissioners. Once appointed the commissioners must act in the interests of the Communities, they are not to be regarded as the representatives of their countries. A commissioner's term of office is five years and the appointment is renewable (EC Treaty, art. 158). The President of the Commission is nominated by common accord of the member States after consulting the European Parliament. The other commissioners are nominated by the member States in consultation with the nominee for President. All of these nominees are subject, as a body, to approval by the European Parliament. After such approval they are formally appointed by common accord of the member States (EC Treaty, art. 158(2)). The Commission may appoint one or two Vice-Presidents (EC Treaty, art. 161).

The Commission is also a civil service. Its officials are organised into directorates-general (DG), headed by a director general (e.g., competition), and other services (e.g., legal). A DG is roughly equivalent to a UK government department. It is misleading to compare a commissioner to a UK minister. While a commissioner has a portfolio of work, this does not entail personal responsibility for the actions of any DG(s) included in that portfolio. The commissioners and directors general, who work closely with each other, are never of the same nationality, though commissioners will usually appoint fellow nationals to their *cabinets*, their support teams of officials and advisers.

The Commission takes the lead in shaping the development of the Communities. While major decisions must be taken by the Council, it will be the Commission which will have submitted proposals and thereby set the agenda. The TEU was an amended version of a plan originally proposed by Jacques Delors, the President of the Commission. The power of initiative comes out of the responsibility to coordinate the work of the Communities and the implementation of rules agreed by the Council. The work of implementation also includes enforcement. If member States are not meeting their treaty obligations then the Commission may act to secure compliance, a process which may lead to an action in the ECJ (EC Treaty, art. 169).

9.3.2 The Council

The Council consists of representatives of the member States (EC Treaty, art. 147). The particular representatives will depend upon the work before the Council. The Foreign Ministers of the member States comprise the General Council. When the business relates to, e.g, finance, agriculture, transport, employment, then the relevant ministers will form a Specialised Council. If the representatives are heads of government or State, then the body is called the European Council (see 9.3.3).

Every six months the presidency of the Council moves from member State to member State according to a rota, under which the UK held the presidency from July to December 1992, and will hold it again in January to June 1998 (Merger Treaty, art. 2, as amended).

The work of the Council involves coordinating member States' general economic policies. It has the power to take decisions, which includes assenting to Regulations, Directives and Decisions (see 9.2.2), and can confer upon the Commission the power to implement rules which it has laid down (EC Treaty, art. 145).

In its work as a legislative body, measures may be approved by unanimity, simple majority or qualified majority. It was originally envisaged that qualified majority voting would become the predominant method. Following particular difficulties with France, the original six agreed the Luxembourg Accords (1966) which stated that unanimity would be required if a member State's vital national interests were at stake. This compromise was not law but a practice and was followed even where the treaties provided for a qualified majority. The SEA has increased the number of areas in which voting is by a qualified majority so that most decisions relating to the completion of the single market may be voted under that method. Unanimity is still required for some matters, e.g., fiscal provisions, measures relating to freedom of movement of persons and the rights and interests of employed persons (EC Treaty, art. 100A(2)).

The qualified majority procedure requires that 62 out of 87 votes are cast in favour of a measure (EC Treaty, art. 148). The votes are distributed amongst the member States so that France, Germany, Italy and the UK have 10 votes, Spain 8, Belgium, Greece, the Netherlands and Portugal 5, Austria and Sweden 4, Denmark, Finland and Ireland 3, and Luxembourg 2. The UK and Spain were opposed to a simple arithmetical change to the number of votes needed to block measures under the qualified majority in the enlarged EU. Previously it had been 23 and now it would be 27. A compromise was agreed at Ioannina in March 1994. This provides that where three member States with a total of 23 to 25 votes oppose the adoption of a proposal, then the Council would do all that it could within a reasonable time, which respects treaty deadlines, to reach a satisfactory solution which would be supported by at least 65 votes.

9.3.2.1 COREPER This body, which is known by its French acronym, is the Committee of Permanent Representatives. It is composed of the member States' ambassadors to the communities and its function is to prepare the work of the Council and to carry out any tasks assigned to it (EC Treaty, art. 151). The need for this body is explained by the fact that the Council is made up of national ministers and accordingly only meets when there is business to transact.

9.3.3 The European Council
The practice of the heads of State or government meeting to discuss Community matters became part of the Communities' institutions by the SEA. The European Council, which consists of member States' heads of State or government and the President of the Commission, and who may be assisted by the foreign ministers of the member States and a member of the Commission, is to meet at least twice a year (TEU, art. D). The aim of this body is that it shall provide the Union with the necessary impetus for its development and shall define the general political guidelines thereof.

9.3.4 The European Parliament
Originally the Parliament was termed an Assembly. The re-naming was effected by the SEA. The Parliament consists of representatives from the member States and their function is to exercise the advisory and supervisory powers conferred by the treaties (EC Treaty, art. 137). Some of the advisory functions relate to the removal of restrictions upon the provision of services (EC Treaty, art. 63), and the competition policy (EC Treaty, art. 87).

The Parliament's major supervisory role refers to the Commission. A motion of censure may be passed against the whole of the Commission which, if passed by a two-thirds majority, would lead to the Commission's resignation (EC Treaty, art. 144). While such motions have been tabled, none have been passed. This control is too much of a blunderbuss to be of any real use though the Parliament does have the power to go to court. The commissioners are subject to questions, both oral and written by MEPs (EC Treaty, art. 140). The President of the Commission and the President of the Council make reports to the Parliament.

Under the TEU the Parliament is consulted over the nomination of the President of the Commission and approves the Commission as a body. When this procedure was first used in January 1995 it was agreed that the nominated Commission members would submit themselves to questioning by the Parliament. Whilst the Parliament did approve the Commission, criticism was expressed of some members and in response the Presidential nominee made various adjustments to the allocation of responsibilities within portfolios.

It was not until 1979 that direct elections to the Parliament were held. The implementing legislation in the UK was the European Assembly Elections Act 1978, now the European Parliament Elections Act 1978, following the SEA (art. 3(1)), incorporated by the European Communities (Amendment) Act 1986, s. 3(2). Prior to this the member States' legislatures appointed their representatives to the Parliament. The term of office is five years. The distribution of the 626 seats amongst the member States is as follows: Germany has 99, France, Italy and the UK have 81; Spain has 60; the Netherlands has 25; Belgium, Greece and Portugal have 24; Sweden has 22; Austria has 21; Denmark and Finland have 16; Ireland has 15; and Luxembourg has 6. At the Edinburgh Summit in December 1992 it was agreed that the number of German representatives in the Parliament would be increased, in order to reflect the greater population in Germany following unification.

Although it is envisaged that elections would be held by a uniform procedure (EC Treaty, art. 138(3)), the elections in 1979, 1984, 1989 and 1994 were conducted according to member States' own arrangements. Varieties of roportional representation were used in 11 of the 12 member States and in Northern Ireland. England, Scotland and Wales retained the first-past-the-post method (see 7.6). Initially the MEPs from Austria, Finland and Sweden will be appointed by their national parliaments. It is expected that by the end of 1995 they will be elected.

The MEPs organise themselves into political groups based on ideology rather than nationality. Much of the work of the Parliament is done by committees which focus on a particular topic. The reports of these committees are the basis for debate. The committees operate even when the Parliament is not in session. The Parliament is only required to meet for one annual session, in March (EC Treaty, art. 139). It does meet on other occasions.

The Parliament has been gaining in power and influence. Despite its name the Parliament is not the major partner in the EU's legislative procedures.

Under art. 189a the Parliament may be consulted about a measure proposed by the Commission, but it is the Council which takes the decision to approve the measure. The essence of the cooperation procedure in art. 189c is that if the Parliament rejects the view of the Council on a measure — the common position — then the measure can only be approved by the Council acting unanimously (for details see figure 9.1).

Some of the topics which may use the art. 189c procedure are implementing the common transport policy (art. 75(1)), Community action on environmental policy (art. 130s(1)), measures assisting developing countries (art. 130w).

The TEU added a new procedure in art. 189b, which is variously known as the joint legislative procedure, the conciliation and veto procedure, or the co-decision procedure. Under this procedure the Parliament has more power, in that it has a veto if it rejects a measure by a majority of its members. Where there is a difference of view between the Parliament and the Council, a Conciliation Committee can be convened which seeks to reach agreement on a joint text. The Council and the Parliament are equally represented on this body. Agreement is reached by both sides, voting separately, on the basis of a qualified majority for the Council's representatives, and a majority of the Parliament's representatives.

Where the Parliament agrees with the Council's common position, or with the joint text produced by the Conciliation Committee, this may be done by a majority of votes cast (see figure 9.2).

Some of the areas which are subject to the art. 189b procedure include single market measures (art. 100a), freedom of movement for workers (art. 49) and incentive measures for public health (art. 129(4)).

Another area in which the Parliament does have real power is that of adoption of the budget for the Communities. The Parliament may refuse to agree the budget, and has refused to do so. These refusals were part of the Parliament's tactics in disputes with other institutions and eventually compromises were agreed and the budgets adopted. The Parliament does have the final say on the non-compulsory section of the budget, which accounted for between 40 and 50 per cent of the total in 1994.

9.3.4.1 The Ombudsman The TEU amended the EC Treaty (art. 138e) to provide for the establishment of an ombudsman, who would be empowered to receive complaints about maladministration from citizens of the EU, or from natural or legal persons residing or having a registered office in a member State. The complaint of maladministration could relate to the activities of any of the Community institutions or bodies apart from the ECJ and CFI acting in their judicial roles.

The ombudsman may also conduct investigations without receiving a complaint which is unlike the jurisdiction of the equivalent officers in the UK (see 15.3). The ombudsman is to be appointed for the life of the Parliament and the appointee is eligible for reappointment. If maladministration is established by the ombudsman then the matter is referred to the institution concerned which has three months to give its views. The ombudsman then

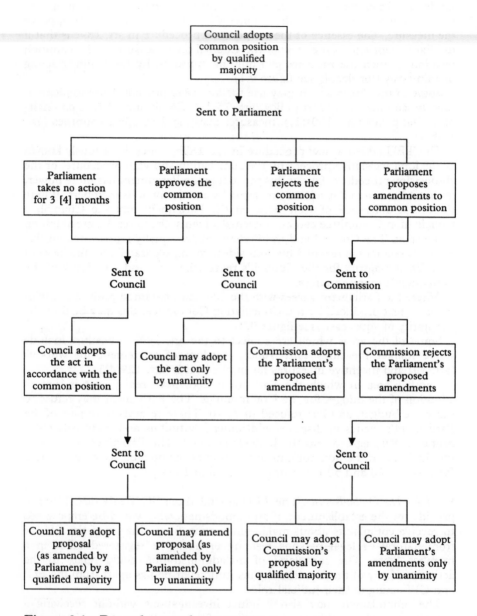

Figure 9.1   Procedure under art. 189c

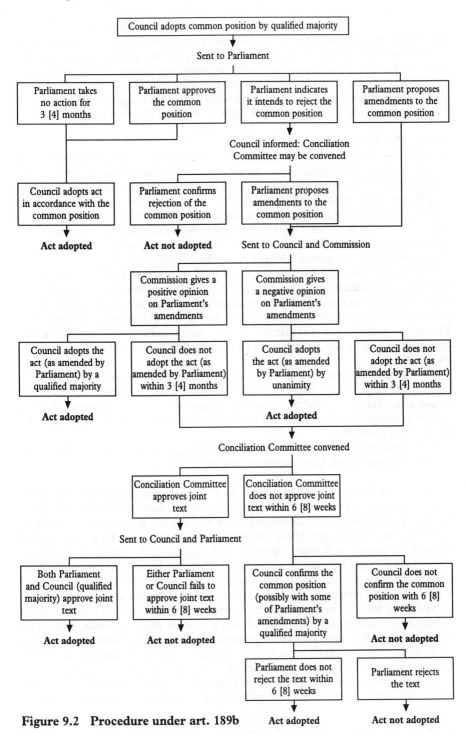

Figure 9.2   Procedure under art. 189b

makes a report to the Parliament and the institution concerned. The person who lodges the complaint must be informed of the outcome of the complaint.

The ombudsman has an independent status, like members of the Commission, so that the ombudsman is neither to seek nor to take instructions from any body. The Parliament may request the ECJ to dismiss the ombudsman if the conditions for performance of the duties are no longer fulfilled or there has been serious misconduct (see Tierney 1996, on the first report).

9.3.5   The Court of Justice

The ECJ is composed of 15 judges (EC Treaty, art. 165), one from each member State. The judges are appointed by the common accord of the governments of the member States for a six-year renewable term of office (EC Treaty, art. 167). Every three years there is a partial replacement of the judges with eight and seven being replaced alternately (EC Treaty, art. 167). Those appointed as judges are to be persons of independence, who possess the qualifications to hold the highest judicial office in their own countries, or are 'jurisconsults of recognised competence' (EC Treaty, art. 167).

The judges elect the President of the ECJ in a secret ballot. This post is held for a renewable three-year term. A judge may resign or be removed from office. Removal can occur if the other judges are unanimously agreed that a colleague no longer meets the conditions for, or the obligations of, office. The President notifies the Presidents of the other institutions and it is the communication to the President of the Council which creates the vacancy in the ECJ.

The judges are assisted in their determination of cases by hearing the opinion of an advocate general. There are nine advocates general who must possess the same qualifications as the judges and are also appointed for a six-year renewable term. They are replaced every three years on an alternating basis of four and five.

The jurisdiction of the ECJ includes actions against the member States and the institutions of the Communities (see further 9.5).

9.3.5.1   *The Court of First Instance*   As the workload of the ECJ increased

something had to be done. The SEA provided for the creation of a new court to determine at first instance certain classes of action, with an appeal lying to the ECJ (EC Treaty, art. 168A inserted by SEA, art. 11). This court would come into existence if the Council acted unanimously following a request from the ECJ and consultations with the Commission and Parliament. This procedure led to a Council Decision (88/591) in November 1988 to create the Court of First Instance (CFI). On 1 November 1989 the CFI began work.

The CFI has 15 judges, one from each member State. They are to be independent and eligible for judicial office in their own countries. Like their more senior colleagues, they are appointed for six-year renewable terms. They elect their own President for a three-year term. The CFI does not have any advocates general but the judges may themselves act in that capacity.

The jurisdiction of the CFI includes disputes between the institutions and their staff, and actions by private individuals or companies for judicial review

(EC Treaty, arts 173, 175), non-contractual liability (EC Treaty, art. 178), and contract (EC Treaty, art. 181). The CFI does not deal with actions brought by the member States or the institutions, or requests for preliminary rulings (EC Treaty, art. 177, see 9.5.6).

9.3.6 The Economic and Social Committee
This committee serves the EC and Euratom (EC Treaty, art. 193). The ECSC has a Consultative Committee. These committees are consulted by the Council and Commission either because the treaties require it, or because it is felt appropriate (EC Treaty, art. 198).

The Council appoints the 222 members of the committee with the following national distribution: France, Germany, Italy and the UK 24; Spain 21; Austria, Belgium, Greece, the Netherlands, Portugal and Sweden 12; Denmark, Finland and Ireland 9; and Luxembourg 6 (EC Treaty, art. 194). Appointments are made from lists submitted by the member States which contain twice as many nominations as their allocations (EC Treaty, art. 195). The members are appointed in their personal capacity but they are representative of various categories of economic and social activity with the treaty specifying producers, farmers, carriers, workers, dealers, craftsmen, professional occupations, and the general public (EC Treaty, art. 193).

The committee is organised into three sections representing employers, workers and various interests which includes, for example, professions and the environmentalist and consumer lobbies.

9.3.7 The Court of Auditors
This body was originally established by the Financial Provisions Treaty of 1975 but was made a formal institution by the TEU (EC Treaty, arts. 4(1) and 188a to 188c). There are 15 members who must have relevant auditing experience. Their terms and conditions of appointment are similar to those of the judges of the ECJ.

They carry out audits of the income and expenditure of the Communities, which are concerned with legality, regularity and sound financial management (EC Treaty, art. 188c) and present an annual report. They may be asked for their opinion on specific questions by other institutions and may assist the Parliament and Council in exercising their power of control over the implementation of the budget (EC Treaty, art. 206A).

9.3.8 The Committee of the Regions
The TEU created another advisory comittee composed of 222 representatives of regional and local bodies (EC Treaty, art. 198a). It advises on education, culture and regional development.

9.4 NATURE AND PRINCIPLES OF COMMUNITY LAW

The Communities are not simply international organisations which have legal personality and powers, they are products of treaties which also created a body of law and a legal order which extends throughout the member States.

This legal order encompasses the legal systems of the member States but is also superior to them. The development of the legal order and its legal principles has come about because of the founding treaties and the interpretation given to them by the ECJ. It has been argued that the ECJ has been very adventurous in its teleological, or purposive, approach to the construction of the treaties. This may well be true but it should not obscure the fact that the treaties do pursue an integrationist objective, the logic of which has been applied by the ECJ.

The development of important principles of Community law by the ECJ will be examined later (see 9.4.3 to 9.4.5.2). Before that, the special nature of some of the treaties' provisions will be outlined in order to show the raw material used by the ECJ.

9.4.1 Incorporation of Community Law in Member States

Treaties are agreements between States. They are part of international law. There are two broad theories which deal with the relationship of treaties and municipal, or national, law: dualism and monism. Basically dualism holds that international law and municipal law are separate systems of law and specific action will have to be taken to make a treaty part of municipal law. On the other hand monism propounds the view that all laws are part of the same system so that a treaty does not require any action to be part of municipal law.

The EC legal order is unusual. The original treaties had to be ratified by the signatories but one of the sources of Community law, the Regulation, is directly applicable, which means that once it is made by the Council it becomes part of the municipal law of all of the member States without them having to take any action. Compare that with the Directive, which gives the member States discretion as to how they incorporate it into their municipal law.

Given that the member States differ in their national structures and institutions as well as specific laws, it was decided that harmonisation of laws and practices was the sensible method by which to seek common conditions throughout the Communities.

The member States have agreed to the taking of 'all appropriate measures' to meet their obligations under Community law (EC Treaty, art. 5).

9.4.2 Enforcement of Community Law

The obligations which the treaties and secondary law impose upon the member States can be enforced at the instigation of the Commission (EC Treaty, art. 169) and member States (art. 170). These procedures are divided into two stages: negotiation and litigation. The Commission discovers the facts and will deliver a reasoned opinion with which the recalcitrant member State is expected to comply. If this does not lead to a resolution of the matter then the member State can be taken to the ECJ as a defendant in an action for failure to fulfil a treaty obligation. If the complaint is upheld then the member State is bound under art. 171 of the EC treaty to implement the ECJ decision.

Usually the first stage brings about a resolution of the dispute. It is very rare for a member State to initiate the art. 170 process. What is more likely is that a member State complains to the Commission which then acts under art. 169 (see Wyatt and Dashwood 1993, pp. 109–21).

These procedures are not open to individuals or companies. They could either complain to the Commission or initiate an action in a national court as, under the doctrine of direct effect (see 9.4.4), they could have a right which is capable of being enforced.

It is not only the member States which have obligations, the Communities' institutions have them too. The ECJ may review the legality of acts of the Council and Commission at the instigation of member States, the Council or the Commission on the grounds of lack of competence, infringement of an essential procedural requirement, infringement of a treaty or of any rule of law relating to its application, or misuse of powers (EC Treaty, art. 173). It seems that the Parliament, despite not being mentioned in art. 173, does have standing to sue in order to annul an act of the commission or Council where its prerogatives are threatened (*Parliament* v *Council* (case C-70/88) [1990] ECR I-2041; see further 9.5.3.2).

Article 173 also permits a natural or legal person to seek review on these grounds but only in respect of a Decision addressed to that person, or a Decision which, although in the form of a Regulation or Decision addressed to another can be shown to have direct and individual concern. Under art. 174 the ECJ may declare the challenged act to be void.

The ECJ not only plays a role in enforcing EC obligations, it also clarifies such matters. This is done through the preliminary ruling procedure (EC Treaty, art. 177). Under this the ECJ may be asked by a national court or tribunal to give a preliminary ruling on the interpretation of the treaty, the validity or interpretation of acts of the institutions, or the interpretation of statutes of bodies established by an act of the Council which provides for this ruling. The national court or tribunal may make the reference if it involves a point of Community law which it is necessary for the court or tribunal to have a ruling on in order to give judgment on the matter before it. Such a ruling must be requested in a case before any national court against which there is no national remedy.

A substantial amount of the development of Community law has been carried out by the ECJ under this provision. The ECJ is the final arbiter of Community law ensuring that there will be uniform interpretation of it throughout the member States. Under this procedure there is a division of labour. The national court asks the questions to which the ECJ gives the answers and these are then used by the national court to decide the case before it.

9.4.3 Supremacy of Community Law

One of the most important doctrines which the ECJ has developed is that of supremacy of Community law. This has been achieved despite the fact that the treaties do not stipulate that Community law should prevail over munici-pal law where they conflict. The ECJ has deduced supremacy from the objectives of the treaties.

The development of this doctrine can be observed passing through various stages. In *Van Gend en Loos* v *Nederlandse Administratie der Belastingen* (case 26/62) [1963] ECR 1, the plaintiff imported goods into the Netherlands from Germany. The customs duty had been 3 per cent before the EC Treaty. Subsequently it was raised following an international agreement. The plaintiff challenged this rise in the Dutch revenue courts on the basis that art. 12 prohibited the introduction of new customs duties and the increase of existing ones. In an art. 177 ruling the ECJ pointed to the policy behind the common market, the creation of institutions with sovereign rights, and the duty of the ECJ to provide a uniform interpretation of Community law:

> The conclusion to be drawn from this is that the Community constitutes a new order of international law for the benefit of which the States have limited their sovereign rights, albeit within limited fields.

The next step in the process concerned a case from Italy, *Costa* v *ENEL* (case 6/64) [1964] ECR 585. The issue was the compatibility between certain treaty provisions and subsequent Italian legislation which nationalised the electricity industry. In its preliminary ruling the ECJ gave the background of the new legal system which 'became an integral part of the legal systems of the member States and which their courts are bound to apply'. The ECJ pointed out that the 'executive force of Community law cannot vary from one State to another in deference to subsequent domestic laws, without jeopardising the attainment of the objectives of the treaty set out in art. 5(2) and giving rise to the discrimination prohibited by art. 7'. This led the ECJ to conclude that the law stemming from the treaty as an independent source of law could not, because of its special and original nature, be overridden by domestic legal provisions, however framed, without being deprived of its character as Community law, and without the legal basis for the Community itself being called into question.

After ruling that Community law prevailed over subsequent municipal law the ECJ further extended this supremacy in *Internationale Handelsgesellschaft mBH* v *Einfuhr- und Vorratsstelle für Getreide und Futtermittel* (case 11/70) [1970] ECR 1125. In this case the German administrative law court thought that Community law conflicted with basic rights in the German constitution. The ECJ reiterated in its preliminary ruling that, due to its special nature, Community law cannot be overridden by municipal law and so 'the validity of a Community measure or its effect within a member State cannot be affected by allegations that it runs counter to either fundamental rights as formulated by the constitution of the State or the principles of a national constitutional structure'. The ECJ then sought to give reassurance that Community law did respect fundamental rights (see 9.4.5.2).

Having shown the extent of the supremacy of EC law the ECJ then gave advice that when national courts are faced with a conflict between municipal and Community law, they can give effect to Community law without waiting for the prior setting aside of inconsistent national provisions by legislation or other constitutional means (*Amministrazione delle Finanze dello Stato* v *Sim-*

menthal SpA (case 106/77) [1978] ECR 629). In Italy it would normally be necessary to wait for the Constitutional Court to set aside Italian legislation, but the ECJ held that a lower court could ignore legislation which conflicted with Community law because of the special nature of Community law.

9.4.4 Direct Effect

The doctrine of direct effect is that Community law can create rights and obligations in municipal law which can be enforced in the national courts. Vertical direct effect refers to obligations which are imposed upon the State and which an individual can enforce against a State body. Horizontal direct effect applies to rights which individuals could enforce against each other.

Van Gend en Loos v *Nederlandse Administratie der Belastingen* (case 26/62) [1963] ECR 1, also played a major part in the development of direct effect. Community law can give rise to rights 'not only where they are expressly granted by the Treaty but also by reason of obligations which the Treaty imposes in a clearly defined way upon individuals as well as upon the member State and upon the institutions of the Community'. The ECJ held that art. 12 could produce direct effects because it was a clear and unconditional prohibition. As it was a negative obligation it was ideally suited to produce a direct effect in the legal relationship between member States and their subjects.

The criteria for Community law to have direct effect are precision and unconditionality so that a member State does not have to decide how to implement it and there is no discretion in implementation. According to *Van Gend en Loos* some treaty provisions meet these criteria. It is clear that Regulations could fulfil them but could the same be said of directives which are implemented in a way that member States can choose? The principle that Decisions and Directives could have direct effect was announced in *Franz Grad* v *Finanzamt Traunstein* (case 9/70) [1970] ECR 825, and *Van Duyn* v *Home Office* (case 41/74) [1974] ECR 1337. In both cases the reasoning of the ECJ was that it would be wrong, given the binding effect of Directives and Decisions under art. 189, to exclude, in principle, the invocation of the obligation by those affected by it.

The ECJ's ruling in *Pubblico Ministero* v *Ratti* (case 148/78) [1979] ECR 1629 shows that if the time-limit for a Directive's implementation by a member State has not expired, the directive cannot have direct effect, and when the time-limit has elapsed, it may have direct effect. Where a member State has implemented the directive it may still have direct effect (*Verbond van Nederlandse Ondernemingen* v *Inspecteur der Invoerrechten en Accijnzen* (case 51/76) [1977] ECR 113).

These cases have dealt with vertical effect, where Community law has imposed obligations upon a member State and individuals have then sought to rely on these obligations in their transactions with State bodies. What of Directives and horizontal effect? The point was firmly answered in *Marshall* v *Southampton and South West Hampshire Area Health Authority (Teaching)* (case 152/84) [1986] QB 401. This case involved the equal treatment Directive 76/207/EEC and the Sex Discrimination Act 1975. The plaintiff contended that the UK statute infringed the Directive by allowing for different retiring ages for men and women. According to art. 189, a Directive is binding only on the member State to which it is addressed. Therefore a Directive cannot impose obligations upon an individual, it can only have vertical direct effect. As the employer was a State body, the plaintiff was successful.

9.4.4.1 Indirect effect The *Marshall* decision is unsatisfactory in that Directives may have direct effect only against State bodies and not private bodies or individuals. It will not always be clear which bodies are State ones. Some guidance was offered in *Foster* v *British Gas plc* (case C-188/89) [1990] ECR I-3133, which dealt with a statutory corporation, British Gas plc. The ECJ held that 'a body, whatever its legal form, which has been made responsible, pursuant to a measure adopted by the State, for providing a public service under the control of the State and has for that purpose special powers beyond those which result from the normal rules applicable in relations between individuals' could be subject to the equal treatment Directive.

The ECJ in *Von Colson* v *Land Nordrhein-Westfalen* (case 14/83) [1984] ECR 1891, and *Harz* v *Deutsche Tradax GmbH* (case 79/83) [1984] ECR 1921, has introduced a principle of 'indirect effect' which could be used to circumvent these problems. In both of these cases the equal treatment Directive was sought to be invoked by the two plaintiffs who had been refused employment on the basis of their gender. The employers were a State body in *Von Colson* and a private company in *Harz*. The plaintiffs contended that the remedies in German law did not meet the obligations in the Directive. The ECJ held that art. 5 of the EC Treaty, which requires member States to take all appropriate measures to fulfil EC obligations, meant that national courts had a duty to interpret municipal law in a way which secured the Directive's objectives.

This 'indirect effect' evades the vertical–horizontal problems but it does depend upon the view which national courts take of their jurisdiction to interpret municipal law in this manner. The ECJ has yet to work out, in detail, the boundaries of 'indirect effect'. In *Officier van Justitie* v *Kolpinghuis Nijmegen* (case 80/86) [1987] ECR 3969, the ECJ held that when a national court is interpreting its national criminal law, it is limited by the Community law general principles of certainty and non-retroactivity. In a recent Spanish case involving a company law Directive which had not been implemented by Spain the ECJ held that the national court in interpreting municipal law must try in every way possible in the light of the text and the aim of the Directive to achieve its envisaged results whether the national law was prior to, or subsequent to, the Directive (*Marleasing SA* v *La Comercial Internacional de Alimentación SA* (case C-106/89) [1990] ECR I-4135).

9.4.4.2 Francovich The ECJ has provided a better way of solving the problems of people who claim to have rights conferred upon them by a Directive which has not been implemented by a member State in its domestic law. This is based, not on direct effect, but on the primary liability of a member State for a failure to fulfil a Community obligation. In *Francovich* v *Italy* (cases C-6 & 9/90) [1991] ECR I-5357, employees were seeking compensation against the Italian authorities regarding their failure to implement Directive 80/987/EEC which concerned the payment of arrears of wages where an employer became insolvent. On an art. 177 reference, the ECJ ruled that a member State could be required to compensate individuals for failure to implement a Directive if three conditions were satisfied. These conditions are (a) the relevant Directive conferred rights upon the individuals; (b) it was possible to identify those rights from the Directive's provisions and (c) there was a causal link between the member State's failure and the damage suffered by the persons affected.

The possibility of such an action for damages against member States may well provide an incentive to them to meet their Community law obligations by implementing Directives. The wording of the ECJ judgment would appear to cover failure to implement, and faulty implementation of, Directives (see Ross 1993; and Steiner 1993).

9.4.4.3 Francovich developed The principle of State liability for breach of Community law encapsulated by *Francovich* where the breach was the non-implementation of a directive has been developed in subsequent cases. In *Brasserie du Pêcheur* v *Germany* (cases C-46 and 48/93) [1996] ECR I-1029, the breach in question was a directly applicable Treaty provision. The ECJ linked the State's liability for breach of Community law to that of the EC under the EC Treaty, art. 215 (non-contractual liability), and pointed out that where the legislature had a wide discretion in taking legislative decisions, then for liability to arise the breach must be sufficiently serious in that the member State had manifestly and gravely disregarded the limits upon its discretion by Community law. It seemed that the ECJ had tightened up the second of the three *Francovich* requirements.

Further elaboration was given in *R* v *HM Treasury, ex parte British Telecommunications plc* (case 392/93) [1996] ECR I-1631. Here British Telecommunications (BT) was arguing that the UK was liable for its incorrect transposition of a Directive. While the ECJ held that this situation was covered by the *Francovich* principle, BT had failed to show that there was a sufficiently serious breach, as the Directive was not worded precisely and was reasonably capable of bearing the meaning given to it by the UK. *R* v *Ministry of Agriculture, Fisheries and Food, ex parte Hedley Lomas (Ireland) Ltd* (case C-5/94) [1996] ECR I-2553 concerned a challenge made to the refusal of export licences because of concern about animal welfare in Spain. The UK justified this apparent breach of art. 34 of the EC Treaty on the basis of art. 36. The ECJ ruled that where the member State was not called upon to make any legislative choices, and had considerably reduced or no discretion, the mere infringement of Community law might be enough to establish the existence of a sufficiently serious breach. Finally in *Dillenkofer* (cases C-178, 179 and 188-190/94) [1996] ECR I-4845, which, like *Francovich*, concerned non-implementation of a Directive, the ECJ said that the requirement of sufficiently serious breach articulated in *Brasserie du Pêcheur, BT* and *Hedley*

Lomas was also required in *Francovich*, even though it was not specifically mentioned. The ECJ ruled that the failure to transpose a Directive within the stipulated time does constitute a sufficiently serious breach, so as to give rise to the member State's obligation to make reparations for losses incurred. All of these cases have made it clear that the national courts assess the amount of damages on the basis of national law, provided that national law does not make it more difficult to obtain reparation or damages for breach of EC law than for similar domestic claims and is not framed so as to make it virtually impossible or excessively difficult to obtain reparation. In the UK this means that reliance upon the tort of misfeasance in public office is not permitted.

9.4.5   General Principles of Community Law

The ECJ, in addition to developing the fundamental doctrines of supremacy and direct effect, has also formulated general principles of law (see Arnull 1989). These are particularly relevant in the enforcement of Community law.

These principles include proportionality, equality, certainty, which encompasses legitimate expectations, and non-retroactivity, natural justice and fundamental human rights. Two of these principles will be briefly discussed.

9.4.5.1   Proportionality   This is a principle which derives from German administrative law. It requires public authorities to ensure that the action which they take to attain objectives is appropriate and necessary. The principle was applied in a case from the UK (*R v Intervention Board for Agricultural Produce, ex parte E. D. & F. Man (Sugar) Ltd* (case 181/84) [1985] ECR 2889). The case concerned the forfeiture of a deposit in connection with an export licence for sugar. The application for the licence was four hours late and the forfeiture amounted to £1,670,370. This penalty was held to be disproportionate given the objectives of regulating the sugar market and the nature of the infringement.

While the UK courts must apply proportionality in Community law, it is unclear if it exists as an independent principle in purely UK administrative law. The House of Lords was divided on the matter in *R v Secretary of State for the Home Department, ex parte Brind* [1991] 1 AC 696, with two of their lordships not ruling it out and two doubting that it was compatible with the nature of the review jurisdiction (see Jowell and Lester 1987 and B. Thompson 1991).

9.4.5.2   Fundamental rights   In *Internationale Handelsgesellschaft* (case 11/70) [1970] ECR 1125, the ECJ held that Community law prevails over conflicting rights in a member State's constitution but it also pointed out that Community law protected fundamental rights as they were part of its general principles. In *J. Nold KG v Commission* (case 4/73) [1974] ECR 491 the ECJ held that in protecting fundamental rights reference would be made to those rights recognised by the member States, not only in their constitutions, but also in international treaties in which they had collaborated or signed. This includes the European Convention on Human Rights (ECHR) (see 12.5). In the UK this means that the ECHR, which has not been incorporated into domestic law, could be invoked in a matter involving Community law. This is what happened in *R v Kirk* (case 63/83) [1984] ECR 2689, where art. 7 of the ECHR, which prohibits the retroactive effect of penal measures, was applied to stop the prosecution of the captain of a Danish vessel fishing in UK waters.

9.5 PROCEDURE AND JURISDICTION OF THE ECJ

9.5.1 Procedure

The ECJ may sit in plenary session with a quorum of seven, or in a chamber. Four chambers of three judges, and two chambers of six judges have been created, each with its own president. Actions brought by member States, and the Communities' institutions, and certain other suits must be heard in a full court.

The written stage of an action plays a more important part in an action before the ECJ than is the case in a UK court. The pleadings are rather substantial containing full argument on the issues as well as indicating the supporting evidence. After the exchange of documents the judge-rapporteur will consider whether or not there is a need for formal proof-taking. This preparatory inquiry is usually conducted by a chamber and includes examination of any witnesses. The oral stage of the proceedings starts from the basis that the parties have read the previously distributed report of the judge-rapporteur in which the case is outlined, arguments summarised and a report made upon the established facts. Counsel make their submissions, reply to questions from the bench and briefly respond to their opponent's address to the court. The advocate general delivers an opinion which provides a detailed survey of the facts and relevant law. This opinion is very influential. The recommendations of the advocates general are not always followed. Their opinions are longer and more discursive than the court's decision and so furnish assistance in the comprehension of the case law of the ECJ. There are no dissenting judgments and no indication that the judges were divided in their views on the case.

9.5.2 Actions against Member States

In 9.4.2 it was pointed out that the Commission and member States could initiate a process of enforcing EC obligations upon member States (EC Treaty, arts. 169 and 170 respectively). If the Commission's reasoned opinion does not elicit a satisfactory response from the recalcitrant member State then the Commission, or the initiating member State in default of the Commission, could begin an action before the ECJ. In such a case all that the ECJ can do is to declare whether or not the member State has failed to fulfil its obligation. If the finding is that there has been such a failure then the member State is obliged to remedy the situation as it is bound by the ECJ's decision (EC Treaty, art. 171). This remedial action should be taken reasonably quickly even though there is no time-limit stipulated in art. 171 (*Commission v Italy* (case 7/61) [1961] ECR 317).

If a member State does not take the appropriate action there was formerly no sanction available to the ECJ. All that could be done was for the art. 169

or 170 procedure to be initiated again for the failure to respond to the judgment. This has happened on some occasions. France on one occasion refused to act upon the judgment that its ban on the import of British lamb and mutton was unlawful and it was not lifted until lengthy negotiations produced an agreement (*Commission* v *France* (case 232/78) [1979] ECR 2729). Since the decision in *Francovich* v *Italy* (cases C-6 & 9/90) [1991] ECR I-5357, it would seem that where individuals can show that a failure to implement a Community obligation has adversely affected them, then they can take an action for damages in their national courts against their national authorities (see 9.4.4.2).

Since the amendment of the EC Treaty by the TEU, the ECJ has the power to impose a fine upon a member State which has failed to comply with a judgment of the court (art. 171).

9.5.3 Judicial Review of Community Acts

The judicial review jurisdiction includes an action to annul Community acts (EC Treaty, art. 173), and an action which alleges that an institution has failed to act (art. 175). The action to annul is discussed first.

9.5.3.1 Reviewable acts Only acts which have legal effect may be challenged. In the EC context this means Regulations, Directives and Decisions. Regard is had to the substance of an act rather than its form, so that if a measure is in the form of a non-binding act, it can be reviewed if it does produce legal effects (*Commission* v *Council* (case 22/70) [1971] ECR 263).

9.5.3.2 Locus standi There are two categories of people who are given the *locus*, or legal interest, to seek to annul an EC act. In the first group are the member States, the Commission and the Council. They are always regarded as having *locus*. The situation is different for the Parliament. The ECJ held in *Parliament* v *Council* (case 302/87) [1988] ECR 5615 that the Parliament could not challenge the decision of the Council on the basis that the Council had unlawfully failed to delegate power to the Commission which had the effect of removing the Parliament's prerogative of political supervision of the Commission in this matter. The ECJ did not think that Parliament was entitled to take an art. 173 action because it was given the same *locus* as the other institutions in an art. 175 action for failure to act. The Parliament's remedy, according to the ECJ, lay in the Commission's responsibilities to protect this prerogative under art. 155.

Subsequently, in *Parliament* v *Council* (case C-70/88) [1990] ECR I-2041, the ECJ backtracked on its earlier view, holding that it was not reasonable for the Parliament to rely upon the Commission in this case. This was because the Council's Regulation, which the Parliament sought to challenge, followed from a Commission proposal, the legal base of which was the subject of disagreement between the Parliament and the Commission. So the Parliament may have standing if it can show an interference with its prerogatives. The TEU amended art. 173 to reflect this position.

Individuals and companies may use art. 173 but they must be able to show either that it is a decision which is addressed to them, or that it is a regulation or decision addressed to another but it is of direct and individual concern to them. Individual concern has been defined as a decision which 'affects them by reason of certain attributes which are peculiar to them or by reason of circumstances in which they are differentiated from all other persons and by virtue of these factors distinguishes them individually just as in the case of the person addressed' (*Plaumann & Co.* v *Commission* (case 25/62) [1963] ECR 95 at p. 107). This is quite a restrictive test and so not many pass it.

9.5.3.3 Time-limit There is a time-limit of two months within which an art. 173 action must be brought. This period will run from (a) the date of publication of a measure; (b) the date of notification of a measure to the plaintiff; or (c) if there was no notification then the date on which the plaintiff became aware of the measure.

9.5.3.4 Lack of competence The first of the four grounds of challenge in an action for annulment is lack of competence. This is similar to substantive *ultra vires* in UK administrative law (see 16.2). The challenge contends that an act was not one which the authority could take because, for example, the body which was given the power wrongly delegated it to another body and so the delegate's exercise of the power is unlawful (*Meroni & Co. Industrie Metallurgiche SpA* v *High Authority* (case 9/56) [1957-58] ECR 133).

9.5.3.5 Infringement of essential procedural requirement Certain procedures are required to be followed before some acts may be carried out and therefore non-compliance with them is unlawful. If the defect is minor then this will not lead to annulment. In *Roquette Frères SA* v *Council* (case 138/79) [1980] ECR 3333, a Council Regulation was annulled on the basis that the Council had failed to consult Parliament as required under art. 43 of the EC Treaty. The Parliament had been consulted but the ECJ held that the time given to the Parliament to make its response was insufficient to allow for a proper consultation.

9.5.3.6 Infringement of the treaty or of any rule of law relating to its application This ground of challenge not only overlaps with the previous two but is also significantly wider. This is because rules of law relating to the application of the treaty include the general principles of law which the ECJ has developed, for example, proportionality (see 9.4.5.1).

9.5.3.7 Misuse of power Where a power is exercised for a purpose which is not one for which the power was conferred then this may be held to be a misuse of power. This ground has not been used much outside the ECSC and even there it has not been raised successfully on many occasions. This may be because it has been interpreted quite narrowly, so that, for example, if a power has been exercised for a mixture of motives, then it is lawful if the dominant motive was proper (*Fédération Charbonnière de Belgique* v *High Authority* (case 8/55) [1954-56] ECR 292).

9.5.3.8 Effect of a successful action   If a claim under art. 173 is made out the ECJ can declare the act void (EC Treaty, art. 174). The ECJ can, in the case of a Regulation, limit the extent of the retroactive effect of such a declaration by indicating those parts which are and are not void. The defendant institution is then required to take action which will comply with the judgment (EC Treaty, art. 176).

9.5.3.9 Failure to act   As with the action for annulment, there are two categories of standing for an action under art. 175 complaining of a failure to act by the Council, Commission or Parliament. In the first category are the member States and the EC institutions. The second group comprises natural and legal persons. So far as both categories are concerned, an art. 175 action cannot be brought unless the defendant institution has been called upon to act and within two months has failed to define its position. The action may then be initiated within two months of the second failure. An example of this involved the Council's failure to produce a common transport policy within the stipulated period under art. 75 of the EC Treaty (*Parliament* v *Council* (case 13/83) [1985] ECR 1513).

Where an individual or company seeks to bring an action for the Council or Commission's failure to act, it would appear that this covers a failure to issue a decision addressed to that person. This is because the provision specifies that the act, other than a recommendation or opinion, must be addressed to the complainant.

Where the complaint is vindicated then the institution must comply with the judgment (EC Treaty, art. 176), and rectify its omission.

9.5.4 Plea of Illegality
Under art. 184 of the EC Treaty a party may raise as a defence in an action the plea of illegality. This operates as a kind of indirect review because it enables the defendant to attack the Regulation, which is the basis for the action he is defending, on the four grounds listed in art. 173. Thus if a person has been fined, then the Regulation which authorised the decision to impose the fine can be challenged, even though the time-limit for a challenge to that Regulation under art. 173 has expired.

The ECJ has held that not only may Regulations be challenged under this action but also any general act which has binding force (*Simmenthal SpA* v *Commission* (case 92/78) [1979] ECR 777).

If the plea of illegality is successful then the Regulation is declared inapplicable thereby rendering the decision based upon it void.

9.5.5 Actions for Damages
The Communities may be held liable in contract and tort. So far as contractual liability is concerned this is generally dealt with in national courts (EC Treaty, arts 181, 215). Claims in tort or non-contractual liability for harm caused by the Communities' institutions, or by their employees in the performance of their duties, are to be heard by the ECJ (EC Treaty, arts 178, 215).

Non-contractual liability is to be determined according to the general principles common to the laws of the member States. Such principles do not, it would appear, have to be recognised in all of the member States.

There has been some difficulty because of the relationship between the judicial review actions (EC Treaty, arts 173, 175) and the action for damages. This is because damages could be sought in respect of legislative or executive acts which are alleged to be wrong but are still lawful because they have not been annulled. The ECJ has accepted that it would be wrong to treat as inadmissible, claims for damages derived from lawful acts because the purposes of the two types of action are different (*Alfons Lütticke GmbH* v *Commission* (case 4/69) [1971] ECR 325).

Where the plaintiff is seeking damages in respect of legislative action involving economic policy, the Communities will not be liable unless the plaintiff 'proves that a flagrant violation of a superior rule of law for the protection of the individual has occurred' (*Aktien–Zuckerfabrik Schöppenstedt* v *Council* (case 5/71) [1971] ECR 975). This is a restrictive test which few plaintiffs have passed.

9.5.6 Preliminary Ruling
As the Communities are a legal order which is above and part of the legal systems of the member States, it is important that there should be uniform interpretation of Community law. This is provided by the ECJ which can be requested by national courts to provide guidance on questions of Community law which arise in cases they are hearing (EC Treaty, art. 177). Having received the guidance on the law it is then applied by the national court. The ECJ is not involved in issues of national law; its role in this jurisdiction is to interpret Community law.

9.5.6.1 Scope of reference A national court or tribunal may seek a preliminary ruling on (a) the interpretation of the Treaty; (b) the validity and interpretation of the acts of the Communities' institutions; and (c) the interpretation of statutes of bodies established by an act of the council where those statutes so provide.

9.5.6.2 Necessity for reference A national court should only make a reference when the determination of a question of EC law is necessary to the case being heard. Some guidance was offered on this in *CILFIT Srl* v *Ministro della Sanità* (case 283/81) [1982] ECR 3415. It will not be necessary to refer if (a) the Community law point is irrelevant; or (b) if the point is materially identical with a question raised in a ruling in a similar case; or (c) if the correct application is so obvious that there is no scope for reasonable doubt, but this assessment must be made bearing in mind the special features and particular difficulties of the interpretation of Community law. Points (b) and (c) are, in effect, aspects of a French administrative law doctrine, *acte clair*. The difficulty is that what is perfectly clear to one court may hold some doubt for another. There is a difference between points (b) and (c) as (b) offers a narrower application of the doctrine which increases the scope for making a request.

In *Foto-Frost* v *Hauptzollamt Lübeck-Ost* (case 314/85) [1987] ECR 4199, the ECJ held that a reference must be made if the national court has doubts about the validity of a Community act, as only the ECJ can declare such an act to be invalid.

9.5.6.3 Mandatory reference   National courts may request a ruling but if the court is one against whose decisions there is no judicial remedy in national law then the court must bring the matter before the ECJ. There is some doubt about the extent of this mandatory jurisdiction to refer. It would seem that it is clear that the court of final appeal must refer, but what of lower courts in which a case might not proceed any further because leave for appeal or judicial review is refused? It is suggested that the nature of the Communities' legal order predicates that, if a court could be the final one to hear the case in the member State, then it should make the reference.

9.5.7   Advisory Opinions

Under art. 228 of the EC Treaty the ECJ may give opinions relating to agreements between the EC and non-member States and international organisations. The Council or Commission or a member State can ask for an opinion before such an agreement is entered into, as to whether or not it is compatible with the Treaty. If the opinion is that the proposed agreement is incompatible then that agreement can only enter into force if the Treaty is amended following the procedure in art. 236.

Usually requests for opinions are made by the Commission. The proceedings before the ECJ are held in private. Each of the advocates general is heard and the member States may be heard. After this the ECJ delivers its reasoned opinion.

The draft agreement to create the EEA was the subject of two opinions after the first one held that the agreement was incompatible with the Treaty (see 9.1.5.3).

9.6   COMMUNITY LAW IN THE UK

The UK joined the Communities with effect from 1 January 1973. Membership has had an impact upon the UK's constitutional arrangements.

9.6.1   The European Communities Act 1972

The signing of treaties is part of the royal prerogative (see 5.5.1). Community law could not become part of UK law unless legislation provided for incorporation. This was done by the European Communities Act 1972. By s. 2(1), Community law, including rights, powers, liability, obligations and restrictions, is to be given legal effect and recognised and enforced in the UK. This also applies to Community remedies and procedures. Thus, existing and future enforceable Community rights are to be given direct effect in UK law.

The arrangements for Community obligations which require implementation are dealt with in s. 2(2). Implementation may be carried out by delegated legislation either by Order in Council or by regulations made by a designated minister or department. This delegated legislation may implement or enable the implementation of any Community obligation; enable the UK to exercise any current and future rights under the treaties; and to deal with the coming into force or operation of s. 2(1). Schedule 2 lists four things that delegated legislation which implements Community obligations cannot do. It cannot: (a) impose or increase taxation; (b) operate retrospectively; (c) confer power to make delegated legislation unless it is to make rules of procedure for courts or tribunals; and (d) create any new criminal offence punishable with more than two years' imprisonment, or on summary conviction with three months' imprisonment or with a fine of more than level 5 on the standard scale (if not calculated on a daily basis), or with a fine of more than £100 a day.

It is made clear in s. 2(3) that, subject to sch. 2, this delegated legislation made under the authority of s. 2(2) may carry out that which may be done by an Act of Parliament. This means that such delegated legislation can amend or repeal statutes which are incompatible with Community law. (See 8.2.8 for arrangements for Parliamentary scrutiny of Community proposals and legislation.)

Under s. 3(1), the meaning, effect and validity of Community law are made a question of law which, if not referred to the ECJ under art. 177, is to be determined according to the principles laid down by the ECJ.

9.6.2 Supremacy

The ECJ has developed the doctrine that Community law prevails over inconsistent national law (see 9.4.3). It would seem that s. 2(4) of the European Communities Act 1972 seeks to ensure the primacy of Community law. It states '. . . any enactment passed or to be passed, other than one contained in this part of this Act, shall be construed and have effect subject to the foregoing provisions'.

It has taken some time for the implications of this to sink in as it would appear to conflict with the traditional understanding of the supremacy of Parliament. Does this provision mean that Parliament has bound its successors so that the doctrine of implied repeal by inconsistent subsequent legislation no longer applies? A fairly definitive answer was provided to this question in litigation over the Merchant Shipping Act 1988. Provision was made in Part II of this statute to deal with the requirements for registering British fishing vessels and the regulations made thereunder stipulated that at least 75 per cent of the beneficial ownership of the vessel must be vested in British citizens or companies. This was challenged by British companies which were mainly owned by Spanish nationals and therefore adversely affected by the regulations. The basis of their challenge was that they were incompatible with, *inter alia*, EC provisions prohibiting discrimination against nationals of other member States. Lord Bridge of Harwich said that s. 2(4) of the European Communities Act 1972:

has precisely the same effect as if a section were incorporated in Part II of the Act of 1988 which in terms enacted that the provisions with respect to registration of British fishing vessels were to be without prejudice to the directly enforceable Community rights of nationals of any member State of the EEC (*R* v *Secretary of State for Transport, ex parte Factortame Ltd* [1990] 2 AC 85 at p. 140).

When the case was heard again in the House of Lords after the ECJ had given a preliminary ruling that national courts could set aside national rules if they were the sole obstacle to the grant of interim relief in a case concerning Community law, Lord Bridge said the terms of the European Communities Act 1972 made it clear that 'it was the duty of a United Kingdom court, when delivering final judgment, to override any rule of national law found to be in conflict with any directly enforceable rule of Community law' (*R* v *Secretary of State for Transport, ex parte Factortame Ltd (No. 2)* [1991] 1 AC 603 at p. 659). (See 17.3.4, for discussion of principles relating to interim relief.)

The situation, then, seems clear that directly enforceable Community law will prevail over inconsistent national law in a UK court. Should the national law expressly and deliberately conflict with the European Communities Act 1972, then it would seem that the traditional view of Parliamentary supremacy would prevail (*Macarthys Ltd* v *Smith* [1979] ICR 785 at p. 789 per Lord Denning MR).

9.6.3 Interpreting Directives

There have been problems with the interpretation of Directives in the UK. It was a case from the UK (*Marshall* v *Southampton and South West Hampshire Area Health Authority (Teaching)* (case 152/84) [1986] QB 401) which established that Directives did not have horizontal direct effect. The aftermath of that case has produced inconsistent decisions by the House of Lords. The first problem arose in *Duke* v *GEC Reliance Ltd* [1988] AC 618, in which the appellant contended that the Sex Discrimination Act 1975, s. 6(4), should be given a purposive interpretation so as to conform with the ECJ's interpretation of the equal pay Directive 76/207/EEC given in *Marshall*. This argument was not successful as their lordships felt that purposive interpretations were only required by the European Communities Act 1972, s. 2(4), in respect of directly effective Community obligations. The Directive could not confer horizontal direct effect. The interpretation asked for would distort the meaning of the British statute which predated the Directive and could not be held to implement it. Their lordships also dismissed the idea that the decision in *Von Colson* (case 14/83) [1984] ECR 1891, was of any assistance to the appellant.

The House of Lords then decided in two cases that it could interpret British legislation so as to give effect to a Directive (*Pickstone* v *Freemans plc* [1989] AC 66; *Litster* v *Forth Dry Dock and Engineering Co. Ltd* [1990] 1 AC 546). It was able to give purposive interpretations because the national legislation had been intended to implement the relevant Directives. Their lordships then reverted to the stance adopted in *Duke* when they decided *Finnegan* v *Clowney Youth Training Programme Ltd* [1990] 2 AC 407. This case from Northern Ireland raised the same issues as in *Duke* but there were two important differences: the relevant Northern Ireland legislation had been passed after the Directive had been issued, and the ECJ had ruled that this Northern Ireland legislation should be interpreted in the light of the Directive (*Johnston* v *Chief Constable of the Royal Ulster Constabulary* (case 222/84) [1986] ECR 1651). These were not accepted by their lordships as being material differences. Again they took the view that the national legislation had not been enacted so as to implement the Directive. They also decided that the case involved no point of Community law which should be referred to the ECJ for a ruling. This latter view is surely wrong. The doctrine of indirect effect is part of Community law but its limits are not clear (see 9.4.4.1). The decision of the ECJ in *Marleasing SA* v *La Comercial Internacional de Almentación SA* (case C-106/89) [1990] ECR I-4135 is quite extensive in suggesting that the national legislation, whether it predates or postdates the Directive, must be construed in the light of the text and the objectives of the Directive. This should be contrasted with *Officier van Justitie* v *Kolpinghuis Nijmegen* (case 80/86) [1987] ECR 3969 which stated that the doctrine was subject to the general principles of Community law, particularly certainty and non-retroactivity. It may be that their lordships were correct in *Duke* v *GEC Reliance Ltd* but for the wrong reasons.

9.6.4 Requests for Preliminary Rulings

Finnegan v *Clowney Youth Training Programme Ltd* [1990] 2 AC 407 shows, it is suggested, a return to older habits with respect to requests for preliminary rulings by UK courts. Under art. 177 the final court in a member State must ask for a ruling if there is a point of Community law which is necessary to the decision in the case before it. In *Finnegan* there was a point of Community law concerning indirect effect and so a request should have been made.

The older, and bad, habit concerning this procedure derived from the guidelines produced by the Court of Appeal in *H. P. Bulmer Ltd* v *J. Bollinger SA* [1974] Ch 401. Lord Denning MR sought to offer this guidance to courts below the House of Lords as they had a discretion whether or not to refer. His guidelines included a version of *acte clair*, as well as factors such as the wishes of the parties, the time, the cost and the workload of the ECJ. These matters are not entirely irrelevant but it is probably preferable that serious Community law points are dealt with sooner rather than later.

Lord Denning's guidance was superseded by the experience of courts in cases involving points of Community law. The House of Lords, before its unfortunate lapse in *Finnegan* sought to educate the Court of Appeal Criminal Division in Community law by making a request (*Director of Public Prosecutions* v *Henn* [1980] 2 CMLR 229 per Lord Diplock at p. 234). Unfortunately Wood J, sitting in the Employment Appeal Tribunal, in *Enderby* v *Frenchay Health Authority* [1991] ICR 382, said that the lower courts in England were bound by the decisions of their superior courts, even on matters of Community law, and therefore they could not make a reference if a higher court had decided a point. Reassuringly the Court of Appeal has made a reference in this case (*Enderby* v *Frenchay Health Authority* (case C-127/92) [1994] ICR 112).

CHAPTER TEN
Local and Quasi-Government

Central government has a prominence in the UK's constitutional arrangements which may partially be explained by the relatively unitary nature of the State. Not all government, however, is carried out by the people's representatives in Parliament and officials in Whitehall. Many tasks of government will be carried out by councils or local government. These authorities are composed of elected representatives and administrators. Local government has a long history but, as we shall see, its scope for freedom of action has been reduced by a centralising trend in government.

The other important sector of government is what in this book will be termed 'quasi-government'. This term is used as it reflects the wide nature of this sector which includes bodies created by the State, as well as private or voluntary bodies which have been given public tasks to perform. The distinguishing feature about such quasi-governmental bodies is that they operate at a distance from elected representatives and so they present problems of control and accountability.

10.1 THE FRAMEWORK OF LOCAL GOVERNMENT

The Local Government Act 1972 created a two-tier system of local government for England and Wales. The upper tier comprised the county council and the lower tier was the district council. In London and the six major conurbations of Greater Manchester, Merseyside, South Yorkshire, West Yorkshire, the West Midlands, and Tyne and Wear there were also two tiers but the allocation of functions between the two tiers was different. The Greater London Council and the six metropolitan county councils were abolished by the Local Government Act 1985 and replaced by a single tier of local government in those areas. These councils are called London borough councils (LBCs) in London, and metropolitan district councils (MDCs) in those conurbations.

There is another, lower, level of local government: the parish council, or in Wales, the Community Council. They have a small range of responsibilities which include cemeteries, footpaths and recreational facilities. Discussion in this chapter will focus upon the county and district councils, or 'principal councils' as they are known. The services provided by these principal councils include arts and libraries, consumer protection, education, environmental health, fire and civil defence, highways, housing, planning, police, refuse collection, social services, and transport.

The government wished to change the structure of local government from mainly two-tier to predominantly unitary. In Wales and Scotland this was announced and with only a little consultation and minimal modification the Wales (Local Government) Act 1994 and the Scotland (Local Government etc.) Act 1994 were passed which created 22 and 32 unitary councils respectively, which have operated from April 1996.

In England it was decided that there should not be a uniform blueprint. In some areas a change to a single tier might lead to the abolition of the county council, in others the district councils might be the only councils for their areas, and in other areas there might be no change from the two-tier structure. The Local Government Commission was established by the Local Government Act 1992 to conduct reviews and make recommendations on structural, boundary and electoral changes. This work includes possible changes from two-tier to unitary authorities, as well as the application at the local government level of the work which the Boundary Commissions carry out in relation to Parliamentary constituencies (see 7.4.1).

Despite central government's preference for a unitary structure, the reports of the Local Government Commission have, on the whole, not recommended much modification to the two-tier structure. Indeed some councils successfully sought judicial review of ministerial guidance to the Local Government Commission which urged a substantial increase in the number of unitary authorities at the expense of existing two-tier structures (*R* v *Secretary of State for the Environment, ex parte Lancashire County Council* [1994] 4 All ER 165). The guidance conveyed more than a hope for a particular result, it expressed an end in itself and was therefore undermining the statutory criteria and adding a further criterion and was therefore beyond the minister's power to give guidance.

Some new counties created in 1972 had not generated local support and were abolished from 1996: these are Avon, Cleveland and Humberside.

10.2 MEMBERS

The members or councillors are the elected local government representatives and the officers are the permanent staff of the authorities. The relationship between members and officers is a little different from the relationship between ministers and their officials.

10.2.1 Elections
The legal framework for elections to local authorities is broadly similar to that established for Parliamentary elections (see 7.3 to 7.7). The system of voting

is also first past the post and the franchise is universal adult suffrage. Peers are eligible to vote in local elections.

Members represent divisions in county councils and wards in district councils. Elections for county councils are held every four years (Local Government Act 1972, s. 7(1)), with the next elections due to be held in May 1997. In the metropolitan districts elections are held for one-third of the members each year except for the year in which county council elections are held (Local Government Act 1972, s. 7(2) as amended). The (non-metropolitan) district councils may choose either (a) elections for the whole of the council every four years or (b) an arrangement for retirement by thirds (Local Government Act 1972, s. 7(4) to (7), s. 26(2) to (5)). Where (non-metropolitan) district councils hold quadrennial elections for the whole of the council, they are held midway between county council elections. Thus the last such non-metropolitan elections were held in 1991 and the next are due in 1995.

Candidates for local elections must have a connection with the area of the authority for which stand. This qualification is met if the candidate is registered as a local government elector, or has occupied premises or land in that area for the previous 12 months, or if the person's principal or only place of work for the previous 12 months was in that area, or if the person has resided in that area for the whole of the previous 12 months (Local Government Act 1972, ss. 79 to 81 as amended).

Individuals are disqualified from being a member if they hold any paid office or employment with the local authority other than the chairman or vice-chairman; or an appointment which is made or confirmed by a local authority (Local Government & Housing Act 1989, s. 1); or they hold a politically restricted post with that or any other local authority in Great Britain (Local Government and Housing Act 1989, s. 1; recommendation of the Widdicombe Committee 1986). Disqualification for five years also results from conviction for an offence with a minimum sentence of three months (Local Government Act 1972, s. 80(1)(d)). Similarly, a five-year exclusion runs if a member was held to have been involved in unauthorised expenditure (Local Government Finance Act 1982, s. 19) or has caused a loss for a local authority through misconduct (Local Government Finance Act 1982, s. 20(1)(b), or is a bankrupt (Local Government Act 1972, s. 80(1)(b)).

As with Parliamentary elections, certain activities are corrupt or illegal practices (see 7.7.3.1). A candidate may spend £205 plus 4.0 pence for every entry in the electoral register on local election expenses. The election of a member may be challenged by presenting an election petition to the Queen's Bench Division of the High Court (Representation of the People Act 1983, ss. 127 to 163 as amended, see 7.7.3). The petition is heard by an election court which consists of a commissioner who is appointed by the judges who are nominated to try election petitions.

10.2.1.1 Remuneration   Payments to members of principal councils are now primarily authorised by the Local Government and Housing Act 1989, s. 18. Regulations have been made under the Act which provide for basic and special responsibility allowances. The basic allowance is the same amount for each member. The special responsibility allowances may vary. They may include attendance allowances which cover the time spent both in the performance of a duty and travelling to and from the place of performance. The relevant regulations are the Local Authorities (Members' Allowances) Regulations 1991 (SI 1991/351) as amended by SI 1995/553.

10.2.1.2 Disclosures of interest Sections 94 to 98 of the Local Government Act 1972 create a regime of duties of disclosure which, if breached, constitute a criminal offence. If members have a direct or indirect pecuniary interest in a contract, or proposed contract, or any other matter which is before the authority, then this interest must be declared by them if they are present at the meeting. They are also required not to vote on these matters or to speak in discussion about them. If a member's spouse has an interest in a contract and the member knows of that interest, then it is an interest which must be declared.

Members may disclose interests generally, or as particular interests arise in council business. The Secretary of State may remove disabilities consequential upon interests if the numbers of members so disabled would impede the business of the authority, or if the Secretary thinks that their removal would be in the best interests of the inhabitants of the area. An example of a general dispensation is to be found in DoE Circular 105/73 which permitted members, who were council house tenants, to speak on general housing policy. The dispensation could remove the bar on speaking but not on voting. It is unclear what the situation is where a member with an interest in a matter votes on it. One view is that the vote could be ignored as it has been cast illegally (*Nell* v *Longbottom* [1894] 1 QB 767; Bailey 1991, para. 4.42).

10.2.1.3 National Code of Local Government Conduct A code of guidance has been available for some time on conduct for members of local authorities and others co-opted on to council committees. It was felt desirable that the code should be put on a statutory basis (Widdicombe 1986, paras 6.7 to 6.23). Under the Local Government and Housing Act 1989, s. 31, the Secretary of State was authorised to prepare a code. Representatives of local government had to be consulted about the code and it had to be approved by both Houses of Parliament.

An example of the code's advice is that clear and substantial personal or non-pecuniary interests should be declared. The suggested criterion for this is whether the public knowing the facts could reasonably think that a person might be influenced by a such an interest (para. 11).

Breaches of the code may be regarded by the Commissioner for Local Administration as maladministration (see generally 15.3). The Nolan committee has made proposals on codes for local government (see 10.8.3.2).

10.3 OFFICERS

10.3.1 Appointment

Local authorities are required to appoint officers as they think necessary to assist in the carrying out of their functions and responsibilities (Local

Government Act 1972, s. 112). Certain officers must be appointed, for example, chief education officers (Education Act 1944, s. 88) and directors of social services (Local Authority Social Services Act 1970, s. 6).

Local authorities must have one of their officers responsible for financial affairs, another who is the head of paid service (responsible for reporting on the authority's organisation, staffing and discharge of functions) and another who is the monitoring officer (who reports on any possible or actual contravention of law, code of practice or maladministration) (Local Government and Housing Act 1989, ss. 4, 5).

Appointments to paid office or employment must be made on merit (Local Government and Housing Act 1989, s. 7(1)).

10.3.2 Terms and Conditions of Employment

Formally, local authorities have a large amount of discretion in determining the reasonable terms and conditions of employment of their officers (Local Government Act 1972 s.112(2)). In practice there is a framework of national negotiating machinery. Some groups employed by local authorities, such as the police and firefighters, have specific statutory provisions relating to their terms and conditions of service (see Police Act 1964 and Fire Services Acts 1947 and 1959).

10.3.3 Political Restrictions

Officers who hold politically restricted posts have limits placed upon their political activities. Examples of these posts are the head of paid service, the statutory and non-statutory chief officers, deputy chief officers, the monitoring officer, political advisers and those officers to whom an authority has delegated some of its powers (Local Government and Housing Act 1989, s. 2). The restrictions upon political activities include disqualification from becoming a member of a local authority or an MP, and prohibitions on taking part in the management of a political party and canvassing for a party. These officers are also forbidden from speaking to the public or writing for publication if these activities are designed to affect public support for a party.

10.4 LOCAL GOVERNMENT PROCESSES

Powers and responsibilities are given to local authorities acting as a corporate body of the members. These powers may be delegated to committees and officers so that, for example, a council's housing responsibilities will generally be regulated by its housing committee, and some powers may be exercised by the officers working in the housing department. It is usual for an authority's standing orders to provide that matters which have been delegated to comittees and officers may be referred back to the full council.

10.4.1 Meetings

Every local authority is required to hold an annual meeting at which a chairman and vice-chairman are appointed. At their other meetings authorities may receive reports from committees and take formal decisions. An authority's standing orders will deal with procedures at meetings and this may include a limit on the length of speeches.

Openness of local authority business was first firmly secured by the Public Bodies (Admission to Meetings) Act 1960 which entitled the public and the press to attend meetings and some committees of local authorities. Admission could be prevented if a resolution was passed to go into closed session. Subsequently a wide range of committees was brought within the scope of this public accessibility (Local Government Act 1972, s. 100).

So far as principal authorities are concerned, the Local Government (Access to Information) Act 1985 has amended the Local Government Act 1972, and provides the public with rights of access to the meetings, committees and papers of local authorities. The public must be excluded if necessary to avoid disclosing information in breach of an obligation of confidence (Local Government Act 1972, s. 100A(2)). If exempt information is to be considered then the public may be excluded (s. 100A(3)). The categories of exempt information are to be found in the Local Government Act 1972, sch. 12A, and they include personal details relating to employees, applicants for, and recipients of, council services (tenants, school pupils), commercial matters and legal proceedings.

Agendas, reports and minutes must be available to the press and public (s. 100B) and are to be kept for a period of six years (s. 100C).

10.4.2 Committees
Councils may delegate their decision-making powers to committees, or they may empower a committee to consider issues and make recommendations (Local Government Act 1972, ss. 101, 102). A council may not delegate a power to raise money (s. 101(6)). Each service administered by a council will have a committee, for example, planning, housing, social services. The composition of some committees, including an education committee, is statutorily prescribed. Other committees may co-opt persons who are not members of the authority up to a maximum of one-third of the committee (s. 102(3)).

10.4.3 Member-Officer Relations
Chief officers in local government are usually highly qualified in a relevant profession, unlike the permanent secretaries in Whitehall. Officers work for the authority rather than any particular member. Chief officers are responsible to the full council and to the person chairing the relevant committee.

In the relationship between members and officers, the officers are bound to play a leading role, especially where technical matters are concerned. Although it is the members as the authority who formally exercise power, the part-time nature of their involvement unsurprisingly leads to the delegation of many routine matters to officers. Whilst most councils are controlled by one political party, officers will advise members of all parties, a consequence of the fact that the authority is composed of all the elected councillors.

This is a contrast to the position of civil servants who work for and are responsible to ministers, with ministers being responsible to Parliament (see 6.4.3).

10.5 LOCAL GOVERNMENT FINANCE

The financing of local government has been a controversial issue. One of the particular features of local government is its ability to produce income by taxation. This revenue-raising power contributed to the autonomy of councils and enabled them to provide services above levels prescribed by legislation. Local taxation does not supply the bulk of local authorities' income, which comes from central government in the form of grants. Concern about total public expenditure has led to control over the amounts both raised in taxes and spent by local authorities.

The community charge or 'poll tax' marked a significant change in local taxation by switching from a property tax to a tax on individuals. There was such a hostile reaction to the tax that in April 1993, after two years of operation in England and Wales, and three in Scotland, it was replaced by the council tax.

10.5.1 Income
There are three sources of income for local authorities: taxes, grants and fees.

10.5.1.1 Taxes The basis for local taxation has been property taxes, apart from the brief interlude of the community charge. Before the community charge local taxes were known as the rates. The foundation of this system was that property was valued on the basis of the rent which it might generate. The local authority would then draw up its budget and calculate how much it would have to raise through taxation. The level of the tax or rate could then be set by dividing the total tax revenues to be raised by the total valuation of the property within the authority's area. Ratepayers would then have to pay a sum calculated by applying the rate to the rateable value of their property. The rate was a multiplier so that, if the rate was £2 and a property's valuation was £300, then the ratepayer would be liable for a rate demand of £600. The higher the valuation of the property then the greater the sum due from the occupier.

This greatly simplifies the system. One of the complicating factors was that different types of property could be subject to a different rate, so that business premises might have a higher rate than domestic properties. Local authorities also had the power to set supplementary rates if they discovered that their expenditure was greater than originally estimated. In order to ensure that local authorities did not spend more than central government felt was appropriate, 'rate-capping' legislation was passed which limited the amount which local authorities could raise (Rates Act 1984).

10.5.1.2 Non-domestic rates When domestic rates were replaced by the community charge, the rating system was retained for non-domestic properties. Local authorities do not set the rate for non-domestic property in their areas; this is done by central government and rises are calculated in accordance with a formula using the retail price index (Local Government Finance Act 1988, sch. 7). The same level is set throughout the country, hence the name 'uniform business rate'. The money raised by this tax is paid into a pool and then distributed to councils according to equalisation rules which allow for payments which may be more or less than the money actually collected in their areas (Local Government Finance Act 1988, sch. 8).

10.5.1.3 Community charge   The community charge, which was abolished after 31 March 1993, did not use property as the basis for liability. Instead it focused upon adults living in local authority areas. One of the reasons for this change was that if more inhabitants paid a contribution to the income of local authorities, then they would be more interested in how this money was spent and so, it was reasoned, the accountability of councils to charge payers would be improved. The difficulty with this tax was that it was not related to income. Certain groups were exempt or only paid a percentage of the charge, otherwise wealthy inhabitants paid the same amount as their poorer neighbours.

The amount of the community charge could vary from council to council but there were capping provisions which could set a maximum to a local authority's expenditure and thus reduce the level of the charge (Local Government Finance Act 1988, Part VII).

As liability for community charge focused upon residence in a council area, a system of registration was required. In practice it has proved difficult to ensure that the register is accurate and it is clear that some people have successfully sought to avoid inclusion in the register so as to evade paying the tax. This has meant that some people have lost their right to vote as the electoral register was a source of information for the community charge registration officers. The critics of the community charge have claimed that they were correct in suggesting that this 'head tax' was, in effect, a tax on voting, justifying the alternative label of the 'poll tax'.

The community charge was not popular. It was perceived by many as unfair by not being sufficiently related to income. It was a difficult tax to collect with people evading it and others refusing to pay. The fact that it did not generate the anticipated revenue in some council areas led to the inclusion of a supplement in the following year's charge to make up the shortfall, thus adding to its unpopularity and attempts to evade it.

10.5.1.4 Council tax   The successor to the community charge is the council tax which came into effect on 1 April 1993 (Local Government Finance Act 1992, s. 1). This tax is primarily a property tax in that liability to pay is based on the value of the property in which the person lives as assessed on 1 April 1991. The amount of tax due will depend upon the particular valuation band in which a dwellinghouse is placed. There are eight bands and their limits are different in England, Scotland and Wales, reflecting national variations in house prices. Each band has a figure, or multiplier, which is applied to the level of each billing authority's tax. People whose house is in the top band, band H, will pay three times as much as people liable in band A, the lowest band (s. 5).

If a dwelling is occupied by one person only, that person may apply for a discount of 25 per cent (s. 11). Certain groups of people are exempt from the tax: people in detention and people who are severely mentally impaired, students, student nurses, and youth training trainees (sch. 1). Recipients of certain social security benefits will be entitled to council tax benefit which may cover the entire council tax liability (sch. 9). Under the community charge such benefit recipients would have been liable for 20 per cent of the tax. There will also be a scheme of transitional relief to assist those whose council tax bills are greater than their previous community charge demands.

Valuation tribunals will hear appeals from those who claim that their property is not a dwelling, and therefore not liable to the tax, or that their dwelling has been placed in the wrong band (s. 16).

Authorities cannot set whatever level of tax they wish – it can be capped by the Secretary of State determining the maximum budgetary requirement (s. 54). The exercise of these powers is subject to approval by a resolution of the House of Commons (ss. 57, 59).

Not every body which provides a local government service is a billing authority, i.e., a council which sets and collects council tax. Services such as fire, civil defence and the police in the areas of metropolitan district councils are not provided by those councils, but by joint boards. These bodies determine how much they need and this precept is added to the amount which the council charges.

10.5.1.5 Grants The grants paid to councils by Whitehall comprise the largest source of local authorities' income. These central government grants may be general or specific. The general grant is known as the revenue support grant. A local government finance report is made to the House of Commons for each financial year. This report will be the basis of distribution of grants to authorities. After it is approved by resolution of the Commons the grant for each authority will be calculated. The calculation of these amounts follows a complicated equalisation formula which seeks to cost the provision of services at a standard level while taking into account relevant variables, such as each authority's total number of inhabitants and the age profile of these people. This is relevant because populations with a substantial number of retired people will have different needs from areas which have large numbers of school-age children.

Local authorities are consulted in the grant determination process but if they are aggrieved with the result they may seek judicial review. Such a challenge will be unlikely to be successful unless it can be shown that the Secretary of State took into account irrelevant factors, or sought to achieve an improper purpose, or acted unreasonably or perversely (*R v Secretary of State for the Environment, ex parte Nottinghamshire County Council* [1986] AC 240). In that decision and in *R v Secretary of State for the Environment, ex parte Avon County Council* (1990) 89 LGR 498, the fact that the Commons approved the minister's decisions was very important. In *Ex parte Avon County Council* it was held that this approval was a strong indication that the minister had not acted unreasonably or perversely.

Examples of specific grants which are made to local authorities are a transport grant (Local Government Finance Act 1988, s. 87) and student grants (Education Reform Act 1988, s. 209).

10.5.1.6 Fees Local authorities may charge for a variety of their services, for example, sport and recreation, rent, fares and tolls. Some of these charges are specifically authorised (for example, planning application fees authorised by the Town and Country Planning Act 1990, s. 303) and others derive from a general power (Local Government Act 1972, s. 111; Local Government and Housing Act 1989, s. 150).

10.5.2 Expenditure

A local authority must be able to point to a statutory authorisation for any expenditure. The authorisation is often specific but there is a general provision permitting expenditure which a local authority thinks is in the interest of its area or of its inhabitants (Local Government Act 1972 s. 137 as amended, see Local Government and Housing Act 1989, sch. 2). Expenditure made under this provision in respect of expenses connected with the 1980 Moscow Olympic Games was approved (*Lobenstein* v *Hackney London Borough Council* unreported, see [1980] LGC 1292 and Bailey 1991, para. 7.13). There is also provision that authorities can do things which are calculated to facilitate, or which are conducive to, the discharge of their functions (Local Government Act 1972, s. 111(1)).

The courts have held that members have a fiduciary duty towards those who contribute to the authorities' income. Sometimes a decision that expenditure was unlawful leads to legislation which permits it (*Prescott* v *Birmingham Corporation* [1955] Ch 210, in which it was held that bus passes for senior citizens were *ultra vires*, reversed by the Travel Concessions Act 1964).

The classic cases on *ultra vires* expenditure were decided in the early years of the 20th century reflecting what was then thought to be the scope of the local authorities' work. In *Attorney-General* v *Fulham Corporation* [1921] Ch 440, it was held that powers to set up places where inhabitants could carry out their washing did not empower the establishment of a laundry where council employees did the work. In a case concerning the wage levels paid to its employees by one council, it was said that it would be wrong to give men and women equal pay (*Roberts* v *Hopwood* [1925] AC 578). More recently, complicated financial transactions, known as interest rate swaps, have been held to be outside local authorities' powers to borrow and to carry out things which are incidental or conducive to the discharge of their functions (*Hazell* v *Hammersmith and Fulham London Borough Council* [1992] 2 AC 1).

Expenditure may be divided between revenue and capital. Construction projects such as housing or swimming-pools cannot be paid for out of revenue income. This sort of capital expenditure is usually met by loans. These may take the forms of overdrafts or loans from a bank, loans from the Public Works Loans Board, or by way of a loan instrument. Local authorities are required to keep their borrowings and other credit agreements within their aggregate credit limit (Local Government and Housing Act 1989, s. 44).

10.5.3 Audit

The Audit Commission was established by the Local Government Finance Act 1982, s. 11. Local authorities' accounts had been subject to audit before the creation of the commission. In addition to checking that accounts meet statutory requirements, the commission may also check upon arrangements for securing economy, efficiency, and effectiveness in the authorities' use of their resources. The commission may also carry out such 'three Es' studies of services provided by the bodies within its supervision with the aim of identifying and promoting best practice.

An audit may be conducted by a member of the commission's staff or by a person in private practice. While authorities are consulted over the selection of an auditor, the final selection is made by the commission. The auditor may make a report on a matter either immediately or at the conclusion of the audit (s. 15(3)). Such a report must be considered by the authority and its details publicised (s. 18).

If the auditor thinks that expenditure was unlawful, the issue may be taken to court for determination. If expenditure is found to be contrary to law then those responsible for it may be ordered by the court to repay it in whole or in part (s. 19(2)(a)). If a member was responsible, and the amount was more than £2,000 then the court can order his or her disqualification from membership of a local authority (s. 20(4)). If the court takes the view that the person responsible for unlawful expenditure had acted responsibly or in the belief that the expenditure was lawful, then penalties may not be imposed (s. 19(3)).

Other irregularities which the auditor may find are that something was not accounted for, or that a loss has been incurred, or a deficiency has been caused by wilful misconduct (s. 20(1)). Auditors must be given access to all of the facilities they require (Local Government Finance Act 1982, s. 16). The public are entitled to inspect the accounts (s. 17).

The work of the commission in improving efficiency has been increased by the Local Government Act 1992. It will oversee the production and publication of performance indicators which will enable comparisons to be made. This will add to the tension which the commission has between its major role as a regulator and as an efficiency consultant (see generally Radford 1991).

10.6   FRAMEWORK OF QUASI-GOVERNMENT

The use of the word 'framework' in relation to quasi-government may suggest rather more order than actually exists. Quasi-government comprises bodies which have been established both by government and private interests. The term 'quango' – 'quasi-autonomous non-governmental organisation' – achieved prominence as the label which could be affixed to bodies as disparate as the British Broadcasting Corporation, the National Consumer Council and the Women's Royal Voluntary Service. The point about these organisations, or non-departmental public bodies (NDPBs) as they now tend to be called, is that they carry out public business at a distance from central and local government.

10.6.1   Classification
It is quite difficult to propose a coherent and comprehensive classification for NDPBs because these bodies do not fall neatly into categories. They may be

placed into broad groupings such as those suggested by Sir Leo Pliatzky (1980). His three suggested classes, which concerned only national bodies and did not deal with local government ones, were executive, advisory and tribunals. This classification was subsequently used by the government in its periodic publication Public Bodies (Cabinet Office 1995 is the most recent) which lists bodies for which ministers have some degree of responsibility. Nationalised industries and National Health Service bodies are included in this list.

The idea of an executive body is quite wide because it includes managerial, regulatory, promotional and trading functions. Executive bodies include the national and regional tourist boards, the food marketing boards, the BBC, the Civil Aviation Authority, the urban development corporations, the National Radiological Protection Board, the Arts Council and the Housing Corporation. Advisory bodies include the Advisory Board for the Research Councils, the Social Security Advisory Committee, the Information Technology Advisory Board, the Medicines Commission, the Royal Fine Art Commission and the Advisory Committee on Pesticides. Examples of tribunals which are not discussed in 15.2 are the Dairy Produce Quota Tribunal, the Data Protection Tribunal, the Financial Services Tribunal and the Traffic Commissioners.

As at 1 April 1996 there were a total of 1,194 NDPBs in the UK, which breaks down into 309 executive bodies, 674 advisory bodies, 75 tribunals, and 136 prisons' boards of visitors (Cabinet Office 1996).

10.6.1.1 Forms There are a variety of forms of quasi-governmental bodies. Many will be corporations created by statute, others can trace their origins to a royal charter (the BBC), a Treasury minute (the National Gallery), or registration as a company (the National Consumer Council). Some private bodies are subsequently given tasks by government (the British Board of Film Classification, see 12.4.2), including the remarkable concept of a charity, the Joseph Rowntree Memorial Trust, being entrusted with the administration of a social benefit, the Family Fund (Bradshaw 1980).

The National House-Building Council appears to be a private body but it resulted from a government initiative to stamp out shoddy house-building in the private sector (see Barker 1982, pp. 14–15).

10.6.2 Rationale

Six reasons were suggested for the development of quasi-governmental bodies by Hague, McKenzie and Barker (1975, p. 362). These were (a) the need to protect some activities from political interference; (b) to avoid the known weaknesses of governmental departments; (c) to place an activity where appropriately skilled people are; (d) the desire to spread power; (e) the creation of a new organisation because the activity could not be conducted within the existing structure; and (f) to combat the perception that there are too many civil servants by creating an NDPB whose staff would not be counted as part of the civil service. Craig (1994, p. 82) adds a further reason, that of central government seeking to immunise itself from criticism in particularly sensitive areas so that possibly unpopular decisions will be associated with the NDPB.

If we take political interference then broadcasting is an example of an activity which, in a liberal democracy, ought to be free from the detailed control of ministers. The BBC was originally a monopoly broadcaster and then limited competition was introduced in television. The Independent Television Authority was created to regulate the new television companies. Its successor is the Independent Television Commission which oversees terrestrial, satellite and cable television services (see 12.4.3). These bodies are responsible for the oversight of broadcasting and so place some distance between the government and this activity. The Home Secretary does, however, have powers to control what may be broadcast (see 12.4.3).

10.7 FROM PUBLIC OWNERSHIP TO PRIVATISATION

One of the significant types of quasi-government in the period from 1945 until the mid 1980s, was the nationalised industry. This often took the legal form of a public corporation, for example, the Post Office, the British Gas Corporation, British Coal (originally the National Coal Board) and British Rail. The Conservative governments embarked in the early 1980s on a programme of privatisation, of returning most of the nationalised industries to the private sector. This whole process of nationalising and then privatising will now be used as a brief case study of quasi-government.

10.7.1 Reasons for Public Ownership
The major reason behind bringing various private companies into public ownership was to ensure that the public interest was protected and promoted. The Labour Party took an ideological view that the cause of workers would be furthered if industries were in public ownership. The public interest may also include social objectives. A private company must make profits or it will not survive and so, for example, a private railway company might reduce the frequency of, or stop operating, uneconomic services even though those services might be vital to rural communities. The very existence of a particular company could be crucial in a community and some companies were placed into public ownership in order to maintain jobs, or to promote a particular industry. The rescue of British Leyland in 1975 was done both to save jobs and sustain a British volume car manufacturer.

10.7.2 Forms of Public Ownership
The public corporation has perhaps been the most widely known form of public ownership. It should be realised that local government as well as central government has played a part in developing public ownership. Many local authorities established utilities companies providing electricity, gas and water services which were subsequently nationalised and then privatised.

Public influence in a company may also be achieved by taking a shareholding rather than owning the whole company. The amount of shares held may vary from a majority through a minority to one, the so-called 'golden share'. The device of a golden share may give the government important controls on particular matters affecting the company (see Graham and Prosser 1988).

10.7.3   The Nationalised Industry Public Corporation

According to one commentator the nationalised industry public corporations shared five common features: (a) they were corporate bodies which could trade and own property; (b) they were created by statute and only legislation could modify them; (c) they were publicly owned; (d) there was a measure of governmental control which could include appointments to the board and a stipulation of various policy and financial matters; and (e) they operated independently of government with their personnel and finances separate from government (Tivey 1973, pp. 33–4).

10.7.3.1 Structure   The classic nationalised industry public corporation would have a board of directors who would be responsible for its operational management. The empowering legislation would give a 'sponsoring minister' the power to appoint (and dismiss) the members of the board. The legislation would often state the term of appointment of board members and might also stipulate their qualifications.

10.7.3.2 Policy and finance   The legislation which created a nationalised industry public corporation stipulated the objectives of the corporation which the board had to pursue. The statutes which nationalised the electricity and gas industries required them to provide efficient, coordinated and economical supplies of electricity and gas (Electricity Act 1947, s. 1(1); Gas Act 1948, s. 1(1)(a)).

As regards their finances the nationalised industry public corporations were meant to be autonomous. The reality has been that ministers have influenced, if not controlled, every financial aspect, from the setting of charges to borrowing. The corporations were required to produce annual reports and accounts.

10.7.3.3 External relations   Ministers, in addition to overseeing these corporations, were usually given the power to make general directives with which the corporations would have to comply. The division of labour between ministers and boards was that the boards were responsible for the day-to-day operations, and the minister set the overall policy framework. In practice ministers intervened in operations and only rarely did they exercise the public power of issuing a directive. Ministerial influence was often exercised informally through the 'lunch-table directive'.

Parliament could require ministers to account for their dealings with these corporations and debate their annual reports and accounts. A Select Committee on Nationalised Industries was created in the 1950s and it usually produced two reports each year. It was abolished in the 1979 reorganisation of the select committee system. The new departmentally specialised select committees could investigate any nationalised industry within the remit of the departments they monitored.

Most of the nationalised industries had a system of consumer representation. There might be a consumer consultative committee or council at both national and regional levels. These bodies could deal with complaints and play a role in formulating policy.

10.7.4 Reasons for Privatisation

A variety of reasons have been put forward to explain why companies and industries should be taken out of public ownership. At the ideological level there are arguments that the boundaries of the State should be rolled back and that popular capitalism should be promoted. The removal of governmental control would mean that market discipline would be the constraining factor, which it was hoped would mean that competition would lead to greater efficiency, benefiting consumers. Popular capitalism encompasses the promotion of an enterprise culture generally, and the encouragement of ownership of shares. Privatisation can also raise money for the government through the sale of shares.

10.7.5 Privatisation of Utilities

The change of ownership from the public to the private does not necessarily mean the end of governmental involvement in an industry. Some of the utilities are still monopolies or dominant suppliers. British Gas plc is still the monopoly supplier to domestic customers and British Telecommunications plc is the dominant supplier of telecommunication services.

In the case of telecommunications, gas, water and electricity it was decided that the newly privatised suppliers of these services should be subject to control by a regulator in order to protect the consumer. A common model has been used in these areas in which a regulatory body headed by a director general has been appointed, which monitors performance, approves pricing structures and seeks to secure efficiency and economy in the provision of these services. The regulatory bodies are OFTEL, the Office of Telecommunications; OFGAS, the Office of Gas Supply; OFWAT, the Office of Water Services; and OFFER, the Office of Electricity Regulation. These new regulators join the already established authorities, the Office of Fair Trading and the Monopolies and Mergers Commission, which have general responsibility for promoting competition.

A striking feature of this regulatory regime for the utilities is its relatively 'light touch', as compared with the equivalent agencies in the United States. The powers of the regulators are limited. A major aspect of their involvement in pricing structures is to police the statutory 'RPI minus X' formula which allows the companies to raise their prices by the amount of retail price inflation minus a specific percentage. The aim of this is to secure efficiency savings to be passed on to consumers. Some costs are permitted to be passed on to consumers. In gas this is known as the Y factor, and in water the cost of compliance with some environmental requirements – the K factor – may also be ignored in the RPI minus X formula (Veljanovski 1991, pp. 18–19).

The telecommunications, gas, water and electricity legislation provides for consumer representation (Telecommunications Advisory Bodies, Gas Consumers' Council, Water Customer Service Committees and Electricity Consumer Committees). These committees originally shared responsibility with the relevant director general for the investigation of complaints. It was felt that the electricity legislation provided better consumer protection and aspects of its provision for specifying standards of service to consumers has been applied to the other utilities (Competition and Service (Utilities) Act 1992, see McHarg 1992). The 1992 statute establishes a three-tier structure for the handling of consumer grievances, in which the initial response is made by the utility company and then it may go to the consumer council committee and then the director general. Special provision is made for disputes over bills (see Lewis and Birkinshaw 1993, and Birkinshaw 1995, for summaries of complaints mechanisms).

10.7.6 Accountability

The rise of quasi-governmental bodies is partially due to the perception that certain tasks are better carried out at a distance from ministers and their departments. This does cause a problem given the importance of ministerial responsibility in the UK's mechanisms of accountability for governmental actions. The following examination of the various means of accountability relating to quasi-government will focus on the example of the regulation of the utilities companies.

10.7.6.1 Ministers   The directors general are appointed by ministers. Ministerial patronage is an important feature throughout quasi-government. There is a long-standing criticism that ministers will appoint persons whose views will not deviate greatly from ministerial opinions. The open and formal powers of general direction over nationalised industries which ministers had were neglected, and instead power was exercised informally and secretly. As the structure for regulation of utilities is not very transparent, this affords great scope for the exercise of discretion and bargaining. It is possible that ministers might seek to bring pressure to bear on the regulators if they were unhappy with their work.

10.7.6.2 Parliament   As ministers have limited formal responsibility for the regulators, it is difficult for Parliament to call ministers to account for the regulators' actions through the normal methods of questions and debate. Operational matters are given to the regulators and the best Parliamentary technique is investigation by a select committee. When there was a select committee dealing with nationalised industries it managed to produce, on average, reports on two of them each year. The remit of the departmental select committees is so wide that it is unlikely that the utilities and their regulators will become a routine subject of inquiry. One of the triggers for select committee interest is political topicality so that their scrutiny will be somewhat intermittent.

10.7.6.3 Audit   When the National Audit Office was created, it was not given jurisdiction over nationalised industries (National Audit Act 1983, sch. 4; see generally 8.4.3). The National Audit Office has carried out value-for-money examinations of the privatisation sales, including those of the utilities (see McEldowney 1989). The regulators, as is the case with most NDPBs, produce annual reports. They are not subjected to scrutiny by the National Audit Office and the Public Accounts Committee. The

Parliamentary Commissioner for Administration has jurisdiction to investi-gate allegations of maladministration leading to injustice made against the regulators (see 15.3).

10.7.6.4 Consumerism The various advisory bodies, consumer and consult-ative committees which have been appointed, allow representatives of the public to play a part in the accountability arrangements for the regulation of the privatised utilities and a rather more limited role in policy formation.

10.7.6.5 Courts There is no doubt that the regulators can be subject to judicial review (see further chapters 16 and 17). There is a problem with this judicial scrutiny in that it is limited, dealing with procedures and process rather than substantive matters. A different regulatory body, the Independent Television Commission, was challenged by an unsuccessful applicant for a Channel 3 licence. The basic rule for the award of licences was the making of the largest bid in a blind auction. The challenge was based on the Commission's discretionary determination that the applicant's business fore-cast was unfeasible so that the licence could be awarded to another applicant who had made a lower bid. The House of Lords decided that there was no basis in law for the application of judicial review. The Commission had correctly exercised its powers following the proper procedures and its deter-minations were not unreasonable (*R v Independent Television Commission, ex parte TSW Broadcasting Ltd* (1992) *The Independent*, 27 March 1992). This decision supports Veljanovski's claim that judicial review will not have much of an impact upon the quality of decision-making by the regulators (1991, p. 17).

10.8 CONSTITUTIONAL ISSUES IN LOCAL AND QUASI-GOVERNMENT

Local authorities and NDPBs raise some important constitutional issues. Discussion of these will be confined to their relationship with central government.

10.8.1 Central-Local Relations

As the discussion of local government finance showed, central government is the dominant partner in central–local relations. There has been a reduction in the responsibilities given to local authorities. The management of the State school system was formerly solely a matter for local education authorities. Schools have been given greater control of their resources through local management and may opt out of local authority control to become grant maintained and receive their funding direct from the Department for Educa-tion (Education Reform Act 1988, s. 52). Provision of housing is another responsibility of local authorities which has been eroded. Council estates may be privatised if tenants opt to change their landlord (Housing Act 1988, Part IV) or by the formation of a housing action trust as a prelude to a change of ownership (Housing Act 1988, Part III).

In addition to consumers opting out of local authority services, the provision of services may be awarded to private companies through compulsory competitive tendering. Initially this was restricted to construction work (Local Government Planning and Land Act 1982, Part III), but it was subsequently extended to services which included refuse collection, cleaning and school meals (Local Government Act 1988, Part I). It has been further expanded to professional services, including those performed by lawyers, architects and information technologists (Local Government Act 1992, s. 8).

Part of the philosophy behind these changes is a desire to reduce the role of the State and a belief that the market is a provider of cheaper services. The major constitutional issue raised by this relationship is the autonomy which a local authority should have. Councils are elected bodies and therefore have some democratic legitimacy for their actions. In the past progressive innovations were pioneered by local authorities. They could carry out such programmes and pay for them because they had a revenue-raising power. A counter-argument to the claim of the local mandate of councils is that it is debased because of the small degree of interest in local government and the low turnout of voters in local elections. Central government seems to claim that its views should prevail because it is elected to govern the country as a whole and that it provides the largest source of finance for local government. It is not clear why local councils should not be able to provide a more expensive level of service if their electorates vote for and pay for it. A possible response is that the people who benefited from these services were not those who actually paid for them. It was reasoning of this type which led to the requirement that the great majority of inhabitants should pay some community charge.

For some people local authorities should be part of a system of checks and balances. It seems that such an idea is a variation upon a federal arrangement where there are two tiers of government elected at different times and given their own particular functions and responsibilities so as to avoid concentration of power. If pluralism, or dispersal of power, is a macro-constitutional issue in central–local relations, then a micro issue is efficiency. It would be inefficient for central government to seek to provide all services, not least because it is too remote from the various localities and less aware of their different circumstances. Local administration can be more responsive to local needs. Yet the role which local authorities can play is being decreased as services for which they were formerly responsible are contracted out. This dispersal means that the public are no longer clear about who is responsible for services. In education there is the Department for Education, the local education authority, the governors of 'State' schools and grant-maintained schools, the Funding Agency for Schools, which not only funds grant-maintained schools, but also shares planning responsibilities with local education authorities until 75 per cent of children in primary or secondary education are in grant-maintained schools. In this situation, as schools leave the supervision of the local authority they enter an area in which accountability will be much reduced. The Department for Education and Employment cannot oversee all of these schools, but how will the Funding Agency for

Schools, an NDPB, be monitored? (See further 10.8.2.) Some commentators argue that these particular arrangements are just part of a trend in which public accountability is being eroded (Stewart 1992, Lewis and Longley 1992).

10.8.2 Ministerial–NDPB Relations

Two connected aspects of the relationship between ministers and NDPBs will be considered: accountability and standards.

10.8.2.1 Accountability Even if it is somewhat weak, local government is accountable to its electorate. The trouble with quasi-government is that it has an accountability gap. NDPBs are meant to have some autonomy from ministers. The examination in 10.7.6 showed that there is both too much and too little autonomy. Ministers can, and do, exercise informal control over NDPBs yet they are not held to account for this. The autonomy which NDPBs ought to have should be sufficient to enable them to discharge their tasks but there should be satisfactory methods of holding them to account.

Johnson (1982) argues that ministerial responsibility will not suffice. He proposes that existing mechanisms should be strengthened. This would include the provision of information by NDPBs, their audit, and the imposition of legal duties directly upon their personnel. Craig (1994, pp. 105-7) offers similar solutions. He advocates that more care be taken in the creation of NDPBs and Next Steps agencies. A permanent body ought to review these bodies, advising which types are best suited to particular tasks. If the legislature which established these bodies paid more attention to aspects of their institutional design then he argues the situation would improve. The NDPBs' relationships with Parliament and ministers could be more clearly specified so that the degree of insulation from a minister was appropriate. If thought was given to NDPBs' decision-making procedures then a balance might be drawn which took full account of the costs and benefits. For example, more open procedures may improve the quality of decisions but add to the length of time taken (see Weir and Hall 1994, Weir 1995).

These general considerations about a better framework for NDPBs can be observed in some of the criticism of the arrangement for the regulation of the privatised utilities. A major complaint is that the regulatory regime is too closed and involves too much discretion, producing a system of regulation by negotiation (Veljanovski 1991).

10.8.3 Standards

One of the three areas considered in the first report of the Committee on Standards in Public Life was that of executive NDPBs and NHS bodies (hereafter quangos) (Cm 2850). Concerns related to two matters in particular: first, the perception that appointment to these bodies was not made on merit, but rather on party political grounds; and second that there were problems of propriety, especially in relation to expenditure (see HC 154 of 1993–4).

Not surprisingly the Committee was clear that merit should be the criterion for appointment and was pleased that the government had publicly committed itself to this. Whilst ministers should continue to make appointments, the area of public appointments should be regulated and monitored by a new Public Appointments Commissioner, who might be one of the Civil Service Commissioners. This Commissioner should take over the running of the Public Appointments Unit from the Cabinet Office and could advise upon best practice. Where departments departed from this, they should produce justification. One element of best practice, which was being introduced into NHS bodies, and which the Committee recommended for universal adoption, was the involvement of an advisory panel. One-third of the membership of such panels should be independent.

The Committee produced a draft code of practice for public appointments. This included the drawing up of a job description and the key qualities sought, which should be publicly available, as should a description of the appointments process. The selection of a short list should be undertaken or overseen by a panel. Any candidate recommended to a minister should have been approved as suitable for the post by the panel, and this could include taking up references where appropriate.

Candidates for public appointment should declare any significant political activity within the previous five years. This would include the holding of office and candidature for election.

In order to improve propriety and accountability, the government should undertake a review which could lead to the production of a more consistent legal framework for quangos and local government. Codes of conduct must be produced, the observance of which would be conditions of appointment for the members of boards, and their staff in quangos. Board members of quangos should, on appointment, give a commitment to undertake induction training, which should include awareness of public sector values and standards of probity and accountability.

Auditing arrangements must be strengthened by better education of quango accounting officers with respect to their responsibility for all aspects of propriety. Best practice in external financial audit should be applied to all quangos.

Quangos should nominate a person who would be entrusted with the task of investigating staff concerns about propriety which have been raised confidentially. The procedures should guarantee anonymity and provide a clear route to the quango's sponsoring department by which unresolved concerns about propriety could be raised. Executive NDPBs should develop codes of openness and ensure that they are brought to the attention of the public. Sponsor departments should work with quangos on this matter and the Cabinet Office should produce and update guidance on good practice for openness in quangos.

The government has committed itself to implementing these recommendations.

10.8.3.1 Local spending bodies In their second report (Cm 3270) the Nolan Committee investigated a sector in which there are over 4,500 bodies in higher and further education, grant maintained schools, training and enterprise councils, the Scottish local enterprise companies, and registered housing associations. These bodies are rarely elected, have some 70,000 board members and are responsible for spending over £15 billion of public funds each year. The committee set out two fundamental propositions:

(a) Where a citizen receives a service which is paid for wholly or in part by the taxpayer, then the government or local authority must retain appropriate responsibility for safeguarding the interests of both user and taxpayer regardless of the status of the service provider.

(b) Central control of autonomous but centrally funded local bodies should be limited as far as possible to setting policy guidelines and operating boundaries, to ensuring an effective audit framework, and to the effective deployment of sanctions. Government and Parliament should aim to ensure that local mechanisms to influence the activities of local bodies exist and should give them the support necessary to ensure accountability.

The committee recommend that principles of good practice on appointments, openness, codes of conduct and conflicts of interest should be adapted with suitable modifications across the sectors covered in their report, and that these local public spending bodies should institute codes of practice on whistle-blowing.

The values which the committee are seeking to promote, then, are generally openness, which helps facilitate appointments on merit, and getting the balance right between local decision-making and a framework for accountability, which is not just concerned with propriety in spending public money but requires that there should be external adjudication of complaints, access to outside impartial assistance in resolving or adjudicating on disputes and a commitment to whistle-blowing which will allow the exposure of malpractice which both respects staff confidentiality and imposes penalties for false accusations.

10.8.3.2 Local government The Nolan Committee in their third report (Cm 3702) found that there was a lack of clarity in the rules dealing with standards of conduct in local government. They took the view that part of the problem was that the responsibility for maintaining standards had moved away from local government and accordingly they wished to return it by requiring all councils to produce their own codes of conduct within a Parliamentary approved framework. Having established its own code each council should have a standards committee, which would deal with issues of propriety and have powers to recommend to the full council that errant members be disciplined. Appeals from councillors (and others) could be heard by independent local government tribunals, which would also be able to deal with other matters arising from a council's code. The system by which councillors are surcharged if found guilty of misconduct should be replaced by a system of penalties involving the courts. The committee are also proposing a new statutory offence of misuse of public office.

The codes should deal with the registration and declaration of pecuniary and non-pecuniary interests. Failure to enter a pecuniary interest on the public register would not be a criminal offence but it would be a breach of the code which the standards committee would consider. A standards committee could be empowered to require withdrawal from certain business and the sanctions it could impose would include the power to suspend a councillor for a maximum of three months.

The local government tribunals, in addition to hearing councillors' appeals, could also determine referrals from the Secretary of State on the issue of whether a council's code, standing orders or other procedures achieved the same effect as the Parliamentary approved model. If the tribunal found the council's arrangements to be deficient then it would have the power to require the council to amend them.

Councils should institute codes to deal with the interests of their officers, and also to prepare protocols on the relationship between officers and councillors, dealing with issues of strife, and 'cosiness'. The special procedures relating to threats of disciplinary action against chief executives should be extended to the other statutory officers (head of paid service, monitoring officer and chief financial officer).

Whistle-blowing procedures should be instituted and staff in organisations which are contracted to provide services to the council ought to be covered by them. These organisations must be subject to a complaints scheme about the services they provide, which must be properly publicised.

The conclusion of this brief excursion into local and quasi-government is that a central plank of our constitutional arrangements, accountability for executive action, is quite weak. This is a consequence of a lack of awareness of constitutional issues within a framework which is inadequately provided with constitutional principles but the work of the Nolan Committee is beginning to redress this.

CHAPTER ELEVEN

The Judicial Power: Personnel and Practice

In the US constitution, art. 4 vests the judicial power in the Supreme Court. The term 'judicial power' is used here to convey a meaning which is wider than the judiciary but not as wide as the whole machinery for, and administration of, justice. The coverage in this chapter is primarily concerned with the position of the judiciary, especially those who sit in the superior courts, in relation to the other two branches of government. One of the most important constitutional principles relating to the judges is that they should be independent. This is usually taken to mean that the only attempts made to influence judicial decisions will be made by the parties arguing their cases in court. The ways in which judicial independence might be threatened include the abuse of the arrangements for the appointment, promotion, remuneration and discipline of the judges. The arrangements for these matters will be outlined and then examined from the perspective of judicial independence. This perspective will also be used in surveying the judiciary's relations with others, both inside and outside the courts. The members of the executive who have responsibilities for legal affairs will also be considered and the final section will discuss proposals for reform.

11.1 THE JUDGES AND THEIR COURTS

The judiciary are organised in grades according to the type of court in which they will sit. The general outline of the public courts system is that there are civil and criminal jurisdictions, both of which have tiers organised on the basis of trial and appeal. The courts of first instance are distributed in a territorial hierarchy according to the importance of the issues which are tried in them.

In England and Wales the lowest tier of the civil courts is the county court, which is staffed by circuit judges and district judges. The magistrates' court also has a small civil jurisdiction. The High Court has three divisions: Queen's Bench, Chancery and Family. Justices of the High Court are known as puisne judges. Members of the Court of Appeal are Lords Justices of Appeal. Leave is required for appeals to the Court of Appeal, Civil Division. A further appeal to the House of Lords also requires leave, as do those appeals which may be made directly to their lordships from the High Court. A magistrates' court tries the less serious criminal offences summarily, while the more serious criminal cases are tried before a jury in the Crown Court. Most magistrates are lay people who are advised by their legally qualified clerk. In some magistrates' courts proceedings are heard by a stipendiary magistrate who is legally qualified. Trials of the less serious offences in the Crown Court may be presided over by recorders and assistant recorders, who are part-time judges. Circuit judges and puisne judges in the Queen's Bench Division conduct the trials of the more serious offences. Criminal appeals may be heard in the Divisional Court of the Queen's Bench Division, and in the Court of Appeal, Criminal Division. A further appeal lies to the Lords, if leave is granted.

The High Court, Crown Court and the Court of Appeal together form the Supreme Court.

In Northern Ireland the same pattern of judges and courts broadly prevails. There are magistrates' courts and county courts. The Supreme Court of Northern Ireland follows the model just described for England and Wales. Appeals may be made from its Court of Appeal, with leave, to the House of Lords. The differences are that legally qualified resident magistrates, rather than lay people, preside in the magistrates' courts, and that trial by a single judge rather than by judge and jury is prescribed for 'scheduled' offences which are mainly terrorist related (Northern Ireland (Emergency Provisions) Act 1996, ss. 1 and 11, and sch. 1, Parts I, III, IV).

The Scottish courts are organised along broadly similar lines to those in England and Wales. The sheriff's court is the lowest tier of the civil courts. The Court of Session is the major civil court which may determine cases both at first instance (the Outer House), and on appeal (the Inner House). The district courts hear the minor criminal offences and the High Court of Justiciary deals with the more serious offences. While the House of Lords may, with leave, hear appeals from the Court of Session, their lordships do not determine criminal appeals from Scotland.

11.1.1 The House of Lords

The judicial work of the House of Lords was formally separated from its other business in the 19th century. Today, only the decision in a case is delivered in the chamber, by handing down the printed speeches of their lordships. Previously, as the term for the opinion of a law lord indicates, they were given orally. Argument before the law lords takes place in a committee room and their lordships are not robed, but wear suits.

The Appellate Jurisdiction Act 1886 provided for the creation of the first life peers, the Lords of Appeal in Ordinary, so as to ensure that there were a sufficient number of properly qualified peers to conduct the judicial work of the House. The current maximum number of Lords of Appeal in Ordinary is 12 and, by convention, two are Scots lawyers. The House of Lords has made significant decisions affecting the common law in the UK in civil appeals from Scotland, e.g., *Donoghue* v *Stevenson* [1932] AC 562.

Other properly qualified peers may assist the law lords but these matters are governed by convention. Former Lord Chancellors may sit when requested to do so by the current Lord Chancellor. The pressure of other duties, acting as Speaker of the Lords and heading the principal government department dealing with legal matters, tends to prevent the Lord Chancellor from sitting as a law lord.

Their lordships usually sit in benches of five, although seven of them have sometimes heard an appeal (e.g., *Pepper* v *Hart* [1993] AC 593, in which their lordships outlined the circumstances in which reference may be had to speeches in Parliament when construing legislation, see 2.2.2.2).

11.1.2 The Judicial Committee of the Privy Council

During the height of the British Empire in the 19th century, the expansion of the number of appeals from the sovereign's overseas dominions led to legislation which created a Judicial Committee of the Privy Council (Judicial Committee Act 1833). The committee's jurisdiction not only included these overseas appeals but also a variety of other matters. The number of these overseas appeals has declined with the transformation of the Empire into a Commonwealth of independent States in which the majority have decided that their final court of appeal should be in their own jurisdiction. New Zealand and a few of the Caribbean States have retained the appeal to the Committee. These overseas appeals may be as of right, with the permission of the national court, or with special leave of the committee. Criminal appeals are by special leave except where they concern fundamental rights provided for in constitutions approved after 1959.

Appeals from the Isle of Man and the Channel Islands may be heard, as may other matters in its miscellaneous domestic jurisdiction which includes, for example, appeals from the ecclesiastical courts and medical disciplinary appeals; applications that an MP is disqualified from membership of the Commons; and the seeking of an advisory opinion by the government.

The membership of the committee includes the Lord President, who never sits, and those Privy Councillors who have held high judicial office. In practice this means the Lords of Appeal in Ordinary, but some judges from Commonwealth countries which retained the appeal have also been invited to sit.

11.2 JUDICIAL APPOINTMENTS AND TERMS OF SERVICE

The greatest number of judges are the 30,000 lay magistrates who try over 95 per cent of criminal cases. The lower ranks of the legally qualified judiciary comprised, on 1 July 1997, some 323 assistant recorders (plus 96 assistant recorders in training), 929 recorders, 89 stipendiary magistrates, 323 district judges (including 19 in the Family Division) and 556 circuit judges (including Official Referees). There are 96 puisne judges, 32 Lords Justices of Appeal, 12 Lords of Appeal in Ordinary plus the Lord Chief Justice, the Master of the Rolls, the Vice-Chancellor and the President of the Family Division.

11.2.1 Appointment

The Lord Chancellor is assisted in the appointment of magistrates by the local advisory committees composed of existing magistrates. Candidates may be nominated by others or propose themselves. Apparently any political affiliations which new magistrates have are known in order that a balance amongst the political parties is maintained. Magistrates must be people of integrity and understanding.

The Lord Chancellor's Department has produced a booklet which outlines the policies and procedures relating to judicial appointments (1990). The practice has evolved that, despite the absence of a career judiciary, there is a kind of apprenticeship. This takes the form of carrying out the part-time duties .of an assistant recorder and moving on to a, similarly part-time, recordership. This could lead to a full-time judicial appointment as a district judge, or a circuit judge or, in the case of high-flyers, to being a justice in the High Court. These judicial appointments are made by, or on the advice of, the Lord Chancellor. The prime minister is responsible for appointments to the Court of Appeal and the House of Lords but takes into consideration the views of the Lord Chancellor. Only High Court justices are appointed to the Court of Appeal, and in turn, its members usually comprise the pool of candidates from which the English and Welsh law lords are chosen, although Lord Slynn of Hadley was appointed to the Lords from the Court of Justice of the European Communities. By convention two of the law lords are Scots. Occasionally a judge from Northern Ireland is appointed to the House of Lords (Lord Hutton succeeded Lord Lowry as Lord Chief Justice of Northern Ireland and then as a law lord).

The Courts and Legal Services Act 1990 has slightly altered the formal criteria for appointments, but the apprenticeship system still operates. The 1990 statute opens up the possibility of solicitors becoming High Court justices. This is because it will be possible for solicitors to obtain an advocacy qualification which will give them a right of audience in the High Court. Before the 1990 statute solicitors could progress to circuit judgeships, but only barristers were appointed to the High Court bench. The great majority of appointments to the High Court were of leading counsel, although some circuit judges have been promoted.

Appointment to the apprenticeship of the junior judiciary begins with lawyers taking the initiative and alerting officials in the Lord Chancellor's Department of their aspirations. Discussions will be had with these people and soundings will be taken amongst the judiciary before whom they have appeared, and their colleagues. Progression will depend upon their performance in the apprenticeship posts. There is no application system for High Court appointments. The Lord Chancellor and relevant officials will review those in recorderships and circuit judgeships, as well as conducting more soundings amongst the judiciary and senior ranks of the profession.

The system, then, is secretive and centralised rather than a formalised one. It has produced a judiciary which under-represents women and minority groups. The Lord Chancellor is concerned about this imbalance and hopes to be able to improve it but this does not appear to mean that positive discrimination will be used to increase the proportion of the under-represented groups. The one change which has been introduced is the use of advertisements seeking applicants for district and circuit judgeships. It may be that this slightly more open approach will encourage under-represented groups to apply.

Formerly, lawyers who had been MPs could expect to be appointed to judicial office. The possibility of appointment to high judicial office of former law officers was particularly marked, indeed, there was supposedly an understanding that they would be considered for the post of Lord Chief Justice. If that was the case, it no longer appears to be so, as the recent appointees were not former law officers (see Griffith 1991, pp. 25–30). One tradition which has been continued with the appointment of Sir John Laws to the High Court, is that those who act as Treasury counsel, representing the government in the courts, become judges.

11.2.2 Remuneration
It has already been mentioned that the remuneration of judges is a Consolidated Fund service (see 8.4.1), which means that there is no Parliamentary scrutiny of this public expenditure. The Lord Chancellor agrees judicial salaries with the Treasury taking into account the recommendations of the Senior Salaries Review Body which in turn draw upon what are considered to be suitable comparisons in the public and private sectors.

The legislation relating to judicial remuneration specifically stipulates that they may be increased but not reduced (Administration of Justice Act 1973, s. 9; Supreme Court Act 1981, s. 12). If a reduction procedure existed it could be used to infringe judicial independence.

11.2.3 Discipline and Termination
Lay magistrates are appointed to serve until they reach the compulsory retirement age of 70, unless the Lord Chancellor has removed them (Justices of the Peace Act 1979, ss. 8(2) and 6).

There is a review process for assistant recorders and recorders. An assistant recorder will be promoted or dropped after serving for three to five years. Recorders' contracts are usually for renewable periods of three years with a retiring age of 72 (Courts Act 1971, s. 21(5)). A circuit judge must retire at 72 but this appointment may be terminated for incapacity or misbehaviour (Courts Act 1971, s. 17(4)).

The arrangements relating to the tenure of the senior judiciary derive from the Act of Settlement 1700. These judges hold their offices during good behaviour but may be removed upon the presentation of an address from both Houses of Parliament (Supreme Court Act 1981, s. 11(3), in relation to High Court judges and Lords Justices of Appeal; Appellate Jurisdiction Act 1886, s. 6, in relation to law lords). They must retire at the age of 75 (Supreme Court Act 1981, s. 11(2); Judicial Pensions Act 1959, s. 2(1)). The retirement age of all of these judges was reduced to 70 upon the implementation of the Judicial Retirement and Pensions Act 1993.

A distinction should be drawn between improper judicial conduct which can be dealt with through the appellate process, and that which leads to disciplinary action. In some appeal cases the trial judge has been criticised for falling asleep and thus missing important points (*R* v *Langham* [1972] Crim LR 457), for excessive interruptions (*Jones* v *National Coal Board* [1957] 2 QB 55), and for warning a jury that unless they delivered their verdict within 10 minutes they would be locked up overnight (*R* v *McKenna* [1960] 1 QB 411).

Formal disciplinary action can follow improper conduct inside and outside the courtroom. The most severe sanction, the removal of a judge, is clearly a very serious matter. The last superior court judge to be removed by a motion in Parliament was an Irish judge, Sir Jonah Barrington in 1830. He had misappropriated money which had been paid into court. A circuit judge was removed after being convicted of smuggling in 1983. This was simply done by the Lord Chancellor.

It might be thought that a criminal conviction would be grounds for removal. However, two senior judges survived drink-driving convictions and were subsequently promoted to the House of Lords and the Court of Appeal (Brazier 1994, p. 294).

In Scotland the junior judges, the sheriffs, may be dismissed under a procedure which involves an investigation into their fitness for judicial office conducted by two of the most senior Scottish judges. This procedure is initiated by the Secretary of State for Scotland to whom the investigating judges report. Should they conclude that the sheriff is unfit, by reason of inability, misbehaviour or neglect of duty, then the minister will lay an order for the removal of the sheriff before Parliament for its approval (Sheriff Courts (Scotland) Act 1971, s. 12). This procedure was invoked in 1977 to remove a sheriff who had persisted, despite a previous warning, in involvement in political life by advocating, both orally and in print, the holding of a referendum on Scottish devolution; and also in 1992 where the reason for removal of the sheriff was inability.

Removal is the final disciplinary action. Other measures include private warnings and public rebukes. The nature of the injudicious conduct will determine the action taken by the Lord Chancellor. When a judge observed, in the course of a trial for rape, that the fact of the victim's hitchhiking by herself amounted to being contributorily negligent to her rape, his comments were repudiated by the Lord Chancellor. Judge Argyle received a severe reprimand following remarks he had made in an after-dinner speech on illegal immigrants, the effectiveness of the government's anti-crime policies and the desirability of judges being able to impose the death sentence on defendants convicted of sentences which carried a sentence longer than 15 years (see Griffith 1991, pp. 37–8).

Openly acknowledged examples of disciplining judges are not many. This may be because the conduct of judges rarely requires such action. The other, and more likely, explanation is that these matters are dealt with privately. Resignation or early retirement may be preferred by both the erring judge and the Lord Chancellor to formal removal. Certainly the Parliamentary address method is very public. There is less publicity attached to the removal of junior judges, especially when, formally, their appointments are not renewed. The case of the non-renewal of an appointment as a recorder of Mr Manus Nunan lifted the veil a little on this area. The case is confused as the parties disagreed about the reason for the decision. The official monitoring procedure in which judges were consulted was confirmed as the basis for such decisions by both the Lord Chancellor and the Attorney-General (see Brazier 1994, p. 291). It may well be that other former recorders are unhappy about the way in which their services were not renewed but, if so, they have not publicised this grievance. The point is that the disciplining of judges is generally carried out in secret by the Lord Chancellor's Department. This may be regarded as a possible threat to judicial independence especially since the Lord Chancellor is a member of the government.

11.3   EXTERNAL RELATIONSHIPS

The judiciary are involved in three relationships with outsiders: Parliament, the government and the public.

11.3.1 Parliament

There is bound to be concern that the independence of the judiciary could be impaired by criticism from MPs. The position according to the Parliamentary rule book seems to be that MPs may refer to individual judges and their decisions when speaking in a debate but that if they wish to criticise a particular judge's motives or character, this may only be done in relation to a motion which specifically criticises them or seeks their removal (Boulton (Erskine May) 1989, pp. 379–80).

Discussion is also limited because the Speaker tends to enforce quite vigorously the *sub judice* rule which prevents discussion of matters which are current or waiting to be heard in court. In criminal cases this period runs from the setting down of the charge until the verdict and, if applicable, sentence have been announced. If there is an appeal the rule applies from the announcement that a notice of appeal has been given until it has been decided. Where a civil case is involved the period runs from the setting down of the trial, or when the issue is first brought before the court, until the decision. Similarly, civil appeals are caught by the rule. If a civil case concerns a matter of national importance, such as the national economy, public order or the essentials of life, or involves the challenging of a ministerial decision on the grounds of misdirection or bad faith, then it may be raised, subject to the discretion of the Speaker, who may refuse permission if there would be prejudice (Boulton (Erskine May) 1989, pp. 377–9).

By convention ministers are required to be even more restrained. Sometimes prime ministers are tempted into discussing a case by a question in the House and on other occasions they resist such ploys (Brazier 1994, pp. 275–6). They may be less restrained in broadcast interviews (Stevens 1997, p. 275).

Insofar as the administration of justice is part of the responsibilities of the government, it is to be expected that Parliament would have some role in scrutinising it. There is some difficulty in establishing the correct balance between proper scrutiny and respecting judicial independence. We have seen (11.2.2) pressure cannot be brought by seeking to reduce judicial remuneration because legislation prevents this. This protects judicial independence but this desirable objective has been used to justify the relatively weak arrangements for the scrutiny of the administration of justice. When the reorganisation of the Commons select committees occurred in 1979, the Lord Chancellor's Department was excluded on the basis that it would be inappropriate to subject the department to this type of Parliamentary oversight. Before this, in 1967, the work of court officials employed by the Lord Chancellor's Department was excluded from the jurisdiction of the Parliamentary Commissioner for Administration, who investigates allegations of maladminstration causing injustice in central governmental agencies (see generally 15.3). A compromise was eventually agreed that the commissioner could investigate the work of these officials, unless it was carried out under the authority or direction of the judges (Courts and Legal Services Act 1990, s. 110, amending the Parliamentary Commissioner Act 1967, s. 5 and sch. 3). This change of mind was also extended to the select committees. The Procedure Select Committee report on the working of the new departmental select committees recommended that the work of the Lord Chancellor's Department be included within the system (HC 19 of 1989–90). The Government accepted this in its response to the report (Cm 1532). The remit of the Home Affairs Select Committee was amended to include the policy, administration and expenditure of the department which would also include the Attorney-General's Office, the Crown Prosecution Service, the Treasury Solicitor's Department and the Serious Fraud Office (Parliamentary Debates (Hansard), Commons, 6th ser., vol. 195, col. 579, 18 July 1991). The new remit does not include the consideration of individual cases and appointments, and neither the policy of, nor advice offered by, the law officers. It was felt that it would be inappropriate for prosecution policy to be considered as this could infringe the independence of the Director of Public Prosecutions and the Serious Fraud Office. Similar amendments were made to the terms of reference of the Scottish Affairs Select Committee.

The relationship between the judiciary and Parliament is not one which should be viewed solely from the perspective of protecting judicial independence. The judiciary do have to interpret legislation made by Parliament. It is improper for the judiciary to offer their opinions on legislation other than a technical assessment given in the course of construing a statute. It is also unbecoming for judges to offer a view in vulgar terms and when Melford Stevenson J said, in 1978, of the Sexual Offences Act 1967 that it was 'a buggers' charter', his comment was, quite rightly, deprecated by the Lord Chancellor (see Brazier 1994, p. 275).

Some of the judiciary are, of course, members of the House of Lords and therefore may play a part in the shaping of legislation. A survey of the Parliamentary activities of the law lords in the period 1952–68 concluded that generally they acted as technical legal consultants (Blom-Cooper and Drewry 1972). There were occasions when some of the law lords dealt with the merits of, and the policies behind, Bills (see Shetreet 1976, pp. 257–8, 345–7, and Griffith 1991, pp. 55–8).

An example of the expression of views on policy and Bills, some of which used extravagant language, is furnished by the reaction to the proposals which subsequently became the Courts and Legal Services Act 1990. The green papers on legal services and the legal profession were debated in the House of Lords on 7 April 1989. The proposals ending the Bar's exclusive rights of audience and a new system for licensing advocates which incorporated an advisory committee in which lay persons were in the majority drew the heaviest criticism. The Lord Chief Justice, Lord Lane, feared executive control over the judiciary, and warned that 'Oppression does not stand on the doorstep with a toothbrush moustache and a swastika armband' (Parliamentary Debates (Hansard), Lords, 5th ser., vol. 505, col. 1331, 7 April 1989). The Master of the Rolls, Lord Donaldson of Lymington, reserved the right to tell the government to 'Get your tanks off my lawn' (col. 1369). Perhaps this reaction led to some of the changes introduced in the white paper and then in the Bill. When the Bill came before the House of Lords, Lords Ackner and Donaldson made the great majority of the contributions to debate from the law lords. Their interventions were made in less colourful language but they were still unhappy with the measure (see Drewry 1991, and Griffith 1991, pp. 66–72).

11.3.2 The Government

The judiciary should be separate from the government as they will have to decide cases in which the government is one of the parties. There is a problem, however, in that whilst the judges are independent of the government, the administration of the courts and the system of justice is part of the work of the executive. The current arrangements are that inside their courtrooms the judiciary should determine issues which come before them in an impartial manner and in accordance with the law. The provision of the courts and the other resources necessary to enable them to conduct trials is made through the Lord Chancellor's Department.

Should the judges have a role in the justice system outside the courtroom? Should they become involved in setting budgets and allocating the resources of the Lord Chancellor's Department? We saw in 6.3.4 that the government is seeking to be more efficient in its administration, concerned that the public service should give value for the taxpayers' money. The Financial Management Initiative was applied to the Lord Chancellor's Department and this involved officials in determining the objectives of the department and planning to achieve them in an efficient and economical way. This process provoked concern in one of the more senior judges, who addressed the topic in 1987 in a public lecture (Browne-Wilkinson 1988). Sir Nicolas (now Lord) Browne-Wilkinson was at that time the Vice-Chancellor and he thought that the distinction between judicial and administrative functions was clearer in theory than in practice. He suggested that it was wrong for officials to set the policy objectives for the courts without consulting the judiciary. This was because the judges determine what is just, subject to legislation, and justice is not easily measured by an accountant's computer. He was of the view that the judiciary should be involved in preparing the estimates for the Lord Chancellor's Department which would then be negotiated with the Treasury by the Lord Chancellor and senior officials. The actual determination of the budget is a political decision, validated by Parliament (see 8.4). Sir Nicolas proposed that once the budget had been set the judiciary should be involved in its allocation. In addition to this he suggested that judges might also be involved in formulating legal policy. This might be done by a body of judges who could act on behalf of the judiciary and their work could be funded by the Lord Chancellor.

These suggestions appear, at first sight, to be compatible with the efficiency ideas which led to the creation of the Next Steps executive agencies, that effective management is carried out by those who are close to the operations of a unit of government. There are, however, problems with this suggestion of actively involving the judiciary in the administration of the department responsible for their work. It would remove them from their sphere, which all agree ought to be insulated from the world of politics. They would be taking down this insulation and becoming part of the hurly-burly of a government's internal politics. If they seek responsibility for what happens outside the courtroom in the justice system then they are losing their independence because they must be accountable. We have already discussed (6.4.3.3) the strain which the Next Steps agencies impose upon the traditional notion of officials accounting to ministers who account to Parliament. The judges must be responsible for their judicial decisions in the conduct of litigation and they should be consulted about proposals affecting the justice system, but for them to take responsibility for matters outside the courtroom removes their independence. The Courts Service became an executive agency in April 1995 with an official from the Lord Chancellor's Department as its chief executive.

Another area of conflict between the judiciary and the government concerns sentencing policy. The judges maintain that they must determine the appropriate sentence, and that guidance from the government could be the thin end of the wedge which would impair their independence. The Home Office, which is responsible for the prison service and which was formerly responsible for criminal legal aid and the management of the magistrates' courts, has taken the view that perhaps the judiciary might be guided towards imposing fewer custodial sentences. The British prison population is rather larger than in comparable countries and objection may be taken to this on grounds of penology and cost. Such has been the sensitivity of the judiciary in this matter that Lord Lane CJ, left a Home Office seminar on the criminal justice system when the topic of sentencing policy was raised (*The Times*, 5 February 1990). Positions were reversed during the period as Home Secretary of Mr Michael Howard, who wished to increase sentences and prescribe mandatory ones (Stevens 1997).

As Allen (1989) has indicated, proposals which have been made about sentencing have sought to offer guidance, to create a coherent sentencing policy and to set the parameters within which the judiciary may exercise their discretion as to the appropriate punishment. To maintain that this could adversely affect their independence is somewhat alarmist. It rather seems in this matter that the judiciary are seeking not only independence from, but primacy over, the government and Parliament (see Munro 1992 on the constitutional position and Ashworth 1992).

While the judiciary have successfully resisted major reform of sentencing policy, such as the creation of a sentencing council, they have lost a few battles. The Criminal Justice Act 1991 has provided a framework for sentencing rather than a coherent policy, in which the seriousness of the offence is a major factor in determining a custodial sentence.

The law lords lost another battle during the passage of the Criminal Justice Act 1991. The upper chamber carried an amendment to the Bill removing the mandatory life sentence for murder. The Commons did not accept the amendment on the basis that it was incompatible with public opinion on the appropriate punishment for this offence. When the Bill was reconsidered by the Lords they did not pursue their amendment (Ganz 1992).

11.3.2.1 Chairing inquiries Governments of all parties have called upon some of the judges to exercise their expertise in the evaluation of evidence, by chairing inquiries into important matters of public concern. Sometimes the format of the inquiry is that of a royal commission, on other occasions it may be a committee of inquiry or an enquiry created under the Tribunals of Enquiry (Evidence) Act 1921. A royal commission is usually regarded as having more prestige than a committee of inquiry. Griffith (1991, p. 47) notes that tribunals created under the 1921 statute tend now to be used to investigate matters which concern the reputation of ministers or officials.

A wide range of events and topics have been subjected to judicially chaired inquiries. There can be no exception taken to those which have dealt with technical legal matters such as defamation (Faulks 1975), or civil liability and compensation for personal injury (Lord Pearson 1978) or into fatal accidents such as the explosion on the Piper Alpha oil rig (Lord Cullen 1990). Concern may be felt when the topic of inquiry is a controversial political one, and as Griffith (1991, pp. 48–55) has pointed out, two such contentious areas are industrial relations and Northern Ireland. Inquiries into such highly charged topics as particular industrial disputes (Grunwick, Scarman 1977) or the actions of the security forces in Northern Ireland ('Bloody Sunday', Lord Widgery CJ, 1972) will never please everyone and the judges who chair them may expect criticism from those who disagree with their reports. Public debate about these matters sometimes using robust language, is desirable, but the participation of a judge exposes the judiciary as a whole to discontent and the perception that they are not impartial in these matters which may then be transferred to their decisions in the courts.

The danger of the public's loss of trust in the impartiality of the judiciary is so harmful that, even if the likelihood of it occurring is not reckoned to be great, it is a risk which should be avoided by using other eminent people to chair such inquiries (Brazier 1994, pp. 285–6). Stevens argues for the same outcome but for different reasons. He believes that the judges should forsake inquiries as they could be interpreting a Bill of Rights. The strong reaction from Conservative politicians against Sir Richard Scott's inquiry into defence equipment exports to Iraq led him to prefer a Parliamentary body to conduct such politically sensitive inquiries. Whilst I agree that the judiciary should be careful, especially in how they debate sentencing policy (indeed it may be questioned whether they should be active in the legislative work of the House of Lords), the public will not trust politicians to police themselves and so it is inevitable, if unfortunate, that judges chair inquiries (Thompson 1997, 182–9).

11.3.3 The Public
The relationship between the judiciary and the public overlaps, to a certain extent, the judiciary's relationships with Parliament and the government. The use of judges to chair inquiries into politically controversial topics runs the risk of damaging the perception that the judiciary are impartial. The behaviour of the judges both in and out of court can also lead the public to form a poor opinion of the judiciary. There was widespread outrage over the remark by a judge that a rape victim had been contributorily negligent by hitchhiking alone. At the other end of the scale some of the public may have been entertained by Judge James Pickles, whose forays into journalism and broadcasting brought him into dispute with Lord Hailsham of St Marylebone LC over the 'Kilmuir rules' which regulate public utterances by the judiciary. These 'rules' required judges to consult the Lord Chancellor upon being approached to take part in radio or television broadcasts. When Lord Mackay of Clashfern became Lord Chancellor he announced that he would leave responses to invitations to broadcast to the judges' discretion.

By and large, few serving judges have entered into public debate, presumably because they feel silence is prudent as it will preserve their independence. Naturally attention is paid when they do comment on public issues, especially when, as in their response to the Green Papers on the legal profession and legal services, they do so in extravagant terms (see 11.3.1).

The maintenance of judicial reserve runs the danger of creating too great a distance between the judiciary and the public, so that the judges are perceived as being aloof from society. Those occasions on which judges display their ignorance of matters of popular culture, such as sports and entertainment personalities, are usually given public prominence in the media and regarded as amusing. If they happened frequently they could give cause for concern that the judiciary are out of touch with the society which they serve. The middle course which the judiciary must steer should include a willingness to participate in serious educational programmes, such as the radio series in which six judges from different levels in the hierarchy discussed their work.

11.4 REGULATION OF JUDICIAL PROCEEDINGS

In this section the focus of attention is on the judge-developed law which seeks to protect the administration of justice. Just as political pressure on the judges could harm the administration of justice, this could also follow from the possibility of their being defendants in legal proceedings. Accordingly, they enjoy certain immunities from legal liability when exercising their judicial duties. They also have powers to deal with behaviour which constitutes an interference with the administration of justice.

11.4.1 Judicial Immunities
The law on the immunities enjoyed by the judiciary is somewhat confused. It does seem clear that all judges in both superior and inferior courts are immune from suits if they have acted within their jurisdiction or powers (*Sirros* v *Moore* [1975] QB 118). The situation is a little more complicated where judges have acted outside their jurisdiction. The judiciary in the superior courts, the High Court, Crown Court, Court of Appeal and House of Lords, will still retain immunity as long as they did not know that they were acting outside their jurisdiction. If magistrates act beyond their jurisdiction, whether innocently or deliberately, then, according to the House of Lords in *McC* v *Mullan* [1985] AC 528, they are not immune from suit. It is not entirely clear from this case if judges in the inferior courts are to be treated like the magistrates or their colleagues in the superior courts.

Where magistrates are successfully sued in respect of their judicial actions, they can be indemnified out of public funds providing that they acted reasonably and in good faith (Justices of the Peace Act 1979, s. 53).

Part of the immunity enjoyed by the judiciary is extended to other participants in judicial proceedings. This relates to the law of defamation so that everything said is absolutely privileged. Proceedings in Parliament also have absolute privilege and for the same reason, that it is in the public interest for participants in these proceedings to be able to speak freely, without fear of adverse consequences, even at the risk of denying a remedy for people who might thereby be defamed.

Juries also enjoy certain protections. They are not required to give reasons for their verdicts, nor may they be punished for failing to give a verdict (*Bushell's Case* (1670) Vaugh 135).

11.4.2 Contempt of Court
We saw in 7.8.3 that Parliament has a penal jurisdiction and may punish people who are adjudged to have committed a contempt of Parliament. In the courts the judges have developed common law principles of civil and criminal contempts of court. A civil contempt is disobedience to a court order, such as an injunction. Criminal contempts have greater constitutional significance and include (a) conduct in the courtroom which interrupts or impedes proceedings, (b) behaviour which scandalises the court, and (c) action which could prejudice proceedings. The last category, which involves restrictions upon media coverage of proceedings, is examined below in the context of freedom of expression (see 12.4.8).

11.4.2.1 Contempt in the face of the court This category of the law of contempt is concerned with situations which occur in the courtroom. If a witness were to refuse to answer a question, for example, a journalist declining to name the source for an article when instructed to do so by a judge, then this constitutes contempt if it is outside the scope of the statutory defence (see 12.4.8).

11.4.2.2 Scandalising the court Where criticism of a judge is regarded as scurrilous, or accusations of partiality are made, this falls within the offence of scandalising the court. The policy behind this offence is concerned with maintaining public confidence in the judiciary which could be eroded by such criticism. In *R* v *New Statesman (Editor), ex parte Director of Public Prosecutions* (1928) 44 TLR 301, criticism which alleged that certain types of people could not hope to obtain a fair trial from a particular judge, and that there were other judges like him, was held to constitute a contempt. If criticism is directed at the sentence, or the repercussions of a case, then it is more likely to be permissible (*R* v *Metropolitan Police Commissioner, ex parte Blackburn (No. 2)* [1968] 2 QB 150, held that very forceful criticisms, including some based on inaccuracies, of the Court of Appeal's decisions in a series of cases, written by Quintin Hogg QC, who became Lord Chancellor in 1970, did not amount to contempt).

11.4.2.3 Scope and procedure There is some uncertainty about which bodies may constitute a court in relation to contempt. This particularly affects administrative tribunals which decide many issues (see 15.2). The Contempt of Court Act 1981, s. 19, defines a court as 'any tribunal or body exercising the judicial power of the State'. This definition does not appear to change the decision in *Attorney-General* v *British Broadcasting Corporation* [1981] AC 303, which held that the functions of a local valuation court in determining appeals against rating valuations were administrative, and so the body was not a court (see Miller 1989, pp. 50–3).

Contempt of court is usually dealt with summarily by superior court judges. They can impose fines and a maximum of two years' imprisonment. If the contempt was in the face of the court, it may be dealt with immediately. The judge may determine that the behaviour was contempt and order that the contemnors be taken directly to prison (*Morris* v *Crown Office* [1970] 2 QB 114, in which protesters interrupted proceedings). In these circumstances the judge is accuser, judge and jury, and there is no statutory provision to ensure that the alleged contemnors can explain their actions, and that there is a delay between determining the issue of contempt and sentence. There is a general right of appeal (Administration of Justice Act 1960, s. 13).

The inferior courts and the magistrates have more limited powers to punish contemnors.

11.5 EXECUTIVE RESPONSIBILITIES

There are many aspects relating to the organisation of government which may be considered to be deficient. One such area concerns the allocation of responsibilities for legal affairs amongst ministers and their departments.

11.5.1 The Lord Chancellor

It was formerly the case that the Lord Chancellor did not have many responsibilities as a government minister. This would have been understandable if matters had been arranged so as to take account of the fact that the holder of this office was the head of the judiciary, as well as the Speaker of the House of Lords. The Lord Chancellor has an enormous amount of patronage because all judicial appointments, except to the Court of Appeal and House of Lords, are effectively made by this minister. The prime minister will consult the Lord Chancellor about filling vacancies in these most senior judicial posts. The Lord Chancellor is also involved in determining the judiciary's remuneration, their promotion, and in their disciplinary procedures, including removal.

Gradually the Lord Chancellor has gathered other responsibilities related to the operation of the courts. The county court system is managed by the Lord Chancellor's Department and it shares responsibility for the Supreme Court with the heads of the court's divisions. Responsibility for the magistrates' courts was transferred from the Home Office as from 1 April 1992 (Parliamentary Debates (Hansard), Commons, 6th ser., vol. 201, written answers, col. 250, 19 December 1991). The Lord Chancellor has overall charge for the system of legal aid which includes determining the fees which barristers and solicitors will receive under it. The distribution of legal aid is in the hands of the Legal Aid Board whose members are appointed by the Lord Chancellor (Legal Aid Act 1988). Following the Courts and Legal Services Act 1990, the Lord Chancellor will play a greater part in regulating the legal profession and allocating civil justice business between the inferior and superior courts. The appointment of people to chair or preside over administrative tribunals is also a responsibility of the Lord Chancellor.

The Law Commission, which has special responsibility for considering law reform, including codification and modernisation, is appointed by the Lord Chancellor. The Scottish Law Commission has the same remit for Scotland and is appointed by the Lord Advocate (Law Commissions Act 1965). The Commission has always been chaired by a judge and the other four Commissioners have usually been drawn from academia and practice with two academics and one representative from the two branches of the profession (see Farrar 1974, Cretney 1985, North 1985 and Zellick 1988).

Until 1992 the Lord Chancellor did not have a junior minister. The appointment of a Parliamentary Secretary now means that there is a representative of the Department in the House of Commons. The current responsibilities of the Parliamentary Secretary include legal aid and the development of legal services, some budget and resource issues, equal opportunities and women's issues (non-judicial).

11.5.2 The Home Secretary

A vast range of activities and responsibilities are allocated to the Home Office, including immigration and citizenship, national security and the fire service. In the field of legal affairs the Home Office plays a major part in the criminal law, being responsible for the prison service and overseeing the police in England and Wales. In addition, the control of dangerous drugs and firearms are administered by the Home Office and it is also concerned with the extradition of accused persons for trial in other countries.

As was mentioned above the Home Office lost its responsibilities for the magistrates' courts from 1 April 1992. The lead position which the Home Office has had in relation to the criminal justice system is also reflected in the fact that it was the Home Secretary who first appointed the Criminal Law Revision Committee in 1959.

The Home Office is also concerned with constitutional matters generally, and specifically with the protection of civil liberties, and the implementation of the Boundary Commission reports (see 7.4.1).

11.5.3 The Law Officers

The Attorney-General and the Solicitor-General are the government's legal advisers. Both of them may represent the Crown in the courts, in both important criminal and civil proceedings. The bulk of this work is conducted by barristers who act as junior counsel to the Treasury.

The Attorney is regarded as the guardian of the public interest and so has standing to appear in proceedings. This standing may be 'extended' to other litigants by means of a relator action (see 17.3.4).

Certain criminal prosecutions may only be commenced if the Attorney has authorised them, for example, official secrets. The Attorney also has the power to stop prosecutions by entering a *nolle prosequi*. In exercising these powers the Attorney is supposed to act without regard to party political considerations. Yet the Attorney is a politician as well as a lawyer and there is a tension between the two roles which it is argued was apparent in the way Sir Nicholas Lyell acted over public interest immunity in the Matrix Churchill affair, which led to Sir Richard Scott's inquiry (Woodhouse 1997a).

The Attorney has responsibility for steering some legal and fiscal measures through the Commons and oversees the work of the Parliamentary counsel who draft legislation for England and Wales.

The Scottish law officers are the Lord Advocate and the Solicitor-General and they have similar responsibilities to their counterparts south of the border.

11.5.4 The Director of Public Prosecutions

The Director of Public Prosecutions is appointed by the Home Secretary but is supervised by the Attorney. The Director of Public Prosecutions is in charge of the Crown Prosecution Service, which is the agency responsible for conducting the vast majority of criminal prosecutions in England and Wales. The service was established by the Prosecution of Offences Act 1985. Before this most prosecutions had been initiated by the police. The Royal Commission on Criminal Procedure had suggested that there should be a separation between the investigation and prosecution of crime. The police still investigate crime and decide to institute prosecutions but it is the Crown Prosecution Service which conducts prosecutions or decides to discontinue them.

The Crown Prosecution Service has a decentralised organisation so that there are various regional units in England and Wales, each of which is headed by a Chief Crown Prosecutor.

11.6 REFORM

The two major proposals for reform in this area concern the judiciary and the allocation of responsibility for legal affairs within government.

11.6.1 The Judiciary

The principal failing of the arrangements relating to the judiciary is the concentration of power in the Lord Chancellor. The Lord Chancellor may be a judge, but, more importantly, he is a minister and therefore the appointment and promotion of all judges, as well as the discipline of the great bulk of the judiciary is susceptible to political patronage.

This is, of course, a very obvious matter, but it is only relatively recently that political parties have decided that this threat to judicial independence should be removed. In the past Labour (1989, 1990) and the Liberal Democrats (1990), proposed commissions which would be responsible for judicial appointments. Their ideas have not been fleshed out whereas the academic and legal communities have put forward more detailed proposals (Institute for Public Policy Research 1991, arts. 102–13 and pp. 80–2, 93–107; Brazier 1991, 152–62; Justice 1992). These three sets of proposals are broadly similar. The major difference amongst them is that the Justice proposals are concerned solely with the judiciary and assume current court structures, whereas the IPPR has proposed a federal-type constitution for the UK which means that there are national and regional aspects to its scheme.

Under these proposals the appointment and disciplining of the judiciary would be the responsibility of specially created bodies comprising both senior judges and lay people. All of these proposals seek the widening of the composition of the judiciary so as to include more women and members of minority ethnic groups. Justice suggests that the qualities and skills required of judges at different levels should be drawn up. This material would then form the basis for the job descriptions of the various judicial appointments which would be advertised. The appointment process would be managed by the Judicial Commission which would have recourse to appropriate tests and interviews, moving away from the present emphasis on experience in advocacy. A report on judicial appointments by the Home Affairs Committee when it had a Conservative majority rejected calls for a commission (HC 52 of 1995–96). The Conservative government agreed (Cm 3387) but the new Lord Chancellor, Lord Irvine of Lairg, has indicated that such a commission will be considered (Parliamentary Debates (Hansard) Lords vol. 580, written answers, col. 145, 23 June 1997.)

Complaints about judges would, in the IPPR plan, be referred to another body, a judicial conduct tribunal; Brazier's judicial service commission and Justice's judicial commission (through a judicial standards committee) would handle this matter. If removal of senior judges was proposed then an order would be laid before Parliament. The difference from current arrangements is that the investigation of all complaints against the judiciary would not be carried out by a minister.

Arrangements for the lower judiciary would be made on a similar basis. There would be regional committees of the English commission in the IPPR plans and Brazier proposes that each of the English and Welsh circuits would have a judicial committee. Again removal of these judges would follow an investigation by the committee.

A new final appellate court, the supreme court, is also suggested in the IPPR and Brazier blueprints. This court would be like the Supreme Court in other common law countries such as Ireland, Canada and the USA. Its members would not also be part of the legislature. Their only duties would be judicial. In the IPPR scheme, the federal constitution would ensure that the supreme court's role was that of a constitutional court. The UK's three jurisdictions of England and Wales, Scotland and Northern Ireland would each have its own court of appeal. Appeals from those courts to the supreme court would only occur in a private law case if it involved an issue of importance for the whole of the UK. The method of appointment to the supreme court is also different from the arrangements for the other courts. Brazier's judicial service commission would still choose candidates but they would be subjected to a confirmation process which would involve an examination by a joint select committee of the two Houses of Parliament. This system is clearly modelled on that of the USA. Brazier argues that the select committee's examination would not mean political interference in the judicial selection process. Once confirmed the judges would be independent and removable only by the two-stage process of the judicial service commission investigation and Parliamentary address. The select committee's examination would allow Parliament and the public to learn something of the attitudes and beliefs of the judges who would be deciding very important cases, which would include civil liberties.

The IPPR proposes a special UK judicial appointments commission which would be composed of representatives from the various judicial service commissions for the UK. The pool of candidates for positions in this court would comprise judges from the superior courts of the UK and people who are outstanding in the practice and teaching of law.

Another IPPR proposal is that the judges should form a judicial council in each of the UK's jurisdictions, which would be composed of judges from all levels in the hierarchy. The role of these councils would be to offer advice to the relevant executive, on the policy for the administration and provision of resources for court services, and also on the administration of justice.

11.6.2 Executive Responsibilities

The muddled allocation of executive responsibility for legal affairs has changed but it has not led to the creation of a single department which Brazier (1991, pp. 143–52) has spelt out in detail.

Since Brazier wrote his proposals the following changes have been implemented: (a) a junior minister has been appointed to represent the Lord Chancellor in the Commons; (b) the Lord Chancellor's Department has taken over responsibility for the operation of the magistrates' courts; and (c) the policy, administration and finances of the Lord Chancellor's Department have been included within the terms of reference of the Home Affairs Select Committee. As Drewry (1992) has remarked, this department is gradually becoming the single ministry of justice which some want.

Brazier would like to see a department of law take responsibility for (a) civil rights, legal services, legal aid and relations with the professions; (b) the reform of civil and criminal law; (c) constitutional development; (d) the provision, administration and procedure of all courts and tribunals; and (e) determination of judicial remuneration. The department's minister would be in the Commons and the post of Lord Chancellor would be abolished. In addition to the tasks already outlined, this department could take over responsibility for overseeing the form of legislation as well as checking it for comprehensibility. This would relieve the law officers and the cabinet's legislation committee.

Brazier's reallocation of responsibilities is very sensible. Currently the Home Office has an incoherent remit with its major role in the criminal justice system including police and prisons as well as internal security on the one hand, and on the other hand its oversight of constitutional matters including civil liberties. Is it really likely that reforms in civil liberties, or the introduction of freedom of information, will be championed by the department so concerned with the police and the security service?

While the incorporation of the Lord Chancellor's Department into the work of the Home Affairs Select Committee is to be welcomed, a better solution would be a new ministry with its own select committee.

The aim of all these reforms is to improve judicial independence and to stop it from being used as an impediment to the proper accountability of the justice system.

PART III
CIVIL LIBERTIES

In this part the law on civil liberties will be examined. As this is rather a large area only part of it will be discussed. The selection will take two broad areas which illustrate some important aspects of the freedom of individuals. In the first of these areas the British approach to civil liberties will be outlined and then some of the detail of the law relating to freedom of association, assembly and expression will be explored. These particular topics have been chosen because they go to the heart of a democratic society. One may be able to judge the health of a country's democracy by inspecting the freedom which its citizens have to demonstrate and protest about important and trivial issues. The law on public order and freedom of speech may therefore be categorised as part of the law relating to the political process, as politics is not just conducted in the chambers and committee rooms of the Houses of Parliament and local authorities. Political discussion and argument can take place on the streets in rallies and processions, in meetings, through the press, and over the television and radio airwaves.

Just as there is a European dimension to the UK's constitutional arrangements through membership of the European Communities, so there is with civil liberties. The UK is a member of the Council of Europe, which is a larger and older organisation of European States than the European Communities. Through the Council of Europe, the European Convention on Human Rights and Fundamental Freedoms (ECHR) was drawn up. The UK signed and ratified this international treaty and citizens of the UK may petition the machinery established under the convention where they believe that they have been victims of breaches of the rights that it guarantees. The approach taken to rights under the ECHR will be examined by focusing on freedom of expression. Finally a comparison between the British and ECHR approaches will be used in considering the issue of a British Bill of Rights achieved through incorporating the ECHR.

In chapter 13 the law relating to arrest, search and seizure, and detention by the police will be outlined. The police have been given the task of dealing with crime, however, the powers which they have and the manner in which they are exercised may encroach upon the citizen's civil liberties. The police are more than 'citizens in uniform' and the chapter will also deal with the arrangements for the funding and overseeing of the police and the machinery for investigating complaints against the police.

CHAPTER TWELVE

Freedom of Association, Assembly and Expression

12.1 THE BRITISH APPROACH TO CIVIL LIBERTIES

In most countries which have a document which is their constitution, there will be a section which will declare the rights enjoyed by the citizens. In the US Constitution the first 10 amendments are known as the Bill of Rights. The first amendment stipulates that the Congress shall pass no law either establishing a particular religion or interfering with the exercise of religion, or abridging the freedoms of speech, the press, peaceful assembly or the right of the people to petition Congress about their grievances.

The UK does not have a constitutional document and therefore no statement of general principle guaranteeing such rights. Dicey wrote, somewhat patronisingly: 'Now, most foreign constitution-makers have begun with declarations of rights. For this they have often been in no wise to blame.'(Dicey 1959, p. 198.) If there are no general declarations of rights, do British citizens enjoy any rights? They do because the approach of British law is to permit something to be done unless there is a legally valid restriction upon it. Thus citizens' rights in the UK may be said to be residual or to consist of what is left after taking into account the lawful limitations. In British law, freedom of speech means that you may say those things which are not prohibited by law. The rights which the citizens have derive from the decisions of the courts in which they found that there was no legitimate bar to what the citizens wanted to do. This approach is the opposite of that where constitutions declare rights. We might contrast the two approaches by saying that in this country we move from the particular to the general, that we induce generalisations about freedom from the various court decisions and legislation, whereas in other countries they move from the general to the particular and deduce the individual right from the broad declaration of principle.

Crucial to both approaches is the availability of a remedy. A declaration of rights will be ineffectual without the provision of machinery for the protection of those rights. In the UK a court may remedy any unlawful encroachments upon a citizen's liberty. Dicey felt that where rights resulted from judge-made law they were more secure than where they derived from a constitutional guarantee. This is debatable but what is true is the importance of remedies to enforce both the judge-made and legislative rights in the UK. This is reflected in the Latin phrase *ubi ius, ibi remedium* which, freely translated, means, where there is a remedy there is a right, and seems to give priority to remedies. While a right may be useless without a means of enforcing it, a remedy will not be of assistance unless there is a right, whether it be in a constitutional declaration or case law.

12.2 FREEDOM OF ASSOCIATION

If a country is truly a democratic one then the freedom to associate with others should be one which is subject to few restrictions. The justification for banning associations must be that they are dangerous. This is the reason behind the proscription of the Irish Republican Army and the Irish National Liberation Army under the Prevention of Terrorism (Temporary Provisions) Act 1989, s. 1 and sch. 1. Because members of these groups engage in acts of terrorism it is an offence to belong to one of them, to solicit or invite support for them, or to arrange or assist in the arrangement of a meeting of three or more persons, knowing that the meeting is to support or further the activities of a proscribed organisation, or will be addressed by a person who belongs to or professes to belong to a proscribed organisation (s. 2(1)). It is also an offence for a person to dress or to display an article in a public place in such a way as to arouse the reasonable apprehension that the person is a member of a proscribed organisation (s. 3; see *Q'Moran* v *Director of Public Prosecutions* [1975] QB 864 for the prosecution of people attending a funeral wearing dark glasses and berets under the Public Order Act 1936, s. 1). Under the Prevention of Terrorism (Temporary Provisions) Act 1989, Part III, various offences are created which involve the soliciting of money, or other property for, or giving money or property to, a proscribed organisation, or as contributions towards acts of terrorism.

In Northern Ireland the Northern Ireland (Emergency Provisions) Act 1996, s. 30 and sch. 2 proscribe the IRA, INLA, and the Irish People's Liberation Organisation, Cumann na mBan, Fianna na hEireann, Saor Eire (republican groups); and the Red Hand Commando, the Ulster Freedom Fighters, the Ulster Volunteer Force and the Ulster Defence Association (loyalist groups). In relation to these organisations it is an offence (a) to be a member; (b) to solicit or invite financial or other support; (c) to solicit or invite membership or to carry out tasks on their behalf.

Prohibition of organisations did not occur for the first time with the current Irish terrorist campaign which began in the 1970s. The British Union of Fascists or the 'Blackshirts' caused problems by, amongst other things, conducting provocative marches in the East End of London. Under the

Public Order Act 1936, s. 2, it is an offence to participate in the control, management, organisation or training of a body which is organised, or trained or equipped for the purpose of enabling it to usurp the functions of the police or the armed forces; or organised, trained, or equipped for the use or display of force in promoting any political object.

12.3 FREEDOM OF ASSEMBLY

Gatherings of people, either in public meetings, or in marches, may lead to problems of public order. Lord Scarman in his report on the disorders in Red Lion Square discussed the relationship between public protest and public order.

> A balance has to be struck, a compromise found that will accommodate the exercise of the right to protest within a framework of public order which enables ordinary citizens, who are not protesting, to go about their business and pleasure without obstruction or inconvenience. The fact that those who at any one time are concerned to secure the tranquility of the streets are likely to be the majority must not lead us to deny the protesters their opportunity to march: the fact that the protesters are desperately sincere and are exercising a fundamental human right must not lead us to overlook the rights of the majority. (Scarman 1975, para. 5.)

Lord Scarman's designation of peaceful assembly and public protest as fundamental human rights does not accurately reflect the law in the UK. There is no general right to hold open-air meetings in public places, which does not mean that every such meeting is unlawful. Meetings in Trafalgar Square must be authorised by the Secretary of State for the Environment (Trafalgar Square Regulations 1952, reg. 3). Over a hundred local authorities have passed by-laws which require that they be notified in advance of any march.

Decisions about what constitutes a threat to public order are made by the police and various additional powers have been conferred upon them by the Public Order Act 1986. This legislation followed a review of public order law. There had been a series of public order problems, particularly the confrontations between rival processions organised by the National Front and anti-fascist groups in the 1970s, which included the disorders in Red Lion Square, and mass pickets during the 1980s at Warrington, Wapping and in the course of the miners' strike. These events raise difficult problems for the police, some calling for judgments to be made very quickly during a march or meeting. How is the balance, which Lord Scarman mentioned, to be drawn between group A, who wish to conduct peaceful meetings or marches, and group B, who are prepared to resort to violence in their opposition to group A? Two cases illustrate the different approaches to this type of situation. In *Beatty* v *Gillbanks* (1882) 9 QBD 308, members of the Salvation Army had organised processions in Weston-super-Mare which provoked violent opposition from a group known as the 'Skeleton Army'. During these incidents none of the

Salvationists committed any violent acts. They disobeyed police instructions to cease marching following an order by the justices prohibiting unlawful assemblies. They were convicted and then appealed to the Divisional Court by way of a case stated. The appeal was successful as the court considered that, in effect, the Salvationists were being punished for acting lawfully if they knew in doing so that others would be induced to act unlawfully, and that there was no authority for such a punishment.

Contrast that case with *Duncan* v *Jones* [1936] 1 KB 218, where a speaker addressed a crowd from a box on the highway and the police feared a breach of peace. The arrest of the speaker for wilful obstruction, by refusing to stop speaking was upheld because this speaker had had a rough reception when speaking a year previously, and the police feared a repetition. This decision weighs the balance between freedom of speech and prevention of disorder too heavily in favour of the latter. It is also remarkable for the views expressed by Lord Hewart CJ. He denied that the case was about the freedom of assembly and that *Beatty* v *Gillbanks* was relevant. He said (at p. 222) that:

> If I thought that the present case raised a question . . . namely, whether an assembly can properly be held to be unlawful merely because the holding of it is expected to give rise to a breach of the peace on the part of persons opposed to those who are holding the meeting – I should wish to hear more argument before I expressed an opinion. This case, however, does not even touch that important question.

It is suggested that the case did touch that important question and that instead of restraining people from lawfully exercising their freedoms because of possible disorderly opposition, the law's approach ought to be that outlined by O'Brien J in another case involving the Salvation Army (*R* v *Justices of Londonderry* (1891) 28 LR Ir 440). He said at p. 450:

> If danger arises from the exercise of lawful rights resulting in a breach of the peace, the remedy is the presence of sufficient force to prevent that result, not the legal condemnation of those who exercise those rights.

12.3.1 Processions

New national powers to control processions were introduced by the Public Order Act 1986. Unless it is not reasonably practicable to do so, advance notice is required in respect of a procession intended to demonstrate support for, or opposition to, the views or actions of a person or body of persons, to publicise a cause or to commemorate an event (Public Order Act 1986, s. 11(1)). If the procession is customarily held in an area then notification is not required. The notice must state the date, starting time and proposed route of the procession, as well as the name and address of an organiser (s. 11(3)). The notice may either be posted to the police, by registered post, at least six days before it is proposed to hold the procession, or delivered by hand six days in advance or as soon as is reasonably practicable. The notification requirement assists the police to exercise their power of imposing conditions on processions (s. 12). The conditions may be imposed prior to, or during the procession. The basis for the imposition of conditions is that the police reasonably believe that the procession may result in serious public disorder, serious property damage or serious disruption to the life of the community, or that the organisers' intention is to intimidate others. The conditions will be such as appear necessary to a senior police officer to prevent disorder, damage, disruption or intimidation and they may include directions as to the route and prohibit the procession from entering a particular public place. Only the chief officer of police may impose conditions on a procession intended to be held and those conditions must be given in writing. Where it is decided to impose conditions during a procession, the senior police officer at the scene may exercise the power.

If the chief officer of police feels that the use of s. 12 powers will be insufficient to prevent serious public disorder resulting from processions, then an application may be made seeking the prohibition of all, or a specified class of processions in an area for a maximum period of three months (s. 13(1)). The chief officer will make the application to the district council which may make the order with the consent of the Home Secretary. In the City of London or the Metropolitan Police District, their Commissioners of Police may make the order with the consent of the Home Secretary. In all cases the prohibition order may be in the terms of the application or as modified by the Home Secretary.

The only way of challenging the police's directions as to processions is by submitting them to judicial review. This, therefore, gives the police a very great power because of the width of the circumstances which may trigger the directions. How serious must the public disorder, or property damage, or disruption to the life of the community be, before the police may impose conditions? What is serious disruption to the life of the community? In the white paper which preceded the 1986 statute an example given of disruption was that of marches held on Saturdays in shopping centres (Home Office 1985, para. 27). Does this kind of inconvenience to the majority justify restricting a minority who wish to protest peacefully? Should those who wish to have provocative marches be restrained because of the concern about the public order consequences of opposition to such marches? The power to ban all marches in a locality for up to three months is very sweeping preventative action. It would seem to indicate that the legal framework prefers the preservation of public order to the protection of protest.

12.3.2 Meetings

There is, in general, no right to hold a meeting, as permission may be refused by the owner of the meeting-place even where a meeting is planned to be held in a publicly owned building. The exception to this is where the meeting is part of a candidate's election campaign and is to be held in a school maintained by the local education authority, or in other publicly owned rooms (Representation of the People Act 1983, ss. 95, 96 and sch. 5).

If a meeting is advertised as being a public one but is to be held in a private building then permission to attend the meeting may be withdrawn and thus a person who does not leave might commit the tort of trespass. It seems that, following *Thomas* v *Sawkins* [1935] 2 KB 249, the police may insist upon being present at such a public meeting on private premises, despite the objections of the promoters of the meeting and the absence of a warrant, where they reasonably apprehend a breach of the peace.

The offence of obstruction of the highway may be committed where the passage and repassage of the highway has been interfered with by a stationary meeting (Highways Act 1980, s. 137). A meeting held without permission on land which is in private ownership would be a trespass. Not every stoppage on the highway will constitute an obstruction. The extent to which stoppages will be considered ancillary to passage is unclear. In *Hubbard* v *Pitt* [1976] QB 142, a majority of the Court of Appeal granted the owner of a section of the highway an interlocutory injunction to stop demonstrators who were picketing his estate agency offices and distributing leaflets in a protest about the way in which he conducted his business. This decision, from which Lord Denning MR dissented powerfully, was reached despite the fact that the police had no objection and no obstruction was caused.

Under the Public Order Act 1986, s. 14, the holding of an assembly of 20 people or more may be subjected to conditions by the police. These powers may be exercised where the police reasonably believe that their directions will help prevent serious public disorder, or serious damage to property, or serious disruption to the life of the community, or deliberate intimidation. The directions can stipulate the location of the assembly, as well as its duration and the number of persons permitted to attend it. Non-compliance with any such directions will be an offence unless the failure to comply can be shown to be outside the defendant's control.

This provision is mainly concerned with a mass picket. Ordinarily an employee or a trade union official may wait at a place of work and, in furtherance of a trade dispute, may obtain or communicate information or peacefully persuade a person to work or refrain from working (Employment Act 1980, s. 16). The police may also prevent people from joining a mass picket because they fear that a breach of the peace will occur. During the miners' strike of 1984–5 the police requested vehicles containing people who wished to join pickets at collieries to turn back. The action of the police in arresting those who ignored this request for obstruction of the police in the execution of their duty was upheld in *Moss* v *McLachlan* [1985] IRLR 76. In this case there had been violence at some nearby collieries and it was accepted by the court that there was a real possibility of immediate and imminent violence, and so the police could exercise their common law power to prevent a breach of the peace. It is less clear that imminence and immediacy of a threat to the peace were present so as to justify the police in turning back intending pickets at the Dartford tunnel, who were at least one hundred miles away from their destination.

As we shall see there are now statutory powers to stop and direct persons not to proceed towards certain types of gatherings.

12.3.3 Trespass and Nuisance

The Criminal Justice and Public Order Act 1994 (CJPOA 1994) is a statute which, in its public order provisions, seems to have arisen from concerns about very particular problems, such as raves, new age travellers, protests by anti-roads campaigners and anti-hunt saboteurs (see Allen and Cooper 1995).

12.3.3.1 Unauthorised camping In order to deal with new age travellers who trespass upon land, the police have been given a power of directing such people to move on (CJPOA 1994, s. 61). The preconditions for the exercise of this power are that the senior police officer at the scene reasonably believes that there are two or more persons trespassing, who have the common purpose of residing on the land, and that reasonable steps have been taken by the occupier to require them to leave, and they have six or more vehicles on the land, or that they have caused damage to the land or to property on the land; or they have used threatening, insulting or abusive words or behaviour towards the occupier or members of the occupier's family, or the employees or agents of the occupier.

The net is wider than the new age travellers who have been in the news over the past few summers, because the duties placed upon local authorities to provide sites for gypsies in the Caravan Sites Act 1968 have been removed, and so gypsies on unauthorised sites could be subjected to this direction.

12.3.3.2 Aggravated trespass If people are trespassing upon land in the open air then they will be guilty of an offence if they do anything: (a) to intimidate others from engaging in a lawful activity, or (b) to obstruct, or (c) to disrupt that lawful activity on that land, or adjoining land (CJPOA 1994, s. 68). This seems to be directed primarily at hunt saboteurs and anti-roads protestors. Subsequent to its enactment there has been a dramatic rise in the number of animal rights protestors, who include people not previously associated with public protest and who have raised the general issue about restrictions on protestors.

As with other provisions in the CJPOA 1994, the drafting seems to have elements of being too wide, as well as allowing for exceptions. Thus it is unclear whether adjoining land includes land separated by a road or a river. If in the course of a hunt, the hunters trespassed then this could provide a defence for hunt saboteurs.

There is a police power to direct people to leave where the senior police officer present reasonably believes that people have committed, are commit-ting, or intend to commit aggravated trespass, or there are two or more trespassers on land and they intend to intimidate persons into ceasing to carry on a lawful activity, or to obstruct or disrupt a lawful activity on the land (s. 69(1)).

12.3.3.3 Trespassory assemblies New powers are inserted into the Public Order Act 1986 which permit the banning of trespassory assemblies (ss. 14A, 14B and 14C). The powers are not unlike those which deal with processions (see 12.2.2). The chief officer of a police force may make an application to the district council in England (outside London), Scotland and Wales, or to the Home Secretary within London, for a prohibition order. The basis for the application is that the officer reasonably believes that it is intended to hold an assembly (of 20 or more persons) in the district on land to which the public has no right of access, or only a limited right of access, and it is likely to be held without permission of the occupier, or to be conducted so as to exceed the limits of the occupier's permission, or the limits of the public's right of access, and may result in serious disruption to the life of the community, or significant damage may be done to the land or to a building or monument on it, which is of architectural, historical, archaeological or scientific importance. Although the application (outside London) is made to the district council, the Home Secretary in England, and the Welsh Secretary in Wales, must consent to the order and any modifications which the council proposes. Scottish councils, however, determine the application without ministerial involvement. The order is limited to a radius of five miles from the anticipated location of the assembly, and to a maximum of four days.

Within an area to which a prohibition order applies, a police officer in uniform who reasonably believes that a person is proceeding towards an assembly in that area, and also believes on reasonable grounds that the assembly is prohibited by the order, may stop such a person and instruct the person not to proceed in the direction of the assembly (s. 14C).

Stonehenge would seem to be one of the sites contemplated by these provisions on trespassory assemblies, but it is not clear what 'significant damage' is, or 'serious disruption to the life of the community' (see 12.3.1). In *R v Chief Constable of Wiltshire, ex parte Arthur Pendragon* (unreported; Klug, Starmer, Weir 1996, p. 197) a prohibition order was granted at Stonehenge. The challenge to this order by King Arthur, who was head of the Glastonbury druids, failed. Thus he and fellow druids could not conduct a ceremony on the grass verge as this would constitute a trespassory assembly. The police had no objection to King Arthur and his colleagues but their concern about, and steps taken by, others adversely affected these 'innocent' druids.

12.3.3.4 Raves Although it is apparent from headings in the CJPOA 1994 that certain powers are directed at raves, this term does not appear in the text of these provisions. Instead reference is made to:

gatherings on land or in the open air of 100 or more persons (whether or not trespassers) at which amplified music is played during the night (with or without intermissions) and is such as, by reason of its loudness and duration and the time at which it is played, is likely to cause serious distress to the inhabitants of the locality (s. 63(1)).

There are further definitions in s. 63(1):

(a)   such a gathering continues during intermissions in the music and, where the gathering extends over several days, throughout the period during which amplified music is played at night (with or without intermissions); and

(b) 'music' includes sounds wholly or predominantly characterised by the emission of a succession of repetitive beats.

And, by s. 63(10):

'land in the open air' includes a place partly open to the air.

Again this does not show off drafting skills, rather the confused thinking which the text is supposed to communicate. What is the problem with raves? Is it noise, which explains the requirements of land in, or partly open to the air, and the likelihood of distress caused to inhabitants in the locality? In which case why specify a minimum number of 100 persons? Perhaps it is felt that the number of those attending is important as it will raise problems of public order other than the amplification of sound wholly or predominantly characterised by the emission of a succession of repetitive beats.

The requirement of 100 persons also affects the preventative powers in ss. 63(2) and 65. The former provision deals with people who are preparing for, or waiting for, such a gathering and provides that such persons may be asked by a police superintendent to leave the land taking their property and vehicles. The latter provision permits an officer in uniform to instruct people who are reasonably believed to be proceeding towards a gathering, to which a s. 63(2) direction is in force, to be stopped and directed not to proceed in the direction of the gathering. These powers depend upon the officers having a reasonable belief that the gathering will have the 100 persons.

12.3.4 Offences

The Public Order Act 1986 and CJPOA 1994 have created a series of offences. Organisers of processions will have committed offences if they have not complied with the notification requirements, or if the procession differs from the details in the notice (s. 11(7)). There is a defence that matters were beyond the defendant's control or that the deviations from the notice resulted from an agreement with a police officer.

The organiser of a procession and a participant commit an offence if they knowingly fail to comply with a condition (s. 12(4), (5)), or if they organise or participate in a procession which is the subject of a prohibition order (s. 13(7), (8)). Again there is a defence of circumstances being beyond the defendant's control. It will also be an offence to incite people to breach a condition or to participate in a prohibited procession (ss. 12(6), 13(9)). On conviction for non-compliance with conditions, or a prohibition order, the organiser and any person who incites others to commit these offences will be liable to a maximum of three months' imprisonment and a £2,500 fine, and a participant to a £1,000 fine. A maximum fine of £1,000 may be levied on participants in processions which were prohibited, or which did not comply with conditions, and on organisers who do not satisfy the notification requirements.

The CJPOA 1994 creates offences of not complying with directions or prohibition notices. If trespassing campers do not comply with the direction to leave within a reasonably practicable time, or leave but return as a trespasser within three months, this is an offence punishable with up to three months' imprisonment or a £2,500 fine or both (s. 61(4)).

The offence of aggravated trespass (s. 68(1)) was mentioned in 12.3.3.2. The punishment on conviction for this is a maximum of three months' imprisonment or a £2,500 fine (s. 68(3)). Where an officer gives a direction to leave land because of a reasonable belief that the offence of aggravated trespass has been committed, is being committed or is intended to be committed, then failure to leave the land as soon as practicable, or leaving but returning as a trespasser within three months, is an offence punishable with up to three months' imprisonment and/or a £2,500 fine (s. 69(3)).

Where directions to leave have been issued to persons who are preparing for, or waiting for, or attending a rave, then if they do not leave within a reasonably practicable time, or leave but return within seven days, then upon conviction a maximum of three months' imprisonment or a £2,500 fine or both may be imposed (s. 63(6)). If a person disregards a direction not to proceed to a rave then this offence may be punished by a fine not exceeding £1,000 (s. 65(4)).

The amendments made to the Public Order Act 1986 in respect of trespassory assemblies follow the format of the offences in relation to processions. Thus to organise a trespassory assembly in defiance of a prohibition is an offence which can lead to up to three months' imprisonment and/or a maximum fine of £2,500 (s. 14B(1) and (5)). The same punishment applies to the offence of inciting a person to participate in a trespassory assembly (s. 14B(3) and (7)). A fine of up to £1,000 is the penalty for both participating in a trespassory assembly (s. 14B(2) and (6)) and for disregarding a direction not to proceed in the direction of one (s. 14C(3) and (5)).

The common law offences of riot, unlawful assembly, and affray have been abolished and replaced with new statutory offences of riot, violent disorder and affray. The offence of riot (s. 1) is committed where a person actually uses violence while being part of a group of 12 people who threaten or use violence for a common purpose, and where any person of reasonable firmness at the scene is caused to fear for his or her personal safety. Violence is defined as violent conduct including violence towards property. If the accused does not intend to use violence the *mens rea* includes an awareness on the part of the accused that his or her conduct may be violent. It is not required that any person actually be at the scene. The seriousness of this offence is reflected in the fact that the Director of Public Prosecution's consent is required for a prosecution and that the maximum sentence is 10 years' imprisonment and a fine.

The offence of violent disorder (s. 2) shares with riot the requirements that a group of people must be together and that they threaten or use violence so that a person of reasonable firmness fears for his or her personal safety. Here the group must number a minimum of three, and the accused must use or threaten violence.

To commit affray (s. 3), a person must use violence towards another, causing a person of reasonable firmness to fear for his or her personal safety.

A threat of violence cannot be constituted by words alone. Both affray and violent disorder are triable either way. On indictment the maximum sentences are five years' imprisonment and a fine for violent disorder, three years' imprisonment and a fine for affray. Where tried summarily the maximum sentences are six months' imprisonment and a £5,000 fine for violent disorder, three months' imprisonment and a £5,000 fine for affray.

12.4 FREEDOM OF EXPRESSION

There are various ways of approaching an examination of the permitted restraints upon expression. One might focus upon the different media, the press, the stage, or one might pay attention to the various categories of restraints such as those relating to morality, which include blasphemy and obscenity. A mixture of these approaches will be used.

12.4.1 Prior Restraint

Whilst Blackstone thought that the freedom of the press 'consists in laying no *previous* restraints upon publications, and not in freedom from censure for criminal matter when published' (Blackstone 1825, p. 151), both prior restraints and subsequent sanctions may restrict freedom of expression in the UK. In the USA the judges prefer Blackstone's antipathy towards prior restraint of speech (Barendt 1985, p. 115). Since licensing and, therefore, censorship of the press stopped in 1694, censorship in the UK has focused mainly upon performances in the theatre, on the cinema screen and over the airwaves. The Theatres Act 1968 abolished censorship of plays on the stage leaving censorship of films and videos and the licensing of broadcasting. Prior restraint may also be achieved through the seeking of injunctions to prevent expression of something which could be sanctioned after publication as, for example, where X becomes aware that Y is planning to say something which could be a breach of confidence which Y owes to X. We may further note that some prior restraints are extra-legal, such as the operation of the D notice system in relation to defence and national security matters. The Defence, Press and Broadcasting Committee, which is composed of officials and journalists, operates informally giving guidance on what may be published or broadcast without prejudicing the State's defence or national security. The issue of a D notice to editors on a topic indicates possible prejudice. Some editors would consult the committee about possible articles and usually its 'approval' was taken to imply that the material could be disclosed. This informal committee's decisions do not always confer official immunity. The BBC discussed a planned radio series *My Country Right or Wrong*, which included interviews with former intelligence service employees, with the committee's secretary who did not object to it. Yet the Attorney-General secured an injunction to prevent its planned transmission. The series was subsequently broadcast unamended.

12.4.2 Film and Video

In the early days of the film industry it was found that the licensing powers of local authorities in respect of cinemas were being used to prevent the exhibition of some films. This came as a surprise because the idea behind the legislation which established cinema licensing had been safety. The film industry in collaboration with the Home Office decided that a voluntary body might issue certificates for films indicating the audience for which they would be suitable. The British Board of Film Censors (BBFC) was established in 1912 and it won acceptance for its decisions so that it became a common condition in cinema licences that films which did not have a BBFC certificate could not be shown without the licensing authority's express consent. This condition was upheld in *Mills* v *London County Council* [1925] 1 KB 213. It had been made clear in *Ellis* v *Dubowski* [1921] 3 KB 621, that the licensing authority could not fetter its discretion by following automatically the BBFC's decisions. In practice everyone complies to a very high degree with the BBFC's decisions despite their lack of statutory authority. The granting of a certificate does not mean that a film will not be banned by a local authority and the absence of a certificate does not mean that a film cannot be shown. Sometimes film-makers will be upset about the particular certificate given to a film as that can affect the potential size of the audiences which may see the film and therefore profits, or they may complain that cuts requested by the BBFC impair a film's artistic integrity.

In 1984 the BBFC changed its name to the British Board of Film Classification and was given a statutory responsibility under the Video Recordings Act of that year. The BBFC is required to classify all video works which are available for sale or hire, with the exception of those which are educational, or concerned with music, sport or religion. However, the exemption from classification does not apply if the work depicts to a significant extent human sexual activity, including associated acts of force; mutilation or torture or acts of gross violence towards humans or animals; or techniques likely to be useful in the commission of offences. Nor can exemption be claimed if the work depicts to any significant extent criminal activity which is likely to any significant extent to stimulate or encourage the commission of offences. It is an offence under the Video Recordings Act 1984 to supply an unclassified video outside the terms of the statute. The genesis of the legislation lay in concern about some so-called 'video nasties' which could be viewed at home by children. Thus the classification system for videos pays attention to their suitability for viewing at home. This does not mean videos which adults might watch at home cannot be classified because of the risk that a child might evade parental supervision and see an unsuitable work.

Originally the statute did not stipulate criteria which the BBFC was to take into account. The CJPOA 1994 inserts a new s. 4A into the 1984 statute which requires that the BBFC, in determining particular classifications for video recordings, is to have special regard to any harm that might be caused to potential viewers or, through their behaviour, to society by the manner in which the work deals with: (a) criminal behaviour, (b) illegal drugs, (c) violent behaviour or incidents, (d) horrific behaviour or incidents, or (e) human sexual activity.

This amending legislation was passed in a period of 'moral panic' about violence in videos and the disputed perception that one such work might have been seen by the young persons convicted of the murder of the toddler James Bulger. These censorship criteria are harm-based, focusing upon their impact upon the viewer and the likelihood of this leading to criminal behaviour (see Stone 1995, p. 393).

Video censorship has been the site of increasing argument between those who feel that the BBFC is, or is not, too strict in its classifications. The statutory specification of criteria might encourage those who feel that the BBFC is too lenient to challenge its decisions by way of judicial review. The courts, however, have tended not to interfere with the exercise of discretionary power by the broadcasting regulators (*Attorney-General, ex rel. McWhirter v Independent Broadcasting Authority* [1973] QB 629 and *R v Independent Broadcasting Authority, ex parte Whitehouse* (1985) Court of Appeal, 3 April 1985).

12.4.3 Broadcasting
The regulation of broadcasting has its origins in the limited number of frequencies available for use, first in radio and then in television. The development of the cable and satellite technologies has increased the opportunities of access for potential broadcasters. Under the Wireless Telegraphy Act 1949 it is an offence to broadcast radio or television signals without a licence. The British Broadcasting Corporation operates under the terms of a licence and agreement with the Home Secretary (Cmnd 8233, 1981) and its income is derived from a licence fee levied on those who have and watch a television set. The BBC is a public corporation and was established under a royal charter. Commercial broadcasting is now regulated by two bodies, the Independent Television Commission (ITC) and the Radio Authority (RA) under the Broadcasting Act 1990. These regulatory bodies issue licences which permit the provision of ordinary 'terrestrial' broadcasting as well as satellite services and local delivery (cable) services. In their oversight of the companies which provide programmes, the ITC (s. 6) and the RA (s. 90) are to ensure that the programmes do not offend against good taste and decency and do not incite to crime and disorder; news is to be given with due accuracy and impartiality; and the use of devices to transmit material without the viewer or listener being fully aware of it is forbidden. The ITC must also ensure that the coverage of items of political and industrial controversy and of current public policy is carried out with due impartiality, and that the presentation of matters relating to religion is to be done with a responsibility to viewers' susceptibilities and sensibilities. The BBC's licence and agreement does not specify these matters but the board of governors of the BBC has undertaken to observe similar obligations. There is provision for the government to be able to require the BBC, ITC and the RA not only to broadcast particular matters (licence and agreement, cl. 13(3); Broadcasting Act 1990, ss. 10(1), 94(1)), but also to refrain from broadcasting material (licence and agreement, cl.13(4); Broadcasting Act 1990, ss.10(3), 94(3)). In 1988, the Home Secretary issued instructions under these powers (the relevant statute was the Broadcasting Act 1981, s. 29(3)) that the words of members or supporters of certain specified groups must not be broadcast. The groups

included those which are proscribed in both the UK as a whole and in Northern Ireland only (see para. 12.2), and groups which are lawful (Sinn Fein, Provisional Sinn Fein and, at that time, the Ulster Defence Association). These instructions were challenged in proceedings for judicial review. The House of Lords upheld them as being reasonable and also ruled that while legislation ought, where possible, to be construed in conformity with obligations derived from international agreements, this did not mean that statutory discretion had to be exercised in accordance with the ECHR (*R v Secretary of State for the Home Department, ex parte Brind* [1991] 1 AC 696). They were rescinded in the autumn of 1994 after the declaration of a cease-fire by the paramilitary organisations.

There is another statutory body concerned with broadcasting. This is the Broadcasting Standards Commission (BSC). It may adjudicate upon complaints made by the public, which comprise complaints relating to unfair treatment of people featured in programmes and of unwarranted intrusions upon privacy, the depiction of violence and sexual conduct, and standards of taste and decency (Broadcasting Act 1996, s. 110). The BSC is also under a duty to draw up and revise codes of guidance on these matters and to monitor and report upon broadcasting standards (Broadcasting Act 1996, ss. 107–9).

12.4.4 Civil Wrongs

In this, the first of our discussions on freedom of expression arranged around a common core, the restrictions derive from civil law. In the subsequent sections the focus is on the criminal law.

12.4.4.1 Breach of confidence This area of law has been developed from one which protected, primarily, trade secrets to one which can prevent disclosure of information which has been obtained in circumstances which gave rise to an obligation of confidentiality. This transition may be said to have begun with *Duke of Argyll* v *Duchess of Argyll* [1967] Ch 302, in which newspaper revelations about the details of a marriage by one of the parties were stopped by an injunction. The government's first attempt to prevent the publication of material using this action was the Crossman diaries case (*Attorney-General v Jonathan Cape Ltd* [1976] QB 752) in which it was held that discussions in cabinet could be regarded as giving rise to an obligation of confidentiality. A subsequent government went to great lengths to stop the publication of a book of memoirs by Peter Wright, a former member of the Security Service (MI5). As he was living in Tasmania and the book was to be published in Australia, criminal charges under the Official Secrets Act 1911, s. 2 could not be brought. Instead the government sought to argue in the Australian courts that those employed in the UK's security and intelligence services owed a lifelong duty of confidentiality in respect of material which they come across in the course of their duties. The action failed, partially because it was not in the Australian public interest to stop the book. While the Australian litigation was in progress, the book, *Spycatcher*, was published in the USA and people imported it into the UK quite freely. The book was the subject of litigation in this country. Some newspapers had carried stories about the book and extracts from it. The House of Lords had approved the granting of an interim injunction against the newspapers but when the substance of the action was heard, the High Court, Court of Appeal and House of Lords all discharged the injunction (*Attorney-General* v *Guardian Newspapers Ltd (No. 2)* [1990] 1 AC 109). Whilst it was held that Mr Wright, as a former MI5 employee, did owe a lifelong duty of confidentiality to the Crown, the House of Lords ruled that there were three principles which limited this. Only confidential material could be protected by this action. As the book had already been published abroad, the material was in the public domain and could no longer be regarded as confidential. The duty of confidence does not apply to useless information or trivia. If disclosure of a matter is in the public interest that may prevail over the public interest in protecting confidential material. This principle includes the defence of iniquity – one cannot be 'the confidant of a crime or fraud' (*Gartside* v *Outram* (1875) 26 LJ Ch 113 at p. 114). It was also said that the disclosure of iniquity may be restricted and that an allegation of iniquity in the security service would be a classic example of this. Lord Goff of Chievely said that the disclosure to the media of an allegation of iniquity in the security service would be justified if:

> following such investigations as are reasonably open to the recipient, and having regard to all the circumstances of the case, the allegation in question can reasonably be regarded as being a credible allegation from an apparently reliable source (at p. 283).

Confidentiality is also limited if the material is stale (*Attorney-General* v *Jonathan Cape Ltd* [1976] QB 736, where the material was some 10 years old).

12.4.4.2 Defamation A person's reputation may be protected against untrue statements. The test of whether or not a statement is defamatory is whether it causes right-thinking people to think less of the plaintiff or would cause others to avoid the plaintiff's company (*Sim* v *Stretch* (1936) 52 TLR 669 at p. 671). Defamation may be either libel, which occurs in a permanent form such as writing, or slander, which is transitory as in speech. This distinction is important because libel is actionable *per se* but in slander the plaintiff must show special damage has been sustained, apart from four exceptions. The requirements for an action in libel and slander are that the statement is defamatory, that it referred to the plaintiff, and that it was published to a third party. A caricature may found an action (*Dunlop Rubber Co. Ltd* v *Dunlop* [1921] 1 AC 367, where it was held that the plaintiff was held up to ridicule or contempt). An action can be successful even if the defendant did not intend the defamation (*Cassidy* v *Daily Mirror Newspapers Ltd* [1929] 2 KB 331). Defences include truth, fair comment on a matter of public interest and occasions of privilege, which may be either absolute or qualified. Following the Bill of Rights 1688 statements made in the course of Parliamentary proceedings are absolutely privileged. If an MP makes a statement outside the House of Commons this privilege will not be available but it does apply to Parliamentary papers ordered to be published by either House of Parliament (Parliamentary Papers Act 1840, s. 1). Statements made in judicial proceedings are also absolutely privileged *(Dawkins v Lord Rokeby* (1873) LR 8 QB 255 at p. 263), and fair and accurate newspaper reports of such proceedings are similarly privileged (Law of Libel Amendment Act 1888, s. 3). Statements by and to officers of State in the course of official duty carry absolute privilege *(Chatterton v Secretary of State for India* [1895] 2 QB 189). Qualified privilege applies to fair and accurate newspaper reports of Parliamentary proceedings, and the proceedings of local authorities, public meetings and statutory tribunals (Defamation Act 1952, s. 7 and sch.). The defence of qualified privilege may be defeated if it can be shown that the defendant acted maliciously.

In the recent past there have been some large awards of damages by juries against newspapers. The balance between freedom of expression and the privacy of people in the public eye may, in the UK, err on the side of protecting privacy which may hinder 'proper investigative journalism'. This situation may be contrasted with that in the USA following the Supreme Court's decision in *New York Times Co. v Sullivan* (1964) 376 US 254, which held that comments may be made about the holder of a public office providing that they are made in good faith.

The House of Lords held in *Derbyshire County Council v Times Newspapers Ltd* [1993] AC 535 that a local authority cannot sue for libel. It would be contrary to the public interest for an institution of government to be able to obstruct the freedom to express criticism of such a body.

12.4.5 Morality

This category of restrictions may be grouped around the idea of morality. There is a mixture of common law and statute.

12.4.5.1 Blasphemy In *R v Taylor* (1676) 1 Vent 293, it was held that the defendant's denunciation of Christ as a whoremonger, and of orthodox religion as a cheat, was a common law offence of blasphemy. Previously such attacks upon Christianity would have been dealt with in the ecclesiastical courts. Gradually the case law developed so that it was the way in which an attack upon Christianity was expressed which breached criminal law. In *R v Hetherington* (1840) 4 St Tr NS 406, Lord Denman CJ contrasted permissible appeals to judgment as opposed to impermissible appeals to the 'wild and improper feelings of the human mind'. Today a jury would be directed that an attack was blasphemous if it was unacceptably 'scurrilous' or 'insulting' or 'abusive'. Following *R v Chief Metropolitan Stipendiary Magistrate, ex parte Choudhury* [1991] 1 QB 429, in which Salman Rushdie's book *The Satanic Verses* was alleged to be insulting to the Islamic religion, it is clear that only the Christian religion is protected from attack by the law on blasphemy. The Divisional Court agreed with the majority view of the Law Commission that the extension of blasphemy to other religions would give rise to practical difficulties (Law Commission 1981). It does seem unfair that only one religion should be protected by the criminal law. The situation should be that all religions are covered by the law on blasphemy or, as the Law Commission recommended, that none are (see also Tregilgas-Davey 1991).

12.4.5.2 Obscenity Common law established the offence of obscenity but now statute plays the leading role. The legislation includes not only the Obscene Publications Acts 1959 and 1964 but also the Theatres Act 1968, the Criminal Law Act 1977 and the Broadcasting Act 1990 which extended the offence beyond texts, art and photographs to plays, films and broadcasts respectively. It is an offence to publish obscene material or to possess it for gain. The test for obscenity in the Obscene Publications Act 1959, s. 1, derives from *R* v *Hicklin* (1868) LR 3 QB 360, and requires the prosecution to show that the material, taken as a whole, would tend to deprave and corrupt those who are likely to come into contact with it. It is not necessary to have the intention to deprave and corrupt in order to be convicted (*R* v *Calder & Boyars Ltd* [1969] 1 QB 151). This case also established that the prosecution must prove that a significant proportion of the people likely to come into contact with the material would have their morals adversely affected. There are defences that a person had not examined the offending material and had no reasonable cause to believe that publication or possession would be an offence, or that publication was for the public good in the interests of science, literature, art or learning, or other objects of public concern. This public-good defence has been used successfully in prosecutions against D.H. Lawrence's *Lady Chatterley's Lover*, and a lesser literary work, *Inside Linda Lovelace*. In the former case the Bishop of Woolwich testified to the book's Christian merit and in the latter case Oxford University's Professor of Jurisprudence testified to the sociological merits of the book. In *Director of Public Prosecutions* v *Jordan* [1977] AC 699, it was held by the House of Lords that the use of what was admitted to be 'hard pornography' for therapeutic purposes did not fall within the 'other objects of public concern' limb of the public-good defence.

12.4.5.3 Common law offences The judges have developed a couple of offences. These are (a) outraging public decency and (b) conspiring to corrupt public morals. The display of a work of art in which two human foetuses were fashioned into earrings is the most recent case in which the outraging of public decency has been found (*R* v *Gibson* [1991] 2 All ER 439). In this case the Court of Appeal held that (a) this common law offence still existed despite the Obscene Publications Act 1959; (b) the prosecution did not have to prove recklessness or intention on the part of the defendant; and (c) that the absence of anything drawing particular attention to this exhibit did not mean that the 'public' nature of the offence was absent as the general invitation to visit the gallery satisfied this requirement (see Childs 1991).

The offence of conspiring to corrupt public morals was, in effect, created by the House of Lords when they approved such a charge in *Shaw* v *Director of Public Prosecutions* [1962] AC 220, in a case which concerned the publication of the *Ladies' Directory* – a list of prostitutes and their services. In *Knuller*

(Publishing, Printing and Promotions) Ltd v *Director of Public Prosecutions* [1973] AC 435, their lordships upheld a conviction for this offence in respect of an agreement under which a magazine accepted advertisements by a man seeking homosexual relationships, and additionally ruled that there could be a conspiracy to outrage public decency, although they did not uphold the conviction for it in this case.

12.4.6 Prejudice to the State
In this category one may group together the law on treason, sedition and official secrecy.

12.4.6.1 Treason The offence of treason is committed if one owes allegiance to the monarch and conspires or incites to kill or overthrow her, or to levy war against her, either by raising an insurrection, or adhering to her enemies. Treason is a capital offence. Treason felony is punishable by life imprisonment and consists of inciting rebellion against the government of the UK, or conspiring to deprive the monarch of her sovereignty in any of her dominions, or inviting a foreigner to invade any of her dominions (Treason Felony Act 1858).

12.4.6.2 Sedition The modern law on sedition relates to the incitement to violence against the laws and institutions of the state (*R* v *Burns* (1866) 16 Cox CC 355). It is unclear whether the incitement to violence against a section of the community is within the scope of sedition. It seemed to be included according to *R* v *Caunt* (1947 unreported), where the section of community attacked was British Jewry. In *R* v *Chief Metropolitan Stipendiary Magistrate, ex parte Choudhury* [1991] 1 QB 429, the applicant for judicial review contended that the publication of the book *The Satanic Verses* constituted sedition because it created discontent amongst Her Majesty's subjects – it had created hostility amongst Her Majesty's subjects, between British Muslims who were deeply offended by the book and those who defended the book as part of the freedom of expression – and because the book had damaged the UK in its international relations with Islamic countries. The Divisional Court ruled that not only must there be proof of incitement to violence, but it must be 'violence or resistance or defiance for the purpose of disturbing constituted authority'.

It can be argued from both *R* v *Caunt* and *Ex parte Choudhury* that sedition resembles blasphemy as the concern now is upon the nature and effects of the attack upon the protected institution, rather than the previous prohibition on any criticism of the institution. This point is important because there are other offences which deal with matters similar to sedition including: incitement to violence; the Incitement to Disaffection Act 1935, which covers the armed forces, and a similar provision referring to the police in the Police Act 1964; and, as in *R* v *Caunt*, incitement to racial hatred (see 12.4.7.2). Thus the Law Commission has suggested the abolition of seditious offences (Law Commission 1977).

12.4.6.3 Official secrecy Everyone in government takes the view that some of the information which they have must not be disclosed to those outside the 'magic circle' of government. It is probable that most people would agree with this but that agreement will depend upon the width of the definition of official secrets. The Official Secrets Act 1989 came about because a series of prosecutions for unauthorised disclosures of official secrets under the Official Secrets Act 1911, s. 2, had been unsuccessful. The most spectacular example being the case brought against Clive Ponting who, as a senior civil servant in the Ministry of Defence, had posted, anonymously, material to an MP which comprised advice to the Secretary of State on answering questions in the House of Commons about the sinking of the *Belgrano* during the Falklands War. Mr Ponting had done this because he believed that the minister was misleading Parliament. The prosecutions had failed despite the wide 'catch-all' nature of s. 2 of the 1911 Act. A committee of inquiry had recommended reform of this provision by narrowing its scope (Franks 1972). Further impetus for change came from the unsuccessful action taken to stop the publication of the memoirs of a former member of the security service using the law on breach of confidence (see 12.4.4.1).

According to its long title the Official Secrets Act 1989 'replaces section 2 of the Official Secrets Act 1911 by provisions protecting more limited classes of information'. Certainly the 1989 statute creates only six classes of protected official information which are: (a) security and intelligence; (b) defence; (c) international relations; (d) crime and special investigation powers; (e) information entrusted in confidence; and (f) information entrusted in confidence to other States or international organisations. Under s. 1 it is an offence for a Crown servant or government contractor to make an unlawful disclosure of security and intelligence material, which is or had been in his or her possession because of his or her position, knowing or having reasonable cause to believe that a disclosure would be damaging, or would be likely to be damaging. The definition of a damaging disclosure is very wide, including actual damage to the work, or any part of the security and intelligence services, as well as materials belonging to a class which would be likely to cause such damage. For current and former members of the security and intelligence services an unlawful disclosure of material will be an offence even if it is not damaging. This provision will also apply to those who are notified that they will be subject to it.

It is an offence for a Crown servant or government contractor to make an unauthorised disclosure of material relating to defence (s. 2) or international relations (s. 3), knowing or having reasonable cause to believe that it would be, or would be likely to be, damaging. Defence material includes information on the size, organisation or operation of the Crown's armed forces, and on their equipment and weapons, defence policy, strategy and planning. Material about international relations will also include that which was obtained from another State or an international organisation. Damage to defence and international relations, which may be actual, or likely to result from the disclosure, includes: affecting the capability of the armed forces to carry out their tasks, or loss of life or injury to the members of the armed forces, or the endangering or obstruction of the UK's interests abroad.

An offence is committed by a Crown servant or government contractor who makes an unlawful disclosure of information knowing or having reasonable cause to believe that it will (a) cause the commission of an offence, (b) facilitate an escape from lawful custody, or (c) impede the prevention or detection of offences or the apprehension of offenders (s. 4).

Where any material described above has come into a person's possession through (a) unlawful disclosure by a Crown servant or government contractor; (b) entrustment on confidential terms by any of these people; or (c) unlawful disclosure by a person to whom the information was entrusted on confidential terms, it will be an offence for that person to disclose the material knowing or having reasonable cause to believe that the disclosure would be damaging (s. 5).

Material relating to intelligence and security, defence and international relations which has been communicated in confidence to another State or an international organisation, and which has been disclosed without the authority of the State or organisation, is protected against disclosure by any person into whose possession it has arrived, if that person knows, or has reasonable cause to believe that such a disclosure would be damaging (s. 6).

In all of these offences it is a defence if the person did not know, or had no reasonable cause to believe that the material belonged to one of these protected classes. Despite claims that this legislation is a liberal reform, the new law on official secrecy is quite restrictive. The government resisted attempts to include a defence that disclosure was in the public interest. This is a very serious matter as some disclosures could be about iniquity which the courts have held would breach confidence. Surely the public interest in secrecy with respect to governmental matters is not absolute so that it can always override a public interest in disclosure? Whilst the classes of protected material are reduced, they are defined quite widely. Material relating to security and intelligence, for example, need not actually cause damage but may belong to a class, the unauthorised disclosure of which might be likely to cause damage. The offence in s. 6 could be committed where an unauthorised leak of the material by a foreign official has been reported in that country. Thus it could be an offence for a British newspaper to carry a story already published in a foreign newspaper.

12.4.7 Public Order
The restrictions in this group are offences to be found in the Public Order Act 1986.

12.4.7.1 Abusive or insulting words It had been an offence at common law to use threatening or abusive words in a public place with intention to provoke a breach of the peace. An extended version of this offence was created in the Public Order Act 1936, s. 5. Its successor is the Public Order Act 1986, s. 4, by which it is an offence to use towards another person threatening, abusive or insulting words, or behaviour, or to display to that person any writing or sign with an intent to cause that person to believe that unlawful violence will be used against that person, or to provoke immediate unlawful violence by that person or another, or whereby that person is likely to believe that such violence will be used or is likely to be provoked. This offence can occur in a public or private place. On summary conviction the maximum sentence is six months' imprisonment and a fine of £5,000. Under the Public Order Act 1986, s. 5, it is an offence to use words or behaviour of the type mentioned in s. 4 within the hearing or sight of a person likely to be caused harassment, alarm or distress by them. It is a defence for the accused to prove that there was no reason to believe that there was a person who would be so alarmed or distressed.

The case law on the previous legislation gives an indication as to how these sections will be interpreted. In *Brutus* v *Cozens* [1973] AC 854, anti-apartheid protesters disrupted a tennis match at Wimbledon by sitting on the court. The House of Lords held that 'insulting' must be given its ordinary meaning, which their lordships did not provide. They held that this was a matter of fact for the jury to decide. They did, however, say that simply because some of the spectators were angered by the protesters did not mean that they were insulted. In *Jordan* v *Burgoyne* [1963] 2 QB 744, a speaker at a rally in Trafalgar Square directed his words against Jews saying that now people understood that Hitler was not our enemy but that world Jewry was. He also addressed himself to people in the crowd who were opposed to his views calling them 'red rabble'. The Divisional Court ruled that speakers will have to take their audiences as they find them. Thus, if an audience is provoked to violence by a speaker's threatening, abusive or insulting words, then it does not matter that this was not the speaker's intention. The principle of taking your audience as you find it could go against the principle in *Beatty* v *Gillbanks* (1882) 9 QBD 308, that the lawful exercise of freedoms should not be prevented because of violent opposition. To protect that principle the speaker's words or actions must be insulting, or threatening or abusive before the audience's reaction can be taken into account.

There is no predecessor to the Public Order Act 1986, s. 5, and so it is difficult to predict how 'distress', or 'alarm', or 'harassment' will be construed. In *Director of Public Prosecutions* v *Clarke* [1992] Crim LR 60, the magistrates held that the photograph of an aborted foetus displayed by anti-abortion protestors was abusive and insulting, but that the defendant could be acquitted as he did not have the *mens rea*, neither intending the photographs to be, nor aware that they were, threatening, abusive or insulting.

The CJPOA 1994 inserts a new s. 4A into the Public Order Act 1986 which creates the offence of using threatening, abusive or insulting words or behaviour, or disorderly behaviour, with intent to cause a person harassment, alarm or distress, or displaying any writing, sign or other visible representation which is threatening, abusive or insulting with intent to cause a person harassment, alarm or distress. The aim behind this provision is to deal with serious racial harassment, although its provisions are wider than that. The difficulty may be that as a person must have been caused harassment, alarm or distress, victims may not be willing to pursue the matter.

12.4.7.2 Incitement to racial hatred There are various offences on this topic in the Public Order Act 1986, ss. 17 to 23. As with ss. 4 and 5, the use of threatening words or behaviour, or the display of signs or writing, constitutes an offence if there is an intention to stir up racial hatred or if, in the circumstances, it is likely that racial hatred will be stirred up (s. 18(1)). Racial hatred is defined as 'hatred against a group of persons in Great Britain defined by reference to colour, race, nationality (including citizenship) or ethnic or national origins' (s. 17). Intention must be proved for this offence (s. 18(5)). It is also an offence to publish or distribute written material which is threatening, or insulting, or abusive with an intent to stir up racial hatred, or if, in the circumstances, it is likely that racial hatred will be stirred up (s. 19(1)). Possession of racially inflammatory material with a view to publishing or displaying it (where it is written), or playing or broadcasting it (if it is a visual or sound recording), is an offence if it is likely that racial hatred would be stirred up, or that was the intention (s. 23(1)).

A Home Office review of the law relating to incitement to racial hatred took the view that its effect had been to change the language of racist propaganda from the crude and abusive towards that which was more moderate in tone and which was, therefore, possibly capable of a greater effect upon public opinion (Home Office 1975).

12.4.8 Contempt of Court
In keeping with British notions of fair trial, there are restraints upon what the media may report about matters which are currently before the courts. The test is whether a publication creates a substantial risk that justice will be seriously impeded or prejudiced. This test derives from the Contempt of Court Act 1981 which followed a finding by the European Court of Human Rights that the previous law was too strict and improperly restricted freedom of expression by its 'likely to prejudice' test (*Sunday Times* v *United Kingdom* (1980) 2 EHRR 245). This case arose from the campaign by the newspaper on behalf of those who had been born deformed because their mothers had taken the drug thalidomide during pregnancy. The newspaper had been subjected to an injunction as the courts felt that the article might lead to public prejudgement of the negligence actions against the manufacturers (*Attorney-General* v *Times Newspapers Ltd* [1974] AC 273). A minority of their lordships felt that it was a contempt to conduct a campaign in order to exert unfair pressure upon the manufacturers to settle the actions against them on possibly disadvantageous terms (see 12.5 for a comparison of the approaches of the British and European courts in this case).

The intention behind the Contempt of Court Act 1981 was that it should be a liberalising measure. A defence is provided where a matter which is before the courts is one of public interest and where its discussion in good faith would only cause an incidental impediment or prejudice (s. 5).

The law on contempt may also pose problems for journalists where they refuse to disclose the source of information for their publications when asked to do so in court proceedings. In such circumstances the statute provides a defence unless the court is satisfied that such disclosure is necessary in the interests of justice, or national security, or for the prevention of disorder or crime (s. 10; see Allan 1991). This defence has received restrictive interpretations from the House of Lords by their giving a wide interpretation to the exceptions. In *Secretary of State for Defence* v *Guardian Newspapers Ltd* [1985] AC 339, the newspaper was required, on the ground of national security, to assist the Ministry of Defence in identifying the person who had leaked information to the paper. This decision was reached by a three to two majority on the basis that the person might *in the future* damage national security. In *Re an Inquiry under the Company Securities (Insider Dealing) Act 1985* [1988] AC 660, the prevention of crime exception in s. 10 was held to encompass the prevention of crime in general. The questions which the journalist refused to answer had not specified any particular allegations of insider dealing, however, their lordships held that the inspectors' inquiries could lead to the prevention of crime and so non-disclosure would be contempt. Finally in *X Ltd* v *Morgan-Grampian (Publishers) Ltd* [1991] 1 AC 1, the interests of justice exception was held to mean that a person should be able to vindicate important legal rights. In this case the journalist should reveal his material to help the employer identify, and thereby dismiss, the employee who was breaching confidences (the journalist was successful before the European Court of Human Rights which held that the action ordered by the British courts was disproportionate (*Goodwin* v *United Kingdom* (1996) 22 EHRR 123); see 12.5 on proportionality in the ECHR).

The width of contempt of court has seemingly been increased by the Court of Appeal in *Attorney-General* v *Newspaper Publishing plc* [1988] Ch 333, when it was held that three newspapers, which were not parties to the injunction against the *Guardian* and *Observer* newspapers in relation to the writings of former MI5 officer Peter Wright (see 12.4.4.1), could be guilty of contempt. This would arise if they knew of the injunctions binding the other newspapers and, by publication, destroyed the subject-matter of those court orders with intent to impede or prejudice the administration of justice. While it must be correct that a third party cannot be permitted to attempt to prejudice proceedings, it is suggested that, in this case, the proper action against the three newspapers lay in breach of confidence rather than contempt (Robertson 1993, p. 335).

12.5 THE EUROPEAN CONVENTION ON HUMAN RIGHTS

The UK, in 1951, was one of the first States to ratify the ECHR. It came into force in 1953, and details various rights and freedoms which ratifying States are to guarantee to everyone within their jurisdiction (art. 1). In the UK this obligation derives from international law as the ECHR has not been incorporated into domestic law. The rights defined in the ECHR include the right to life (art. 2); freedom from torture or inhumane or degrading treatment or punishment (art. 3); freedom from slavery or compulsory labour (art. 4); the right to liberty and security of the person (art. 5); the right to a fair trial by an impartial tribunal (art. 6); the prohibition of retrospective criminal laws (art. 7); the right to respect people's privacy including their homes and correspondence (art. 8); the right to freedom of thought, conscience and religion (art. 9); freedom of expression (art. 10); freedom of peaceful assembly and association including the right to join trade unions (art. 11); the right to marry and found a family (art. 12). The enjoyment of these rights is to be secured without discrimination on any ground such as sex, race, colour, language, religion, political or any other opinion, national, or social origin, association with a national minority, property, birth or other status (art. 14).

There are a number of protocols to the ECHR, some of which protect additional rights. The UK has not ratified all of these. The rights to peaceful enjoyment of possession and to participate in free elections by secret ballot in the First Protocol have been ratified. The Fourth Protocol protects freedom of movement and this has not been ratified by the UK. If it were in force then the legislation providing for exclusion orders (Prevention of Terrorism Act (Temporary Provisions) Act 1989, Part II) could be in breach of it. An exclusion order can require a person to be removed from England, Scotland and Wales to Northern Ireland, and vice versa. It has been called a kind of internal exile.

Terrorism can be considered to justify recourse to ECHR, art. 15, which allows a State to derogate from its obligations under the ECHR. This may happen in time of war or other public emergency threatening the life of the nation. Such a derogation must only be as is strictly required by the exigencies of the situation. Derogations are not permitted in respect of torture, slavery, retrospective criminal law, or the right to life, except where death results from lawful acts of war. The UK has entered derogations in the past but only in respect of Northern Ireland. Following *Brogan* v *United Kingdom* (1988) 11 EHRR 117, which held that the power of detention in the Prevention of Terrorism (Temporary Provisions) Act 1984, s. 12 (see now Prevention of Terrorism (Temporary Provisions) Act 1989, s. 14), breached the ECHR, art. 6, a derogation was, for the first time, entered for the whole of the UK.

The procedure for determining complaints about breaches of the ECHR may be invoked in two ways: the first is where a State complains about another State (art. 24), and the second, and more common, is a petition by an individual (art. 25). The UK only accepted the right of individual petition as from 1966. In either case the complaint is investigated by the European Commission on Human Rights. After determining that the case is admissible, which in the case of an individual petition would mean checking, for example, that the complainant had exhausted all domestic remedies, the facts will be verified and the Commission will try to obtain a friendly settlement. If that is not secured the Commission will deliver its opinion on whether there has been a violation of the ECHR. This opinion is given to the State and the Council of Europe's Committee of Ministers. The complaint may then be referred to the European Court of Human Rights, within three months, by the Commission or the State but only if the State has accepted the Court's compulsory jurisdiction (art. 46), or has agreed to the Court hearing the particular case (art. 47). The decision of the Court is final and implementation of judgments is supervised by the Committee of Ministers, the court having no coercive powers.

Where no reference is made to the Court, the Committee of Ministers will determine, by a two-thirds majority, whether or not there was a breach of the ECHR. As with decisions of the Court, the Committee's decisions are final and States undertake to regard them as binding.

There will be changes to the institutions and procedures of the ECHR when the Eleventh Protocol takes effect (see the text in (1994) 17 EHRR 501 and for comment Mowbray 1994). The amendments have been designed to streamline operations, to reduce the backlog which is otherwise likely to increase with the expansion in membership of the Council of Europe and the consequent number of complaints taken to Strasbourg. There is to be a new court which will be organised differently. The full court is the Plenary Court but it will not determine cases. The great bulk of the work will be carried out by chambers of seven judges which will decide admissibility, seek a friendly settlement, and failing that determine the application. In applications from individuals, one member of the chamber dealing with the case will always be of the same nationality as the applicant. A chamber can relinquish jurisdiction to the Grand Chamber, which consists of 17 judges, where an application raises a serious question involving the interpretation of the Convention or where a judgment could be inconsistent with earlier decisions. Such relinquishment must be agreed by both parties. The Grand Chamber may rehear a case if an application has been made by any party to the case within three months of the chamber's determination. The application is determined by a panel of five judges of the Grand Chamber and they will accept the case if it raises (a) a serious question of interpretation or application of the ECHR, or (b) a serious issue of general importance.

The Court has found that the UK has breached the ECHR in more than 40 cases, and in other cases a friendly settlement has been agreed between the UK and a complainant (see Bradley 1991 and Constitution Unit 1996b). Some of the areas in which UK domestic law has failed to protect rights guaranteed by the ECHR include prisoners' rights (*Golder* v *United Kingdom* (1975) 1 EHRR 524; *Silver* v *United Kingdom* (1983) 5 EHRR 347); corporal punishment in schools (*Campbell* v *United Kingdom* (1982) 4 EHRR 293); telephone tapping (*Malone* v *United Kingdom* (1985) 7 EHRR 14); and immigrants' rights (*Abdulaziz* v *United Kingdom* (1981) 4 EHRR 38). In order to rectify these breaches the UK has had to pass legislation (see Churchill and Young 1992, for a survey of the UK's implementation of Court and Committee decisions between 1975 and 1987).

The issue of contempt of court within freedom of expression may be used to compare the approaches of the law in the UK and under the ECHR. In *Attorney-General* v *Times Newspapers Ltd* [1974] AC 273, the *Sunday Times* was prevented from publishing an article in a series about the drug, thalidomide. As the manufacturers of the drug were defending personal injury actions it was considered that the article constituted a possible prejudgment of that litigation, and also that the public pressure generated by the article might force the defendants to settle on terms disadvantageous to them. The newspaper complained that this decision breached the freedom of expression in the ECHR, art. 12. The way in which the right is framed is typical of the ECHR. The right is declared broadly: 'Everyone has the right to freedom of expression'. Thereafter particular aspects of the right are stated including, 'This right shall include freedom to hold opinions and to receive and impart information and ideas without interference by public authority and regardless of frontiers'. Finally, art. 10(2) lists the specific restrictions upon the right which are permitted. These include national security, prevention of disorder or crime, the protection of health or morals and, the one relevant to this case, the maintenance of the authority and impartiality of the judiciary. It must be noted that the restrictions must be prescribed by law and be necessary in a democratic society. The Court has ruled that 'necessary in a democratic society' means that there must be a pressing social need and that the restriction must be proportionate to the desired objective. The Court accepts that a State must have a discretion or margin of appreciation in determining these matters but that it is subject to the Court's supervision (*Handyside* v *United Kingdom* (1976) 1 EHRR 737).

If we compare the judgments of the House of Lords and the majority of the European Court of Human Rights, we can discern differences of approach and tone. In the House of Lords all of their lordships accepted that freedom of speech is important but that it is not absolute. It might come into conflict with the fair administration of justice. Lords Reid and Cross of Chelsea said that it may only be abridged by the law on contempt when reasonably necessary. Two principles of the law on contempt were discussed by their lordships: 'pressure' and 'prejudgment'. Only Lords Diplock and Simon took the view that the article constituted unfair pressure. Lord Diplock distinguished between private pressure on a litigant to desist from pursuing an action and the public abuse of a party continuing an action. The holding up of litigants to public obloquy amounted to contempt. The majority of their lordships did not find the article constituted unfair pressure. They considered that the views were expressed in moderate terms. As to the issue of prejudgment, because the article dealt with the manufacture, testing and marketing of the drug, it touched upon the issue of the negligence of the manufacturers which was an important part of the pending litigation between the victims and the manufacturers. Their lordships felt that the publication of this material could lead to the publication of further information intended to be a rebuttal. This opened up the possibility of a gradual slide towards trial by newspaper or television. This was wrong because, in Lord Diplock's view, it was a usurpation of the role of the courts to which the task of administering justice is given. For Lord Reid the prospect of media campaigns in which responsible argument could be joined by ill-informed and 'prejudicial attempts to inform the public' could result in 'disrespect for the processes of law . . . and if mass media are allowed to judge unpopular people and causes could fare badly'. This line of reasoning can be brought within the ECHR's exception of 'maintenance of the authority of the judiciary', which the Attorney-General sought to uphold in arguing the UK's case before the European Court of Human Rights. The approach of the European Court to this issue was described by the majority as follows (*Sunday Times* v *United Kingdom* (1980) 2 EHRR 245):

> The Court is faced not with a choice between two conflicting principles, but with a principle of freedom of expression that is subject to a number of exceptions which must be narrowly interpreted (at p. 281).

They also stated that:

> Article 10 guarantees not only the freedom of the press to inform the public but the right of the public to be properly informed (at p. 281).

The majority were outlining the content of the freedom of expression and emphasising it whereas the law lords appeared to focus on the rationale for the law on contempt.

In their examination of the application of the 'authority of the judiciary' exception, the majority of the European Court reiterated the interpretation of 'necessary in a democratic society' as requiring a pressing social need and that the curtailment of the right must be proportionate to the legitimate aim pursued. They acknowledged that a State had a margin of appreciation in determining restrictions upon the freedom of expression, but held that the 'authority of the judiciary' exception was sufficiently objective, and enjoyed such substantial common ground in the law and practice of the contracting States, that the Court could supervise its application by the House of Lords. This was in contrast to the exception 'for the protection of morals' which was more variable so that its applicability was a matter which a State authority was better placed to determine than an international judge. After taking into account all of the circumstances of the case, including the fact that the thalidomide tragedy was a matter of 'undisputed public concern', the majority did not find that the permitted exception of maintaining the authority of the judiciary supported restraint of the newspaper article. Whilst they were aware of the possibility of the unfortunate aspects of trial by newspaper, they did not find that persuasive. Indeed, they took the view that the making of counter-arguments by the manufacturers could put a brake upon speculation in the media.

The ECHR approach, then, is to formulate rights quite broadly and to construe restrictions upon them quite narrowly, with the Court giving the case for restrictions a penetrating examination. In the UK the residual nature of liberties, coupled with a less exacting judicial scrutiny seems to suggest that the protection of rights in UK domestic law is less secure than under the ECHR.

12.6 A BILL OF RIGHTS FOR THE UK

This brief overview of the freedom of association, assembly and expression in the UK has indicated that the extent of these liberties is not as great as it should be. There are a variety of reasons which may explain this situation.

First, there is the residual nature of individual liberty in British law. This precarious quality means that the common law cannot adequately develop liberty. The right to personal privacy, in common with freedoms of assembly and expression can be described as that which remains after accounting for the permissible infringements upon it. Thus prisoners had to have recourse to the ECHR to protect their correspondence. In *Malone v Metropolitan Police Commissioner* [1979] Ch 344, Megarry V-C lamented the fact that there was nothing that could be done in domestic law about the tapping of Mr Malone's telephone by the police. He too had to protect his privacy by going to Strasbourg (*Malone v United Kingdom* (1985) 7 EHRR 14). The second point is that legislation may be passed which may restrict the individual's liberty. We have seen examples of this in the Public Order Act 1986 (see 12.3.1) and the Official Secrets Act 1989 (see 12.4.6.3). A third factor is that the judiciary may not interpret the law in a way which maximises liberty. An example of this in common law is the decision in *Duncan v Jones* [1936] 1 KB 218 (see 12.3), which restricted the right to a meeting whilst denying that this point was at issue. The decisions on the scope of the defence which journalists have to charges of contempt where they refuse to disclose their sources demonstrate inadequate interpretations of statutory rights (e.g., *X Ltd v Morgan-Grampian (Publishers) Ltd* [1991] 1 AC 1, see 12.4.8).

There are a number of groups which argue that liberty is insufficiently protected in the UK. One of the most damning critiques of the position in the UK was carried out by Klug, Starmer and Weir (1996). Their audit concluded that there was not a culture of liberty in the UK. The public were not very aware nor concerned about rights and one looked in vain to Parliament. They use the passage of the CJPOA 1994 as a case study. They do acknowledge that the House of Lords does have experts in its membership, in particular Lord Lester of Herne Hill QC, but conclude that their efforts are insufficient. To be fair the House of Lords emerges with credit over the passage of the Police Act 1997. Led by Liberal Democrat peers, the House of Lords was able to ensure that the provisions relating to the powers of the police to enter or interfere with property and in relation to wireless telegraphy would be subject both to authorisation from a very senior police officer and review by, and appeal to, commissioners who hold or have held high judicial office, along the lines of the arrangements in the Interception of Communications Act 1985, the Security Service Act 1989 and the Intelligence Services Act 1994. The Bill was being considered in the pre-election period when the Conservative and Labour parties were competing to show their toughness on crime and their support for the police. Nor did the courts fare well in this audit. Given that the scope afforded to the courts is small, as the ECHR is not incorporated, they felt that the use made of this opportunity was disappointing. In cases on the LEXIS database between 1972 and 1993 there were only 64 references to the ECHR in the judgments and only in 11 did the Convention play a significant part. Subsequently this analysis was expanded to 1996, which increased the significant references to 16. The strong rise in total references in the 5 years 1991–7 has not led to what is called 'back-door incorporation' (Klug and Starmer 1997).

Some feel that a Bill of Rights should be enacted into domestic UK law and others prefer to create a series of specific statutes which would deal with particular problems, such as race and sex discrimination. Those who advocate a Bill of Rights argue that fundamental rights should be protected as they may be said to constitute the rules of the game in a democracy. They also contend that the British approach is inadequate and that the protection offered by the ECHR is flawed by the delay and expense involved. Most groups seeking a Bill of Rights take the view that incorporation of the ECHR into the UK would be satisfactory. Instead of going to Strasbourg to enforce the ECHR rights this could be done in the UK's courts, although the authoritative interpretation of the ECHR would remain that of the European Court of Human Rights.

The arguments against a Bill of Rights, whether it be the ECHR or an entirely British model, include the difficulty of entrenchment because of Parliamentary sovereignty, and the appropriateness of entrusting important decisions to a group of people which is neither elected nor accountable for their decisions. As a Bill of Rights will usually be drafted in broad terms it will be open to the judiciary to decide if they will approach its interpretation in an activist or conservative manner. Indeed, they could choose to be activist in some areas and conservative in others (Ewing and Gearty 1990, p. 269). An argument related to the previous one is that the record of the UK judiciary does not inspire confidence that a Bill of Rights would be 'safe in their hands'. It is somewhat ironic that the decisions of the Judicial Committee of the Privy Council are referred to both by those who are pessimistic (Ewing and Gearty 1990, pp. 271–3) and those who are optimistic (IPPR 1990, p. 12) about the judges.

Advocates of a Bill of Rights who consider that there is some force in the point about judges being unelected, respond by suggesting that there should be reform of the judicial appointments system and propose commissions which would seek to make the judiciary more representative (Charter 88 1990; Liberal Democrats 1990, p. 32; IPPR 1990, p. 13). It is interesting that all of these groups seek a new constitutional settlement involving a written constitution interpreted by a supreme court.

Those who are sceptical about a Bill of Rights tend to view the judges as the wrong group to deal with what are political questions (Griffith 1979) and they suggest that political reform is required (Ewing and Gearty 1990, p. 275).

One group which is committed to the protection of rights and democracy is the National Council for Civil Liberties (1991). They propose a Bill of Rights which would be an improvement upon the ECHR and which would be 'semi-entrenched'. By this they mean that legislation could be passed which was contrary to the Bill of Rights. They propose that this could happen not only after a decision by the courts that legislation or action was contrary to the Bill of Rights, but also when a new Bill was going through Parliament thereby preventing the courts from striking it down. The suggested procedures for this are quite complicated and involve a two-thirds majority vote in favour, a new committee in Parliament as well as an advisory human rights commission (pp. 106–22). They argue that semi-entrenchment of a Bill of Rights through the political process recognises that in some instances determining whether a measure breaches rights is more of a political assessment than a legal interpretation. Accordingly it is better for such decisions to be taken under the democratic process rather than the judicial process (pp. 26–9).

Their proposal also calls for changes in the appointment and removal of the judiciary; and improved training and education in human rights law for them (pp. 104–7), and society as a whole. A society which is better educated about human rights will have a greater awareness and this will produce a climate of opinion which will be very sensitive to possible abuses of rights (pp. 14, 28).

The debate about a Bill of Rights now changes given the commitment of the Labour government to incorporate the ECHR. A white paper is promised before the Bill is presented to Parliament. The major issue now is what will the judges be entitled to do under the incorporating legislation? Will they, as in Canada, be enabled not only to declare that legislation is incompatible and offer a remedy, or will they, as in New Zealand, only be empowered to declare that legislation is incompatible if they cannot interpret it to compatible? In a speech Lord Irvine of Lairg (1997) the Lord Chancellor, who chairs the cabinet committee on incorporating the ECHR, mentioned both of these models but his insistence on legislative supremacy leads some to think that he, at least, is inclined to the New Zealand model. Lord Irvine also referred to Parliamentary scrutiny and seemed to hint at a preference for a Joint Human Rights Committee of the Commons and Lords to check Bills raising significant ECHR issues. He spoke of a previous Labour policy paper on a Human Rights Commission which might have four functions: scrutinising legislation, taking test cases, producing policy papers and providing education. He also alluded to the relationship that a Human Rights Commission might have with the Commission for Racial Equality and the Equal Opportunities Commission. The idea of an umbrella body has been advanced, but there is a concern that this might adversely affect the work of the individual elements, e.g., the Equal Opportunities Commission.

Lord Irvine also said that the task force within his department is considering the impact of incorporation upon the courts and this will include the training which the judiciary would need, consideration if existing procedures should continue or if a special cause of action should be introduced and whether it would be useful to establish a special court.

Whichever of the various options is pursued it is absolutely clear that incorporation of the ECHR will be a fundamental change in our constitutional arrangements with an impact going beyond the better protection of human rights. It could give birth to greater public appreciation not only of human rights but about constitutionalism and will change the balance in the relationships amongst the executive, the legislature and the judiciary.

CHAPTER THIRTEEN
Police Powers

13.1 INTRODUCTION

Deprivation of liberty and property are two of the most invasive of interferences with a person's freedom but the ability to inflict them is something which we have allowed in certain circumstances. The justification for this is the enforcement of law, particularly the criminal law. The tasks of maintaining law and order and investigating crime have been given to the police and in order to perform them the police must have the necessary powers. Given that we want the police to be able to apprehend those who commit crimes, we must also consider the consequences for those who are subjected to the exercise of police powers. Not every person suspected of having committed a crime is guilty, and neither is every person convicted in the courts. What we must bear in mind is the idea of a balance between 'the interests of the community in bringing offenders to justice and the rights and liberties of persons suspected or accused of crime' (Philips 1981, p. iv). This balance was fundamental to the Report of the Royal Commission on Criminal Procedure (Philips 1981), which was the basis for the legislation which codified the law on police powers – the Police and Criminal Evidence Act 1984.

Dicussion in this chapter will focus on those powers which the police exercise 'on the street', i.e., arrest and search, and in the police station, detention and interrogation of suspects. The significant variations to those powers where terrorist offences are concerned will also be outlined.

13.1.1 General Background
The police, as we shall see, do have particular powers which enable them to arrest those suspected of criminal offences. The general law has developed so that individuals are either free to go or have been arrested and therefore deprived of their freedom. There is no intermediate position of detention

short of arrest. An officer may ask an individual to answer questions but there is no legal duty to answer them. If the individual does answer the questions, that voluntary cooperation can cease at any time and the individual is free to walk off. This can only be stopped by the officer making an arrest. The case of *Rice v Connolly* [1966] 2 QB 414, illustrates this position. Officers on the beat came across Mr Rice. As there had been burglaries in the area he was asked to account for his movements. He gave some answers which the officers considered to be unhelpful. They then asked if he would come with them to the police station in order to check his answers. He refused and was arrested for wilfully obstructing the police in the execution of their duty. Mr Rice sued for false imprisonment claiming that the arrest was unlawful. The court ruled that Mr Rice was not obstructing the officers because he was under no legal duty to answer the questions, and he did not have to accompany them to the station unless arrested.

Just as the citizen is entitled not to answer questions, the officer is entitled to ask them when seeking cooperation. Indeed, an officer is permitted to attract the attention of an individual in order to ask questions. In *Donnelly v Jackman* [1970] 1 WLR 562, an officer had tapped a man on the shoulder in order to speak to him about an offence. The man turned round and tapped the officer on the chest. The officer again tapped the man on the shoulder and the subsequent blow dealt to the officer was held to be an assault on an officer in the execution of his duty. The court held that the officer's tapping of the shoulder was 'a trivial interference' with a citizen's liberty. Thus the triviality of this interference did not take the officer beyond his duty. Contrast that case with *Bentley v Brudzinski* (1982) 75 Cr App R 217, in which an officer stopped and questioned two men who fitted the general description of people allegedly involved in the taking away of a car without consent. Another officer arrived who wished to question the men. They were moving away and so the officer placed his hand on the shoulder of one them and was then punched. The defendant was acquitted of assaulting an officer in the execution of his duty because the action of the officer was held to be outside his duty. The Divisional Court noted that much would depend upon circumstances in deciding whether interference was trivial or not. The theory is, however, clear in that personal liberty includes the freedom not to cooperate with the police.

13.1.2 The Royal Commission on Criminal Procedure

The Royal Commission on Criminal Procedure was established in 1978 as a response to an inquiry into a miscarriage of justice when three youths had been convicted of murder on the strength of false confessions (Fisher 1977). Its remit was very wide, covering the investigation and prosecution of criminal offences and related features of criminal procedure and evidence. The concept of a balance between bringing offenders to justice and the rights and liberties of those suspected or accused of crime was also part of the remit given to the commission. It was a matter which the commission took very seriously and they felt that they should seek to create an evaluative framework of first principles within which they could analyse the existing law and practice and suggestions for reform.

The commission was of the view that the police needed the support and confidence of the public in investigating crime. They proposed that principles of fairness, openness and workability should underpin the arrangements for the investigation of crime. The commission's recommendations in this area may be summarised as follows:

(a)   Police powers should be used only where there are reasonable grounds for suspecting that an offence has been committed and that a person subjected to them has committed an offence.

(b)   Police powers should only be exercised when justified by the circumstances and decisions to use them must be capable of review.

(c)   Those taking such decisions must have clear powers and responsibilities and, where practicable, reasons should be recorded.

(d)   The powers to search persons and property must be subject to substantial safeguards.

(e)   The power to arrest without a warrant should only be exercised upon the basis of necessity for specified offences.

The commission's recommendations sought to rationalise the variety of powers, many of which were conferred by local legislation, and to balance greater powers for the police with greater safeguards for the individual.

13.2   ARREST

Arrest means that a person has been deprived of liberty. A deprivation of liberty will be lawful if an arrest power provided by law has been exercised correctly. The use of the arrest power has changed over the years. It used to be the case that an arrest would be made in order to bring a person to court to answer charges following the investigation of a crime which had resulted in that person being reasonably suspected of the crime. Today it is not uncommon for the police to arrest someone, not as the culmination of their investigation of a crime, but as part of the investigative process. In *Holgate-Mohammed* v *Duke* [1984] AC 437, the House of Lords held that it was lawful for the officer who arrested Mrs Holgate-Mohammed to take into account the consideration that there was a greater likelihood of her answering questions truthfully while under arrest at the police station than if she were at home.

There are two basic ways in which an arrest may be made. These are (a) under a warrant, and (b) without a warrant under legislation or the common law.

13.2.1   Arrest under a Warrant

A magistrate has a power under the Magistrates' Courts Act 1980, s. 1, to issue a warrant for the arrest of a person upon being satisfied with the case proposed by the police. An arrest under warrant may only be in connection with an arrestable offence (defined in 13.2.2). The police case must be in writing and substantiated on oath. The warrant will name the person to be arrested and specify the offence. Cases in the 18th century established that general warrants are unlawful (e.g., *Leach* v *Money* (1765) 19 St Tr 1002). An officer executing the warrant for arrest need not be in possession of the warrant at the time of the arrest, but it must be produced as soon as possible after a request to see it (Magistrates' Courts Act 1980, s. 125 as amended by the Police and Criminal Evidence Act 1984, s. 33).

13.2.2 Arrest without a Warrant

The usual basis for arrest without a warrant, or summary arrest, will be the Police and Criminal Evidence Act 1984, ss. 24–25, although this Act preserves some other statutory powers to arrest without a warrant (s. 24(2) and (3)). The common law power to arrest without a warrant for a breach of the peace also remains. The power to arrest without a warrant under the Police and Criminal Evidence Act 1984 may be exercised if an offence is an arrestable offence. An arrestable offence is defined as any offence for which the sentence is fixed by law, and those offences in respect of which a person aged 21 or over may be sentenced to a five-year term of imprisonment (s. 24(1)). The definition also includes specific offences listed in s. 24(2) and (3).

Having set out the offences which carry the possibility of arrest without a warrant, s. 24 then provides for different categories of the arrest power. In some circumstances anyone may exercise the power; in other circumstances it may only be exercised by a police officer. Anyone may arrest a person who is committing an arrestable offence, or a person who is suspected on reasonable grounds of committing an arrestable offence (s. 24(4)). Where an arrestable offence has been committed, any person may arrest anyone who is guilty of the offence, or any person who is suspected on reasonable grounds of having committed the offence (s. 24(5)). A police officer may arrest any person who is about to commit an arrestable offence, or any person who is suspected on reasonable grounds to be about to commit an arrestable offence (s. 24(7)). Where a police officer reasonably suspects that an arrestable offence has been committed, then the officer may arrest anyone suspected on reasonable grounds of having committed the offence.

There are important differences between the powers of arrest given to the police and to any person. Only an officer may arrest where a person is about to commit an arrestable offence. Where an officer reasonably suspects that a person has committed an arrestable offence it does not matter that such an offence has not been committed, provided that the officer has reasonable grounds for suspecting that such an offence has been committed (s. 24(6)). Where any person reasonably suspects that an individual has committed an arrestable offence, the arrest will be unlawful if the person did not commit such an offence, or no such offence had been committed. Thus the decision in *Walters* v *W. H. Smith and Son Ltd* [1914] 1 KB 595, is still good law. In that case a store detective thought that a person had stolen something. As no offence had been committed the arrest was unlawful despite the fact that there did seem to be grounds for suspecting Mr Walters.

The definition of an arrestable offence includes serious offences, defined in terms of the possible sentence which a court might impose. There are circumstances in which it is possible for an officer to carry out an arrest without a warrant even though the offence is not an arrestable one. If an officer reasonably suspects that a 'relevant person' has committed or attempted, or is committing or attempting, to commit an offence which is not an arrestable offence, then an arrest may be carried out if the service of a summons appears to the officer to be impracticable or inappropriate because one of the general arrest conditions is satisfied (s. 25(1)). These conditions are (s. 25(3)):

(a)   that the name of the relevant person is not known and is not readily ascertainable by the officer;

(b)   that the officer has reasonable grounds for doubting that the name given by the relevant person is not that person's real name;

(c)   that the address given by a relevant person is either unsatisfactory, or is reasonably doubted by the officer to be satisfactory for the purpose of serving a summons;

(d)   that the officer reasonably believes that arrest is necessary to prevent the relevant person from:

(i)   harming himself or others;
(ii)   suffering physical injury;
(iii)   causing loss of, or damage to, property;
(iv)   committing an offence against public decency; or
(v)   causing an unlawful obstruction of the highway;

(e)   that the officer reasonably believes that arrest is necessary to protect a child or other vulnerable person from the relevant person.

The effect of s. 25 is to widen the power of arrest without a warrant to cover *all* offences, provided one of the general arrest conditions is satisfied. Reasonable suspicion of a minor offence can lead to summary arrest if the relevant person is, for example, homeless, as service of a summons could be difficult. In one case an officer exercised the s. 25 arrest power because he did not believe the name and address given to him. The basis for this was his assertion that 'suspects usually gave false names and addresses', which the Divisional Court felt was insufficient to justify the arrest (*G* v *Director of Public Prosecutions* [1989] Crim LR 150).

The royal commission recommended that summary arrest should only take place where the offence could give rise to a term of imprisonment and that detention upon arrest must be necessary. The elements of its necessity principle were (a) that the suspect would not give a name and address for service of a summons; (b) the need to prevent continuation or repetition of the offence; (c) the need to protect the suspect, or other people or property; (d) the need to preserve evidence relating to the offence, or to obtain it through questioning the suspect; and (e) to ensure that the suspect would appear at court to answer the charge. The legislation is both narrower and wider than these recommendations. The scope of an arrestable offence is narrower as the Police and Criminal Evidence Act 1984 defines it as one where the sentence is fixed by law or where a 21-year-old person could be sentenced to imprisonment for five years or more, compared to the commission's recommendation of any offence which could lead to a sentence of imprisonment. This was to be restricted by the operation of the necessity principle. Its elements relating to concern about service of a summons, the safeguarding of people, property and evidence are to be found in the legislation but their function is not to restrict but to *widen* the power of summary arrest. The general arrest conditions go further than the commission's elements of necessity by including powers to deal with offences against public decency, obstruction of the highway and the protection of children and other vulnerable people. It might seem that the effect of s. 25 is to widen summary arrest from specific and fairly serious offences to any offence where the police feel it would be convenient to make an arrest.

13.2.3 The Elements of Arrest
Whether an arrest is made with or without a warrant it must contain certain elements. The person arrested must understand that arrest has a compulsory nature, that liberty has been deprived, and must be given certain information.

13.2.3.1 Compulsion Arrest means the detention of a person by the police officer or citizen making the arrest, usually against the wishes of the arrested person. It seems that if a person reasonably believes that compliance with a request to accompany an officer to a police station is voluntary then that will not be arrest. In *Alderson* v *Booth* [1969] 2 QB 216, a motorist took a breathalyser test which proved positive. He was asked to go to the station which he did. He thought that his action was voluntary and this was one of the magistrates' findings of fact. As he had been given no other indication that he had been arrested the police were found to have made an unlawful arrest.

One way of indicating the compulsion involved in an arrest is to touch the body of the arrested person in a restraining manner. Sometimes the person will resist arrest and force may be used to subdue the person (see 13.2.4).

13.2.3.2 Information to be given Before the enactment of the Police and Criminal Evidence Act 1984, the House of Lords decision in *Christie* v *Leachinsky* [1947] AC 573, stipulated what information should be given to an arrested person. The propositions in Viscount Simon's speech required that the arrested person be told of the fact of arrest and the grounds for arrest, though this need not be done if the circumstances made these things obvious or difficult to communicate. The reason why this information should be given is that a person is free unless there is a valid arrest. The provision of the information could enable the arrested person to decide to submit or to resist depending upon whether or not there were valid grounds justifying the arrest.

The Police and Criminal Evidence Act 1984 requires that, subject to the exception of the person arrested escaping before the information could be communicated (s. 28(5)):

(a)   the person making the arrest must inform the arrested person of the fact of, and reasons for, arrest, either immediately or as soon as is reasonably practicable afterwards (s. 28(1) and (3)),

(b)   a police officer making an arrest must inform the person arrested of these matters even if they are obvious (s. 28(2) and (3)).

There are various questions which can be posed about the requirements of s. 28 and the legality of an arrest. How specific and precise should the information be? What counts as reasonably practicable for the purpose of permitting a delay in giving the information? What is the legal status of the period between arrest and the provision of the required information?

In *Christie* v *Leachinsky* Viscount Simon said that precise or technical language need not be used. Subsequently the courts have given the police a large degree of latitude. *Gelberg* v *Miller* [1961] 1 WLR 153 concerned a person who would not move his car. He had removed the rotor arm from the car's engine and refused to replace it. He also refused to give his name and address. He was told that he was being arrested for obstruction by refusing to move a vehicle. These facts could found two different offences: (a) obstructing the police in the execution of their duty, and (b) obstruction of the highway. The important point was that the police, at that time, did not have the power of summary arrest for offence (a). The court held that the arrest was lawful as the information given to the person arrested was sufficient to explain 'in substance' why the arrest was made.

This judicial attitude of not requiring the particular power of arrest to be specified was maintained in a Court of Appeal decision on an arrest made under the law before the Police and Criminal Evidence Act 1984 (*Abbassy* v *Commissioner of Police of the Metropolis* [1990] 1 WLR 385). In this case the court overturned the decision of the judge at first instance that the explanation by one of the arresting officers that the arrest was for 'unlawful possession' was insufficient in law. The officers were not satisfied with the driver's statements about the ownership of the car. There were at least three offences which might have led to arrest. Woolf LJ said that *Christie* v *Leachinsky* still provided good guidance on the information to be provided upon arrest.

Information upon arrest may be delayed because of the conduct of the person arrested. In *Director of Public Prosecutions* v *Hawkins* [1988] 1 WLR 1166, a violent struggle by the arrested person delayed the giving of reasons, but they were not given when the person was subdued. The court held that it was reasonable not to give the information until the violent conduct had stopped. At that point the reasons should have been given. Since they had not been given the arrest only became unlawful then and not when the person was apprehended by the police.

Although *Murray* v *Ministry of Defence* [1988] 1 WLR 692, is a decision relating to the exercise of arrest powers given to the army in Northern Ireland by anti-terrorist legislation, it is a pointer to the thinking of the House of Lords on arrest. Briefly the facts were that a patrol entered Mrs Murray's house with the intention of arresting her in connection with an IRA-related offence. The army personnel followed standing instructions which were to carry out a search for people in the house and to collect the people into one room. Only when the person to be arrested had been identified would they announce that an arrest had been made and then leave immediately with their captive. While Mrs Murray was dressing she asked the corporal with her if she was under arrest. The officer did not answer that question. The court held that, as Mrs Murray knew from the entry of the soldiers into the house that she was no longer at liberty, the arrest began at that point even though it was not until 30 minutes later that she was formally told that she was under arrest. This delay was held to be reasonable because in the circumstances of such house arrests it was advisable that soldiers had standard procedures which took into account the need to prevent the alarm being raised and to minimise the possibility of any shooting. Under the Northern Ireland (Emergency Provisions) legislation (currently the Northern Ireland (Emergency Provisions) Act 1996) a soldier does not have to state the ground of arrest. This decision has been criticised (Williams 1991). Professor Williams is unhappy about the definition of arrest relied upon by their lordships, that arrest occurs when liberty is deprived. Surely arrest only occurs when there is a lawful deprivation of liberty? He also thinks that their lordships' upholding of the delay in informing of the fact of arrest as being reasonably practicable is somewhat unfortunate. This is because their lordships went beyond getting through the fact of arrest to the person arrested to strategic considerations about how such an arrest might best be conducted.

If we take the *Murray* decision in conjunction with *Lewis v Chief Constable of the South Wales Constabulary* [1991] 1 All ER 206, we can see a basis, favourable to the police, on which the courts decide when and if an arrest is lawful. In *Lewis* two people were arrested and were not given the reasons for arrest until 10 and 23 minutes, respectively, after arrest. The Court of Appeal upheld the decision of the circuit judge, in an action for false imprisonment, that the arrests were unlawful until the reasons were given but once the reasons were given the arrests were lawful. The courts seem to be taking the view that arrest is a continuing act in which a person is deprived of liberty. Where delay in providing information occurs this will not make the arrest unlawful where it is not reasonably practicable for the information to be given. Where it is practicable to give the information at the time of arrest the arrest is unlawful until it is regularised by the provision of the information. Therefore so long as the arrestor is intending to follow the requirements for a proper arrest this will ensure legality. This would also seem to explain the decision in *R v Kulynycz* [1971] 1 QB 367, in which the person was given the wrong reason for arrest, that there was a warrant for arrest. At the station it became clear that there was no warrant and the person was then told that he was reasonably suspected of having committed an offence. The court held that the person had been lawfully arrested throughout even though, initially, the wrong reason was given.

What if the arrested person has difficulty in understanding the information given by the person making the arrest? It seems that the duty is to do what is reasonable in the circumstances. In *Wheatley v Lodge* [1971] 1 WLR 29, the person arrested was deaf and did not realise that he was required to go to the police station under arrest. The arresting officer did not appreciate that the person was deaf and it was not until they were in the police station that the person disclosed his deafness. The actions of the officer in stating that the person was being arrested and taking the person to a car to go to the station were held to be reasonable.

13.2.4 The Use of Force
A person making an arrest may use reasonable force against the person arrested (Criminal Law Act 1967, s. 3). The reasonableness of force will depend upon the circumstances. The sorts of consideration which can be relevant are the nature of resistance to arrest, the seriousness of the offence which has led to the arrest, and the nature and degree of risk which making the arrest poses to third parties. One case in which it was held that the police used unnecessary force was *Sturley* v *Metropolitan Police Commissioner* (1984) *The Times*, 27 June 1984. In this case a female officer twisted the arm of a middle-aged woman behind her back whilst making an arrest for assault. This broke the woman's wrist. The court held that this use of force was too strenuous and also unnecessary as there was another officer present. Two officers should have been able to arrest one woman without breaking her wrist.

If one officer is arresting a very strong person, or two or more people, then a greater degree of force may be reasonable.

The use of force may include the use of handcuffs. Again the circumstances must be such that their use is reasonable, as, for example, where the prisoner is being violent. Force may sometimes mean the use of firearms. Fortunately this is rare in Great Britain but does occur in Northern Ireland where the Royal Ulster Constabulary carry weapons. The police have internal guidelines on the use of firearms as do members of the armed forces serving in Northern Ireland where the guidance is known as the 'yellow card'. All of this guidance on the use of lethal force is secret. The relevant law is the same as that for non-lethal force. Juries and the judiciary are reluctant to convict officers of murder unless the case is very clear. A case from Northern Ireland shows the considerations involved. In *R* v *MacNaughton* [1975] NI 203, a soldier was accused of attempted murder and grievous bodily harm. The defendant was a member of a patrol operating in the dangerous area near to the border with the Irish Republic. The patrol was investigating an explosion which they had heard and they received a radio message that there had been military casualties. They came upon Mr Walsh whom they arrested on suspicion of being involved in the bombing of an army vehicle. Subsequently Mr Walsh was shot and wounded. He said that he was ordered to climb a fence and then he was shot. The defendant said that Mr Walsh was escaping and on refusing to stop he shot him to prevent an escape. The court preferred the evidence of the defendant. On appeal Lowry LCJ listed the factors which made the use of a firearm reasonable. The patrol was operating in hostile territory, with the threat of an ambush. There was also the danger of booby traps. Mr Walsh was suspected of terrorist acts and if he escaped then he might carry on such activity. Lowry LCJ also pointed out that the soldier had to make a decision on the use of deadly force very quickly. He said that the law expected soldiers to act reasonably but also responsibly.

When the House of Lords had the opportunity to offer guidance on deadly force in Northern Ireland they declined to take it. Instead, the leading speech given by Lord Diplock provides guidance which is both convoluted and general so that it would not be of any real assistance. The facts of *Attorney-General for Northern Ireland's Reference (No. 1 of 1975)* [1977] AC 105, were that a soldier was on a farm and approached Mr McElhone, a farmhand, in order to detain him for questioning. Mr McElhone ran off and the soldier shouted at him to stop. He did not stop and the soldier opened fire and killed him. The soldier was acquitted of murder, mainly on the basis that he genuinely believed that he was shooting at an escaping suspected terrorist, and that he had no method of stopping him other than opening fire. When he was shot Mr McElhone was unarmed and the defendant, while he believed that Mr McElhone was a member of the IRA, did not have a belief that Mr McElhone had been involved in acts of terrorism or was likely to be involved in such activity in the immediate future. The decision was greeted with concern and this caused the Attorney-General to ask the Northern Ireland Court of Appeal if it was a crime for a member of the security forces to shoot to kill or seriously wound a person believed to be a member of a proscribed organisation in the course of his attempted escape; and if it was a crime, was it murder or manslaughter? Jones and Gibson LJJ did not disapprove of the trial judge's finding of fact and held that it was a triable issue as to whether the Crown had proved that the soldier's use of force was excessive. McGonigal LJ dissented from his colleagues. He decided that shooting an escaping member of a proscribed organisation who posed no immediate threat was excessive force and therefore unlawful. The law lords did not follow this approach. Instead Lord Diplock's question for a jury was this :

Are we satisfied that no reasonable man (a) with knowledge of such facts as were known to the acccused or reasonably believed by him to exist (b) in the circumstances and time available for reflection (c) could be of the opinion that the prevention of the risk of harm to which others might be exposed if the suspect were allowed to escape justified exposing the suspect to the risk of harm that might result from the kind of force that the accused contemplated using? (at p. 137).

Perhaps it is understandable that the courts do not wish to restrict unduly members of the security forces who have to operate in difficult circumstances. However, it should be remembered that the situation in this case was not one of self-defence but rather one where the question posed asks if it is permissible to arrest a person by shooting him. (See Spujt 1986 for cogent criticism of the courts.)

Contrast *R* v *Clegg* [1995] 1 AC 482, which concerned a soldier, also on patrol in Northern Ireland, who fired four shots at an escaping joyrider. As the final shot could not be regarded as effecting an arrest or self-defence, it was excessive force and a conviction for murder was correct.

It should be noted that art. 2 of the European Convention on Human Rights permits only force which is absolutely necessary in making an arrest, or preventing an escape, or quelling a riot or insurrection. This standard would seem to be more stringent than British law.

13.2.5 Removal to a Police Station

Where a person has been arrested other than in a police station, then the person should be taken to a station as soon as is reasonably practicable (Police and Criminal Evidence Act 1984, s. 30(1)). This is required because there are various safeguards relating to police detention which operate upon arrival at a station. The arrested person may be taken to another place first but only if that is necessary to carry out investigations which it is reasonable to conduct immediately (s. 30(10)). The reasons for any delay in removal to a police station must be recorded on arrival at the station (s. 30(11)).

In order to comply with the safeguards for detention at a station, chief constables have to designate some stations as ones where detention is carried out (s. 35). Accordingly an arrested person should be taken to such a designated station (s. 30(2)). There are exceptions to this. First, if an officer is based at a non-designated station, the arrested person may be brought to that station, unless it appears that he or she will be held for more than six hours (s. 30(3) and (4)). A suspect who is to be held for more than six hours but who is taken to a non-designated station must be removed to a designated one unless released (s. 30(6)). The second and third exceptions are similar: an arrested person need not be taken to a designated police station if arrested by a single officer having no other officer to assist (s. 30(5)(a)(i)), or taken into custody following arrest by a citizen (s. 30(5)(a)(ii)), and it appears to the officer that removal to a designated station will lead to injury to the suspect, the officer or someone else (s. 30(5)(b)).

13.2.6 Reasonable Suspicion

One of the preconditions for the exercise of the power of summary arrest conferred by the Police and Criminal Evidence Act 1984 is that of reasonable suspicion. This is also required for the powers of search which are discussed below beginning at 13.3. It is convenient to discuss this concept of reasonable suspicion for both sets of powers here.

One can only arrest under the Police and Criminal Evidence Act 1984, s. 24, someone who is committing or has committed an arrestable offence or is reasonably suspected of these things. The occasions on which a person is caught 'red-handed' will be fewer than those in which arrest is carried out because of reasonable suspicion. What is reasonable suspicion? Guidance from the courts has been somewhat general. Two of the better known judicial statements were made by Scott LJ in *Dumbell* v *Roberts* [1944] 1 All ER 326, and Lord Devlin in *Hussien* v *Chong Fook Kam* [1970] AC 942. Both of them indicate that suspicion is at the opposite end of a line from prima facie proof. Lord Devlin pointed out that while prima facie proof consists of admissible evidence, 'Suspicion can take into account matters that could not be put in evidence'. The two judges also agree that where there is no danger of escape by the person who has aroused suspicion, then enquiries should be made which can assist the decision as to whether or not an arrest should be made. Scott LJ said that the police 'should act on the assumption that their prima facie suspicion may be ill-founded'.

There is guidance on reasonable suspicion in one of the codes of practice issued by the Home Office. It deals with the power of stop and search which is discussed below (13.3.1). The guidance states that there must be an objective basis for reasonable suspicion and that to rely solely on personal factors, such as an individual's age, colour, hairstyle or manner of dress, or knowledge of a relevant conviction will be insufficient. With respect to the power to stop and search for a prohibited or stolen article, the code states that the nature of the article suspected to be carried should be considered in the context of factors such as the time and place and the behaviour of the person. If information has been received about an article describing it, or a person suspected of carrying it, and that person is observed acting warily or covertly or attempting to hide something; or a person is carrying a certain type of article at an unusual time or in a place where it is known that a number of thefts have recently taken place, then grounds for reasonable suspicion may exist.

This advice is quite general. Perhaps assistance may be gained from cases in which the courts have ruled on whether suspicion was reasonable or not. Unfortunately, as the following cases demonstrate, the courts may take differing views about broadly similar situations. In *R v Prince* [1981] Crim LR 638, the defendant was observed going into two post offices where he discussed with counter staff a document which he was holding. The police officer who saw this recognised the document as a giro cheque. The officer felt that his observations and a hunch were sufficient grounds to exercise a power granted by the Metropolitan Police Act 1839, s. 66 (repealed by the Police and Criminal Evidence Act 1984, s. 7(1)(b)), which allowed for the stopping and searching of a person who is reasonably suspected of having or carrying something stolen or obtained unlawfully. At trial the judge disagreed that the officer did have the necessary reasonable suspicion. Contrast that case with *Pedro v Diss* [1981] 2 All ER 59, where the question on appeal to the Divisional Court concerned other aspects of the validity of an arrest. The facts were that officers in a police car had observed three youths who were standing in a doorway. They walked away following the approach of the police car. One of the youths was questioned. He refused to answer in an abusive manner. The magistrates made a finding that the police observations, combined with a hunch, were sufficient grounds to suspect reasonably that the youth could have stolen goods or housebreaking implements.

Despite the requirement that there should be an objective basis to the reasonableness of suspicion, it would appear that officers do not always reach that particular standard. Sometimes the courts acquiesce in this, and on other occasions they do not.

13.2.6.1 Reasonable belief Some police powers may only be exercised where the officer has reasonable grounds for believing that a certain state of affairs exists. For example, if an officer wishes to stop and search a person in a garden because of a reasonable suspicion that the person is carrying stolen articles, then the officer must also reasonably believe that the person does not live in the dwelling or have permission to be there from someone who does live in the dwelling (Police and Criminal Evidence Act 1984, s. 1(4); see 13.3.3. for general discussion of this power). It seems that there is a difference between suspicion and belief, that belief is a higher standard than suspicion. In a case involving road traffic legislation (*Baker* v *Oxford* [1980] RTR 315), the Divisional Court accepted this distinction without elaborating on it. Argument before the court had suggested that 'suspect' implied an imagination to exist without proof, whereas 'belief' impied an acceptance of what was true (see further Bailey and Birch 1982).

13.3 SEARCH

English common law has not developed much protection for privacy but the privacy of an individual's home or office does enjoy the strong protection afforded to property. Some 18th century cases established that property could not be seized under a general warrant, i.e., a warrant which did not specify the items sought, and that only the correct legal authority could provide for the entry and search of premises, so that a government minister was not permitted to send in people to search the house of a person believed to have committed the offence of sedition (*Entick* v *Carrington* (1765) 19 St Tr 1029; *Wilkes* v *Wood* (1763) 19 St Tr 1153; *Leach* v *Money* (1765) 19 St Tr 1002; *Wilkes* v *Lord Halifax* (1769) 19 St Tr 1406).

Developments since the 18th century have led to giving powers to persons other than the police which permit them to enter premises and to search and seize property (e.g., Customs and Excise, see Stone 1989). The Police and Criminal Evidence Act 1984 provides the police with powers to search people and property. People may be searched after arrest or may be stopped and searched without arrest. Similarly, property may be searched following the arrest of a person there or after the granting of a search warrant.

13.3.1 Search under a Warrant
Under the Police and Criminal Evidence Act 1984 the magistrates may be asked to grant a search warrant in respect of evidence of a crime, and the Crown Court hears applications for special procedure material and certain excluded material. Only items which are subject to legal professional privilege are outside the scope of these powers.

One difference between the powers for searches conducted under warrant and those following arrest or under the power to stop and search is that warrants deal with serious arrestable offences. Serious arrestable offences include treason, murder, manslaughter, rape, kidnapping, drug-trafficking, hostage-taking and some sexual offences (s. 117, sch. 5). An arrestable offence may become a serious arrestable offence if it has led or is intended to lead to any of the following consequences: serious harm to the security of the State or public order, serious interference with the administration of justice or investigation of offences, death or injury to a person, substantial financial gain or serious financial loss to a person (s. 116(3) and (5)).

The police apply to a magistrate for a search warrant where they reasonably believe that a serious arrestable offence has been committed, and that there is on the specified premises material which is likely to be of substantial value to the investigation of the offence and likely to be relevant evidence. The police must also show that one of the following conditions is fulfilled: that it is not practicable to communicate with a person entitled to grant entry to the premises or access to the evidence; that entry will not be granted without a warrant; or that the purpose of the search will be frustrated or seriously prejudiced unless the police can gain immediate entry once they are at the premises (s. 8). If the magistrate is satisfied on these points a warrant can be granted (s. 8(1)).

The magistrate does not have the jurisdiction to grant a warrant (s. 8(1)(d)) where material is subject to legal privilege (communications between a professional legal adviser and client or person representing the client in respect of legal advice or concerning or contemplating legal proceedings) (s. 10); or is excluded material (personal records made or acquired for the purpose of a trade, business or profession, human tissue or tissue fluid held in confidence for diagnosis or medical treatment, journalistic material comprising documents, or other material held in confidence) (s. 11)). Where there were powers prior to the Police and Criminal Evidence Act 1984 which would have enabled the granting of search warrants for evidence now defined as excluded material then this becomes special procedure material which can be the subject of a warrant granted by a circuit judge (s. 9, sch. 1). Otherwise excluded material cannot be the subject of a search warrant under the Police and Criminal Evidence Act 1984.

The application for a warrant to search for special procedure material is normally heard by the judge in the presence of the police and the person against whom the warrant is sought. This is different from the ordinary warrant application where only the police are present with the magistrate. There are two sets of access conditions, either of which must be satisfied in order for the warrant to be granted. The first set requires reasonable belief that a serious arrestable offence has been committed, and that material including special procedure material, but not excluded material, is on the specified premises; that this material is likely to be of substantial value to the investigation and that it is likely to be relevant evidence; and that other methods of obtaining the material were tried unsuccessfully or not pursued because they appeared to be bound to fail; and that it is in the public interest that the material should be produced or access to it granted having regard to the benefit likely to accrue to the investigation and to the circumstances under which the person in possession of the material holds it (sch. 1, para. 2). The second set of conditions require reasonable belief that special procedure material is on the specified premises; and that, but for s. 9(2), a search warrant under another enactment could have been authorised and this would have been appropriate (sch. 1, para. 3).

The legislation also stipulates how the warrant should be executed (s. 16). This includes the requirements that (a) entry and search should take place within one month of issue (s. 16(3)); (b) the search should be at a reasonable hour unless that would frustrate the search (s. 16(4)); (c) the officer shall provide documentary evidence of status and a copy of the warrant to the occupier of the premises (s. 16(5)); the search shall only be of the extent required for the purpose for which the warrant was issued (s. 16(8)); and the warrant shall be endorsed with a statement of the result of the search including whether seized articles were other than those sought (s. 16(9)).

The code of practice requires that applications should normally be made with the authority of an inspector for an ordinary warrant, and a superintendent for a special procedure material warrant. Care should be taken to check that the information on which an application is based is recent and accurate, and where it comes from an anonymous source some corroboration should have been sought. The occupier is to be provided with a notice providing information about the grounds for, and powers of, a search; and the occupier's rights, including that of compensation where damage was caused in entering the premises or during the search. In addition to the endorsement of the warrant a full record of the search shall be made on return to the station and the record shall be entered into the subdivisional station's search register.

The legislation and code on entry, search and seizure would appear to provide that proper authorisation is required before the police execute a search warrant and that the material covered is restricted. Research had shown that the magistrates hardly ever refuse an application for a warrant, indeed that they rarely ask questions about the information on which the application is based (Lidstone 1984, p. 450). Subsequent research in two cities has shown that only 12 per cent of searches were made under a warrant, with 47 per cent carried out under s. 18 after arrest (Bevan and Lidstone 1991, para. 4.07). The safeguards would seem to be undermined, if not rendered impotent, by the general power of seizure (s. 19). Under this provision where an officer is lawfully on premises an article may be seized if there are reasonable grounds for believing (a) it has been obtained as a consequence of the commision of an offence, or it is evidence relating to the offence under investigation or any other offence; and (b) that it is necessary to seize it in order to prevent its concealment, loss, alteration or destruction. While it might seem odd not to permit such evidence to be seized in the course of a search, this power has the potential to turn a search for specified items into a general fishing expedition.

13.3.2 Search on Arrest
The Police and Criminal Evidence Act 1984 provides powers of search of the person and property following arrest.

13.3.2.1 Search of the person If a person has been arrested at a place other than a police station, a search may be conducted if the officer reasonably believes that the person presents a danger to anyone (Police and Criminal Evidence Act 1984, s. 32(1)). Where articles are found they may be seized if the officer reasonably believes that the person might use them to cause physical injury to anyone (s. 32(8)).

A search is also permitted for (a) anything which could be used to make an escape; (b) evidence relating to any offence (s. 32(2)(a)). The officer may seize any item not subject to legal privilege if there are reasonable grounds for believing: (a) that the person might use it to make an escape; or (b) that it is evidence of an offence, or that it has been obtained as the result of an offence (s. 32(9)).

13.3.2.2 Search of premises There are two powers of search of premises following arrest. One deals with premises where the person was at the time of, or immediately before, arrest. Such premises may be entered and searched for any evidence relating to the offence for which the arrest was made if the officer reasonably believes such evidence to be there (s. 32(2)(b) and (6)).

The other power of search following the arrest of a person for an arrestable offence is wider but normally requires authorisation. This power permits an officer to enter and search any premises occupied or controlled by that person if there are reasonable grounds for suspecting that the premises contain evidence or other items relating to that offence, or some other arrestable offence connected with, or similar to, that offence (s. 18(1)). If any such material is found then it may be seized by the officer (s. 18(2)).

Ordinarily there must be written authorisation by an inspector or more senior officer (s. 18(4)). The search may be conducted without such authorisation if the person has been taken directly to the premises because the presence of the person at a place other than a police station was necessary for the effective investigation of the offence (s. 18(5)). Where a search has been conducted without the inspector's authorisation, then such an officer must be informed of the search as soon as is practicable afterwards (s. 18(6)).

The officer who authorises the search or is informed of one afterwards is to make a written record of the grounds for the search and the nature of the material sought (s. 18(7)).

13.3.3 Stop and Search

The Royal Commission on Criminal Procedure was divided on the issue of conferring on the police a nationwide uniform power of stopping individuals and searching them for stolen items and offensive weapons. The two dissenting commissioners feared that such a random power would do little to improve relations between the police and young people, particularly black youth. As we have seen (13.2.6), the code's advice on what constitutes reasonable suspicion seeks to prevent the use of stereotypes as a criterion for the exercise of the power.

Under the Police and Criminal Evidence Act 1984, s. 1, an officer may stop and search a person, or a vehicle, if it is reasonably suspected that a stolen or prohibited article will be found. A prohibited article is defined as being (a) an offensive weapon, or (b) an article which was made or adapted for use, or intended to be used, in connection with burglary, theft or offences under the Theft Act 1968, s. 12 (taking away a vehicle without authority), s. 15 (obtaining property by deception) (Police and Criminal Evidence Act 1984, (s. 1(7)). This power also includes searching for an article which is covered by the Criminal Justice Act 1984, s. 139 (the possession of an article with a blade or point in a public place) (Police and Criminal Evidence Act 1984, s. 1(8A)). The search may be conducted in a place (a) where the public may be as of right, or with express or implied permission or (b) where people have ready access at the time of the proposed search, but is not a dwelling (s. 1(1)). If the search of the person or vehicle is to be carried out in a garden or yard, or on land occupied with and used for the purposes of a dwelling, then the officer must believe on reasonable grounds that (a) the person does not reside in that dwelling or (b) the person or vehicle is not in the place in question with the express or implied permission of the person who does reside in the dwelling (s. 1(4) and (5)).

13.3.3.1 Stop and search procedure   The Police and Criminal Evidence Act 1984 stipulates the procedures for (a) a stop and search under s. 1, and (b) under other powers of search which may be exercised without making an arrest. Before an officer exercises the stop and search power certain steps must be taken. If the officer is not in uniform then the person should be shown documentary evidence of the officer's status, i.e., the officer's warrant card (s. 2(2)). The officer must then provide certain information before conducting the search. This includes the officer's name and 'home' station, the object of the search and the grounds for it (s. 2(3)). Ordinarily the officer will make a record of the search (s. 3(1)), and so must give notice of the right to obtain a copy of the record of the search within 12 months of the search (ss. 2(3), 3(7), (8) and (9)). If it is not practicable to make a record of the search then no such notice need be given (s. 2(4)). If it is not practicable to make a record on the spot then one should be made as soon as is practicable afterwards. A search record must state the object of the search; the grounds for making it; the date and time when it was made; what, if anything, was found; what, if any, injury to a person or damage to property resulted from the search; and the identity of the officer who conducted the search (s. 3(6)). The record should also include a note of the name of the person searched if known, but the officer may not detain the person in order to find that out (s. 3(3)). Where the officer does not know the name of the person searched then a description of that person is to be included in the record (s. 3(4)).

The officer may search the person or vehicle where first detained or nearby, and the detention shall last as long as is reasonably required for the conduct of the search (s. 2(8)). The officer may not require the person to remove, in public, any clothing other than an outer coat, jacket or gloves (s. 2(9)(a)).

The code of practice on stop and search, in addition to restating the requirements prescribed by the Police and Criminal Evidence Act 1984, also offers guidance to officers on what they should do. One note of guidance states that the power should be exercised responsibly and sparingly. If it is misused then this could lead to mistrust of the police by the community. Officers should be courteous and considerate to those who are stopped and searched.

The code recommends officers to ask questions before conducting the stop and search, as an explanation might render the search unnecessary. This reflects the Police and Criminal Evidence Act 1984, s. 2(1), which makes it clear that the power is one of *stop* as well as of search. It is still the law that the person need not answer the officer's questions which may lead to the officer conducting the search.

In making the record of the search the code states that the person's ethnic origin should be included. Perhaps this has been included so that the supervision of officers' stops and searches could pick up on those who, wrongly, use racial stereotyping as the basis for exercising this power. Certainly the aim of the royal commission in recommending the giving of reasons and the making of records was to provide a safeguard (Philips 1981, paras. 3.24 to 3.28).

13.3.3.2 Vehicle searches Where an officer searches an unattended vehicle a note should be left stating (a) that the vehicle has been searched; (b) the name and home station of the officer; (c) that an application for compensation for any damage may be made to that police station; and (d) that a request may be made within 12 months for a record of the search (Police and Criminal Evidence Act 1984, s. 2(6)). This note should be left inside the vehicle unless it is impracticable to do so without damaging the vehicle (s. 2(7)).

The police can set up roadblocks under the Road Traffic Act 1988, s. 163, for the general purpose of checking all vehicles in an area, or for checking vehicles selected by any criterion. Where the particular objective of such a check is to search vehicles for a person (a) who has committed an offence other than a road traffic or vehicle excise offence; (b) who is a witness to such an offence; (c) intending to commit such an offence; or (d) who is unlawfully at large, then special rules apply (s. 4(1)). Normally a check with these objectives must be authorised in writing by a superintendent or more senior officer (s. 4(3)). The authorising officer must have reasonable grounds to believe that the offence is or would be a serious arrestable offence, and must reasonably suspect that the person, but not the witness in (b), is or is about to be in a vehicle which would be stopped if the check were authorised (s. 4(4)).

Authorisation may be given by an officer below the rank of superintendent if the permitted objective is urgent (s. 4(5)). The officer who gives such an authorisation must record it in writing at the time it is given and inform a superintendent or more senior officer of the authorisation (s. 4(6)). This more senior officer may authorise, in writing, the continuation of the check (s. 4(8)). Alternatively, this officer may decide that the check should not continue, in which case a written record of the fact that the check took place and its purpose shall be made (s. 4(9)). Where a superintendent or more senior officer authorises the initiation or continuation of a check, this authorisation must include the period of its duration, up to a maximum of seven days, and whether it is to be continuous or to be conducted at specified times during that period (s. 4(11)). Extensions of the period of the check, not exceeding seven days, may be authorised by a superintendent or more senior officer (s. 4(12)). All written authorisations must name the officer giving it, specify its purpose, including the relevant serious arrestable offence, and designate the locality of the check (s. 4(13) and (14)).

The person in charge of a vehicle when it is stopped is entitled to have a written statement detailing the purpose of the check if the request is made within 12 months of the check (s. 4(15)).

Chief constables are required to include in their annual reports statistical information about road checks and recorded searches (s. 5).

13.3.3.3 Anticipation of violence   A new power to conduct a stop and search of (a) pedestrians and (b) vehicles including their drivers and passengers has been conferred to deal with anticipated violence (CJPOA 1994, s. 60). If a police superintendent reasonably believes that incidents involving serious violence may occur in any area of that officer's locality, and it is expedient to prevent them, then authorisation may be given which will permit this search power to be exercised within the locality for a period of up to 24 hours. The authorisation is to be issued in writing and signed by the authorising officer, specifying the locality and the period of operation. Where such authorisation has been issued then an officer in uniform may stop and search pedestrians and vehicles for offensive weapons or dangerous instruments. In doing this the officer need not have any grounds for suspecting that such weapons or instruments are being carried by the persons or vehicles (s. 60(5)). If such items are found then they may be seized.

It is worth emphasising that s. 60(5) does not require any suspicion to carry out the stop and search. Once the s. 60 authorisation has been given, however, a driver or pedestrian who has been stopped and searched may receive a written statement that such an action occurred under this power if an application is made within 12 months.

13.4 DETENTION, TREATMENT AND QUESTIONING

Once a person has arrived at a police station either voluntarily or under arrest, the police will wish to question that person. If the person came along voluntarily and wishes to stop that cooperation then the police must make an arrest in order to detain the person. The Police and Criminal Evidence Act 1984 stipulates certain safeguards for persons who are detained under arrest and questioned. Normally only designated stations will be places where detention and questioning should be carried out. At such stations special officers known as custody and review officers will exercise supervision over persons brought to the station. These officers are not directly involved with the investigation of the offence which has led to the person's arrival at the station. They will maintain the custody record for the person. Minimum ranks are specified for these officers: a sergeant for a custody officer, an inspector for a review officer. Where another officer of a rank higher than the custody or review officers gives instructions relating to a suspect which are at variance with the decisions of these statutory officers exercising their statutory duties, they are to take the matter up immediately with the officer responsible for the station (ss. 38(6) and 40(11)).

13.4.1 Detention

The framework of supervision of a person in police detention is that, at certain intervals, a decision must be made to charge or release the person, or to continue detention without charge. The points at which these determinations are to be made are:

(a) on arrival at the station (s. 37);

(b) at reviews made six hours later, and then subsequently every nine hours (s. 40);

(c) at 24 hours a more senior officer may authorise continued detention beyond the 24 to 36 hours (s. 42);

(d) at 36 hours the magistrates decide whether or not to grant a warrant of further extension which permits a maximum of a further 36 hours' detention (s. 43);

(e) an extension of a warrant of further detention of up to 36 hours may be granted by the magistrates with the upper limit on police detention without charge being 96 hours (s. 44).

The criteria for these decisions are as follows. At stages (a) and (b), the initial decision and review are made by the custody officer. Detention without charge may be carried out if there are reasonable grounds to believe that this is necessary to secure or preserve evidence of the offence, or to obtain such evidence by questioning. At stage (c), the review is by an inspector, at (d) and (e) by a magistrates' court. Detention without charge may be continued using the previous criteria and also that the decision-makers are satisfied that the offence is a serious arrestable offence, and that the investigation is being conducted diligently and expeditiously.

Records must be kept of the decisions and the grounds for them, and the arrested person should be given this information. At stages (b) and (c) the officer may permit the arrestee or the arrestee's solicitor, if available at the time of the decision, to make representations about the detention (ss. 40(12) and 42(6)). At the hearings before the magistrates, the person is entitled to be legally represented and the hearing may be adjourned to enable this (ss. 43(3) and 44(6)).

This structure is designed to facilitate the approach to the investigation of crime which relies upon questioning in police detention. The maximum duration of detention without charge is 96 hours even though research for the Royal Commission on Criminal Procedure indicated that 95 per cent of suspects had been charged or released within 24 hours (Philips 1981, para. 3.96). Beyond 24 hours more stringent criteria are required to justify detention, and after 36 hours the magistrates determine if the person's detention is to continue.

Some of the safeguards may be completely or partially overridden. It is permissible to postpone reviews of detention where it would not be practicable to conduct them at the stipulated latest time. Two examples given are that the person is being questioned and the review officer is satisfied that a review would prejudice the investigation of the offence; or no review officer is readily available (s. 40(4)(b)). When postponed, the review must be carried out as soon as practicable after the latest stipulated time (s. 40(5)).

Detention is permitted after the person has been charged where the custody officer (a) cannot ascertain the name and address of the suspect, or has reasonable grounds for doubting that any name and address given are correct; (b) reasonably believes that detention is necessary to prevent the suspect from injuring anyone, or causing loss of, or damage to, property; or (c) reasonably believes that the suspect will not appear in court to answer bail, or that detention is necessary to prevent the suspect interfering with the administration of justice or the investigation of any offences (s. 38(1) and (2)).

Any person who is detained after being charged must be brought to the magistrates' court as soon as practicable (s. 46). During the period between charge and appearance before the magistrates, the person's detention will be subject to review (s. 40).

13.4.2 Treatment and Questioning

Research for the Royal Commission on Criminal Procedure indicated that questioning was a crucial element in the investigation of crime. It could lead to confessions or to information which provided evidence about offences. One of the fundamental tenets of the English criminal justice system is the right of a person to say nothing, either to the police or in the course of a trial, without any adverse inferences being drawn from that silence. This is the so-called right to silence and while the royal commission had research evidence which indicated that very few people actually exercised this right, it decided not to recommend its abolition. This right has been removed in Northern Ireland by the Criminal Evidence (Northern Ireland) Order 1988 (SI 1988/1987) and in England and Wales by CJPOA 1994, ss. 34–38.

The commission did recommend that there should be a right to have someone informed of an arrest, and a right to consult a solicitor. These were enacted as ss. 56 and 58, respectively, of the Police and Criminal Evidence Act 1984. A person may be denied the immediate exercise of these rights. In both cases the delay may last for up to 36 hours of detention. Once the reason for delay ceases to exist then the exercise of the rights must be allowed. In order to delay the exercise of these rights, the detention must be in connection with a serious arrestable offence and the authorising officer must reasonably believe that the exercise of the rights would (a) lead to interference with or harm to evidence connected with a serious arrestable offence, or interference with, or injury to, other persons; (b) lead to the alerting of other persons suspected of having committed such an offence but not yet arrested; and (c) hinder the recovery of any property obtained as a result of such an offence (ss. 56(5) and 58(8)). Delay may also be authorised in connection with a drug trafficking offence where the officer reasonably believes that the exercise of the right by a person will hinder the recovery of that person's proceeds arising from the offence. The person must be informed of the delay and this must be entered into the custody record.

It is clearly a serious matter to deny access to legal advice because it is feared that a solicitor might deliberately, or even inadvertently, hinder the investigation of a crime by providing information to accomplices. The criterion for this is reasonable belief and so there must be stonger grounds than suspicion. The code makes it quite clear that the likelihood of a solicitor advising exercise of the right to silence cannot justify denial of access to a solicitor. The consultation with the solicitor is to be held in private.

Where a detainee has requested a solicitor, and the police are not delaying this right, questioning by the police should not begin before the solicitor's arrival. This may be overruled if the person consents in writing or on tape, or a superintendent reasonably believes that the waiting period would cause unreasonable delay to the investigation, or that delay would involve a risk of harm to persons or of loss of, or damage to, property.

13.4.2.1 Searches When a person is arrested, the custody officer is to obtain a list of possessions of the person and this may be done by a search if that is felt to be necessary (Police and Criminal Evidence Act 1984, s. 54(1) and (6)). The police may seize clothes or personal effects if they reasonably believe that they are evidence of the offence, and they may also seize any items which they believe the person could use (a) to cause injury to any person, (b) to damage property, (c) to interfere with evidence, and (d) to make an escape (s. 54(4)). Under s. 54(3) other items may be seized.

Intimate searches, i.e., of body orifices, may be carried out either for protective purposes or to obtain drugs (s. 58). Such a search may be authorised where a superintendent reasonably believes that the person has concealed (a) items which could be used to injure people whilst in detention or (b) class A drugs (e.g., heroin). Normally these searches are to be carried out by registered medical practitioners or nurses, but if a superintendent considers this to be impractical then a search for a protective purpose may be conducted by an officer. Drug searches can be conducted only at a hospital or doctor's surgery or other place used for medical purposes, whereas a protective search may be carried out a police station.

The provisions for search also include a strip search, which includes the removal of more than outer clothing. The code stipulates that such a search should only be conducted where the custody officer considers it necesssary to remove an article which the person would not be allowed to keep, such as weapons or evidence of crime.

13.4.2.2 Fingerprinting A person's fingerprints may be taken without consent if the person has been convicted of a recordable offence or a superintendent authorises it. This authorisation is conditional on the officer reasonably suspecting that the person is involved in a criminal offence and reasonably believing that the fingerprints will tend to confirm or disprove such involvement. The fingerprints and any copies are to be destroyed if the person is cleared of the offence, or is not to be prosecuted, or the person is not suspected of having committed the offence (s. 64). According to Lidstone and Palmer this means that as a matter of routine fingerprints will be taken of detained people who may be prosecuted (1996, para. 7.99).

13.4.2.3 Questioning Confessions play a crucial role in the criminal justice system. The law of evidence seeks to exclude confessions which were not made voluntarily by the defendant but resulted from oppression, coercion or inducement. It has not been unusual for a judge, in the course of a trial, to determine the admissibilty of confessions where the defendant claimed to have been 'verballed', i.e., the police made up the confession. The government decided that the best method of dealing with this was by tape recording interviews. Initially this was done on a trial basis, the success of which led to its introduction throughout England and Wales by 1991. There is a code for taping of interviews and one of the prescribed safeguards is the making of two recordings. One is the working copy and the other is a sealed master tape to prevent allegations of tampering by the police. It has been suggested that there is a practice of conducting interviews in a police car on the way to the station, which short-circuits both recording and access to legal advice (Robertson 1993, p. 35). In *R v Maguire* (1981) Cr App R 115 the Court of Appeal held that a conversation in a car on the way to the police station and which did not comply with code on interviewing could still be admitted as evidence at trial.

One of the codes stipulates the physical conditions for questioning by the police. Interview rooms should be adequately lit, heated and ventilated. There should be breaks for meals, refreshments and sleep which should be an uninterrupted eight-hour period normally at night. The breaks and sleep period may be interrupted or delayed where it is reasonably believed that they would involve a risk of injury to anyone or damage to property, or would unnecessarily delay the person's release from custody, or otherwise prejudice the outcome of the investigation. A suspect may sit when questioned and have his or her lawyer present. The code allows for the police to remove a solicitor from an interview for misconduct. An example of this is the solicitor answering on behalf of the client or writing down answers for the client to use. It is stated not to be misconduct for the solicitor to seek to challenge improper questions or to advise a client not to answer any question.

13.5 ANTI-TERRORISM PROVISIONS

The activities of terrorists have led to the enactment of legislation which increases the powers of the police when investigating terrorist offences. Northern Ireland has legislation which applies only in that jurisdiction, with one of the most significant differences being trial without a jury for particular 'scheduled offences' (Northern Ireland (Emergency Provisions) Act 1996, s. 1 and sch. 1). Following the Birmingham pub bombs of 1974 special legislation applying to the whole of the UK has been enacted. The current statute is the Prevention of Terrorism (Temporary Provisions) Act 1989. All police powers vary where terrorist offences are under investigation.

13.5.1 Arrest
Special offences have been created and therefore there are additional powers of arrest. Some of these offences, e.g., membership of or contributing to the

resources of proscribed organisations, could come within the scope of an arrestable offence. The power to arrest without a warrant, on reasonable suspicion, a person who is or has been concerned in the commission, preparation or instigation of an act of terrorism (Prevention of Terrorism (Temporary Provisions) Act 1989, s. 14(1)(b)) is a power to arrest where no actual offence may have been committed. A preparatory act is not the commission of an offence nor an attempt to, nor incitement to, commit an offence. The statute provides a very wide definition of terrorism: 'the use of violence for political ends, and includes any use of violence for the purpose of putting the public or any section of the public in fear' (Prevention of Terrorism (Temporary Provisions) Act 1989, s. 20(1)).

13.5.2 Entry, Search and Seizure

A search warrant may be granted by a magistrate to enable an officer to enter premises to search and arrest a person who is reasonably suspected of being there and whom an officer believes is liable to arrest under the Prevention of Terrorism (Temporary Provisions) Act 1989, s. 14(1)(b) (a person concerned with preparation, commission or instigation of acts of terrorism) (Police and Criminal Evidence Act 1984, s. 51(1)). Where there is a power to arrest under the Prevention of Terrorism (Temporary Provisions) Act 1989, s. 14, an officer may stop and search a person to ascertain if that person possesses any document or article which could constitute evidence of liability to arrest under s. 14. A search for the same purpose may be carried out where a person has been arrested under s. 14 other than for the commission of a crime.

The powers and procedure relating to search warrants are altered where a terrorist investigation is underway. Such an investigation is concerned with acts of terrorism, or acts done in furtherance of, or in connection with, acts of terrorism s. 17(1)). Search warrants under the Police and Criminal Evidence Act 1984 are available only in respect of serious arrestable offences. Not every act of terrorism will constitute such an offence and so the Prevention of Terrorism (Temporary Provisions) Act 1989 search powers are wider. The major difference is that some searches may be authorised by the Secretary of State or a police officer. The Secretary of State may authorise searches in relation to offences concerned with financial assistance for terrorism (Prevention of Terrorism (Temporary Provisions) Act 1989, sch. 7, para. 8). This may be done if the Secretary of State is satisfied of the requirements which must be met in an application to magistrates or circuit judges, and believes that disclosure of information in such applications would prejudice the investigation by the Royal Ulster Constabulary or prejudice the safety of persons in Northern Ireland. This power only applies in Northern Ireland.

There is no such territorial restriction upon the provision which allows a superintendent to authorise searches for any material related to the offence apart from that subject to legal privilege (sch. 7, para. 7). The conditions for this are that the case is one of great emergency and it is in the interests of the State that immediate action be taken. The Secretary of State is to be notified of such authorisations.

In non-urgent cases applications are made to the magistrates and circuit judges as in Police and Criminal Evidence Act 1984 cases. Where the search is for ordinary material, not excluded or special procedure material, the only major difference from applications under the Police and Criminal Evidence Act 1984, s. 8, is the point just noted about the serious arrestable offence condition not applying (Prevention of Terrorism (Temporary Provisions) Act 1989, sch. 7, para. 2). Not only may special procedure material be sought, but also excluded material. Only one set of access conditions have to be satisfied. These are the same as the second set in the Police and Criminal Evidence Act 1984, sch. 1, which refer to powers granted under pre-1984 legislation. The Prevention of Terrorism (Temporary Provisions) Act 1989 application, unlike a Police and Criminal Evidence Act 1984 one, is made without the presence of those who would be subjected to the warrant.

Examining officers on port and border control duty have powers of search which enable them to search aircraft, ships and vehicles for people who may be examined to determine if they have any connection with acts of terrorism (Prevention of Terrorism (Temporary Provisions) Act 1989, sch. 7, para. 6). Baggage to be loaded or unloaded may also be searched.

The Prevention of Terrorism (Additional Powers) Act 1996 adds new search powers to the 1989 Act (see Reid 1996). A new para. 2A in sch. 7 to the 1989 Act enables the police to ask magistrates for a warrant to search non-residential premises rather than identified premises. To grant the warrant the magistrate must be satisfied that there are reasonable grounds to believe that items on the premises will be of substantial value to a terrorist investigation. The application is to be made by a superintendent and it must be executed within 24 hours. A superintendent may authorise a search in an emergency and it can cover items which under the Police and Criminal Evidence Act 1984 would be excluded or special procedure material. New powers to search goods by an examining officer at a port are given by sch. 5, para. 4A of the 1989 Act. The power permits the detention of goods for examination up to a maximum period of seven days, and the goods need not have anything to do with terrorism.

13.5.2.1 Stop and search power

The Criminal Justice and Public Order Act 1994 has amended the Prevention of Terrorism (Temporary Provisions) Act 1989 by inserting a new s. 13A. This permits an officer in uniform to stop persons or vehicles (which include ships and aircraft) in order to search for articles of a kind which could be used for a purpose connected with the commission, preparation or instigation of acts of terrorism. In exercising this power the officer is not required to have any grounds for suspecting that the person or vehicle is carrying such articles. The power may only be exercised if an assistant chief constable, or commander in the Metropolitan or City of London police forces, thinks it expedient to prevent acts of terrorism in that officer's area or a specific locality and has issued a written authorisation for the power. The authorisation must specify the locality and its duration which is a maximum of 28 days. This may be extended for a further maximum of 28 days.

A written statement that a pedestrian or driver was subjected to the exercise of this power may be applied for within 12 months of the stop and search.

The Prevention of Terrorism (Additional Powers) Act 1996 inserts a new s. 13B in the 1989 Act to cover the search of pedestrians and any items which they are carrying. This is authorised separately from the s. 13A power but the authority may be given orally and then confirmed in writing as soon as possible thereafter. The safeguards which attach to the power are that the Secretary of State is to be informed of it quickly and may cancel or shorten the duration of the order and must in any event confirm it within 48 hours. When conducting a search in public all that the officer may require to be removed by the person is headgear, footwear, outer coat, jacket or gloves. As with s. 13A, no suspicion is required to initiate a search under the order but searches are subject to the PACE Code A on stopping and searching.

Failure to stop when requested and wilful obstruction of an officer exercising these powers are offences, the prosecution of which requires the consent of the Director of Public Prosecutions.

13.5.2.2 Police cordons and parking restrictions   The Prevention of Terrorism (Additional Powers) Act 1996 inserts new ss. 16C and 16D in the Prevention of Terrorism (Temporary Provisions) Act 1989, allowing for cordons and parking prohibitions and restrictions. A cordon may be authorised by a superintendent, or junior officer in an emergency, for a maximum period of 14 days. The basis for making the order is that it is expedient to do so in connection with an investigation into the commission, preparation or instigation of an act of terrorism. Schedule 6A allows the police to order a person to leave and to move vehicles, and officers may remove or move any vehicle. The parking prohibitions and restrictions are authorised on the basis of preventing acts of terrorism and require authorisation by an assistant chief constable, or a commander in London. It is an offence to leave a vehicle, or to permit a vehicle to remain at rest on a road in an area subject to prohibition or restriction but the leave of the Director of Public Prosecutions is required to commence a prosecution.

13.5.3 Detention

The examination of people at ports of entry may involve their detention. This examination may last for 24 hours but detention may be extended by the officer to 48 hours pending a decision on prosecution by the relevant authorities. The Secretary of State may authorise further detention of up to five days.

Where a person has been arrested under Prevention of Terrorism (Temporary Provisions) Act 1989 powers, detention may extend to a total of seven days which is authorised by the Secretary of State and not the magistrates (s. 14(5)). The rights of informing someone about arrest, and access to legal advice may both be delayed for up to 48 hours (annex B to code on detention, treatment and questioning). This may be done on the same basis as the Police and Criminal Evidence Act 1984 where a serious arrestable offence is involved (Police and Criminal Evidence Act 1984, ss. 56(5) and (5A), 58(8) and (8A)), or where a superintendent reasonably believes that their exercise would lead to interference with the gathering of information about acts of terrorism, or the alerting of any person would make it more difficult to prevent an act of terrorism or secure the apprehension, prosecution or conviction of a person in connection with an act of terrorism (Police and Criminal Evidence Act 1984, ss. 56(11) and 58(13)). Consultation by a person detained under anti-terrorism provisions with a solicitor may be required to be conducted within the sight and hearing of an officer. This is to be authorised by a commander or assistant chief constable on the same basis as that used to delay access to legal advice (Police and Criminal Evidence Act 1984, s. 58(14) to (17)).

13.6 REMEDIES

There are various remedies which an individual aggrieved at treatment by the police may use. Where the complaint concerns arrest there is the ancient writ of habeas corpus. In tort one may sue for false imprisonment. This is one of the torts dealing with trespass to the person. Trespass to property may be used where it is alleged that a search was unlawful. It might be possible to sue for a breach of statutory duty in respect of Police and Criminal Evidence Act 1984 duties. Individuals may also make a complaint to the Police Complaints Authority which was established under the Police and Criminal Evidence Act 1984.

13.6.1 Habeas Corpus
The writ of habeas corpus was used to determine the validity of a detention. The writ required that the person detained be brought to the court and a justification given for the detention. Its development by the judges was hailed by Dicey as one of the virtues of the English common law, providing a means of ensuring that the authorities did not exercise their powers in an arbitrary and unfair fashion. The provisions in the Police and Criminal Evidence Act 1984 which deal with police detention and, in particular, require the authorisation of detention without charge beyond 36 hours by the magistrates, have reduced the need for habeas corpus applications. They are more likely to occur where the detainee is challenging (a) extradition to another country to face criminal proceedings there, or (b) deportation because of breach of the immigration legislation.

Unless it is impossible, the application for habeas corpus is made by, or with the consent of, the detainee. If the application establishes a prima facie case that the detention is unlawful then the person who ordered detention, or has custody of the detainee (e.g., a prison governor), must come to the court to show cause why the writ should not be issued and the detainee released. Both the grant and refusal of the writ may be appealed, with leave, direct to the House of Lords.

13.6.2 Tort
Detailed discussion of the law on false imprisonment and trespass may be found in tort textbooks (see, e.g., Jones 1996). Suffice to say that those

subjected to unlawful arrest may seek damages. The amount of the award will vary depending upon the duration of detention. The Police Act 1964 stipulates that the chief constable of the relevant police force will be the defendant but that any award will be paid by that force's police authority.

13.6.3 Complaints

Part IV of the Police Act 1996 deals with police complaints and discipline. Under it, the Police Complaints Authority supervises the handling of some complaints against officers. It must supervise serious complaints, such as those alleging that death or serious injury was caused by an officer, and has a discretion to direct referral of complaints which are not legislatively prescribed to be referred. The authority does not conduct the investigation itself but supervises an investigating officer from a different police force. The authority reports to the chief constable of the officer complained against. The chief constable's decision on whether or not to refer to the Director of Public Prosecutions for a possible criminal prosecution, or to initiate, or dispense with, disciplinary proceedings, is subject to review and the direction of the Authority.

Disciplinary proceedings may result in a reprimand, fine, reduction in rank, requirement to resign or dismissal.

This structure was created because there was disquiet about the previous arrangements which had a minimal independent involvement so that police officers investigated complaints against other officers. It seems that a consensus is forming to create an entirely independent system, certainly this is the view of the Police Federation which represents junior and middle-ranking officers (see Goldsmith 1991 for a general account of British and foreign experience of complaints against the police).

13.7 CONCLUSIONS

This survey has shown some of the powers of the police and the safeguards which it is hoped will maintain an appropriate balance between society's interest in combating crime and the liberty of the individual. Opinions differ as to whether the balance achieved through the Police and Criminal Evidence Act 1984 favours the police or the citizen. Certainly disquiet about the serious miscarriages of justice such as the Guildford Four and the Birmingham Six, and the activities of some of the detectives in the West Midlands, created a climate which led to the establishment, in 1991, of the Royal Commission on Criminal Justice chaired by Lord Runciman of Doxford. The remit of this commission was wide, including events leading up to trial, the conduct of trials, and the appeal process. The commission reported in the summer of 1993 (Runciman 1993). One important topic was the right to silence. The commission decided not to recommend restricting this right. The government, however, took the opposite view and the major Bill for that session of Parliament, the Criminal Justice and Public Order Bill, included proposals to restrict the right to silence but omitted to deal with the problem of miscarriages of justice. Indeed the Criminal Appeal Bill proposing the creation of a

Criminal Cases Review Authority was not presented to Parliament until 1995.

This order of priorities flourishes because the UK does not have a written constitution with a declaration of rights, there is no culture of rights. Instead there is a tendency to compartmentalise so that the criminal justice system is thought of with the emphasis upon the criminal. This colours perceptions of the rights of the citizen and weakens their content. It is right that people should be concerned about crime, but this concern seems to tip the balance away from the liberty of the citizen. If people were more aware of rights generally, then there might be less reluctance to see that, while the police may not be organised on a national basis, they are still agents of the State, and agents of the State with significant powers to encroach upon individuals' liberty. To give an example of what I mean, one academic observed that when he went to the USA to teach criminal procedure, he was surprised to see that it was regarded as a part of constitutional law. I would suggest that if we thought of our relationship with the police as one involving constitutional rights, this would make a difference. To associate something with a constitution is to give it more weight, more significance, and this is so even in the UK with its lack of a written constitution. Debating rights in the context of a constitution would be very different from the current thinking prevalent in the UK where criminal justice is rooted in ideas of law and order, which I suggest limits the scope of a citizen's liberty.

PART IV

ADMINISTRATIVE LAW

Part IV deals with administrative law, which may be defined as the law relating to public administration. Administrative law is concerned with the way in which government carries out the tasks given to it, and this includes the nature of powers and duties as well as the means by which they may be controlled. For some scholars administrative law is really about the control of the administration and the protection of individual liberty, with the focus of attention being the case law of judicial review of administrative action. Harlow and Rawlings have termed this a red-light theory of administrative law (1984). This perspective is important but it should not dominate our view of administrative law. It should be remembered that citizens have an interest not only in lawful administration, but also in effective and efficient administration. Administrative law is, therefore, also concerned with enabling administrators to conduct government, which has been called a green-light theory (Harlow and Rawlings 1984).

In order to understand the law relating to public administration, one must have an appreciation of what administrators do. Chapter 14 seeks to provide a context by outlining aspects of the administrative process, and the values and techniques of administrators, which are somewhat different from lawyers' ways of doing things. The chapter will give examples of agencies and institutions which have been created to discharge governmental tasks, and focus on the public local inquiry as a case-study.

In chapter 15 two of the methods by which citizens may seek redress of grievances against government are examined. These are tribunals, and commissioners who deal with citizens' complaints. Both of these methods of redress were established because of perceived advantages compared with the courts. The merits of these extra-judicial institutions will be assessed.

The next two chapters, 16 and 17, are concerned with judicial review of administrative action, the grounds of challenge and the available remedies, respectively.

Finally, chapter 18 is concerned with the liability of the Crown and other public authorities in contract and tort. The special position of the Crown in ordinary litigation is outlined, as well as certain rules of evidence.

CHAPTER FOURTEEN

The Administrative Process

14.1 ADMINISTRATORS' TASKS AND TOOLS

Public administration is, broadly, the implementation of governmental policies. This definition would not satisfy scholars in political science because it would suggest that officials, be they civil servants, local government officers, or those working in non-departmental public bodies, simply carry out a mechanical function, which equates policy implementation to turning the rudder in order to steer a boat. It is now recognised that officials do play a part in formulating policy. A role which is shared with our elected representatives – MPs and councillors. This is not properly reflected in our constitutional arrangements, in particular the convention of ministerial responsibility, which we saw in 6.4.3.4, fails adequately to take into account the changes which resulted from the creation of executive agencies as offshoots of central government departments.

For our purposes of explaining the context of administrative law, we must have some idea of the activity subjected to this body of law and the broad perception of policy implementation will suffice.

It is suggested that there are seven functions or tasks of government. These are (a) defence, law and order; (b) taxation; (c) provision of welfare services; (d) protection of individuals; (e) regulating the economy; (f) provision of certain economic services; and (g) development of human and physical resources (Beloff and Peele 1985, pp. 42–4). Public servants, then, are involved in implementing policies relating to these areas. Let us examine the provision of cash welfare benefits as an example of public administration. The aim of the benefits system is to assist people with particular needs. The need may be that a person or a family have no income because of unemployment or sickness. Another need might be associated with disability as where, for example, a person requires modifications to be made to a car in order to be able to drive it. The government has to decide which needs will be met with cash benefits and then devise a scheme which will prescribe the eligibility conditions for receipt of the benefit. Having created the scheme it will then be used to process claims for the benefit. The contact the public will have with the administration of most cash benefits will be the making of a claim at the local office of the Social Security Benefits Agency. The policy decisions about which benefits there will be are taken by the ministers and officials in the Department of Social Security. Parliament must approve of this and so legislation must authorise the provision of the benefit. The usual pattern for this is that a statute creates a benefit and then statutory instruments contain the detailed rules about those who may be eligible to receive the benefit.

From this example we can see that the classic activity of an administrator is the making of decisions. We can observe a hierarchy of decision-making. At the top are policy decisions about which benefits to create, then lower-level policy decisions about eligibility, and finally deciding if a claim for benefit is successful.

Decisions made by officials in response to action by a member of the public comprise a very large proportion of public administration. It is possible to divide this decision-making into two broad categories: claims for benefit and applications for a licence. The benefits which officials decide include not only welfare cash benefits but also grants awarded to students in higher and further education to cover their fees and part of their maintenance, and employers may receive grants in respect of trainees whom they employ. Benefits may take the form of services such as the provision of home helps to the elderly and infirm, or exemption from taxes which bodies such as the Scottish and Welsh Development Agencies may offer to companies in order to persuade them to locate their businesses in an economically deprived area. Aiding the profitability of companies can also result from governmental licensing schemes. A company which is awarded a licence by the Independent Television Commission hopes to be able to make a healthy profit, as would an airline company which seeks permission from the Civil Aviation Authority to operate a service. Other licensing decisions include permission to construct buildings, to discharge effluent into rivers, to drive a vehicle.

Licensing is itself part of the process of regulation which involves a governmental agency setting limits and conditions upon the freedom of action of individuals and companies. In addition to licensing particular activities, the agency will set standards and also enforce the system of controls where there is non-compliance. If we take the task of environmental protection, the setting of standards is concerned with the quality of the environment. The Environment Agency (EA), in association with the Department of the Environment and the EC Council and Commission, sets a standard for the quality of surface water (Water Resources Act 1991, Directive 75/440/EEC). It is possible for effluent to be discharged into rivers but consent must be obtained from the EA and the consent will stipulate conditions about the discharge. Enforcement of river pollution control by the EA involves its officers in checking that discharges are authorised. Unauthorised discharges are those where either there is no consent, or non-compliance with the terms of a consent. Enforcement can mean that those responsible for unauthorised discharges may be prosecuted as this is a criminal offence.

Decision-making in public administration includes initial determinations such as a benefit claim or an application for planning permission, and also appeals against an adverse determination. This leads us into a very broad area of public administration, that of dispute resolution. The disputes may be between individuals as well as between an individual and a government agency. Disputes between individuals could be in the field of industrial relations. An employee might allege that dismissal was unfair and this would be adjudicated by an industrial tribunal. Public administration also concerns itself with collective disputes in industrial relations. The Advisory Conciliation and Arbitration Service (ACAS) may be called upon to attempt to resolve a dispute between an employer and a trade union representing employees. Other disputes between private bodies which may be resolved by those working in the public service include disputes about the amount of rent charged to a tenant by a landlord; disputes about the service offered to a customer by a privatised utility company, e.g., the Director General of Telecommunications deals with British Telecom and its customers; disputes about broadcast material which may be referred to the Broadcasting Standards Commission (see 12.4.3); complaints of unlawful discrimination on the grounds of sex or race which may be pursued with assistance from the Equal Opportunities Commission (EOC) or the Commission for Racial Equality (CRE).

Disputes between individuals and governmental agencies may be resolved by administrative tribunals. Social security, immigration, patents and council tax valuations are some examples of areas in which appeals against adverse decisions may be made to appeal tribunals. Some appeals against adverse decisions are determined by ministers or persons appointed by them. In land use planning these appeals may be disposed of by using a written representations procedure, or by holding a public local inquiry, or a hearing. Another method of challenging an initial decision is to have it reviewed. The machinery for review does not follow a uniform model, for example, Social Fund payments are reviewed by a single official whereas Housing Benefit is reviewed by a Review Board.

Where there is no provision for appeal a citizen may complain to a commissioner about treatment received from some public bodies. Commissioners have been appointed to investigate allegations of injustice caused by maladministration in central government, the health service and local government.

14.1.1 Discretion

It has been suggested that decision-making is an important aspect of the work of officials engaged in public administration. Any person given decisionmaking powers will appreciate discretion as an aid to the exercise of those powers. One definition of discretion states that 'a public officer has discretion whenever the effective limits of his power leave him free to make a choice among possible courses of action and inaction' (Davis 1971, p. 4). The discretion may arise, for example, from the application of a standard. If an official is authorised to meet expenses arising from an emergency, or as a consequence of a disaster, then the officer has discretion in determining what constitutes an emergency or a disaster. Discretion allows for the shaping of the official's powers to the particular circumstances of the case. Another form of discretion consists of a power to give a consent subject to conditions. This occurs in land use planning where the local planning authority has the choice of rejecting, or permitting unconditionally or conditionally, an application for planning permission. This discretionary power benefits both the applicant and the planning authority by providing a means whereby an unsatisfactory proposal can be made acceptable to the authority by the granting of a conditional consent. Take the example of a planning authority in a rural area. One of its plans or policies for its area is to safeguard visual amenity from scattered development. People's enjoyment of the landscape will be spoilt if buildings can be erected anywhere in the countryside. An applicant seeks permission to build a house on a remote rural site. The planning authority's plans and policies create a presumption of refusal. This might be rebutted if it is possible to screen the house by planting trees and shrubs. It may be that the adverse visual impact of the proposed house could be reduced if its position on the site was changed. The planning authority could grant permission which requires the applicant to carry out a scheme of planting and so there is a compromise which gives the applicant permission and meets the planning authority's concern of protecting visual amenity.

While discretion can be helpful to administrators it can also cause problems. Officials may be unhappy with wide discretion as it can make decision-making difficult. To return to the example used above of meeting expenses arising from an emergency or a disaster, how does an agency set about ensuring consistency amongst officials who have to exercise this discretionary power? The answer is to structure the discretion by providing rules and guidance for officials who determine such benefit claims. During the 1980s social security legislation both reduced the amount, and narrowed the width, of discretion conferred upon officers who determined claims. The reasons for this were that the officials who exercised this wide discretion found it difficult and this also led to a lack of consistency in such determinations throughout the country. The discretion was replaced with rules and the guidance for officials was published. Income Support and the Social Fund also have this framework of rules reducing discretion, and guidance which assists officials to apply the rules. In the Social Fund there is provision for crisis loans to meet expenses accruing from an emergency or a disaster. As this is a benefit which secures for individuals what may be regarded as the State's minimum standard of living, it is understandable that the key terms 'emergency' and 'disaster' are not defined. However, guidance is given to officials in the Social Fund Manual in the form of examples of situations in which it would be appropriate to make a crisis loan. Other aspects of these loans are defined, such as the conditions for eligibility, which includes the specification of some expenses as short-term financial difficulties.

Wide discretionary power has the potential of being abused by officials. This is a major concern of those who espouse red-light theories of administrative law. The differences in values between lawyers and administrators will be discussed below (see 14.3)

14.2 ADMINISTRATIVE PRACTICES

There are various practices which have been developed by administrators to assist them in implementing policy. It was suggested that much of what administrators do involves decision-making. Good decision-making is related to the quality of the information upon which the decision is based. Some administrative practices are methods of gathering information: consultation, inquiry, inspection, investigation and public participation. Rule-making, which serves as an aid to decision-making, is a practice which employs consultation and public participation. The task of dispute resolution may be discharged through adjudication or conciliation but may also use investigation and inquiry to collect data. Decisions about enforcing standards or permissions will rely upon discovering if they are being breached, and inspection is one method of acquiring such information.

Eight types of administrative practice are outlined below, with examples of the tasks to which they are put, and the agencies which use them.

14.2.1 Adjudication

The major type of dispute resolution in public administration is the determining of appeals against adverse initial decisions on benefit claims and licence applications. Such appeals are most frequently dealt with by administrative tribunals such as social security appeal tribunals. The significance of these tribunals in administrative law is such that fuller discussion about them is to be found in chapter 15. In this context it is sufficient to say that they operate as court substitutes. The type of procedure followed by the tribunal is modelled on that of the courts, so that the appellant and the respondent public agency are adversaries. The tribunal relies upon the parties for the provision of information about the dispute which is to be resolved, and the determination must be based on the submissions made by the parties. The typical composition of these tribunals is a legally qualified chair and two members drawn from panels of people who have relevant experience in the field of the tribunal's work. As will be seen later, tribunals are used as substitutes for courts because they are regarded as having advantages over courts which include expertise, cheaper operating costs, quicker disposal of cases and a less intimidating atmosphere for appellants.

This form of administrative tribunal is also used in disputes between individuals. The largest number of such disputes occur in industrial relations. Industrial tribunals are also composed of a lawyer chair and two members drawn from panels of those experienced in industrial relations from both of the major groups: employers and employees.

Rent control has been another area in which administrative tribunals have resolved disputes between private individuals. Legislation in the 1980s has diminished the number of disputes over fair rents which rent assessment committees will determine. They still have a role in determining rents. As with other tribunals, rent assessment committees draw their members from lawyers and those with relevant expertise, such as valuers. They have tended to visit the property which is the subject of the rent dispute but do not always hear oral argument made by the disputing parties.

In the declining number of cases where a rent assessment committee hears appeals from a rent officer, it is like an administrative appeal tribunal. The great majority of its case-load, like that of the industrial tribunals, is the first attempt at dispute resolution by a third party.

Another appeal mechanism concerned with disputes between the individual and a public authority is the inspector in land use planning. Again the appeals procedure is adversarial but the system has developed from the use of a different technique – the public inquiry – which is discussed below (see 14.2.4).

Formally, all appeals against the decisions of local planning authorities are to the Secretary of State but there is provision for this jurisdiction to be transferred to an appointed person, one of the members of Her Majesty's Planning Inspectorate. The inspectorate is composed of people who have expertise in relevant occupations, such as land use planning, surveying, civil engineering, architecture and law.

A planning appeal may be disposed of by using one of three methods: a written representation procedure, the holding of a public local inquiry, or an informal hearing. The written representation procedure can be opted for by the appellant and the local planning authority if there is no significant third-party interest, i.e., where other people who may be neighbours, or belong to residents' associations or amenity groups, have not already played a part in the process which led to the planning authority's decision on the application for planning permission. In the written representations procedure the parties reduce their arguments to writing and submit them to the inspector who then determines the appeal. Where a public local inquiry is held, the appellant and the planning authority make their cases orally and the inspector may allow third parties to give evidence and indeed to cross-examine the other parties and any witnesses they may call. The inspector usually visits the site to which the appeal relates and then determines the appeal. The informal hearing starts with an exchange of written representations and then a hearing is held which is subject to much more direction by the inspector than is the case in an inquiry (see further 14.3.1.1).

A common factor, then, in adjudication in public administration is the involvement of people who have either expertise in, or experience of, the topic. As many of the dispute resolution tribunals are court substitutes, it is not surprising that the adversarial mode of procedure, in which the adjudicators exercise little initiative in the gathering of information, has been adopted.

14.2.2 Conciliation

A conciliator attempts to assist disputants to come to a resolution of their own devising. Unlike an adjudicator or arbitrator, a conciliator cannot impose a decision upon the parties. A conciliator does not seek to declare a winner and a loser but to help the parties come to their own compromise.

The Advisory, Conciliation and Arbitration Service (ACAS) is a body which operates in the sphere of industrial relations, ready to assist parties resolve individual and collective grievances. Individual grievances may relate, for example, to dismissal or to complaints of unlawful discrimination on the ground of sex or race. Collective complaints involve trade disputes between trade unions and an employer over matters such as pay, and terms and conditions of employment.

While ACAS deals with disputes between citizens, there are officers who are concerned with citizens' grievances against public bodies, and who have a small conciliation role. These commissioners' basic technique is investigation (see 14.2.3) but conciliation may occur. This is more likely with the local government commissioners who have to ensure that local authorities have been given an opportunity to consider a complaint before the commissioner has jurisdiction to accept it. The annual reports of the commissioners for local administration state the number of complaints which resulted in a local settlement. Such settlements are not imposed by the commissioners and so may be said to be conciliation. This is because it can be argued that the making of the complaint to the commissioners led to the complainant and the local authority agreeing to a mutually satisfactory resolution.

14.2.3 Investigation
Where an adjudicator resolves a dispute, the parties have agreed to be bound by the decision which will create a winner and a loser. Conciliation, as we have seen, depends upon agreement. The commissioners investigate complaints of injustice caused by maladministration on the part of central and local government and the National Health Service. Strictly speaking the parties are not bound to accept the commissioner's finding but in the great majority of cases it is accepted.

The commissioner is different from both an adjudicating administrative tribunal and ACAS, in that the technique of investigation involves an active approach. The commissioner may wait for a complaint to be made but once it has been accepted the commissioner takes the initiative and decides what files should be examined and which people should be interviewed as witnesses. To assist this investigative process the commissioners have been given the powers of the High Court to order the production of papers and persons, so that non-compliance can amount to contempt of court.

Two other public bodies with significant powers of investigation are the Commission for Racial Equality and the Equal Opportunities Commission. Their powers to conduct formal investigations follow on from the assistance which they can give to individuals who complain of unlawful discrimination. The Commissions have also a strategic role through which they may investigate particular companies or sectors of work in order to ascertain if unlawful discriminatory practices occur.

14.2.4 Inquiry
In public administration the public inquiry is used for two main purposes. The first of these is the gathering of information as part of the consideration of a proposal. The second purpose is to discover the causes of an event of public concern.

Proposals which are concerned with the environment comprise the majority of the matters subjected to a public inquiry. Some examples of these proposals are the route of a motorway, or the siting of a new coal mine, or a new nuclear power station. The usual procedure is that a public authority makes a proposal about which comments will be invited. Quite often the reaction to the proposal will include dissatisfaction, if not outright opposition to it. At the inquiry the promoters of the proposal or scheme will make representations, as well as the objectors. The inspector compiles a report based upon the submissions made during the inquiry. The report is given to the minister who then decides whether or not to confirm, modify or reject the scheme.

This procedure sounds as if it conforms to the adversarial model and this is so, but in a qualified way. If we consider the example of a 'big public inquiry' such as the one into the proposal to construct the Sizewell B nuclear power station, it will deal with technical matters including the safety aspects of such an installation. To assist the inspector in evaluating such evidence specialist assessors are appointed. In addition, a counsel to the inquiry may be appointed whose function it will be to cross-examine the various witnesses and this serves to test their evidence. The counsel to the inquiry may be said to act as a kind of proxy inquisitor. The major departure from the adversarial mode of procedure is that the inspector does not decide the matter, but reports and recommends to the minister. This is confusing for many participants in inquiries, especially if the inspector recommends against a scheme but the minister decides to confirm it.

One type of environmental decision which a minister may take after a public inquiry is the determination of a planning appeal. This was once the usual way in which planning appeals were determined. As we saw in 14.2.1, planning inspectors can act as single-person appeal tribunals and this happens in the vast majority of planning appeals. Accordingly the continued use of the term 'public inquiry' for the hearing which the planning inspector holds before deciding the appeal is anomalous.

The other use to which a public inquiry is put is to attempt to discover the cause of a serious event. This can include accidents in which there were many fatalities, such as those involving aircraft, shipping and trains. Under the Police Act 1964, s. 32, inquiries into public disorder have been established. Two such inquiries were conducted by Lord Scarman. These concerned Red Lion Square in 1974 and Brixton in 1981. Inquiries may also be created to deal with matters of 'urgent public importance' created under the Tribunals of Inquiry (Evidence) Act 1921. The inquiry into the Aberfan disaster was conducted under this statute.

Inquiries may also be relatively informal as with departmental or interdepartmental committees of inquiry, or take the rather more grand form of a royal commission.

14.2.5 Consultation

This technique is used both in legislative or rule-making activity, and in licensing determinations. When central governmental departments are creating the flesh of schemes outlined in statutes, this is done by delegated legislation and those bodies which are representative of established interests in the relevant area will be given the opportunity to comment on drafts of the statutory instruments (see 8.2.6).

In land use planning most local planning authorities invite comments about most applications for planning permission. This may be done generally by the placing of lists of planning applications in local newspapers, or more specifically by writing to neighbours to bring to their attention the planning application proposed on a site adjacent to them.

Sometimes consultation through the use of publicity is required by legislation and imposed upon the applicant. This is the case with what is known as 'bad neighbour development', where, for example, applications for cinemas, bingo halls, or use of land for the disposal of waste materials, are to be publicised by a notice on the site, and in a local newspaper (Town and Country Planning Act 1990, s. 65).

Where an applicant appeals the refusal of a planning permission, notification of the appeal may be given so as to allow those who have an interest in the matter to make representations.

14.2.6 Public Participation

Whereas much consultation by public authorities, particularly in respect of draft statutory instruments, is selective and somewhat secretive, the consultation exercise required in the making of development plans by local planning authorities is more open and wide-ranging. Development plans contain the planning policies for an area. The plans are formulated at two levels: broad strategies, and detailed proposals. In a structure plan, policies on matters such as shopping and housing provision will be outlined. A local plan will indicate how the policies will be implemented in an area. Industrial zones and residential areas will be proposed. The aim of the development plans is to provide an indication to the public and developers of the pattern of land use which the planning authority envisages. The plans and policies form the background against which planning applications are decided.

Before the plans are drafted, planning authorities are required to give adequate publicity to the matters proposed to be included; they must consider the people and groups likely to want to make representations about the draft plans and ensure that they are informed of their right to do so. The planning authority may hold exhibitions and conduct surveys as part of its programme of public participation in the preparation of development plans.

14.2.7 Inspection

Inspection may seem to differ little from investigation, but inspection involves the idea that standards for a particular area or activity have been set and a failure to meet them will result in action to remedy the defects. Providing personal social services and the police service are the responsibilities of the social services and police authorities throughout the country. The relevant central government departments, the Department of Health and the Home Office, can ensure that the appropriate standards are met following visits by their inspectorates.

Another form of inspection of public administration is the work of the National Audit Office and the Audit Commission. These bodies deal with central and local government respectively and the audit they conduct is not just a straightforward financial one in which the accounts are examined for accuracy and to ensure that the expenditure was in respect of permissible matters, but can also check that resources are used economically, efficiently and effectively (see further 8.4.3).

The enforcement of standards is not just restricted to the service provided by parts of public administration, it also applies in the private sector. In the field of pollution control inspectors check that emissions into the atmosphere and discharges into rivers meet the standards specified in consents. It is possible that a breach of control can lead to the individual or company responsible being prosecuted. The Shell Oil company was prosecuted and fined over £1 million for a leak from one of its pipelines into the River Mersey in 1989.

Other regulatory schemes involving inspection to check compliance with standards or permissions relate to environmental health (e.g., hygiene in shops and restaurants), consumer protection, land use planning and health and safety at work.

14.2.8 Rule-making

Rule-making has been described as the process by which administrators lay down prescriptions to govern the future conduct of those subject to their authority (Schwartz and Wade 1972, p. 93). This is narrower than the classification of functions of administrative rules suggested by Baldwin and Houghton (1986). Their list includes:

(a) procedural rules (e.g., the Police and Criminal Evidence Act 1984 code of practice on detention, treatment and questioning of suspects);

(b) interpretative guides (e.g., social security guidance);

(c) instructions to officials (e.g., Prison Department circulars);

(d) prescriptive evidential rules, where the objective is to influence people's behaviour and breach of the rules is not unlawful but may have an evidential role in determining issues of legal liability (e.g., the Highway Code);

(e) commendatory rules, which also seek to influence behaviour but, unlike (d), carry no indirect sanction for non-compliance (e.g., Health and Safety Commission and Executive guidance notes);

(f) voluntary codes, issued by private bodies (City Code on Takeovers and Mergers);

(g) rules of practice, management or operation (e.g., Inland Revenue's extra-statutory concessions); and

(h) consultative statements: a safety-net class which could include a draft outline of a policy inviting comment.

This classification shows a wide range of functions which administrative rules can fulfil. It is important to bear in mind that governmental agencies can also promote legislation, and that public administration will involve the making of general rules which will be applied by reference to interpretive rules, group (b) in Baldwin and Houghton's classification. The Social Fund officers have a hierarchy of rules within which they may make a crisis loan to a claimant in respect of expenses arising out of an emergency or a disaster. First, there is the statute which creates the benefit and prescribes some of the eligibility conditions. Regulations concerning the way in which applications are to be made are contained in statutory instruments. Then there are directions which are made by the Secretary of State, are binding upon the officer and set out in more detail the circumstances of entitlement to a loan. Finally, the officer has guidance in the Social Fund Manual. As these rules are all published, claimants and their advisers have an indication of how determinations are made and the Social Fund officers have a framework which assists them in making determinations and which promotes consistency.

Unlike the situation with most benefits, a dissatisfied claimant to the discretionary Social Fund cannot appeal the determination to the independent social security appeal tribunals. Instead there is a system of review which may be conducted by the same, or another Social Fund officer, or a Social Fund inspector. The Social Fund commissioner has the task of supervising a scheme of quality control for the decisions.

The development plans discussed in 14.2.6, are also a variety of administrative rule. They seek to influence behaviour, to guide certain types of development to particular areas, and so give an indication of how the local planning authority will determine planning applications.

14.2.9 Contract

The quest for efficiency in government has led to the idea that while a governmental body may be responsible for a particular service, this does not mean that it is the service provider. In the metaphor of two influential American writers government bodies should be 'steering rather than rowing' (Osborne and Gaebler 1992). This is part of the 'new public management' and contract plays a very important role in governing the relationship between the body responsible for the service and the body which actually delivers it. The service deliverer could be a private or public sector body. For some services it was expected that the service would be delivered by the private sector. Whilst in-house bodies could bid, it was envisaged that for some services, especially those which were included in the first wave of compulsory competitive tendering, private-sector businesses in catering, buildings maintenance and cleaning would have economies of scale which would probably make their bids the ones with the lowest costs and therefore more likely to be successful. In central government we have noted the programme of market testing, which decides if a function should be provided by the public sector at all and, if it is, whether it is suitable for delivery by an executive agency. A framework agreement would be the contract between the department and its agencies.

One area which has really made large strides is the National Health Service and its internal market with the purchaser – provider split. The health authority decides which clinical and non-clinical services it wants to purchase and who is going to provide them, which in the case of clinical services, means which hospital(s). A variant on this is the idea of the fund-holder general practice in which the doctors might contract with a particular hospital for a particular service and which led to the accusation of a two tier health service, in which patients from fund-holding practices would gain priority over patients from non fund-holding practices because of the contract.

The use of contract has always been a major part of public administration, that part known as procurement is of long standing and can be illustrated by the relationship between the Ministry of Defence and the industry which has grown up to conduct the research and development of sophisticated weapons systems such as fighters and bombers, warships, tanks and artillery and ordnance which it sells to the armed forces (see 18.3).

Contract has also been used to do more than secure the simple provision of goods and services. Other policy goals can also be achieved although this has been statutorily reduced for local government (see 18.3.1).

14.3   A CLASH OF VALUES

Two views of administrative law may be broadly classified as the red and green-light theories which seek to control and enable, respectively, the action of administrators in implementing government policy. The tension between these views may be seen in two significant reports which shaped the development of administrative law in the 20th century. These were the Donoughmore Report on Ministers' Powers (1932), and the Franks Report on Tribunals and Enquiries (1957). Both were established because of public unease about the exercise of power by ministers and their officials. The impetus for the Donoughmore Committee was the scathing attack upon bureaucracy by the then Lord Chief Justice, Lord Hewart, in his book published in 1929 entitled *The New Despotism*. The Franks Committee was created in the aftermath of the Crichel Down affair (see Griffith (1955) and Nicolson (1986)). Briefly, the affair concerned the treatment of relatives of people who had had some land compulsorily acquired by the Air Ministry. The property was later transferred to the Ministry of Agriculture and it was the way in which the land was sold by the Agriculture Ministry which provoked the disquiet. An inquiry into the sale was held which criticised its handling by officials, and the minister, Sir Thomas Dugdale, resigned. Ironically although Crichel Down was a major factor in the establishment of the Franks Committee, its terms of reference, administrative tribunals and enquiries, excluded the procedures and processes involved in that affair, which were non-statutory. The remit of the Donoughmore Committee was to investigate ministers' powers in relation to delegated legislation and the making of judicial and quasi-judicial decisions.

The two committees seem to have been imbued with the views of Dicey. This is especially true of the Donoughmore Committee, given that it was to consider these ministerial powers while having regard to the constitutional principles of the sovereignty of Parliament and the supremacy of law.

The Donoughmore Committee, in considering ministerial powers of judi-cial and quasi-judicial decision-making, proposed a definition of these decisions. Judicial decisions in disputes involved four aspects: (a) the presentation of arguments by the parties which dealt with disputed questions of (b) fact; and (c) law; and (d) the decision which made a finding on the facts, to which the law was applied, and which could include a ruling on any disputed matters of law (p. 73). The committee defined quasi-judicial decisions as those which comprised points (a) and (b), not necessarily (c) and never (d). A quasi-judicial decision was administrative action by a minister derived from discretionary power. Equipped with this classification of decisions the committee then proposed a somewhat circular allocation of decisions and functions. Decisions were analysed and if found to be judicial then they were said to be decisions which should be taken by the courts. As Jennings (1932) pointed out they failed to identify functions which might best be served by a particular decision-making process. Jennings denied that there was a clear distinction between judicial and administrative decisions based on law and policy, with judges being concerned only with law and administrators only with policy. His view was that judicial, quasi-judicial and administrative decisions involved facts, law and the policy behind the law. In coming to the decision one sought to further the policy behind the law. Jennings was in favour of activist government, and could be expected to advocate that the policy behind law should be furthered. Those, like Dicey, who favour a more restricted role for government, would prefer a less policy-oriented approach to judicial decision-making.

The Franks Report inclines towards the red-light end of the spectrum, stating that administrative tribunals were not part of the machinery for administration but part of the machinery for adjudication and so should be the responsibility of the Lord Chancellor's Department rather than the department conducting administration in that topic. The committee understood the reasons why tribunals had been created but in general felt that courts should be allocated judicial decision-making unless there were good reasons to the contrary. They seemed to agree with the Donoughmore classification but accepted that it could not provide a wholly satisfactory principle on which to allocate adjudicatory functions as between the courts and tribunals.

The Franks Committee did not, however, take an either/or, judicial/administrative view of enquiries, indeed the committee said that it would be wrong to emphasise one at the expense of the other. A balance should be struck between the administration carrying out its tasks and 'the rights and feelings of citizens who find their possessions or plans interfered with by the administration' (para. 276).

In the following section the public local inquiry will be used as a case study to illustrate the different uses to which an administrative technique may be put and the values which lie behind such allocative decisions.

14.3.1 The Public Local Inquiry

As was pointed out in 14.2.4, there are two basic purposes for which an inquiry is used: the gathering of information in a decision-making process and the uncovering of the causes of an accident or other disquieting incidents.

Our concern here is with inquiries which inform decision-making. Most inquiries of this type are to be found in the environmental sphere, especially planning, where they are used to determine appeals against refusal of planning permission, and to consider objections to development plans, motorways, and controversial proposals such as nuclear power stations. The inquiry has evolved to meet the nature of these particular tasks under the influence of different purposes or ideologies. Table 14.1 presents a classification of inquiries according to their functions.

Task	Nature	Technique	Perspective
Planning appeal	Bi-polar	Tribunal	Judicial
Structure plan	Polycentric	Examination in public	Administrative
Motorway scheme	Medium polycentric	Traditional inquiry	Administrative/ political
Major proposal	Polycentric	Investigative inquiry	Political/ administrative

Table 14.1 Types of Inquiry

The nature of the task can vary from being bi-polar, that is, a dispute between two parties, to polycentric, which is a topic which is composed of several inter-connected matters which it is not possible to isolate from each other. A structure plan is a good example of a polycentric topic. Such a plan will present policies related to the allocation of land use in an area. Examples of such policies include industrial location, transportation, housing, offices, retailing provision, leisure facilities, mineral working and waste disposal.

The factors which can influence the choice of inquiry type for a task have been termed 'perspectives'. Those used here are derived from analyses conducted by McAuslan (1980) and O'Riordan, Kemp and Purdue (1988). The judicial perspective is influenced by the procedures and values of the courts which, in the field of planning law, have been associated with the protection of private property. The administrative perspective is the approach adopted by public administration and it promotes the public interest which may prevail over the interest of private property. The political perspective seeks to inject direct public participation into decision-making. Four tasks dealt with by land-use inquiries will now be examined in order to understand how the different perspectives have influenced the selection of the particular inquiry type.

14.3.1.1 Appeals When a planning authority refuses planning permission, or grants it conditionally, the applicant may appeal to the Secretary of State (Town and Country Planning Act 1990, s. 78). Such an appeal must, if it is the wish of either of the parties, provide an opportunity for a hearing before an inspector (s. 79(2)). Formerly, it was the case that the hearing was conducted by the inspector as a public local inquiry at which the appellant, planning authority and other third parties could make representations and the inspector would report to the minister with a recommendation. The determination would then be made by the minister. This situation prevailed until the end of the 1960s when the inspector was given the power to determine appeals. At first this was limited, but by 1981 the rules which transferred the minister's powers to the inspector covered almost all types of appeal (Town and Country Planning (Determination of Appeals by Appointed Persons) (Prescribed Classes) Regulations 1981 (SI 1981/840)). The current practice is for around 85 per cent of appeals to be determined without a hearing, using the written representations procedure.

The evolution of the planning appeal process since the Franks Report began initially with the publication of the inspector's report of the inquiry to the minister and the introduction of rules of procedure. These rules had the effect of transforming the inquiry into a proceeding which was modelled on the adversarial process to be found in the courts. The inquiry was divided into stages to which rules were applied. At the pre-inquiry stage adequate notice of the date of the inquiry was to be given and a written statement of the planning authority's case was to be provided in advance to the appellant and other interested persons. During the inquiry the inspector was given discretion as to how proceedings were to be conducted. The order of the proceedings was that the appellant was to make the opening and final statements. The inspector determined the order in which other participants appeared and had discretion to permit appearances by parties who had no formal right to participate. The appellant and the planning authority could give evidence and call their own witnesses, all of whom could be subject to cross-examination. The inspector could extend these procedural rights to other parties. The inspector could make an unaccompanied visit to the site of the appeal to inspect it, before or during the inquiry. If one of the parties requested that a visit during the inquiry be made in the presence of the parties then this had to be done. A visit after the inquiry had to be an accompanied one. After the inquiry the inspector was to make a report and recommendation to the minister but if the minister took into consideration any new evidence, or any new fact which had not been raised at the inquiry, then if the minister was minded to disagree with the inspector by relying upon that new material, the appellant, planning authority and others who had appeared at the inquiry should be given the opportunity to comment upon it, or request that the inquiry be reconvened. When the minister had decided the appeal the decision letter was to be served on the parties who were entitled to appear at the inquiry and who had requested a copy.

Inquiries into appeals became more and more like a court as appellants, especially in cases where planning permission would be valuable, employed lawyers to present their case. This transformation into a court did not occur by accident. The Franks Report clearly preferred adjudicatory procedures where the rights of the citizen were at stake and the system of planning control restricts what may be done with property. McAuslan suggests that the common law has traditionally been concerned with the protection of private property. Therefore court processes were imported to continue the inquiry's role of protecting the interest of private property.

The inquiry as a planning tribunal has continued to evolve. As interest in environmental matters increased, people other than the appellant and the planning authority were gradually allowed to participate as third parties. The adversarial character of the proceedings could cope with this as most third parties objected to the proposed development and so the bi-polar nature of an appeal as a dispute between two sides was unaffected. The involvement of these third parties brings in, to a limited extent, the political perspective affording to these parties participation in the proceedings which the procedural rules could accommodate.

The widespread take-up of the written determinations method of determining appeals does allow for some third-party involvement. This method is popular because it is cheaper and quicker than an inquiry.

Finally, an informal hearing may be used as the mode of procedure. This is intermediate between written representations and an inquiry. It begins with an exchange of written representations and then at a hearing the inspector leads the discussion and there is no cross-examination by the parties.

14.3.1.2 Structure plans The control of development is carried out against a background of policy. Such policy may be incorporated in either development plans or non-statutory policies. In the 1960s it was decided that the plans which would seek to guide development would follow a two-tier pattern (Planning Advisory Group 1965). One tier would deal with the strategy for an area (the structure plan) and the second tier would implement the broad strategy into detailed guidance (the local plan, see now Town and Country Planning Act 1990, Part II). This pattern still applies in England and Wales in the non-metropolitan counties. The two-tier approach is now carried out in a unitary development plan in London and the metropolitan districts.

The preparation of structure plans involves surveying the area in order to have a basis on which to draw up the policies which the plans contain. The plans are subject to public participation and consultation. It had been thought that the consideration of objections and representations about structure plans would be carried out by a traditional inquiry as they were to be approved or modified or rejected by the minister. The minister would oversee the plan-making process for the country within a context of any national policies and seek to ensure that there was, for example, compatibility between structure plans for different areas within the same region. The experience of a prototype structure plan at an inquiry changed that. The Greater London Development Plan Inquiry dealt with 28,000 objectors and lasted over two years. This led to the design of the examination in public. Its major purpose was to make the scrutiny of a structure plan a manageable exercise and this was achieved by giving the minister the power to select both the participants and the issues to be studied. This was justified on the basis that since the structure plan was written at a certain level of abstraction it was a document unsuited to the cut and thrust of an inquiry. An appropriate procedure for a subject with a complex structure, like a spider's web with all its interconnections, was a process like a seminar. This limited examination would not prejudice people because there would be an inquiry for local plans which implemented the policies in the structure plan.

The examination in public was used to scrutinise the first round of structure plans and it will be used to investigate alterations of, and replacements for, structure plans.

The administrative perspective therefore influenced the creation of this new type of inquiry which reflects both the public interest, which administrators seek to advance, and the pragmatic and practical concern with the workability of a task.

14.3.1.3 Motorways One of the environmental topics which has been the subject of controversy is the road construction programme. Objections have been made against the principle of extra roads on the basis that catering for an increase in the use of motor vehicles will harm the environment. At a local level some people's property may be within the 'land-take' of the scheme and therefore be required in order for the road to be built, and there may also be concern about the adverse effect on the area's amenities. It is not then surprising that motorway inquiries have been disrupted by people objecting to a particular scheme.

The process by which road schemes are made is that the Department of Transport will carry out surveys to try to forecast traffic volumes and then seek to ensure that the road system can cope with that demand. A policy framework for major roads, such as motorways, will be presented to Parliament. After approval, work will be carried out implementing the policy by determining priorities and then planning the route or line which the motorway will take. Often a number of lines will be prepared as each will have advantages and disadvantages. The options will be published for consultation and then a scheme will be proposed and publicised. Objections to it will be heard at an inquiry which has the classic function of gathering information to assist the minister in deciding whether or not to approve the scheme.

Formal procedural rules for highways inquiries were not issued until 1976. Before that proceedings had been conducted in a fashion which followed the planning inquiries. This meant that the procedure was mainly adversarial in character, although the nature of the consideration of a road scheme was not simply an issue of whether the line of the road would be approved or rejected. As it could be modified that meant consideration of proposed alternatives. The inquiry also offered a forum for those who were against the principle of more road construction and who would seek to oppose the road by questioning the need for it. This introduced a dimension to the proceedings which the administrative perspective preferred not to see and which was backed up by the House of Lords in *Bushell* v *Secretary of State for the Environment* [1981] AC 75. In this case objectors at an inquiry complained that they were not allowed to cross- examine witnesses on the methods which they had used to forecast the traffic volumes which were part of the case for the need for the motorway. By a majority the House of Lords held that the inspector had not acted unfairly. It was emphasised that the focus of the inquiry was on local matters, with the considerations of objections to the scheme, and not with issues of national policy. The policy framework for the motorways programme could not be discussed at an inquiry, and matters relating to the methods used to produce the forecasts of traffic volume were also inappropriate for discussion at an inquiry because of the wider range of issues which this encompassed.

Lord Diplock warned against 'applying to procedures involved in the making of administrative decisions concepts that are appropriate to the conduct of ordinary civil litigation between private parties'. It would be wrong, he said, to 'over-judicialise' the inquiry so that in ascertaining matters of fact and expert opinion, it would be fair not to resort to oral testimony of witnesses who would then be subjected to cross-examination. This was a technique peculiar to the courts which follow the common law system.

The objectors' assault on the traditional administrative perspective was based on the idea that since the inquiry was adversarial it should follow completely the court model and allow them to put the case against the scheme, even if that did go to national policy. The court-like atmosphere led them to think that if they presented good arguments, which might even draw some support from the inspector, then it would be illegitimate for the minister to go against them and approve the scheme. As the process was adjudicatory they could participate and they felt that by confining policy to Parliament, they were being denied a say in this decision-making process. Their lordships reaffirmed that our system is one of representative democracy rather than a participatory democracy. The point about citizens' involvement is important because the administrative perspective should take the political context into account so that decisions and actions can be accepted. In practice, inspectors at highways inquiries will hear evidence about need as objectors do want to raise it. There is some judicial support for this view from Woolf LJ in *R v Secretary of State for Transport, ex parte Gwent County Council* [1988] QB 429, who said that it was permissible for objectors to have examined the case for departing from national policy in their locality. Given the context of the process, which means that the minister's officials will have been fairly committed to a scheme in order to propose it, this will not adequately address the concerns of such inquiry participants. The result of this can be that the inquiry is regarded as symbolic reassurance, a chance for objectors to vent their grievances. The current motorway process is one which is political, yet the public are only involved in a judicial type forum, whereas the decision is taken in the political sphere to which they have limited access.

14.3.1.4 Sizewell B The inquiry into the Central Electricity Generating Board's application for planning permission to construct a pressurised water reactor nuclear power station at Sizewell in Suffolk is an example of the big public inquiry, an inquiry which focuses upon a major proposal. The Sizewell inquiry lasted for 340 days and as the team who researched it say, it 'is likely to be the first and last of its kind' (O'Riordan, Kemp and Purdue 1988,

p. 399). It was unusual because it was given a wide remit to deal with policy which included matters which had not previously been properly subjected to debate in any public forum. It was also unusual in that the consideration of the particular reactor was the first of a kind.

The conclusions drawn by O'Riordan, Kemp and Purdue are that, so far as inquiries into major proposals are concerned, there is no blueprint (1988, p. 400). The views they offer will be very briefly summarised. The work of the inquiry ought to be preceded and followed by debate and review by Parliament. The work of the inquiry must be sensibly organised so that the parties can make their cases effectively. Pre-inquiry meetings ought to set a timetable; parties ought to exchange information thereby avoiding duplication and reducing oral proceedings. Accredited parties should enjoy equal procedural rights to enable them to present relevant submissions. This may mean that some public funding of groups is required but it should be on the basis that it matches funds raised by the groups.

Only rarely will it be desirable to consider policy. This may occur if policy is crucial to a proposal and is also unsettled and controversial. In normal circumstances it would be better to leave policy to a select committee which can clarify matters before an inquiry. Technical matters should be dealt with in a specially constituted commission rather than take up time in an inquiry. The work of such a commission must be seen to be fair, open and impartial, especially if the subject-matter is something which is part of a programme of work rather than a one-off. Finally they note that the judicial, administrative and political perspectives should influence the inquiry where appropriate. Thus if conflicts of interest are involved then the adversarial procedure is applicable. If an examination of a wide range of information is necessary to serve the public interest then inquisitorial methods would be desirable. Should the political dimension be important then there should be a mix between adversarial and inquisitorial techniques.

14.3.1.5 Summary This survey of types of inquiries has shown the different tasks to which this instrument of government has been applied. The variation in inquiry types has also been influenced by the judicial, administrative and political perspectives. These perspectives emphasise different procedures and values. Sometimes, as in motorway inquiries, the dominant perspective is at odds with the perceptions and expectations of the majority of participants, and so the inquiry loses authority. This may be regained by adjusting the mixture of perspectives but there may be limits to this if the changes amount to a fundamental challenge to the basis of the existing constitutional order – representative democracy.

CHAPTER FIFTEEN
Remedying Grievances out of Court

15.1 INTRODUCTION

In chapter 14, elements of the administrative process were described. It was shown that tasks which might have been allocated to courts were given to other bodies as these had perceived advantages. In this chapter two such institutions or offices are discussed, administrative tribunals and the ombudsmen, or commissioners, which is the term which will be used here.

The tribunals with which we will be concerned here are those which deal with disputes between the citizen and a governmental agency. The dispute will usually have derived from a decision made under a governmental scheme by an agency. Tribunals are also used to determine disputes where the parties are both private persons. The State's involvement is that the dispute concerns rights conferred by statute, and it provides the machinery to adjudicate on contested claims, as in industrial relations.

These tribunals have been called court-substitutes and distinguished from policy-oriented ones (Abel-Smith and Stevens 1968, p. 220) such as the Monopolies and Mergers Commission and the Civil Aviation Authority (CAA). It is said that in these policy-oriented tribunals there is a greater concern with the policy behind the legislation than is the case with the court-substitute ones (see Farmer 1974 for a general discussion of tribunals; and Baldwin 1985, for a study of the CAA).

It could be said that tribunals and the commissioners dispense administrative justice. That term sounds strange. It seems to suggest that the use of administrative as an adjective to describe justice alters it somehow and this alteration implies that it is inferior to the justice dispensed in the courts. There is a difference but this does not mean that there is inequality. Justice is not an absolute, its content will vary with the context. Courts are said to dispense justice according to law. What that means is that the law is a framework within which the judges determine the issues brought before them.

This framework may produce a particular result which could be thought to be unjust or unfair. We are here entering the territory of jurisprudence or philosophy of law, in which the search to understand justice is a key issue. For our purposes it is enough to note that justice is an objective which should be strived for but it is not the same thing in every context. We shall see at 16.7, that the lawyers' term, 'natural justice', embodies ideas which others would not necessarily say were natural to their ideas of justice.

The evaluation of tribunals and commissioners will be conducted from the perspective of administrative justice, but, before analysing these alternatives to the courts, let us describe their origins, composition, procedures and supervision.

15.2   ADMINISTRATIVE TRIBUNALS

15.2.1   Origins

Part of the legacy of Dicey was the conception of the legal system as the work of the ordinary courts staffed by the judiciary who were drawn from the Bar. Law was the province of lawyers. In fact the legal system has always been more diverse than that. It is probably more accurate to speak of legal systems, each with their own specialist courts. An early example of a specialist court is the Court of Star Chamber which developed as an offshoot of the Royal Council. The Star Chamber acquired a reputation as a tyrannical tribunal which was derived from the exercise of its criminal jurisdiction, part of which concerned public order offences such as riot. It was notorious for its imposition of harsh punishments, including whipping and the pillory as well as heavy fines. The Star Chamber became a factor in the constitutional upheavals of the 17th century. As it was objected to by the common lawyers who played a prominent part in the shaping of the constitutional settlement at the end of that century, the Star Chamber has been represented as an embodiment of the executive's arbitrary power which is contrary to the rule of law to be found in the common law courts.

Various bodies which could be said to be administrative tribunals were created in the 19th century, e.g., the Board of Railway Commissioners (1846) or the Railway and Canals Commissioner (1873). It is in the 20th century that we see a proliferation in tribunals which is accounted for by the creation and growth of the welfare State. The National Insurance Act 1911 was an early landmark in the social security sector of the welfare state. Disputes about benefits were to be determined by umpires and referees rather than by courts. This was partially because German arrangements served as a model for the UK legislation, and partially because of dissatisfaction by those in public administration with the performance of the courts in the operation of the Workmen's (Compensation for Injury) Act 1897. Under this statute unresolved disputes about entitlement to, and amount of, compensation for injuries sustained at work were given to the county court. This was regarded as unsuccessful because the courts were not equipped to further the social policy underpinning the legislation. The courts focused on each individual dispute and the procedures and values of lawyers led to technical arguments before the appellate courts on statutory interpretation (Bell 1969, p. 18).

15.2.2   Characteristics of Tribunals
The tribunal which is used to determine appeals arising out of a governmental
scheme is, perhaps, the archetypal administrative tribunal. The reasons for its
creation are cheapness, accessibility, freedom from technicality, expedition
and expert knowledge of their particular subject (Franks 1957, para. 38).
What are the factors which lead to these advantages over courts? They derive
from the composition and procedures of tribunals.

15.2.2.1   Composition   Following from the recommendations of the Franks
Report most of the court-substitute tribunals have a legally qualified chair and
the other ('wing') members are drawn from people who have experience of
the subject-matter of the tribunal. The Lord Chancellor's Department is
usually responsible for the compilation of the list of lawyers (solicitors,
barristers or advocates usually of seven years' standing), while the relevant
government department organises the panels of wing-members. Social security appeal tribunals must have a lawyer chair but rent assessment committees
may be chaired by a valuer or surveyor. Doctors sit on medical appeal
tribunals and people who may be said to be representatives of employers and
employees sit on national insurance appeals, while persons having a knowledge of the social conditions of the area will sit on income support appeals.
Wing-members are required to be impartial so that their representativeness
relates to their knowledge and experience which is relevant to the work of the
tribunal.
    If we turn to the more policy-oriented tribunals, which include the Civil
Aviation Authority (CAA), the Independent Television Commission (ITC)
and the Gaming Board, we can see that they have a much wider range of work
than the court-substitute tribunals. This is especially true of the CAA which
deals with safety, air traffic control and the licensing of operators on routes
as well as the oversight of fares. The CAA's members rely upon their staff
who have backgrounds in relevant disciplines, especially economics.

15.2.2.2   Procedure   There are a variety of procedures which the tribunals
may adopt. The Franks Report (1957, para. 63) recommended that a
procedure for a tribunal ought to be laid down in legislation. The committee
realised that informality was often an important consideration but it should
not be at the expense of an orderly procedure. Its general proposal was that
a Council on Tribunals should be consulted about procedural matters. More
specific recommendations on procedure were divided into before, during and
after the tribunal hearing. Citizens ought to be made aware of their right to
apply to a tribunal, and where this right has been exercised it is crucial that
they know the case they will have to meet. This could be done by providing
the citizen in good time with a list of the main points of the opposing case.
Generally hearings should be public, but if national security considerations
are involved, or intimate personal or financial details are to be disclosed, or
professional reputation or capacity is at stake, then it would be more
appropriate to hear such cases in private. The committee accepted that,
whilst a prescribed order of events promotes clarity and regularity, this might

not be suitable for unaided citizens. The tribunal ought to have a discretion to vary procedure. The committee recommended that bans on legal representation before tribunals should be exceptional. It also recommended that only where a citizen employed a legal representative should the opposing government department be permitted to do so. It suggested that legal aid might be available before formal and expensive tribunals as well as those which hear final appeals. As for post-hearing procedure, here the Committee recommended that parties receive notification of the findings of fact, the decisions and the reasons.

It is clear that the Franks Committee had the court model of procedure at the forefront of its deliberations on tribunal procedure. The recommendations detailed above were implemented, apart from the availability of legal aid. The only tribunal in recent times in which the citizen may have a legal representative paid for through the green form scheme is the Mental Health Review Tribunal. This is a special case because it is a body which takes decisions concerning the liberty of the citizen.

15.2.2.3 Organisation Some of the tribunals are national bodies and others are organised on a regional basis. The presidential system provides a hierarchy in which there are some chairs who work full time. Their role is a managerial and training one. In the case of the industrial and social security appeal tribunals there is not only a national president, but also regional chairs. Industrial tribunals also have full-time chairs who do not have regional responsibilities. The immigration adjudicators have a chief adjudicator and a mixture of full and part-time adjudicators located in the major towns and ports of entry. The Immigration Appeal Tribunal has a president who must be legally qualified. The other members are a mixture of lawyers and lay people. This tribunal has four divisions and each chair is always legally qualified.

15.2.2.4 Advantages As most of the tribunal members are part-time, their remuneration is not a significant cost. The chairs are paid a fee which is either a half-day or a daily one. Generally the wing-members claim only expenses. The parties bear their own costs although some tribunals award travelling expenses to the citizen, e.g., the SSATs, and some, such as the Lands Tribunal and industrial tribunals, do award costs.

Expenditure is also reduced because of the tribunals' expertise. Familiarity with the subject-matter means that cases can be considered fairly quickly. There is some evidence from industrial tribunals (Dickens 1985) to suggest that where legal representation is used, the proceedings are longer than where it is absent. As the atmosphere of the tribunals is supposed to be such that citizens should not be intimidated, and should feel able to represent themselves, attendance at tribunals should be promoted. In other words these features are designed to encourage citizens to exercise their right of resort to the tribunals. The reality is, however, that a sizeable number of citizens do not attend so that their cases are determined in their absence.

15.2.3 Supervision

The work of the tribunals is subject to two different kinds of supervision. The Council on Tribunals reviews the constitution and working of some of the tribunals as was recommended by the Franks Committee. It was also recommended by the committee that there should be appeals to the courts on a point of law from tribunals. This was implemented slowly. Immigration is one area in which such an appeal is not available. The decisions of the adjudicators and the tribunal may be the subject of an application for judicial review.

Some of the tribunals are part of a two-tier system. Thus appeals on a point of law lie to the Employment Appeal Tribunal and the Social Security Commissioners from the industrial tribunals and the SSATs, and then from these bodies to the Court of Appeal.

The major area of the Council on Tribunals' supervisory work is the consultation on procedural rules which departments are required to conduct when a new tribunal is proposed. Under a code of practice it is recommended that departments should consult the Council generally when they are considering the creation of a new tribunal. This does not always happen and the statutory consultation does not mean that the department accepts the Council's views.

The Council visits tribunals when they are sitting as part of its monitoring responsibilities. These responsibilities do not extend to a specific power to investigate complaints about tribunals, a matter which the Council would like to see amended (Council on Tribunals 1980). Where a complainant has no reasonable access to another remedy, the Council will follow up the complaint with the relevant authorities but will not act until after a decision has been given.

15.2.4 Evaluation

The system of tribunals processes a large number of cases every year. Details are given in table 15.1 of five subject areas, in three of which there is provision for an appeal on a point of law: (a) the Mental Health Review Tribunal (MHRT); (b) the rent assessment committees (RAC); (c) the industrial tribunals (IT) (appeal to the Employment Appeal Tribunal but this body is not subject to supervision by the Council as it is a court); (d) the immigration adjudicators (IA), and Immigration Appeal Tribunal (IAT); and (e) the social security appeal tribunals (SSAT) and the Social Security Commissioners (SSC).

Tribunal	Brought forward	Received	Withdrawn or settled	Decided	Carried forward
MHRT	1,441	12,746	6,683	6,784	721
RAC	5,357	14,239	2,380	13,989	3,380
IT	N/A	108,962	43,389	21,828	N/A
IA	12,813	29,347	—*	20,875	21,285
IAT	1,486	9,350	—*	9,922	914
SSAT	108,000	116,000	21,900	63,500	118,100
SSC	3,640	11,899	274	5,418	9,851

Table 15.1 Case-loads of certain tribunals 1995

Sources: *Annual Report of Council on Tribunals 1995–96* (HC 114 of 1996–97) and, for EAT and SSC, *Judicial Statistics 1995* (Lord Chancellor's Department 1996, Cm 3290). SSAT data 1 Jan–30 Sept 1995, the *DSS*.
* Number included in 'Decided' total.
Statistics are for England, Scotland and Wales, except that Scotland is not included in the MHRT or SSC figures.

Clearly the adjudicatory work of tribunals is very significant in terms of case-load. The disputes which they decide can also have a very important impact upon the individuals who appear before them. In immigration cases the person may be refused leave to enter the country; in MHRT cases the person may continue to be detained in a mental hospital and in employment cases a person may be claiming that a dismissal was unfair or that unlawful discrimination on grounds of sex or race has been suffered. The SSATs deal with people who are dissatisfied with the adjudication of their claims for benefit and this tribunal will be used as a case-study to determine how effectively tribunals operate.

15.2.4.1 Context The SSATs were formed by combining national insurance tribunals with supplementary benefit appeal tribunals (Health and Social Services and Social Security Adjudication Act 1983, sch.8). Research carried out in the 1970s had indicated that while the national insurance benefits system (e.g., unemployment benefit) was operating fairly satisfactorily, the same could not be said of the safety-net benefit, supplementary benefit. The appeal tribunals were found to be poor at distinguishing between questions of law and questions of policy in a benefit which contained a large amount of discretion. This discretion, which was meant to tailor the benefits to the needs of claimants, resulted in inconsistent decisions and was felt to demean claimants because their entitlement was not a right. The solution to these problems was (a) the reduction of discretion and (b) improving the standard of people appointed to tribunals. The reduction of discretion was brought about by the increased use of rules, or 'legalisation'. The standard of tribunals was to be improved by appointing legally qualified chairs, a practice which was felt to have contributed to the better performance of national insurance benefits appeals, and by providing chairs and wing-members with better training. The 'judicialisation' of tribunals through legally qualified chairs reinforced the legalisation of the benefits system. As the complexity of the rules of entitlement increased, there was a greater need to have lawyers chairing tribunals.

15.2.4.2 Procedure The first president of the SSATs, Judge Byrt QC, promoted, through the training of chairs, a move away from the traditional adversarial nature of the courts and their substitutes (Baldwin, Wikeley and Young 1992, p. 97). This was felt to be necessary as many appellants do not have a representative to help them to present their appeal. Chairs are encouraged to help appellants feel at ease and to draw out the basis for their appeal by asking questions. This is not a transformation from adversarial to an inquisitorial mode of procedure, rather a grafting on of inquisitorial elements to an adversarial process. The tribunals are still dependent upon the parties to furnish them with information. The appellants can provide details about their circumstances, and the respondent, the Department of Social Security, through its presenting officer, gives a report about the determination of the application, the relevant rules and case law, if any, from the SSC and the courts. The Department's written submissions, it seems, are not designed to help the tribunal but to explain and justify decisions, and their effect can be that they set the agenda and define the issues in the appeal for the tribunal (Baldwin, Wikeley and Young 1992, p. 103).

Research indicates that the great majority of chairs are competently performing the various aspects of their roles which seek to put appellants at ease and enable them to have a fair hearing (Baldwin, Wikeley and Young 1992, p. 114; Potter 1992, p. 342). It appears that the standard of the wing-members has improved but not all of them play an active part in the conduct of the appeal (Baldwin, Wikeley and Young, 1992, pp. 143–51; Potter 1992, pp. 348–50).

15.2.4.3 Appellants The changes to the tribunals have not addressed some of the problems which appellants face. If claimants are unhappy about determinations to whom can they turn for advice? The Citizens Advice Bureaux (CAB) are the major source of advice and assistance for claimants throughout the country as the provision of specialist legal advice centres is restricted. Whilst State-funded legal advice and assistance cover welfare benefit problems, the number of legal practitioners providing this advice is not very large. It may well be that the absence of expert advice plays a part in the large proportion of appeals, about 50 per cent, where the appellant fails to attend. A consensus appears from the research studies carried out into non-attendance that some appellants do not really understand what it means to lodge an appeal and that it can involve attending the tribunal. Thus non-attendance can be explained by practical reasons such as illness, caring for a relative, travel problems or an alternative appointment (Bell 1975; Farrelly 1989). The documentation which appellants are sent also seems to play a part in causing non-attendance. These papers include a somewhat technical submission by the adjudication officer, which is intimidating for some, and for others it serves to bring home to them the fact that their appeal is not well-founded and is unlikely to succeed (Baldwin, Wikeley and Young 1992, p. 158). The papers also state that attendance is advisable, and so some appellants may feel that it is not necessary for them to attend.

Another factor which contributes to non-attendance is delay in the hearing of appeals. In 1990 the average wait between the lodging of the appeal and the hearing was 23 weeks (Parliamentary Debates (Hansard), Commons, vol. 186, written answers col. 26, 18 February 1991). Whilst acknowledging that their sample is small, Baldwin, Wikeley and Young suggest that delay is not as important a factor in explaining non-attendance as appellants' ignorance about the appeals process (1992, p. 166).

Baldwin, Wikeley and Young report that non-attendance does mean that the appeal will tend to be given a more cursory examination than would be the case if the appellant did attend (1992, pp. 108–9).

Appellants who are represented at tribunals have a higher success rate than those who are unrepresented. Again the absence of advice and assistance means that some appellants are not prepared for the tribunal's formal procedure. Even with the enabling role which the SSAT chairs are expected to play, some appellants find it difficult to express themselves and present information which is relevant to the appeal. The issue of representation has long been debated in the context of tribunals. The Franks Committee recommended the provision of legal aid for individuals appearing before tribunals (1957, para. 89). Other advocates of legal aid include the Lord Chancellor's Advisory Committee on Legal Aid (HC 20 of 1974–5, paras 35–41 and subsequent annual reports) and Justice-All Souls Committee (1988, paras 9.29 to 9.67). Research conducted for the Lord Chancellor's Department not only affirmed the importance of representation but suggested the creation of a tribunal representation service (Genn and Genn 1989; see Young 1990 for a critical review of this report). This report was endorsed by the Council on Tribunals who (not for the first time) strenuously urged the provision of advice, assistance and representation at tribunals (HC 64 of 1989–90, paras 1.35 to 1.50). The government's position would appear to be that such provision is not a priority and that existing lay agencies can continue to provide appellants with help.

It should not be thought that representation is a guarantee of success. Baldwin, Wikeley and Young report that some tribunal chairs and wing-members take an adversarial view of proceedings so that if the appellant's representative is not very good then they will not intervene to assist the drawing out of relevant points (1992, p. 109). The nature of the benefit rules also means that many appeals cannot succeed. This is appreciated by tribunal chairs and members as well as by appellants who draw the distinction between a fair hearing and being fair to the appellant. They acknowledge that they are dealt with courteously and sympathetically by the SSAT but realise that the regulations are not generous.

Prosser has written about this aspect of appeals, as being a device which promotes the acceptance of unpopular benefits (1977). The government is responsible for the conditions of entitlement to benefit which determine the range of successful claimants. The creation of an independent appeal mechanism offloads responsibility for unpopular decisions and enables the government to claim that the system must be fair because of the involvement of an impartial independent tribunal. This does not mean that tribunals are a sham. Baldwin, Wikeley and Young suggest that the tribunals have more discretion to vary decisions than many chairs and wing-members appear to appreciate (1992, pp. 98–103), and that the complexity of the rules in combination with the conditions of work and culture of the Benefits Agency local offices mean that errors are made which can be rectified on appeal (pp. 26–64).

15.2.4.4 Conclusions It would seem that, compared with the operation of the supplementary benefit appeals tribunals in the 1970s, the SSATs are a considerable improvement. The quality of those who sit on tribunals has been raised so that the standard of decision-making is higher. Appellants who attend appeals believe that they are treated satisfactorily in what can be a stressful situation. The problem is that while tribunals may be substitutes for courts they are not really alternatives in that they still conform to the adversarial approach (see Genn 1993, 1994). Therefore appellants require advice, assistance and representation. The greater degree of inquisitorial-type intervention in proceedings which tribunal members may carry out cannot offset the reinforcing trends of judicialisation and legalisation in welfare benefits.

15.3 COMMISSIONERS

15.3.1 Origins

In the UK the idea of a grievance officer can certainly be traced back to a 1961 report by Justice, *The Citizen and the Administration*. This report identified a gap in the redress of citizens' complaints against public authorities. Neither political channels nor the courts were satisfactory. The Parliamentary devices such as questions and adjournment debates did not really penetrate the department. The relevant files were not made available to the MP and there was no independence in any investigation. On the other hand access to the courts was at that time difficult, due to a restricted view of *locus standi*, or the legal interest necessary for an applicant to demonstrate in the issue for which judicial review was sought. Even if a court would entertain a challenge, the likelihood of success was not high as the grounds of judicial review were not as developed as they are now.

The Justice report recommended the establishment of a commissioner who would be an officer of Parliament able to assist MPs in seeking redress for their constituents' complaints. The Justice committee recognised that MPs were jealous of their function of assisting constituents and realised that supplementation and not substitution of MPs was a realistic proposal.

It took some time before a government accepted that there was such a need and the first grievance officer was created by the Parliamentary Commissioner Act 1967. By this time New Zealand had become the first common law jurisdiction to have imported this Scandinavian official.

The 1967 statute was a modified form of the Justice recommendations. An important development was the creation of a House of Commons select committee to oversee the work of the commissioner. This committee has given support to the Parliamentary Commissioner for Administration and argued for improvements in law and practice.

The next stage of the development of this remedial technique occurred in Northern Ireland. The devolved governmental departments there were subjected to their own commissioner (Parliamentary Commissioner Act (Northern Ireland) 1969, now Ombudsman (Northern Ireland) Order 1996) and another office was created to deal with the region's local government and health authorities (Commissioner for Complaints Act (Northern Ireland) 1969, now Commissioner for Complaints (Northern Ireland) Order 1996). These two offices have always been held by one person. Initially, the work of the commissioners was conducted by two separate sections in the same building. Subsequently an integrated organisation was implemented (Hayes 1990).

The health authorities in Great Britain were the next sector of public administration to have a grievance investigator. The new Health Service Commissioner created by the Health Service (Scotland) Act 1972 and the National Health Service Reorganisation Act 1973, has always been the person appointed to be the Parliamentary Commissioner for Administration. This involvement of the Parliamentary Commissioner for Administration in new areas continued with the arrangements for local government. Under the Local Government Act 1974, Commissions for Local Administration in England and Wales were created. The English Commission has three Commissioners for Local Administration, one of whom chairs the Commission. The Welsh Commission has one Local Commissioner. Both of these commissions have, as an ex officio member, the Parliamentary Commissioner for Administration. In Scotland, the Local Government (Scotland) Act 1975 created a Commissioner for Local Administration.

All of the UK commissioners share similarities, as the Parliamentary Commissioner for Administration served as the model. Thus, the remit of all of them is to investigate complaints of injustice arising out of maladministration. There are some differences which reflect the particular context of their area of work, whether it be the sector of public administration, central or local government, or the locality, as in the special circumstances of Northern Ireland.

15.3.2 Access

The point has already been made that the conception of the Parliamentary Commissioner for Administration was of someone who assisted MPs. This was reflected in the legislation by the requirement that complaints had to be referred to the Commissioner by an MP (Parliamentary Commissioner Act 1967, s. 5(1)), thereby giving the MP a chance to pursue the matter first. There should be the consent of the complainant to refer to the Commissioner as well as the willingness of the MP to do so.

This MP filter has caused problems because citizens tended to complain direct to the Commissioner. It would be explained to these complainants that they must approach their MPs first, but it was clear that most of those who complained direct did not then contact their MP. In 1978 it was agreed that the Parliamentary Commissioner for Administration could forward the complaint to the complainant's MP in order for it to be referred back.

Currently the Health Service Commissioner can accept complaints direct from citizens as can the commissioners for local administration (LO) in England, Scotland and Wales (Local Government Act 1974, s. 26(2) as amended by the Local Government Act 1988, sch. 3, para. 5). Originally complaints about local authorities would first have to be raised with a councillor. The reason again being the constituency work role of an elected representative, and also the opportunity for the matter to be resolved. If the councillor refused to refer the complaint to the LO then the complaint could be taken directly to the commissioner. Not surprisingly this reduced the number of complaints which the LOs received. After a long campaign waged by the LOs and bodies such as Justice, and the adoption by the LOs of a practice similar to that of the Parliamentary Commissioner for Administration, there is now direct access to the LOs as an alternative to referral through a councillor. Unsurprisingly, direct access has led to an increase in complaints received by the LOs.

In Northern Ireland there never was a 'filter' for the Commissioner for Complaints, whereas the Parliamentary Commissioner for Northern Ireland was to receive complaints from MPs of the Northern Ireland Parliament. Since the proroguing of that legislature in 1972, complaints are to come from Westminster MPs. As most complaints are made direct to the Parliamentary Commissioner for Northern Ireland, the practice is to screen them and, if they seem to be within jurisdiction, then the complainant is asked to have an MP refer it.

15.3.3 Jurisdiction
It is a feature of all of the commissioners that their annual reports present statistics indicating that a large number of complaints have not been accepted because they are outside their jurisdiction. Before dealing with some of the matters which are specifically excluded, we will detail the requirements which must be met. Complaints are to be in writing (Parliamentary Commissioner Act 1967, s. 5(1)(a) Local Government Act 1974, s. 26(2)) and must be made by the person who claims to have suffered injustice through the maladministration caused by the public authority. A representative may submit the complaint where the complainant has died or is otherwise incapable of acting unaided (Parliamentary Commissioner Act 1967, s. 6(2)). The complaint is to be made within 12 months of the day on which the person aggrieved first had notice of the matters alleged in the complaint. However, this time limit may be waived at the discretion of the commissioners where they believe there are circumstances which make it proper or reasonable to conduct an investigation (Parliamentary Commissioner Act 1967, s. 6(3)); Local Government Act 1974, s. 26(4)).

The Parliamentary Commissioner for Administration's jurisdiction did not initially extend beyond the UK. Complaints had to relate to matters in the UK and the complainants had to reside there unless the complaint had occurred in the UK (Parliamentary Commissioner Act 1967, s. 6(4)). Subsequently the complaints about the work of UK consul officials abroad was included (s. 6(5), added by the Parliamentary Commissioner (Consular Complaints) Act 1981).

The LO is not able to accept complaints which affect the locality as a whole (Local Government Act 1974, s. 26(7)). The thrust of all of the commissioners' legislation is the investigation of complaints affecting individuals.

15.3.3.1 Contractual or commercial matters The Parliamentary Commissioner for Administration and the LOs are not permitted to deal with complaints about commercial or contractual matters of bodies which are otherwise subject to their investigation. This exclusion has been criticised by the commissioners, the Parliamentary Commissioner for Administration select committee and organisations such as Justice. Government has been firm in maintaining this restriction, justifying it by contending that governmental contracting should not be subject to a type of examination which is not applied to other contractors. In other words, only matters which are unique to government should be within the commissioners' jurisdiction. This argument is also applied to the situation where government is an employer, which is considered next.

15.3.3.2 Public service personnel matters The inclusion of public service personnel matters is resisted by the government on the basis that there are mechanisms for resolving such grievances. The commissioners' legislation was intended to deal with citizen–public authority relations and not as employee–employer. Yet this is not the case in Northern Ireland. Concern about religious discrimination in local government job appointments led to the Commissioner for Complaints Act (Northern Ireland) 1969, containing a provision which made it clear that complaints about these matters were within jurisdiction (s. 5(1)). Subsequently a body, the Fair Employment Commission, was created specifically to deal with such discrimination in the workplace (see now the Fair Employment (Northern Ireland) Act 1989). Another point is that citizens can complain to the commissioners because it is felt correct that public authorities should behave in an exemplary fashion. It is not clear why this should not be the case in respect of their actions as an employer.

15.3.3.3 Alternative remedy If there is an alternative remedy by way of an appeal to a minister or a tribunal, or by initiating court proceedings, then the complaint is excluded unless the commissioner is of the opinion that it would be unreasonable for the complainant to resort to that remedy (Parliamentary Commissioner Act 1967, s. 5(2); Local Government Act 1974, s. 26(6)). To judge from the annual reports of the commissioners, they are more likely to exercise this discretion in favour of the complainant where the alternative remedy entails going to court. The Parliamentary Commissioner for Administration has outlined the sort of factors which lead towards deciding to investigate a complaint despite a possible court action. These are that the legal process would be too cumbersome, slow and expensive to achieve the desired objective (Parliamentary Commissioner for Administration 1981). A study of the Scottish LO suggests that in addition to the point about the proportionality of the effort to the objective, the following considerations are taken into account when a court action is available to the complainant: the nature of the complaint, any possible hardship to the complainant and the action of the authority concerned (Logie and Watchman 1990, pp. 104–9). The Scottish LO, it seems, is reluctant to deal with issues of legal liability raised in complaints, apart from those arising in council tenancies. Thus in one case, that part of the complaint which related to damage of the complainant's boundary wall was not accepted for investigation as being appropriate for settlement by a court.

As the commissioners' waiver is a discretionary power, they must not automatically apply a policy which says that it is unreasonable to expect a citizen to seek judicial review. The point was made in the Divisional Court that there must be a genuine exercise of discretion in waiving the exclusion of a complaint which has an alternative remedy (*R* v *Commissioner for Local Administration, ex parte Croydon London Borough Council* [1989] 1 All ER 1033).

15.3.3.4 Crime or court proceedings Where a complaint relates to crime or the initiation of court proceedings these are matters outside jurisdiction. It was formerly the case that investigation of crime was also outside all of the commissioners' jurisdiction. This exclusion was used by some local authorities as a defence to the LOs when they proposed to investigate complaints relating to enforcement action. The enforcement process in planning, consumer protection or environmental health may result in a criminal prosecution where an offender has failed to comply with specified requirements. Some authorities, for example, contended that their action taken as part of the enforcement of planning control was outside the LOs' jurisdiction on the basis that it involved the investigation of crime. This view has not found favour with the LOs who have accepted various types of enforcement complaints for investigation. The LOs took the view that the administrative arrangements which surrounded a decision to initiate a criminal prosecution were not caught by the exclusion. Only the actions of the police and police authorities in connection with the investigation of crime are now outside jurisdiction (Parliamentary Commissioner Act 1967, sch. 3, para. 9; Local Government Act 1974, sch. 4, para. 3).

15.3.3.5 Access to government information In preference to enacting a Freedom of Information Act which would confer a statutory right to official information enforced by the courts, the government announced in 1993 that it would prepare a code of practice on government information which would be supervised by the PCA (Cm 2290, see Birkinshaw 1993). In effect, for those bodies subject to the PCA, failure to follow the code would amount to maladministration and injustice. The code was promulgated in 1994, taking effect as from April. It does not give persons the right to see 'pre-existing documents', rather information, and the greater part of the document deals with exemptions, some of which include: (a) defence, security and international relations; (b) internal discussion and advice; (c) communications with the royal household; (d) law enforcement and legal proceedings; and (e) privacy.

15.3.3.6 Jurisdictional sieve The reason why most complaints are rejected is not because of the limits on the commissioners' jurisdiction but because there appears to be no maladministration. In 1995–6, 8,534 investigations were terminated at the discretion of the English LOs out of a total of 13,079 which were concluded after initial enquiries. This is to be compared with the total of investigation reports issued in that period which was 486, of which 410 found maladministration causing injustice.

It is not clear from the annual reports whether the complainant is aggrieved by the merits of a decision, which the commissioners cannot question unless there is maladministration, or whether the complaint is trivial. In some local government cases the initial exchange between the LO and the council leads to a settlement of the complaint and a local settlement may also be obtained during the investigation which often leads to discontinuation.

15.3.4 Investigation Process
The commissioners' staff screen complaints, i.e., they check if the complaint is within jurisdiction. If it is not, then this is explained to the complainant, or the referring MP in the case of the Parliamentary Commissioner for Administration. Where a complaint is accepted for investigation the head of the body concerned, a permanent secretary in a central government department or chief executive of a council, is informed of the complaint and given the opportunity to make preliminary comments. The investigation then proceeds with an examination of the various files and any interviews which the investigators feel are required. For example, it is the practice of the Scottish LO to interview officials and the complainant when the complaint involves a disputed conversation between an official and the complainant. Planning provides examples of such complaints in which the complainant made a telephone enquiry and recollects that particular advice was given. Then, after following the advice the council state that the action taken was wrong and that such advice would not have been given. It may be that it is not clear which official spoke to the complainant, in which case the investigators interview other officials in order to determine who did speak to the complainant.

After the files have been examined and interviews conducted, a draft report is drawn up and shown to the parties to check for factual accuracy. The final version of the report with its finding is produced and sent to the authority and the complainant or referring MP.

15.3.5 Maladministration and Injustice
The two key terms in the commissioners' legislation, 'maladministration' and 'injustice', are undefined. They are the heart of the matter. In the course of the second reading of the Parliamentary Commissioner for Administration Bill, the minister who was introducing the measure, Mr Crossman, gave some examples of what might constitute maladministration. This is known as the Crossman catalogue and includes 'bias, neglect, inattention, delay, incompetence, ineptitude, perversity, turpitude, arbitrariness and so on'. In a sense maladministration is what the commissioners say it is. Here are some examples from the 1995–96 annual report of the English LOs. Housing: two tenants requested a transfer on medical grounds, unsuitable offers made and delays in processing housing benefit applications (94/A/156); an enquiry about a renovation grant was not processed and this was not maladministration, the council did not have sufficient funds to meet the demand for grants, but the failure to inspect the house and see if it was unfit, which could lead to the issue of a repair notice, was maladministration (91/C/3521), council

did not inform a tenant that sand blasting of the flat was about to occur and failed to ensure that the windows were sealed during the process (92/A/3949)

Planning: a neighbour was not notified by the council of a planning application for the adjacent property, even though notification was council policy, — the complainant received compensation for the loss in value of his property (93/C/3209); the complainant claimed to have incurred lost expenditure after being incorrectly advised by the council — the LO did not find that this loss was caused by or could be attributed to the council's error, but delay in dealing with the complainant's written enquiry constituted maladministration and injustice (94/A/3229).

Education: following the issue of a draft statement of education needs there was a delay in the issue of an education needs statement, because of misunderstanding between the Council and the mother. The delay resulted in the mother paying unneccesary school fees. One term's school fees and compensation for time and trouble in making the complaint were paid (92/A/3201).

Highways: when the council closed a road to effect repairs in village, it did not have a road closure order. The failure to apply for one meant that the opportunities for objection were removed (93/B/2569).

Council tax: the council failed to take action after phone calls and correspondence about a person's council tax. As it was not resolved a summons for non-payment was wrongly issued and caused the complainant to attend the court hearing, which could have been avoided. The council paid the person's court costs as well as a sum of compensation (93/B/2058).

Environmental health: the council delayed in dealing with a person's complaint about pollution from a neighbour's septic tank (94/C/460).

These examples give some idea of the commissioners' conception of maladministration. Some studies (Crawford and Thompson 1987; Logie and Watchman 1990) concluded that it is not possible to identify principles of maladministration from the commissioners' reports. A partial explanation for this is that the main purpose of the commissioners is redressing grievances, not the development and articulation of the concept of maladministration.

Does maladministration cover only the manner in which authorities carry out their tasks or does it also include what might be called 'bad decisions' or 'bad rules'? This was a matter which was raised by the select committee on the Parliamentary Commissioner for Administration. The committee defined a bad decision as one which, judged by its effect upon the aggrieved person, appears to be so thoroughly bad in quality that the Parliamentary Commissioner for Administration might infer that maladministration had been involved. A 'bad rule' is one which has been properly applied but has caused hardship. Here the committee wanted the Parliamentary Commissioner for Administration to enquire if the department had undertaken a review and, if so, to what effect. The Parliamentary Commissioner for Administration has regarded these matters as falling within his jurisdiction and so have the other commissioners.

We can obtain an idea of what the commissioners consider to be injustice by referring to the examples of maladministration listed above. There we can see what injustice might have been caused, e.g., delay, damage to property, inconvenience, unnecessary expense. The issue of the identification of injustice was raised in *R v Local Commissioner for Administration, ex parte Eastleigh Borough Council* [1988] QB 855. In this case the LO had made a finding of maladministration causing injustice in a complaint concerning drains. The authority challenged this finding and Nolan J held that the commissioner had erred by (a) questioning a decision taken without maladministration by an authority in the exercise of discretionary power (contrary to the Local Government Act 1974, s. 34(3)), and (b) making a report when it had not been established that the complainant had suffered injustice (contrary to the Local Government Act 1974, s. 26(1)). Despite finding for the council Nolan J did not quash the commissioner's report or grant a declaration that he had exceeded his jurisdiction. The council appealed and the commissioner cross-appealed the finding that he had exceeded his powers. The Court of Appeal, by a majority, found for the council and upheld Nolan J's finding that the wording of the commissioner's report did not support the conclusion that the complainant had sustained injustice.

This case illustrates a difference between the courts and the commissioners. It has already been suggested that the commissioners' reports are not drafted with a view to developing the concept of maladministration. The concern is to redress complainants' grievances. Lord Donaldson of Lymington MR said that the reports are neither statutes nor judgments, and therefore not intended to be subjected to legalistic analysis. They were written in everyday language to convey a message to the council and the public. Despite this sympathy for the commissioner, Lord Donaldson did have to suggest significant additions to the report in order to demonstrate the meaning which he thought was intended by the commissioner. Taylor and Parker LJJ could not construe the report's paragraph on injustice in the way contended by the commissioner.

15.3.6 Outcomes of Reports
Where the commissioner finds that the complainant has sustained injustice as a result of maladministration, the offending authority generally accepts the decision and offers a remedy. There is usually no difficulty in the Parliamentary Commissioner for Administration's reports being accepted by central government departments. Occasionally the department will disagree that maladministration has occurred but offers recompense. This has happened in two major investigations involving a number of complainants. The first of these concerned the non-payment of compensation by the Foreign Office to those who had been prisoners of war in the Sachsenhausen camp, and in the second case the regulation of financial institutions by the Department of Trade and Industry was found to have been at fault and to have played a part in the losses sustained by investors when the Barlow Clowes group of companies collapsed. The former Department of Transport resisted for some time compensating people whose property had been blighted due to delay over the Channel Tunnel Rail Link. It is likely that the robust support of the select committee helped persuade the department to move from its initial

rejection of the Commissioner's special report (HC 193 of 1994–95, special report; HC 270 of 1994–95, select committee's reaction; HC 819 of 1994–95, department signals change of heart, HC 453 of 1996–97, proposals for redress, see James and Longley, 1996).

The LOs have found that some authorities have not accepted their reports and provided a remedy for the complainant. The original version of the Local Government Act 1974 provided for a further report by the LOs where they were unhappy with the council's response to the first report. Neither the initial nor the further report could be enforced against an unwilling council. This situation aggrieved the LOs. They thought it unfair that a council could accept a report which found no maladministration, but could reject one which found that they had caused injustice through maladministration. They looked jealously at the situation in Northern Ireland. Under the Commissioner for Complaints (Northern Ireland) Order 1996, art. 16, it is possible for a complainant to go to the county court to seek, as it were, judicial enforcement of the commissioner's report. The court could award damages or make an order against the authority which the commissioner had found to have caused injustice through maladministration. (The 1996 Order also confers a power on the Commissioner to ask the Attorney-General to apply to the High Court to grant an injunction, declaration or other relief. The basis for this is that because of a vindicated complaint the Commissioner is aware that the body had previously engaged in conduct which was of the same or a similar kind to that which amounted to the maladministration, and it is likely to continue unless the High Court grants relief.) This solution of judicial enforcement was advocated in the report of the Committee on the Conduct of Local Authority Business (Widdicombe 1986) and in the review of administrative law in the UK conducted by a committee of Justice and All Souls College, Oxford (Justice–All Souls 1988). The government did not accept this advice and instead amended the legislation so that an authority must inform the LO of the action which it proposes to take following an adverse report. This would also apply if a second report was issued. Where an authority does not intend to accept the LO's recommendations in a further report, the authority, as a whole, must consider that further report and if the commissioner is not satisfied with the response to it he may require that a notice is published in a local newspaper in a form agreed with the authority. This notice will state the action recommended by the LO and the authority may include its reasons for not complying with those recommendations (Local Government Act 1974, s. 31 as amended by Housing and Local Government Act 1989, ss. 26 and 28).

The government decided against extending the Northern Ireland provisions on judicial enforcement on the basis that the prospect of court proceedings would adversely affect the generally very good relationship between the LOs and the councils. Certainly this was the view of some academics (Lewis, Seneviratne and Cracknell 1987; Crawford and Thompson 1987). Some doubt whether the reforms which use publicity to exert pressure as a sanction will really achieve anything (Jones 1988). It remains to be seen what effect the reforms will have. It should be realised, however, that the number of cases in which the LOs have been dissatisfied with the councils' response amounts to 5 per cent of those reports which found maladministration causing injustice.

There has been little research conducted on further reports issued by the LOs. One study reported that the two largest categories of reasons given for non-compliance in the further reports were disagreement with (a) the finding of maladministration and (b) the proposed remedy. Interestingly in many of the second category cases the disagreement was not total, as the authority was prepared to comply partially with the suggested remedy (Crawford and Thompson 1987). This point was still found to exist in research by the English LOs into cases in 1993/4–1994/5. The largest source of disagreement was over whether the conduct amounted to maladministration (Annual Report 1995–96, p. 4 also CLA 1995).

In *R v Parliamentary Commissioner for Administration, ex parte Dyer* [1994] 1 WLR 621, a complainant whose complaint had been upheld by the PCA sought judicial review because the PCA (a) had not investigated what she felt were some of the most important aspects of her case; (b) had followed the established practice of giving the department, but not the complainant, a draft of the facts in the report for comment; (c) had not reopened the investigation after she had pointed out deficiencies; and (d) claimed to be precluded from reopening an investigation once a report had been issued. In rejecting her application, Simon Brown J did hold that the PCA was subject to judicial review but such was the amount of discretion conferred upon the PCA by the legislation that a court would not readily interfere with the PCA's decision to continue or discontinue an investigation. To show a draft of the report only to the department was not to breach fairness or natural justice. It gave the department the opportunity provided for in the Parliamentary Commissioner Act 1967, s. 11(3), to notify the PCA if the disclosure of any information could be contrary to the public interest, and also to propose a remedy which the PCA could declare to be satisfactory or unsatisfactory in the final report.

In *R v Parliamentary Commissioner for Administration, ex parte Balchin* [1996] EGCS 166, Balchin did not receive any compensation from the local highways authority when the Secretary of State confirmed a road order. The failure to evaluate the stance of the local body, even though outside the PCA's jurisdiction, was a failure to consider a relevant fact so that the PCA had omitted a potentially decisive element in determining whether the minister caused Balchin injustice by maladministration in its dealing with the local authority. The minister could have drawn the power of compensation to the local authority's attention. The case was remitted to the PCA for reconsideration.

15.3.7 Evaluation
In order to evaluate properly the commissioners, we must first identify their objectives. Some writers have suggested a variety of tasks which the commissioners are to fulfil. These include the remedying of wrongs, the humanising of bureaucracy, the reduction of public alienation from government, the

prevention of abuses by government, the vindication of officials unjustly accused of wrongdoing, and the stimulation of administrative reform (Hill 1976). To these may be added, the opening up of government to public scrutiny, the stimulation of internal grievance procedures, the furthering of central or managerial control by feedback about actual conduct of administration by 'street-level' officials, and the representation of the citizen within the administrative system (Rawlings 1987). These tasks are quite wide. We can see that there is a certain amount of overlap with objectives stated by the commissioners themselves: the encouraging of the development and publicising of internal procedures for the settlement of grievances, the encouragement of settlement of complaints referred to the commissioners, to increase the public awareness of the commissioners and to give advice on how to make complaints, to publicise the lessons to be learnt from complaints, to give guidance to those whose complaints are outside the commissioners' jurisdiction and to support the work of other commissioners. Logie and Watchman (1990) suggest that it is possible to reduce the essence of most of these various objectives to two major tasks, remedying grievances and improving administration. They also argue that the remedying of grievances is the task to which the commissioners devote the most time and effort.

15.3.7.1 Awareness All commissioners are concerned about publicising their existence. They produce leaflets, give talks and issue press releases on the publication of their annual reports. Yet it would appear that the public in general do not know much, if anything, about them. If there was a greater public awareness would this lead to a flood of complaints and would an increase in workload lead to a decrease in the efficiency and effectiveness of the commissioners? Would it be the case that an increase in complaints would lead to an increase in complaints within the commissioners' jurisdiction? The advent of direct access to the English LOs led to an initial 44 per cent increase in complaints received but it does not seem that this has improved the ratio of acceptable to rejected complaints. Anyway, is a large number of complaints rejected as being outside jurisdiction a good or bad indicator of the quality of administration? Some rejected complaints will concern the merits of a decision. In planning, for example, it is recognised that a large number of complaints about planning permissions are made by neighbours who do not think that consent should have been given. The planning appeals system does not provide for appeal against the grant of permission, or for appeal by such third parties, and so a complaint to the LO is a surrogate appeal. Yet there may well have been some maladministration in the processing of the planning decision. The LOs have repeatedly held that a failure to consult neighbours about planning applications, even where this is not required by legislation, amounts to maladministration and that injustice is the sense of grievance at the loss of an opportunity to give one's view.

The MP filter to the Parliamentary Commissioner for Administration has been examined by Drewry and Harlow (1990) and they conclude that some MPs are unclear about the jurisdiction of the Parliamentary Commissioner for Administration, and others tend not to refer because they think that investigations take far too long. This, Drewry and Harlow suggest, is because there is a lack of fit between the way in which MPs work and the Parliamentary Commissioner for Administration's 'house-style' (1990, p. 766).

The filter has also been examined by the Select Committee on the Parliamentary Commissioner for Administration which has recommended its retention on the basis that abandoning it could lead to the PCA being overwhelmed with cases and that the decrease in the MPs' work would mean that they would be less effective in holding the government to account because of a decrease in their knowledge and experience of constituents' grievances (HC 33 of 1993–4, paras 53–76). The committee did, however, call for the enlarging and strengthening of access to the PCA.

15.3.7.2 Effectiveness The majority of commissioners in the UK have evolved in a direction which is different from that of their Scandinavian forebear. The Parliamentary Commissioner for Administration was envisaged as an adjunct to Parliament and the grievance redress function of MPs. This was carried over into the LO with the initial requirement of referring complaints to councillors. In Northern Ireland it was intended that complainants would approach the Commissioner for Complaints directly. The deviation from the UK's normal constitutional basis in Northern Ireland was because it was so different, with the governmental institutions lacking legitimacy in the eyes of a significant minority of the population. The problem of religious discrimination, especially in local government (allocation of housing, appointments and promotions), led to the provision for direct access, the inclusion of public service personnel complaints within jurisdiction, and judicial enforcement of the commissioner's report finding injustice arising out of maladministration. The majority of cases in which a court has awarded damages have involved public service personnel complaints (Crawford and Thompson, 1987; see also White 1994), and these declined with the enactment of the Fair Employment (Northern Ireland) Act 1976 (see now the Fair Employment (Northern Ireland) Act 1989).

There has been a tradition of innovation amongst the Northern Ireland commissioners and they have conducted 'outreach' work by travelling around towns and 'setting up their stall' in community centres in order to advertise their existence to the public. They will also deal with some complaints by telephone, in effect providing a two-tier system of investigation, with some matters dealt with by telephone between the commissioner's staff and the body complained against; and others subjected to a full investigation and report (HC 182 of 1990–1). Perhaps these developments owe much to the direct access to the commissioner, the need to 'drum up business', which can produce 'minor' complaints which are capable of quick resolution.

The developments in Northern Ireland have not amounted to a fundamental change in the nature of the UK commissioners, as numbers of complaints are not very high and a large proportion are not accepted for investigation.

There has not been much research into consumer satisfaction. A study conducted for Justice (1980) showed that many complainants who had their complaint vindicated by the LO were satisfied with the service, and that those who had their complaint rejected or not accepted for investigation were dissatisfied. Yet 21 per cent of those whose complaint was investigated were very dissatisfied and 16 per cent were dissatisfied. When one looks at complainants whose complaints were upheld by the LO, 10 per cent were very dissatisfied, and 11 per cent were dissatisfied. In some cases the dissatisfaction arose because of the action of the council. Some complainants were unhappy because they only received an apology. Further analysis suggested that some areas of council responsibilities may be more likely to have dissatisfied complainants. In planning 47 per cent of complainants were dissatisfied compared with an average of 37 per cent of all complainants. If it is found that a building is not constructed in accordance with approved plans so that a view is impaired, an apology or a small sum of compensation is not likely to satisfy the complainant, yet it is unlikely that demolition of the building would be ordered.

These statistics must be studied with caution as the sample size was not large and the survey was carried out within the first five years of operation of the LOs in England. It might be thought that these data may add to the arguments which the LOs in England, Scotland and Wales made in the 1980s for a provision similar to that in Northern Ireland allowing for judicial enforcement. It is certainly the case that the complainant and the LO will feel very aggrieved when the council does not comply with the investigation report. Yet maladministration is not always a straightforward issue. It is sometimes a fault which could be remedied in the courts or elsewhere and sometimes it is not. It seems to be better suited to a negotiated process for resolving a grievance. The point that judicial enforcement would cast a long and unhelpful shadow over this process is not controverted by the views of successive Northern Ireland commissioners who claim that it does not have to be resorted to because the threat of its use is sufficient to achieve a satisfactory result. Councils will, it is suggested, be somewhat wary and even if, as Justice–All Souls proposed, the findings of the LO were to be conclusive for the court proceedings, this would not stop councils seeking judicial review. The majority attitude of the courts in *R v Local Commissioner for Administration, ex parte Eastleigh Borough Council* [1988] QB 855, indicates that the drafting of reports would have to change to reflect their new status as a text which would be subject to legalistic scrutiny, rather than the basis for negotiation. This would add to the duration of investigations and is surely undesirable. The commissioners' wish to have the possibility of judicial enforcement suggests that they perceive their work as being quasi-judicial (see also Drewry and Harlow 1990, p. 765).

The relationship between the courts and the commissioners as redressers of grievances is curious. The logic of the Justice report and the Parliamentary Commissioner Act 1967 is that maladministration is different from a breach of law. The discretionary waiver to accept complaints for which there may be an alternative remedy opens up the possibility of overlap between the courts and the commissioners. The possibility of overlap could lead to similar issues being treated differently, thereby creating confusion for all concerned (see Bradley 1980). Overlapping jurisdiction does offer advantages for complainants, allowing them to choose commissioners whose services are free, who can conduct a penetrating investigation, and whose involvement may lead to financial compensation being made to complainants. On the other hand there are types of case which the courts can deal with very quickly as, for example, where the care of children is involved, and the court's decision is binding.

The Justice–All Souls report took the view in relation to the Parliamentary Commissioner for Administration, that the overlap should be left allowing complainants to choose their remedy (1988, paras 5.25 to 5.29). It also recommended that the commissioners should not have a power to refer to the courts on a point of law which arises during an investigation (paras 5.31 to 5.35). On this latter point Sir Harry Woolf took a contrary view, arguing that it is preferable for the courts to deal with significant points of law and to deal with cases where they are better placed to provide a remedy (1990, pp. 89–91). He also wondered if it might not be advantageous to give the courts a power to refer a case to the commissioner whose investigation might be more satisfactory. The commissioners' investigation could probe into areas denied to the court, such as public interest immunity (on this immunity see further 18.6).

It is the case that the scope of judicial review has expanded since the Justice report (1961) and the Parliamentary Commissioner Act 1967 so that the potential overlap has increased. It may be that the pragmatic view of leaving things as they are is sensible. Both remedies have their advantages and disadvantages and the real, as opposed to the potential, overlap may not be great.

There is a concern that dissatisfied complainants may seek judicial review of commissioners' decisions and risk a clash between the different values of the two systems of redress.

15.3.7.3 Audit While the predominant conception of the commissioners is that of redressers of individuals' grievances, there is a concern that this may prevent the commissioners from grasping the opportunities to improve the standards of administration. In a study of the Scottish LO, K. Thompson feared that the growth of local settlements, or conciliation, might allow authorities to 'buy off' complainants and avoid a full, and possibly undesirable, investigation (1991, p. 25). In Northern Ireland the commissioner says that if the fast-track investigation indicates a systemic weakness then this is brought to the attention of the permanent secretary or chief officer with an invitation to review procedures. If serious maladministration or a persistent failure to observe reasonable standards is disclosed, then a full investigation will be mounted. This seems to be edging towards the view advocated by some (including this particular commissioner: Hayes 1990, p. 50), that commissioners should be able to initiate investigations instead of waiting for a complainant, and widen an investigation beyond the terms of the complaint. The government has rejected the repeated recommendations of the Select Committee on the Parliamentary Commissioner for Administration that the commissioner be able to carry out inspections and initiate investigations without receiving a complaint, holding that it would be a distraction from the central purpose of investigating individual complaints (Cmnd 7449; HC 619 of 1993–4.

The LOs in England now prepare guidance for local authorities. The first two sets of guidelines they produced were on the creation of internal complaints systems and good administrative practice. It is difficult to know how far the ripples from a commissioner's investigation travel across the administrative pond. The former civil servant Parliamentary Commissioners have indicated that they regard the lessons for an improvement in standards as an important part of their thorough, if lengthy, investigations. It does seem that the commissioners' experience of administration places them in a good position to promote higher standards and that allowing them to initiate investigations would enable them to perform this role more effectively.

15.3.7.4 Charters It may be that the government feels there is no need to have commissioners distracted from their central task of redressing individuals' grievances because the improvement of standards in the public service will be achieved by the Citizen's Charter initiative (see Barron and Scott 1992). This was launched in July 1991 (Cm 1599). There are many themes to this programme. It declares that the principles of public service will include:

(a)   Standards. There should be explicit and prominently displayed standards of performance with a presumption that they will be progressively improved.

(b)   Openness. There should be no secrecy about how services are run and officials should be identified by name badges unless there is a threat to their safety.

(c)   Information. There should be clear, full information about provision of services; targets should be published and compared with results achieved.

(d)   Choice. The public sector should provide choice wherever practicable; people affected by services should be consulted regularly and systematically to inform decisions about service provision.

(e)   Non-discrimination. Services should be available regardless of race or sex and where there is a need leaflets should be published in minority languages.

(f)   Accessibility. Services should be run to suit the convenience of customers so there should be flexible opening hours and inquiry service points for telephone callers.

(g)   And if things go wrong? Explanations and apologies should be given when things go wrong, there should be a well-publicised and available complaints procedure.

In the section of the white paper which dealt with complaints, the first point was that there should be clear and well-publicised internal complaints procedures. Where these fail then there should be independent complaints machinery. Reference was made to the Parliamentary, health and local government commissioners, indeed the government indicated that if difficulties continued in the local government area, legislation would be introduced to make the LO's recommendation legally enforceable as in Northern Ireland. Consultation was promised on a scheme of lay adjudicators who would be appointed to deal with minor claims for redress which the body complained against has not settled in a speedy and satisfactory way.

The Parliamentary Commissioner for Administration select committee considered this proposal and made a guarded response. Whether or not the concern of the commissioners was a factor in the fate of this proposal, there was no mention of lay adjudicators in the first report on the Citizen's Charter (Cm 2101, 1992). Instead a list of principles was announced for internal complaints systems: they should be effective, readily accessible, simple to operate, speedy, confidential, integrated with the organisation's management information systems, and objective, with provision for an independent investigation if necessary. A complaints task force would examine whether current arrangements met these principles, and would identify, if appropriate, if more is needed in the longer term to provide more satisfactory ways of resolving individuals' problems with public services (p. 49). The task force did produce guidance for internal complaints systems. Failure to have such a system would disqualify a body from being awarded a Chartermark, which rewards high standards of service. The Inland Revenue in their Taxpayer's Charter refer to the Complaints Adjudicator, to whom taxpayers may refer grievances without prejudicing their right to invoke the assistance of the PCA. The Adjudicator is independent of the Inland Revenue. The person holding the post has also been appointed to a similar position by Customs and Excise (see Morris 1996). Similar appointments have been made for Companies House, and the prison services in England and Wales, and Scotland. This might result in fewer complaints being made to the PCA. This was what happened in Northern Ireland with the Commissioner for Complaints when the Northern Ireland Housing Executive improved its own complaints service. In the annual report for 1994 the PCA noted the appointment of these adjudicators (implying criticism of the title of Prisons 'Ombudsman' for England and Wales) and stated that complaints concerning the actions of these adjudicators were now being received (HC 307 of 1994–5, para. 13).

A review of the English LOs took the view that with a requirement to have internal complaints systems, the need for the LOs as an investigatory body was not justified (DoE 1996a). This view was not accepted and so the LO faced an efficiency review (DoE 1996b and DoE 1996c).

15.4 CONCLUSIONS

The Citizen's Charter initiative suggests that the government is not in favour of increasing the powers and resources of the Council on Tribunals, or creating a new body like the Australian Administrative Review Council as recommended by the Justice–All Souls report (1988, pp. 75–83). It seems likely that the Council on Tribunals, which is not an expensive body, will continue with (a) its general remit of supervising tribunals and inquiries, and

(b) its support of the Franks Committee's views that in administrative justice, acting justly means acting judicially, that is, operating an adversarial process which concentrates on form and requires equality of resources of advice, assistance and representation, which not all citizens are likely to enjoy.

There is some linkage between service targets and the PCA and maladministration, with the PCA taking the view that if the target is mandatory, or the citizen has an expectation of compensation when it is not met, then a failure to meet the target may amount to maladministration and injustice which could lead to compensation. In the 1993 annual report the PCA reported agreement with the Department of Social Security on the issue of service targets in charters (HC 290 of 1993–4, para. 8). Relations between these parties subsequently deteriorated. The PCA records in the 1994 annual report that there was disagreement between them on the manner in which the department's compensation scheme was to be applied which had first been flagged the previous year (see HC 307 of 1994–5, paras 46–9; Thompson 1995a).

The issue of maladministration and redress was the subject of a special report by the select committee which found that government guidance on this was directed more to protecting the public purse than the rights of citizens (HC 112 of 1994–5). It is also the case that inadequate resources and preparation have caused injustice through maladministration for citizens in two aspects of the work of the Department of Social Security. These failures were pointed out by the PCA in the special report on complaints about disability living allowance (HC 652 of 1992–3), but it seemed that they were repeated in the creation of the Child Support Agency (HC 135 of 1994–5).

The guardians of administrative justice, the commissioners and the members of tribunals, do their best, within the scope allowed to them, to ensure that citizens are dealt with fairly. It may be that the Citizen's Charter programme will improve the standards of the public service, filter out and resolve minor complaints, and direct those with more serious cases to the commissioners. This hierachy occurs in the National Health Service. The first stage is internal. The second stage operates with a panel of external people and there may then be recourse to the Health Service Commissioner.

CHAPTER SIXTEEN

The Principles of Judicial Review of Administrative Action

16.1 INTRODUCTION

16.1.1 Constitutional Role

A constitution with the characteristics discussed in 1.2 provides a higher law to which legislation and governmental actions should conform. Disputes about such conformity are heard by the courts and if they find that legislation or action does not conform to the constitution, they may strike them down. This is known as judicial review. In the UK the scope of judicial review is narrower as, apart from Community law (see 3.3.3 and 9.6), the courts may not deprive legislation of legal effect. This is because of the doctrine of the supremacy of Parliament, the fundamental rule in the UK's constitutional arrangements (see 3.2).

While the doctrine of Parliamentary supremacy restricts review, it also supports it in the sense that, when the courts are examining the actions of public bodies, they usually do so with a view to upholding the will of Parliament, because legislation is the most common source of legal authority for the activities of public bodies. The major judicial review doctrine of *ultra vires* is founded on the idea of bodies keeping within the powers they have been given. Acting outside those powers is not only flouting Parliamentary intention, but it is also a breach of law. Accordingly there are two bases for judicial review. These bases are not unproblematic. The idea of Parliamentary will does not encompass bodies which are not statutory in origin, but the judges have expanded the scope of review from source of power to nature of function. If, therefore, a body is carrying out what may be regarded as a public function then it may be subject to judicial review. This fits in with the broader political-doctrine aspect of the rule of law discussed in 3.4.2.2.

Where the courts are dealing with a statutory source of power, it must be realised that their policing of Parliamentary intention by the interpretation of legislation is not a mere technical exercise. Legislative language is not precise and so construing statutes is a creative endeavour. While the courts acknowledge the primacy of legislation in the hierarchy of legal norms, their canons of interpretation include points derived from legal policy which they devise, the authority for which is that they have not been changed by legislation (Bennion 1992, pp. 531–96). One such principle is the presumption that legislation does not make changes in the common law (*Attorney-General, ex rel. Yorkshire and Derwent Trust Ltd* v *Brotherton* [1992] 1 AC 425 at p.439; see Bennion 1992, p. 563). Sometimes even express words in legislation are not given effect to by the court as the example of clauses which purport to oust the jurisdiction of the courts shows (see 17.5).

If broader ideals such as the rule of law and the liberal democratic nature of the State inform developments in judicial review which seek to subject legislation to scrutiny this may also be justified by the fact that Parliamentary oversight is not necessarily rigorous when the executive dominates the House of Commons through party discipline. On the other hand, the convention of ministerial responsibility can sometimes play a part in the courts' refusal to review action which they think is more properly suited to political accountability as with, for example, national security (see 17.2.5 on justiciability).

16.1.2   The Distinction between Appeal and Review

The distinction between appeal and review is both very important and somewhat difficult to maintain in practice. If one appeals a decision, one is claiming that it is wrong, or incorrect, and that the appellate authority should change the decision. Thus if X was found to have defamed Y, X might appeal that finding, or the amount of damages which the court awarded to Y. The Court of Appeal, if it is persuaded of the merits of the case, may allow X's appeal and so it substitutes its view for that of the court of first instance. In review the court is not concerned with the merits of the case, whether the decision was right or wrong, but whether it was lawful or unlawful. In the words of Lord Brightman: 'Judicial review is concerned, not with the decision, but with the decision-making process' (*Chief Constable of the North Wales Police* v *Evans* [1982] 1 WLR 1155 at p. 1173).

The consequence of finding that the decision or action was unlawful is that it is invalidated. This means in the case of a decision that it will have to be taken again, but this time it must be taken in accordance with the law. It would be possible for the decision-maker to come to the same decision providing that the law was respected.

While most people who challenge decisions do so because they think that they are decided incorrectly, i.e., not in their favour, they hope that ultimately the decision will be different. In other words most people's concept of challenge is that of appeal. Yet this will not necessarily be the final outcome of a challenge by way of judicial review.

16.1.3   Resort to Judicial Review

Why should people resort to judicial review if they cannnot be certain that the decision or action which they challenge will be changed? Some challengers will hope that review will lead to a more favourable decision. It may be that review is the only avenue of redress left to them. Going to court may be a tactic in a struggle between two parties which offers delay or publicity. There is concern that public authorities should not be delayed by mere busybodies and this is reflected in judicial review procedures (see 17.2 to 17.4).

Research into who seeks judical review, against whom and in respect of what, is not substantial. Sunkin (1987, 1991, 1995) has found that while the numbers of applications for judicial review have increased, this is mainly accounted for by a few areas of governmental action. These areas can change, for example, the number of reviews sought by prisoners dropped between his two surveys, whereas reviews of planning and environmental issues, and local government and rating matters increased. In the area which has the most reviews, immigration, there are trends in different types of case. Most cases refer to refusal of entry but there was a decline of such cases around the time of an increase in reviews of refusal of asylum cases. The rise in asylum cases was caused by the Tamils who feared for their lives in Sri Lanka.

Sunkin points out that two factors which will play a part in surges of particular review applications are the availability of legal aid and the existence of alternative means of redress.

16.2 GENERAL OUTLINE OF GROUNDS FOR REVIEW

In *Council of Civil Service Unions* v *Minister for the Civil Service* [1985] AC 374, Lord Diplock restated the grounds of judicial review using the three broad classes of illegality, irrationality and procedural irregularity. These classes differ from earlier attempts at classification carried out by academics. Lord Diplock's first class contains the fundamental doctrine of judicial review: *ultra vires*. The idea underlying this principle is that administrative authorities are given grants of power in order to carry out their tasks, and if they act beyond their powers, then they act illegally. The concept of jurisdiction is often used in respect of bodies which hear and determine issues, such as tribunals.

Jurisdiction may be said to amount to a power to decide. The body can only determine those matters which are within the grant of power. If the body mistakenly thinks that a particular issue is within its power, and then proceeds to determine that issue, it will have acted without jurisdiction. The errors which have this drastic effect of depriving the body of jurisdiction may be ones of law or of fact. In addition to making a jurisdictional error before the determination of an issue, such an error may also be made in the way in which the jurisdiction to decide is exercised.

Authorities may also be given powers by legislation to take actions. These powers are often discretionary and so the authority has a choice of possible actions and, indeed, inaction. The courts have developed two broad grounds relating to illegality in the exercise of discretionary power. The first is that there has been a restriction upon the exercise of discretionary power so that it cannot truly be said to be lawfully exercised. Such restrictions include the rigid adherence to policies or actions taken because of an agreement. In addition to these grounds it is also illegal if discretion is exercised by someone other than the person conferred with it, either through unauthorised delegation or because it was done under the dictation of another person or body.

The second class of illegal exercise of discretionary power has as its core idea the abuse of the power. This may be because the power is used to attain an objective for which that power was not conferred or because bad faith motivated the authority in its exercise of the power. The courts have also held that it is wrong to have regard to irrelevant matters and to fail to take into account relevant matters.

Irrationality was Lord Diplock's second class of the grounds of review. By this he meant 'a decision so outrageous in its defiance of logic or of accepted moral standards that no sensible person who had applied his mind to the question to be decided could have arrived at it'. This ground of review was first articulated under the title of unreasonableness by Lord Greene MR in *Associated Provincial Picture Houses Ltd* v *Wednesbury Corporation* [1948] 1 KB 223, and is frequently referred to as *Wednesbury* unreasonableness. It was often grouped with those grounds of review dealing with abuse of discretionary power.

The third class identified by Lord Diplock is that of procedural irregularity. This contains what might be called procedural *ultra vires*. Some administrative authorities are required, by the terms of their grant of power, to follow certain procedural requirements. If they fail to comply with such a requirement then that may mean that they have acted outside their powers and this illegality may be dealt with by the courts.

Procedural irregularity also contains the judicially created rules of procedural fairness known as natural justice. Unlike the other grounds of review outlined above, in which the courts might be said to be holding administrative authorities within the boundaries of the powers conferred upon them by Parliament, natural justice is entirely a creation of the judiciary. At first they held that it should only apply to those who were under a duty to act judicially, but gradually that classification restriction has been relaxed. The courts have also developed a duty to act fairly. As we shall see, while both fairness and natural justice are concerned with procedural safeguards, they do not appear to require the same safeguards.

16.3   JURISDICTION

What are the criteria used to determine whether an error of law or fact is so serious that its commission means that the administrative body has thereby lost its power to decide or act? Unfortunately an examination of the case law does not provide a clear answer to this question.

16.3.1   Errors of Fact

One criterion may be more easily recognised than others. This is the idea that in order for the power to be exercised there must be a factual precondition. This is illustrated in *White and Collins* v *Minister of Health* [1939] 2 KB 838, which concerned the exercise of powers of compulsory purchase of land.

Under the authorising legislation land could be acquired through the compulsory purchase powers so long as it did not form 'part of any park, garden or pleasure ground'. The minister's confirmation of a compulsory purchase order was quashed because the court held that the land in question was part of a park. It should be noted that, generally, the courts are more reluctant to review errors of fact rather than errors of law. This is because the procedure before the court is not particulary well suited to the determination of disputed facts (per Devlin J in *R v Fulham, Hammersmith and Kensington Rent Tribunal, ex parte Zerek* [1951] 2 KB 1). Factual issues which are precise are more suited to judicial review. If the issue is ambiguous so that it is reasonable for different views to be held, then it is less likely that review based on jurisdictional error will be successful. In *Dowty Boulton Paul Ltd v Wolverhampton Corporation (No. 2)* [1976] Ch 13, the dispute concerned land which was used as an aerodrome. Under legislation the local authority could re-appropriate land if it was no longer required for the purpose for which it had been acquired. The council wished to put the land to housing use and its exercise of the statutory re-appropriation power was challenged on the basis that the land was still required for use as an aerodrome. The court held that the council's exercise of this power in good faith could not be challenged, partially because the legislation envisaged choice between competing requirements and the court was not as well placed as the local authority to make such a choice.

A variation upon this approach to questions of fact is to make a distinction between those situations in which a precedent fact must exist and the court checks this requirement, and circumstances in which the court examines the evidence in order to determine if it was reasonable for the administrative authority to act as it did. This approach was used in *Zamir v Secretary of State for the Home Department* [1980] AC 930, in which the question of fact – whether an immigrant's entry certificate had been obtained by fraud – was determined by the immigration officer at the point of entry. As there were a wide variety of factors to be taken into consideration on such a matter it was felt that this factual issue was not really suitable for classification as a question which the officer must answer correctly as interpreted by the court. This decision was criticised and, to an extent, it was reversed in *R v Secretary of State for the Home Department, ex parte Khawaja* [1984] AC 74, where it was held that, in matters of personal liberty, the courts must ensure that factual questions on which a detention order depends are answered correctly rather than reasonably. So the approach in *Zamir v Secretary of State for the Home Department* was upheld but the allocation of that particular context to reasonableness was wrong.

16.3.2 Distinguishing Law from Fact
A point of general relevance to jurisdictional review is made by the change made from *Zamir v Secretary of State for the Home Department* [1980] AC 930, to *R v Secretary of State for the Home Department, ex parte Khawaja* [1984] AC 74, which is that the courts do have a choice in deciding how they are going to categorise the matter before them. Traditionally, they have been more wary

about holding questions of fact to be jurisdictional errors. Therefore, if they did not wish to intervene in a case, the issue might be categorised as being one of fact rather than law. This device assumes that the distinction between law and fact is not entirely straightforward so as to afford the courts this flexibility. It might be thought that construction of statutes would always be regarded as a question of law but there is some inconsistency in the case law. For example, in planning law, permission must be sought for a 'material change of use' and this has been construed as a question of fact and degree, the determination of which will only be interfered with if it is unreasonable (*Bendles Motors Ltd* v *Bristol Corporation* [1963] 1 WLR 247).

There is clearly a difference between questions relating to the need for planning permission and those affecting personal liberty. The latter are much more serious and perhaps it is therefore constitutionally appropriate that the courts retain their review jurisdiction. Perhaps we can say that reasons of principle and pragmatism are combined by the courts when they distinguish law from fact. Where matters are serious then the law category is more likely to be applied but where extensive examination of evidence is required, or differing views may reasonably be arrived at, or the court is happy with the expertise of the body whose decision is challenged, matters are more likely to be designated as questions of fact.

The situation is further confused by the judicial development of saying that factual matters may become errors of law. There is a trend in some decisions which suggests the development of a substantial evidence rule which holds that the evidence before the decision-maker must be able to support the conclusions reached from it. In the context of statutory applications to quash, some of these decisions (*Ashbridge Investments Ltd* v *Minister of Housing and Local Government* [1965] 1 WLR 1320 and *Coleen Properties Ltd* v *Minister of Housing and Local Government* [1971] 1 WLR 433) may be said to incorporate into this statutory challenge the equivalent of jurisdictional error of fact. In general, this line of development has been restricted and does not seem to invalidate the tentative conclusions drawn on the categorisation of questions as fact or law.

16.3.3   Errors Of Law

A very important case concerning jurisdictional error of law is *Anisminic Ltd* v *Foreign Compensation Commission* [1969] 2 AC 147. The commission was empowered to compensate former owners of land which had been national-ised by the Egyptian government. In its construction of the delegated legislation which authorised the payment of compensation, the commission decided that it was a condition that the successors in title of applicants had to be British nationals. On this basis Anisminic's claim for compensation was rejected by the commission. Anisminic challenged this and the House of Lords, by a majority, ruled that this decision by the commission was an error of law which deprived it of jurisdiction to determine the compensation claim. The approach of the majority seems to suggest that any error of law will have the effect that the body subsequently acts without power and so denying that some errors may be made within jurisdiction and therefore immune from judicial review. The *Anisminic* decision also seems to hold that not only errors with respect to preconditions to the exercise of power may lead to acting without jurisdiction, but also errors made in the course of exercising the power.

This issue is very important because if every error of law goes to jurisdiction, this expands the scope of judicial review and the possibility of intervention by the courts. The expansion seems to arise because questions about the exercise of the power may deal with the merits of an issue, and only appeal provides for interference with the merits. The review/merits distinction is a difficult one to draw and the approach of the majority in *Anisminic* appears to obscure it.

The decision also raises an argument about respecting the will of Parliament. If Parliament has created bodies to carry out specified tasks and it is not clear from the legislation that any particular error of law should deprive the body of the power to act, why should the courts, which do not have the specialist knowledge of the administrative body, be able to invalidate its acts? On the other hand it is presumably to be assumed that Parliament did not intend administrative authorities to act outside the law, in which the courts are expert. The courts could ensure uniformity of law and their proceedings are suited to disputes over questions of law.

There has been some doubt about whether or not *Anisminic* has abolished entirely the distinction between jurisdictional and non-jurisdictional errors. This appears to have been resolved by the House of Lords in *R v Lord President of the Privy Council, ex parte Page* [1993] AC 682 so that '. . . in general any error of law made by an administrative tribunal or an inferior court in reaching its decision can be quashed for error of law' (per Lord Browne-Wilkinson at p. 702), however, the distinction may remain when one is dealing with the jurisdiction of a visitor of a university, who determines disputes concerning 'domestic laws' in a university, as in *Page*, or the Inns of Court, as in *R v Visitors to the Inns of Court, ex parte Calder* [1994] QB 1. The ground for this is the *ultra vires* doctrine, that these bodies had been conferred their decision-making power on the basis that it would be exercised on the correct legal basis (see Craig 1994a, pp. 372–83 for suggestions for reform of review of jurisdiction).

The decision in *Ex parte Page* would seem to spell the end of the head of review for error of law on the face of the record which was 'rediscovered' in *R v Northumberland Compensation Appeal Tribunal, ex parte Shaw* [1952] 1 KB 338. This allowed for the possibility of errors of law within jurisdiction to be reviewed if they were on the face of the record. The record included the pleadings and the decision, and might also include the reasons for the decision.

16.4   FETTERING OF DISCRETIONARY POWER

16.4.1   Rigid Adherence to Policy
This is the first of the four grounds of review which deal with a fetter or restriction upon the exercise of discretionary power. The courts are

concerned that such power should be genuinely exercised, as the purpose of discretionary power is to provide for full consideration of each case.

As we saw in 14.1.1, discretionary power can provide too much scope for action, so that it is desirable to reduce it to more manageable proportions. This may be achieved by drawing up policies. As well as assisting staff, policies are useful to people who make applications covered by them, as they have an indication of likely success. Consistency will be promoted by adherence to policies.

The clearest guidance for staff who process claims or applications involving decision-making is formulated as a rule, e.g., if circumstance X occurs then the decision is to be outcome Y. Is the automatic application of a policy rule compatible with the genuine exercise of discretion? It would seem not, as the particular case has not been considered fully. Yet, if a policy cannot be followed then what is the point of drawing up a policy?

The classic dictum on policy was given by Bankes J in *R v Port of London Authority, ex parte Kynoch Ltd* [1919] 1 KB 176, where he drew a distinction between the rejection of an applicant's case in accordance with the policy, and the situation where a body has resolved not to hear particular types of application, no matter who the applicant is. It seemed to be part of the judge's approval of the former situation that the applicant was informed of the policy and had been given a hearing before the decision was made. An illustration of the illegality of not hearing anyone is provided by *R v Secretary of State for the Environment, ex parte Brent London Borough Council* [1982] QB 593, in which the minister refused to meet a delegation of representatives of local authorities who wished to discuss the calculation of their rate support grant. The minister regarded his policy on the matter as final. Ackner LJ said that the minister did not have to have an open mind on the matter, but it must be ajar.

In *British Oxygen Co. Ltd v Minister of Technology* [1971] AC 610, some of the dicta of the law lords show the difficulty they have in drawing the line between the lawful and illegal adherence to policy. The case concerned the Board of Trade's policy of not making a grant for the purchase of items costing less than £25. A company had bought containers worth more than £4 million in total, but each individual container cost about £20. The company challenged the policy underlying the rejection of its grant application. The Board's decision was upheld by the House of Lords. Lord Reid said that he could see no great difference between a rule and a policy, and Viscount Dilhorne said that it seemed pointless for the Board to have to consider an application which was bound to fail because of the policy. Yet both of them were of the view that the Board must be willing to consider anything new or representations to change the policy.

In these cases the judges understand the need for policies and the reality that their utility is increased if they are adhered to quite strictly. Yet they feel that it is in the nature of the grant of the discretion, and for reasons of acting fairly (*R v Secretary of State for the Environment, ex parte Brent London Borough Council*), that a case should be considered fully, which includes the possibility of an exception being made or the policy changed.

These views seem to be mutually exclusive. You can have the policy but every case is a possible exception. Perhaps they can be reconciled by the metaphor of scales. The scales are tipped in favour of decision-makers because they can enjoy the advantages of a policy, and if it is publicised, some of those who fall outside it may not apply. The scales swing away from the decision-makers because applicants who are outside the policy are entitled to make out a case.

An inferior understanding of the place of policies in the exercise of discretionary powers was displayed in *Sagnata Investments Ltd* v *Norwich Corporation* [1971] 2 QB 614 and *Stringer* v *Minister of Housing and Local Government* [1970] 1 WLR 1281. In those cases the view was propounded that a policy is only one of a range of factors to be considered, and should not be given more weight than other factors. This view robs a policy of a great deal of its utility. (On *Sagnata Investments Ltd* v *Norwich Corporation*, see Galligan 1976.)

16.4.2 Contracts or Undertakings

If an administrative body has made an agreement about how it will exercise its discretionary power, this can amount to an unlawful fetter. In *Stringer* v *Minister of Housing and Local Government* [1970] 1 WLR 1281, a local planning authority had entered into an agreement with Manchester University which sought to safeguard the Jodrell Bank radio telescope by discouraging development within a specified area. An application for housing development was rejected by the authority in accordance with the agreement. This decision was appealed to the minister who also refused to grant permission. The disappointed developer challenged the minister's decision in court. The challenge was unsuccessful but the judge did hold that the agreement between the university and the authority was an unlawful fetter upon the authority's exercise of its discretionary power to determine planning applications. The minister's decision was lawful because, while he did take account of the objective in the agreement, which was a relevant consideration, he also considered fully the developer's case before rejecting it.

Stringer v *Minister of Housing and Local Government* concerned a positive obligation in an agreement which was held to prevent the authority from properly discharging its statutory duties. In *William Cory and Son Ltd* v *City of London Corporation* [1951] 2 KB 476, a company tried to argue that the agreement it had with a local authority contained an implied term that the authority should not have exercised its public health powers in the way that it did. This was rejected because such a construction would have impaired the authority's performance of its statutory duties.

Does this mean that contracts can be broken if they interfere with statutory responsibilities? The answer seems to be that if the interference is significant then it amounts to an impermissible fetter. The following two cases illustrate where the courts have drawn the line on this issue. In *Ayr Harbour Trustees* v *Oswald* (1883) 8 App Cas 623, the trustees had powers of compulsory land acquisition which could be used for the construction of harbour works. They had compulsorily acquired some land and agreed with its former owner not to construct works on it in a way which would adversely affect other land owned by that person. The agreement was held to be a significant interference with the duties of the trustees. The power to acquire land was for the purposes of improving the harbour and the agreement hindered that purpose. The purpose, or statutory birthright, was found not to have been impaired in *Birkdale District Electric Supply Co. Ltd* v *Southport Corporation* [1926] AC 355. The electricity company had contracted with the local authority to supply electricity at a price which was less than the statutory maximum. Basing its argument on *Ayr Harbour Trustees* v *Oswald*, the company argued that the contract fettered its statutory power to set its supply rates. This was rejected by the House of Lords. The contract related to a matter of commercial judgment which did not mean that the company had renounced its statutory birthright.

16.4.3   Dictation

The previous grounds of review are based on the idea that the exercise of discretionary power has not been genuine because rigid aherence to policy or contract has acted as a fetter. Where a decision-maker allows someone else to have the dominant influence so that the other person or authority is, in effect, dictating the outcome, this too is regarded as an unlawful fettering of discretion. In *H. Lavender and Son Ltd* v *Minister of Housing and Local Government* [1970] 1 WLR 1231, an application for planning permission was refused and the appeal was disallowed by the minister. From the minister's decision letter it was clear that the reason for rejection was that the site of the application was in an area of good-quality agricultural land. In these circumstances the Ministry of Agriculture was consulted and if they objected to the grant of planning permission then the appeal was disallowed. In other words the minister who was supposed to decide the appeal did not really make the decision but left it to officials in another ministry.

This example overlaps with the rigid adherence to policy. In *R* v *Stepney Corporation* [1902] 1 KB 317, the council had a duty to compensate a part-time clerk who was made redundant. Legislation listed the various considerations which should be taken into account when calculating the compensation. The council decided not to calculate the compensation itself but to ask the Treasury for its assessment and then apply it. This was held by the court to be unlawful. The duty was placed on the council and therefore it should have made the calculation.

16.4.4   Unauthorised Delegation

Where an authority acts under the dictation of another this is an implicit transfer of the power. Therefore if there is an explicit transfer, or delegation of the power, it is not surprising that the resulting decision or act is unlawful. Where a power has been conferred upon a person or authority, this is because it is thought appropriate that the exercise of the power is carried out by that person or authority. It must be noted that only unauthorised delegations are unlawful.

Two cases involving the National Dock Labour Board illustrate the basic idea of this ground of review. The National Board was not only authorised but encouraged to delegate powers to local boards. In *Barnard* v *National Dock Labour Board* [1953] 2 QB 18, the local board delegated disciplinary powers to a port manager, and in *Vine* v *National Dock Labour Board* [1957] AC 488, disciplinary powers had been delegated to a committee of the local board. Disciplinary actions taken by the port manager and the committee were successfully challenged because the delegations were not authorised. In *Barnard* Denning LJ also held that the only permissible relationship between the local board and the manager was for the manager to have recommended disciplinary action to the board which could then exercise the power which had been properly delegated to it.

The courts have tended to be quite strict where delegations of disciplinary or judicial power are concerned. In *R* v *Gateshead Justices, ex parte Tesco Stores Ltd* [1981] QB 470, magistrates had improperly delegated some decisions in connection with the issue of summonses. The delegation by the Director of Public Prosecutions of the initial screening of prosecutions to ordinary civil servants rather than legally qualified Crown prosecutors was successfully challenged on the basis that the work was appropriate only for lawyers in the new independent Crown Prosecution Service (*R* v *Director of Public Prosecutions, ex parte First Division Association* (1988) 138 NLJ Reports 158).

Local government legislation provides that some of the powers conferred upon the councillors or members of the local authority may be delegated to the officers (Local Government Act 1972, s. 101). Powers relating to the raising of money or the levying of precepts are not to be delegated.

Within central government there is no general statutory provision for delegating powers to officials. There are some specific authorisations as, for example, the determination of planning appeals by inspectors. The general position is covered by *Carltona Ltd* v *Commissioners of Works* [1943] 2 All ER 560, in which a challenge was made unsuccessfully against the requisitioning of property by a civil servant acting on behalf of the minister. The Court of Appeal held that it was not possible for a minister to discharge personally all of the powers and duties vested in the office. Constitutionally, the action of the official is the action of the minister, so that it can be said that there is no delegation as the official is a facet of the ministerial personality. The accountability of the minister to Parliament meant that the courts need not exercise the same amount of supervision here as they would in the case of an administrative authority. It is questionable whether such faith in Parliamentary control is justifiable.

In *R* v *Secretary of State for the Home Department, ex parte Oladehinde* [1991] 1 AC 254, it was said that the *Carltona* principle could be negatived by statute.

16.5 MISUSE OF DISCRETIONARY POWER

16.5.1 Improper Purpose
This ground is the first of four which involve the notion of abuse or misuse of a discretionary power. It is unlawful to use a discretionary power to achieve a purpose other than that for which the power was conferred. The courts can

refer to the legislation which bestowed the power in order to ascertain the purpose to be pursued through its exercise. In *Westminster Corporation* v *London and North Western Railway* [1905] AC 426, it was clear that the purpose of the challenged power was the construction of public conveniences by the council. The challenge was based on the fact that underground public conveniences had been constructed on both sides of a street and were linked by a subway. The council did not have a specific power to build a subway. However, as it had not been shown that the construction of the lavatories was a pretext, or that they were not needed at that place, the construction of the slightly wider connecting subway was not an improper purpose for the exercise of the power to construct conveniences.

The *Westminster* decision shows that the courts do allow some latitude and accept that powers may be exercised for a mixture of motives. As long as the dominant motive is the one which is the specified purpose of the power, it will not matter that an ancillary purpose is also achieved. The drawing of the line between lawful and unlawful can be quite difficult as inferences have to be drawn from the evidence. Compare *Westminster Corporation* v *London and North Western Railway* with *Lynch* v *Sewers Commissioners of London* (1886) 32 ChD 72 and *Webb* v *Minister of Housing and Local Government* [1965] 1 WLR 755. In *Lynch* v *Sewers Commissioners of London* the authority had the power to acquire land for street widening but not for altering the level of a street. It was held that, as the widening was only about 12 inches, and the level of the street was to be altered, the latter purpose was dominant. Compulsory purchase powers were also present in *Webb* v *Minister of Housing and Local Government*, where they could be used in order to facilitate the construction of sea defences. A challenge to a compulsory purchase was allowed because the majority in the Court of Appeal held that because the sea wall was wider than necessary, and was also paved, it was really a promenade. As the construction of a promenade was held to be the real purpose, the exercise of the sea defence compulsory purchase powers was unlawful.

If it is the case that a good and an improper purpose are so entwined together then the improper purpose will be inferred to be the dominant one by the courts. Where a council decided to boycott Shell Oil products because of the company's associations with South Africa, it was held that the desire to put pressure upon the company to end those associations played a prominent part in the decision, in addition to the reason that the council was attempting to fulfil its duty of promoting good race relations in its area (*R* v *Lewisham London Borough Council, ex parte Shell UK Ltd* [1988] 1 All ER 938).

The *Lewisham* case is one of a category of cases in which councils have taken action which they hoped might persuade others to adopt a particular view, or seek to disadvantage those who do not agree with them, or show support for a particular group. In *Wheeler* v *Leicester City Council* [1985] AC 1054, as in the *Lewisham* case, the council claimed that its action was designed to promote good race relations. The council withdrew permission for a rugby club to use council recreation facilities after the club declined to adopt as strong a stance against sporting links with South Africa as the council wished. Some of the club's players had accepted the invitation to join the Rugby Football Union's tour of South Africa. This case is very interesting because the council only lost in the House of Lords, where some extravagant rhetoric was employed by Lord Templeman. (For opposing views on this case see Turpin 1985, Allan 1985 and Hutchison and Jones 1988).

Some councils banned their libraries from taking certain newspapers, it was held, out of solidarity with dismissed workers in their dispute with their former employer, rather than for the promotion of their statutory duty with respect to the provision of a good library service (*R v Ealing London Borough Council, ex parte Times Newspapers Ltd* (1986) 85 LGR 316).

A council decided to oppose the Employment Training Scheme. Part of its opposition took the form of refusing to give financial assistance to voluntary organisations which participated in the scheme. The court held that the object was to coerce or punish those who disagreed with the council's view (*R v Liverpool City Council, ex parte Secretary of State for Employment* (1988) *The Times*, 12 November 1988).

These cases all have a high political content. The justification for the courts' interference was that the powers had been given to the councils for purposes which could be inferred from the legislation and these permitted purposes were not pursued by the councils. Whilst political considerations may lie behind the attainment of improper objectives, this ground of review attacks the deviation from the grant of power rather than the reasoning which led to the improper action. Relevance (see 16.5.2) deals with the factors which may and may not be considered in making decisions.

On the whole it seems that political considerations are regarded as 'pre-eminently extraneous' (*R v Board of Education* [1910] 2 KB 165 per Farwell LJ at p. 181). The courts have, however, been inconsistent in cases where action has been justified by reference to an electoral mandate. This is the idea that a party campaigned upon a particular topic and its victory authorises the implementation of the policy. This argument was accepted in *Secretary of State for Education and Science v Tameside Metropolitan Borough Council* [1977] AC 1014 and rejected in *Bromley London Borough Council v Greater London Council* [1983] 1 AC 768 (for discussion see McAuslan 1983).

16.5.2 Relevance

Just as grants of power may specify the purposes to which they may be applied, so they may also indicate considerations which are to be taken into account in the exercise of the powers. A failure to take those considerations into account can be *ultra vires*. The courts have also held that the taking into account of irrelevant considerations can render the exercise of power unlawful. This aspect of relevance is closely related to the ground of improper purposes.

Whilst a statute may declare that certain factors are to be taken into account, this may not be done with a high degree of precision. For example, a local planning authority in determining planning applications is to have regard to 'material considerations'. This can be interpreted widely or narrowly. One judge ruled that it could include considerations which 'relate to the use and development of land' (*Stringer* v *Minister of Housing and Local Government* [1970] 1 WLR 1281). Does that definition cover the economics of development? The answer to this is unclear as judges have disagreed on the point. Clearly the judges have the opportunity for creativity. One consideration which the courts have held to be relevant is the idea that a council owes a fiduciary duty to those who contribute to its income. This arose in *Roberts* v *Hopwood* [1925] AC 578, in which the district auditor's decision that a council's wage agreements were contrary to law was upheld by the courts. The council decided (a) to pay wages at a level which was higher than the average in the area and (b) that men and women should have equal pay. Despite the fact that the legislation empowered the council to pay such wages as it thought fit, the court felt that the desire of the council to be a model employer was in conflict with the duty it owed its ratepayers.

Some cases on this fiduciary responsibility involve transport. In *Prescott* v *Birmingham Corporation* [1955] Ch 210, the proposal to give old people free travel was challenged successfully on this ground. Subsequently legislation was passed to authorise such concessionary arrangements. The Greater London Council's 'Fares Fair' scheme, which sought to increase the number of passengers using public transport by cutting fares and paying for this by means of a higher subsidy to the London Transport Executive, was held to be *ultra vires* (*Bromley London Borough Council* v *Greater London Council* [1983] 1 AC 768). This was partially because of the fiduciary duty owed to ratepayers, which had to be balanced against its responsibilities to transport users. A similar type of arrangement was upheld in *R* v *Merseyside County Council, ex parte Great Universal Stores Ltd* (1982) 80 LGR 639, but the legislation was different. An amended fares reduction scheme for London received judicial approval (*R* v *London Transport Executive, ex parte Greater London Council* [1983] QB 484).

After the political stir caused by the 'Fares Fair' case, it has been stated that fiduciary duty is only one relevant factor and not something which the courts will use to interfere with the exercise of discretionary power by local authorities (*Pickwell* v *Camden London Borough Council* [1983] QB 962).

What is the basis on which a failure to consider a relevant matter, or the taking into account of an irrelevant one, will lead to illegality? The courts will only intervene if the decision was materially affected by the relevant or irrelevant point. If the decision would have been the same had the relevant matter been considered, or the irrelevant one ignored, then the decision is lawful (*R* v *Broadcasting Complaints Commission, ex parte Owen* [1985] QB 1153).

16.5.3 Bad Faith

As a finding that an administrative authority has not acted in good faith is such a serious thing, it is not surprising that it is a rare ground of review. Megaw LJ has suggested that bad faith involves dishonesty (*Cannock Chase District Council* v *Kelly* [1978] 1 WLR 1). Yet it is difficult to think of an example in which a dishonest exercise of power would not also be the consideration of an irrelevant purpose, or the seeking of an improper purpose.

Certainly, some of the earlier cases appeared to proceed on the basis that these faults were part of bad faith (*Associated Provincial Picture Houses Ltd* v *Wednesbury Corporation* [1948] 1 KB 223; *Smith* v *East Elloe Rural District Council* [1956] AC 376).

16.5.4 Unreasonableness or Irrationality

One of the most frequently cited cases in judicial review of administrative action is *Associated Provincial Picture Houses* v *Wednesbury Corporation* [1948] 1 KB 223. In this decision Lord Greene MR defined unreasonableness. He gave a general definition which included misdirection on points of law, relevance and bad faith, but he also said that a conclusion was unreasonable if no reasonable authority could come to it. It is this aspect of the definition which has come to be referred to as '*Wednesbury* unreasonableness', or what Lord Diplock renamed 'irrationality'.

In Lord Greene MR's definition what is striking is its circular nature: something is unreasonable if no reasonable person could come to it. He also categorised it as something so absurd that nobody could think that it was within the authority's power to act in that way. This sounds as if it is part of the general definition of unreasonableness, specifically improper purposes or relevance, however, Lord Greene MR did state that if irrelevant considerations had been ignored the court might still strike down the action as being unreasonable. How can a decision be said to be unreasonable if the relevance and improper purpose and bad faith tests have been passed? If a court can say that an administrative body's exercise of the power given to it by Parliament is absurd, does that not amount to judges substituting their view, something which is outside the scope of review? Assuming that *Wednesbury* unreasonableness, or irrationality, is a dubious ground of review, is that offset by the very high threshold which must be passed in order for such a challenge to be successful? It is true that many challenges alleging unreasonableness or irrationality are unsuccessful, and that in decisions which find unreasonableness there are other faults which have led to the courts' holding of *ultra vires*.

There have been some *dicta* suggesting that the threshold of *Wednesbury* review may be lowered when dealing with fundamental rights (*per* Simon Brown LJ in *R* v *Ministry of Defence, ex parte Smith* [1995] 4 All ER 427, 441 and 445 and in *R* v *Coventry Airport, ex parte Phoenix Aviation* [1995] 3 All ER 37, 62). This was rejected in a lecture by Lord Irvine of Lairg when he was still the Shadow Lord Chancellor (1996), who pointed out that the constitutional basis for review required judicial restraint because the judges are not qualified technically or democratically. He was therefore concerned by extra-judicial writing hinting at judicial supremacism which would allow the judges to strike down statutes (Laws 1995, Sedley 1995, Woolf 1995). In the extreme situations in which democracy would be under the type of assault which would prompt judges to deny legislation validity, Lord Irvine of Laing feels it would be judicial romanticism to think that a judicial decision could hold back a revolution. He also wrote that his party, when in government, would incorporate the ECHR and this would give significant power to the judges. As was discussed in 12.6 it seems his views on the nature of incorporating legislation appear to favour a situation similar to that in New Zealand, where the judges may not strike down legislation which they find is incompatible with a Bill of Rights.

16.5.5 Proportionality

One other point mentioned by Lord Irvine of Lairg is the incoming tide of European law which has brought significant changes. This body of law allows for a principle of substantive review, proportionality which is lower than the *Wednesbury* threshold (see 9.4.5.1). While Lord Diplock mentioned it as a possible future addition to the review categories of illegality, irrationality and procedural irregularity, Lord Irvine of Lairg is happy that it has not been explicitly recognised by the courts as a separate head of review in domestic law (*R* v *Secretary of State for the Home Department, ex parte Brind* [1991] 1 AC 697) although British courts must apply it in Community law. Jowell and Lester (1987, 1988) have argued that proportionality should become part of domestic law but their analysis has been subject to criticism (Craig 1989, Boyron 1992). Craig (1994a) suggests a kind of matrix involving the steps to be taken in applying proportionality, and the types of case in which it could be applied. The suggested steps are:

(a) Identify the relevant interests.

(b) Ascribe weights to those interests.

(c) Take a view on whether some interests may be traded off to achieve other goals (e.g., trade a fundamental right to achieve an improvement of the general economic good).

(d) Decide whether the action or decision was disproportionate using the following formulations:

(i) Is the disputed measure the least restrictive which could be used in the circumstances?

(ii) Do the means adopted to achieve the aim correspond to the importance of the aim, and are they necessary for its achievement?

(iii) Is the challenged act suitable and necessary for the achievement of its objective and one which does not impose excessive burdens on the individual?

(iv) What are the relative costs and benefits of the disputed measure?

(e) Determine the intensity with which these suggested tests are to be applied.

Craig suggests that there are three types of case in which proportionality could be applied. The first is where the exercise of power clashes with a civil liberty or fundamental right. He states that this may be easier to decide as the calculation in step (c) has already been made. For example, if we are dealing with freedom of speech, then we have some idea of the weight which we attach to it. A second situation is where a penalty or punishment is regarded as disproportionate to the offence committed. The third situation differs from the other two as neither fundamental rights nor excessive penalties are involved, but rather a claim that the authority's balancing of interests was in some way disproportionate. This is more difficult. In Craig's example of *Bromley London Borough Council* v *Greater London Council* [1983] 1 AC 768, the interests to balance were those of the users of London buses and trains and the ratepayers of Bromley. What is the appropriate intensity of review? How much leeway should the court permit the authority before substituting its own view? How difficult is it for the court which will not be experienced in a particular topic to be able to carry out the balancing operation involved? Should the court consider the matter narrowly, or seek to take into account alternative policy strategies. Craig suggests that it would be possible, but not easy, to divide the third type of situation into those in which the courts felt able to conduct a more searching scrutiny and those where a lower intensity of review is appropriate.

We may conclude from this that there are difficulties with proportionality and that care must be taken. We must learn from our EU partners who have developed it in their domestic law and also in Community law where it is a head of review which can be used in our courts. This makes it likely that it will eventually be adopted in our domestic law. Craig has sensitised us to some of the range of considerations to be taken into account. Failure to break proportionality down could mean that it might become a catch-all category facilitating judicial intervention when no other basis will suffice.

16.6 PROCEDURAL REQUIREMENTS

A piece of legislation may state procedural requirements which the administrative authority is to follow. Non-compliance with such requirements may lead to the quashing of decisions or action which should have been preceded by the procedural requirement. The basis on which the court will intervene because of non-compliance would appear to have changed. In the 19th century the consideration appeared to be the nature of the requirement: if it could be interpreted as being mandatory then the court could strike down the decision. This then raises the issue of how a mandatory requirement could be distinguished from a directory one. Lord Penzance stated that one should 'consider the importance of the provision which has been disregarded and the relation of that provision to the general object to be secured by the Act' and this would assist the decision on the classification of the procedural requirement (*Howard* v *Bodington* (1877) 2 PD 203).

In *London and Clydeside Estates Ltd* v *Aberdeen District Council* [1980] 1 WLR 182, Lord Hailsham of St Marylebone LC, stated that the 'use of rigid legal classifications' was not desirable in dealing with questions of non-compliance with procedural requirements. The court should use its discretion to decide what to do bearing in mind the particular circumstances of the case. This seems to be quite a change from the certainty which resulted from classification, to the uncertainty which may ensue from discretion. The change is less marked than that categorisation of it would suggest. Lord Penzance referred to the object of the particular procedure from which its importance can be assessed and then its classification made. An analysis of purpose must be made in order to establish the particular circumstances of the case in which the judicial discretion is to be exercised. In addition, the circumstances of the case include the consequences of the non-compliance with the procedure. Generally speaking it seems that the courts take the view that procedures involving consultation, and notification of appeal or objection rights ought to be followed.

The case law indicates that if the procedure requires consultation then not only should it take place, but it should be adequate. Giving people involved in the government of a school only a few days in which to make representations about a proposal to change to the comprehensive system was inadequate (*Lee* v *Department of Education and Science* (1967) 66 LGR 211). Similarly a failure to give an accused officer timely notice of the subject-matter of police disciplinary proceedings led to the chief constable's decision being struck down (*R* v *Chief Constable of the Merseyside Police, ex parte Calveley* [1986] QB 424). In other cases partial compliance has been deemed sufficient and the non-compliance challenge has failed. For example, in *Coney* v *Choyce* [1975] 1 WLR 422, public notification of proposals was to be given in three places; in fact it was only given in two but those making the challenge did know about the proposals. The point about nobody being prejudiced by non-compliance with notification requirements was crucial in *Main* v *Swansea City Council* (1985) 49 P & CR 26. Despite the fact that two separate notifications had not been carried out, the court decided the challenge would fail because those who should have been notified had not been adversely affected, and there was a considerable delay in the initiation of the proceedings.

In one case it was felt that there would be more prejudice caused if the challenge on non-compliance with procedure was upheld (*R* v *Bradford-upon-Avon Urban District Council, ex parte Boulton* [1964] 1 WLR 113). An ownership certificate required in a planning matter was inaccurate and the court took the view that, so long as there was a genuine certificate signed by, or on behalf of, a genuine owner, this would suffice. If it were otherwise this would increase the checks which prospective purchasers of property would have to undertake causing great public inconvenience.

16.7 NATURAL JUSTICE AND FAIRNESS

Natural justice refers to the rules governing procedures which have been developed by the courts. These rules are (a) *nemo iudex in causa sua,* and (b) *audi altem partem.* Freely translated, these rules require (a) that procedures must be free from bias, and (b) that a person should not be denied the opportunity to make representations, or to a fair hearing. These rules take as their model for good procedure that of the court in which the judge is impartial and makes a decision based upon the material presented by the adversaries. Indeed for a period the courts would not apply the principles of natural justice where there was no duty to act judicially. This use of classifications, as has already been noted (see 14.3), has played a significant role in the development of administrative law. In this area of procedural safeguards, the classification of a procedure as judicial or administrative was crucial for the applicant for review. If the court designated the matter as judicial this opened up the possibility of the applicant obtaining the procedural protections which the courts had devised. To have the matter classed as administrative meant the end of the applicant's challenge. Not surprisingly, the judges were unhappy with the formalism which they had created and tried to ameliorate it by creating the quasi-judicial category to which the principles of natural justice would apply. Eventually, the abolition of the effects of the distinction was set in train by the House of Lords in the landmark case of *Ridge* v *Baldwin* [1964] AC 40. In this case a chief constable had been dismissed by the watch committee (the supervisory authority for a police force, now called the police authority). Although it was held that the action of the committee was not judicial, natural justice was to apply as it was held that a chief constable was the holder of an office from which dismissal had to be for cause. Therefore the chief constable could not be dismissed without first informing him of the case against him and then considering his defence or explanation. In other words, the safeguard of the second rule of natural justice, or a fair hearing, should have been observed.

Lord Reid's examination of the cases led him to declare that a duty to act judicially was not a precondition for the application of natural justice, but the authority in question must have a power to determine a question affecting a person's rights. This removal of difficulty was followed by the creation of another source of confusion, the duty to act fairly. This duty was promulgated by Lord Parker CJ in *Re H. K. (An Infant)* [1967] 2 QB 617. An immigrant had been refused entry to the country by an immigration officer because the officer did not believe the immigrant to be under 16 years of age. According to Lord Parker CJ, the officer should have told the immigrant what his impression was, which would have permitted the immigrant to disabuse him. Lord Parker CJ described this course of action thus: 'That is not, as I see it, a question of acting or being required to act judicially, but of being required to act fairly'. The confusion which arises is that if *Ridge* v *Baldwin* meant that natural justice was not confined to judicial-type procedures, why was there a need for a duty to be fair, which was first applied in a procedure where a decision-maker was not acting judcicially? The subsequent case law has referred to both natural justice and a duty to be fair or fairness. There appears to be a tendency for the courts to apply natural justice in circumstances which are rather more judicial in character, and fairness for situations which would formerly have been described as administrative. This suggests that the law on procedural safeguards has changed from a position in which protection was required only if there was a duty to act judicially, to a situation in which all procedures are to observe safeguards, but that these will vary in intensity, with more being required where rights are at issue.

Perhaps we can best make sense of natural justice and fairness by regarding it as a flexible concept which takes into account all of the circumstances of each case and then provides the appropriate procedural protection. The circumstances will include the interest which the individual has in the proceedings, the nature of the procedure, and the benefits and costs which would ensue from a greater degree of procedural protection.

16.7.1 Bias

Several types of bias have been identified as breaching natural justice. These are pecuniary, or financial, bias, and other non-financial interests which include personal relationships and institutional opinion.

16.7.1.1 Pecuniary interest Where a decision-maker has a pecuniary interest in the subject-matter of a determination, then this is considered to be so undesirable that the decision must be invalidated. The classic illustration of this involves a Lord Chancellor. In *Dimes* v *Grand Junction Canal* (1852) 3 HL Cas 759, Lord Cottenham LC affirmed some decrees relating to a company in which he was a shareholder. The House of Lords acknowledged that there was no actual bias on the part of the Lord Chancellor but because the financial interest was a direct one, albeit small, the rule against bias would be strictly applied. Accordingly the decrees were invalidated.

16.7.1.2 Personal interest The Latin formulation of the rule against bias, *nemo iudex in causa sua* (no one to be a judge in his own cause) indicates one type of prohibited personal relationship, where the conflicting roles of prosecution and judge are combined in the same person or body. In one case some members of a bench of magistrates heard criminal proceedings against a person whose prosecution had been initiated by the town clerk on the instructions of a council committee. These magistrates were also members of that committee and it was held they should not have heard the case (*R* v *Lee, ex parte Shaw* (1882) 9 QBD 394). Compare that with another case, *Leeson* v *General Council of Medical Education and Registration* (1889) 43 ChD 366, in which two members out of 29 sitting on a medical disciplinary committee were also members of the organisation which had initiated a complaint to be determined by the committee. This was not held to amount to bias. The explanation for the difference is probably that the magistrates as members of the council committee were much more involved in initiating the prosecution than was the case with the doctors and the 'tainted magistrates' could have more influence on their colleagues than could the two doctors. As we shall see in 16.7.1.4, there was a little confusion about the test used to determine non-pecuniary bias.

Personal bias may be found where the judge has a relationship or connection with one of the parties. This occurred in *Metropolitan Properties Co. (FGC) Ltd* v *Lannon* [1969] 1 QB 577, where Mr Lannon, the chairman of the committee, lived with his father in property owned by a company which was in the same group of companies as the landlord whose appeal Mr Lannon was to determine. In addition, Mr Lannon had also assisted his father in a dispute with their landlord.

The courts have been very concerned about the presence of persons other than the decision-makers during their deliberations. Where the 'extraneous' person is a party to the proceedings then this, quite clearly, is undesirable. These circumstances led to findings of bias in police and fire service disciplinary proceedings (*Cooper* v *Wilson* [1937] 2 KB 309; *R* v *Leicestershire Fire Authority, ex parte Thompson* (1978) 77 LGR 373), and in the revocation of a market licence (*R v Barnsley Metropolitan Borough Council, ex parte Hook* [1976] 1 WLR 1052). Bias was also found where the extraneous person had a more remote personal interest. In *R v Sussex Justices, ex parte McCarthy* [1924] 1 KB 256, Mr McCarthy had been involved in a road accident for which he was prosecuted. The magistrates' clerk had joined the magistrates when they had retired. This was held to invalidate the trial because the clerk was a member of a firm of solicitors which was acting on behalf of a plaintiff who was suing Mr McCarthy for personal injuries arising from the accident.

16.7.1.3 Institutional bias We have seen that decision-makers may have policies which assist them in the exercise of their discretionary powers. Could it be argued that a policy predisposes the decision-maker and thus amounts to bias? This has been rejected. In *R v Amber Valley District Council, ex parte Jackson* [1984] 3 All ER 501, Woolf J said, at p. 509, that it is to be expected that authorities will have policies but that does not mean that they will be biased. They will be expected to exercise their discretion according to law and that means considering any objections. In this case objectors to a particular planning application feared that the district council's planning committee would be biased in favour of the application. The fear arose because both the district and county councils were under Labour Party control and the Labour group on the county council had voted to support the application.

A similar type of institutional bias was alleged in *Franklin v Minister of Town and Country Planning* [1948] AC 87. The statutory procedure for the establishment of new towns began with the minister making a proposal to which objections could be heard at a public local inquiry. After considering the inspector's report the minister would decide to confirm or reject the proposal. Objectors to the designation of Stevenage as a new town alleged that the minister was biased, not least because at a public meeting he had said that the designation would go ahead. The court had recourse to the administrative/judicial distinction saying that in this process the minister was not acting judicially when deciding to confirm or reject a new town order. The court also found that the minister had not foreclosed his mind and had genuinely considered the objections.

The existence of policy or the initiation of a process can lead to a decision-maker being predisposed on a particular matter but that does not necessarily amount to a predetermination of the issue. One case which does indicate that a policy did operate to prejudge an issue is *R v Secretary of State for the Environment, ex parte Brent London Borough Council* [1982] QB 593, in which it was held that it was unlawful for the minister not to listen to representatives who wished to argue for a change in policy on local authority finances.

16.7.1.4 The test for non-pecuniary bias Some confusion has arisen over the test to be applied in determining if a non-pecuniary interest amounts to bias. Two tests have been formulated: one asks whether there is a real likelihood of bias; and the other inquires if there is a reasonable suspicion of bias. It has been suggested that the real likelihood test is a more difficult hurdle to surmount. Perhaps it is significant that the reasonable suspicion test emerged in *R v Sussex Justices, ex parte McCarthy* [1924] 1 KB 256, which is famous for the dictum of Lord Hewart CJ 'that justice should not only be done but should manifestly and undoubtedly be seen to be done'. The personal connection was remote but the proceedings were judicial.

The House of Lords has now ruled in *R v Gough* [1993] AC 646 that a test of 'real danger' as opposed to 'real likelihood' should apply, thereby indicating that the court is thinking in terms of possibility and not probability of bias. Their lordships held that this test should apply to justices, members of inferior tribunals, jurors and arbitrators. Their lordships did not say that the perspective from which the test is applied should be that of the reasonable man as the court personifies this legal character.

It was unclear whether it is significant that the list of those to whom the test applies is not exhaustive, and that its members are more concerned with 'judicial' rather than 'administrative' decisions. Certainly there are earlier cases which suggested that planning decisions might be subjected to the former real likelihood test (*Steeples* v *Derbyshire County Council* [1985] 1 WLR 256). Planning authorities can make decisions in which they have a corporate interest and these will only be set aside if their actions prior to making such decisions impeded the proper exercise of their discretion (*R v Sevenoaks District Council, ex parte Terry* [1985] 3 All ER 226; *R v St Edmundsbury Borough Council, ex parte Investors in Industry Commercial Properties Ltd* [1985] 1 WLR 1168).

Sedley J has ruled in *R v Secretary of State for the Environment, ex parte Kirkstall Valley Campaign Ltd* [1996] 3 All ER 304, that the 'real danger' test is of general application in public law and not limited to judicial or quasi-judicial bodies or proceedings. In this case the grant of a planning permission by an urban development corporation was challenged unsuccessfully. The argument that the authorities supported a different test in planning was rejected by Sedley J who said that the true situation in *Ex parte Terry* was the surrender of judgment by a decision-making body rather than the disqualification of a member of a decision-making body through personal interest.

16.7.1.5 Exceptions There are some circumstances in which the rule against bias will not apply. The first of these is necessity and is demonstrated by the position of Lord Cottenham LC in *Dimes v Grand Junction Canal* (1852) 3 HL Cas 759. Despite his involvement in the case, the Lord Chancellor's signature was essential to the procedures which led to the hearing of the case by the House of Lords.

Statute may create exceptions to bias but they are strictly construed. For example, in *R v Lee, ex parte Shaw* (1889) 9 QBD 394, the court decided that the statutory provision which permitted members of local authorities to sit as magistrates could apply where the magistrate also acted as a prosecutor.

It is possible for a person to waive the interests of a decision-maker and it seems that the courts will be careful in accepting this, especially if an individual was unaware that an objection could have been made at that time (*R v Essex Justices, ex parte Perkins* [1927] 2 KB 475).

16.7.2 Hearings
It is the second rule of natural justice which has been the subject of the developing law on fairness. The approach will be to consider the factors which the courts have decided make a hearing fair. These factors derive from the court model of adversarial procedure and so some proceedings have not been deemed appropriate for the incorporation of these safeguards. 16.7.3 will deal with some areas of administration and the procedural protection provided there under the title of fairness.

16.7.2.1 Should there be a hearing? The case of *Cooper* v *Board of Works for Wandsworth* (1863) 14 CB NS 180 involved the power of the board to require the demolition of property. In finding that this was a situation in which the owner should be given an opportunity to make representations, the judges were split on the basis for requiring a hearing. Some were of the view that the board's power of requiring demolition was a judicial act, others looked to the effect which the action would have on the owner. The effect upon the owner could be an interference with a right, or a privilege or licence. Some decisions have indicated that this is a crucial difference. In *Schmidt* v *Secretary of State for Home Affairs* [1969] 2 Ch 149, two US students of scientology were not permitted to remain in the country beyond the expiry of the period determined when they arrived. They were not permitted to make representations to the Home Office and it was suggested that this was an important matter affecting the liberty of the person. Lord Denning MR pointed out that the students were aliens, they had no right to be in the country, only a licence. He then proceeded to point out that there was a difference between the revocation of their licence to be in the country before its expiry, and their plea to have that licence extended. The former situation gave rise to an opportunity of being heard because of the legitimate expectation that they could remain in the country for the duration of the licence, whereas the latter situation did not.

Having given birth to the idea of legitimate expectation, Lord Denning used it again in *Cinnamond* v *British Airports Authority* [1980] 1 WLR 582, in a case in which six cab drivers had been banned under a by-law from operating taxis in the area of Gatwick airport. Lord Denning MR said that in view of the history of persistent breaching of rules applying to taxis, these drivers could have had no legitimate expectation of being heard. The authority did have a duty to act fairly and had done so in Lord Denning's view.

In between these two cases Megarry V-C had also invoked this doctrine of legitimate expectations in a case of a non-statutory body (*McInnes* v *Onslow-Fane* [1978] 1 WLR 1520). The body was the British Boxing Board of Control and the case concerned its power to issue licences, without which it was impossible to work in the boxing world. Megarry V-C ruled that where a person was applying for a renewal of a licence there was a legitimate expectation that it would be granted. This situation and one in which a licence was revoked would be matters in which a hearing would be required.

The use of legitimate expectation indicated that a hearing might be required because a decision might remove a licence. The doctrine has also been used to require a hearing where there was a legitimate expectation that a hearing would be given. This second aspect is illustrated by *Council of Civil Service Unions* v *Minister for the Civil Service* [1985] AC 374. Here there had always been a practice of consultation with the unions when changes were proposed to contracts of employment. This practice gave rise to a legitimate expectation that consultation would be carried out over such proposals. Here that legitimate expectation of a hearing was defeated because the civil servants in question worked in Government Communications Headquarters Cheltenham, and this raised the non-justiciable topic of national security, which prevailed.

This sense of legitimate expectations had been developed earlier in a Privy Council case *Attorney-General of Hong Kong* v *Ng Yuen Shiu* [1983] 2 AC 629, and drew on the case of *R* v *Liverpool Corporation, ex parte Liverpool Taxi Fleet Operators' Association* [1972] 2 QB 299. In both cases an authority had given undertakings about how they proposed to deal with illegal immigrants, and the granting of taxi licences, respectively. In both cases it was held that the failure to honour those undertakings was unlawful. In the *Liverpool* case the undertaking was broken without giving the interested parties a hearing, and in *Ng Yuen Shiu* while the immigrant was interviewed, he was not given an opportunity to make representations about the change in policy which adversely affected him.

16.7.2.2 Notice of hearing Where there is a hearing it can be regarded as unfair if insufficent notice of it is given, as this reduces the time in which a defence can be prepared. A conviction was quashed on this basis (*R* v *Thames Magistrates' Court, ex parte Polemis* [1974] 1 WLR 1371).

The presence of a person at a hearing or the adequacy of a person's representations may be improved if an adjournment is granted. In two cases the refusal of an adjournment was held to be unfair. The reasons which should have secured adjournments were that the time clashed with a job appointment (*R* v *South West London Supplementary Benefits Appeal Tribunal, ex parte Bullen* (1976) 120 SJ 437) and a breakdown in communication about the suitability of the hearing date between an appellant and her adviser which meant that the appellant was absent (*R* v *Diggines, ex parte Rahmani* [1985] 1 QB 1109). The decision of the Court of Appeal in *Ex parte Rahmani* was overruled by the House of Lords in *Al-Mehdawi* v *Secretary of State for the Home Department* [1990] 1 AC 876, on the basis that it was the fault of the legal advisers that the party was denied a hearing rather than anything done by the decision-maker (see Herberg 1990).

Where there had been adequate prior notice of a public local inquiry, a late application to defer it on the basis that an individual would not be able to attend on those dates was not granted (*Ostreicher* v *Secretary of State for the Environment* [1978] 1 WLR 810). Here the court found that the balance weighed more heavily in favour of the general public inconvenience which would be caused by a change than the individual's loss of an opportunity to attend the inquiry, especially as her written objections would be taken into account.

16.7.2.3 Notice of case to answer If a procedure is a disciplinary one then the person who is facing charges should have knowledge of them in order to prepare a defence. In *Glynn* v *Keele University* [1971] 1 WLR 487, the student learnt of his disciplinary offence, nude sunbathing on campus, in a letter from the Vice-Chancellor which informed him that he had been fined for it. This was a breach of natural justice.

Proceedings may not be disciplinary but they may affect a person's interests, and so a fair hearing requires that some indication of the authority's views is made in order that a response can be made. We have seen that this was at issue in *Re H. K. (An Infant)* [1967] 2 QB 617, in which it was found that the immigration officer had said that he was not satisfied that the immigrant was under 16 years of age. In *R* v *Gaming Board for Great Britain, ex parte Benaim and Khaida* [1970] 2 QB 417, the Gaming Board refused a certificate of consent which was a prerequisite for an application to the magistrates for a gaming licence. The disappointed applicants' request for further details about the board's objections did not provide material which was new to the applicants, or give details about any sources of information relied upon in their decision. It was held that the board was subject to the rules of natural justice but that it had obeyed them. Bearing in mind the desire that only suitable people be permitted to operate casinos the board might have to be reticent about its sources of information. Its dealings with these applicants successfully charted the correct course between protecting confidentiality of sources and permitting applicants to make effective representations.

Note that the board was not making charges against the applicants. A case which revolved around an investigation of a company takes us closer to a process in which charges are made. In *Re Pergamon Press Ltd* [1971] Ch 388, the company's directors were to be interviewed and they wished to see the transcripts of evidence of other witnesses and so be able to respond to any allegations. This was refused and a challenge was made. The Court of Appeal stated that the effect of the directors' challenge, if successful, would be to require the inspectors to act as if they were a court. As the inspectors were conducting an investigation which would result in a report which might be made public, the inspectors should give an outline of the charges made so as to allow for correction or contradiction by the directors.

There are some topics in which the courts give a great deal of latitude to the government, of which national security is one. A case of deportation shows the deference given to the authorities at the expense of the individual. In his attempt to challenge a deportation order Mr Hosenball was disadvantaged by the fact that in his non-statutory hearing with the 'security advisers' he was not provided with much information on which to respond to the Home Secretary's conclusion that his deportation was conducive to the interest of national security. His contention that the lack of details breached the duty to be fair was rejected, as the minister's sources were confidential and were connected with national security (see also *R* v *Secretary of State for the Home Department, ex parte Cheblak* [1991] 1 WLR 890, arising out of the Gulf War, and Leigh 1991).

16.7.2.4   Should the hearing be oral?   The right to be heard does not mean that there is a right to make oral representations, as written ones may be sufficiently fair. In *Lloyd* v *McMahon* [1987] AC 625, it was argued that the district auditor's failure to invite oral representations, in response to his notification of intent to issue a certificate stating that financial loss had been caused by the councillors' misconduct, was contrary to a legitimate expectation of an oral hearing. The expectation was based on the fact that in such circumstances there had only been one previous occasion on which an oral hearing had not been offered. The House of Lords ruled that fairness was the point of a legitimate expectation and there had been no unfairness in the use of the written procedure.

16.7.2.5   Conduct of the hearing   Where an oral hearing is held, is there an expectation that it should be conducted like a trial, so that parties can call witnesses and carry out cross-examinations? The general answer appears to be yes, but it is subject to reservations. The Prison Rules provide that, in proceedings before a board of visitors, evidence may be called which can establish facts. In *R* v *Board of Visitors of Hull Prison, ex parte St Germain (No. 2)* [1979] 1 WLR 1401, it was held that there was a discretion to refuse to call a witness. This could be done if it was felt that calling a large number of witnesses was a ploy to disrupt the hearing.

Cross-examination will be allowed where it is felt to be fair and relevant. In *Ex parte St Germain (No. 2)* it was held that hearsay evidence was admissible, but that where it had been admitted, fairness might require cross-examination of those witnesses who had given it.

Two cases involving public local inquiries provide different rulings on cross-examination. In *Nicholson* v *Secretary of State for Energy* (1977) 76 LGR 693, the inspector permitted the plaintiff to cross-examine the departmental witnesses, but not the local authority ones. This was done because it was feared that it would be repitious. As the evidence of the local authority witnesses was germane to the plaintiff's case, it was held that he had been disadvantaged. In *Bushell* v *Secretary of State for the Environment* [1981] AC 75, objectors at a motorway inquiry were prevented from cross-examining departmental witnesses on the subject of the predictions of traffic flows. The objectors' case was that there was no need for the road. This decision by the inspector was challenged unsuccessfully. The majority of the House of Lords held that this subject was policy, which had been approved in Parliament. It was not appropriate that it be dealt with in an inquiry which was concerned about the application of the policy, the route of the motorway.

Resort was had to the judicial/administrative distinction in *R* v *Commission for Racial Equality, ex parte Cottrell and Rothon* [1980] 1 WLR 1580. The commission notified a company of its decision to issue a non-discrimination notice and offered it the opportunity to make representations. The offer was accepted but the company was dissatisfied because the hearing was not attended by witnesses who had provided evidence which the commission relied upon in its decision about the non-discrimination notice. The company argued that the hearing was flawed as they did not have the chance to cross-examine the witnesses. This argument was based on *R v Board of Visitors of Hull Prison, ex parte St Germain (No. 2)* [1979] 1 WLR 1401. The court ruled that, whereas the proceedings in the Hull prison case were judicial, and evidence as to identity was crucial to the matter, these considerations were absent here.

16.7.2.6 Should there be legal representation? The case law appears to be clear that there is no right to legal representation. It is less clear what the circumstances are in which legal representation may be granted. We can distinguish between statutory bodies governed by statutory rules, and domestic bodies operating under contract. Statutory proscription of legal representation will be upheld, even, it seems, when a very serious matter is involved (*Maynard v Osmond* [1977] QB 240). Where a non-statutory body is concerned, Lord Denning MR suggested in *Enderby Town Football Club Ltd v Football Association Ltd* [1971] Ch 591, that it is wrong for it to have a rule excluding legal representation, but his colleagues, Fenton Atkinson and Cairns LJJ disagreed.

What are the considerations which are to be taken into account where legal representation is requested and the rules do not exclude it? Regard will have to be had to the nature of the proceedings. In prison disciplinary proceedings, it would appear that a distinction may be drawn between hearings before the governor of the prison and the board of visitors. It is, apparently, extremely difficult to think of circumstances in which it would be appropriate to allow legal representation before the governor, even where the charge could also constitute a criminal offence (*R v Board of Visitors of HM Prison, The Maze, ex parte Hone* [1988] AC 379). This is because of convenience. Most of the hearings before governors are much more regular occurrences and deal with more minor matters than those before boards of visitors. These boards, in exercising their discretion on this topic, should have regard to the following criteria: (a) the seriousness of both the charge and the potential penalty; (b) whether any points of law are likely to arise: (c) the educational capacity of prisoners, relating to their ability to present their own cases; (d) procedural difficulties – has the prisoner been able to interview relevant witnesses prior to the hearing; (e) the need for reasonable speed in making the adjudication; and (f) the need for fairness as between the prisoners and prison officers (per Webster J in *R v Secretary of State for the Home Department, ex parte Tarrant* [1985] QB 251).

In the field of non-statutory bodies it had been said that issues relating to livelihood and reputation might justify legal representation (*Pett v Greyhound Racing Association Ltd* [1969] 1 QB 125), but this was later disapproved of (*Pett v Greyhound Racing Association Ltd (No. 2)* [1970] 1 QB 46). It might be thought that if questions of law were involved, this would indicate the suitability of legal representation. This contention was not accepted in *Enderby Town Football Club v Football Association Ltd*, where it was suggested that the courts would be the appropriate place to deal with such points. Having chosen to use the Football Association's appeal procedures, legal representation was not really appropriate.

Perhaps we can conclude that, whatever the body, legal representation will only be justified if the matter is sufficiently serious and there are no compelling objections based upon convenience, speed and general suitability.

16.7.2.7 Reasons The common law has not imposed a duty to give reasons for decisions. Such is the trend in the case law that this position may be overthrown in the not too distant future (Craig 1994b).

One House of Lords decision which points in the direction of a change to the requiring of reasons is *R v Secretary of State for the Home Department, ex parte Doody* [1994] 1 AC 531. In this case prisoners were serving mandatory life sentences for murder. Parole arrangements for such prisoners were that the minister, after consulting with the judiciary, set the penal element of the sentence and then assessed the risk to society posed by release. A review by the Parole Board would be set after these calculations. The applicants were of the view that the minister had lengthened the penal element, which had the effect of delaying a Parole Board review. In their application for judicial review the prisoners contended that they were entitled to make representations to the minister before the decision was made about the date of the first review; that they should be informed of any material on which the minister would make this decision; and that they should know of the judiciary's views on the penal element and, where this was departed from by the minister, the reasons for it. Lord Mustill, while still accepting that there was no general duty to give reasons, stated that reasons should be provided here. This was because the minister's decision seriously affected the prisoners' future, and so fairness required that they be informed about these matters. Another aspect of fairness underpinned the decision that reasons should be given, namely, that of the operation of the parole scheme. If the reasons for decisions were not given then it would not be apparent if there were errors in the process. In order to be able to mount a challenge alleging error, the reasons for the decision would have to be given.

These points have been the foundations of previous decisions — the obstacle to appeal or review in *Minister of National Revenue v Wright's Canadian Ropes Ltd* [1947] AC 109 and *Norton Tool Co. Ltd v Tewson* [1973] 1 WLR 45, and fairness in *R v Civil Service Appeal Board, ex parte Cunningham* [1991] 4 All ER 310 and *R v Parole Board, ex parte Wilson* [1992] QB 740 — and both have a potential for widening the requiring of reasons.

The pattern of formally upholding the lack of a duty to give reasons whilst detailing exceptions was followed in *R v Higher Education Funding Council, ex parte Institute of Dental Surgery* [1994] 1 WLR 242 where the assessment of the Institute's quality of research was given without reasons. Sedley J, in denying that there was a duty to give reasons where the matter being challenged was an exercise of academic judgment, did hold that, where serious interests are at stake, or where the decision being challenged appears to be aberrant, then fairness requires the provision of a reasoned explanation. Failure to give this will render the decision a nullity. He was also of the view that where there was a duty to provide reasons, non-compliance was a breach of law independent of the irrationality head of review.

16.7.2.8 Appeals Can an appeal cure a defective initial hearing? This was the question raised in a case, concerning the Australian Jockey Club, before the Privy Council (*Calvin* v *Carr* [1980] AC 574). Lord Wilberforce suggested that there were three categories of situation which could be discerned from the cases. In the first category the rules provide for a rehearing by the original body or a fuller form of it, and this hearing is taken to have superseded the first one. Social clubs often fall into this category. In the second category are those cases where a fair hearing is required at the original stage and on appeal. It was suggested that trade union matters and the subjects of planning and employment belonged to this category. The third category was stated to be intermediate to the first two, and comprises cases where parties may be said to have agreed to a fair end result despite some initial defect. Domestic disputes were placed in this category. So, where people joined organisations and agreed to be bound by their rules any disputes would be regarded as domestic ones. The Australian Jockey Club was put into the third category. At race meetings stewards' inquiries had to operate very quickly, but there was a full appeal process in which legal representation and cross-examination of witnesses were permitted and a transcript of the original hearing was available.

This case shows the flexibility of fairness and what has been called 'transaction-typing' so that different degrees of fairness are applied in different contexts (Elliott 1980).

16.7.3 Fairness in Administration

The point has been made that the closer proceedings are to the court model of procedure, the more likely it is that safeguards derived from that model will be applied. Fairness has to be observed but it will be different in contexts dissimilar from the courts. Two examples will now be presented in order to give an indication of the courts' views on fairness in sections of the administrative process.

16.7.3.1 Licensing The law relating to licensing is a good example of an area which has always been regarded as administrative but the development of the duty to act fairly means it is subject to review for procedural protection (*R* v *Liverpool Corporation, ex parte Liverpool Taxi Fleet Operators' Association* [1972] 2 QB 299), whereas in the days of natural justice only, this was not so (*R* v *Metropolitan Police Commissioner, ex parte Parker* [1953] 1 WLR 1150). We have seen distinctions drawn by Megarry V-C between forfeiture, renewal and applications (*McInnes* v *Onslow-Fane* [1978] 1 WLR 1520). Forfeiture is serious and should command a hearing. A renewal case might require a hearing if the licensor was minded not to grant the reapplication. The situation regarding a mere application was quite different. There would not be the automatic assumption that a hearing should be granted. Megarry V-C was quite careful not to rule out hearings for all applications.

There appears to be a difference between the opportunity to speak in support of one's application and responding to any objections to an application. It is unfair to decide a licence application without informing the applicant that objections have been made. However, it is permissible to provide that representations about those objections may be made in writing (*R v Huntingdon District Council, ex parte Cowan* [1984] 1 WLR 501). In *R v Gaming Board for Great Britain, ex parte Benaim and Khaida* [1970] 2 QB 417, the context and statutory purpose of the board were such that full details of the opposing case need not be provided to the applicant as an outline would be sufficient.

What of the rights of objectors? There is a decision which ruled that objectors should not have been denied a hearing when the applicant was, unusually, allowed to speak in support of the planning application (*R v Great Yarmouth Borough Council, ex parte Botton Brothers Arcades Ltd* (1987) 56 P & CR 99).

16.7.3.2 Initiating or investigatory procedures   Where procedures are the start of a process then fairness may not require much in terms of notice of the material gathered by the investigators. There are some cases on the investigation of companies which illustrate this point. When it is decided to appoint inspectors to conduct an investigation it is not required that a hearing be given to consider representations about that decision (*Norwest Holst Ltd v Secretary of State for Trade* [1978] Ch 201). The inspectors in their fact-finding are not obliged to give directors of a company details of evidence from other witnesses, but where they are minded to make a critical report, they should give an outline or impression of what might be called 'charges' in order that representations may be made (*Re Pergamon Press Ltd* [1971] Ch 388).

In tax matters procedures may be conducted in order to determine if there is a liability for unpaid tax. The taxpayer may not see the evidence provided to the tribunal by the Inland Revenue (*Wiseman v Borneman* [1971] AC 297). This is because the nature of these procedures is preparatory, involving a decision as to whether the evidence amounts to a prima facie case. At this stage it is not unfair that the taxpayer does not see the Revenue's case. Material will be available if proceedings are initiated.

16.7.4   Fairness in Sentencing

As fairness has substantive aspects as well as procedural, we consider these in a few recent cases in which decisions taken by the Home Secretary on sentencing matters have been challenged by way of judicial review.

16.7.4.1 Legitimate expectations   In *R v Secretary of State for the Home Department, ex parte Hargreaves* [1997] 1 WLR 906 a policy on the earliest date on which applications for home leave could be made was changed. The prisoners challenged this claiming that they had a legitimate expectation of an earlier date for consideration of home leave applications. The Court of Appeal held that, as in *Re Findlay* [1985] AC 318, the prisoners' legitimate expectation was that their cases would be considered fairly in the light of current lawful policies. Policies could change. The court held that the notice and compact on which they based their claim for an earlier date, could not be held to be valid representations for the purpose of creating a legitimate expectation as it was not a clear and unambiguous representation. The court overruled Sedley J in *R v Ministry of Agriculture, Fisheries and Food, ex parte Hamble (Offshore) Fisheries Ltd* [1995] 2 All ER 714 on the correct test for determining if the change in policy had frustrated a substantive legitimate expectation. The correct test was that of *Wednesbury* unreasonableness and not a balancing exercise.

16.7.4.2 Setting the adult tariff A mandatory life sentence is imposed on those convicted of murder. Those prisoners may not spend life in prison as there is provision to release them on licence (Criminal Justice Acts 1967 and 1991). The Home Secretary takes advice on release from the Parole Board, but if the Board recommends release it is still within the minister's discretion not to release. The practice has grown up that the Home Secretary will not refer a case to the Parole Board until a certain period has elapsed. This period is known as the tariff and the Home Secretary sets it so as to impose the appropriate period for punishment (retribution and deterrence) in the particular case. Various Home Secretaries have issued policy statements about the tariff, which is non-statutory. Some of the policy statements have been made in response to court decisions. A 1987 policy implemented the requirement in *R v Secretary of State for the Home Department, ex parte Handscomb* (1987) 86 Cr App R 59 that the tariff should be set as soon after conviction and sentence as possible. *R v Secretary of State for the Home Department, ex parte Doody* [1994] AC 531 required that prisoners should be able to make representations about the tariff before it was fixed by the Home Secretary, and that to facilitate this, they should be informed of the judicial advice received on the tariff, and of any other relevant considerations. Another aspect of the policy statement, issued in 1993, was challenged in *Pierson v Secretary of State for the Home Department* [1997] 3 All ER 577. The challenged provision indicated that the tariff set at the start of the mandatory life sentence was only an initial view and exceptionally it could be revised if it was not thought to be adequate. The prisoner challenged the increase of his tariff. By a 3–2 majority the House of Lords upheld the challenge. Lord Goff of Chieveley took the view that the 1993 policy could not have retrospective effect. Lords Steyn and Hope of Craighead thought the Home Secretary's acts in deciding the tariff period were analogous to the judicial sentencing function and were accordingly subject to a common law principle that a sentence once lawfully pronounced could not be retrospectively increased. The dissenting members of the House Lords Browne-Wilkinson and Lloyd of Berwick, did not accept that there were common law rules of non-aggravation so that a penalty could not be increased. Lord Lloyd did not accept that the Home Secretary's actions were analogous to a judge when imposing a sentence.

16.7.4.3 Setting the tariff for children In *R v Secretary of State for the Home Department, ex parte Venables* [1997] 3 WLR 23, two boys aged 10 were convicted of murder and given the mandatory sentence of detention during

Her Majesty's pleasure. The trial judge set a tariff of eight years' detention, but the Lord Chief Justice advised 10 years. Following a public campaign involving petitions, and coupons in a national newspaper, the Home Secretary decided to set a tariff of 15 years. This tariff was successfully challenged. The House of Lords held by a majority that there was a difference between a mandatory life sentence for an adult murderer and children who were sentenced to mandatory detention during Her Majesty's pleasure. Periodically a review must be carried out to determine if detention is still justified, whereas with a life sentence, review concerns the questions of whether and when release is justified. Lords Browne-Wilkinson and Hope of Craighead took the view that the Children and Young Persons Act 1933 required the Home Secretary to pay attention to the welfare of children. The application of the tariff of 15 years had the effect of rendering irrelevant the progress and development of a detained child offender, and so it was a failure to consider the duty imposed by the 1933 Act. A different majority ruled that the minister, when determining the tariff, was acting like a judge when sentencing and so must be detached from the pressure of public opinion. The public protests about the tariff were irrelevant and ought not to have been taken into account by the minister.

16.7.4.4 Analysis In these cases we can see how fairness changes depending upon the particular context. We saw earlier in 16.7.2.1 the first sense of legitimate expectation, that a person could expect to have a procedural benefit, a hearing. In other words it would be unfair not to provide it. This expectation may also give rise to substantive benefit. The question in *Hargreaves* is: if the policy changes, can it be relied upon? By preferring the *Wednesbury* test to one of balancing to determine if it is unfair to the citizen to supersede the earlier policy, the courts are favouring the policy-maker (although the applicants were not successful in *ex parte Hamble (Offshore) Fisheries Ltd*, in which the balancing test was applied). The balancing test was drawn from European case law and is a test which is found in proportionality, which is still not a separate ground of review in English law. A European influence can also be detected in the majority stance on retrospective increase of penalties. The principle of legal certainty was used to support the majority position. Both of these principles, it is suggested, permit a greater intensity of review and more scope for interference by the judges than *Wednesbury* unreasonableness, which seeks to ensure respect for legislative supremacy.

The difference of opinion about the claim that the ministerial setting of the tariff is analogous to a judge exercising the power to pass sentence is important and could be based on a separation of powers point, although none of the judges mentioned it explicitly. Thus, judges must be independent and impartial, so they are detached from public opinion and ought not be able to make retrospective increases in penalties. The minority, by denying the analogy, were seeking to allow the minister to take public opinion into account, which is more in tune with a more restricted intensity of judicial review.

It may be that the incorporation of the ECHR will give the judiciary clearer guidelines for the increase in their power which it will confer. At the moment the development of judicial review of administrative action is in flux as its exercise is tending towards a greater intensity than that allowed for in the current constitutional basis of legislative supremacy and rule of law.

CHAPTER SEVENTEEN
The Remedies of Judicial Review of Administrative Action

17.1 INTRODUCTION

The law relating to remedies in English common law has sometimes played a disproportionate role in the development of the substantive principles. It is perhaps not a gross exaggeration, in discussing the relationship between remedies and substantive principles, to refer to the metaphor of the tail wagging the dog and to allocate the role of the tail to remedies. The development of the equitable remedies in the Court of Chancery, and the 19th-century fusion of the common law and equity jurisdictions, were partially driven by the rigidity in the common law. Writing after these reforms had been made, one of the foremost legal historians remarked, 'Although we have buried the forms of action, they still rule us from their graves' (Maitland 1909, p. 296). It is probably the case that this was an overstated observation, but the general point about the influence of remedies is, surely, correct.

In administrative law the remedies have caused, and continue to pose, problems. It will be recalled that the development of the law on natural justice had, for a time, been restricted to situations in which it could be said that there was a duty to act judicially (see 16.7). It seems that this could be traced back to a dictum of Atkins LJ about the circumstances in which the remedy of certiorari might be available (*R* v *Electricity Commissioners, ex parte London Electricity Joint Committee Co. (1920) Ltd* [1924] 1 KB 171 at p. 204). Lord Reid showed how this was incorrect in his speech in *Ridge* v *Baldwin* [1964] AC 40, thus paving the way for an activist judicial development of a requirement for fair hearings.

Certiorari, prohibition and mandamus are prerogative orders and comprise the specialised public law remedies. In private law the major remedy is damages. Currently a public law wrong alone will not lead to an award of damages. A person cannot seek damages simply because it is alleged that a tribunal exceeded its jurisdiction, or a minister acted *ultra vires*. Only if it can be shown that a private law right was also breached can a person seek damages in respect of a public law wrong.

The other private law remedies of an injunction and a declaration may be awarded by the court in a public law action.

17.1.1 Statutory Actions

Judicial review is part of the High Court's inherent supervisory jurisdiction, however, there are statutory remedies which may be pursued. The legislation which creates tribunals also often provides that an appeal will lie to the High Court or the Court of Appeal on a point of law. The decisions and actions of ministers, especially on environmentally related topics, such as planning, motorways and compulsory acquisition of land, may be subject to a statutory application to quash. Such challenges may be based on the grounds that the matter is outside the powers of the statute, or that substantial prejudice was sustained by someone because of non-compliance with a procedural requirement. In *Ashbridge Investments Ltd v Minister of Housing and Local Government* [1965] 1 WLR 1320, Lord Denning MR suggested that there was little difference between the grounds of review developed by the courts in inherent review jurisdiction and the grounds in a statutory application to quash. The person who may apply for this statutory remedy is to be a person aggrieved. Initially this was interpreted narrowly, but it has been widened as has been the case with the standing requirements for the other public law remedies. The widening of the availability of the statutory application to quash may be illustrated by comparing two cases. In the first, the owner of land adjoining that for which planning permission had been granted was held not to be a person aggrieved because no legal right of his had been affected. Only planning authorities and applicants were regarded as having a legal interest under the planning legislation (*Buxton v Minister of Housing and Local Government* [1961] QB 278). The second case involved members of an amenity society who had been permitted to participate in the public local inquiry part of a planning appeal by the inspector who had conducted the proceedings. These people wished to challenge the minister's decision on the appeal and the court held that, as they had participated in the inquiry, they could be regarded as persons aggrieved (*Turner v Secretary of State for the Environment* (1973) 28 P & CR 123). This inclusion of third parties in planning matters as people having a sufficient legal interest in order to be able to mount a challenge, is also to be found in inherent judicial review (*Covent Garden Community Association Ltd v Greater London Council* [1981] JPL 183). Where the planning matter is the scheduling of an ancient monument, third parties do not have standing to challenge the minister's decision (*R v Secretary of State for the Environment, ex parte Rose Theatre Trust Co.* [1990] 1 QB 504).

The bulk of this chapter will be taken up with the application for judicial review and the remedies available in that procedure. 17.5 will deal with the courts' response to statutory exclusions of judicial review.

17.2 THE APPLICATION FOR JUDICIAL REVIEW

17.2.1 Background

Each of the different public law remedies was subject to particular conditions. The rules on standing and the scope of the remedies varied. Applications for the prerogative orders of certiorari, prohibition and mandamus were quite different from seeking a declaration or an injunction. If a person chose the wrong remedy then the proceedings would have to be started over again, assuming that the time-limit had not expired for the 'correct' remedy. If damages were also sought, then the applicant would have to demonstrate that a private right had been breached in addition to the alleged public law wrong. If the relief sought for the public law wrong was a prerogative order then a completely different action would have to be commenced in respect of the claim for damages. In these circumstances it is not surprising that the Law Commission should have suggested that a thorough examination of administrative law be conducted. The government rejected the idea of a royal commission on administrative law and instead the Law Commission was asked to consider the desirability of changes in the form and procedures of the judicial remedies. Eventually the Law Commission (1976) produced its report in which it recommended that there should be a uniform procedure in which all of the public law remedies might be sought. No change was suggested with respect to the requirement that the leave of the court was a precondition. These aspects of the report were put into effect, first, by amending ord. 53 of the Rules of the Supreme Court 1965 (SI 1977/1955; SI 1980/2000; SI 1982/1111), and then by placing the new procedure, called an application for judicial review, on a statutory basis (Supreme Court Act 1981, s. 31).

17.2.2 Procedure

Before one may make an application for judicial review, leave to make such an application must be granted by the court. The application for leave is usually made *ex parte*, i.e., in the absence of the respondent. In the leave application the applicant must state the relief sought, the grounds on which it is sought and include an affidavit which verifies the facts relied upon. The leave application will not be granted if the court thinks that the action is 'vexatious or frivolous'. In *R v Secretary of State for the Home Department, ex parte Doorga* [1990] COD 109, Lord Donaldson of Lymington MR suggested that there were three categories of leave cases: (a) those in which there are prima facie reasons for granting judicial review; (b) cases that are wholly unarguable and so leave should be refused; and (c) an intermediate category where it was not clear and so it might be appropriate to adjourn the application and hold a hearing between the parties.

Research has shown that around a third of leave applications are rejected and that applications dealt with on paper have a lower success rate than oral leave applications (Le Sueur and Sunkin 1992). It is the case that some important cases are initially refused leave but a renewal of the application is successful (e.g., *R v Panel on Take-overs and Mergers, ex parte Datafin plc*

[1987] QB 815). Le Sueur and Sunkin would prefer the leave stage to be abolished but think this is unlikely. Therefore they wish to see the test for leave changed from one of arguability, to 'a serious issue to be tried'. This should help keep the leave stage confined to a 'quick look', reserving for the full hearing difficult points. They also wish reasons to be given for refusals.

Where leave has been granted to the applicant, the new procedure allows for amendments to be made to the grounds and the relief sought, as well as providing enhanced rights of discovery, interrogatories and cross-examination, although the tradition of review proceedings relying predominantly upon documentary evidence is still maintained.

The time-limits in which the application must be brought are defined differently in ord. 53 and the statute. The House of Lords gave guidance on these time-limits in *R* v *Dairy Produce Quota Tribunal for England and Wales, ex parte Caswell* [1990] 2 AC 738:

(a) The court decides at the leave application stage if the application has been made promptly. Applying within three months does not necessarily guarantee promptness.

(b) If the application has not been made promptly or within three months then the court decides if there is good reason for the delay.

(c) A finding of promptness at the leave stage does not preclude a finding of undue delay at the substantive hearing.

(d) Whenever there is a failure to act promptly or within three months there is undue delay, and the court may either refuse to grant leave or, at the substantive hearing, refuse to grant relief if it considers that the granting of the relief sought would be likely to cause substantial hardship to, or substantially prejudice the rights of, any person or would be detrimental to good administration.

The Law Commission (1994) in its report thinks that leave should be retained, although renamed preliminary consideration, and that it should be determined on the papers unless the case is one which should have an oral hearing either because it includes a claim for immediate interim relief, or because a hearing would be in the interests of justice (paras 5.8–5.11). An application would proceed to a substantive hearing if there was a serious issue which ought to be determined (para. 5.15). It would still be possible to renew a refused application (para. 5.12).

On time-limits the Law Commission decided that the statute should provide for them to be specified in the rules of court, thereby removing the current confusing situation. Otherwise the three-month limit is retained as are the grounds for both undercutting it on promptness, and extending it for good reasons, provided this would not cause substantial hardship to, or substantially prejudice the rights of, any person, or be detrimental to good administration (para. 5.26).

Brief reasons for not permitting an application to proceed to a substantive hearing should be given (para. 5.36).

17.2.3 What Is a Public Law Issue?

The public law remedies are only available in respect of public law issues. It is therefore important to know whether or not an issue involves public law. There appear to be two bases for this: the source of power, and the nature of the function.

17.2.3.1 Source of power For most administrative authorities the source of their power will be legislation, but for others it could be the prerogative. Legislation can confer upon a private body a public law element in respect of which judicial review can be sought (*R v Statutory Committee of the Pharmaceutical Society of Great Britain, ex parte Pharamaceutical Society of Great Britain* [1981] 1 WLR 886, disciplinary powers). So far as the prerogative is concerned the reasoning in *Council of Civil Service Unions v Minister for the Civil Service* [1985] AC 374, made it clear that not only was judicial review available where the source of power was the prerogative, but that review could deal with the exercise of the prerogative-based power, and not just its existence and extent. The issue of passports has been held to be an exercise of the prerogative which is subject to judicial review (*R v Secretary of State for Foreign and Commonwealth Affairs, ex parte Everett* [1989] QB 811), and the creation of the Criminal Injuries Compensation Board to administer the Criminal Injuries Compensation Scheme was held to have been carried out under the prerogative, and amenable to review (*R v Criminal Injuries Compensation Board, ex parte Lain* [1967] 2 QB 864).

The fact that the source of power is statutory does not automatically mean that judicial review will be available, as public sector employment cases show. In *R v East Berkshire Health Authority, ex parte Walsh* [1985] QB 152, the court held that judicial review of the dismissal of a nurse was not a public law matter as, despite the statutory origin of the authority, its relationship with its employees was based on contract. Accordingly, public and private sector employment are usually matters of private law.

Some general guidance about the exceptions to the non-availability of judicial review in public sector dismissal cases has been provided by *obiter dicta* of Woolf LJ in *McClaren v Home Office* [1990] ICR 824. If a disciplinary or other body has been created by statute or prerogative to which the employer or employee are entitled or required to refer employment disputes then that creates a public law element (*R v Civil Service Appeal Board, ex parte Bruce* [1988] 3 All ER 686, body created under the prerogative). If an employee is affected by a decision of general application made by the employer then judicial review may be available to challenge flaws in that decision (*Council of Civil Service Unions v Minister for the Civil Service* [1985] AC 375, decision to restrict some civil servants from membership of trade unions).

The courts are now more willing to find that civil servants may be employed under a contract of employment (*R v Lord Chancellor's Department, ex parte Nangle* [1991] ICR 743), but this can have unfortunate consequences for civil servants (see Fredman and Morris 1991).

It has been held that commercial decisions of a public body are not susceptible to judicial review. In *R v National Coal Board, ex parte National*

Union of Mineworkers [1986] ICR 791, it was said of a decision to close a colliery by the board that it 'was an executive, business, or management decision in exactly the same category as a decision in similar circumstances made by a public company' (per Macpherson J at p. 795). This decision has been doubted by Glidewell LJ in *R v British Coal Corporation, ex parte Vardy* [1993] ICR 720, where the Divisional Court upheld a challenge to the decision to close collieries by the minister and British Coal on the basis that they had been made without consultation with the unions and breached the Trade Union and Labour Relations (Consolidation) Act 1992, s. 188. His lordship held that if British Coal did not comply with its obligations under the Coal Industry Act 1946 then this was a matter of public law.

17.2.3.2 Nature of function Part of the reasoning of the decision in *R v Criminal Injuries Compensation Board, ex parte Lain* [1967] 2 QB 864, was that the High Court's supervisory jurisdiction had been held to apply to inferior courts and tribunals created under the prerogative and therefore this body, which acted as a tribunal, was within the scope of review. Part of this reasoning refers to the nature of the power which the body exercises. In *Ex parte Lain* the Board was determining claims, which was a public function. This criterion of exercising a public function was extended somewhat in *R v Panel on Take-overs and Mergers, ex parte Datafin plc* [1987] QB 815. Donaldson MR observed that the Panel, in its role of overseeing compliance with the City Code on Take-overs and Mergers, 'performs this function without any visible means of legal support'. Neither the Panel nor the Code were created by statute; they were elements in a system of self-regulation. The court had no doubt that the Panel performed a public function. It was clear that the government used the Panel as its centrepiece in regulating take-overs and mergers. Sir John Donaldson MR said that the Panel's source of power was only partly voluntarism: the bottom line was the statutory powers exercised by the Department of Trade and Industry and the Bank of England. His lordship also said that it did not appear that private law remedies were available to those who were dissatisfied with the Panel's decisions. During argument counsel had been invited to draft a writ, and all were agreed that it was inadequate to the task.

In *Ex parte Datafin plc* the context of the Panel's work made it clear that it was conducting a function with a public element. It has been suggested (Pannick 1992) that some bodies which exercise monopolistic powers should be subject to judicial review because, in their field of work, people have no choice but to comply with their rules. When this type of argument was presented to the Court of Appeal in a challenge to a decision of the Jockey Club, it was held that while the Club regulates racing, it had not been woven into any system of governmental control for horse racing. In this particular case the Club's jurisdiction derived from contract and was not subject to judicial review, however, Bingham MR said it was unnecessary in that case to determine whether the Club's decisions might ever be challenged by judicial review (*R v Disciplinary Committee of the Jockey Club, ex parte Aga Khan* [1993] 1 WLR 909).

17.2.4 Exclusivity in Public Law Issues

The Law Commission's report on remedies in administrative law (1976) did not recommend, and the rules relating to ord. 53 of the Rules of the Supreme Court 1965 do not specify, that the application for judicial review should be the sole method of seeking all types of relief in public law. Certainly, the prerogative orders may only be sought by ord. 53, but does that apply to a declaration or an injunction? Declarations had been used by many litigants to overcome the difficulties involved in seeking the other public law remedies. In *O'Reilly* v *Mackman* [1983] 2 AC 237, prisoners sought a declaration by a writ that disciplinary proceedings had been conducted in a manner that breached natural justice. This was successfully countered by the argument that the writ should be struck out as an abuse of the process of the court because it was a public law matter and should only have been brought under ord. 53. Lord Diplock said that the ordinary action would avoid the 'safeguards imposed in the public interest against groundless, unmeritorious or tardy attacks on the validity of decisions made by public authorities in the field of public law'. His lordship reached that conclusion by comparing the application for judicial review with the ordinary writ procedure. He found that there were two important differences. First, ord. 53 was subject to a leave requirement, whereas the ordinary writ was not. A person seeking judicial review had to persuade a judge that the issue was a public law one and that it was a serious matter affecting the applicant. This distinction was justified on the basis that administrative authorities required protection from 'mere busybodies'. The second difference was that ord. 53 had a three-month time-limit and the ordinary writ could be commenced within three years. Again, the special position of an administrative authority provided the explanation for the disparity. There was a need for certainty in the work of administrative authorities. It would be contrary to the public interest if challenges could be mounted to decisions or orders when the action which they authorised had already begun. Unlawful administrative action should not be free from review but this must be balanced against the public interest in certainty and so immunity arises after a period. As ord. 53 sets a three-month limit, which may be extended, why should an administrative authority not be able to rely upon it?

The House of Lords, despite the absence of an express provision, ruled that the seeking of declarations or injunctions in public law matters should only be done by ord. 53 proceedings. The basis for this exclusivity could be inferred from the differences in the two procedures. The House indicated that there were two exceptions to this exclusivity principle: where the public law issue was a collateral one, and where the parties had agreed to the writ procedure. Other exceptions could be decided on a case-by-case basis.

17.2.4.1 The application of O'Reilly v Mackman   The very first application of the exclusivity principle stated in *O'Reilly* v *Mackman* [1983] 2 AC 237, occurred in a case decided on the same day . In *Cocks* v *Thanet District Council* [1983] 2 AC 286, the council's decision not to house a person was challenged as being a breach of the statutory duty to house homeless people. The House divided this issue into two parts. There was the private law right to be housed under the statutory duty, but the steps taken in reaching the decision whether to carry out that duty were public law matters. As the challenge related to the making of the decision, rather than the executive function of carrying out the duty, this action should have been brought under ord. 53.

A different conclusion was reached in *Davy v Spelthorne Borough Council* [1984] AC 262. The council and Davy had agreed that an enforcement notice which sought to restrain a breach of planning control would not be pursued for three years if Davy did not exercise the right to appeal the notice to the minister. Davy did not appeal the notice but, after two years, he claimed that the agreement was *ultra vires* the council, and that the advice which the council had given him breached the duty of care owed to him. He brought an action in negligence and also sought to have the enforcement notice invalidated. The Court of Appeal struck down his claim to have the notice set aside but permitted him to proceed with his negligence action. The council contended that this action was an abuse of process and should have been brought under ord. 53. The House of Lords held that Davy was not seeking to challenge the enforcement notice but to establish that the council had breached a private law duty owed to him. He was seeking to vindicate private, and not public law rights. The test in *O'Reilly v Mackman* is: could and should the action be brought in an application of judicial review? The answer here was no.

The next case involves an action initiated by an authority. In *Wandsworth London Borough Council v Winder* [1985] AC 461, the defendant refused to pay an increase in rent imposed by the landlord, the council. Eventually the council sued for recovery of arrears and for possession of the flat. The defendant counterclaimed that the decision to increase the rent was unlawful and sought a declaration that the increase was of no legal effect. The House of Lords held that it was permissible to raise this public issue as a collateral challenge in defending a private law action. The defendant was trying to fend off an allegedly unlawful claim by the council which was quite different from the purpose of ord. 53, the protection of an administrative authority from unmeritorious claims.

Another distinction was drawn in *Waverley Borough Council v Hilden* [1988] 1 WLR 246, in which the council wished to obtain an injunction to stop land being used as a gypsy caravan site in breach of planning law. The defence claimed that the decision to institute proceedings was unlawful. The court ruled that this challenge to the decision of the council could only be raised in an application for judicial review. Scott J pointed out that, in order for the contention that the council's decision was unlawful to succeed, the court would have to make a favourable exercise of its discretion, which was not certain. In *Wandsworth London Borough Council v Winder* the situation was different as finding that the rent increase was unlawful would mean the defeat of the council's action for arrears and possession.

Another distinction between these two cases is that in *Wandsworth London Borough Council v Winder* it was held that a private right was being defended, whereas in *Waverley Borough Council v Hilden*, the claim that the council's action was *ultra vires* was not a substantive defence of a private law right.

In *Roy* v *Kensington and Chelsea and Westminster Family Practitioner Committee* [1992] 1 AC 624, Lord Lowry discussed two interpretations of the exclusivity rule. The 'broad approach' was that ord. 53 was to be used only if there were no private rights at issue. The 'narrow approach' requires ord. 53 to be used if public law acts are challenged (even collaterally) subject to some exceptions involving private law rights. While Lord Lowry seemed to incline towards the 'broad approach', suggesting that the courts should not debate the form of the proceedings provided that they were not unsuited to the disposal of the issue, the House did not state a preference. *Roy* therefore seems to be another case in which the private rights at issue constitute an exception to the exclusivity rule (see comments by Fredman and Morris 1992).

17.2.4.2 Rationale of the exclusivity principle The procedural distinction drawn in *O'Reilly* v *Mackman* [1983] 2 AC 237 between public and private law is out of keeping with the general development of English common law. For Dicey it was a glory of the common law that it did not have a separate system of administrative law. The use of declarations in public law matters was not new. Indeed, applicants had increasingly turned to declarations because it was felt to have advantages over the other public law remedies, not the least of which was the longer time-limit. Therefore the courts had experience of balancing the considerations mentioned by Lord Diplock. The leave requirement was justified on a couple of points. First, it weeds out the 'frivolous and vexatious' litigants, and secondly, it is convenient for both applicant and authority as it is usually an *ex parte* application. Therefore the authority will only have to defend actions which have some merit, and the applicant learns quite quickly and at lower cost if the case is without worth. This does mean that a meritorious applicant is forced through two hoops. As we have seen the application of *O'Reilly* v *Mackman* means that some authorities will have to face a public law issue in an ordinary writ action in cases where there is a public law element, but one which is regarded as peripheral to the private law issue. Similarly, some public law points may be raised in an ordinary writ and so outside ord. 53's three-month time limit. Perhaps the three-month period is too short. Before the changes to ord. 53 there was a six-month limit in respect of certiorari. If it is felt that some administrative matters should have a shorter period in which they may be challenged, then they could be identified and provided for in legislation. This is done in the case of the statutory applications to quash, where the time-limit is often six weeks, and the courts usually respect that period for challenge (see 17.5).

17.2.4.3 Reform The Law Commission (1994, para. 3.15) takes the view that the operation of procedural exclusivity following *Roy* v *Kensington and Chelsea and Westminster Family Practitioner Committee* [1992] 1 AC 624 is satisfactory, so that (a) a litigant only resorts to ord. 53 when the challenge is on public law grounds, i.e., the challenge is solely on the validity or legality of a public authority's acts or omissions, and (b) the litigant does not seek either to enforce or to defend a completely constituted private law right. As there are some topics, such as housing law, in which it is difficult to disentangle public and private law, the Law Commission also recommends that as well as the possibility of transferring an action out of ord. 53, a litigant should be able to transfer into ord. 53, provided the leave criteria are satisfied (paras 3.16, 3.21).

17.2.5 Justiciability

A matter may seem to be pre-eminently one of public law, but the courts may decline to exercise review because it is felt that the matter is not justiciable, i.e., not suitable to judicial determination. The reason for the non-justiciability may be that the judges are not expert enough to deal with the matter, or perhaps it would be constitutionally inappropriate. This latter reason is to be found in *Gouriet* v *Union of Post Office Workers* [1975] AC 435, in which the House of Lords held that the Attorney-General's decision to grant or deny permission for a relator action was unreviewable (see 17.3.4). Constitutionally, the Attorney answered to Parliament.

Issues relating to national security are usually felt to be non-justiciable as the courts have neither the expertise to assess such matters nor the constitutional authority. Again it is felt to be appropriate that ministers decide these points and answer for them in the political arena (*Council of Civil Service Unions* v *Minister for the Civil Service* [1985] AC 374). Some of the judges are inclined to be less deferential to the executive's claims of national security in peacetime (e.g., Lord Scarman in *Council of Civil Service Unions* v *Minister for the Civil Service* and Taylor J in *R* v *Secretary of State for the Home Department, ex parte Ruddock* [1987] 1 WLR 1482), but this attitude generally ceases in wartime.

17.2.6 Sufficient Interest

Prior to the changes in ord. 53, one of the difficulties for applicants was that there were different tests for standing for each of the remedies. Standing, or *locus standi*, refers to the close connection between the applicant and the subject of the action which the court requires in order for the applicant to be heard by the court. The rule for standing in making a leave application for ord. 53 is that the applicant should have a sufficient interest in the matter to which the application relates (Supreme Court Act 1981, s. 31(3)). This raises the question whether or not the sufficient interest test applies to all of the remedies. Unfortunately, no clear answer was given to that question in the leading case on sufficient interest (*Inland Revenue Commissioners* v *National Federation of Self-Employed and Small Businesses Ltd* [1982] AC 617, hereafter the *Fleet Street Casuals* case; although in *R* v *Felixstowe Justices, ex parte Leigh* [1987] QB 582, it seems that the position was stated to be that standing is related to the applicant's interest in a case, rather than the remedy sought).

In the *Fleet Street Casuals* case the applicant sought to challenge an agreement between the Revenue and casual workers on the national newspapers, which were at that time mainly located on Fleet Street. The agreement required the workers to declare fully their earnings in the future, in consideration of which the Revenue would grant them an amnesty in respect of past unpaid tax.

The House of Lords' decision is clear that the applicant did not have a sufficient interest in other taxpayers' affairs. There is some confusion over the test which was formulated for determining a sufficient interest. The House held that the question of sufficient interest is not simply a threshold issue, a preliminary point arising before, and independent of, the merits of the action. Only in the simplest of cases is the issue of standing clear-cut. At p. 630, Lord Wilberforce said of the less straightforward cases that:

> it will be necessary to consider the powers or the duties in law of those against whom the relief is asked, the position of the applicant in relation to those powers or duties, and to the breach of those said to have been committed. In other words, the question of sufficient interest cannot, in such cases, be considered in the abstract, or as an isolated point: it must be taken together with the legal and factual context.

The House held that it was correct for leave to have been granted as, on the information available, the judge could not determine finally the sufficient interest of the applicants. The legal context of the case was that the dealings between the Revenue and taxpayers were confidential and so one taxpayer could not complain about the treatment given to another taxpayer. The House also held that there was no enforceable duty upon the Revenue to collect every penny of tax. They had a managerial discretion in tax collection and the decision here, which referred to cost-effectiveness, was not an abuse of that discretion.

As some of their lordships did refer to the earlier case law on the differences in standing for the prerogative orders, it is unclear if those variations have been swept away by the statutory sufficient interest test. The courts now seem to operate a less restrictive standing test for the prerogative orders. It would appear that the legislation has relaxed the standing requirements for a declaration and an injunction which were stricter than for the prerogative orders, because the court may now grant a declaration or an injunction where a prerogative order could be awarded (s. 31(3)).

Standing, like leave, is a filter to remove cases without any merit. Public law wrongs may affect an individual or a whole community. Should only those who have been directly affected be entitled to seek judicial review or should a wider view be adopted which suggests that any citizen has an interest in correcting unlawful administrative action? It seems that the test in the *Fleet Street Casuals* case, with its focus on the legal and factual context, will be individualistic and flexible, however, this means that an applicant may not find out until the determination of the application for judicial review that the test for standing has not been passed even though, in the legislation, the test relates only to the leave application.

The Law Commission (1994), in its recommendations on standing propose a two-track system. One track would cover those who have personally been adversely affected by the decision or action which they seek to challenge.

Unless a statutory power or duty concerns, or is owed to, an individual or a narrow group to which the applicant does not belong, standing should be accorded as a matter of course. The second track deals with public-interest and group challenges, where applicants have not been personally adversely affected by a decision. The denial of sufficient interest to a group who wished to challenge a ministerial decision not to schedule as a monument of national importance the site of a Shakespearean theatre (*R v Secretary of State for the Environment, ex parte Rose Theatre Trust Co.* [1990] 1 QB 504) had concerned many, including the Law Commission in its consultation paper (1993, paras 9.17, 9.18, 9.27). Subsequently more liberal standing decisions have been made (*R v Secretary of State for Employment, ex parte Equal Opportunities Commission* [1995] 1 AC 1, challenge to the incompatibility of legislation on part-time employees' rights with European Community law; *R v HM Inspectorate of Pollution, ex parte Greenpeace Ltd* [1994] 1 WLR 570, challenge to variation on authorisations at Sellafield; *R v Secretary of State for Foreign and Commonwealth Affairs, ex parte World Development Movement Ltd* [1995] 1 WLR 386, challenge to payment of aid in respect of the Pergau Dam Hydroelectric project).

The second track proposed by the Law Commission would be discretionary and is intended to cover challenges which (a) affect the public interest generally, and (b) by groups where a specific individual has been particularly affected (1994, paras 5.20–5.22). The Commission decided not to specify in the rules factors which would be taken account of in public-interest challenges. The report did note that the following factors would be relevant: the importance of the legal point; the chances of the issue being raised in any other proceedings; the allocation of scarce judicial resources; the concern that in the determination of issues the courts should have the benefit of conflicting points of view of those most directly affected by them (para. 5.22).

The Law Commission recommends that unincorporated associations should be permitted to make applications for judicial review where they meet the criteria for standing (para. 5.41). This would reverse the decision in *R v Darlington Borough Council, ex parte Association of Darlington Taxi Owners* (1994), *The Times*, 21 January 1994.

17.3 SCOPE OF THE REMEDIES

17.3.1 Mandamus
The order of mandamus requires the carrying out of a public duty which has been imposed by law. It developed as a means for returning to public office those people who had been wrongfully deprived of such a position (*Bagg's Case* (1615) 11 Co Rep 93b).

The duty must be a public one. Not every duty owed by a public body amounts to a public duty (*R v Industrial Court, ex parte A.S.S.E.T.* [1965] 1 QB 377). Some public duties are possibly too wide for them to be enforced by mandamus. For example, the obligations on the former nationalised industries, now privatised utilities companies, to provide economic and efficient supplies of water, gas and electricity.

If the duty is owed by the Crown or a Crown servant then mandamus cannot issue (*R v Powell* (1841) 1 QB 352; *R v Secretary of State for War* [1891] 2 QB 326). This does not mean that a government minister, who is an officer of the Crown, cannot be compelled to carry out public duties. Enforcement will depend upon whether the duty is imposed upon a named Crown servant and owed to another person (*Padfield v Minister of Agriculture, Fisheries and Food* [1968] AC 997).

Mandamus has traditionally only been issued where a duty is owed and a request to perform it has been refused. Craig (1994a, pp. 528–9) thinks this is a formalistic requirement and that a request to perform the duty will not be insisted upon. Examples of the use of mandamus to enforce performance of a duty include: requiring a tribunal to determine a case which it had wrongfully claimed was outside its jurisdiction (*R v Paddington South Rent Tribunal, ex parte Millard* [1955] 1 WLR 348), requiring a body to consider matters according to law where a discretionary power had been fettered by overly rigid adherence to a policy (*R v London County Council, ex parte Corrie* [1918] 1 KB 68), and requiring a body to exercise a power according to law where the power had been abused (*Padfield v Minister of Agriculture, Fisheries and Food* [1968] AC 997).

It seems that *ex gratia* payments are outside the scope of mandamus (*R v Criminal Injuries Compensation Board, ex parte Lain* [1967] 2 QB 864), however, the Board could be compelled to adhere to its proper procedures even though it was not a statutory body at that point (*R v Criminal Injuries Compensation Board, ex parte Clowes* [1977] 1 WLR 1353).

One duty which is owed to a significant number of people is the duty of a chief constable to enforce the law. It has been held that mandamus can compel performance of this duty. Mr Blackburn was an applicant in several public law cases. Some of his actions were against the Metropolitan Police. In the first of these actions Mr Blackburn challenged a policy decision which seemed to provide for the non-enforcement of certain aspects of the gaming legislation (*R v Metropolitan Police Commissioner, ex parte Blackburn* [1968] 2 QB 118). Before the action came to trial the policy was changed. The court held that a chief constable had a wide managerial discretion in carrying out the duty of law enforcement, but made it clear that mandamus could lie against a chief constable operating a policy of non-enforcement. In another police case Mr Blackburn was concerned about the enforcement of the law relating to obscene publications. Again mandamus was not issued, but the court said that an order would lie only in an extreme case (*R v Metropolitan Police Commissioner, ex parte Blackburn (No. 3)* [1973] QB 241). The court seemed to be making it clear that it would be a rare event for the court to interfere with the chief constable's discretion by issuing mandamus.

The old case law on the *locus standi* for the public law remedies made it clear that a greater interest was needed for mandamus than for certiorari. A very strict formulation of the test was proposed in *R v Lewisham Union* [1897] 1 QB 498, which required that the applicant have a 'legal specific right' to the duty in question. This formulation was criticised in the *Fleet Street Casuals* case [1982] AC 617. An example of a less strict test is that ratepayers have a sufficient interest in the financial affairs of their council (*R v Hereford Corporation, ex parte Harrower* [1970] 1 WLR 1424). In the *Fleet Street Casuals* case Lord Diplock pointed out that people other than ratepayers may have an interest in the work of a council, but their lordships also held that taxpayers do not have an interest in the Revenue's dealing with other taxpayers.

17.3.2 Certiorari

The order of certiorari quashes or nullifies an action or decision. The point has already been made that the dictum of Atkin LJ in *R v Electricity Commissioners, ex parte London Electricity Joint Committee Co. (1920) Ltd* [1924] 1 KB 171 at p. 204, on the scope of certiorari delayed the development of natural justice (see 17.1). The dictum stated that certiorari could control 'any body of persons having legal authority to determine questions affecting the rights of subjects, and having the duty to act judicially'. The duty to act judicially was misinterpreted to mean that it was added to the determination of questions affecting rights, rather than being regarded as a consequence of such determinations.

The dictum therefore stipulates that there should be a body having legal authority for the determination of questions affecting rights. If we examine first, bodies having legal authority, this includes inferior courts and tribunals created by statute. The Criminal Injuries Compensation Board derived its legal authority from the prerogative. If the body is a private one and its legal authority is grounded in contract, and even though its decisions can have significant effects, certiorari may not lie (*Law v National Greyhound Racing Club Ltd* [1983] 1 WLR 1302). It is unclear if the Panel on Take-overs and Mergers, a body without any visible means of legal support would be controllable by certiorari as Donaldson MR said that it was more appropriate that the courts' relationship with the Panel be historic rather than contemporary, and relief being by declaratory order (*R v Panel on Take-overs and Mergers, ex parte Datafin plc* [1987] QB 815 at p. 842).

The rights which are at stake may include common law rights (*R v Barnsley Metropolitan Borough Council, ex parte Hook* [1976] 1 WLR 1052), real property (*R v Agricultural Land Tribunal for the Wales and Monmouth Area, ex parte Davies* [1953] 1 WLR 722). There has been an expansion from rights into interests. *R v Criminal Injuries Compensation Board, ex parte Lain* [1967] 2 QB 864, held that *ex gratia* payments could be covered and in *R v Board of Visitors of Hull Prison, ex parte St Germain (No. 2)* [1979] 1 WLR 1401, the fact that there was no right to remission of sentence was not held to be a bar to certiorari. If remission was denied to the prisoners, this amounted to a penalty.

The pre-1978 standing requirement for certiorari distinguished between a 'person aggrieved' and a 'stranger'. Mention has already been made of the widening of standing to include third parties and interest groups (see 17.1.1). While a group of taxpayers were denied standing for a mandamus and a declaration in the *Fleet Street Casuals* case, it seems that where a taxpayer is seeking a declaration about the legality of the procedure by which the

Treasury may make payments to the European Communities, a point of constitutional importance, then sufficient interest might be made out (*R* v *Her Majesty's Treasury, ex parte Smedley* [1985] QB 857). The point was not actually determined in the case but there were dicta to that effect.

Certiorari is not available against the Crown but usually a declaration suffices.

17.3.3 Prohibition

Whereas certiorari is sought after an alleged unlawful decision or act, prohibition is sought to prevent such actions. Accordingly its award will depend upon there being knowledge that an unlawful act will be carried out. It was sought successfully in *R* v *Kent Police Authority, ex parte Godden* [1971] 2 QB 662, to stop a doctor carrying out an examination to determine a person's fitness for work, on the basis that this doctor had already formed a view on the matter and so was biased.

In *R* v *Liverpool Corporation, ex parte Liverpool Taxi Fleet Operators' Association* [1972] 2 QB 299, a prohibition was granted to stop the council from granting additional taxi-cab licences without first giving a hearing to existing taxi-drivers.

An unsuccessful application for prohibition was made in *R* v *Boundary Commission for England, ex parte Foot* [1983] QB 600. A challenge was mounted to the recommendations of the Commission on amendments to the boundaries of electoral constituencies. The court held that, had the application been successful, it would have prevented the consideration of the proposals by the House of Commons and so a declaration would have been more appropriate relief.

17.3.4 Injunction

Relief in the form of a court order restraining action (prohibitory), or requiring something to be done (mandatory), is a remedy which was developed in equity. It is less likely that a mandatory injunction will be awarded as this would necessitate close supervision by the court. Thus a ferry service was not ordered to be restarted (*Attorney-General* v *Colchester Corporation* [1955] 2 QB 207). An injunction may be granted to restrain the *ultra vires* exercise of a power (*Attorney-General* v *Fulham Corporation* [1921] Ch 440).

In public law matters an ordinary individual could only show standing prior to 1978 if a private law right was being infringed, or if special damage was sustained, i.e., damage greater than that sustained by others. The Attorney-General always has standing in public law matters. An individual could try to secure the Attorney's consent, or fiat, to a relator action. This simply means that the action is actually brought by the individual but it is in the Attorney's name, thus giving standing. The decision of the Attorney on the issue of consent to a relator action is unreviewable. In *Gouriet* v *Union of Post Office Workers* [1975] AC 435, the applicant's attempts to obtain an injunction to stop the union from participating in an international boycott of mail from South Africa failed. The Attorney refused consent for a relator action and the House of Lords overruled the Court of Appeal which had held that the

Attorney's decision was justiciable. The House of Lords pointed out that the Attorney answered to the House of Commons.

Gouriet also provides some guidance on the use of injunctions to assist the criminal law. In this case a criminal offence had not yet been committed. It was held that the grant of an injunction to restrain criminal action should be a rare occurrence as the use of civil proceedings was inappropriate. The civil standard of proof is lower than in criminal proceedings and, bearing in mind that contempt of court is the sanction against non-compliance with an injunction, the penalties imposed could be greater than those stipulated for the offence by Parliament.

The Attorney has secured injunctions where there has been deliberate and repetitious flouting of the criminal law (*Attorney-General* v *Harris* [1961] 1 QB 74), and where there was urgency in stopping the breach of fire safety regulations in a hotel (*Attorney-General* v *Chaudry* [1971] 1 WLR 1614).

European Community law has played a part in developing the law on injunctive relief. Injunctions are not available against the Crown, however, declarations may be awarded instead (Crown Proceedings Act 1947, s. 21(1)). A minister or other officer of the Crown who is empowered in his or her own name is susceptible to injunctive and interim relief (*Re M* [1994] 1 AC 377). As a result of the *Factortame* litigation (*R* v *Secretary of State for Transport, ex parte Factortame Ltd (No. 2)* [1991] 1 AC 603), an injunction against the Crown is also available in respect of Community law matters. This includes an interlocutory injunction which may be awarded where it would be wrong to defer the making of an injunction until the final determination of the case. In *Factortame (No. 2)* there is guidance to the effect that, in deciding if there is some merit in the plaintiff's case, consideration must also be given to whether damages could be awarded. If a plaintiff could not obtain damages then it might be correct to award the interim relief. In this case neither the plaintiffs (the Spanish fishermen) nor the defendant (the Secretary for Transport) could obtain damages and it was decided that the balance of convenience lay with the fishermen, i.e., that whatever the final outcome it would be better to award the interlocutory injunction than to refuse it (see Oliver 1991a).

It is often the case that a plaintiff who is awarded an interim injunction is required to indemnify the defendant in respect of any resulting losses. This does not apply where the Crown or a local authority is engaged in enforcing the law (*Kirklees Metropolitan Borough Council* v *Wickes Building Supplies Ltd* [1993] AC 227).

The Law Commission (1994, para. 6.13) recommended that, for the avoidance of doubt, there should be provision for interim relief in judicial review proceedings against ministers in their official capacity and against government departments.

17.3.5 Declaration

A remedy which simply declares the rights of the parties but has no coercive force might not appear to be very useful. In public law the declaration's popularity rose because the Crown and other public authorities would regard themselves as bound by the declaration, and it had a longer time-limit than the prerogative orders.

The range of public law faults in which the remedy of declaration has been held to be available include unreasonable planning conditions (*Hall and Co. Ltd v Shoreham-by-Sea Urban District Council* [1964] 1 WLR 240), jurisdictional error by a tribunal (*Anisminic Ltd v Foreign Compensation Commission* [1969] 2 AC 147), and breach of natural justice (*Ridge v Baldwin* [1964] AC 40).

Administrative authorities can find it useful to discover if their proposals are lawful or not. The Greater London Council, following its defeat in the Fares Fair case (*Bromley London Borough Council v Greater London Council* [1983] 1 AC 768), successfully sought a declaration that its second attempt at a fare reduction scheme was lawful (*R v London Transport Executive, ex parte Greater London Council* [1983] QB 484).

The remedy is not available if a statutory regime is regarded as being exclusive in that it both creates rights and provides for their determination (*Barraclough v Brown* [1897] AC 615). If it can be shown that the statutory scheme is not exclusive then a declaration may be given (*Pyx Granite Co. Ltd v Ministry of Housing and Local Government* [1960] AC 260). If the question is hypothetical, as where the issue has not yet arisen, then the remedy will be refused. One of the cases brought by the litigious Mr Blackburn was an action for a declaration that it would be unconstitutional for the Queen to sign the Treaty of Accession to the European Communities. Amongst the reasons for dismissing his case was the fact that the point had not yet occurred (*Blackburn v Attorney-General* [1971] 1 WLR 1037).

The case of *Punton v Ministry of Pensions and National Insurance (No. 2)* [1964] 1 WLR 226, illustrates a couple of points about the scope of the declaration. The public law defect in this case was an error of law on the face of the record. A declaration would be of no assistance because such an error is within jurisdiction and it could not remove the error. Only certiorari or a successful appeal under the statutory procedure could change the decision. The better course would have been to appeal under the statutory procedure. It has been suggested that *Punton* is not a well-founded decision (Cane 1980). It should be recalled that in an application for judicial review an applicant can change the remedy sought so that a switch may be made from a declaration to certiorari.

The Law Commission (1994, paras 8.12, 8.14) has recommended that the courts should be able to grant advisory declarations where there is no decision to be impugned, with the safeguard that the point concerned must be of general public importance.

17.4 DISCRETIONARY NATURE OF THE REMEDIES

All of the public law remedies are discretionary, so that it is possible for an applicant to show that a public law wrong did occur but still be denied relief. The court may take the view that the motives of the applicant were suspect, as in *R v Commissioners of Customs and Excise, ex parte Cook* [1970] 1 WLR 450, where it appeared that the applicants wished to force competitors out of business. In a case involving a dispute between local authorities, the court inferred that making political capital was a motive (*R* v *Greater London Council, ex parte Royal Borough of Kensington and Chelsea* (1982) *The Times*, 7 April 1982).

The court may disapprove of the behaviour of the applicant. Students are not a group who usually gain the beneficial exercise of judicial discretion. There is a group of cases in which students successfully alleged breaches of natural justice, but no remedy was given. In two of these cases the courts took a dim view of the disciplinary offences of (a) a female student sharing a room in a hall of residence with a man (*Ward* v *Bradford Corporation* (1971) 70 LGR 27), and (b) nude sunbathing (*Glynn* v *Keele University* [1971] 1 WLR 487). In *Ward* v *Bradford Corporation* there seemed to be a clear case of a body being prosecutor and judge (contrast the comparable case of *Hannam* v *Bradford Corporation* [1970] 1 WLR 937 which was not cited in *Ward* v *Bradford Corporation*). It seems that the court disapproved of the student's conduct. In *Glynn* v *Keele University* the court said that the absence of a hearing only deprived the student of the chance to make a plea in mitigation. In other words to grant the remedy would be a useless formality.

The legislation requires the courts to consider if the grant of relief in an application for judicial review would be detrimental to good administration (Supreme Court Act 1981, s. 31(6)). This is clearly a broad ground. Some indication of what it might mean is given by Donaldson MR in *R* v *Monopolies and Mergers Commission, ex parte Argyll Group plc* [1986] 1 WLR 763, when he discussed the requirement that the court should have 'a proper awareness of the needs of public administration'. The case concerned the decision to set aside a reference to the Commission, which was made solely by its chairman and held to be unlawful by the court. According to the Master of the Rolls good administration is concerned with substance not with form and it seemed that the decision would have been the same if the matter had come before the whole Commission. Speed is another important consideration. To grant relief would be to delay matters. The general public interest could be safeguarded by the minister and he had consented to the decision. As for the interest of the applicant in this process, it was of a commercial nature which was not the purpose of this particular administrative process. Good administration is always served by finality. The financial market had been entitled to rely on the decision and there was no compelling reason to prolong the uncertainty.

The Master of the Rolls there engaged in what amounted to a cost-benefit calculation. In another case the cost of requiring a meeting to be reconvened and to vote again on resolutions thereby causing financial problems, outweighed the benefit to be gained (*R* v *Brent Health Authority, ex parte Francis* [1985] QB 869). The claim that financial problems would follow if relief was granted failed to convince the court in *R* v *Hillingdon Health Authority, ex parte Goodwin* [1984] ICR 800.

17.4.1 Alternative Remedies

A major consideration in the exercise of judicial discretion is the availability of an alternative remedy. One test was whether the alternative remedy was as effective as judicial review. This test was applied in a planning case where there was the alternative of a statutory appeal to the minister whose decision could be subject to a statutory application to quash (*R* v *Hillingdon London Borough Council, ex parte Royco Homes Ltd* [1974] QB 720). This system would usually be preferable as all issues could be considered by the minister on appeal. Review would only deal with questions of law. Lord Widgery CJ identified a proper case for judicial review 'as being a case where the decision in question is liable to be upset as a matter of law because on its face it is clearly made without jurisdiction or made in consequence of an error of law'. Thus questions of law are more suited to review, especially if an important point of law is at issue (*R* v *Huntingdon District Council, ex parte Cowan* [1984] 1 WLR 501). Conversely if the matter is one which involves facts, or its subject-matter is better considered by a specialist body, then the alternative remedy will be preferred (*R* v *Inland Revenue Commissioners, ex parte Preston* [1985] AC 835).

Lord Widgery CJ in *R* v *Hillingdon London Borough Council, ex parte Royco Homes Ltd* felt that judicial review was quicker than the alternative remedy. Speed was a factor in a police disciplinary case, in which it was held that the delay in that procedure, which had been initiated, justified seeking judicial review (*R* v *Chief Constable of the Merseyside Police, ex parte Calveley* [1986] QB 424).

If the alternative remedy is not a true remedy, as in the possibility of a prisoner petitioning the Home Secretary, who could not quash the governor's decision, then it is not an alternative (*Leech* v *Deputy Governor of Parkhurst Prison* [1988] AC 533).

An analysis (Collar 1991) suggests that there is a trend in the case law of the courts becoming stricter and requiring that alternative remedies be exhausted. Two types of policy considerations are identified: external and internal. External policy considerations refer to the desire of the courts to respect Parliamentary intention in allocating matters to particular bodies. Internal policy factors include the point that an advantage of the application of judicial review is that it is quick. If the volume of cases is increased then the benefit of speed is lost and judicial resources are misapplied. Collar suggests that in a highly political topic such as immigration both the internal and external policy considerations may explain the decision in *R* v *Secretary of State for the Home Department, ex parte Swati* [1986] 1 WLR 477, where the immigrant could only exercise the appeal outside the country. The number of immigration applications for judicial review did decline after that decision. It is also the case that homeless person cases used to comprise a significant number of judicial review applications but the House of Lords 'shut the door' to such applicants in *Puhlhofer* v *Hillingdon London Borough Council* [1986] AC 484, despite there being no alternative remedy.

The Law Commission (1994, para. 5.35) proposes that normally an application for judicial review should not proceed to a substantive hearing unless the applicant has exhausted all alternative legal remedies or demonstrates that, despite the existence of such a remedy, judicial review is an appropriate procedure. Accordingly the pursuit of an alternative remedy is a factor which a court can take into account when faced with an application which was made after the three-month time-limit.

17.5 EXCLUSION OF REVIEW

Parliament is sovereign. The courts will obey Parliament. Therefore legislation which excludes the courts from reviewing decisions of administrative authorities will be obeyed. The foregoing syllogism may be logical but it is not the law. This is not to say that the courts will never give effect to legislative attempts to immunise an administrative authority from judicial review, nor that Parliament will always try to oust the review jurisdiction of the courts.

Traditionally the courts have not been willing to deny citizens recourse to the courts. Legislation which has included phrases such as 'any decision on a claim or question . . . shall be final' has not been interpreted as an effective exclusion of judicial review. Denning LJ construed such a clause in *R v Medical Appeal Tribunal, ex parte Gilmore* [1957] 1 QB 574 at p. 583:

> . . . I find it very well settled that the remedy by certiorari is never to be taken away by any statute except by the most clear and explicit words. The word 'final' is not enough. That only means 'without appeal'. It does not mean 'without recourse to certiorari'. It makes the decision final on the facts, but not final on the law. Notwithstanding that the decision is by a statute made 'final' certiorari can still issue for excess of jurisdiction or for error of law on the face of the record.

This decision should be contrasted with a House of Lords ruling which held that the clause 'shall not be questioned in any legal proceedings whatsoever' would defeat a plaintiff seeking a declaration that a compulsory purchase order had been obtained through fraud (*Smith v East Elloe Rural District Council* [1956] AC 736). The legislation, the Acquisition of Land (Authorisation Procedure) Act 1946, provided for a challenge in the High Court within a six-week period, after which the clause ousted or excluded the jurisdiction of the courts. The action for the declaration was brought some five years after the order had been confirmed.

The Franks Committee (1957) had criticised the exclusion of the prerogative orders with respect to some tribunals, and the Tribunals and Inquiries Act 1958, s. 11(1), provided that any provision in legislation enacted before 1 August 1958 which sought to exclude the High Court should not prevent removal of proceedings to the High Court by an order of certiorari, or prejudice the powers of the High Court to make orders of mandamus. Exceptions were made to this in subsection (3) which dealt with circumstances in which a statute made provision for application to the High Court within a specified period, and determinations of the Foreign Compensation Commission. This provision seemed to approve of the decision in *R v Medical Appeal Tribunal, ex parte Gilmore* and *Smith v East Elloe Rural District Council*, and the scope of legislative limitation upon review was reduced.

The decision of the House of Lords in *Anisminic Ltd* v *Foreign Compensation Commission* [1969] 2 AC 147, evaded the attempt in two legislative provisions (Foreign Compensation Act 1950, s. 4(4); Tribunals and Inquiries Act 1958, s. 11(3)) to immunise the Commission from review. The House of Lords held that the Commission had made an error of law in asking if the successor in title of the applicant was a British national. This error went to the jurisdiction of the Commission. Such a fundamental error meant that the Commission's determination was a nullity. Since it was a nullity, there was no determination which was not to be questioned in a court of law. Lord Reid said, 'if one seeks to show that the determination is a nullity one is not questioning the purported determination – one is maintaining that it does not exist as a determination'.

If the courts had evaded one of the exceptions in the Tribunals and Inquiries Act 1958, would they also ignore the exception relating to a provision which limited judicial consideration to an application to the High Court within a specified period? This question arose in *R* v *Secretary of State for the Environment, ex parte Ostler* [1977] QB 122. The situation was similar to that in *Smith* v *East Elloe Rural District Council* in that a plaintiff sought to challenge a compulsory purchase order some 18 months after it had been confirmed. The basis for the challenge was that a secret agreement between an official and another person had only just been revealed thus preventing an earlier objection. The period in which an application could be made to the High Court was six weeks. The applicant argued that *Anisminic* prevailed over the ouster clause and the *East Elloe* decision. The claim failed. The Court of Appeal pointed out significant differences between *Anisminic* and *East Elloe*. The Commission's determination could be characterised as judicial, whereas the minister's confirmation of the compulsory purchase order is an administrative act. In *Anisminic* there was a fundamental error which deprived the Commission of jurisdiction but in *East Elloe* the minister's action was within jurisdiction, the point was that fraud was alleged to have procured the order. In *Anisminic* there was a total ouster of the courts, but in *East Elloe* it was partial, as there was a six-week period in which an application could be made to the High Court.

The attempt in *Ostler* to find reasons of principle underlying the differences between *Anisminic* and *East Elloe* is, it is suggested, not very convincing. Pragmatism provides a better explanation. The fact was that the road works scheme, which was the reason for the compulsory purchase, had begun. This was a case in which administrative certainty and convenience prevailed over injustice to an individual caused by possible administrative illegality.

Mr Ostler subsequently complained to the Parliamentary Commissioner for Administration who found that justice had not been seen to be done. The department made an *ex gratia* payment which covered the reasonable costs in going to the Court of Appeal and also acquired Mr Ostler's land paying the proper compensation.

In *R* v *Cornwall County Council, ex parte Huntington* [1994] 1 All ER 694, a partial ouster under the Wildlife and Countryside Act 1981 was upheld by the Court of Appeal based upon *Ostler* and the construction of the legislation.

The position regarding statutory exclusion of review seems to be a truce between the courts and Parliament based on the tribunals and inquiries legislation, now the Tribunals and Inquiries Act 1992 (s. 12). Thus Parliament concedes the amendment of the earlier ouster clauses, and the courts accept that where there is provision for a challenge, then its time-limit exclusion will be respected. The Foreign Compensation Act 1969 was passed after *Anisminic Ltd* v *Foreign Compensation Commission* and it provides that the Court of Appeal can consider questions of law on the Commission's determinations but apart from that and issues of natural justice, the Commission's determinations, including purported determinations, should not be questioned in a court of law. This truce does not preclude Parliament from enacting total ouster clauses. One example was in the Interception of Communications Act 1985. Determinations of the tribunal 'shall not be subject to appeal or liable to be questioned in any court' (s. 7(8)). This might not be immune from an *Anisminic*-type attack. It is unlikely, however, that the courts would defy Parliament over this provision, bearing in mind that matters of national security could be involved.

17.6 CONCLUSIONS

The Law Commission has produced a report which, within its limits of improving the framework for judicial review and statutory appeals, is commendable (see Gordon 1995). There is, however, a much wider aspect to this which requires us to look at the whole *system* of administrative justice, recognising that the courts deal with only a small number of citizens' grievances (see Cane 1993 on the Commission's 1993 Consultation Paper). Indeed there was a perception that a concern which prompted the Law Commission's work here was one of managing the increasing volume of judicial review cases. The empirical research carried out by Sunkin et 'al. (1995) has shown that two areas, homeless persons and immigration, account for the majority of applications for judicial review. The Law Commission has taken this into account and has recommended that there should be an appeal on a point of law to a tribunal or court in homelessness cases (1994, paras 2.26–27).

This point and other Law Commission recommendations (including leave or preliminary consideration and standing) were endorsed in Lord Woolf 's report *Access to Civil Justice* which had a chapter on judicial review (1996, pp. 250–59). In general, Lord Woolf preferred litigation to be a matter of last resort and this was also true for judicial review. He wished to see claimants use alternative dispute resolution methods and in public law this included the various Ombudsmen. He wished to see an exchange of cases between the Ombudsmen and the courts so that, for example, a case might start off with an Ombudsman but then be referred to the courts for the determination of a legal issue. Accordingly he was happy that the Local Ombudsmen were using their discretion to accept cases for investigation which could be remedied in the courts. Lord Woolf first made this point in his Hamlyn Lectures (1990, p. 90–1) and it may be that his decision *R* v *Commissioner for Local*

Administration, ex parte Croydon London Borough Council [1989] 1 All ER 1033, was an example of a situation in which it was unfortunate that there is a lack of flexibility between the courts and the Ombudsmen (see 15.3.3.3).

Lord Woolf also recommended that some judicial review cases could be determined outside London and proposed an experiment. He also thought that some cases, with the agreement of the parties, might be determined without a hearing.

The data collected and analysed by Sunkin et al. (1995, p. 197) also indicate that some public bodies appear to be using applications for judicial review as a way of deciding which complaints they will treat seriously. So that if leave is granted then there may be a resolution of the matter which is satisfactory to the complainant which leads to the case being withdrawn. This is not surprising as it is what happens with civil litigation, but given the findings on the somewhat arbitrary nature of determinations for leave, one wonders if the recommendations for leave or preliminary consideration will improve matters. Perhaps they will as they reflect many of the suggestions of Le Sueur and Sunkin (1992).

As Cranston observes lawyers' focus upon judicial review diverts them from more fundamental, if less glamorous, mechanisms to redress citizens' grievances (1994, p. 80). Indeed apart from Sunkin's work (1987, 1991, 1995) we know very little about judicial review in action. More of this type of research must be carried out but it must be integrated with the rest of the administrative justice system. The UK requires a programme of work similar to, but more extensive than, that conducted in Australia which began with the appointment of the Commonwealth Administrative Review Committee (see Cane 1993, p. 895) rather than the predominantly court-focused Justice-All Souls project (1988) which was, unfortunately, a wasted opportunity (McAuslan 1988).

CHAPTER EIGHTEEN
Liability of The Crown and Public Authorities

18.1 GENERAL PRINCIPLES

It is, perhaps, still correct to state that the starting-point for a consideration of the liability of the Crown and other public authorities is that the general principles are the same as for private individuals and companies. Whilst there are some differences, there has not, for example, been a development of an entirely separate set of principles for contracts involving public authorities, as is the case in France.

There are good reasons why public bodies should be treated differently. They have been given tasks to do and these public responsibilities may justify the imposition of a narrower range of liability than would apply to a private individual. On the other hand, such is the power of government, especially in contractual matters, that it might be appropriate to create protection for citizens in their relations with government.

The Crown's position is still quite special. The maxim that 'the King can do no wrong' expanded from the personal immunity of the sovereign to the actions of central government, which is composed of Crown servants whether they be ministers or officials. This protective barrier surrounding central government was not uniform. It was, for example, stronger in tort than in contract. It was possible to seek redress for an alleged breach of contract by means of a petition of right. The individual as a subject petitioned the sovereign to do right in the matter. The sovereign would permit the matter to be heard in the courts and, as an exercise of grace and favour, the court's declaration of the rights of the parties would be respected. The route to the court was regulated by the Attorney-General who determined whether or not consent would be given to the bringing of the petition. This practice was formalised by the Petition of Right Act 1860.

As it was clear that there was no bar to the personal liability of Crown servants for infringements of rights (*Entick* v *Carrington* (1765) 19 St Tr 1030), the Crown agreed to pay, *ex gratia*, any damages awarded against the defendant Crown servant. The practice developed that a person would be nominated by a department as the defendant in an action. Such a nominee might not have had any connection at all with the alleged tort. Judicial disapproval of this 'palpable fiction' (*Adams* v *Naylor* [1946] AC 543) led to a reconsideration of the issue which produced the Crown Proceedings Act 1947. This statute provided that where claims could previously have been pursued by a petition of right, they could now be taken as of right to the courts. For some aspects of tortious liability the Crown was placed in the position of a 'private person of full age and capacity'. Fuller discussion of the statute now follows in 18.2 and 18.3 dealing with liability in tort and contract.

18.2 TORT

18.2.1 Liability

18.2.1.1 The Crown Under the Crown Proceedings Act 1947, s. 2(1), the Crown is made liable for (a) torts committed by its servants or agents (vicarious liability); (b) breaches of its duty to employees or agents (employer's liability); and (c) breaches of duty owed by occupiers of property (occupier's liability).

Where a statutory duty binds both other persons and the Crown then liability for a breach of such a duty is imposed upon the Crown (s. 2(2)). The range of Crown employees for which the Crown may be vicariously liable includes those who have been appointed directly or indirectly by the Crown and who are paid for their Crown employment out of the Consolidated Fund, or money provided by Parliament, or a fund certified by the Treasury (s. 2(6)). There is no Crown liability for action of a judicial nature taken by officers of the Crown (s. 2(5)).

The major exclusion from the 1947 statute was the armed forces. Section 10 provided that neither the Crown nor a member of the armed forces would be liable for death or personal injury caused by acts or omissions of a member of the armed forces while on duty, if the deceased or injured person was also a member of the armed forces on duty, or was on land, premises, ships, aircraft or in vehicles used for the purposes of the armed forces and if the injury was certified by the Secretary of State as attributable to service for entitlement to a pension. This exclusion was regarded as unfair, especially as it operated even if a pension was not awarded (*Adams* v *War Office* [1955] 1 WLR 1116). The government cooperated in the passage of a private member's Bill which reformed the situation. The Crown Proceedings (Armed Forces) Act 1987 repealed s. 10 of the 1947 statute but not with retrospective effect and it was also provided that it could be revived by the Secretary of State if it was expedient to do so because of imminent national danger, or great emergency, or warlike preparations outside the UK. This reviving power was not used during the period of the preparations for, and the conduct of, the United Nations action to expel Iraq from Kuwait in 1990–91.

18.2.1.2 Liability of public authorities Unlike the Crown, public authorities never had immunity in tort. While the vicarious liability of the Crown for the torts of its employees was only formally recognised in the Crown Proceedings Act 1947, the courts had decided that vicarious liability applied to public authorities (*Mersey Docks and Harbour Board Trustees* v *Gibbs* (1866) LR 1 HL 93). Vicarious liability only occurs where the employee's tort arose out of and in the course of the employment. A disapproved method of carrying out the employment may be within the scope of vicarious liability (*Limpus* v *London General Omnibus Co. Ltd* (1862) 1 Hurl & C 526), however, it must be shown that the prohibited act was done for the employer's purposes (*Rose* v *Plenty* [1976] 1 WLR 141). Since the introduction of the Police Act 1964, s. 48, a chief constable may be vicariously liable for the torts of police officers, and where a plaintiff is successful in an action, the damages are paid out of the police force's funds.

18.2.2 Statutory Authority Defence

This defence applies particularly in the context of the tort of nuisance. This tort seeks to balance the uses to which land may be put with the enjoyment of property. Major construction works can be a nuisance to a neighbouring landowner, as can, for example, the operation of a railway. If something has been authorised by legislation and this inevitably means that there will be interference with private rights, then the courts will hold that the statutory authorisation will constitute a good defence. Thus in *Allen* v *Gulf Oil Refining Ltd* [1981] AC 101, a local Act of Parliament which provided for the construction of an oil refinery at Milford Haven, was held to be a good defence even though the Act did not expressly empower the company to build and operate the refinery or define the site. This may be contrasted with *Metropolitan Asylum District* v *Hill* (1881) 6 App Cas 193, in which hospital trustees were authorised to build hospitals. An action brought against the trustees in respect of the alleged nuisance caused by the construction of a smallpox hospital in Hampstead was successful because the court held that the legislation only authorised the building of hospitals, leaving the trustees a discretion which must be exercised in a manner respecting private rights. The hospital was not required by the legislation to be on that particular site. Therefore it could have been located in a place which would not have created a nuisance.

If the injury caused by the authorised project is not inevitable then it is not protected by the authorisation. In *Manchester Corporation* v *Farnworth* [1930] AC 171, the defendants were authorised to construct an electricity generating station on a particular site. They could not show that the inevitable result would be the particular fumes which were emitted from the station, as they had not established that they had done all that was reasonable to reduce the fumes.

Clearly, the wording of the statute is crucial. Some statutes will stipulate that there will be no exoneration for nuisance caused by the works, but this will not prevail if it can be shown that there is a duty to execute those works (*Department of Transport* v *North West Water Authority* [1984] AC 336). Some legislation does provide for compensation, for example, the Land Compensation Act 1973.

18.2.3 Negligence

The defence of statutory authorisation does not apply if the work has been negligently conducted. The relationship of the tort of negligence with statutory powers is complicated. The law seeks to draw a line between those circumstances in which it is, and is not, appropriate to declare that a duty of care is owed by one person to another. The fact that a public authority exercising its statutory powers is involved is another factor to be taken into account in drawing this line. Matters are further complicated where the public authority is exercising a statutory discretionary power. In administrative law the courts may only interfere with such actions where they are *ultra vires* (see generally chapter 16). Would it be correct to allow the courts to interfere more extensively with an authority's exercise of such discretion in a private law action? In *Dorset Yacht Co. Ltd* v *Home Office* [1970] AC 1004, and *Anns* v *Merton London Borough Council* [1978] AC 728, it was established that a precondition for liability in a negligent exercise of statutory powers, was a finding that this exercise was *ultra vires*. In *Anns* reference was made to a distinction between policy or planning decisions and operational matters. The issue in the case was whether the authority, which had powers to inspect buildings, had (a) negligently failed to inspect or (b) negligently inspected the foundations of a building which subsequently exhibited structural damage. It was held that the taking of decisions about inspections involved discretion and this policy decision could be attacked only upon public law grounds, thereby protecting the statutory discretion. If it appeared that the actual inspection was negligent, then this operation would be governed by principles relating to negligence. One might say that a negligent exercise of an operational matter under a statutory power is itself *ultra vires* as the legislation would not usually permit the authority to be negligent.

The distinction between policy and operations has been subject to criticism (for a summary see Cane 1996, pp. 250–5). It has also been doubted by Lord Keith in *Rowling* v *Takaro Properties Ltd* [1988] AC 473 at p. 501, as the touchstone of liability. He took the view that the important point was that some questions on whether decisions were taken negligently were not suitable for judicial resolution. Examples of such decisions were those relating to the allocation of scarce resources or the distribution of risks. If such a policy decision was to be excluded from liability in negligence, this did not mean that an operational matter could automatically give rise to a duty of care.

In *Caparo Industries plc* v *Dickman* [1990] 2 AC 605, the factors relevant to the establishment of a duty of care were listed as foreseeability of damage, proximity of relationship between the parties, and that it was just and reasonable to impose the duty. It is easier to show that it may be foreseeable that the action or omission of a public authority could cause harm to an individual, than it is to establish the necessary degree of proximity or that the imposition of a duty is just and reasonable. The case of *Hill* v *Chief Constable of West Yorkshire* [1989] AC 53, illustrates several reasons which may lead to the denial of a duty of care. There was insufficent proximity for the police to owe a duty of care to a member of the public when the police were searching for a criminal. Secondly, it would be counter-productive for the police to have the possibility of a negligence action in relation to their investigation of crime, in that it might induce defensive practices. Thirdly, there was the possibility of another source of compensation for victims of crime – the Criminal Injuries Compensation Scheme (see also *Jones* v *Department of Employment* [1989] QB 1, in which it was held that no duty of care is owed in determining a claim for unemployment benefit as there is a right of statutory appeal). The courts will examine carefully the legislation under which the authority operates in order to determine if the imposition of a duty of care is appropriate. In *Curran* v *Northern Ireland Co-ownership Housing Association Ltd* [1987] AC 718, and *Yuen Kun Yeu* v *Attorney-General of Hong Kong* [1988] AC 175, it was held that the defendant public authorities were not intended to protect individuals from losses, and additionally that negligence for omissions, whether by public authorities or others, will be restricted (see Jones 1996, pp. 67–73).

In *X* v *Bedfordshire County Council* [1995] 2 AC 633, Lord Browne-Wilkinson sought to provide guidance on the third requirement for a duty of care, that it is just and reasonable. Is the imposition of a duty of care compatible with the statute? Was the discretion exercised unreasonably in the *Wednesbury* sense, and if it had been, would this lead the court, in deciding if there was breach, into considering non-justiciable issues? In *X* v *Bedfordshire County Council* the authority's social services department and its child abuse responsibilities were at issue. It was held the imposition of a duty of care would 'cut across the whole statutory system set up for the protection of children at risk'. It is not entirely clear what is meant by non-justiciable, as policy matters, or decisions on use of resources, are not always regarded as non-justiciable (see, e.g., *R* v *Sefton Metropolitan Borough Council, ex parte Help the Aged* (CA July 1997) on duties of a local authority towards the elderly).

18.2.4 Breach of Statutory Duty

An action for a breach of statutory duty is different from an action alleging negligent exercise of statutory powers. In statutory duty proceedings the court examines to discover if the breach of such a duty can properly found an action. Sometimes the legislation will expressly state whether or not a breach will be actionable (Nuclear Installations Act 1965 – yes; Guard Dogs Act 1975 – no). Generally the legislation is silent on the matter and the courts will have to divine the will of Parliament. If a penalty is provided for in the statute this will usually preclude a civil action. In *Atkinson* v *Newcastle and Gateshead Waterworks Co.* (1877) 2 ExD 441, the plaintiff sued the water-works company for fire damage as it had not maintained the water supply to the proper pressure. As the Waterworks Clauses Act 1847 stipulated a £10 fine for such a failure, this defeated the plaintiff's claim. Contrast that case with an action alleging a breach of a different duty under the same statute, the provision of a supply of pure and wholesome water (*Read* v *Croydon Corporation* [1938] 4 All ER 631). In this case the plaintiff was successful despite the stipulation of a penalty. Stable J distinguished the earlier case on the basis that the maintenance of water pressure was for the benefit of the community whereas the supply of pure water was a matter which affected each householder individually. Various factors can help to explain these conflicting decisions. One is that it is too much to expect the waterworks company to act, in effect, as an insurer against fire damage, as that could easily be done by occupiers of property, however, it would be more appropriate for the company rather than householders to insure against contracting typhoid (Jones 1996, p. 360). This would appear to fit in with some dicta which allow for exceptions to the general rule that if there is a specified means of enforcing performance then a civil action is not permitted. Lord Diplock in *Lonrho Ltd* v *Shell Petroleum Co. Ltd (No. 2)* [1982] AC 173, stated these exceptions to be (a) where an obligation was imposed for the benefit or protection of a particular class of individuals; and (b) when an individual member of the public sustains particular damage to a statutory right. Matters are somewhat complicated because there are cases in which the prescribed remedy is held to be inadequate (*Groves* v *Lord Wimborne* [1898] 2 QB 402). This tends to occur in cases dealing with industrial safety legislation, and it could be argued that employees are the particular group who are meant to be protected by such legislation. In another case the statutory enforcement was sidestepped as the action was an application for mandamus and Veale J said that an action would lie where there was no penalty for the breach (*Refell* v *Surrey County Council* [1964] 1 WLR 358 which concerned an education authority's duty in relation to safety of students at its schools).

If there are existing remedies then they may preclude a civil action (*Phillips* v *Britannia Hygienic Laundry Co.* [1923] 2 KB 832).

The Crown will only be liable for breach of statutory duty if the duty is binding on others. Usually the Crown will have immunity as it is not bound by legislation except by express words or necessary implication (see 5.4.2). This common law position was maintained by the Crown Proceedings Act 1947, s. 40(2)(f).

18.2.5 Misfeasance in Public Office

Misfeasance in public office is a tort which is confined to public officers, so it may be described as a public law tort. The definition of the tort is quite restrictive and, like the bad faith ground of judicial review, it will rarely be available (see 16.5.3). The tort consists either of a person discharging powers of public office maliciously so as to inflict damage upon another, or knowing both that an act will harm another and that there is no lawful power to carry out that act (*Bourgoin SA* v *Ministry of Agriculture, Fisheries and Food* [1986] QB 716). It will be very difficult to establish malice, and it can be just as difficult to show that a public officer knew that an act was *ultra vires*.

It seems that it would be possible for a minister to be vicariously liable for the malicious actions of an official so long as those actions can be regarded as improper modes of carrying out acts authorised by the minister (*Racz* v *Home Office* [1994] 2 AC 45, acts of a prison officer).

As this liability has a higher test than 'serious breach' it is not to be used in EU member State liability cases (*Francovich* v *Italy* (cases C-6 & 9/90) [1991] ECR I-5357; see 9.4.4.3).

18.3 CONTRACT

18.3.1 Capacity to Contract

The Crown has a greater capacity to contract than have public authorities, such as councils, which have been created by legislation. Such bodies are restricted to their statutory purposes. Legislation has narrowed the objectives which councils and other bodies may seek by use of contract. Powers of contract may not be exercised by reference to non-commercial grounds (Local Government Act 1988, s. 17, but s. 18 permits councils to promote good race relations).

The seeking of collateral objectives by governmental bodies through the use of contract was formerly more extensive. One example which lasted from 1891 until 1983 was the Fair Wages Resolutions. These were resolutions of the House of Commons, the purpose of which was to include a term in central government contracts requiring the contractor to pay a minimum wage to employees. One controversial example of the use of government contracting power to implement government policy was the threat to blacklist companies from those approved to tender for contracts if they did not conform to a non-statutory wages policy which sought to limit pay increases (see Daintith 1979, 1994).

Contract continues to play a major part in government policy. The current aim is to improve value for money which is being pursued by the programme of securing the delivery of a greater proportion of services by the private sector. This takes the form of compulsory competitive tendering by local authorities (see 10.8.1), and market testing by central government (see 6.3.4.3; see generally on the increasing use of contract as a public law device Harden 1992).

18.3.2 Governmental Effectiveness

One of the differences between private contracts and government contracts is that governmental bodies must not act in a way which can impair the discharge of their tasks.

18.3.2.1 Legislation As we have seen (16.4.2) bodies which have had discretionary power conferred by statute are not permitted to fetter their exercise of it by making agreements which have the effect of binding them to act in a particular way, for example, *Stringer* v *Minister of Housing and Local Government* [1970] 1 WLR 1281, in which the planning authority had agreed to exercise its planning powers so as to protect the Jodrell Bank radio telescope). Commercial contracts tend not to fall foul of this restriction but only if the authority's statutory purposes are not prejudiced. The test for this is one of incompatibility (*R* v *Inhabitants of Leake* (1833) 5 B & Ad 469). This was strictly applied in *Ayr Harbour Trustees* v *Oswald* (1883) 8 App Cas 623, thereby invalidating an agreement with the former owner of a compulsorily acquired site not to construct works on it in a way which would adversely affect other land owned by that person. This should be contrasted with *Birkdale District Electric Supply Co. Ltd* v *Southport Corporation* [1926] AC 355, in which the electricity company was held to its contract to supply electricity at a price lower than the statutory maximum. The House of Lords held that this was a matter of commercial judgment. This case was endorsed in *British Transport Commission* v *Westmorland County Council* [1958] AC 126 and their lordships referred to reasonable foreseeability as the appropriate test to determine any incompatibility with statutory purposes.

18.3.2.2 Common law The exercise of the power to contract is not permitted to impair the Crown's exercise of its common law powers. An important, if not entirely clear, case on this point is *Rederiaktiebolaget Amphitrite* v *The King* [1921] 3 KB 500. The facts were that Swedish shipowners sought assurances that their ship would not be seized on reaching its British destination during the First World War. Assurances had been sought from the British legation in Stockholm and, in the belief that these had been given, the ship set sail. In an action following the seizure of the ship at its British destination, the trial judge appeared to hold that there was no contract as there had been no intention to create legal relations. Rowlatt J said that the undertaking had been no more than 'an expression of intention to act in a particular way in a certain event'. The government 'cannot by contract hamper its freedom of action in matters which concern the welfare of the State' (at p. 503).

How wide is this principle? The wartime context of the case and the unusual nature of the undertaking given on behalf of the Crown would indicate that the scope is not that wide. This would appear to be backed up by the use of the phrase 'welfare of the State'.

Not only can this rule of public policy deprive of legal effect a purported contract which would fetter the Crown, but it can also override a provision in an otherwise valid contract. In *Commissioners of Crown Lands* v *Page* [1960] 2 QB 274, the commissioners had leased premises to the defendant. A minister acting under statutory authority requisitioned the premises and took possession. When the commissioners sued for rent the defendant claimed that the lease had an implied covenant of quiet enjoyment which had been breached by the exercise of the requisitioning power. This argument was rejected as the 'Crown's future proper exercise of its powers and duties under statute' could not be limited (per Lord Evershed MR at p. 287). Devlin LJ was of the view that even if there had been an express covenant of quiet enjoyment, it could not have fettered the Crown in the exercise of its power to requisition.

There is concern that this rule is unjust and unnecessary (Hogg 1971, pp. 129–40). As it invalidates contracts which would fetter the Crown, the other party is deprived of damages for the Crown's breach of the contract. Turpin (1989, p. 90), reports that the usual situation in government contracts is that there is a standard clause which enables the Crown to end the contract in the public interest but permits the other party to obtain some compensation if this happens.

18.3.3 Agency

It is possible for the employees of public authorities to bind their principals, including the Crown, provided that they have actual or ostensible authority.

Ministers will have authority to enter into contracts and so may officials but this will depend upon the organisation within a department, its rules, delegations of responsibility and practices. If an official acts outside actual authority then the principal will not be bound unless it can be shown that there was ostensible authority. By this is meant that the principal has by words or conduct represented that the agent has the necessary authority to contract and the other party has entered into a contract with the agent on the basis of that representation. This may arise because the agent has been placed in a position where it is reasonable for outsiders to regard the agent as having authority to enter into the transactions. Ostensible authority could also arise from a course of dealing between a contractor and the agent where the principal has acquiesced to this and honoured the transactions. If, however, the contractor knows that the agent's authority does not cover the particular transaction then there cannot be reliance upon any contrary representation by the principal (*Armagas Ltd* v *Mundogas SA* [1986] AC 717 per Lord Keith of Kinkel at p. 777). Turpin suggests that ostensible authority can be invoked against the Crown and cites a Canadian case, *J. E. Verreau et Fils Ltée* v *Attorney-General for Quebec* (1976) 57 DLR (3d) 403. A Privy Council decision seems to imply that it is possible for an agent of the Crown to have ostensible authority, even though the agent was not found to have it. In *Attorney-General of Ceylon* v *Silva* [1953] AC 461, the authority of the Collector of Customs to offer goods for sale at an auction was at issue. The Collector became aware after the auction that some goods had already been included in a contract. The buyer at the auction sued for breach of contract when the Collector refused to deliver the goods. It was held that the Customs Ordinance provision for sale did not bind the Crown. The argument that, as a public officer, the Collector could act on behalf of the Crown in Crown matters was rejected, as such a right had to be expressly conferred by statute or otherwise. The court also held that the Collector had no ostensible authority. An agent who had no authority to act in a particular matter could not make a representation binding upon the principal that such authority had been conferred. Only the principal could do this (see further estoppel 18.4).

Normally a person may have an action against an agent for breach of warranty where the agent has wrongfully claimed authority to enter into contracts on the principal's behalf. This is not the case with an agent of the Crown (*Dunn* v *Macdonald* [1897] 1 QB 401).

18.3.4 The Crown
The position of the Crown in contract is special in a couple of respects. We have already seen that employees of the Crown are, at common law, dismissable at pleasure (see 6.2.3). In fact, and in law, such employees have much greater job security than this formal position would suggest. The Employment Protection (Consolidation) Act 1978 applies the legislation on unfair dismissal and recourse to industrial tribunals to Crown employees. The legislation does not apply to the armed forces (s. 138), and it is possible for others to be denied this protection by the issue of a ministerial certificate of exclusion in the interests of national security (s. 138(4)). This was done in

respect of employees at Government Communications Headquarters, Cheltenham, and was challenged unsucessfully due to the non-justiciability of national security (*Council of Civil Service Unions* v *Minister for the Civil Service* [1985] AC 374).

18.3.4.1 Parliamentary spending authority There has been some confusion about the *ratio* of *Churchward* v *R* (1865) LR 1 QB 173, which has been suggested to hold that a contract is invalid if there is no explicit approval of the expenditure by Parliament. The better view of this case seems to be that no such prior aproval is required but that if Parliament specifically excluded a contract from the spending authority of the Appropriation Acts then the contract would be unenforceable (see generally on Parliamentary financial procedures 8.4).

18.3.5 Government Contracting

In delivering services to the public, central and local government will be involved in purchasing goods and engaging the services of personnel. Turpin, the pioneer of studies in the area of government contracting and procurement, notes (1989, p. 10) that the Ministry of Defence is the largest customer of British industry. Despite the large amounts of money involved, the world of the 'procurement community' is one which is generally hidden from view. While the general law of contract applies, there is not much case law on government contracting. This is because of the preference of the parties to these contracts for negotiation over litigation (Turpin 1989a, p. 102). Usually these contracts have an arbitration clause to determine disputes. Resort to arbitration means that decisions are private and do not provide precedents.

There has also been little judicial review in this area, but as the prerogative is, in principle, amenable to review, the situation could change (see Arrowsmith 1990a, 1990b for argument that it could and should).

Procurement is probed by the Public Accounts Committee but the area is so large that its scrutiny can only be episodic (see 8.4.3 and Turpin 1989, ch. 2 and 9).

Government procurement is becoming increasingly regulated under Community law. Measures include (a) the requirement of common advertisement procedures and award criteria; and (b) the prohibition on discrimination against contractors from other member States in the award of contracts (Public Supply Contract Regulations 1991 (SI 1991/2679) and Public Works Contracts Regulations 1991 (SI 1991/2680)).

18.4 ESTOPPEL

Estoppel is a private law doctrine which serves to stop X benefiting from the strict legal rights of a situation where Y, relying upon X's representations, has acted and suffered detriment. There are difficulties in transposing a private law doctrine to a public law context. As public authorities are limited to the powers conferred upon them, they should not be able to increase them by estoppel. On the other hand, an authority should not be prevented from performing its statutory powers and duties because of estoppel (*Maritime Electric Co. Ltd* v *General Dairies Ltd* [1937] AC 610). Can a public authority be estopped by unlawful representations by its officials? This question was answered in *Western Fish Products Ltd* v *Penwith District Council* [1981] 2 All ER 204, where a planning officer indicated that some land had existing use rights. This was relied upon but it was incorrect. Therefore an application for planning permission was required. One was submitted but it was refused and enforcement action was taken against the breaches of planning control. In the ensuing action the court held that the representation by the officer should not stop the planning authority from exercising its statutory duties or powers. There were, however, two exceptions to this general principle. The first was where the person to whom the representation was made could think that the representor had authority to make decisions and that there had been a lawful delegation of power. The court did not give much guidance in setting criteria for the identification of such delegates. The court did say that the seniority of the officer was, by itself, insufficient. There had to be evidence of a practice of delegation of the powers as in *Lever Finance Ltd* v *Westminster (City) London Borough Council* [1971] 1 QB 222. The second exception was where a public authority waived a particular formality, then it was estopped from relying upon the lack of that formality.

These are essentially procedural variations to the *ultra vires* doctrine. This doctrine may be upheld because there are limits to statutory powers and it would be wrong for the courts to permit authorities to act beyond their powers. This has the consequence of allowing an individual to suffer an injustice because that is to be preferred to prejudicing the public interest.

Lord Denning has been consistent in seeking to mitigate the injustice to an individual who has acted upon representations and suffered detriment (see, for example his judgments in *Robertson* v *Minister of Pensions* [1949] 1 KB 227, *Falmouth Boat Construction Co. Ltd* v *Howell* [1950] 2 KB 16, and *Lever Finance Ltd* v *Westminster (City) London Borough Council*). One approach which he has proposed involves what Craig (1977; 1994a, pp. 663–70) terms 'judicial balancing'. In *Laker Airways Ltd* v *Department of Trade* [1977] QB 643 Lord Denning said at p. 707:

> The underlying principle is that the Crown cannot be estopped from exercising its powers . . . when it is doing so in the proper exercise of its duty to act for the public good, even though this may work some injustice or unfairness to the private individual . . . .. It can, however, be estopped when it is not properly exercising its powers, but is misusing them; and it does misuse them if it exercises them in circumstances which work injustice or unfairness to the individual without any countervailing benefit for the public.

There has been an indication that this approach could be used in situations where the decision of the authority is *ultra vires*. In *R* v *Inland Revenue Commissioners, ex parte Preston* [1985] AC 835, there appeared to be an agreement between a tax inspector and a taxpayer, which was ignored some four years later. It was held that the taxpayer could not be allowed to say that the Revenue could bind themselves for the future, but judicial review could restrain the Revenue if their action amounted to an abuse of power. Breach of a representation could amount to an abuse of power and estop the public authority from saying that the representation was *ultra vires*. In *Ex parte Preston* new material had come to light and so there was no abuse of power. The case can be reconciled with legitimate expectation cases in which a change of policy is announced but those affected by it should be permitted to argue why the new policy should not apply as per a representation made when the change was announced (*Attorney-General of Hong Kong* v *Ng Yuen Shiu* [1983] 2 AC 629).

Cane, who thinks that judicial balancing is not to be accepted in cases of *ultra vires* action, suggests that the effect of the balancing approach is to dispense with unlawful acts of public authorities, and this is quite different from saying that an apparently lawful decision is unfair. In other words balancing could undermine the *ultra vires* doctrine, allowing courts greater scope to interfere with the actions of public authorities. Perhaps the way to deal with this problem where an individual suffers from an unlawful act or representation, is by maintaining the *ultra vires* doctrine but compensating the individual. This could be done by conferring rights to an action through legislation or by giving the Parliamentary or Local Government Commissioners jurisdiction to deal with such cases.

18.5   CROWN PROCEEDINGS

The Crown Proceedings Act 1947 imposed a large degree of liability in contract and tort upon the Crown. This affected the government rather than the personal liability of the sovereign (s. 40). Actions are to be brought against the relevant department from a list of authorised departments compiled by the Minister for the Civil Service. If there is doubt about the appropriate department, then the Attorney-General is the defendant.

It has been noted that an injunction is not available against the Crown in the person of the sovereign, but that a declaration can issue (s. 21(1)). If the effect of granting an injunction against a Crown servant or officer would, in effect, give an injunction not available under s. 21(1) then such an injunction cannot be awarded (s. 21(2)). Injunctive relief can be sought against an officer of the Crown in his or her own capacity as, for example, a minister (*Re M* [1994] 1 AC 377). Where damages are awarded against the Crown the department should pay the amount following a specified procedure, otherwise it is not possible to enforce judgment against the Crown (s. 25). Unsurprisingly the Crown can enforce orders made in its favour in the same way as is possible in an action between ordinary litigants (s. 26).

18.6   PUBLIC INTEREST IMMUNITY

In an action each party can, before trial, obtain a list of documents held by the other side which are relevant to the dispute. These documents may then be inspected or copied. This procedure is known as discovery. A party may refuse to disclose something and the court may then be asked to determine what should be disclosed. The criteria for disclosure are that it is necessary for the fair disposal of the case, or because it will save costs (Rules of the Supreme Court 1965, ord. 24). Discovery and the making of interrogatories (the submission of questions to one party by the other which are answered on oath) may be ordered against the Crown (Crown Proceedings Act 1947, s. 28), but the Crown still enjoys an immunity against the production of documents, or the exclusion of oral evidence about the existence of a document where this would be injurious to the public interest. This was formerly known as Crown privilege but is now generally known as public interest immunity. This name change signifies two points: first, that the immunity is not limited to the Crown; and secondly, that it is not a privilege which may be waived. Indeed, it is a matter which, if facts are disclosed upon which it could arise, must be considered (*Air Canada* v *Secretary of State for Trade (No. 2)* [1983] 2 AC 394). According to Bingham LJ, where a document is prima facie immune, the person who possesses the document can waive the immunity only in an exceptional case (*Makanjuola* v *Commissioner of Police of the Metropolis* [1992] 3 All ER 617 at pp. 623–4).

18.6.1 Contents Claims

The immunity from discovery may be claimed on two grounds. The first of these relates to the contents of the documents. In *Duncan* v *Cammell Laird and Co. Ltd* [1942] AC 624, an action was brought against the builders of the submarine *Thetis* in respect of the deaths of sailors who were serving on the vessel when she sank during sea trials in Liverpool Bay. The Admiralty issued a certificate claiming that disclosure of the plans of the *Thetis* would be injurious to the public interest. As the proceedings took place during the Second World War it can be understood why documents relating to national defence should not be ordered to be disclosed. The House of Lords also instanced diplomatic relations as being another area where the contents of documents would not be disclosed where there was a claim about injury to the public interest.

18.6.2 Class Claims

The second type of claim laid down in *Duncan* v *Cammell Laird and Co. Ltd* [1942] AC 624, could be based on a class of documents. The contents of a particular document might not cause harm if revealed but, because the document belonged to a class the disclosure of which could impede the proper functioning of the public service, a successful claim for immunity could be raised. If documents exchanged between ministers, or between ministers and officials, or between officials and the public could be disclosed, then the candour with which views might be expressed would be jeopardised if the person expressing the view thought that it might be read by people other than the intended recipients.

18.6.2.1 Confidentiality This is a major strand in the case law on class claims and is not a separate basis for a claim to public interest immunity. It featured in the first major case in which the judiciary indicated their unhappiness about the use of the term 'Crown privilege' (*Rogers* v *Home Secretary* [1973] AC 388). In this case an unsuccessful applicant to the Gaming Board for a certificate of consent began an action for criminal libel against the Chief Constable of Sussex Police. The chief constable had been consulted by the board as part of its determination of the application for the certificate. The House of Lords held that the chief constable's letter should not be produced as it belonged to a class of documents which should be immune from disclosure. This was because the board, in carrying out its statutory duty, should be able to respect the confidentiality of information submitted to it, otherwise such information might not be provided. An analogy was drawn with the rule of public policy which protected the identity of police informers.

The major step in the development of public interest immunity was *D* v *National Society for the Prevention of Cruelty to Children* [1978] AC 171. This was because the claim for immunity was not made by a minister or an official but by a voluntary organisation. The NSPCC had followed up an allegation that the plaintiff was maltreating her child. The visit by an NSPCC inspector established that the accusation was untrue. The plaintiff decided to sue the NSPCC and sought discovery of documents from which the identity of the maker of the false accusation could be learnt. The NSPCC did not wish to breach the confidentiality between it and its informant, and contended that the public interest could be adversely affected. Although the NSPCC is a private body, it does have the power, granted by statute, to initiate child care proceedings. The House of Lords found in favour of the NSPCC, taking the view that the police informant analogy which had been applied to the statutory Gaming Board could also be extended to the NSPCC. The welfare of children was clearly a matter of public interest.

The status of public body is by itself not enough to justify a claim of public interest immunity. Where the claim of confidentiality related to unlawful discrimination and discovery was sought of personnel records, it was held that the interest at stake was a private one of an employer. Therefore the public body's claim of immunity failed (*Science Research Council* v *Nassé* [1980] AC 1028).

18.6.2.2 Proper functioning of the public service   A restrictive interpretation is provided by *Ellis* v *Home Office* [1953] 2 QB 135, in which a prisoner on remand was attacked by a mentally disturbed patient in the prison hospital. As part of his personal injuries action, the plaintiff sought discovery of medical reports made about the assailant. The Home Office's class claim was successful, although the judges voiced some disquiet about the justice of this state of affairs. This may be contrasted with *Campbell* v *Tameside Metropolitan Borough Council* [1982] QB 1065, in which a teacher was attacked by a pupil. The court held that psychologists' reports which the council had commissioned as part of its statutory responsibilities, should be disclosed as the writers would not thereby be inhibited in making their reports.

In another local authority case, *Gaskin* v *Liverpool City Council* [1980] 1 WLR 1549, it was held that the proper functioning of the child care service required confidentiality for records and so discovery of them was not allowed. Mr Gaskin then successfully petitioned the European Court of Human Rights in Strasbourg for breach of the European Convention on Human Rights, art. 8 (right to respect for private and family life, home and correspondence (*Gaskin* v *United Kingdom* (1989) 12 EHRR 36; see now Access to Personal Files Act 1987).

Cane (1996, pp. 286–7) suggests that the difference between these two local authority cases is that the courts took a sympathetic view to Campbell's action but not to Gaskin's.

Two contrasting decisions involving business documents may now be considered. In *Norwich Pharmacal Co.* v *Customs and Excise Commissioners* [1974] AC 133, the plaintiffs held patents for a chemical. The commissioners had records which could identify firms which had imported the chemical from an undisclosed source in breach of the patents. The plaintiffs wished to identify the importers in order to protect their rights and sought discovery from the commissioners who claimed that the information was confidential and that it had been provided to them under a statutory duty. The court held that even if the records were confidential, the customs service would not be harmed if the names of wrongdoers were disclosed.

The commissioners were also involved in another case in which they had obtained records from third parties in order to determine the correct tax liability in respect of gaming machines. This information had been supplied voluntarily by third parties, although the commissioners could have exercised powers to obtain it. The court upheld the immunity claim stating that while confidentiality alone would not suffice, it was an important consideration in a class claim. The work of the commissioners would be impaired if confidentiality could not be guaranteed to their informants (*Alfred Crompton Amusement Machines Ltd* v *Customs and Excise Commissioners (No. 2)* [1974] AC 405).

Perhaps the distinction between these two cases is that in *Norwich Pharmacal* the plaintiff was seeking to protect a legal right, the patent, and as the information sought had not been supplied on a confidential basis, the interest in the administration of justice outweighed any interest in preventing disclosure (see further on the balancing of these interests 18.6.3).

18.6.2.3 Police matters In a number of cases involving tort actions against the police, material which has come into their possession has been held to be protected from disclosure. In *Neilson* v *Laugharne* [1981] QB 736, the material sought had been originally obtained by the police in the conduct of an investigation into a complaint against the police. The Court of Appeal held that the effectiveness of the statutory police complaints procedure would be impaired if disclosure of those documents was possible (also applied by the majority of the Court of Appeal in *Halford* v *Sharples* [1992] 1 WLR 736, where such documents were sought in the context of a claim alleging unlawful sex discrimination). There is an exception to this general rule where the allegation is of a serious crime committed by the police (*Peach* v *Metropolitan Police Commissioner* [1986] QB 1064).

In *R* v *Chief Constable of the West Midlands Police, ex parte Wiley* [1995] 1 AC 274, the House of Lords ruled that *Neilson* and the cases in which it was subsequently applied should be regarded as having been wrongly decided. Their Lordships did not, however, rule that material which came into being as a result of an investigation into a complaint against the police under the Police and Criminal Evidence Act 1984 could never be entitled to class immunity. The Court of Appeal ruled in *Taylor* v *Anderton* [1995] 2 All ER 420 that reports and working papers produced by officers carrying out an investigation into police conduct under the 1984 Act were entitled to immunity.

It would seem that communications between the police and the Crown Prosecution Service are also protected as disclosure could impair the functioning of the service (*Evans* v *Chief Constable of Surrey* [1988] QB 588).

A very important decision on immunity concerned internal police documents which were reports on a probationer constable (*Conway* v *Rimmer* [1968] AC 910). The officer had been acquitted of a theft charge and then had been dismissed from the police. He brought an action for the tort of malicious prosecution and requested the probation reports and the reports into the investigation of the alleged theft. The House of Lords held that these were routine documents and doubted that candour in them would be adversely affected, which would be the only injury to the public interest.

18.6.3 Judicial Balancing

Duncan v *Cammell Laird and Co. Ltd* [1942] AC 624 was an important case, not only for laying down the types of claim of immunity from discovery, but also because their lordships held that the issue of a certificate claiming immunity was conclusive. The courts would accept the certificate at face value. The combination of judicial deference to the executive, and the potentially very wide class claim caused disquiet. The dicta in *Ellis* v *Home Office* [1953] 2 QB 135, about the unfairness of prison hospital medical reports being kept secret helped to create a climate in which the government felt it prudent to make concessions, undertaking that certain documents would not be the subject of immunity claims.

The judicial dissatisfaction in *Ellis* v *Home Office* also had a basis in decisions in Scots law (*Glasgow Corporation* v *Central Land Board* 1956 SC (HL) 1) and Australian law (*Robinson* v *South Australia (No. 2)* [1931] AC 704). The law lords as the final court of appeal in those jurisdictions had held that the courts had an inherent power to inspect claims of immunity for discovery. In *Conway* v *Rimmer* [1968] AC 910, the House of Lords decided that such a power was also to be found in English common law. The reasoning was that the immunity claim was based on the public interest, however, the public interest had several aspects. Just as there was a public interest in ensuring that documents relating to national defence were not disclosed, so there was also a public interest in the administration of justice. The issue in *Conway* v *Rimmer* posed a conflict between these two aspects of the public interest. Their lordships held that they could balance these competing considerations. It was clear that where a certificate was issued, it would be given great weight. The judges would not say that they were competent to weigh every consideration. Certainly contents claims would rarely be overridden by the judges. If a court was in doubt about a claim for immunity, or minded to overrule it, then it would order the party to provide the documents for judicial inspection. After inspection the court would decide whether or not to order disclosure. If disclosure was ordered, it could be partial, or made on the condition that only the legal advisers and not the party, could read the documents.

This decision seemed to herald a breakthrough but the case law appears to have limited the relaxation. The criterion for discovery is relevance. The courts do not want plaintiffs to use discovery to engage in 'fishing expeditions' in order to determine if they have a good case. Order 24 of the Rules of the Supreme Court 1965 stipulates that the fair disposal of the issue is a guide to the relevance of documents. When presented with an immunity claim the court should determine if the documents properly fall into the ground of claim made and that the appropriate person has considered the matter.

In *Air Canada* v *Secretary of State for Trade* [1983] 2 AC 394, a group of airlines suspected that the raising of landing charges at Heathrow airport by the British Airports Authority (BAA) had been unlawfully instigated by the minister. The minister handed over some documents which had been exchanged between his staff and the BAA, but claimed immunity for documents relating to the formulation of governmental policy on the BAA, the public sector borrowing requirement, and ministerial control of the BAA. In upholding the minister's claims, their lordships were divided over the criterion which should be used to decide whether or not to inspect documents. The majority, comprising Lords Wilberforce, Fraser and Edmund-Davies ruled that it must be reasonably likely that the documents would assist the party seeking discovery, or damage the case of the party opposing disclosure. The minority, Lords Scarman and Templeman, held that the test asks if it is likely that the documents are necessary for the fair disposition of the case.

Where a party knows of some documents, the burden of proof established in *Air Canada* v *Secretary of State for Trade (No. 2)* may be met, but if a party has not seen documents it will be difficult to show that it is reasonably likely that they will support the person's case or damage that of the opponent. It must be remembered that this test is used to decide if the documents are to be inspected, as inspection is the necessary precursor to disclosure.

There is a problem for the courts in correctly balancing the competing aspects of the public interest. There must be some deference to the executive in matters which are non-justiciable such as defence, but deference does not mean unqualified acceptance. Inspection by the court is a safeguard to those claiming immunity but the test for inspection errs too much in favour of government secrecy than the administration of justice.

18.6.4 The Scott Report
Most of the case law on public interest immunity has been in civil law, but it can be raised in criminal law. As prosecutions may result in conviction and

deprivation of liberty, the ability to have access to relevant documents is of great importance. In the Matrix Churhcill prosecution for breach of an export ban on defence equipment, it was the rejection of most of the public interest immunity certificates by the trial judge which enabled counsel to run the defence which led to the collapse of the case. It was understandable that the terms of reference of Sir Richard Scott's inquiry into the export of defence equipment to Iraq also included the prosecutions related to the policy. Sir Richard was very critical of the government's recourse to public interest immunity. Too much was covered and ministers were wrongly advised about their duties in relation to their consideration of certificates (HC 115 of 1995–96, see also Scott 1996b).

The recommendations which Sir Richard made on claims of public interest immunity in criminal cases were:

(a) Documents need only be disclosed if they meet the criteria on materiality in *R* v *Keane* [1994] 1 WLR 746 and *R* v *Brown* [1994] 1 WLR 1599.

(b) Class claims should not be made, and contents claims should not be made if it is apparent that the documents might be of assistance to the defence.

(c) In contents claims consideration should be given to redaction (editing) so that the claim can be confined to redacted parts of the documents.

(d) Contents claims should only be made if the minister is of the view that the 'disclosure will cause substantial harm' (per Lord Templeman in *R* v *Chief Constable of the West Midlands Police, ex parte Wiley* [1995] 1 AC 247).

(e) A claim should not be made if the minister thinks that notwithstanding the sensitivity of the documents, the public interest requires disclosure.

(f) Ministers asked to sign certificates must be given adequate time to consider the matter unless circumstances render that impracticable.

(g) On a disclosure issue which goes before a judge, unless the parties are in agreement, the judge should be asked to determine first if the documents are material and thus disclosable.

(h) If documents are material then the judge should be asked to determine if they might help the defence and if they might then they ought not to be withheld from the defence on public interest immunity grounds as there is no true balance to be struck. Where disclosure is to be withheld, the defendant should know whether the decision was based on the judge's conclusion that the document would not be of any assistance, or, despite meeting that test, the public interest precluded disclosure. This latter conclusion is, in Sir Richard's view, wrong in principle and contrary to authority.

(i) The defendant should, in argument about the assistance which a document might give, specify the line(s) of defence which in the defendant's view give it materiality.

(j) If the documents are relevant and prima facie helpful to the defence, the judge may still conclude, in the light of the public interest factors underlying the claim, that the documents need not be disclosed.

Following the report, the government conducted a public consultation and announced a change in policy by Sir Nicholas Lyell, then Attorney-General (Parliamentary Debates (Hansard) Commons vol. 287, cols 949–52, 18 December 1996). The policy applies to civil and criminal law. Ministers would only make a claim if they believed that the disclosure of a document would cause real damage or harm to the public interest. The former division between class and contents claims would no longer be applied. Certificates will specify in greater detail what the document is and the damage its disclosure would be likely to do, unless to do so would itself cause the damage which the certificate seeks to prevent. Examples of harm include the safety of an informant, or safety of a regulatory process, or the damage to international relations which could be caused by disclosure of confidential diplomatic communications. Claims will not be made in relation to internal advice or national security material simply because of their class — there must be a belief that disclosure will cause real harm. Claims in criminal cases are always determined by the judge.

This policy only applies to government documents. Other bodies can claim public interest immunity, but the withering of the class claim derives from *ex parte Wiley* rather than the government's new policy and should therefore be generally applicable. The result of this policy should be that there are fewer public interest immunity claims made by the government and the assistance given to citizens in litigation against the Crown provided by the Crown Proceedings Act 1947 will be less likely to be reduced through routine (and unnecessary) claiming of public interest immunity.

Bibliography

Abel-Smith, B., and Stevens, R. (1968) *In Search Of Justice: Law, Society and the Legal System* (London, Allen Lane).

Alder, J. (1989) *Constitutional and Administrative Law* (Basingstoke: Macmillan).

Allan, T.R.S. (1985) 'Rugby, Recreation Grounds and Race Relations: Punishment for Silence' 48 *Modern Law Review* 448.

Allan, T.R.S. (1986) 'Racial Harmony, Public Policy and Freedom of Speech' 49 *Modern Law Review* 121.

Allan, T.R.S. (1991) 'Disclosure of Journalists' Sources, Civil Disobedience and the Rule of Law' 50 *Cambridge Law Journal* 131.

Allen, M.J. (1989) 'Sentencing Guidelines: Lessons To Be Learned?' 39 *Northern Ireland Legal Quarterly* 313.

Allen, M.J., and Cooper, S. 'Howard's Way — A Farewell to Freedom?' 58 *Modern Law Review* 364.

Armitage, Sir A. (1978) *Report of the Committee on the Political Acitivities of Civil Servants* (Cmnd 7057) (London: HMSO).

Armstrong, Sir R. (1986) 'The Duties and Responsibilities of Civil Servants in Relation to Ministers' in *The Duties and Responsibilities of Civil Servants in Relation to Ministers. Government Response to the Seventh Report from the Treasury and Civil Service Committee Session 1985–6.* (Cmnd 9841) (London: HMSO).

Arnull, A. (1990) *The General Principles of EEC Law and the Individual* (London: Leicester University Press).

Arrowsmith, S. (1990a) 'Judicial Review and the Contractual Powers of Public Authorities' 106 *Law Quarterly Review* 277.

Arrowsmith, S. (1990b) 'Government Contracts and Public Law' 10 *Legal Studies* 231.

Ashworth, A. (1992) *Sentencing and Criminal Justice* (London: Weidenfeld & Nicholson).

Bagehot, W. (1867) *The English Constitution* (Oxford).

Bailey, S.H., and Birch, D.J. (1982) 'Recent Developments in the Law of Police Powers' *Criminal Law Review* 475.

Bailey, S.H. (1991) *Cross on Local Government Law*, 8th ed. (London: Sweet & Maxwell).

Baldwin, J., Wikeley, N., and Young, R. (1992) *Judging Social Security: The Adjudication of Claims for Benefit in Britain* (Oxford: Clarendon Press).

Baldwin, R. (1985) *Regulating the Airlines* (Oxford: Clarendon Press).

Baldwin R., and Houghton, J. (1986) 'Circular Arguments: The Status and Legitimacy of Administrative Rules' *Public Law* 239.

Barendt, E. (1985) *Freedom of Speech* (Oxford: Clarendon Press).

Barendt, E. (1995) 'Separation of Powers and Constitutional Government' *Public Law* 599.

Barker, A. (1982) 'Governmental Bodies and the Networks of Mutual Accountability' in Barker. A. (ed.) *Quangos in Britain: Government and the Networks of Public Policy-Making* (London: Macmillan) p. 3.

Barron, A., and Scott, C. (1992) 'The Citizen's Charter' 55 *Modern Law Review* 526.

Bell, K. (1969) *Tribunals in the Social Services* (London: Routledge & Kegan Paul).

Bell, K. (1975) *Research Study on Supplementary Benefit Appeal Tribunals: Review of Main Findings, Conclusions and Recommendations* (London: HMSO).

Beloff, M., and Peele, G. (1985) *The Government of the UK: Political Authority in a Changing Society*, 2nd ed. (London: Weidenfeld & Nicolson).

Benn, T. (1980) 'Manifestos and Mandarins' in *Policy and Practice: The Experience of Government* (London: Royal Institute of Public Administration).

Bennion, F.A.R. (1992) *Statutory Interpretation, a Code*, 2nd ed. (London: Butterworths).

Bevan, V., and Lidstone, K. (1991) *The Investigation of Crime: A Guide To Police Powers* (London: Butterworths).

Birkinshaw, P. (1993) 'I Only Ask for Information — The White Paper on Open Government' *Public Law* 557.

Birkinshaw, P. (1995) *Grievances, Remedies and the State*, 2nd ed. (London: Sweet & Maxwell).

Blackstone, Sir W. (1825) *Commentaries on the Laws of England*, 16th ed. (London).

Blom-Cooper, L., and Drewry, G. (1972) *Final Appeal: a Study of the House of Lords in its Judicial Capacity* (Oxford: Clarendon Press).

Bogdanor, V. (1997) 'Ministerial Accountability' in Thompson, B., and Ridley, F.F. *Under the Scott-light: British Government Seen Through the Scott Report* (Oxford: Oxford University Press 71; also published in 50 *Parliamentary Affairs* 71.

Boulton, C.J. (1989) *Erskine May's Treatise on the Law, Privileges, Proceedings and Usage of Parliament*, 21st ed. (London: Butterworths).

Boyron, S. (1992) 'Proportionality in English Administrative law: A Faulty Translation?' 12 *Oxford Journal of Legal Studies* 237.

Bradley, A.W. (1980) 'The Role of the Ombudsman in Relation to the Protection of Citizens' Rights' 39 *Cambridge Law Journal* 304.

Bradley, A.W. (1991) 'The United Kingdom before the Strasbourg Court 1975–1990' in Finnie, W., Himsworth, C., and Walker, N. *Edinburgh Essays in Public Law* (Edinburgh: Edinburgh University Press) p. 185.

Bradley, A.W. (1992) 'Justice, Good Government and Public Interest Immunity' *Public Law* 514.

Bradley, A.W. (1994) 'The sovereignty of Parliament – in Perpetuity?' in Jowell, J., and Oliver, D., *The Changing Constitution*, 3rd ed. (Oxford: Clarendon Press) p. 79.

Bradley, A.W., and Ewing, K.D. (1993) *Wade and Bradley Constitutional and Administrative Law*, 11th ed. (London: Longman).

Bradshaw, J. (1980) *The Family Fund: on Initiative in Social Policy* (London: Routledge, Kegan Paul).

Brazier, R., (1994) *Constitutional Practice* (Oxford: Clarendon Press).

Brazier, R. (1991) *Constitutional Reform: Reshaping the British Political System* (Oxford: Oxford University Press).

Brazier, R. (1992) 'The Non-Legal Constitution: Thoughts on Convention, Practice and Principle' 43 *Northern Ireland Legal Quarterly* 262.

Browne-Wilkinson, Sir N. (1988) 'The Independence of the Judiciary in the 1980s' *Public Law* 44.

Browne-Wilkinson, Lord. (1992) 'The Infiltration of a Bill of Rights' *Public Law* 397.

Bryce, J. (1901) *Studies in History and Jurisprudence* (Oxford: Clarendon Press).

Butler-Sloss, Dame E. (1988) *Report of the Inquiry into Child Abuse in Cleveland 1987* (Cm 412) (London: HMSO).

Cabinet Office (1992) *Questions of Procedure for Ministers* (London: Cabinet Office).

Cabinet Office (1995) *Public Bodies 1994* (London: HMSO).

Cabinet Office (1997) *A Ministerial Code: A Code of Conduct and Guidance on Procedures for Ministers* (London: Cabinet Office).

Campaign for a Scottish Assembly (1988) *A Claim of Right for Scotland* (Edinburgh).

Cane, P. (1980) 'A Fresh Look at Punton's Case' 43 *Modern Law Review* 266.

Cane, P. (1993) 'The Law Commission on Judicial Review' 56 *Modern Law Review* 887.

Cane, P. (1996) *An Introduction to Administrative Law*, 3rd ed. (Oxford: Clarendon Press).

Charter 88 (1990) *A Bill of Rights* (London: Charter 88).

Childs, M. (1991) 'Outraging Public Decency: The Offence of Offensiveness' *Public Law* 20.

Churchill, R.R., and Young, J.R. (1992) 'Compliance with Judgments of the European Court of Human Rights and Decisions of the Committee of Ministers: the Experience of the United Kingdom' 62 *British Yearbook of International Law* (Oxford: Clarendon Press) p. 283.

CLA (1995) *Remedies: Non-compliance* (London: Commission for Local Administration in England).

Coleman, F. (1993) 'All in the Best Possible Taste: The Broadcasting Standards Council' *Public Law* 488.

Collar, N. (1991) 'Judicial Review and Alternative Remedies – An Analysis of Recent English Decisions' 10 *Civil Justice Quarterly* 138.

Committee of Privileges (1938) *Case of Duncan Sandys MP* (HC 146 of 1937–8) (London: HMSO).

Committee of Privileges (1957) *Report* (HC 305 of 1956-7) (London: HMSO).

Committee of Privileges (1985) *Second Report: Premature Disclosure of Proceedings of Select Committees* (HC 555 of 1984-5) (London: HMSO).

Constitution Unit (1996a) *Scotland's Parliament: Fundamentals for a New Scotland Act* (London: Constitution Unit).

Constitution Unit (1996b) *Human Rights Legislation* (London: Constitution Unit).

Council on Tribunals (1980) *The Functions of the Council on Tribunals: Special Report* (Cmnd 7805) (London: HMSO).

Council on Tribunals (1990) *Annual Report* (HC 64 of 1989-90) (London: HMSO).

Craig, P.P. (1977) 'Representations By Public Bodies' 99 *Law Quarterly Review* 398.

Craig, P.P. (1989) *Administrative Law*, 2nd ed. (London: Sweet & Maxwell).

Craig, P.P. (1990) *Public Law and Democracy in the United Kingdom and the United States of America* (Oxford: Clarendon Press).

Craig, P.P. (1994a) *Administrative Law*, 3rd ed. (London: Sweet & Maxwell).

Craig, P.P. (1994b) 'The Common Law, Reasons and Administrative Justice' 53 *Cambridge Law Journal* 282.

Cranston, R. (1994) 'Reviewing Judicial Review' in Richardson, G., and Genn, H. *Administrative Law and Government Action* (Oxford: Clarendon Press) p. 45.

Crawford, C., and Thompson, B. (1987) *Decisions of Local Ombudsmen* (unpublished report for the Department of the Environment).

Cretney, S. (1985) 'The Politics of Law Reform – A View from the Inside' 48 *Modern Law Review* 493.

Crossman, R.H.S. (1975) *The Diaries of a Cabinet Minister*, vol. 1 (London: Hamilton).

Cullen, Lord (1990) *Report of the Public Inquiry into the Piper Alpha Disaster* (Cm 1310) (London: HMSO).

Daintith, T. (1979) 'Regulation by Contract: the New Prerogative' *Current Legal Problems* 41.

Daintith, T. (1982) 'Legal Analysis of Economic Policy' 9 *Journal of Law and Society* 191.

Daintith, T. (1994) 'The Techniques of Government' in Jowell, J. and Oliver, D. *The Changing Constitution*, 3rd ed. (Oxford: Clarendon Press) p. 209.

Davis, K.C. (1969) *Discretionary Justice: A Preliminary Inquiry* (Baton Rouge: Louisiana State University Press).

De Smith, S., and Brazier, R. (1994) *Constitutional and Administrative Law*, 7th ed. (Harmondsworth: Penguin).

Dearlove, J., and Saunders, P. (1991) *Introduction to British Politics*, 2nd ed. (Cambridge: Polity).

Deregulation Committee (1995) *First Report. Consideration of Deregulation Proposals and Draft Orders: The Government's Reply to the First Special Report from the Committee. Deregulation (Greyhound Racing) Order 1995.* (HC 409 of 1994-5). (London: HMSO).

Dicey, A. V., (1959) *An Introduction to the Study of the Law of the Constitution*, 10th ed. with an introduction by E.C.S. Wade (London: Macmillan).

Dickens, L. (1985) *Dismissed: A Study of Unfair Dismissal and the Industrial Tribunal System* (Oxford: Blackwell).

DoE. (1996a) *Financial and Management Review of the Commission for Local Administration: Stage I* (Sir G. Chipperfield) (London: Department of the Environment).

DoE. (1996b) *Financial Management and Policy Review of the Commission for Local Administration: Stage II* (A. Whetnall) (London: Department of the Environment).

DoE. (1996c) *Government Response to the Financial Management and Policy Review of the Commission for Local Administration* (London: Department of the Environment).

Donoughmore, Earl of (1932) *Report of the Committee on Ministers' Powers* (Cmd 4046) (London: HMSO).

Drewry, G. (1989) 'The Committees Since 1983' in Drewry, G. (ed.) *The New Select Committees*, 2nd ed. (Oxford: Clarendon Press) p. 397.

Drewry, G. (1991) 'Judicial Independence in Britain: Challenges Real and Threats Imagined' pp. 37–57 in Norton, P. (ed.) *New Directions in British Politics?* (Aldershot: Edward Elgar).

Drewry, G. (1992) 'Ministers, Parliament and the Courts' 142 *New Law Journal* 50.

Drewry, G., and Harlow, C. (1990) 'A "Cutting Edge"? The Parliamentary Commissioner and MPs' 53 *Modern Law Review* 745.

Drewry, G. and Butcher T. (1991) *The Civil Service Today*, 2nd ed. (Oxford: Blackwell).

Duchacek, I.D. (1991) 'Constitution/Constitutionalism' in Bogdanor, V. (ed) *Blackwell's Encyclopaedia of Political Science* (Oxford: Blackwell) p. 142.

Edwards, D.J., (1992) 'The Treaty of Union: More Hints of Constitutionalism' 12 *Legal Studies* 34.

Efficiency Unit (Jenkins, K., Caines, K., and Jackson, A.) (1988) *Improving Management in Government: The Next Steps* (London: HMSO).

Elliott, M. (1980) 'Appeals, Principles and Pragmatism in Natural Justice' 43 *Modern Law Review* 66.

Ewing K.D. and Gearty C.A. (1990) *Freedom Under Thatcher: Civil Liberties in Modern Britain* (Oxford: Oxford University Press).

Farmer, J.A., (1974) *Tribunals and Government* (London: Weidenfeld & Nicolson).

Farrar, J.H. (1974) *Law Reform and the Law Commission* (London: Sweet & Maxwell).

Farrelly, M. (1989) *The Reasons Why Appellants Fail To Attend their Social Security Appeal Tribunals'* unpublished PhD thesis (University of Birmingham) cited in Baldwin, J., Wikeley, N. and Young, R. (1992) *Judging Social Security* (Oxford: Clarendon Press).

Farran, C.d'O. (1951) 'The Royal Marriages Act 1772' 14 *Modern Law Review* 53.

Faulks, Sir N. (1975) *Report of the Committee on Defamation* (Cmnd 5909) (London: HMSO).

Finer, S.E. (1956) 'The Individual Responsibility of Ministers' 34 *Public Administration* 377.

Finer, S.E. (1979) *Five Constitutions* (Harmondsworth: Penguin).

Fisher, Sir H. (1977) *Report of an Inquiry into the Death of Maxwell Confait* (HC 90 of 1977–8) (London: HMSO).

Foreign Affairs Select Comittee (1981) *First Report: British North America Acts: The Role of Parliament* (HC 42 of 1980–1) (London: HMSO).

Franks, Sir O. (1957) *Report of the Committee on Administrative Tribunals and Enquiries* (Cmnd 218) (London: HMSO).

Franks, Sir O. (1972) *Report of the Committee on Section 2 of the Official Secrets Act 1911* (Cmnd 5104) (London: HMSO).

Fredman, S., and Morris, G. (1991) 'Judicial Review and Civil Servants: Contracts of Employment Declared to Exist' *Public Law* 484.

Fredman, S., and Morris, G. (1992) 'A Snake or a Ladder? *O'Reilly* v *Mackman* Reconsidered' 108 *Law Quarterly Review* 353.

Friedrich, C.J. (1963) *Man and his Government* (New York: McGraw-Hill).

Fulton, Lord (1968) *Report of the Committee on the Civil Service* (Cmnd 3638) (London: HMSO).

Galligan, D. (1976) 'The Nature and Function of Policies within Discretionary Power' *Public Law* 332.

Ganz, G. (1992) 'The War Crimes Act 1991 – Why No Constitutional Crisis?' 55 *Modern Law Review* 87.

Genn, H. (1993) 'Tribunals and Informal Justice' 56 *Modern Law Review* 393.

Genn, H. (1994) 'Tribunal Review of Administrative Decision-Making' in Richardson G., and Genn, H. *Administrative Law and Government Action* (Oxford: Clarendon Press) p. 249.

Genn, H., and Genn, Y. (1989) *The Effectiveness of Representation at Tribunals* (London: Lord Chancellor's Department).

Goldsmith, A. (1991) *Complaints against the Police: The Trend To External Review* (Oxford: Clarendon Press).

Gordon, R. (1995) 'The Law Commission and Judicial Review: Managing the Tensions Between Case Management and Public Interest Challenges' *Public Law* 11.

Graham, C., and Prosser, T. (1988) 'Golden Shares: Industrial Policy by Stealth?' *Public Law* 423.

Graham, E. (1984) 'The Armagh Election Petition' 35 *Northern Ireland Legal Quarterly* 76.

Greenwood, J.R., and Wilson, D.J. (1989) *Public Administration in Britain Today*, 2nd ed. (London: Unwin Hyman).

Greer, P. (1994) *Transforming Central Government: The Next Steps Initiative* (Milton Keynes: Open University Press).

Griffith, J.A.G. (1955) 'The Crichel Down Affair' 18 *Modern Law Review* 557.

Griffith, J.A.G. (1979) 'The Political Constitution' 42 *Modern Law Review* 1.

Griffith, J.A.G. (1991) *The Politics of the Judiciary*, 4th ed. (London: Fontana).

Griffith, J.A.G. and Ryle, M. (1989) *Parliament: Functions, Practice and Procedures* (London: Sweet & Maxwell).

Gunn, E. (1993) *Vacher's Parliamentary Companion* (Berkhamsted: Vacher).

Hadfield, B. (1983) 'Learning from the Indians? The Constitutional Guarantee Revisited' *Public Law* 351.

Hadfield, B. (1984) 'Whether or Whither the House of Lords?' 35 *Northern Ireland Legal Quarterly* 313.

Hadfield, B. (1989) *The Constitution of Northern Ireland* (Belfast: SLS Legal Publications).

Hadfield, B. (1990) 'Direct Rule, Delegated Legislation and the Role of Parliament' in Hayes J., and O'Higgins, P., (eds) *Lessons from Northern Ireland* (Belfast: SLS Legal Publications) p. 9.

Hague, D.C., McKenzie, W.J.M., and Barker, A. (1975) *Public Policy and Private Interests: The Institutions of Compromise* (London: Macmillan).

Haldane, Lord (1918) *Report of the Machinery of Government Committee* (Cd 9230) (London: HMSO).

Hansard Society (1991) *Agenda for Change: Report of the Hansard Society Commission on Election Campaigns* chaired by Chataway C. (London: Hansard Society).

Hansard Society (1993) *Making the Law: Report of the Hansard Society Commission on the Legislative Process* chaired by Rippon, Lord. (London: Hansard Society).

Harden, I. (1991) 'The Constitution and its Discontents' 21 *British Journal of Political Science* 489.

Harden, I. (1992) *The Contracting State* (Milton Keynes: Open University Press).

Harlow, C., and Rawlings, R. (1984) *Law and Administration* (London: Weidenfeld & Nicholson).

Harris, B.V., (1992) 'The "Third Source" of Authority for Government Action' 108 *Law Quarterly Review* 626.

Hart, H.L.A., (1961) *The Concept of Law* (Oxford: Clarendon Press).

Hartley, T.C. (1992) 'The European Court and the EEA' 41 *International and Comparative Law Quarterly* 841.

Hayes, M. (1990) 'The Ombudsman' in Hayes, J., and O'Higgins, P. (eds) *Lessons from Northern Ireland* (Belfast: SLS Legal Publications).

Heard, A. (1991) *Canadian Constitutional Conventions* (Toronto: Oxford University Press).

Heath, E. (1977) in Expenditure Committee *Eleventh Report. The Civil Service* vol. II *Minutes of Evidence (Part II)* (HC 535-II of 1976–7) (London: HMSO) Q. 1877 at p. 764.

Hennessy, Sir J. (1984) *Report of an Inquiry by HM Chief Inspector of Prisons into the Security Arrangements at HM Prison, Maze* (HC 203 of 1983–4) (London: HMSO).

Hennessy, P. (1985) 'The Quality of Cabinet Government in Britain' 6 *Policy Studies*, Part 2, 15.

Hennessy P. (1986) *Cabinet* (Oxford: Basil Blackwell).

Herberg, J. (1990) 'The Right to a Hearing: Breach Without a Fault?' *Public Law* 467.

Heuston, R. (1964) *Essays in Constitutional Law*, 2nd ed. (London: Stevens).

Hewart, Gordon, Baron Hewart (1929) *The New Despotism* (London: Benn).

Hill, L., (1976) *The Model Ombudsman: Institutionalizing New Zealand's Democratic Experiment* (Princeton: Princeton University Press).

Hogg P. W. (1971) *Liability of the Crown in Australia, New Zealand and the United Kingdom* (Melbourne: Law Book Co.).

Hogwood, B.W., and Mackie, T.T. (1985) 'The United Kingdom; decision sifting in a secret garden' in Mackie, T.T. and Hogwood B.W. (eds), *Unlocking the Cabinet: Cabinet Structures in Comparative Perspective* (London: Sage), p. 36.

Home Office (1975) Racial Discrimination (Cmnd 6234) (London: HMSO).

Home Office (1985) *Review of Public Order Law* (Cmnd 9510) (London: HMSO).

Hood, Phillips, O. (1970 *Reform of the Constitution* (London: Chatto & Windus).

Hood, Phillips, O., and Jackson, P. (1987) *O. Hood Phillips' Constitutional and Administrative Law*, 7th ed. (London: Sweet & Maxwell).

House of Lords (1997) The House of Lords maintains a Website. The homepage is to be found at <www.the-stationery-office.co.uk/pa/ld/info.htm> and from there one can move to pages giving 'Membership information and attendance statistics' and on to the 'Composition of the House'. These statistics are updated monthly. The URL to the source of statistics given in the text was <www.the-stationery-office.co.uk/pa/ld199697/ldinfo/ld03mem/inf3e.htm>

House of Lords Committee on the Scrutiny of Delegated Powers (1995) *Fourth Report: Special Report on Deregulation Orders* (HL 48 of 1994–5) (London: HMSO).

Hunt, Lord (1982) 'Access to a Previous Government's Papers' *Public Law* 514.

Hutchinson A., and Jones, M. (1988) '*Wheeler*-Dealing: An Essay on Law, Politics and Speech' 15 *Journal of Law and Society* 263.

Institute for Public Policy Research (1990) *A British Bill of Rights* (London) chaired by Lester A.

Institute for Public Policy Research (1991) *The Constitution of the United Kingdom* (London: Institute for Public Policy Research).

Irvine of Lairg, Lord. (1996) 'Judges and Decision-Makers: The Theory and Practice of *Wednesbury* Review' *Public Law* 59.

Irvine of Lairg, Lord. (1997) 'Keynote Address to Conference on A Bill of Rights for the United Kingdom' delivered at University College, London 4 July 1997 text at Lord Chancellor's Department Website < www.open.gov.uk/lcd/speeches/lc4jy97.htm >

James, R., and Longley, D. 'The Channel Tunnel Rail Link, the Ombudsman and the Select Committee' *Public Law* 38.

Jennings, W.I. (1932) 'The Report on Ministers' Powers' 10 *Public Administration* 333.

Jennings, W.I. (1959) *The Law and the Constitution*, 5th ed. (London: University of London Press).

Johnson, N. (1982) 'Accountability, Control and Complexity: Moving beyond Ministerial Responsibility' in Barker, A. (ed.) *Quangos in Britain: Government and the Networks of Public Policy Making* (London: Macmillan) p. 206.

Jones, B. (1989) *Garner's Administrative Law*, 7th ed. (London: Butterworths).

Jones, M. (1988) 'The Local Ombudsman and Judicial Review' *Public Law* 608.

Jones, M.A. (1996) *Textbook on Torts* 5th ed. (London: Blackstone).

Jones, T. (1997) 'Scottish Devolution and Demarcation Disputes' *Public Law* 283.

Jowell, J., and Lester, A. (1987) 'Beyond *Wednesbury*: Substantive Principles of Administrative Law' *Public Law* 368.

Jowell, J., and Lester, A. (1988) 'Proportionality: Neither Novel Nor Dangerous' in Jowell, J. and Oliver, D. *New Directions in Judicial Review* (London: Stevens) p. 51.

Jowell, J., and Oliver, D. (1994) *The Changing Constitution*, 3rd ed. (Oxford: Clarendon Press).

Judge, D. (1992) 'The "Effectiveness" of the Post-1979 Select Committee System: The Verdict of the 1990 Procedure Committee' 63 *Political Quarterly* 91.

Justice (1961) *The Citizen and the Administration: The Redress of Grievances* chaired by Whyatt, Sir J. (London: Stevens).

Justice (1980) *The Local Ombudsmen: A Review of the First Five Years* (London: Justice).

Justice (1992) *The Judiciary in England and Wales* chaired by Stevens, R. (London: Justice).

Justice–All Souls (1988) *Administrative Justice: Some Necessary Reforms* chaired by Neill, Sir P. (Oxford: Clarendon Press).

Kavanagh, D. (1987) 'Margaret Thatcher: a Case of Prime Ministerial Power? in Robins, L. *Political Institutions in Britain* (London: Longmans) p. 9.

Kellner, P., and Crowther-Hunt, Lord (1980) *The Civil Servants: an Inquiry into Britain's Ruling Class* (London: Macdonald Futura).
Kilbrandon, Lord (1973) *Report of the Royal Commission on the Constitution* (Cmnd 5460) (London: HMSO).
Klug, F., Starmer, K., and Weir, S. (1996) *The Three Pillars of Liberty: Political Rights and Freedoms in the United Kingdom* (London: Routledge).

Labour (1990) *Looking to the Future* (London: Labour Party).
Law Commission (1976) *Remedies in Administrative Law* (Law Com No. 73, Cmnd 6407) (London: HMSO).
Law Commission (1977) *Treason, Sedition and Allied Offences* (Working Paper No. 72) (London: HMSO).
Law Commission (1981) *Offences against Religion and Public Worship* (Working Paper No. 79) (London: HMSO).
Law Commission (1993) *Administrative Law: Judicial Review and Statutory Appeals* (Consultation Paper No. 126) (London: HMSO).
Law Commission (1994) *Administrative Law: Judicial Review and Statutory Appeals* (Law Comm No 226, HC 669 of 1993–4) (London: HMSO).
Laws, Sir J. (1993) 'Is the High Court the Guardian of Fundamental Constitutional Rights?' *Public Law* 59.
Laws, Sir J. (1995) 'Law and Democracy' *Public Law* 72.
Le Sueur A. P., and Sunkin, M. (1992) 'Applications for Judicial Review: The Requirement for Leave' *Public Law* 102.
Leigh, I. (1991) ' The Gulf War Deportations and the Courts' *Public Law* 331.
Leigh, I., and Lustgarten, L. (1991) 'Employment, Justice and Détente: the Reform of Vetting' 54 *Modern Law Review* 613.
Lewis, N., and Birkinshaw, P. (1993) *When Citizens Complain* (Buckingham: Open University Press).
Lewis, N., Seneviratne, M., and Cracknell, S. (1987) *Complaints Procedures in Local Government* (Sheffield: University of Sheffield Centre for Criminological and Socio-Legal Studies).
Lewis, N., and Longley, D. (1992) 'Accountability in Education, Social Services and Health' in *Accountability to the Public* (London: European Policy Forum) p. 14.
Liberal Democrats (1990) *We, the People*, Federal Green Paper No. 13 (London: Liberal Democrats).
Lidstone, K.W. (1984) 'Magistrates, the Police and Search Warrants' *Criminal Law Review* 449.
Lidstone, K.W., and Palmer, C. (1996) *Bevan and Lidstone's The Investigation of Crime: A Guide to Police Powers,* 2nd ed (London: Butterworths).
Logie, J.G., and Watchman, P.Q., (1990) *The Local Ombudsman* (Edinburgh: T&T Clark).
Lord Chancellor's Advisory Committee on Legal Aid (HC 20 of 1974–5) (London: HMSO).
Lord Chancellor's Department (1990) *Judicial Appointments: The Lord Chancellor's Policies and Procedures* (London: HMSO).

Lustgarten, L., and Leigh I. (1989) 'The Security Service Act 1989' 52 *Modern Law Review* 801.

Lustgarten, L., and Leigh I. (1994) *In From the Cold: National Security and Parliamentary Accountability* (Oxford: Clarendon Press).

Mackie T.T., and Hogwood, B.W. *Unlocking the Cabinet: Cabinet Structure in Comparative Perspective* (London: Sage).

Mackintosh, J.P. (1977) *The British Cabinet*, 3rd ed. (London: Stevens).

Maitland, F.W. (1909) *Equity also the Forms of Action at Common Law* ed. Chaytor, A.H., and Whittaker, W.J. (Cambridge: Cambridge University Press).

Markesinis, B.S., (1972) *The Theory and Practice of Dissolution of Parliament* (London: Cambridge University Press).

Marquand, D. (1989) 'Regional Devolution' in Jowell J., and Oliver, D. *The Changing Constitution*, 2nd ed. (Oxford: Clarendon Press) p. 385.

Marshall, G. (1971) *Constitutional Theory* (Oxford: Clarendon Press).

Marshall, G. (1984) *Constitutional Conventions* (Oxford: Clarendon Press).

Masterman, J.C. (1949) *Report of the Committee on the Political Activities of Civil Servants* (Cmd 7718) (London: HMSO).

McAuslan, P. (1980) *The Ideologies of Planning Law* (Oxford: Pergamon).

McAuslan, P. (1983) 'Administrative Law, Collective Consumption and Judicial Policy' 46 *Modern Law Review* 1.

McAuslan, P. (1988) 'Administrative Justice — A Necessary Report? *Public Law* 402.

McAuslan, P., and McEldowney J.F. (1985) *Law, Legitimacy and the Constitution* (London: Sweet & Maxwell).

McCrudden, C., (1989) 'Northern Ireland and the British Constitution' in Jowell, J., and Oliver, D. *The Changing Constitution*, 2nd ed. (Oxford: Clarendon Press) p. 297.

McCrudden, C. (1994) 'Northern Ireland and the British Constitution' in Jowell, J., and Oliver, D. *The Changing Constitution*, 3rd ed. (Oxford: Clarendon Press) p. 323.

McEldowney, J.F. (1985) 'Dicey in Historical Perspective – A Review Essay' in McAuslan, P., and McEldowney, J.F., *Law, Legitimacy and the Constitution* (London: Sweet & Maxwell) p. 39.

McEldowney, J.F. (1989) 'The National Audit Office and Privatisation' 54 *Modern Law Review* 933.

McHarg, A. (1992) 'The Competition and Service (Utilities) Act 1992: Utility Regulation and the Charter' *Public Law* 385.

Miers, D.R., and Page, A.C. (1990) *Legislation*, 2nd ed. (London: Sweet & Maxwell).

Miller, C.J. (1989) *Contempt of Court*, 2nd ed. (Oxford: Clarendon Press).

Mitchell, A. (1994) 'Backbench Influence: A Personal View' 47 *Parliamentary Affairs* 687.

Mitchell, J.D.B., (1968) *Constitutional Law*, 2nd ed. (Edinburgh: Green).

Morris (1996) 'The Revenue Adjudicator — The First Two Years' *Public Law* 309.

Mount, F. (1992) *The British Constitution Now* (London: Heinemann).
Mowbray, A.R. 'A New European Court of Human Rights' *Public Law* 540.
Munro, C. (1987) *Studies in Constitutional Law* (London: Butterworths).
Munro, C, (1992) 'Judicial Independence and Judicial Functions' in Munro, C., and Wasik, M. *Sentencing, Judicial Discretion and Training* (London: Sweet & Maxwell).

National Council for Civil Liberties (1991) *A People's Charter* (London: National Council for Civil Liberties).
Nicolson, I.F. (1986) *The Mystery of Crichel Down* (Oxford: Clarendon Press).
North, P. (1985) 'Law Reform: Processes and Problems' 101 *Law Quarterly Review* 338.
Northcote and Trevelyan (1854) *Report on the Organisation of the Permanent Civil Service* (C 1713) (London: HMSO).
Norton, P. (1981) *The Commons in Perspective* (Oxford: Robertson).
Norton, P. (1985) *Parliament in the 1980s* (Oxford: Blackwell).
Norton-Taylor, R. (1990) *In Defence of the Realm? The Case for Accountable Security Services* (London: Civil Liberties Trust).

O'Leary, C., Elliott, S., and Wilford, R.A. (1988) *The Northern Ireland Assembly 1982-1986: A Constitutional Experiment* (London: Hurst).
Oliver, D. (1991a) 'Fishing on the Incoming Tide' 54 *Modern Law Review* 442.
Oliver, D. (1991b) *Government in the United Kingdom: The Search for Accountability, Effectiveness and Citizenship* (Milton Keynes: Open University Press).
O'Riordan, T., Kemp, R., and Purdue, M. (1988) *Sizewell B: An Anatomy of the Inquiry* (Basingstoke: Macmillan).
Osborne, D.E., and Gaebler, T. (1992) *Reinventing Government: How the Entrepreneurial Spirit is Transforming the Public Sector* (Reading (Mass): Addison-Wesley).
O'Toole, B., and Chapman, R.A. (1995) 'Parliamentary Accountability' in O'Toole, B. and Jordan G. *Next Steps: Improving Management in Government?* (Aldershot: Dartmouth) p. 118.

Page, A. (1985) 'MPs and the Redress of Grievances' *Public Law* 1.
Pannick, D. (1992) 'Who is Subject to Judicial Review and in Respect of What?' *Public Law* 1.
Parliamentary Commissioner for Administration (1981) Annual Report for 1980 (HC 148 of 1980–1) (London: HMSO).
Parliamentary Commissioner for Administration (1995) *Third Report. Investigation of Complaints Against the Child Support Agency.* HC 135 of 1994–5 (London: HMSO).
Pearson, Lord (1978) *Report of the Royal Commission on Civil Liability and Compensation for Personal Injury* (Cmnd 7504) (London: HMSO).
Philips, Sir C., (1981) *Report of the Royal Commission on Criminal Procedure* (Cmnd 8092) (London: HMSO).

Planning Advisory Group (1965) *The Future of Development Plans* (London: HMSO).

Pliatzky, Sir L. (1980) *Report on Non-Departmenal Public Bodies* (Cmnd 7797) (London: HMSO).

Potter, J.C. (1992) 'Adjudication by Social Security Appeal Tribunals: A Research Study' 21 *Anglo-American Law Review* 341.

Prosser, T. (1977) 'Poverty, Ideology and Legality: Supplementary Benefit Appeal Tribunals and their Predecessors' 4 *British Journal of Law and Society* 39.

Radcliffe, Lord (1962) *Report of the Committee on Security Procedures in the Public Service* (Cmnd 1681) (London: HMSO).

Radcliffe, Lord (1976) *Report of the Committee of Privy Counsellors on Ministerial Memoirs* (Cmnd 6386) (London: HMSO).

Radford, M. (1991) 'Auditing for Change: Local Government and the Audit Commission' 54 *Modern Law Review* 912.

Rawlings, H.F. (1988) *Law and the Electoral Process* (London: Sweet & Maxwell).

Rawlings, R. (1986) 'Parliamentary Redress of Grievance' in Harlow, C. (ed.) *Public Law and Politics* (London: Sweet & Maxwell) p. 118.

Rawlings, R. (1987) *Grievance Procedure and Administrative Justice: A Review of Socio-Legal Research* (London: Economic and Social Research Council).

Rawlings, R. (1994) 'Legal Politics: the United Kingdom and the Ratification of the Treaty on European Union' *Public Law* 254, and 367.

Raz, J. (1977) 'The Rule of Law and its Virtue' 93 *Law Quarterly Review* 195.

Reid, K. (1996) 'Prevention of Terrorism (Additional Powers) Act 1996' 4 *Web Journal of Current Legal Issues*.

Ridley, F.F. (1988) 'There is no British Constitution: A Dangerous Case of the Emperor's Clothes' 41 *Parliamentary Affairs*, 340.

Ridley, F.F. (1991) 'Defining Constitutional Law in Britain' 20 *Anglo-American Law Review* 101.

Robertson, G. (1993) *Freedom, the Individual and the Law*, 7th ed. (Harmondsworth: Penguin).

Robinson, A. (1989a) 'The Treasury and Civil Service Committee' in Drewry G. (ed.) *The New Select Committees* 2nd ed. (Oxford: Clarendon Press) p. 268.

Robinson, A. (1989b) 'The Financial Work of the Select Committees' in Drewry, G. (ed.) *The New Select Committees* 2nd ed. (Oxford: Clarendon Press) p. 307.

Ross, M. 'Beyond *Francovich*' 56 *Modern Law Review* 55.

Runciman, Viscount (1993) *Report of the Royal Commission on Criminal Justice* (Cm 2263) (London: HMSO).

Sampford, C.J.G, (1987) 'Recognize and Declare: An Australian Experiment in Codifying Constitutional Conventions' 7 *Oxford Journal of Legal Studies* 369.

Scarman, Sir L. (1975) *Report of the Inquiry into The Red Lion Square Disorders 15 June 1974* (Cmnd 5919) (London: HMSO).

Scarman, Sir L. (1977) *Report of a Court of Inquiry into a Dispute between Grunwick Processing Laboratories Ltd and Members of the Association of Professional, Executive, Clerical and Computer Staff* (Cmnd 6922) (London: HMSO).

Schwartz, B., and Wade, H.W.R. (1972) *Legal Control of Government: Administrative Law in Britain and the United States* (Oxford: Clarendon Press).

Scott, Sir Richard. (1996a) 'Ministerial Accountability' *Public Law* 410.

Scott, Sir Richard. (1996b) 'The Acceptable and Unacceptable Use of Public Interest Immunity' *Public Law* 427.

Scottish Constitutional Convention (1990) *Towards Scotland's Parliament* (Edinburgh: Scottish Constitutional Convention).

Scottish Office (1993) *Scotland in the Union: a Partnership for Good* (Cm 2225) (Edinburgh: HMSO).

Sedley, Sir S. (1995) 'Human Rights: A Twenty-First Century Agenda' *Public Law* 386.

Select Committee on Privilege (1968) *Report* (HC 34 of 1967–8) (London: HMSO).

Select Committee on Procedure (1978) *First Report* (HC 588 of 1977–8) (London: HMSO).

Select Committee on Procedure (1986) *Second Report: The Use of Time on the Floor of the House* (HC 350 of 1985–6) (London: HMSO).

Select Committee on Procedure (1989) *Fourth Report: The Scrutiny of European Legislation* (HC 622 of 1988–9) (London: HMSO).

Select Committee on Procedure (1990) *Second Report: The Working of the Select Committee System* (HC 19 of 1989–90) (London: HMSO).

Select Committee on Procedure (1991) *Third Report: Parliamentary Questions* (HC 178 of 1990–1) (London: HMSO).

Select Committee on Procedure (1992) *First Report: Review of the European Standing Committees* (HC 31 of 1991–2) (London: HMSO).

Select Committee on Procedure (1994a) *First Report. Parliamentary Scrutiny of Deregulation Orders* (HC 238 of 1993–4).

Select Committee on Procedure (1994b) *First Special Report. Parliamentary Scrutiny of Deregulation Orders: Government Response to the Fifth Report* (HC 404 of 1993–4) (London: HMSO).

Shaw, M. (1991) *International Law*, 3rd ed. (Cambridge: Grotius).

Shetreet, S. (1976) *Judges on Trial* (Amsterdam: North-Holland).

Simcock, A.J.C. (1992) 'One and Many – The Office of Secretary of State' 70 *Public Administration* 535.

Social Security Committee (1992) *First Special Report: The Conduct of Mr Ian Maxwell and Mr Kevin Maxwell* (HC 353 of 1991–2) (London: HMSO).

Social Security Committee (1994) *Fifth Report: The Operation of the Child Support Act: Proposals for Change* (HC 470 of 1993–4) (London: HMSO).

Spujt, R.J. (1986) 'The Official Use of Deadly Force by the Security Forces against Suspected Terrorists' *Public Law* 38.

Starr, W.C. (1977) 'Hart's Rule of Recognition and the EEC' 28 *Northern Ireland Legal Quarterly* 258.

Steiner, J. (1993) 'From Direct Effect to *Francovich*: Shifting Means of Enforcement of Community Law' 18 *European Law Review* 3.

Stevens, R. (1997) 'Judges, Politics, Politicians and the Confusing Role of the Judiciary' in Hawkins, K. (ed) *The Human Face of Law: Essays in Honour of Donald Harris* (Oxford: Clarendon Press) 245.

Stewart, J. (1992) 'The Rebuilding of Public Accountability' in *Accountability to the Public* (London: European Policy Forum) p. 3.

Stone, R. (1989) *Entry, Search and Seizure*, 2nd ed. (London: Sweet & Maxwell).

Stone, R. (1995) 'Extending the Labyrinth: Part VII of the Criminal Justice and Public Order Act 1994' 58 *Modern Law Review* 389.

Sunkin, M. (1987) 'What Is Happening To Applications For Judicial Review?' 50 *Modern Law Review* 432.

Sunkin, M. (1991) 'The Judicial Review Case-load 1987–1989' *Public Law* 490.

Sunkin, M., Bridges, L., and Mészáros, G. (1995) 2nd ed. *Judicial Review in Perspective* (London: Cavendish).

Thompson, B. (1991) 'Broadcasting and Terrorism in the House of Lords' *Public Law* 346.

Thompson, B. (1995a) 'The Parliamentary Commissioner for Administration and Social Security' 2 *Journal of Social Security Law* 24.

Thompson, B. (1995b) 'Whitehall's Cultural Revolution' 1 *Web Journal of Current Legal Issues*.

Thompson, B. (1997) 'Judges As Trouble-Shooters' in Thompson, B., and Ridley, F.F. *Under the Scott-light: British Government Seen Through the Scott Report* (Oxford: Oxford University Press) 182; also published in 50 *Parliamentary Affairs* 182.

Thompson, K. (1991) 'Conciliation or Arbitration?' *Local Government Studies* 15.

Tierney, S.J.A. (1996) 'European Citizenship in Practice? The First Annual Report of the European Ombudsman' 2 *European Public Law* 517.

Tivey, L. (1973) *Nationalisation in British Industry*, revised ed. (London: Cape).

Tomlin, Lord (1931) *Report of the Royal Commission on the Civil Service* (Cmd 3909) (London: HMSO).

Treasury (1992) *Budgetary Reform* (Cm 1867) (London: HMSO).

Treasury and Civil Service Committee (1986) *Seventh Report. Civil Servants and Ministers: Duties and Responsibilities* (HC 92 I–II of 1985–6) (London: HMSO).

Treasury and Civil Service Committee (1991) *Seventh Report. The Next Steps Initiative* (HC 496 of 1990–1) (London: HMSO).

Treasury and Civil Service Select Committee (1994) Fifth Report *The Role of the Civil Service* (HC 27 of 1993–4) (London: HMSO).

Tregilgas-Davey, M. (1991) '*Ex Parte Choudhury* – An Opportunity Missed' 54 *Modern Law Review* 394.

Turpin, C. (1985) 'Race Relations, Rugby Football and the Law' 44 *Cambridge Law Journal* 333.

Turpin, C. (1989) *Government Procurement and Contracts* (Harlow: Longman).

Turpin, C. (1990) *British Government and the Constitution*, 2nd ed. (London: Weidenfeld & Nicholson).

Turpin, C. (1994) 'Ministerial Responsibility: Myth or Reality?' in Jowell, J. and Oliver, D., *The Changing Constitution*, 3rd ed. (Oxford: Clarendon Press) p. 109.

Veljanovski, C. (1991) 'The Regulation Game' in Veljanovski, C. (ed.) *Regulators and the Market* (London: Institute of Economic Affairs) p. 3.

Wade, E.C.S. (1934) 'Act of State in English Law: Its Relations with International Law' 15 *British Yearbook of International Law* 98.

Wade, H.W.R. (1955) 'The Basis of Legal Sovereignty' 14 *Cambridge Law Journal* 172.

Wade, H.W.R. (1980) *Constitutional Fundamentals* (London: Stevens).

Walker, C., and Weaver, R.L., (1994) 'A Peace Deal for Northern Ireland? The Downing Street Declaration of 1993' 8 *Emory International Law Review* 817.

Wass, Sir D. (1984) *Government and the Governed* (London: Routledge & Kegan Paul).

Watkins, A. (1992) *The Observer*, 2 February.

Weir, S. (1995) 'Quangos: Questions of Democratic Accountability' 48 *Parliamentary Affairs* 306.

Weir, S., and Hall, W. (1994) *EGO Trip: Extra-governmental Organisations in the UK and their Accountability* (London: Charter 88 Trust).

Welsh Office (1993) *Local Government in Wales: a Charter for the Future* (Cm 2155) (Cardiff: HMSO).

Wheare, K.C. (1953) *The Statute of Westminster and Dominion Status*, 5th ed. (London: Oxford University Press).

Wheare, K.C. (1966) *Modern Constitutions*, 2nd ed. (London: Oxford University Press).

White, C. (1994) 'Enforcing the Decisions of Ombudsmen — The Experience of the Northern Ireland Local Government Ombudsman' 45 *Northern Ireland Legal Quarterly* 395.

Widdicombe, D. (1986) *Report of the Committee on the Conduct of Local Authority Business* (Cmnd 9797) (London: HMSO).

Widgery, Lord (1972) *Report of the Tribunal Appointed to Inquire into the Events on Sunday 30 January 1972 which led to Loss of Life in Connection with the Procession in Londonderry on that Day* (HC 220 HL 101 of 1971–2)(London: HMSO).

Willetts, D. 'The Role of the Prime Minister's Policy Unit' 65 *Public Administration* 443.

Williams, G. (1991) 'What Is an Arrest?' 54 *Modern Law Review* 408.

Woodhouse, D. 'Ministerial Responsibility in the 1990s: When Do Ministers Resign?' (1993) 46 *Parliamentary Affairs* 277.

Woodhouse, D. (1997a) 'The Attorney General' in Thompson, B., and Ridley, F.F. *Under the Scott-light: British Government seen through the Scott Report* (Oxford: Oxford University Press) 97 also published in 50 *Parliamentary Affairs* 97.

Woodhouse, D. (1997b) 'Ministerial Responsibility: Something Old, Something New' *Public Law* 262.

Woolf, Sir H. (1990) *Protection of the Public — A New Challenge* (London: Stevens & Sons).

Woolf of Barnes, Lord (1995) '*Droit Public* — English Style' *Public Law* 57.

Woolf of Barnes, Lord (1996) *Access to Justice: Final Report to the Lord Chancellor on the Civil Justice System in England and Wales* (London: The Stationery Office).

Wyatt, D., and Dashwood, A. (1993) *Wyatt and Dashwood's European Community Law*, 3rd ed. (London).

Young, H., and Sloman, A. (1982) *No, Minister* (London: British Broadcasting Corporation).

Young, R. (1990) 'The Effectiveness of Representation at Tribunals' 9 *Civil Justice Quarterly* 16.

Zellick, G. (1988) *The Law Commission and Law Reform* (London: Sweet & Maxwell).

COMMAND PAPERS

C 1713 (1854) *Report on the Organisation of the Permanent Civil Service* chaired by Northcote and Trevelyan.

Cd 9230 (1918) *Report of the Machinery of Government Committee* chaired by Lord Haldane.

Cmd 3909 (1931) *Report of the Royal Commission on the Civil Service* chaired by Lord Tomlin.

Cmd 4046 (1932) *Report of the Committee on Ministers' Powers* chaired by Lord Donoughmore and then Sir Leslie Scott.

Cmnd 7718 (1949) *Report of the Committee on Political Activities of Civil Servants* chaired by J.C. Masterman.

Cmnd 218 (1957) *Report of the Committee on Administrative Tribunals and Enquiries* chaired by Sir O. Franks.

Cmnd 1681 (1962) *Report of the Committee on Security Procedures in the Public Service* chaired by Lord Radcliffe.

Cmnd 3301 (1967) *Legal and Constitutional Implications of United Kingdom Membership of the European Communities.*

Cmnd 3638 (1968) *Report of the Committee on the Civil Service* chaired by Lord Fulton.

Cmnd 5104 (1972) *Report of the Committee on Section 2 of the Official Secrets Act 1911* chaired by Lord Franks.

Cmnd 5460 (1973) *Report of the Royal Commission on the Constitution* chaired by Lord Kilbrandon.

Cmnd 5909 (1975) *Report of the Committee on Defamation* chaired by Sir N. Faulks.

Cmnd 5919 (1975) *Report of the Inquiry into the Red Lion Square Disorders 15 June 1974* chaired by Sir L. Scarman.

Cmnd 6234 (1975) *Racial Discrimination.*
Cmnd 6386 (1976) *Report of the Committee of Privy Counsellors on Ministerial Memoirs* chaired by Lord Radcliffe.
Cmnd 6407 (1976) *Remedies in Administrative Law* (Law Com No. 73), Law Commission.
Cmnd 6922 (1977) *Report of a Court of Inquiry into a Dispute between Grunwick Processing Laboratories Ltd and Members of the Association of Professional, Executive, Clerical and Computer Staff* chaired by Sir L. Scarman.
Cmnd 7057 (1978) *Report of the Committee on the Political Activities of Civil Servants* chaired by Sir A. Armitage.
Cmnd 7449 (1979) *Observations on the Fourth Report of the Select Committee on the Parliamentary Commissioner for Administration* (1977–8).
Cmnd 7504 (1978) *Report of the Royal Commission on Civil Liability and Compensation for Personal Injury* chaired by Lord Pearson.
Cmnd 7797 (1980) *Report on Non-Departmental Public Bodies* chaired by Sir L. Pliatzky.
Cmnd 7805 (1980) *The Functions of the Council on Tribunals: Special Report.*
Cmnd 8092 (1981) *Report of the Royal Commission on Criminal Procedure* chaired by Sir C. Philips.
Cmnd 8233 (1981) *Licence and Agreement between HM Secretary of State for the Home Department and the British Broadcasting Corporation.*
Cmnd 9510 (1985) *Review of Public Order Law.*
Cmnd 9657 (1985) *Agreement between the Government of the United Kingdom and the Republic of Ireland.*
Cmnd 9797 (1986) *Report of the Committee on the Conduct of Local Authority Business* chaired by D. Widdicombe.
Cmnd 9841 (1986) *The Duties and Responsibilities of Civil Servants in Relation to Ministers: Government Response to the Seventh Report from the Treasury and Civil Service Committee Session 1985–6.*
Cm 412 (1988) *Report of the Inquiry into Child Abuse in Cleveland 1987* chaired by Dame Butler-Sloss.
Cm 1081 (1990) *The Scrutiny of European Legislation: Government Response.*
Cm 1310 (1990) *Report of the Public Inquiry into the Piper Alpha Disaster* chaired by Lord Cullen.
Cm 1532 (1991) *The Working of the Select Committee System.*
Cm 1599 (1991) *The Citizen's Charter: Raising the Standard.*
Cm 1867 (1992) *Budgetary Reform.*
Cm 2101 (1992) *The Citizen's Charter: First Report.*
Cm 2155 (1993) *Local Government in Wales: A Charter for the Future.*
Cm 2225 (1993) *Scotland in the Union: a Partnership for Good.*
Cm 2263 (1993) *Report of the Royal Commission on Criminal Justice* chaired by Viscount Runciman.
Cm 2290 (1993) *Open Government.*
Cm 2434 (1993) *Compensating Victims of Violent Crime: Changes to the Criminal Injuries Compensation Scheme.*
Cm 2442 (1994) *Joint Declaration by the Prime Minister Rt Hon John Major MP and the Taoiseach Mr. Albert Reynolds TD.*

Cm 2627 (1994) *The Civil Service: Continuity and Change.*

Cm 2748 (1995) *The Civil Service: Taking Forward Continuity and Change.*

Cm 2750 (1994) *Next Steps Agencies in Government Review 1994.*

Cm 2850 (1995) *First Report of the Committee on Standards in Public Life* chaired by Lord Nolan.

Cm 3232 (1996) *Northern Ireland: Ground Rules for Substantive All-Party Negotiations.*

Cm 3270 (1996) *Second Report from the Committee on Standards in Public Life: Local Public Spending Bodies.*

Cm 3387 (1996) *Government Response to the Third Report from the Home Affairs Committee 1995–6.*

Cm 3658 (1997) *Scotland's Parliament.*

Cm 3702 (1997) *Third Report from the Committee on Standards in Public Life: Local Government, England, Scotland and Wales.*

Cm 3718 (1997) *A Voice for Wales.*

HOUSE OF COMMONS PAPERS

HC 146 of 1937–8 (1938) *Report from the Committee of Privileges.*

HC 118 of 1946–7 *Report from the Committee of Privileges.*

HC 305 of 1956–7 (1957) *First Report from the Committee of Privileges.*

HC 34 of 1967–8 (1968) *Report from the Select Committee on Privilege.*

HC 29 of 1971–2 (1971) *Report from the Select Committee on the Civil List.*

HC 220, HL 101, of 1971–2 (1972) *Report of the Tribunal Appointed to Inquire into the Events on Sunday 30 January 1972 which Led to Loss of Life in Connection with the Procession in Londonderry on that Day* chaired by Lord Widgery.

HC 20 of 1974–5 (1974) *Annual Report of the Lord Chancellor's Advisory Committee on Legal Aid.*

HC 535–II of 1976–7 (1977) *Eleventh Report. The Civil Service Expenditure Committee. Volume II Minutes of Evidence (Part II).*

HC 90 of 1977–8 (1977) *Report of an Inquiry into the Death of Maxwell Confait* chaired by Sir H. Fisher.

HC 588 of 1977–8 (1978) *First Report from the Select Committee on Procedure.*

HC 42 of 1980–1 (1981) *First Report from the Foreign Affairs Select Comittee: British North America Acts: The Role of Parliament.*

HC 148 of 1980–1 (1981) *Annual Report of the Parliamentary Commissioner for Administration.*

HC 203 of 1983–4 (1984) *Report of an Inquiry by HM Chief Inspector of Prisons into the Security Arrangements at HM Prison, Maze* chaired by Sir J. Hennessy.

HC 555 of 1984–5 (1985) *Second Report from the Committee of Privileges: Premature Disclosure of Proceedings of Select Committees.*

HC 92 I–II of 1985–6 (1986) *Seventh Report from the Treasury and Civil Service Committee: Civil Servants and Ministers: Duties and Responsibilities.*

HC 350 of 1985–6 (1986) *Second Report from the Select Committee on Procedure: The Use of Time on the Floor of the House.*

HC 622 of 1988–9 (1989) *Fourth Report from the Select Committee on Procedure: The Scrutiny of European Legislation.*

HC 19 of 1989–90 (1990) *Second Report from the Select Committee on Procedure: The Working of the Select Committee System.*

HC 64 of 1989–90 (1990) *Annual Report of the Council on Tribunals.*

HC 178 of 1990–1 (1991) *Third Report from the Select Committee on Procedure: Parliamentary Questions.*

HC 182 of 1990–1 (1991) *Annual Report of the Parliamentary Commissioner of Administration for Northern Ireland and Commissioner for Complaints.*

HC 496 of 1990–1 (1991) *Seventh Report from the Treasury and Civil Service Committee: The Next Steps Initiative.*

HC 20 of 1991–2 (1992) *Report from the Select Committee on Sittings of the House.*

HC 31 of 1991–2 (1992) *First Report from the Select Committee on Procedure: Review of the European Standing Committees.*

HC 353 of 1991–2 (1992) *First Special Report from the Social Security Committee: The Conduct of Mr Ian Maxwell and Mr Kevin Maxwell.*

HC 652 of 1992–3 *Sixth Report from the Parliamentary Commissioner for Administration. Delays in Handling Disability Living Allowance Claims.*

HC 33 of 1993–4 (1993) *First Report from the Select Committee on the Parliamentary Commissioner for Administration: The Powers, Work and Jurisdiction of the Ombudsman.*

HC 154 of 1993–4 *Eighth Report from the Committee of Public Accounts: The Proper Conduct of Public Business.*

HC 155 of 1993–4 *Seventeenth Report from the Committee of Public Accounts: Pergau Hydro-Electric Project.*

HC 290 of 1993–4 (1994) *Annual Report of the Parliamentary Commissioner for Administration 1993.*

HC 619 of 1993–4 (1994) *Fifth Report from the Select Committee on the Parliamentary Commissioner for Administration: Government Reply to the Committee's First Report on The Powers, Work and Jurisdiction of the Ombudsman.*

HC 112 of 1994–5 (1995) *First Report from the Select Committee on the Parliamentary Commissioner for Administration: Maladministration and Redress.*

HC 135 of 1994–5 (1995) *Third Report from the Parliamentary Commissioner for Administration: Investigation of Complaints Against the Child Support Agency.*

HC 193 of 1994–5 (1995) *Fifth Report from the Parliamentary Commissioner for Administration: The Channel Tunnel Rail Link and Blight.*

HC 270 of 1994–95 (1995) *Sixth Report from the Select Committee on the Parliamentary Commissioner for Administration: The Channel Tunnel Rail Link and Exceptional Hardship.*

HC 816 of 1994–5 (1995) *Second Report from the Select Committee on Standards in Public Life.*

HC 307 of 1994–5 (1995) *Annual Report of the Parliamentary Commissioner for Administration 1994.*

HC 819 of 1994–5 (1995) *Fifth Special Report from the Select Committee on the Parliamentary Commissioner for Administration: The Channel Tunnel Rail Link and Exceptional Hardship: The Government Response.*

HC 52 of 1995–6 (1996) *Third Report from the Home Affairs Committee: Judicial Appointments Procedures.*

HC 115 of 1995–6 *Report of the Inquiry into the Export of Defence Equipment and Dual-Use Goods to Iraq and Related Prosecutions.*

HC 313 of 1995–6 (1996) *Second Report from the Public Service Committee: Ministerial Accountability and Responsibility.*

HC 323 of 1996–7 (1997) *First Report from the Liaison Committee: Work of Select Committees.*

HC 455 of 1996–7 (1997) *Second Report from the Select Committee on the Parliamentary Commissioner for Administration: The Channel Tunnel Rail Link and Exceptional Hardship — Government Proposals for Redress.*

HC 30 of 1997–8 (1997) *First Report from the Committee on Standards and Privileges: Complaints from Mr Mohamed Al Fayed and The Guardian and others against 25 Members and Former Members.*

HC 190 of 1997–8 (1997) *First Report from the Select Committee on the Modernisation of the House of Commons: The Legislative Process.*

HC 240 of 1997–8 (1997) *Seventh Report from the Committee on Standards and Privileges: Complaints from Mr Mohamed Al Fayed and The Guardian and others against 25 Members and Former Members: Further Report.*

Index